THE NEGRO
AMERICAN

The Daedalus Library

Each of these volumes is available as a Beacon Paperback.

THE NEGRO AMERICAN

EDITED AND WITH INTRODUCTIONS BY
TALCOTT PARSONS AND KENNETH B.
CLARK AND WITH A FOREWORD BY
LYNDON B. JOHNSON

Illustrated with a 32-page portfolio
of photographs by Bruce Davidson
selected and introduced by
Arthur D. Trottenberg

BEACON PRESS   BOSTON

The Introductions by Talcott Parsons, Kenneth B. Clark, and
Arthur D. Trottenberg, "Negro Fertility and Family Size
Preferences" by Adelaide C. Hill and Frederick S. Jaffe,
and "The Civil Rights Movement and the Frontiers of
Law" by Paul A. Freund are here published for the first
time. The other essays in the book appeared originally,
some of them in slightly different form, in the Fall 1965
and Winter 1966 issues of *Dædalus*, the Journal of the
American Academy of Arts and Sciences.

Printed in the United States of America
Standard Book Number: 8070–4183–1

Fifth printing, April 1970

LYNDON B. JOHNSON

Foreword

NOTHING IS of greater significance to the welfare and vitality of this nation than the movement to secure equal rights for Negro Americans.

This Administration is dedicated to that movement. It is also dedicated to helping Negro Americans grasp the opportunities that equal rights make possible.

Much has been done—within government and without—to secure equal rights. Much remains to be done if a people enslaved by centuries of bigotry and want are to realize the opportunities of American life.

In June 1965 I spoke to the graduating class of Howard University about the condition of most Negroes in America. Before me were those for whom the future was illuminated with hope. My thoughts were of the others—those for whom equality is now but an abstraction.

I said, "You do not take a person who for years has been hobbled by chains and liberate him, bring him up to the starting line of a race, and say, 'you are free to compete with all the others,' and still justly believe that you have been completely fair.

"Thus it is not enough to open the gates of opportunity. All our citizens must have the ability to walk through those gates.

"This is the next and more profound stage of the battle for civil rights . . . the task is to give 20 million Negroes the same choice as every other American to learn and work and share in society, to develop their abilities—physical, mental, and spiritual—and to pursue their individual happiness."

No one who understands the complexity of this task is likely to promote simple means by which it may be accomplished. The papers that follow testify to the inter-locking effects of deprivation —in education, in housing, in employment, in citizenship, in the entire range of human endeavor by which personality is formed.

It will not be enough to provide better schools for Negro children, to inspire them to excel in their studies, if there are no decent jobs waiting for them after graduation. It will not be enough to open up job opportunities, if the Negro must remain trapped in a jungle of tenements and shanties. If we are to have peace at home, if we are to speak with one honest voice in the world—indeed, if our country is to live with its conscience—we must affect every dimension of the Negro's life for the better.

We have begun to do that—sometimes haltingly and in great trepidation, sometimes boldly and with a high heart. The will of government and of the people has been committed to resolving the long, bitter trial of the Negro American in the only way that was ever really possible: by including him in our society.

Some of these papers instruct us in the means by which that may be done. They are invaluable source materials for the White House Conference, which I have called "To Fulfill These Rights." For this contribution by the American Academy of Arts and Sciences, the participants in that conference—and all those who work for a just society—are profoundly grateful.

CONTENTS

III. Diagnostic Factors:
Personality, Identity, and Attitudes

IV. Sectors of the Society in Process of Change

V. *Fields and Proposals for Policy*

VI. *Two Sources of Pressure for Change: Internal and External*

VII. *Some General Perspectives and Prospects*

CONTENTS

*A photographic essay by Bruce Davidson, with
an Introduction by Arthur D. Trottenberg, will
be found following p. 448*

KENNETH B. CLARK

Introduction

The Dilemma of Power

THE NEW American Dilemma is one of power. The dilemma is a confrontation between those forces which impel a society to change and those which seek to maintain the past. This volume, in all of its essays, may be seen as a reflection of this theme.

Some chapters describe the nature of American racial patterns and their consequences. These are essentially diagnostic. They tell us what the past has bequeathed in terms of the symptoms of social and racial instability. The contributions, for example, by John Hope Franklin, St. Clair Drake, Daniel Patrick Moynihan, Lee Rainwater, and Rashi Fein, highlight for us the historical basis of the power conflict and the broad social and economic consequences of this particular form of institutionalized injustice. The contributions of Erik Erikson, Robert Coles, and Thomas Pettigrew, in particular, make clear for us the more personal anguish, the human meaning of racism in terms of the struggle for personal power, effectiveness, and identity. In Paul Sheatsley's essay, we find that white attitudes, too, reflect the subtle problem of identity, and the schizophrenia inherent in the struggle of human beings for belief in their goals of equality, liberty, and justice, in conflict with their desire to maintain a privilege, power, and status which are in conflict with their ideals.

But this problem is more than a rational dilemma; it is a deeper one reflecting the ethical confusion of man, a struggle similar to the attempt of Christianity to justify itself by what at times has been the raw exercise of naked power, as in the Inquisition, the Crusades, and in the plague of anti-Semitism. The fact is that man has never effectively resolved the issue of power versus ideals, or of power as an instrument of the maintenance of ideals, or of ideals themselves as a form of power, or of fundamental emotions, such as love and hatred, as primary sources of power. The American racial dilemma is merely one of the more recent manifestations of this prolonged confusion of man.

This dilemma is focused in America, particularly, because America has dared to attempt to develop a political system, which is essentially a power system, on the basis of ideals. This attempt has tended to sharpen the dilemma and the contradiction. The issues have been more consciously drawn and therefore have required the mobilization and use of machinery of government in seemingly endless attempts at reconciliation or resolution of those issues. Those essays in this volume on the question of the role of the federal government show the extent to which political, legislative, and judicial power have been used in attempts to bring about desired change.

Change has been defined, in American thought, as progress in the direction of America's ideals. American political machinery is therefore required to use its assumed power to move the society toward these ideal goals. The conflict between the ideal and the practice is seen throughout the various stages of American history. John Hope Franklin quotes Professor Rayford Logan, who described the post-Reconstruction period as the "nadir" of American race relations. In this period the power of the American political system was directed away from American ideals; the inferior status of the Negro and the privileged status of the white were articulated and enforced by political power.

Since the 1930's, American society has made an increasingly successful attempt to reverse this regression. In the New Deal, Franklin Roosevelt set in motion those forces of federal power which made inevitable the eventual federal intervention in problems of race. But the fact that even as great a liberal as Roosevelt had to be forced to express his general liberalism in the specific terms of race, indicates the basic and perennial contest between the power of maintaining the racial *status quo* and the power of liberal ideals.

The racial confrontation of the 1940's and 1950's was, nevertheless, precipitated by the Depression when masses of American whites found themselves economically deprived and abused. Out of their search for economic equity, when America came closer than it ever has before to overt class conflict, came the realization that political power had to be utilized to repair and set in motion an economic system that had broken down. Roosevelt was sufficiently free of the constraints of the past and the alleged constrictions of his "class" to use the power of the federal government for dramatic attempts at remedy. Thus the New Deal committed itself to economic justice, and set the stage for the present drama and movement toward racial justice.

It was an indication of the folk wisdom on the part of Negroes that they worshipped the Roosevelts in spite of the fact that FDR never clearly defined civil rights goals. This might be a reflection of their intuitive understanding that problems of racial equality had their roots in economic problems, and that, once the political power of the federal government had been harnessed for the attainment of economic equity, its use for the attainment of racial justice became inevitable. The 1940's and 1950's represent a concerted attempt on the part of civil rights workers, Negro and white, to facilitate that further use of power.

During the New Deal, economic justice was advanced through executive and legislative power, a reflection of the fact that the white majority—and even the South, which in some ways was the more liberal in matters of general economic equity—perceived that its fundamental interest was at stake. When the power of the majority faced the demand for racial justice, however—the demand of a minority for redress—the confusion of power versus ideals once again emerged. Those branches of government most responsive to the need for economic justice proved more resistant to the need for racial justice. To translate economic gains into racial gains, American society required another kind of confrontation. Therefore, that branch of government least responsive to the masses—the judiciary —was the most likely to respond—and did respond, particularly in the 1954 decision—to resolve the ambivalence of the society. Ironically, it was the judicial branch of the federal government which was least responsive to the people's demand for economic equity in the early years of the Roosevelt New Deal era.

Today, the civil rights movement has clearly been successful in terms of attaining the limited goals of enlisting all branches of the federal government in the commitment to use the power of the federal government in the struggle for the ideals of racial equality. In a sense, the ideals stated by Jefferson in terms of the nation as a whole were being met, as the white society had to accept, or certainly not resist massively and systematically, the attainment of these goals. The majority had now committed itself verbally to the redress of the grievances of the minority and accepted the re-

KENNETH B. CLARK

sponsibility of the federal government to include the Negro within the advantages and the promises of the American political system.

We could speculate why, at this juncture in world history, America has moved toward that goal which seemed so obvious in terms of its own ideals but which was so long in coming. One could point to the role of the two world wars, the role of industrialization and urbanization, the growing sense and need of national purpose, to the practical consequences of a unified country rather than a schizophrenic one at an awesome, complex, and challenging period of world history. But these speculations do not really contribute full understanding of the fact itself.

There was one thing it could *not* have been, however. The ideals *alone* could not and did not force their own transformation into constructive and consistent power for social change. Ideals, at best, are part of a constellation of practical power imperatives and sometimes have sufficient strength to require at least the verbal commitment to change in their direction. Yet the constellation of power is not itself an adequate explanation, for the same constellation of federal power, economic and industrial power, religious power, and even the influence of Negro leaders like Booker T. Washington in the latter part of the nineteenth century and the early part of the twentieth century, was mobilized for the retention of the *status quo,* served to maintain the racial *status quo.* For power in its various forms and configurations is amoral and can be used for the attainment of contradictory goals. That same constellation of power which once kept America at the "nadir" of race relations is now redirected to the opposite goal.

The missing ingredient that has forced the redirection of American power is not reflected in any of the papers contributed to this volume. It is not clear what that missing ingredient is. Not that one can accept the semi-mystical notion that right or justice tends, in the end, to prevail in terms of itself. Perhaps rather, America may have been caught with its ideals exposed by a new type of challenge in the world at large, by the emergence of an adversary which offered effective ideological, psychological, and military competition.

From this perspective, it is fascinating to inquire why Communism never was successful in appealing to large masses of American Negroes, even at the depths of the Depression. One possible explanation was the psychological mistake made by American Communists, who suggested a form of black nationalism, a new and naked segregation, as a solution. Another more subtle explanation may have been the fact that the Negro, since the Emancipation, had become immunized and somewhat cynical to egalitarian promises which had never been fulfilled for him within the American system. He had no more reason to expect them to be fulfilled in the white-dominated Soviet system. Despite all of its attempts to be raceless, American Communism was racist. This fact was evident and probably was intuitively felt by the Negro masses.

Still another factor affecting the present momentum in the use of federal power for positive change toward racial justice is the rise of nationalism in Asia and Africa. The whole world, in fact, has been undergoing a racial revolution, a breakdown in imperialism and a change in the relationship between white Europeans and the colored peoples of the world. White and Negro Americans could not escape the impact of this world-wide racial revolution. The irony is that this revolution reflected the basic power of the ideals of American, French, and Marxist thought—white European in origin. These essentially European ideas caused the overthrow of European-spawned imperialism. The ideals of justice cannot be contained by one culture or one race, by one privileged hierarchy or by geographic limitation. The democratic ferment unleashed in Europe in two world wars within one generation had to spill over in a demand for justice that was not to the limited advantage of the privileged creators of the ideals themselves.

The psychological and political realities force one to see that this type of revolutionary process could not proceed without profound ambivalence. Such manifestations of ambivalence are not to be found only on the international level but must be expected within America itself. No group of human beings can easily and graciously give up power and privilege. Such change can come only with conflict and anguish and the ever present threat of retrogression.

The ultimate power is the power of force, the power of the military, but military power can no longer alone determine decisions in the realm of national or racial status. America and the nations of Europe, and more recently Communist China, which control the ultimate military power, are restrained by the fact that they are not allied either ideologically or racially; their military nuclear power is balanced by differences and by the realization that the use of this ultimate power can destroy all human society. This balance and inhibition of power and its realization lead to a real advantage for the colored and lower-status peoples of the world. The world is now thrown back on other determinants of status. What has happened, whether we are now fully aware of it or not, is that the use of force for the maintenance of class, racial, economic, or national distinctions is no longer tolerable or possible. The revulsion against international war has infected the domestic society, as well, and we are no longer willing to allow violence to be the determinant of status in American society. Violence in the world and violence in the nation have become nonadaptive with the risk, in the world, of total conflagration, and the risk, at home, of destructive turmoil. So, even quasi-military power will not likely ever be used again in America for the maintenance of racial injustice. Even its use *for* the achievement of justice is seen as limited—the mobilization of military force at the University of Mississippi was transitional only and effected no basic change.

In America, during the last ten years, there has been a thrust, a new militance on the part of American Negroes determined to settle for nothing less than unqualified application of the American promise to them. They have been willing to risk everything by stark confrontation, and so, in the fascinating obbligato of nonviolence, Negroes employed a form of psychological power in confrontation with contrary power. The strategy of nonviolence reflects most obviously the fact that Negroes, in the minority, could not afford to be violent—except for the unplanned Watts type of violence, itself suicidal or a reflection of racial desperation. The historical and contemporary predicament of the Negro in America provides no basis for systematic military revolution. But beyond that lies the fact that violence, as a means of changing or maintaining status, is no longer acceptable in the latter part of the twentieth century. So, one finds in America the growing use of federal power to investigate and overthrow those last organized remnants of guerrilla warfare at home—the Ku Klux Klans, the White Citizens Councils, and allied groups.

The Negro, like the white, is forced to press his case by the use of techniques of power short of violence. In a sense this is the predicament of all the peoples of the world—but in the case of the oppressed, the predicament is a welcome one, for at this period of world history if violence is unavailable to the victim, so it is unavailable to the oppressor. Negroes at home, like the new nations of Asia and Africa, *could* be most effectively contained by unleashing violence against them, but the chance of this kind of barbaric retrogression has been severely lessened by the risk of larger impersonal forces that seem to restrict the forms and uses of available military power.

So a sophisticated concept of power countenancing only the use of more civilized forms has coincided with pragmatic needs. Even in the new nations of Africa, the attempts of Communist China to sell its perspective of the inevitability of a military confrontation between the two major competitive ideologies are resisted and are generally seen as inconsistent with the economic and industrial growth of these new nations or as the attempt on the part of the Chinese to substitute their form of racial arrogance, domination, and control—or as a combination of both.

In the United States, the Negro is exploring forms of power other than violence, or its counter, nonviolence, which tends to be most effective in the presence of imminence of violence. One can therefore understand the direction the civil rights movement is now taking, with Negroes demanding to be included in political decision-making or power positions. The sit-in demonstrations have given way to more specifically-oriented types of efforts, such as voter registration drives and campaigns for political office. Negroes, for the first time since Reconstruction are running for and winning seats in state legislatures and are competing for state-wide offices in Northern and Southern states. A Negro has been brought into the President's Cabinet without a single Southern vote against confirmation, though a few years ago the Cabinet position itself was defeated by a Congress which feared the prospect of a Negro's appointment. Negroes are also looking toward the goal of membership in the Supreme Court. All of these can be viewed as demands for inclusion in the political system. Nor can these goals be denied if the Negro is not forced back into the older and less adaptive forms of power-seeking. Should Negroes like Julian Bond be elected legitimately to office, only to be denied their post by sabotage of the democratic process, the Negro would lose hope in the potential of legal, non-violent means to achieve justice—and could be thrown back into a nadir of silent or strident despair.

The Negro must now be aware that no fundamental change in his status can come about through deference to or patronage from whites. He cannot have rights that are given as a gesture of good will (with the implication of the right to withdraw those rights). He is using the fuel of protest, formerly directed to demonstrations, to win inclusion in the power system itself. The recent activities of SNCC in political education, voter registration, and the formation of the Mississippi Freedom Democratic party are highly focused examples of this most recent civil rights development. The Negro is struggling to participate in the processes of democracy, convinced that the nation has gone beyond the stage when only the judiciary would sustain the minority toward a stage in which the executive and the legislative majority recognize his rights as just. The Negro, further, has gone beyond the level of the melting pot, beyond pluralism, beyond a sterile coexistence; he wants to participate fully in and to share the possibilities and the responsibilities of the American system. Although a political reality, it seems psychologically repugnant that this goal of inclusion be determined by ideological consensus among the white majority. Like every other group that has moved into a status of equality, the Negro has to be willing to accept all of the risks of the confrontation of power, including the risks of failure and retrogression. The alternative to these risks is a continuation of subtle or flagrant forms of tokenism and racism—or the transparent disguise of condescension.

What evidence is there that meaningful social change will be successful? The imperatives of world and national economic and political reality may have resulted in the conjunction of the practical and the ideal goals. My collaborator and co-editor, Professor Parsons, begins his introductory statement to this volume with a reference to Gunnar Myrdal's thesis as stated in *An American Dilemma* which was published in 1944. Given the eons of change which have taken place in the two crucial and turbulent decades since, I believe that it is appropriate and relevant for me to end my introductory essay with the words of Myrdal published in 1963 in his *Challenge to Affluence.* "Never in the history of America [and I should like to add in the history of the world] has there been a greater and more complete identity between the ideals of social justice and requirements of economic progress." This observation, if proven to be accurate, provides a substantive basis for optimism for the resolution of the American racial dilemma. The Myrdal of the 1960's appears to be dealing with a more substantive aspect of power as a factor in social change than the Myrdal of the 1940's. Ideals, alone, as demonstrated by this and similar volumes, do not bring justice. Ideals, combined with necessity, may.

TALCOTT PARSONS

Introduction
Why "Freedom Now," Not Yesterday?

THE EDITORS of this volume have been favored with something of a sinecure, since most of the ordinary editorial work has been done for them by the Editor and staff of *Dædalus* and by the Planning Group which met in the spring of 1964 to start the project. Indeed, our editorial functions have been confined to helping to work out the organization of the volume—given the papers already available and, with two exceptions, included in the two issues of *Dædalus* on which this book is based—and to writing these introductory statements. It is important to note that the editors had written their papers before they were invited to serve as editors.

The present project constitutes the most comprehensive survey of the problems and status of the Negro in American society since *An American Dilemma,* written by Gunnar Myrdal and his associates nearly a generation ago. It differs from the Myrdal study in one respect which must be made clear at the outset. It is not, and in the circumstances of its genesis could not be, the product of a unified research effort such as a responsible director and a professional staff could produce on the basis of several years' work. The coordination—dare we say "integration"?—brought about by the Planning Conference in the spring of 1964, by the larger conference more than a year later (when drafts of most of the papers had been circulated to the participants), and by the careful editorial work of the *Dædalus* staff, is necessarily not of the same order as that to be expected from a unified research project. In a sense not true of the Myrdal effort, each chapter in the present volume is the personal contribution of its author.

Not only is the present volume a different kind of study than Myrdal's, but much has changed in the subject matter itself in the intervening years, which will help explain the difference in tone as well as intellectual organization. Critical discussion of the Myrdal study involved disagreement about the importance of the "American Creed," which Myrdal thought significant for his expectation of improvement in the Negro's situation. Indeed the controversy continues in the present volume, with a minority asserting that *only* power can effect improvement. However this may be, there is a sense in which the issue was predominantly a moral one in the Myrdal period; despite the climate of social reform in the New Deal era, relatively little happened in the field of race relations. In the past few years, however, the situation has come "unstuck" in a way that makes us aware that not since Abolition have we witnessed such fundamental change. The legal implications of the 1954 Supreme Court decision on school desegregation, the bus boycotts, the lunch-counter sit-ins, the freedom rides, and the other protest demonstrations—these have accompanied and contributed to the emergence of a newly strong and organized civil rights movement. In 1964 and 1965, there were two major acts of Congress; the Executive Branch has been no less resolute. The nation's moral commitments have been immensely activated; it has been a time of action, and not only of moral stocktaking.

If the moral sentiments Myrdal described were really present, the problem of why so long a period elapsed before things began to happen is important. Indeed, this long "latency" has led some to deny that appreciable moral sentiments existed at all. The latency, in fact, extended for more than a generation before Myrdal wrote; there is a sense in which his book marked the beginning of change.

Though little happened in the field of civil rights as such, enormous changes occurred in American society and in the world at large during the latency period. Many of the salient facts are succinctly summarized in Mr. Drake's and Mr. Hauser's papers. They relate in the first instance to industrialization and urbanization, a process by which the structure of the society became increasingly differentiated and in certain senses pluralistic. The New Deal brought the first major governmental entry into the field of guaranteeing the *social* components of citizenship[1] through labor and social welfare legislation, establishing a trend which could readily be extended into the field of protecting minority groups. Combined with various other measures of governmental control, this entailed both a general strengthening of the federal government's administrative machinery and a general increase in popular support for such strengthening. Although it has been a bone of political contention ever since, this trend was a necessary prelude to the role recently assumed by the federal government in civil rights matters, as well as its support of large-scale education and anti-poverty programs. It is notable that this issue, so important in national politics, has forced the right wing of the Republican Party and the old-line Southern Democrats into an electoral coalition in Presidential politics, the consequences of which have broken the power of the Congressional coalition of Republicans and Southern Democrats, which for so many years effectively barred federal measures in the civil rights field.

Occurring at the same time were developments in the legal system, some of whose more recent phases are elegantly traced by Mr. Freund. These had their roots in the New Deal era and before. Yet, as Mr. Freund remarks, the courts had never before taken so strong an initiative in introducing changes over such a broad front. It is important to recognize that the recent innovations regarding civil rights are part of a much broader stream, one principal aspect of which has been the increasingly systematic extension of the Bill of Rights to the states through reinterpretation of the 14th Amendment. In our view, this broad legal development is part of a more general development of American society toward emancipating the individual from older types of particularistic involvement and toward making the individual's involvements in the various contexts of social relations increasingly independent of each other. For example, the white immigrant groups, notably the "new immigration" of the turn of the century, have been rapidly diffusing themselves through the social structure in this way; it is no longer safe to infer that a person has a working-class occupation from knowing that he is a Catholic of Irish descent. In the present situation, the special position of the Negro, as occupying a "total" status by virtue of his race, has become increasingly anomalous.

Two specific features of change in the position of the Negro community are particularly important. The first is the massive migration from the rural South to the cities, particularly to the Northern cities, but also, because of the South's general modernization, to the Southern cities. The political developments which Mr. Wilson illustrates with Atlanta would have been inconceivable in the South only a short time ago. The great Northern "ghettos" seem to be the focus of the most acute distress and tension now that the phase of concern with legal and voting rights has begun to reach the stage of "mopping-up operations" in the South. This is not to say that bitter die-hard resistance in the South will not be encountered.

In spite of enormous distress, the migration to the cities has led to a very substantial upgrading of the Negro in many respects. Recently, there has been a lag in the rate of upgrading Negroes compared to that of the white population in fields like health and education, but the trend of Negro "welfare" has certainly been upward. That is clear even in the relatively "pessimistic" papers of Messrs. Moynihan and Fein. In our view the most important consequences of this change derive from the release of the Negro masses from the social isolation of the rural South, and their exposure to the main absorptive forces of the larger society. As part of this exposure, increasing proportions of Negroes have, as people whose position has recently improved substantially, become more acutely aware than before of their *relatively* disadvantaged position. Indeed this general situation has had much to do with the activation of the issue in the nation as a whole, on both sides of the racial line.

The second major change in the position of the Negro community is the emergence of an increasingly large and competent Negro "middle class," especially as participants in the higher reaches of the occupational system where substantial educational qualifications are required. As Mr. Foley shows, the participation of Negroes in the business world has been minimal at the entrepreneurial and executive levels—partly as a result of white discrimination. Therefore, it may be significant that the society has been moving away from the former predominance of business and toward greater prominence of the professional and government sectors, where Negroes are far less handicapped. Several of the papers refer to the rapid development of this Negro middle-class and the good prospects for its growth and further inclusion in the national community. A major worry, however, has been occasioned by the tendency for these successful groups to become dissociated from the Negro masses.

Not the least of the changes occurring since Myrdal wrote *An American Dilemma* have been those outside the United States. These have enormously enhanced the American position of power and its symbolic importance in the world. The breakdown of the colonial system, the emergence into independence, and the beginning of "development" in so many formerly colonial societies has, as Messrs. Emerson and Kilson so strongly emphasize, enormously changed the world-wide symbolic significance of the American color problem. In particular, the political independence of so many sub-Saharan Africans nations has provided a considerable symbolic stimulus to the Negro movement in this country. Diplomatic representation of the new nations in Washington and the presence of the United Nations headquarters in New York has underlined the new situation and acutely posed the international significance of problems of discrimination.

However incomplete the above sketch of changes in the last generation may be (many are discussed much more fully in papers in this volume), we think that factors of this kind explain why the status of the Negro American has now become so much more than "only" a moral issue. Our emphasis is on the "more than." It surely is just as much a moral issue now as it was in the 1930's and early 1940's, as (among others) Father Fichter has indicated in outlining the involvement of religious groups with these matters. The importance of its moral aspects is underlined by the fact that American society is not only complex and changing, but also pluralistic in a manner making it impossible for many—even (or especially) very vital—problems to be in the forefront of public attention and generalized political action at any one time. In recent decades, the problems of two world wars, the Great Depression with its complex relations to the New Deal, the Cold War with its culmination in the Berlin airlift and the Korean War, the serious internal crisis of McCarthyism, again directly related to the Cold War, have all commanded attention. Hence, it is possible to argue that the latency of even a very major issue is not necessarily abnormal; all issues have been subject to severe competition for the center of the stage. Without its strong *moral* resonance, it is possible that civil rights might even now have great difficulty in capturing attention.

The racial issue had been generating pressure for a considerable time. Its emergence now as a principal concern is in part at least the result of the nation's having cleared away its preoccupations with the Second World War and its aftermath, which included Korea and McCarthyism, and the end to the political quietism characteristic of the Eisenhower administration. The first major break came with the 1954 Supreme Court decision; then occurred Little Rock with its dramatization not only of Southern resistance, but of the federal government's passivity. With the election of a liberal Democratic administration in 1960, expectations began to mount rapidly.

Indeed, the emergence of the problem into prominence, even on this level, seems to have depended, in addition to its inherent pressure for attention, on *two* independent sets of circumstances. First, there developed at least a temporary easing of the political tensions resulting from the new American position in the world power system—tensions which, except for the brief period of the early New Deal, had long inhibited domestic reform. Second, a new postwar generation, impatient with the cautious conservatism typified by Eisenhower, began to press for a program of active change. The election of Kennedy in 1960 was certainly a turning point. The moral sentiments, particularly strong among the activists of the younger group of both races, began to have an effect.

It is our view, as social scientists, that the type of social change now occurring, which involves a new level of institutionalization of the values of equality in our society (as Mr. Moynihan so clearly stated in the 1965 Conference), requires a complex combination of conditioning factors. The papers in this volume consider the whole range of such factors; they analyze the actual processes of, and prospects for, change. They suggest that the state of American society, probably as late as Myrdal's study and certainly at the turn of the century, was such that a powerful movement toward inclusion of the Negro *could not* have been generated despite the egalitarian moral standards which were widespread and genuine for most of the nation.[2]

Only in a highly urbanized, hence individualized and pluralized, society does the opportunity emerge for a saliently different minority group to diffuse itself through the society. Only then does its position become so anomalous as to activate strong pressures to break up its monolithic separateness, even if, as in some historic cases (for example, certain Jewish communities), it is a privileged separateness.

There has been much controversy about whether the processes of inclusion of the earlier Jewish and Catholic immigrants and those of Negroes are in any way comparable. Certainly, there are many differences. One, emphasized particularly by Mr. Hughes at the 1965 Conference, was that, at the turn of the century, a huge demand existed for unskilled labor. There is no equivalent need now. Another is the sheer magnitude of the problem created by the size of the Northern urban concentrations of Negroes. It must be remembered, in this connection, that the whole society has grown enormously. Moreover, the federal government now constitutes a far more powerful agency of collective action than any which existed in the earlier period. Popular support has articulated a very far-reaching commitment of that agency to advance the process of inclusion.

The most serious difference of all, perhaps, is not color, as such, but the fact that historically the Negro has served as the primary *symbol* of inferiority. As Mr. Franklin makes clear, this meaning has by no means been confined to the South, but has been widespread among even the "best people," at least until very recently, in the North. As my co-editor tries to make clear in his paper, the very definition of a *category* of citizens as inherently inferior is an anomaly which the developments sketched above have increasingly revealed as basically incompatible with our social principles and organization. The type of modern society which we have been developing has for *both* moral and structural reasons *no* legitimate place for such a category.

Because of this factor, symbolized by differences of color, inclusion of the Negro seems to constitute the most difficult problem of this character ever faced by our nation. This is partly responsible for, and is vastly complicated by, other differences, such as the low demand for Negro labor, stressed by Mr. Tobin, and the problems of the urban Negro family, emphasized by Messrs. Moynihan and Rainwater. The principal counter to the pessimism readily generated by these and certain other difficulties weighed by the authors of various papers in this volume, lies in the strength of a *combination* of factors which have already begun to promote inclusion, and which almost certainly will be greatly strengthened in the coming years, unless the main developmental trend of the society is unexpectedly interrupted.

Not the least of these factors is the civil rights movement itself. Mr. Freund, at our conference, spoke of the legally acceptable type of civil disobedience as that which was "nonviolent," "symbolic," "aimed at the conscience."[3] This formula can perhaps be generalized to characterize the role of the movement as a whole. Particularly in the accelerating phase of the last five years, it has provided, along with the Supreme Court, the most important single link between the moral values which Myrdal emphasized and the present processes of implementation of those values. The movement has certainly been a direct agent for bringing about certain specific changes, such as the desegregation of schools, lunch counters, and bus stations. However, its more important function has been symbolic; it has dramatized the moral issue in terms which make concrete continuance of the old practices morally intolerable.

In doing so, it has benefited not only from the federal government, to which it has quite self-consciously appealed, but also from the mass media, which have spread its message far and wide, not only in this country but throughout the world. The movement brought together considerable, though still "token," elements of both races in a *common* moral cause, perhaps most conspicuously in the Selma episode of the spring of 1965. This has been particularly poignant in those instances where white persons have given their lives for the common cause. Not least important among the consequences of the movement has been its contribution to the current moral "reenergizing" of American society.

Although the problem of such reenergizing goes somewhat beyond our direct concern, a brief discussion may contribute to an understanding of the setting of the racial issue in American society. Mr. Freund has spoken of the legal "pour-over." Among its most important aspects, as mentioned above, is the generalized clarification of the legal status of civil disobedience. Beyond this, however, the civil rights issue could not have become nearly so general an issue for the American system if it had not engaged very large and diverse elements of the population in one way or another. We have emphasized the participation of many categories of whites in the movement itself, and in various kinds of support of the "cause." Indeed, the prominent role of the federal government would not be understandable without this, for the American system requires strong political "pressure" from *various* sectors of the public to generate this magnitude of governmental action. The very genesis of such strong political support, however, serves to activate resistance. So far this has been most conspicuous in the South, and has in turn stimulated the genesis of the more radical elements in the civil rights movement itself.

Here we have an important example of the generalization of movements for social change, a process which matches that of the generalization of support (as well as resistance) on a particular issue, such as civil rights. The shape that the so-called "New Left" will take is still far from clear. On two points, however, there seems to be agreement among interpreters who would differ greatly in other respects: its centering on youth and the salience of civil rights problems as its point of departure. Besides the involvement of these elements in the movement itself, as (in Mr. Clark's description) embodied first in CORE and then more radically in SNCC, the most important point here is that the same groups, by and large, have now taken up protest in two other important contexts, namely, higher education (most conspicuously at Berkeley) and the American involvement in the war in Viet-Nam.[4]

Extended discussion of these latter issues is not appropriate here. The main point we wish to make is that they constitute a generalization of an attitudinal complex beyond its original focus. This phenomenon may be interpreted in the context of American pluralism. On the one hand, the effectiveness of the civil rights movement has depended directly upon coalitions between various elements, Negro and white, radical and "conservative," "Establishment" and "anti-Establishment." As Dr. Coles has suggested,[5] the more radical elements of the movement have shown much ambivalence about the high degree of involvement with the federal government. Indeed, getting the government to act has been the principal aim of protests, yet the government has been, for the radicals, the primary symbol of a corrupt system. On the other hand, the broader coalitions constitute a threat to the independence of such a radical movement. The generalization to other *issues* may then be interpreted as a "compensatory" mechanism, to preserve the integrity of its radicalism and to tap sources of support which are not particularly resonant to the civil rights issue.

If continued indefinitely, such a process would result in the polarization of the society between the "radicals" and their opponents. American society, however, seems to have reached a level of pluralization which makes it unlikely that any polarization process can get so far. After a point, generalization is likely to be checked on both sides of the issue by the involvement of the relevant population elements in other issues which cannot be identified too directly with the initial point of reference.

The *timing* of the salience of a major issue—the problem with which this introductory discussion started—therefore points to certain major features of the society. The process of social change which characterizes this type of society is not "total revolution," but focus on one or a few salient "problems" at any one time. The status of the Negro American is probably *the* salient internal problem of this period in our history. The prospects for its relatively satisfactory resolution depend on a combination of factors. Not least among these are the pluralistic institutional frameworks of the society, which make such processes of change procedurally possible with quite limited violent overturn, and the moral values characterized by Myrdal as the American creed.

REFERENCES

1. Cf. my own paper, "Full Citizenship for the Negro American," in this volume, pp. 709–754; and T. H. Marshall, *Class Citizenship and Social Development* (Garden City, N. Y., 1964) Ch. IV.

2. See C. Vann Woodward's remarks in "Transcript of the American Academy Conference on the Negro American—May 14–15, 1965," in *Dædalus* (Winter 1966), pp. 379 ff.

3. See Paul Freund's remarks in *ibid.*, p. 379.

4. This generalization may well not redound to the benefit of the civil rights movement because it disperses forces and activates other forms of resistance.

5. "Transcript of the American Academy Conference," *op. cit.*, pp. 381 ff.

ACKNOWLEDGMENTS

The Editors wish to express their appreciation to the authors included in this volume and also to the following people who participated in the conferences held at the House of the American Academy of Arts and Sciences, and without whose counsel and cooperation this volume could not have been produced: Daniel Bell, Edwin C. Berry, Wiley Branton, James P. Breeden, Oscar Cohen, Ralph Ellison, Clifford Geertz, Hudson Hoagland, Carl Kaysen, Max Lerner, Edward H. Levi, Hylan Lewis, Jean Mayer, Robert Merton, Guichard Parris, Saunders Redding, Peter H. Rossi, William M. Schmidt, and C. Vann Woodward.

To Professor Stephen R. Graubard, the Editor of the Academy and of the journal *Dædalus*, we wish to express our special thanks for the devoted and effective help which he has so willingly given on all questions related to this project. A great portion of any success with which this volume meets will be owing to his thoughtful efforts in its preparation.

Finally, the Carnegie Corporation is to be thanked for its generous grant to the American Academy of Arts and Sciences for this undertaking.

I

GENERAL BACKGROUND

ST. CLAIR DRAKE

The Social and Economic Status of the Negro
in the United States

Caste, Class, and "Victimization"

DURING THE 1930's, W. Lloyd Warner and Allison Davis developed and popularized a conceptual scheme for analyzing race relations in the Southern region of the United States which viewed Negro-white relations as organized by a color-caste system that shaped economic and political relations as well as family and kinship structures, and which was reinforced by the legal system. Within each of the two castes (superordinate white and subordinate Negro), social classes existed, status being based upon possession of money, education, and family background as reflected in distinctive styles of behavior. "Exploitation" in the Marxist sense was present within this caste-class system, but also much more; for an entire socio-cultural system, not just the economic order, functioned to distribute power and prestige unevenly between whites and Negroes and to punish any individuals who questioned the system by word or behavior.[1]

Students of the situation in the North rarely conceptualized race relations in terms of caste, but tended rather to view specific communities as areas in which *ethnic* groups were involved in continuous competition and conflict, resulting in a hierarchy persisting through time, with now one, and again another, ethnic group at the bottom as previous newcomers moved "up." Each ethnic group developed a social class structure within it, but as individuals acquired better jobs, more education, and some sophistication, they and their families often detached themselves from immigrant colonies (usually located in slum areas) and sometimes from all ethnic institutions as well. They tended to become a part of the middle class. The Negroes who migrated North in large numbers during World War I were the latest arrivals in this fluid and highly competitive situation, but their high visibility became a crucial factor limiting their upward mobility. Upwardly mobile Negroes could not "dis-

3

appear" into the middle class of the larger society as did European ethnics.[2]

Thus, on the eve of World War II, students of race relations in the United States generally described the status of Negroes as one in which they played subordinate roles in a caste system in the South and an ethnic-class system in the North. The actions of persons toward those of another race were explained not in terms of some vaguely defined emotions connected with "prejudice," but rather in terms of the behavior they felt was expected of them by others in various positions within the social structure, and as attempts to protect and maximize whatever power and prestige accrued to them at their locus in the system. John Dollard, a psychologist, in his *Caste and Class in a Southern Town,* added an additional dimension. He analyzes the situation in terms of the "gains" and "losses"—sexual, psychological, economic, and political —which both Negroes and whites sustained at different levels in the Southern caste-class system.[3]

The caste-class analysis still provides a useful frame of reference for studying the behavior of individuals and groups located at various positions in the social structure. It can also serve as a starting point for viewing the *processes* of race relations in terms of their consequences. Of the racial and ethnic groups in America only Negroes have been subjected to caste-deprivations; and the ethnic-class system has operated to their disadvantage as compared with European immigrants. In other words, Negroes in America have been subject to "victimization" in the sense that a system of social relations operates in such a way as to deprive them of a chance to share in the more desirable material and non-material products of a society which is dependent, in part, upon their labor and loyalty. They are "victimized," also, because they do not have the same degree of access which others have to the attributes needed for rising in the general class system—money, education, "contacts," and "know-how."

The concept of "victimization" implies, too, that some people are used as means to other people's ends—without their consent—and that the social system is so structured that it can be deliberately manipulated to the disadvantage of some groups by the clever, the vicious, and the cynical, as well as by the powerful. The callous and indifferent unconsciously and unintentionally reinforce the system by their inaction or inertia. The "victims," their autonomy curtailed and their self-esteem weakened by the operation of the caste-class system, are confronted with "identity problems." Their social condition is essentially one of "powerlessness."

Individual "victims" may or may not accept the rationalizations given for the denial to them of power and prestige. They may or may not be aware of and concerned about their position in the system, but, when they do become concerned, victimization takes on important social psychological dimensions. Individuals then suffer feelings of "relative deprivation" which give rise to reactions ranging from despair, apathy, and withdrawal to covert and overt aggression. An effective analysis of the position of the Negro in these terms (although the word "victimization" is never used) may be found in Thomas F. Pettigrew's *A Profile of the Negro American* (1964).

Concepts developed by Max Weber are useful for assessing the degree of victimization existing within the American caste-class system.[4] Individuals and groups can be compared by examining what he refers to as "life chances," that is, the extent to which people have access to economic and political power. *Direct victimization* might be defined as the operation of sanctions which deny access to power, which limit the franchise, sustain job discrimination, permit unequal pay for similar work, or provide inferior training or no training at all. *Indirect victimization* is revealed in the consequences which flow from a social structure which decreases "*life chances,*" such as high morbidity and mortality rates, low longevity rates, a high incidence of psychopathology, or the persistence of personality traits and attitudes which impose disadvantages in competition or excite derogatory and invidious comparisons with other groups. Max Weber also compared individuals and groups in terms of differences in "*life styles,*" those ways of behaving which vary in the amount of esteem, honor, and prestige attached to them. Differences in "life chances" may make it impossible to acquire the money or education (or may limit the contacts) necessary for adopting and maintaining prestigious life styles. The key to understanding many aspects of race relations may be found in the fact that, in American society, the protection of their familiar and cherished life styles is a dominating concern of the white middle classes, who, because many Negroes have life styles differing from their own, have tried to segregate them into all-Negro neighborhoods, voluntary associations, and churches.[5] (Marxist sociologists tend to overemphasize protection of economic interests as a dynamic factor in American race relations, important though it is.)

The "Ghettoization" of Negro Life

Pressure upon Negroes to live within all-Negro neighborhoods has resulted in those massive concentrations of Negro population in Northern metropolitan areas which bitter critics call "concentration camps" or "plantations" and which some social scientists refer to as "Black Ghettos."[6] Small town replicas exist everywhere throughout the nation, for the roots of residential segregation lie deep in American history. In older Southern towns slave quarters were transformed into Negro residential areas after Emancipation—a few blocks here, a whole neighborhood there, often adjacent to white homes. In newer Southern towns and cities a less secure upwardly mobile white population usually demanded a greater degree of segregation from ex-slaves and their descendants. Prior to World War I, the residential patterns did not vary greatly between North and South, but the great northward migration of Negroes between 1914 and 1920 expanded the small Negro neighborhoods into massive Black Belts. Middle-class white neighbors used "restrictive-covenants" as their main device for slowing down and "containing" the expansion of Negro neighborhoods. Thus, with continued in-migration and restricted access to housing in "white neighborhoods," the overcrowded Black Ghetto emerged with its substandard structures, poor public services, and high crime and juvenile delinquency rates.

Scholars know from careful research, and increasingly wider circles are becoming aware of the fact, that Negroes do not depress property values, but that middle-class white attitudes toward Negroes do.[7] As long as Negroes, as a group, are a symbol of lower social status, proximity to them will be considered undesirable and such social attitudes will be reflected in the market place. The problem is complicated by the fact that a very high proportion of Negro Americans actually does have lower-class attributes and behavior patterns. The upward mobility of white Americans, as well as their comfort and personal safety, is facilitated by spatial segregation. (Older cities in the South have been an exception.) The white middle class could protect its values by acting solely in terms of class, letting middle-class Negro families scatter into white neighborhoods irrespective of race. Instead, the white middle class in American cities protects its own neighborhoods from behavior patterns it disapproves of and from chronic social disorganization by "ghettoizing" the Negro. Real-estate operators, black and white, have exploited the fears of the white middle class from the beginning of the northern migration by "block busting," that is, by buying property for less than its normal market value and reselling it at a higher price to Negroes barred from the open market or by charging them higher rentals. Eventually the profit-potential in residential segregation was maximized by the institutions which controlled mortgage money and refused to finance property for Negro residence outside of the Black Belts except under conditions approved by them.

In 1948, the Supreme Court declared racial restrictive covenants unenforceable in the courts, but this action tended to accelerate rather than reverse the process of ghettoization, for many whites proceeded to sell to Negroes at inflated prices and then moved to the suburbs, or they retained their properties, moved away, and raised the rents. The Court's decision was based partly upon a re-evaluation of the concept of civil rights and partly upon a recognition of the fact that serious economic injustice was a by-product of residential segregation, a situation summed up by Thomas Pettigrew:

> While some housing gains occurred in the 1950's, the quality of Negro housing remains vastly inferior relative to that of whites. For example, in Chicago in 1960, Negroes paid as much for housing as whites, despite their lower incomes. . . . This situation exists because of essentially two separate housing markets; and the residential segregation that creates these dual markets has increased steadily over past decades until it has reached universally high levels in cities throughout the United States, despite significant advances in the socio-economic status of Negroes. . . .[8]

The trend has not yet been reversed despite F.H.A. administrative regulations and Supreme Court decisions.

The spatial isolation of Negroes from whites created Negro "communities." Within these Negro neighborhoods, church and school became the basic integrative institutions, and Negro entrepreneurs developed a variety of service enterprises—barbershops and beauty parlors, funeral homes and restaurants, pool parlors, taverns, and hotels—all selling to what came to be called "The Negro Market." Successful banking and insurance businesses also grew up within some Negro communities. A Negro "subculture" gradually emerged, national in scope, with distinctive variations upon the general American culture in the fields of literature, art, music, and dance, as well as in religious ritual and church polity.

The spatial isolation of Negroes from whites in "Black Belts" also increased consciousness of their separate subordinate position, for no whites were available to them as neighbors, schoolmates, or friends, but were present only in such roles as school teachers, policemen, and social workers, flat janitors and real-estate agents, merchants and bill collectors, skilled laborers involved in maintenance, and even a few white dentists and doctors with offices in the Black Belt. Such a situation inevitably generated anti-white sentiments (often with anti-Semitic overtones), and the pent-up feelings have occasionally erupted in anti-white riots. Normally, however, this intense racial consciousness finds expression in non-violent forms of social protest and is utilized by Negro leaders to sanction and reinforce Negro institutions and their own personal welfare. It has also lent powerful support to the segments of municipal political machines existing within Negro neighborhoods. As long as ghettos remain, race consciousness will be strong.

Residential segregation created the demographic and ecological basis for "balance of power" politics, since the possibility of a Negro bloc vote had to be recognized by both political parties. Northern Black Belt voters are not only occasionally the decisive factor in municipal elections, but have also sent a half-dozen Negroes to Congress. Indeed, it is ironic that one of the most effective weapons against segregation and discrimination in the South has been the political power generated in Negro precincts and wards of Northern Black Ghettos, thus reinforcing the direct action tactics of the civil rights movement. In the South, too, with the passage of the Civil Rights Act of 1964 and subsequent legislation, the political strength of newly enfranchised voters lies in their spatial concentration. There is some evidence that fear of this strength may operate as a factor in Northern cities to support "open occupancy," desegregation being considered preferable to Negro dominance.[9]

While the development of machine politics has brought some gains to Negro communities, it has also resulted in various forms of indirect victimization. Local Negro leaders often co-operate with the city-wide machine in the protection of "the rackets"—policy, dope, and prostitution—and sacrifice group welfare to personal gain for self and party. They have not hesitated, in some places, even to drag their heels in the fight for residential desegregation rather than risk wiping out the base of their power. Being saddled with a "bought leadership" is one of the greatest burdens Black Ghettos have had to bear. Economic victimization is widespread, too. In the "affluent society" of the sixties, consumption-oriented and given to the "hard sell," Negroes like other Americans are under social pressure to spend beyond their means. Given the lack of sophistication of many recent migrants and the very low median income of those with less than a high-school education, it is not surprising that loan sharks and dubious credit merchants (of all races) make the Black Ghetto a prime target. Negroes pay a high price for "protection" of the white middle-class way of life, since those who aspire to leave the ghetto are trapped, and those who are content to stay develop a limited and restricted view of the world in which they live.

Folkways and Classways Within the Black Ghetto

Black Ghettos in America are, on the whole, "run down" in appearance and overcrowded, and their inhabitants bear the physical and psychological scars of those whose "life chances" are not equal to those of other Americans. Like the European immigrants before them, they inherited the worst housing in the city. Within the past decade, the white "flight to the suburbs" has released relatively new and well-kept property on the margins of some of the old Black Belts. Here, "gilded ghettos" have grown up, indistinguishable from any other middle-class neighborhoods except by the color of the residents' skin.[10] The power mower in the yard, the steak grill on the rear lawn, a well stocked library and equally well stocked bar in the rumpus room—these mark the homes of well-to-do Negroes living in the more desirable portions of the Black Belt. Many of them would flee to suburbia, too, if housing were available to Negroes there.

But the character of the Black Ghetto is not set by the newer "gilded," not-yet run down portions of it, but by the older sections where unemployment rates are high and the masses of people work with their hands—where the median level of education is just above graduation from grade school and many of the people are likely to be recent migrants from rural areas.[11]

The "ghettoization" of the Negro has resulted in the emergence of a ghetto subculture with a distinctive ethos, most pronounced, perhaps, in Harlem, but recognizable in all Negro neighborhoods. For the average Negro who walks the streets of any American Black Ghetto, the smell of barbecued ribs, fried shrimps, and chicken emanating from numerous restaurants gives olfactory reinforcement to a feeling of "at-homeness." The beat of "gut music" spilling into the street from ubiquitous tavern juke boxes and the sound of tambourines and rich harmony behind the crude folk art on the windows of store-front churches give auditory confirmation to the universal belief that "We Negroes have 'soul.'" The bedlam of an occasional brawl, the shouted obscenities of street corner "foul mouths," and the whine of police sirens break the monotony of waiting for the number that never "falls," the horses that neither win, place, nor show, and the "good job" that never materializes. The insouciant swagger of teen-age drop-outs (the "cats") masks the hurt of their aimless existence and contrasts sharply with the ragged clothing and dejected demeanor of "skid-row" types who have long since stopped trying to keep up appearances and who escape it all by becoming "winoes." The spontaneous vigor of the children who crowd streets and playgrounds (with Cassius Clay, Ernie Banks, the Harlem Globe Trotters, and black stars of stage, screen, and television as their role models) and the cheerful rushing about of adults, free from the occupational pressures of the "white world" in which they work, create an atmosphere of warmth and superficial intimacy which obscures the unpleasant facts of life in the overcrowded rooms behind the doors, the lack of adequate maintenance standards, and the too prevalent vermin and rats.

This is a world whose urban "folkways" the upwardly mobile Negro middle class deplores as a "drag" on "The Race," which the upper classes wince at as an embarassment, and which race leaders point to as proof that Negroes have been victimized. But for the masses of the ghetto dwellers this is a warm and familiar milieu, preferable to the sanitary coldness of middle-class neighborhoods and a counterpart of the communities of the foreign-born, each of which has its own distinctive subcultural flavor. The arguments in the barbershop, the gossip in the beauty parlors, the "jiving" of bar girls and waitresses, the click of poolroom balls, the stomping of feet in the dance halls, the shouting in the churches are all *theirs*— and the white men who run the pawnshops, supermarts, drug stores, and grocery stores, the policemen on horseback, the teachers in blackboard jungles—all these are aliens, conceptualized collectively as "The Man," intruders on the Black Man's "turf." When an occasional riot breaks out, "The Man" and his property become targets of aggression upon which pent-up frustrations are vented. When someone during the Harlem riots of 1964 begged the street crowds to go home, the cry came back, "Baby, we *are* home!"

But the inhabitants of the Black Ghetto are not a homogeneous mass. Although, in Marxian terms, nearly all of them are "proletarians," with nothing to sell but their labor, variations in "life style" differentiate them into social classes based more upon differences in education and basic values (crystallized, in part, around occupational differences) than in meaningful differences in income. The American caste-class system has served, over the years, to concentrate the Negro population in the low-income sector of the economy. In 1961, six out of every ten Negro families had an income of less than $4000.00 per year. This situation among whites was just the reverse: six out of every ten white families had *over* $4000.00 a year at their disposal. (In the South, eight out of ten Negro families were below the $4000.00 level.) This is the income gap. Discrimination in employment creates a job ceiling, most Negroes being in blue-collar jobs.

With 60 per cent of America's Negro families earning less than $4000.00 a year, social strata emerge between the upper and lower boundaries of "no earned income" and $4000.00. Some families live a "middle-class style of life," placing heavy emphasis upon decorous public behavior and general respectability, insisting that their children "get an education" and "make something out of themselves." They prize family stability, and an unwed mother is something much more serious than "just a girl who had an accident"; pre-marital and extra-marital sexual relations, if indulged in at all, must be discreet. Social life is organized around churches and a welter of voluntary associations of all types, and, for women, "the cult of clothes" is so important that fashion shows are a popular fund raising activity even in churches. For both men and women, owning a home and going into business are highly desired goals, the former often being a realistic one, the latter a mere fantasy.

Within the same income range, and not always at the lower margin of it, other families live a "lower-class life-style" being part of the "organized" lower class, while at the lowest income levels an "unorganized" lower class exists whose members tend always to become *dis*organized—functioning in an anomic situation where gambling, excessive drinking, the use of narcotics, and sexual promiscuity are prevalent forms of behavior, and violent interpersonal relations reflect an ethos of suspicion and resentment which suffuses this deviant subculture. It is within this milieu that criminal and semi-criminal activities burgeon.

The "organized" lower class is oriented primarily around churches whose preachers, often semi-literate, exhort them to "be in the 'world' but not of it." Conventional middle-class morality and Pauline Puritanism are preached, although a general attitude of "the spirit is willing but the flesh is weak" prevails except among a minority fully committed to the Pentecostal sects. They boast, "We *live* the life"—a way of life that has been portrayed with great insight by James Baldwin in *Go Tell it on the Mountain* and *The Fire Next Time.*

Young people with talent find wide scope for expressing it in choirs, quartets, and sextets which travel from church to church (often bearing colorful names like The Four Heavenly Trumpets or the Six Singing Stars of Zion) and sometimes traveling from city to city. Such groups channel their aggressions in widely advertised "Battles of Song" and develop their talent in church pageants such as "Heaven Bound" or "Queen Esther" and fund-raising events where winners are crowned King and Queen. These activities provide fun as well as a testing ground for talent. Some lucky young church people eventually find their fortune in the secular world as did singers Sam Cooke and Nat King Cole, while others remain in the church world as nationally known gospel singers or famous evangelists.

Adults as well as young people find satisfaction and prestige in serving as ushers and deacons, "mothers," and deaconesses, Sunday-school teachers and choir leaders. National conventions of Negro denominations and national societies of ushers and gospel singers not only develop a continent-wide nexus of associations within the organized lower class, but also throw the more ambitious and capable individuals into meaningful contact with middle-class church members who operate as role models for those talented persons who seek to move upward. That prestige and sometimes money come so easily in these circles may be a factor militating against a pattern of delaying gratifications and seeking mobility into professional and semi-professional pursuits through higher education.

Lower-class families and institutions are constantly on the move, for in recent years the Negro lower class has suffered from projects to redevelop the inner city. By historic accident, the decision to check the expansion of physical deterioration in metropolitan areas came at a time when Negroes were the main inhabitants of substandard housing. (If urban redevelopment had been necessary sixty years ago immigrants, not Negroes, would have suffered.) In protest against large-scale demolition of areas where they live, Negroes have coined a slogan, "Slum clearance is Negro clearance."

They resent the price in terms of the inconvenience thrust upon them in order to redevelop American cities,[12] and the evidence shows that, in some cities, there is no net gain in improved housing after relocation.

At the opposite pole from the Negro lower class in both life styles and life chances is the small Negro upper class whose solid core is a group in the professions, along with well-to-do businessmen who have had some higher education, but including, also, a scattering of individuals who have had college training but do not have a job commensurate with their education. These men and their spouses and children form a cohesive upper-class stratum in most Negro communities. Within this group are individuals who maintain some type of contact—though seldom any social relations—with members of the local white power élite; but whether or not they participate in occupational associations with their white peers depends upon the region of the country in which they live. (It is from this group that Negro "Exhibit A's" are recruited when white liberals are carrying on campaigns to "increase interracial understanding.") They must always think of themselves as symbols of racial advancement as well as individuals, and they often provide the basic leadership at local levels for organizations such as the N.A.A.C.P. and the Urban League. They must lend sympathetic support to the more militant civil rights organizations, too, by financial contributions, if not action.[13]

The life styles of the Negro upper class are similar to those of the white upper *middle* class, but it is only in rare instances that Negroes have been incorporated into the clique and associational life of this group or have intermarried into it. (Their participation in activities of the white upper class occurs more often than with those whites who have similar life styles because of Negro upper-class participation as members of various civic boards and interracial associations to which wealthy white people contribute.) Living "well" with highly developed skills, having enough money to travel, Negroes at this social level do not experience victimization in the same fashion as do the members of the lower class. Their victimization flows primarily from the fact that the social system keeps them "half in and half out," preventing the free and easy contact with their occupational peers which they need; and it often keeps them from making the kind of significant intellectual and social contributions to the national welfare that they might make if they were white. (They are also forced to experience various types of nervous

strain and dissipation of energy over petty annoyances and deprivations which only the sensitive and the cultivated feel. Most barbershops, for instance, are not yet desegregated, and taxi drivers, even
in the North, sometimes refuse Negro passengers.)

The Negro upper class has created a social world of its own in
which a universe of discourse and uniformity of behavior and outlook are maintained by the interaction on national and local levels
of members of Negro Greek-letter fraternities and sororities, college
and alumni associations, professional associations, and civic and
social clubs. It is probable that if all caste barriers were dropped, a
large proportion of the Negro upper class would welcome complete
social integration, and that these all-Negro institutions would be
left in the hands of the Negro middle class, as the most capable
and sophisticated Negroes moved into the orbit of the general society. Their sense of pride and dignity does not even allow them to
imagine such a fate, and they pursue their social activities and play
their roles as "race leaders" with little feeling of inferiority or deprivation, but always with a tragic sense of the irony of it all.

The Negro middle class covers a very wide income range, and
whatever cohesion it has comes from the network of churches and
social clubs to which many of its members devote a great deal of
time and money. What sociologists call the Negro middle class is
merely a collection of people who have similar life styles and aspirations, whose basic goals are "living well," being "respectable,"
and not being crude. Middle-class Negroes, by and large, are not
concerned about mobility into the Negro upper class or integration
with whites. They want their "rights" and "good jobs," as well as
enough money to get those goods and services which make life
comfortable. They want to expand continuously their level of consumption. But they also desire "decent" schools for their children,
and here the degree of victimization experienced by Negroes is
most clear and the ambivalence toward policies of change most
sharp. Ghetto schools are, on the whole, inferior. In fact, some of
the most convincing evidence that residential segregation perpet-
uates inequality can be found by comparing data on school districts in Northern urban areas where *de facto* school segregation
exists. (Table 1 presents such data for Chicago in 1962.)

Awareness of the poor quality of education grew as the protest
movement against *de facto* school segregation in the North gathered momentum. But while the fight was going on, doubt about the
desirability of forcing the issue was always present within some sec-

tions of the broad Negro middle class. Those in opposition asked, "Are we not saying that our teachers can't teach our own children as well as whites can, or that our children can't learn unless they're around whites? Aren't we insulting ourselves?" Those who want to stress Negro history and achievement and to use the schools to build race pride also express doubts about the value of mixed schools. In fact, the desirability of race consciousness and racial solidarity seems to be taken for granted in this stratum, and sometimes there

TABLE 1.   Comparison of White, Integrated and Negro Schools in Chicago: 1962

	Type of School		
Indices of Comparison	*White*	*Integrated*	*Negro*
Total appropriation per pupil	$342.00	$320.00	$269.00
Annual teachers' salary per pupil	256.00	231.00	220.00
Per cent uncertified teachers	12.00	23.00	49.00
No. of pupils per classroom	30.95	34.95	46.80
Library resource books per pupil	5.00	3.50	2.50
Expenditures per pupil other than teachers' salaries.	86.00	90.00	49.00

Adapted from a table in the U. S. Commission on Civil Rights report, *Public Schools, Negro and White* (Washington, D. C., 1962), pp. 241–248.

is an expression of contempt for the behavior of whites of their own and lower income levels. In the present period one even occasionally hears a remark such as "Who'd want to be integrated with *those* awful white people?"

Marxist critics would dismiss the whole configuration of Negro folkways and classways as a subculture which reinforces "false consciousness," which prevents Negroes from facing the full extent of their victimization, which keeps them from ever focusing upon what they could be because they are so busy enjoying what they are—or rationalizing their subordination and exclusion. Gunnar Myrdal, in *An American Dilemma*, goes so far as to refer to the Negro community as a "pathological" growth within American society.[14] Some novelists and poets, on the other hand, romanticize it, and some Black Nationalists glorify it. A sober analysis of the civil rights movement would suggest, however, that the striking fact about all levels of the Negro community is the absence of "false consciousness," and the presence of a keen awareness of the extent of their victimization, as well as knowledge of the forces which maintain it. Not lack of knowledge but a sense of powerless-ness is the key to the Negro reaction to the caste-class system.

Few Negroes believe that Black Ghettos will disappear within the next two decades despite much talk about "open occupancy" and "freedom of residence." There is an increasing tendency among Negroes to discuss what the quality of life could be within Negro communities as they grow larger and larger. At one extreme this interest slides over into Black Nationalist reactions such as the statement by a Chicago Negro leader who said, "Let all of the white people flee to the suburbs. We'll show them that the Black Man can run the second largest city in America better than the white man. Let them go. If any of them want to come back and integrate with *us* we'll accept them."

It is probable that the Black Belts of America will increase in size rather than decrease during the next decade, for no city seems likely to commit itself to "open occupancy" (although a committee in New York has been discussing a ten-year plan for dismantling Harlem).[15] And even if a race-free market were to appear Negroes would remain segregated unless drastic changes took place in the job ceiling and income gap. Controlled integration will probably continue, with a few upper- and upper-middle-class Negroes trick-ling into the suburbs and into carefully regulated mixed neighbor-hoods and mixed buildings within the city limits.[16] The basic prob-lem of the next decade will be how to change Black Ghettos into relatively stable and attractive "colored communities." Here the so-cial implications of low incomes become decisive.

Social Implications of the Job Ceiling and the Income Gap

Nowhere is direct victimization of Negroes more apparent than with respect to the job ceiling and the income gap; but indirect victimization which is a consequence of direct victimization is often less obvious. For instance, it has been mentioned that family in-comes for Negroes are lower than for whites; but family income figures are inadequate tools for careful sociological analysis unless we know which, and how many, members of a family labor to earn a given income. In 1960, half of the white families were being sup-ported by a husband only, while just a few more than a third of the Negro families could depend solely upon the earnings of one male breadwinner. In six out of ten nonwhite families where both a hus-band and wife were present, two or more persons worked; yet less than half of the white families had both husband and wife working. But even in those families which commanded an income of over $7,000.00 a year, twice as many nonwhite wives had to help earn it as white.[17] One not unimportant consequence is that a smaller proportion of Negro than white wives at this income level can play roles of unpaid volunteers in civic and social work, a fact which should be remembered by those who criticize Negroes in these income brackets for not doing more to "elevate their own people."

One of the most important effects of the income gap and the job ceiling has been the shaping of social class systems within Negro communities which differ markedly in their profiles from those of the surrounding white society. Negro class structure is "pyramidal," with a large lower class, a somewhat smaller middle class, and a tiny upper class (made up of people whose income and occupations would make them only middle class in the white society). White class profiles tend to be "diamond shaped," with small lower and upper classes and a large middle class. Unpromising "life chances" are reflected in inferior "life styles," and Black Ghettos are on the whole "rougher" and exhibit a higher degree of social disorganization than do white communities.

The job ceiling and the income gap do not create classways—for these reflect educational levels and cultural values, as well as the economic situation—but job ceiling and income gap do set the limits for realization of class values. It is a fact of American life (whether one approves of it or not) that as long as Negroes are predominantly lower-class they will, as a group, have low esteem. Yet, Negroes are victimized in the sense that the job ceiling and the income gap make it more difficult for them than for whites to maintain middle-class standards equivalent to those obtaining among whites. A given life style demands a minimum level of income, but it is evident that Negroes are victimized in the sense that their effort as reflected in the acquisition of an education does not bring equal rewards in terms of purchasing power, for they have less to spend than their white counterparts at any given educational level. Nonwhite family heads in 1960 had a smaller median income than whites for every educational level. (See Table 2.)[18]

In a sense, getting an education "pays off" for Negroes as for all other Americans; but while some individuals "get ahead" of other Negroes, education has not yet raised their earning power to the level of whites with equivalent training. In fact, the average income for a nonwhite family with a male head who had finished high

TABLE 2. White and Nonwhite Median Family Income by Educational Level, 1960: U.S.A.

Amount of Education in Yrs. of School Completed	White	Nonwhite
Elementary School		
Less than 8 years	$3,656	$2,294
8 years	4,911	3,338
High School		
1–3 years	5,882	3,449
4 years	6,370	4,559
College		
1–3 years	7,344	5,525
4 or more years	9,315	7,875

school was less than that of a white male head who had finished only the eighth grade. Since any aspects of the caste-class system which make it more difficult for Negroes than for whites to achieve middle-class norms of family behavior retard the process of eventual "integration," the income differential and the necessity for more members of the family to work operate in this negative fashion. Even more serious in determining deviations from general middle-class family norms is the manner in which both income distribution and the occupational structure function to reinforce the number of families without fathers and to lower the prestige of Negro males *vis-à-vis* their mates, prospective mates, and children. Thus a pattern of male insecurity which originated under slavery persists into the present. In fact, the struggle of Negro men, viewed as a group, to attain economic parity with Negro women has, up to the present, been a losing fight. Norval Glenn, in an exhaustive study of this problem,[19] has concluded that "Among full-time workers, non-white females were, in 1959, less disadvantaged relative to whites than were non-white males." Women were obtaining employment at a relatively faster rate than men and sustained a more rapid proportionate increase in income between 1939 and 1959. According to Glenn, there was an actual reversal in the income growth pattern of Negro males and females during a twenty-year period, and he notes that if their respective rates remain the same it will take twice as long for Negro males to catch up with white males as for Negro women to catch up with white women (93 years to achieve occupational equality and 219 to achieve equality of income). This is a case of *relative* deprivation, of course, but is significant nevertheless. An impressive body of evidence indicates that rather serious personality distortions result from the female dominance so prevalent in the Negro subculture, since the general norms of the larger society stress the opposite pattern as more desirable.

The interplay between caste evaluations and economic and ecological factors has tended not only to concentrate a low-income Negro population within ghettos, but has also concentrated a significant proportion of them in vast public housing projects—sometimes "high rise." In the 1930's public housing projects were often exciting experiments in interracial living, but there has been a tendency in many cities for them to become ghettos within ghettos. Within housing projects as well as out, a small hard core of mothers without husbands and a larger group of youth without jobs are developing a pattern which social psychologist Frederick Strodtbeck has called "the poverty-dependency syndrome." Here and there an integrated program of professional family services has proved its usefulness, but, in general, family case-work becomes a mere "holding operation."

Only the future will tell whether a large-scale "Poverty Program" coordinated through federally sponsored agencies will break the interlocking vicious circles which now victimize urban Negro populations. The dominant pattern in the American economic system has never been one of racial segregation. In fact, the racial division of labor has always involved considerable close personal contact, while demanding that Negroes play subordinate occupational roles carrying the lesser rewards in terms of economic power and social prestige. Doctrines of racial inferiority originated as dogmas to defend the use of African slave labor and were later used by white workers to defend their own privileged position against Negro competition. Trade union restrictionism reinforces employer preference in maintaining a job ceiling. Often, even when an employer decided it was profitable to use Negro labor, white workers used intimidation or violence against both white employer and black employee.

Access to new roles in the economic structure has occurred during periods of a great shortage of labor, as in the North during both world wars. Negroes entered at the bottom of the hierarchy, but were "last hired and first fired." Yet the job ceiling *was* raised, and, beginning with the organization of industrial unions in the 1930's and reaching a climax in the civil rights movement of the 1960's, ideological factors have reinforced economic interest in breaking the job ceiling. Now, for the first time in American history the full weight of top leadership in labor, industry, and government has been thrown in the direction of "fair employment practices," and public opinion is tolerating an all-out drive against job discrimination (partly because the economy is still expanding). Yet so drastic are the effects of the past victimization of the Negro that any decisive alteration in the caste-class structure without more drastic measures seems remote. Thomas Pettigrew, after an analysis of recent changes, concludes:

At the creeping 1950-1960 rate of change, non-whites in the United States would not attain equal proportional representation among clerical workers until 1992, among skilled workers until 2005, among professionals until 2017, among sales workers until 2114, and among business managers and proprietors until 2730![20]

"In Sickness and in Death"

The consequences of being at the bottom in a caste-class system are revealed clearly in comparative studies of morbidity, mortality, and longevity, the latter being a particularly sensitive index to the physical well-being of groups. Comparing Negroes and whites with respect to longevity, Thomas Pettigrew notes that:

At the turn of this century, the average non-white American at birth had a life expectancy between 32 and 35 years, 16 years less than that of the average white American. By 1960, this life expectancy had risen from 61 to 66 years. . . . But while the percentage gain in life expectancy for Negroes over these sixty odd years has been twice that of whites, there is still a discrepancy of six to eight years. . . .[21]

In other words, Negroes were "catching up," but, as a Department of Labor study pointed out in 1962, they ". . . had arrived by 1959 at about the longevity average attained by whites in 1940."[22] They were twenty years behind in the race toward equality of longevity.

Differences in longevity reflect differences in morbidity rates. Among the communicable diseases, for instance, the Negro tuberculosis rate is three times greater than that of whites, and the rates for pneumonia and influenza are also higher. The incidence of venereal disease is substantially higher among Negroes, although the Public Health Service figure of a syphilis rate ten times larger than that for whites has been questioned in Dr. Ann Pettigrew's study.[23] Twice as many Negro children per thousand as white children suffer from measles, meningitis, diphtheria, and scarlet fever. Given such differences between Negroes and whites in the incidence of specific diseases, it is not surprising to find that the *death* rate from childhood diseases is six times higher among Negroes than whites and that the tuberculosis death rate is four times higher in all age-groups.[24]

The analysis of mortality rates provides one tool for studying the effects of the caste-class system which victimizes the Negro population. A United States government report for the year 1963 noted that "The age pattern of mortality . . . as in previous years, is similar for each of the color-sex groups—high rates in infancy, lower rates until the minimum is reached during grade-school age, then rising rates for the older age-groups."[25] Although the *pattern* was the same, there were racial differentials in the actual rates; for instance, "The relative increases in the 1963 death rates over the prior years were slightly greater for non-white persons than for white. . . ." There were other differentials too.

The death rate among mothers at childbirth in 1963 was four times greater for nonwhites than for whites (96.9 deaths per 100,000 live births to 24.0). The death rate of nonwhite babies during the first year after birth was almost double the rate for white babies (46.6 per thousand to 25.3 per thousand for males and 36.7 to 19.0 for females.) Prenatal hazards were, as in previous years, greater for nonwhites than for whites. Up to the age of five the nonwhite death rate was twice that for whites, and for older age-groups varied from two to four times the white rate.

Using broad categories of classification, the U. S. National Center for Health Statistics reported in 1963 that "the three chief causes of death—diseases of heart, malignant neoplasms [Cancer], and vascular lesions affecting central nervous system account for three fifths of all deaths. They are also the chief causes of death for each color-sex group."[26] Here, too, racial differentials exist, the non-white to white death ratios being: (a) diseases of heart (333.9/ 100,000 to 277.9); (b) malignant neoplasms (145.2/100,000 to 123.7); (c) vascular lesions of central nervous system (133.4/ 100,000 to 71.3). A comparison of deaths from specific diseases and from other causes also reveals racial differentials and the pattern of indifferences suggests a relationship between high rates and low socio-economic status.

If the ten leading causes of death in 1963 for nonwhites and whites are compared by sex, the results of indirect victimization of Negroes are apparent: Those diseases which rate highest as causes of death are found disproportionately among lower-class families, those who suffer from poor nutrition, overcrowded housing, hazardous occupations, and inadequate medical care. Table 3 presents rates for ten leading causes of death for males:

TABLE 3.   The Ten Leading Causes of Death: Males, U.S.A., 1963

Causes of Death	Nonwhite		White	
	Rate	Rank	Rate	Rank
Diseases of the heart	330.6	1	444.8	1
Vascular lesions of Central Nervous System	116.8	2	100.5	2
Certain diseases of early infancy	81.8	3	34.3	7
Influenza and pneumonia	70.6	4	39.3	5
Hypertensive heart disease	61.1	5	24.1	9
Accidents other than motor vehicle	57.9	6	37.8	6
Cancer of digestive organs	51.1	7	54.1	3
Symptoms-senility and ill-defined conditions	42.1	8	10.9†	—
Motor vehicle accidents	36.7	9	34.4	8
Homicide	35.7	10	3.9†	—
Cancer of respiratory system	34.5*	—	43.7	4
Diabetes mellitus	13.9*	—	14.2	10

* Not among first ten for nonwhites
†Not among first ten for whites

Among males, certain causes of death directly related to standard of living affect nonwhites two to four times more frequently than whites: (a) certain diseases of early infancy (2.38×); (b) influenza and pneumonia (1.79×); and (c) "symptoms-senility and ill-defined conditions" (3.86×). The last named "cause" does not even appear among the first ten for whites. (See Table 4.)

Two causes of death on the list for nonwhite males are probably directly related to the caste situation. The death rate for hypertensive heart disease is over twice that for whites and ranks fifth as a cause of death, compared to ninth for whites. Thomas Pettigrew, commenting on all types of hypertension, notes that some students feel that it is related to "psychosocial influences" and that, with regard to the high rates for Negroes, " . . . the problem of repressing hostility against whites . . . may be an important factor."[27] A homicide death rate nine times higher than that for whites, and appearing among the ten leading causes of death for nonwhite males, reflects the overt terror in the Black Belt, the explosions of in-caste aggression, and the anomic lower-class situation, as well as the distinctive ethos of the Negro subculture where crimes of passion among the lower-class are not condemned to the extent that they are in some other segments of American society.

Of the ten leading causes of death among nonwhite males, eight are also leading causes of death for white males, but in the case of six of these the nonwhite rate is higher (diseases of the heart and cancer of digestive organs being the exceptions). The extent of the difference is indicated in Table 4.

TABLE 4. Comparison of Death Rates for Nonwhites and Whites, by Sex, for the Ten Leading Causes of Death for Each Color-Sex Group

Degree of Difference Between Rates	*Males*		*Females*	
	Cause of Death	*Ratio of Nonwhite to White Rates*	*Cause of Death*	*Ratio of Nonwhite to White Rates*
Very much higher for Nonwhites	Homicide†	9.14	None	
Considerably higher for Nonwhites	Symptoms— Senility, and ill-defined conditions†	3.86	Symptoms— Senility, and ill-defined conditions†	4.35
	Certain diseases of early infancy	2.38	Certain diseases of early infancy	2.56
	Hypertensive heart disease	2.12	Hypertensive heart disease	2.09
Somewhat higher for Nonwhites	Influenza and pneumonia (except pneumonia of newborn)	1.79	Influenza and pneumonia (except pneumonia of newborn)	1.68
	Accidents other than motor vehicle accidents	1.37	Diabetes mellitus	1.38
	Vascular lesions affecting central nervous system	1.16	Cancer of genital organs	1.17
	Motor vehicle accident	1.07	Accidents*	1.15
			Vascular lesions affecting central nervous system	1.08
Lower for Nonwhites	Diabetes mellitus*	.97	Diseases of the heart	.84
	Cancer of digestive organs	.94	Cancer of digestive organs†	.71
	Cancer of respiratory system*	.78	Cancer of the breast	.67
	Diseases of the heart	.73		

* Among ten top-ranking causes for whites but not for nonwhites
† Among ten top-ranking causes for nonwhites but not for whites

The perinatal period is much more serious for nonwhite male babies than white, death rates for "certain diseases of infancy" (birth injuries, infections, and so forth) ranking seventh as a cause of death for white males, but only third for nonwhites.

The section of Table 4 dealing with females indicates that nonwhite women are also more vulnerable to death from pneumonia and influenza, hypertension, diseases of early infancy, and "senility and ill-defined conditions" than are white women and to the same degree as nonwhite males. Deaths from "deliveries and complications of pregnancy, childbirth, and the puerperium" are not a major cause of death for any American women but for the 1,466 cases reported for 1963 the nonwhite rate was over five times that for whites (5.6 to 1.0). Anemias, too, are not prime killers, but nonwhite women have more than their share of death from this cause (3.0/1,000 to 1.7), with the same situation obtaining from asthma (3.2 to 1.8), and gastric ailments (7.2 to 3.9). Table 5 summarizes the data for the ten leading causes of death among women. The diseases of infancy rank fourth as a cause of death among nonwhite women and ninth among white women, a similar situation to that involving males. On the other hand, while the nonwhite female hypertension rate is twice that of whites, the rank order as a cause of death is not very different.

TABLE 5. The Ten Leading Causes of Death: Females, U.S.A., 1963

	Nonwhite		White	
Causes of Death	Rate	Rank	Rate	Rank
Diseases of the heart	262.2	1	312.1	1
Vascular lesions of central nervous system	120.4	2	110.9	2
Hypertensive heart disease	67.0	3	32.0	5
Certain diseases of early infancy	58.1	4	22.7	9
Influenza and pneumonia	51.0	5	30.3	6
Accidents	38.1	6	33.0	4
Cancer of digestive organs	32.1	7	45.5	3
Symptoms-Senility, and ill-defined conditions	30.9	8	7.1†	—
Cancer of genital organs	28.2	9	24.0	8
Diabetes mellitus	25.4	10	19.2	10
Cancer of the breast	18.2	—*	27.0	7

* Not among first ten for nonwhites
† Not among first ten for whites

In addition to an analysis of the ten leading causes of death, other 1963 death rates reflect the low socio-economic status and the influences of the Negro subculture. Of the 6,835 who died from tuberculosis, three and one-half times as many nonwhites as whites succumbed. Only about 2,000 deaths from syphilis occurred, but nonwhites were over-represented four to one.

As for a group of deaths from children's diseases, the pattern of over-representation for nonwhites also prevails. (See Table 6.)

TABLE 6. Number of Deaths and Rates for Whites and Nonwhites, for Certain Children's Diseases: U.S.A., 1963

Diseases	Cases	Nonwhite	White
Whooping Cough	115	.3	.0
Scarlet Fever	102	.1	.0
Diphtheria	45	.1	.0
Measles	364	.4	.2

It was once both fashionable and scientifically respectable to explain these differences in terms of differential racial susceptibility to various diseases, but as Thomas Pettigrew points out:

The many improvements in his situation since 1900 rendered a dramatic increment in the Negro's health, providing solid evidence that corrosive poverty and inadequate medical care were the reasons for his short life span in the past. . . . this difference [between Negro and white rates] can be traced to the diseases which are treatable, preventable and unnecessary.[28]

This is now the generally accepted view among serious students of the problem, and "corrosive poverty" and "inadequate medical care" are aspects of the victimization to which Negroes have been subjected. Further improvement in the health status of Negroes depends upon the eradication of poverty and all its accompanying side effects as well as upon access to adequate medical care.

Much of the "corrosive poverty" has been associated with life in the cotton fields, the logging camps, the mines, and the small-town slums of a poverty-stricken South. Conditions were bad for most people, and the caste-system made them worse for the Negro. Dr. Ann Pettigrew has presented convincing evidence that the massive shift of Negro population into Northern and Western cities during the past two decades has resulted in some health gains for the Negro, and these gains have been due largely to greater access to medical advice and medical care.[29] But, the differentials are still large, even in the North, especially for tuberculosis, pneumonia, and venereal diseases. "Ghettoization," with its associated overcrowding, has been one important factor in keeping these rates high; but for these, as well as for other ailments, hospital discrimination is a primary factor limiting access to adequate medical care.

Patterns of discrimination and segregation by hospitals are prevalent throughout the country. A report prepared in 1962 for circulation to members of the National Medical Association (an organization of Negro physicians)[30] summarized the hospital situation in a sentence, "Things are bad all over," and the report included the bitter comment that "Hospitals under religious auspices have been the most vicious in discrimination." Conditions were worst in the South where the caste-system has not yet been shattered. In Birmingham, Alabama, for instance, a city of 750,000 people half of whom are Negro, only 1,100 beds were available for whites, and only 500 for Negroes. In Atlanta, Georgia, the South's most progressive city, 4,000 beds were available for whites, but only 600 for Negroes. (Nonwhites were 22.8 per cent of the population of the metropolitan area.) In Augusta, Georgia, a smaller city, twelve beds were set aside for Negroes in the basement of the white hospital but there were no beds for Negro pediatrics or obstetrics patients. The Hill-Burton Act under which federal funds may be secured for aid in building hospitals has a non-discrimination clause, but, generally, it has been evaded or ignored in the South. In one large Texas city a new $6,000,000 hospital constructed with federal aid refused to admit any Negroes until threatened with a suit. (The National Medical Association report emphasized that it was a Catholic hospital.) In Richmond, Virginia, a new "treatment center" accepted Negroes only as out-patients. By 1962, about 2,000 hospitals had been built in the South with federal assistance, and of these 98 would accept no Negroes, while the others stayed within the letter of the law by providing as little space for them as possible. In the few places where Negro physicians are practicing, they usually find it impossible to have their patients hospitalized under their own care since they cannot become members of hospital staffs. (In Elizabeth City, North Carolina, a Negro physician was recently taken on a staff after thirty-two annual applications.) Most Southern local medical societies bar Negroes from membership. (In South Carolina, however, twenty-five of the sixty-five Negro doctors belong to the state medical association, but must hold separate sessions. They can join local societies only if they will agree in advance to stay away from social functions.)

In the more fluid ethnic-class system in the North, patterns of discrimination and segregation vary from city to city. At one extreme is Pittsburgh, Pennsylvania, of which the National Medical

Association report simply says, "No hospital problems." A similar assessment is made of Philadelphia. In Gary, Indiana, after a prolonged fight, 85 per cent of the Negro physicians were placed on the staff of some formerly all-white hospitals. When the National Medical Association says that "There is no hospital problem" in these cities, what it really means is that Negro physicians no longer find it difficult to have their patients hospitalized. But the Negro masses still face other problems; for, insofar as they are disproportionately represented in low-income groups, more of them are "charity" patients and must face the more subtle forms of victimization which the poor face everywhere in American hospitals—less careful attention to their needs, psychological and physical, than private patients receive. There is substantial evidence from studies made in one Northern city that such patients are more frequently handled by medical students and interns than by fully trained doctors, and there is reliable statistical evidence indicating that more infants die on the wards than in the rooms of private patients. As important as it is to insist upon the right of Negro doctors to take their patients into hospitals which formerly barred them, other aspects of the Negro health problem must be dealt with, too.

The city of Chicago, with its 900,000 Negroes rigidly segregated into ghettos, reveals the full dimensions of the problem. As recently as 1960 there were no more than 500 beds available to Negroes in private hospitals—one-half bed per 1000 Negroes as compared with 4.5 beds per 1000 whites. A distinguished Negro physician serving as Chairman of a Committee to End Discrimination in Medical Institutions released a statement to the press in October, 1963, in which he said that only thirty-three out of eighty private hospitals admitted Negroes and that:

Many of these do so on a segregated and discriminating basis. . . . Some hospitals which do admit Negroes place them in the oldest rooms, in basements, in all-Negro wings and often have a quota system limiting the number of Negro patients they will accept. . . . when a Negro becomes ill, he knows he will be accepted at County hospital and is in no mood to have to fight to gain admittance to a private hospital where he will be discriminated against.[31]

The Negro physicians, however, did take up the issue by insisting upon staff appointments so they could take their own patients into these hospitals and insure adequate care for them.

The fight began seriously in 1955 with the passage of an antidiscrimination bill in the City Council and a plea for compliance by

Cardinal Stritch. In 1960, after five years of publicity and pleading, only twenty-one of the two hundred fifteen Negro physicians in Chicago held appointments on any private hospital staff outside of the Black Belt, these being at twenty-one of the sixty-eight hospitals of this type. At this point the Mayor appointed a special committee to work on the problem, and a group of ten Negro doctors filed suit under the Sherman and Clayton anti-trust acts against fifty-six hospitals, the Illinois Hospital Association, the Chicago Medical Society, the Chicago Hospital Council, and the Illinois Corporations operating Blue Cross and Blue Shield medical prepayment plans. They took this action, they said, "to thwart the more subtle and sophisticated techniques" being used to evade the issue.[32]

In response to these pressures (and to the general atmosphere regarding civil rights), forty-two of the sixty-eight hospitals in the city had given one hundred two staff appointments to sixty-four of the city's two hundred twenty-five Negro doctors by 1965. (Only eighty-eight of these, however, "permit the physician to admit his private patients.") The downward trend in the number of Negro physicians choosing to practice in Chicago was arrested. For a city which ranked only fourth from the bottom among fourteen cities on degree of hospital integration, the breakthrough has been a major victory.[33] One measure of the extent of the Negro's victimization is the fact that scores of physicians had to spend their money and invest time which could have been devoted to research or professional development in fighting for access to hospital facilities.

The victory of the Chicago Negro doctors has alleviated the plight of paying patients who now have a wider choice of hospitals, though not necessarily closer to their homes. (Because of the fear of being "swamped" by Negro patients, some hospitals near the Black Belt have interposed stronger barriers against Negro doctors than have those farther away.) As early as 1949, a health survey of Chicago pointed out that "A serious problem faced by the Blue Cross Plan for hospital care in this area is its inability to fulfil its obligations to the 50,000 Negro subscribers, since they are not accepted by all the member hospitals. . . . Many of the subscribers must be admitted to Cook County Hospital under the guise of emergencies. . . ." Six years later, the Packinghouse Workers Civic and Community Committee complained that "Our union has struggled and won hospital benefits for all our members, but a great number of UPWA-CIO members who are Negroes are being cheated out of those benefits. . . ." With over 100,000 insured Negroes and less than 1,000 beds available to them in private hospitals they are still being cheated, and not they alone.[34]

Chicago Negroes have been forced by hospital discrimination to use the facilities of four or five hospitals within the Black Belt and the large but overcrowded Cook County Hospital which should be serving only those who cannot pay and emergency cases. By 1960, almost two-thirds of all the Negro babies delivered in a hospital were being born at Cook County. Some white hospitals near the Black Ghetto closed down their maternity wards rather than serve Negroes. A prominent white physician delivering an address in 1960 in favor of widening access to hospital care stressed that this was unfair both to the paying patients who were denied the right to choose and to the indigent who were being deprived of space at the Cook County Hospital by Negroes who could pay. He said:

Cook County Hospital is even being used to absorb a large number of Negro patients unwanted by the voluntary hospitals even though they may be able and willing to pay . . . the Chicago public would not tolerate this misuse of a tax-supported hospital. . . . for an equivalent number of non-Negro patients. . . .[35]

Placing Negroes on the hospital staffs has not solved the fundamental problem of the shortage of beds available to a rapidly expanding Negro population. To build new hospital facilities in the Black Belt *before* eliminating segregation in *all* hospitals would be considered bad strategy by most Negro leaders and a "sell-out" by the militants. The Chicago paradigm has general relevance and is not applicable only to the local scene.

Hospital discrimination is only one facet of a complex process involving both direct and indirect victimization which leads to a lower level of physical and mental well-being among Negroes and which is reflected in morbidity and mortality rates. Health hazards for most of the Negro population begin even before birth, and they affect both mother and child. These hazards are greatest in the rural South, but they exist in urban situations as well, both Northern and Southern. Premature births occurred 50 per cent more frequently among Negroes than among whites during 1958-1959 and maternal mortality rates among Negroes were four times higher.[36] A higher proportion of Negro mothers failed to receive prenatal care, and a higher proportion died in childbirth. The most authoritative testimony on the disadvantaged position of the Negro expectant mother has been supplied by an eminent obstetrician, Dr. Philip F. Williams, who has called attention to the fact that "one survey of maternal mortality is cited which found errors in judgment and technique as well as neglect on the part of the physician, as much as fifty per cent more frequently in the case of Negro than white mothers." He pointed out, too, that Negro women who were pregnant and those who had babies were victims of a set of interlocking conditions which included a lack of concern by husbands and putative fathers, a relatively high exposure to gonorrhea and syphilis, and, in the South ". . . a scarcity of physicians that has resulted in an inferior grade of attendance at birth (the untrained midwife). . . ."[37] In both North and South, hospital facilities are still inadequate and all of these factors combine to create a situation " . . . more or less adversely affecting the chances of survival of the Negro mother at childbirth." They affect the chances of the baby's surviving, too. Studies made soon after World War II revealed that, for Negroes as compared with whites, fewer Negro babies were delivered in hospitals and therefore more of them died at birth or during the first year after (and more died before they could be born, too). Immunization of children was less common among Negroes and childhood diseases more prevalent and more often fatal.[38] Negro children, on the average, received fewer of the benefits of deliberately planned feeding, and fewer parents, in proportion, ate according to the more advanced nutritional standards.

Insofar as the job ceiling, the income gap, and Ghettoization preserve and reinforce lower-class behavior patterns among Negroes to a greater extent than in the general society, the general health status of the Negro will be affected. For instance, a less adequate nutritional level than is found among whites is one factor often cited in accounting for the poorer average health status of Negroes. It is conceivable that Negroes could improve their nutritional status immediately by altering their present patterns of food consumption, but this is likely to occur less as a result of education and propaganda than as a by-product of changes in the caste-class situation. Except in wartime or during depressions, food habits are among the most difficult to change, unless change is related to mobility strivings. Maximizing the opportunity for Negroes to achieve the values and norms of the general American middle class is likely to do more to change the eating habits of the Negro population than all of the written or spoken exhortations of home economists or the most seductive of television commercials. A shift in social class supplies the motivation to change, and such a shift is dependent upon an increase in the number and proportion of Negroes entering white-collar occupations.

Maintaining a style of living consonant with any occupational roles demands a minimum level of income. Success in improving the health status of the Negro population may ultimately depend upon an indirect rather than a frontal assault. One student of the problem gives us a clue to the strategy when he observes that ". . . the much lower income level of the American Negro, to the extent that it is a measure of standard of living, explains, in part at least, the differences in health status and longevity between whites and non-whites in the United States."[39] Carefully controlled studies "point up the intimate relationship between physical illness and economic . . ."[40] to use Dr. Ann Pettigrew's expression. Economic factors not only partially explain, or serve as indices of, the causes of divergent morbidity and mortality rates, but they also give us the clues to a strategy for change, namely, working toward a continuously rising standard of living. Whether hope or pessimism is warranted depends upon the possibility of drastically changing the economic status of the Negro over the next decade, of eliminating economic "victimization."

Closing the income gap is crucial, or alternatively, the provision of a subsidy for medical services. Large masses of Negroes will never become members of the white-collar class, but better job opportunities in commerce and industry will place many of them in a position to benefit from privately sponsored health and insurance plans. These will be of maximum benefit, however, only if hospital discrimination is eliminated. Also, the wider extension of adequate medical care to all citizens through the use of public funds, and the more effective use of social workers and educators, will automatically benefit those Negroes who are not upwardly mobile.

Chronic illness, as well as frequent periods of sickness, not only results in loss of man-hours of production, but also increases stress and strain in interpersonal relations and deprives individuals of the maximum amount of pleasure to be derived from a sense of physical well-being and from recreation and pleasurable interaction with other human beings. Insofar as the general health level of Negroes is lower than that of whites they suffer more from these deprivations. Tendencies to escape from pain and its consequences by habitual use of alcohol and drugs, or the anodyne of excessive preoccupation with the supernatural world, may be related to the general health situation within the Negro lower class. These less tangible and immeasurable disabilities are as real as the financial burdens imposed by sickness.

The Identification Problem

Some of the most damaging forms of indirect victimization manifest themselves at the psychological level. The Black Ghetto and the job ceiling are the key variables in accounting for differences in morbidity and mortality rates, and for the persistence of subcultural behavior patterns which deviate from middle-class norms. At the subjective level they also determine the crucial points of social reference for the individual Negro when answering the questions "Who am I today?" and "What will I be tomorrow?" The Black Ghetto forces him to identify as a Negro first, an American second, and it gives him geographical "roots." The job ceiling is an ever present reminder that there are forces at work which make him a second-class American. But the Black Ghetto and the job ceiling are only two components of a caste-class system now undergoing revolutionary transformation—an institutional complex which includes the courts, schools, churches, voluntary associations, media of mass communication, and a network of family units. Like all other persons, the individual Negro receives his orientation to this social nexus first from his family and later from his peer group. Exposure to schools and the mass media continues the process of socialization and personality formation while membership in voluntary associations provides a tie to the class system and constitutes an aid to upward mobility.

The white middle class is the reference group for those who are mobile; yet the entire system operates to emphasize identity with "The Race," since defensive solidarity must be maintained against the white world. Inner conflicts are inevitable; and conventional, as well as idiosyncratic, adjustments to this situation have been thoroughly studied. Ann Pettigrew suggests that ". . . the perception of relative deprivation, the discrepancy between high aspirations and actual attainments . . . is a critical psychological determinant of mental disorder. And certainly racial discrimination acts to bar the very achievements which the society encourages individuals to attempt."[41] A disparity in psychosis rates reflects this discrepancy, but for most Negroes the reaction to oppression is less severe. Neither insanity nor suicide is a *typical* Negro reaction.

Both Negroes and whites are "victims" of one persisting legacy of the slave trade—the derogation of "negroidness." The idea that a dark skin indicates intellectual inferiority is rapidly passing, but at the esthetic level derogatory appraisal of thick lips, kinky hair, and very dark skin is still prevalent. That many Negroes reject their own body image is evident from advertisements for skin lighteners in the major Negro publications,[42] and Negro children in experimental situations begin to reject brown dolls for white ones before the age of five.[43] The ever present knowledge that one's negroid physiognomy is evaluated as "ugly" lowers self-esteem and, therefore, weakens self-confidence. The rise of the new African states has given a psychological "lift" to those American Negroes who still look more African than *metis,* but extreme Negro physical traits are still a source of inner disquiet—especially for women. (There is no equivalent in America of the African cult of *negritude* whose poets idealize the black woman.) These negative esthetic appraisals are part of a larger stereotype-complex which equates Africa with primitiveness and savagery and considers Negro ancestry a "taint." A frontal assault on a world-wide scale is necessary to undo this propaganda of the slave era which still exists as a form of cultural lag which has lost even the excuse of the functional utility it once had in rationalizing an integral part of the Western economic system—Negro slavery.[44]

Negroes in America, as a numerical minority, always have a feeling of being "on the outside looking in," of not being "in the main stream." Yet, the mere fact of being only one in ten does not automatically generate this feeling; the "victimization" flows, rather, from the values of the majority who refuse to accept every individual upon his own merit, but insist upon ascription of status on the basis of membership in a racial group. (Bahia, Brazil, presents an interesting case where the opposite is true, where individual achievement can almost completely over-ride racial origin.)[45] This sense of alienation is reinforced by traditional or deliberate omission of Negroes from the decision-making process. That they are absent from the boards of major corporations is not surprising; but it is surprising that they are virtually absent from the boards of foundations and professional associations. Only in the realm of public administration and the world of sports and entertainment are Negroes present in sufficient numbers to be "visible," and to serve as role models for Negro youth.

These omissions are particularly crucial in a society where

numerous illustrated publications function as the image-makers. A Negro child seldom sees a person like himself in an advertisement or in illustrations accompanying fiction. The children in the text-books are all white. The image of the powerful, the desirable, the admirable is set very early as "white." There is an increasing aware-ness of the seriousness of this problem, and by 1964 the television industry was making a half-hearted attempt to use a few Negroes in commercials, and one or two Northern cities were experimenting with "integrated textbooks." But still, Negro newspapers and maga-zines alone cater to this hunger to see the Negro image in print. These publications also give prominence to whatever interracial participation is taking place, but they cannot eliminate the feeling of resentment over exclusion from the collective representations of the larger society.

Leaders in the civil rights movement frequently refer to the process of desegregation and integration as having the goal of "bringing Negroes into the main stream." This sense of isolation from "the main stream" was given poetic expression by the late Dr. W. E. B. Du Bois in the 1890's when he spoke of living be-hind, or within, "The Veil." This isolation not only generates dis-torted perceptions of the total society and occasionally bizarre definitions of situations, but it also results in cognitive crippling. The communication flow needed to provide data for rational decision making is often impeded. Incomplete information is available for "playing the game" the way it is played in various segments of the larger society, and in a highly mobile society it is all-important to know "who is who" and "what is what." There is some evidence, for instance, to indicate that lower-middle-class and lower-class Negro parents often have high aspirations for their children but have no clear idea how to realize them. Negro students in segre-gated colleges and high schools are also often woefully ignorant of opportunities and techniques for succeeding.[46]

One cannot be mobile without learning the professional codes and the folkways of other social strata. It was this which the Supreme Court had in mind when it ruled some years ago that a separate law school for Negroes cut the student off from those con-tacts which were necessary to make a person a first-class lawyer and therefore could not meet the criterion of equality. It is this contact which most Negro physicians are denied. Also, in a society where the social ritual is so much a part of the business world, Negroes are generally not in a position to secure the cues and tips needed for competition on a basis of complete equality. If they cannot meet their peers at professional meetings and in the informal gatherings of persons who pursue similar occupations and professions, they, of necessity, will see only "through a glass darkly." Very clever and ambitious individuals (and persistent ones) sometimes rip aside "The Veil," but such persons are rare within any ethnic group. Most individuals remain victims of the communication blockage, and special efforts will be necessary to open the channels of communication. Participation across race lines with persons in similar occupations is the first step toward structural integration.

In a social system which forces Negroes to think of themselves *first* as Negroes and only second as Americans, a problem of "double identification" is posed for those who are partially integrated. Guilt feelings sometimes arise over the charge hurled by others that they are "running away from the Race." Negroes who represent the country abroad are exposed to the criticism of Africans and Asians as being "the tool of the white man." Personnel officers, political leaders, and work-supervisors are always open to the charge that they are "Uncle Toms," have "sold out," or have "forgotten the Race." This problem will be intensified if the process of integration at upper levels of power and prestige is not accompanied by the complete disappearance of racial barriers to upward mobility, or if the masses of Negroes are doomed to be America's permanent lower class. In the meanwhile, the rise of Malcolm X and the appeal of the Black Muslims and various local Black Nationalist groups suggest that the lower classes and lower middle classes can work their way out of the problem of double identification by rejecting "white" values and by proudly proclaiming their psychological independence. Such a solution is not available to the more sophisticated Negroes, but the possibility is not to be excluded that, since America insists upon limited integration rather than complete acceptance, increased identification of educated Negroes with some aspects of the Negro subculture and with the cultural renaissance taking place in Africa may become the norm.[47]

The Condition of Powerlessness

The problem of "identification" is crucial, but Charles Silberman in, *Crisis in Black and White*, puts his finger upon the most critical aspect of Negro-white relations in the United States when he stresses the psychological effect of being "powerless." Negroes realize that, as a minority in "the white man's country," they do not set the rules of the game. Unlike Negroes in Africa and the West Indies they do not fight for national independence, but rather for "desegregation" and "integration," and they can attain these goals only if the white majority sanctions them as legitimate and desirable. "Integration," in the final analysis, also means that the Negro community must increasingly become more middle-class in values and behavior if it is to win respect and approval. Negroes do not determine the ends for which they struggle, nor the means. The most they can expect is an increasingly greater share in the *joint* determination of their future. The problem of maintaining dignity and some autonomy in such a situation is, for sensitive personalities, a continuous one, even within the civil rights movement, for white friends, even in liberal-left circles, often strive to bend Negroes to their will and not to ask their advice as co-workers.

In the past, this sense of "powerlessness" to determine their own destiny or to change their position in the caste-class system has been one important factor in accentuating in-group aggression among lower-class Negroes, in the diversion of energy and financial resources into the over-elaboration of the church-voluntary association complex, and in the development of those styles of life which E. Franklin Frazier portrayed so unsympathetically in *Black Bourgeoisie*. Black Belt crime, juvenile delinquency, and cynical exploitation have also been interpreted by some sociologists as one reaction to a state of "powerlessness." Within the lower class and lower middle class, hostility and resentment become "socialized" for a few in the form of Black Nationalism and take organized form in movements such as the Black Muslims.[48] Among the rootless masses, the anger flowing from frustration bursts forth periodically in verbal abuse and violent assault, in arson and looting, in attacks upon policemen and property—thus the tragedy of Harlem, Rochester, and Philadelphia in 1964 and of Los Angeles and Chicago in 1965. The feeling of having made the conquest of power, of being in control of their own fate, if only for a moment, is symbolized in a widely circulated photograph of jubilant Negroes giving the V-for-Victory sign on top of a shattered police car in Los Angeles. But these Black Belt explosions underscore a basic fact—that no revolution can follow the storming of the Bastille by Negroes in America. Camus and Sartre, not Marx, provide the key for understanding these events.

Conventional politics has been the most realistic approach to gaining at least the semblance of power. Recent demographic trends, including the flight of whites to the suburbs, have placed some Negro communities in a strategic position to play "balance of power" politics more effectively, and the civil rights movement may result in increased political power for Negroes in the South. Yet, all Negro leaders know the limits of their ability to wield decisive political influence. (And in the world of "big business" their influence is even less.) Silberman has suggested the importance—cathartic and practical—of grass-roots movements, with "middle-level" leadership, fighting for limited goals where results can be achieved, and Thomas Pettigrew has stressed the psychologically liberating effect of participation in the civil rights movement.[49] The feed-back in terms of an increased incentive to secure more education or to get better jobs can be sustained only if society actually provides the rewards in terms of expanded occupational mobility. The sense of being powerless can disappear, however, only if the social system eventually changes to the extent that Negroes will not need to organize *as Negroes* to defend their interests and if color ceases to be a factor in membership in the "power structure." Riots will cease only when Americans allow Black Ghettos to dissolve.

The Myth of "Separate but Equal"

Negroes have been "victimized" throughout the three hundred fifty years of their presence on the North American continent. The types of social systems which have organized their relations with whites have been varied—over two hundred years of slavery and indenture, ten years of post-Civil War Reconstruction in the South, and eighty years of experimentation with a theory of "separate but equal" ostensibly designed to replace caste relations with those of class. The "separate but equal" doctrine has now been repudiated by the federal government and a broad section of public opinion as unjust and inimical to the national welfare. The period of desegregation has begun. Yet, the legacy of the past remains. As a transition to some new, and still undefined system of race relations takes place, it is relevant to examine the extent to which victimization persists, probing for its more subtle and covert manifestations. An estimate, too, should be made of whether or not what Merton has called "the unintended consequences of purposive social action" carry a potential for new forms of victimization.

By 1900 the doctrine had become firmly established that it was desirable for Negroes and whites to be members of two functionally related segments of a bi-racial society in which families, intimate friendship groups, and voluntary associations (including churches) would be separate, although members of both races were participating in a common economic system and political order. Both Negro and white leaders emphasized the point that "social equality" was not a Negro aspiration, and Booker T. Washington's famous Atlanta Compromise address delivered in 1895 made this point very explicit with his symbolism of the five fingers, separate and distinct, but joined together at the palm.

The theory of "separate but equal" visualized a future in which Negroes would gradually acquire wealth and education on such a scale as to develop a social-class system within the Negro community paralleling that of the white community. Then, as the sociologist Robert Park once phrased it, Negroes and whites would "look over and across" at each other, not "up and down." Defenders of "bi-racialism" believed that although institutional life—including schools and neighborhoods—should remain separate, Negroes should be allowed to compete freely for jobs and should gradually acquire the full voting rights which they had lost in the South after 1875. It was considered unwise, however, to make a frontal assault upon segregation in public places since the key to the ultimate dissolution or transformation of the caste system lay in the acquisition of education and economic well-being—not in protest. The "correct" behavior of an enlarged Negro middle class would eventually win acceptance by the white middle class. The doctrine of "separate but equal" was given legal sanction in a number of Supreme Court decisions, the most famous being that of *Plessy vs. Ferguson*, and it became the operating ideology among Southern white liberals between the two world wars.

During the first decade after World War II the doctrine of "separate but equal" was abandoned as a guide to the formulation of public policy insofar as the armed forces, public transportation, public accommodations, and public schools were concerned. Experience between the two world wars had demonstrated that, while it might be theoretically possible to achieve equality within the framework of a segregated school system in the South, it seemed impossible in actual practice. In the field of public transportation, no matter how many shiny new coaches replaced the old rickety "Jim Crow" coaches, Negroes did not consider them "equal," and they never ceased to be resentful that there were two American armies instead of one. The cost of duplicating facilities to make public accommodations and schools truly equal would have been exorbitant even if Negroes welcomed the idea. Thus, a demand for change was in the air when the historic 1954 decision requiring school desegregation was taken, and the Court cut through to a fundamental question which had often been evaded: whether or not it was possible to maintain any kind of *forced* segregation in an open society without perjorative implications. Did not the very insistence upon separation imply inferiority? The caste-class system organizing race relations was recognized for what it really was—a system which, irrespective of the intent of individuals, resulted in the victimization of Negroes. Makers of national policy have now embarked upon a thoroughgoing program of desegregation coupled with an assault upon all institutionalized forms of racial discrimination. But the white public has not accepted the concept of "total integration."

Some Paradoxes of Progress

The abandonment of the doctrine of "separate but equal" has forced consideration of many provocative questions, such as: "Can the victimization resulting from unequal treatment of Negroes in the past be eliminated without preferential treatment for present-day victims?" There are those who contend that justice demands more than equality, that it requires a "revolutionary break-through" in the form of preferential hiring, distinctive programs of education, and special scholarship schemes. The existence of entrenched patterns of residential segregation also raises the question of the desirability and probability of the persistence of Negro neighborhoods and institutions. If *forced* separation eventually disappeared would separateness cease to be an index of victimization? Would it then lose its pejorative implications? Would the right to choose, if it ever came, mean that some Negroes will choose *not* to be "integrated" except in the economic and political order?

New types of victimization are emerging which are not only indirect but are also unintended consequences of actions designed to eliminate victimization. For instance, in several Northern cities an earnest effort is being made to facilitate and speed up the process of residential desegregation at the middle-class level. Negroes whose incomes and life styles approximate those of the white middle class are accepted into neighborhoods and apartment buildings in limited numbers in order not to excite fear and panic among white residents.

The goal, as one Chicago neighborhood association states it, is "an integrated neighborhood with high community standards," to reverse the process of ghettoization. However, without a commitment to "open occupancy" at the city level, attainment of this goal demands a neighborhood-by-neighborhood approach, which calls for studying "tipping points" and setting up "benign quotas" in order to maintain a "racial balance." It may also involve a program which forces all lower-class residents to leave irrespective of their color, while integrating a small number of middle-class Negroes into neighborhoods or specific apartment buildings. One effective technique has been clearance of slums followed by rebuilding at a high enough rent level to keep the proportion of Negroes automatically very low. This process is frequently called "controlled integration."[50] Actions such as these often result in the concentration of many lower-class Negroes into almost completely segregated public housing projects. What is gained for some in terms of better physical surroundings is lost in increased "ghettoization." Other displaced persons increase the degree of overcrowding in already overcrowded neighborhoods or filter into middle-class Negro neighborhoods and disorganize them.

Serious problems also arise within the middle class at the psychological level. Insofar as Negro families have to cooperate actively in setting and maintaining quotas on the number of Negroes who enter, and in eliminating lower-class Negroes from the neighborhood, they become vulnerable to attack by other Negroes. Some sensitive individuals suffer from a feeling of guilt over manipulating the situation to maintain exclusiveness; others feel a loss of dignity in carrying on continuous discussion about race with white people. They dislike dealing with themselves as "a problem." A few people simply withdraw from such "integrated" situations into the comfort of the middle-class "gilded ghetto." This situation is only a special case of a more general problem confronting some Negroes in this Era of Integration—how to reconcile being a "loyal Negro" or a "Race Man" with new middle-class interracial relations or new occupational roles.

Rapid and fairly complete "integration" of middle-class Negroes into neighborhoods, churches, educational, and voluntary associations could have a profound effect upon Negro institutional life, "skimming off the cream" of the Negro élites to the disadvantage of the larger Negro community. This would result in a kind of victimization of the Negro masses which would be permanent unless the conditions of life for the lower classes were drastically changed.

Unfortunately there are few signs of hope that the Negro masses will profit from current economic changes, for at the very moment when the civil rights movement has been most successful, and when access to training is being made more widely available to Negroes, forces are at work which could render these gains meaningless. Whitney Young, Jr., of the National Urban League, emphasizing economic problems facing Negroes, stated upon one occasion: "Unless we identify these problems and take steps to meet them, we will find the masses of Negroes five years from today with a mouthful of rights, living in hovels with empty stomachs."[51] About 12 per cent of the nonwhite labor force were unemployed in 1960, twice the rate for white workers.[52] In some urban areas it was between 15 and 20 per cent. It was higher for Negro men than for women. Unemployment rates are particularly high for Negro youth. In 1961, nonwhite boys and girls between fourteen and nineteen had the highest unemployment rate of any age-color group in the nation, while the unemployment rate for Negro high-school graduates between the ages of sixteen and twenty-one was twice that for white youth and higher than the rate for whites who had *not* attended high school. One out of five Negro high-school graduates were unable to find jobs.[53] If high-school graduates face such a situation, the plight of the untrained Negro is likely to be even worse. It was estimated in 1964 that automation was wiping out about 40,000 unskilled jobs a week, the sector of industry where Negro workers are concentrated. This trend is likely to continue for some time.[54]

If Negroes are not to become a permanent *lumpen-proletariat* within American society as a result of social forces already at work and increased automation, deliberate planning by governmental and private agencies will be necessary. Continued emphasis upon "merit hiring" will benefit a few individuals, but, in the final analysis, structural transformations will have to take place.[55] There are those who feel that only a radical shift in American values and simultaneous adjustments of economy and society will wipe out, forever, the victimization of the Negro. If such a situation does occur it is not likely to be the result of any cataclysmic proletarian upheaval, but rather through drift and piece-meal pragmatic decisions. One straw in the wind has been raised to test the temper of the time. Gunnar Myrdal and twenty-nine other scholars, writers, and political scientists have released a statement on "The Cybernation Revolution, the Weaponry Revolution, and the Human Rights Revolution." In discussing the need for adjustment to the effects of largescale automation, they made a revolutionary suggestion:

We urge, therefore, that society, through its appropriate legal and governmental institutions, undertake an unqualified commitment to provide every individual and every family with an adequate income as a matter of right. . . .

Should this ever happen, Negroes would, of course, profit even more than whites, but demands for radical reforms of this type have not arisen from within the Civil Rights Movement whose leaders generally accept a middle-class work ethic which is incompatible with such a solution.

The author wishes to acknowledge with gratitude the assistance of Miss Odessa D. Thompson.

REFERENCES

1. The first systematic formulation of a caste-class hypothesis to explain American race relations appeared in an article by W. Lloyd Warner and Allison Davis, "A Comparative Study of American Caste," one of several contributions to a volume edited by Edgar Thompson, *Race Relations and The Race Problem* (Raleigh, N. C., 1939). The field research upon which much of the article was based was published later as Allison Davis, Burleigh Gardner, and Mary Gardner, *Deep South* (Chicago, 1941). For a Marxist criticism of the caste-class interpretation of American race relations see Oliver Cromwell Cox, *Caste, Class and Race* (New York, 1948).

2. Analysis of inter-ethnic mobility in terms of conflict, accommodation, and assimilation characterized the work of "The Chicago School" of Sociology during the 1920's and early 1930's. For more sophisticated analysis, note W. L. Warner and Leo Srole, *The Social Systems of American Ethnic Groups* (New Haven, Conn., 1946), in which studies of comparative mobility rates of various ethnic groups are made. Nathan Glazer and Patrick D. Moynihan, in *Beyond The Melting Pot* (Cambridge, Mass., 1963), have recently suggested that ethnic solidarities are much more enduring than earlier sociologists had expected them to be.

3. John Dollard, in association with Allison Davis, has added other dimensions to his analysis in *Children of Bondage* (Washington, D. C., 1940).

4. For a discussion of these concepts see Hans Gerth and C. Wright Mills, *From Max Weber: Essays in Sociology* (New York, 1946), chapter on "Caste, Class and Party."

5. The distinguished psychotherapist, Bruno Bettelheim, of the Orthogenic School of the University of Chicago, in a provocative and perceptive article

in *The Nation,* October 19, 1963 ("Class, Color and Prejudice"), contends that protection of social class values is a more important variable than race prejudice in structuring relations between Negroes and whites in the North of the U.S.A.

6. St. Clair Drake and Horace R. Clayton, in *Black Metropolis* (New York, 1962), use the term "Black Ghetto" to refer to the involuntary and exploitative aspect of the all-Negro community and "Bronzeville" to symbolize the more pleasant aspects of the segregated community. Robert C. Weaver, another Negro scholar, called his first book *The Negro Ghetto* (New York, 1948). The term is widely used by contemporary Negro leaders with pejorative implications. See also Kenneth Clark, *Dark Ghetto* (New York, 1965).

7. The most careful study of the effect of Negro entry into all-white neighborhoods is to be found in a book published by the University of California Press in 1961 which reports upon the results of research in Detroit, Chicago, Kansas City, Oakland, San Francisco, Philadelphia, and Portland, Oregon— Luigi Laurenti's *Property Values and Race* (Berkeley, Calif., 1961).

8. Thomas F. Pettigrew, *A Profile of the Negro American* (Princeton, N. J., 1964), p. 190. His wife, Dr. Ann Pettigrew, M.D., collaborated with him on the chapter dealing with health.

9. Though based upon only one community in Chicago, *The Politics of Urban Renewal,* by Peter Rossi and Robert A. Dentler (Glencoe, Ill., 1961) analyzes basic processes to be found in all Northern cities.

10. Professor Everett C. Hughes makes some original and highly pertinent remarks about new Negro middle-class communities in his introduction to the 1962 edition of Drake and Cayton's *Black Metropolis.*

11. Pettigrew, *op. cit.,* pp. 180-181.

12. The issue of the extent to which Negroes have been victimized by urban redevelopment is discussed briefly by Robert C. Weaver in *The Urban Complex: Human Values in Urban Life* (New York, 1964). See also Martin Anderson, *The Federal Bulldozer: A Critical Analysis of Urban Renewal: 1949-1962* (Cambridge, Mass., 1964).

13. Drake and Cayton, *op. cit.,* Chap. 23, "Advancing the Race."

14. See section on "The Negro Community as a Pathological Form of an American Community," Chap. 43 of Gunnar Myrdal, *An American Dilemma* (New York, 1944), p. 927.

15. A report appeared on the front page of *The New York Times,* April 5, 1965, stating that a commission was at work trying to elaborate plans for "integrating" Harlem by 1975. Columbia University was said to be co-operating in the research aspects of the project.

16. A successful experiment in "controlled integration" has been described by Julia Abrahamson in *A Neighborhood Finds Itself* (New York, 1959).

17. Jacob Schiffman, "Marital and Family Characteristics of Workers, March,

1962," in *Monthly Labor Review*, U. S. Department of Labor, Bureau of Labor Statistics, Special Labor Force Report No. 26, January 1963.

18. *Ibid.*

19. Norval D. Glenn, "Some Changes in the Relative Status of American Non-whites: 1940-1960," *Phylon*, Vol. 24, No. 2 (Summer 1963).

20. Pettigrew, *op. cit.*, p. 188.

21. *Ibid.*, p. 99; see also Marcus S. Goldstein, "Longevity and Health Status of Whites and Non-Whites in the United States," *Journal of the National Medical Association*, Vol. 46, No. 2 (March 1954), p. 83. Among other factors, the author emphasizes the relationship between nutrition and racial mortality differentials.

22. Marion Haynes, "A Century of Change: Negroes in the U. S. Economy, 1860-1960," *Monthly Labor Review*, U. S. Department of Labor, Bureau of Labor Statistics, December 1962.

23. Pettigrew (*op. cit.*, p. 87) comments that some research indicates that ". . . these group differences are inflated through disproportionate under-reporting of whites. . . ."

24. The rates cited are from Pettigrew, *op. cit.*, Chap. 4, "Negro American Health."

25. *Monthly Vital Statistics Report*, National Center for Health Statistics, U. S. Department of Health, Education and Welfare, Public Health Service, Vol. 13 (November 2, 1964), p. 8.

26. *Ibid.*, p. 7.

27. Pettigrew, *op. cit.*, p. 96.

28. *Ibid.*, p. 99.

29. *Ibid.*, pp. 82-94, "Communicable Diseases," and pp. 97-98, "Economics and Physical Health."

30. It has been demonstrated with data drawn from six Southern states that Negro mothers occupying private rooms in hospitals had a lower death rate among their infants than white mothers on the wards. See H. Bloch, H. Lippett, B. Redner, and D. Hirsch," Reduction of Mortality in the Premature Nursery," *Journal of Pediatrics*, Vol. 41, No. 3 (September 1952), pp. 300-304.

31. Dr. Arthur G. Falls' statement was released through the Chicago Urban League on October 20, 1963, having been sent out on October 16th with a "hold." (Copy in files of Chicago Urban League, C.E.D.)

32. These actions are discussed in the Presidential Address delivered to the Institute of Medicine of Chicago, January 14, 1960, by Dr. Franklin C. McLean, "Negroes and Medicine in Chicago." (Mimeographed copy in files of Chicago Urban League).

33. The 1965 assessment is from a statement by Dr. Robert G. Morris, circulated in mimeographed form by the Chicago Urban League. The standard work on the problems facing Negro physicians in Dietrich C. Reitzes, *Negroes and Medicine* (Cambridge, Mass., 1958).

34. Summarized from documents on file with Chicago Urban League.

35. Dr. F. C. McLean, cited in 32 *supra*.

36. Note Pettigrew, *op. cit.*, p. 97, which cites "lack of prenatal care, poor family health education, inadequate diet and inexpert delivery" as factors.

37. Philip F. Williams, "Material Welfare and the Negro," *Journal of American Medical Association*, Vol. 132, No. 11 (November 16, 1946), pp. 611-614.

38. M. Gover and J. B. Yaukey, "Physical Impairments of Members of Low-Income Farm Families," *Public Health Reports*, Vol. 61, No. 4 (January 25, 1946), and Marion E. Altenderfer and Beatrice Crowther, "Relationship Between Infant Mortality and Socio-economic Factors in Urban Areas," *Public Health Reports*, Vol. 64, No. 11 (March 18, 1949), pp. 331-339.

39. Marcus S. Goldstein, *op. cit.*, p. 93.

40. Dr. Ann Pettigrew cites a study carried out in Chicago, using 1950 data, in which, when Negroes and whites of the same economic level were compared, mortality rates were about the same although the rates for Negroes as a group when compared with those for whites as a group were higher. Other studies using the same body of data indicate sharp differences in mortality rates as between laborers and skilled workers among Negroes, a situation similar to that found among whites (Pettigrew, *op. cit.*, p. 98).

41. *Ibid.*, p. 80.

42. *Ebony*, a well-edited, widely circulated, popular weekly magazine which concentrates upon the display of what its editor calls "Negro achievement" carries skin-lightener advertisements routinely. *Ebony*'s African imitator, *Drum*, also carries such advertisements.

43. The classical study in this field is Kenneth B. Clark and Mamie P. Clark, "Racial Identification and Preference in Negro Children," which has been made widely accessible through T. M. Newcomb and E. L. Hartley's *Readings in Social Psychology* (New York, 1947), pp. 169-178.

44. Analyses of the genesis of the derogatory stereotypes of Africa and Africans may be found in Kenneth Little, *Negroes in Britain* (London, 1948), and Philip Curtin, *The Image of Africa* (Madison, Wisc., 1964). See also "Toward an Evaluation of African Societies," by St. Clair Drake, in *Africa Seen by American Negro Scholars* (New York, 1958).

45. The extent to which the pattern in Bahia, Brazil, differs from that in the United States is analyzed by Donald Pierson in *Negroes in Brazil* (Chicago, 1942).

46. Wilson Record, "Counseling and Communication," *Journal of Negro Education*, Vol. 30, No. 4 (Fall 1961).

47. Note Harold Isaacs, *The New World of Negro Americans* (New York, 1963), and St. Clair Drake, "To Hide My Face? An Essay on Pan Africanism and Negritude," in Herbert Hill (ed.), *Soon One Morning* (New York, 1963).

48. See Essien-Udom, *Black Nationalism: A Search for an Identity in America* (Chicago, 1962); and Charles Eric Lincoln's *The Black Muslims in America* (Boston, 1961). Reactions to the deaths of Patrice Lumumba and Malcolm X among a segment of the Negro American lower-class reveal the not-to-be-ignored depth of Black Nationalist feeling in the U.S.A.

49. Pettigrew, *op. cit.*, pp. 161-168, "The New Role of the Equal Citizen."

50. Peter Rossi, *op. cit.*

51. Quoted by James Reston in a column, "The Ironies of History and the American Negro," *The New York Times,* May 15, 1964.

52. See Glenn, *op. cit.*, and Haynes, *op. cit.*

53. See Schiffman, *op. cit.*

54. Pettigrew, *op. cit.*, p. 169.

55. *Ibid.*, "Some Needed Societal Reforms," pp. 168-176.

JOHN HOPE FRANKLIN

The Two Worlds of Race: A Historical View

I

MEASURED BY universal standards the history of the United States is
indeed brief. But during the brief span of three and one-half centuries of colonial and national history Americans developed traditions and prejudices which created the two worlds of race in modern America. From the time that Africans were brought as
indentured servants to the mainland of English America in 1619, the
enormous task of rationalizing and justifying the forced labor of peoples on the basis of racial differences was begun; and even after
legal slavery was ended, the notion of racial differences persisted as
a basis for maintaining segregation and discrimination. At the same
time, the effort to establish a more healthy basis for the new world
social order was begun, thus launching the continuing battle between the two worlds of race, on the one hand, and the world of
equality and complete human fellowship, on the other.

For a century before the American Revolution the status of Negroes in the English colonies had become fixed at a low point that
distinguished them from all other persons who had been held in
temporary bondage. By the middle of the eighteenth century, laws
governing Negroes denied to them certain basic rights that were
conceded to others. They were permitted no independence of
thought, no opportunity to improve their minds or their talents or to
worship freely, no right to marry and enjoy the conventional family
relationships, no right to own or dispose of property, and no protection against miscarriages of justice or cruel and unreasonable
punishments. They were outside the pale of the laws that protected
ordinary humans. In most places they were to be governed, as the
South Carolina code of 1712 expressed it, by special laws "as may
restrain the disorders, rapines, and inhumanity to which they are
naturally prone and inclined. . . ." A separate world for them had

47

been established by law and custom. Its dimensions and the conduct of its inhabitants were determined by those living in a quite different world.

By the time that the colonists took up arms against their mother country in order to secure their independence, the world of Negro slavery had become deeply entrenched and the idea of Negro inferiority well established. But the dilemmas inherent in such a situation were a source of constant embarrassment. "It always appeared a most iniquitous scheme to me," Mrs. John Adams wrote her husband in 1774, "to fight ourselves for what we are daily robbing and plundering from those who have as good a right to freedom as we have." There were others who shared her views, but they were unable to wield much influence. When the fighting began General George Washington issued an order to recruiting officers that they were not to enlist "any deserter from the ministerial army, nor any stroller, negro, or vagabond, or person suspected of being an enemy to the liberty of America nor any under eighteen years of age." In classifying Negroes with the dregs of society, traitors, and children, Washington made it clear that Negroes, slave or free, were not to enjoy the high privilege of fighting for political independence. He would change that order later, but only after it became clear that Negroes were enlisting with the "ministerial army" in droves in order to secure their own freedom. In changing his policy if not his views, Washington availed himself of the services of more than 5,000 Negroes who took up arms against England.[1]

Many Americans besides Mrs. Adams were struck by the inconsistency of their stand during the War for Independence, and they were not averse to making moves to emancipate the slaves. Quakers and other religious groups organized antislavery societies, while numerous individuals manumitted their slaves. In the years following the close of the war most of the states of the East made provisions for the gradual emancipation of slaves. In the South, meanwhile, the antislavery societies were unable to effect programs of state-wide emancipation. When the Southerners came to the Constitutional Convention in 1787 they succeeded in winning some representation on the basis of slavery, in securing federal support of the capture and rendition of fugitive slaves, and in preventing the closing of the slave trade before 1808.

Even where the sentiment favoring emancipation was pronounced, it was seldom accompanied by a view that Negroes were the equals of whites and should become a part of one family of

Americans. Jefferson, for example, was opposed to slavery; and if he could have had his way, he would have condemned it in the Declaration of Independence. It did not follow, however, that he believed Negroes to be the equals of whites. He did not want to "degrade a whole race of men from the work in the scale of beings which their Creator may *perhaps* have given them. . . . I advance it therefore, as a suspicion only, that the blacks, whether originally a distinct race, or made distinct by time and circumstance, are inferior to the whites in the endowment both of body and mind." It is entirely possible that Jefferson's later association with the extraordinarily able Negro astronomer and mathematician, Benjamin Banneker, resulted in some modification of his views. After reading a copy of Banneker's almanac, Jefferson told him that it was "a document to which your whole race had a right for its justifications against the doubts which have been entertained of them."[2]

In communities such as Philadelphia and New York, where the climate was more favorably disposed to the idea of Negro equality than in Jefferson's Virginia, few concessions were made, except by a limited number of Quakers and their associates. Indeed, the white citizens in the City of Brotherly Love contributed substantially to the perpetuation of two distinct worlds of race. In the 1780's, the white Methodists permitted Negroes to worship with them, provided the Negroes sat in a designated place in the balcony. On one occasion, when the Negro worshippers occupied the front rows of the balcony, from which they had been excluded, the officials pulled them from their knees during prayer and evicted them from the church. Thus, in the early days of the Republic and in the place where the Republic was founded, Negroes had a definite "place" in which they were expected at all times to remain. The white Methodists of New York had much the same attitude toward their Negro fellows. Soon, there were separate Negro churches in these and other communities. Baptists were very much the same. In 1809 thirteen Negro members of a white Baptist church in Philadelphia were dismissed, and they formed a church of their own. Thus, the earliest Negro religious institutions emerged as the result of the rejection by white communicants of their darker fellow worshippers. Soon there would be other institutions—schools, newspapers, benevolent societies—to serve those who lived in a world apart.

Those Americans who conceded the importance of education for Negroes tended to favor some particular type of education that would be in keeping with their lowly station in life. In

1794, for example, the American Convention of Abolition Societies recommended that Negroes be instructed in "those mechanic arts which will keep them most constantly employed and, of course, which will less subject them to idleness and debauchery, and thus prepare them for becoming good citizens of the United States." When Anthony Benezet, a dedicated Pennsylvania abolitionist, died in 1784 his will provided that on the death of his wife the proceeds of his estate should be used to assist in the establishment of a school for Negroes. In 1787 the school of which Benezet had dreamed was opened in Philadelphia, where the pupils studied reading, writing, arithmetic, plain accounts, and sewing.

Americans who were at all interested in the education of Negroes regarded it as both natural and normal that Negroes should receive their training in separate schools. As early as 1773 Newport, Rhode Island, had a colored school, maintained by a society of benevolent clergymen of the Anglican Church. In 1798 a separate private school for Negro children was established in Boston; and two decades later the city opened its first public primary school for the education of Negro children. Meanwhile, New York had established separate schools, the first one opening its doors in 1790. By 1814 there were several such institutions that were generally designated as the New York African Free Schools.[3]

Thus, in the most liberal section of the country, the general view was that Negroes should be kept out of the main stream of American life. They were forced to establish and maintain their own religious institutions, which were frequently followed by the establishment of separate benevolent societies. Likewise, if Negroes were to receive any education, it should be special education provided in separate educational institutions. This principle prevailed in most places in the North throughout the period before the Civil War. In some Massachusetts towns, however, Negroes gained admission to schools that had been maintained for whites. But the School Committee of Boston refused to admit Negroes, arguing that the natural distinction of the races, which "no legislature, no social customs, can efface renders a promiscuous intermingling in the public schools disadvantageous both to them and to the whites." Separate schools remained in Boston until the Massachusetts legislature in 1855 enacted a law providing that in determining the qualifications of students to be admitted to any public school no distinction should be made on account of the race, color, or religious opinion of the applicant.

Meanwhile, in the Southern states, where the vast majority of the Negroes lived, there were no concessions suggesting equal treatment, even among the most liberal elements. One group that would doubtless have regarded itself as liberal on the race question advocated the deportation of Negroes to Africa, especially those who had become free. Since free Negroes "neither enjoyed the immunities of freemen, nor were they subject to the incapacities of slaves," their condition and "unconquerable prejudices" prevented amalgamation with whites, one colonization leader argued. There was, therefore, a "peculiar moral fitness" in restoring them to "the land of their fathers." Men like Henry Clay, Judge Bushrod Washington, and President James Monroe thought that separation—expatriation—was the best thing for Negroes who were or who would become free.[4]

While the colonization scheme was primarily for Negroes who were already free, it won, for a time, a considerable number of sincere enemies of slavery. From the beginning Negroes were bitterly opposed to it, and only infrequently did certain Negro leaders, such as Dr. Martin Delany and the Reverend Henry M. Turner, support the idea. Colonization, however, retained considerable support in the most responsible quarters. As late as the Civil War, President Lincoln urged Congress to adopt a plan to colonize Negroes, as the only workable solution to the race problem in the United States. Whether the advocates of colonization wanted merely to prevent the contamination of slavery by free Negroes or whether they actually regarded it as the just and honorable thing to do, they represented an important element in the population that rejected the idea of the Negro's assimilation into the main stream of American life.

Thus, within fifty years after the Declaration of Independence was written, the institution of slavery, which received only a temporary reversal during the Revolutionary era, contributed greatly to the emergence of the two worlds of race in the United States. The natural rights philosophy appeared to have little effect on those who became committed, more and more, to seeking a rationalization for slavery. The search was apparently so successful that even in areas where slavery was declining, the support for maintaining two worlds of race was strong. Since the Negro church and school emerged in Northern communities where slavery was dying, it may be said that the free society believed almost as strongly in racial separation as it did in racial freedom.

II

The generation preceding the outbreak of the Civil War witnessed the development of a set of defenses of slavery that became the basis for much of the racist doctrine to which some Americans have subscribed from then to the present time. The idea of the inferiority of the Negro enjoyed wide acceptance among Southerners of all classes and among many Northerners. It was an important ingredient in the theory of society promulgated by Southern thinkers and leaders. It was organized into a body of systematic thought by the scientists and social scientists of the South, out of which emerged a doctrine of racial superiority that justified any kind of control over the slave. In 1826 Dr. Thomas Cooper said that he had not the slightest doubt that Negroes were an "inferior variety of the human species; and not capable of the same improvement as the whites." Dr. S. C. Cartwright of the University of Louisiana insisted that the capacities of the Negro adult for learning were equal to those of a white infant; and the Negro could properly perform certain physiological functions only when under the control of white men. Because of the Negro's inferiority, liberty and republican institutions were not only unsuited to his temperament, but actually inimical to his well-being and happiness.

Like racists in other parts of the world, Southerners sought support for their ideology by developing a common bond with the less privileged. The obvious basis was race; and outside the white race there was to be found no favor from God, no honor or respect from man. By the time that Europeans were reading Gobineau's *Inequality of Races,* Southerners were reading Cartwright's *Slavery in the Light of Ethnology.* In admitting all whites into the pseudo-nobility of race, Cartwright won their enthusiastic support in the struggle to preserve the integrity and honor of *the* race. Professor Thomas R. Dew of the College of William and Mary comforted the lower-class whites by indicating that they could identify with the most privileged and affluent of the community. In the South, he said, "no white man feels such inferiority of rank as to be unworthy of association with those around him. Color alone is here the badge of distinction, the true mark of aristocracy, and all who are white are equal in spite of the variety of occupation."[5]

Many Northerners were not without their own racist views and policies in the turbulent decades before the Civil War. Some, as Professor Louis Filler has observed, displayed a hatred of Negroes that gave them a sense of superiority and an outlet for their frustrations. Others cared nothing one way or the other about Negroes and demanded only that they be kept separate.[6] Even some of the abolitionists themselves were ambivalent on the question of Negro equality. More than one antislavery society was agitated by the suggestion that Negroes be invited to join. Some members thought it reasonable for them to attend, but not to be put on an "equality with ourselves." The New York abolitionist, Lewis Tappan, admitted "that when the subject of acting out our profound principles in treating men irrespective of color is discussed heat is always produced."[7]

In the final years before the beginning of the Civil War, the view that the Negro was different, even inferior, was widely held in the United States. Leaders in both major parties subscribed to the view, while the more extreme racists deplored any suggestion that the Negro could ever prosper as a free man. At Peoria, Illinois, in October 1854, Abraham Lincoln asked what stand the opponents of slavery should take regarding Negroes. "Free them, and make them politically and socially, our equals? My own feelings will not admit of this; and if mine would, we well know that those of the great mass of white people will not. Whether this feeling accords with justice and sound judgment, is not the sole question, if indeed, it is any part of it. A universal feeling, whether well or ill founded, cannot be safely disregarded. We cannot, then, make them equals."

The Lincoln statement was forthright, and it doubtless represented the views of most Americans in the 1850's. Most of those who heard him or read his speech were of the same opinion as he. In later years, the Peoria pronouncement would be used by those who sought to detract from Lincoln's reputation as a champion of the rights of the Negro. In 1964, the White Citizens' Councils reprinted portions of the speech in large advertisements in the daily press and insisted that Lincoln shared their views on the desirability of maintaining two distinct worlds of race.

Lincoln could not have overcome the nation's strong predisposition toward racial separation if he had tried. And he did not try very hard. When he called for the enlistment of Negro troops, after issuing the Emancipation Proclamation, he was content not only to set Negroes apart in a unit called "U. S. Colored Troops," but also to have Negro privates receive $10 per month including clothing, while whites of the same rank received $13 per month plus clothing. Only the stubborn refusal of many Negro troops to accept discriminatory pay finally forced Congress to equalize compensation for white and Negro soldiers.[8] The fight for union that became also a fight for freedom never became a fight for equality or for the creation of one racial world.

The Lincoln and Johnson plans for settling the problems of peace and freedom never seriously touched on the concomitant problem of equality. To be sure, in 1864 President Lincoln privately raised with the governor of Louisiana the question of the franchise for a limited number of Negroes, but when the governor ignored the question the President let the matter drop. Johnson raised a similar question in 1866, but he admitted that it was merely to frustrate the design of radical reformers who sought a wider franchise for Negroes. During the two years following Appomattox Southern leaders gave not the slightest consideration to permitting any Negroes, regardless of their service to the Union or their education or their property, to share in the political life of their communities. Not only did every Southern state refuse to permit Negroes to vote, but they also refused to provide Negroes with any of the educational opportunities that they were providing for the whites.

The early practice of political disfranchisement and of exclusion from public educational facilities helped to determine subsequent policies that the South adopted regarding Negroes. While a few leaders raised their voices against these policies and practices, it was Negroes themselves who made the most eloquent attacks on such discriminations. As early as May 1865, a group of North Carolina Negroes told President Johnson that some of them had been soldiers and were doing everything possible to learn how to discharge the higher duties of citizenship. "It seems to us that men who are willing on the field of battle to carry the muskets of the Republic, in the days of peace ought to be permitted to carry the ballots; and certainly we cannot understand the justice of denying the elective franchise to men who have been fighting *for* the country, while it is freely given to men who have just returned from *four* years fighting against it." Such pleas fell on deaf ears, however; and it was not until 1867, when Congress was sufficiently outraged by the inhuman black codes, widespread discriminations in the South, and unspeakable forms of violence against Negroes, that new federal legislation sought to correct the evils of the first period of Reconstruction.

The period that we know as Radical Reconstruction had no significant or permanent effect on the status of the Negro in American life. For a period of time, varying from one year to fifteen or twenty years, some Negroes enjoyed the privileges of voting. They gained political ascendancy in a very few communities only temporarily, and they never even began to achieve the status of a ruling class. They made no meaningful steps toward economic independence or even stability; and in no time at all, because of the pressures of the local community and the neglect of the federal government, they were brought under the complete economic subservience of the old ruling class. Organizations such as the Ku Klux Klan were committed to violent action to keep Negroes "in their place" and, having gained respectability through sponsorship by Confederate generals and the like, they proceeded to wreak havoc in the name of white supremacy and protection of white womanhood.[9]

Meanwhile, various forms of segregation and discrimination, developed in the years before the Civil War in order to degrade the half million free Negroes in the United States, were now applied to the four million Negroes who had become free in 1865. Already the churches and the military were completely segregated. For the most part the schools, even in the North, were separate. In the South segregated schools persisted, even in the places where the radicals made a half-hearted attempt to desegregate them. In 1875 Congress enacted a Civil Rights Act to guarantee the enjoyment of equal rights in carriers and all places of public accommodation and amusement. Even before it became law Northern philanthropists succeeded in forcing the deletion of the provision calling for desegregated schools. Soon, because of the massive resistance in the North as well as in the South and the indifferent manner in which the federal government enforced the law, it soon became a dead letter everywhere. When it was declared unconstitutional by the Supreme Court in 1883, there was universal rejoicing, except among the Negroes, one of whom declared that they had been "baptized in ice water."

Neither the Civil War nor the era of Reconstruction made any significant step toward the permanent elimination of racial barriers. The radicals of the post-Civil War years came no closer to the creation of one racial world than the patriots of the Revolutionary years. When Negroes were, for the first time, enrolled in the standing army of the United States, they were placed in separate Negro units. Most of the liberals of the Reconstruction era called for and worked for separate schools for Negroes. Nowhere was there any extensive effort to involve Negroes in the churches and other social institutions of the dominant group. Whatever remained of the old abolitionist fervor, which can hardly be described as unequivocal on the question of true racial equality, was rapidly disappearing. In its place were the sentiments of the business men who wanted peace at any price. Those having common railroad interests or crop-marketing interests or investment interests could and did extend their hands across sectional lines and joined in the task of working together for the common good. In such an atmosphere the practice was to accept the realities of two separate worlds of race. Some even subscribed to the view that there were significant economic advantages in maintaining the two worlds of race.

III

The post-Reconstruction years witnessed a steady deterioration in the status of Negro Americans. These were the years that Professor Rayford Logan has called the "nadir" of the Negro in American life and thought. They were the years when Americans, weary of the crusade that had, for the most part, ended with the outbreak of the Civil War, displayed almost no interest in helping the Negro to achieve equality. The social Darwinists decried the very notion of equality for Negroes, arguing that the lowly place they occupied was natural and normal. The leading literary journals vied with each other in describing Negroes as lazy, idle, improvident, immoral, and criminal.[10] Thomas Dixon's novels, *The Klansman* and *The Leopard's Spots,* and D. W. Griffith's motion picture, "The Birth of A Nation," helped to give Americans a view of the Negro's role in American history that "proved" that he was unfit for citizenship, to say nothing of equality. The dictum of William Graham Sumner and his followers that "stateways cannot change folkways" convinced many Americans that legislating equality and creating one great society where race was irrelevant was out of the question.

But many Americans believed that they *could* legislate inequality; and they proceeded to do precisely that. Beginning in 1890, one Southern state after another revised the suffrage provisions of its constitution in a manner that made it virtually impossible for Negroes to qualify to vote. The new literacy and "understanding" provisions permitted local registrars to disqualify Negroes while permitting white citizens to qualify. Several states, including Louisiana, North Carolina, and Oklahoma, inserted "grandfather clauses" in their constitutions in order to permit persons, who could not otherwise qualify, to vote if their fathers or grandfathers could vote in 1866. (This was such a flagrant discrimination against Negroes, whose ancestors could not vote in 1866, that the United States Supreme Court in 1915 declared the "grandfather clause" unconstitutional.) Then came the Democratic white primary in 1900 that made it impossible for Negroes to participate in local elections in the South, where, by this time, only the Democratic party had any appreciable strength. (After more than a generation of assaults on it, the white primary was finally declared unconstitutional in 1944.)

Inequality was legislated in still another way. Beginning in the 1880's, many states, especially but not exclusively in the South, enacted statutes designed to separate the races. After the Civil Rights Act was declared unconstitutional in 1883 state legislatures were emboldened to enact numerous segregation statutes. When the United States Supreme Court, in the case of Plessy *v.* Ferguson, set forth the "separate but equal" doctrine in 1896, the decision provided a new stimulus for laws to separate the races and, of course, to discriminate against Negroes. In time, Negroes and whites were separated in the use of schools, churches, cemeteries, drinking fountains, restaurants, and all places of public accommodation and amusement. One state enacted a law providing for the separate warehousing of books used by white and Negro children. Another required the telephone company to provide separate telephone booths for white and Negro customers. In most communities housing was racially separated by law or practice.[11]

Where there was no legislation requiring segregation, local practices filled the void. Contradictions and inconsistencies seemed not to disturb those who sought to maintain racial distinctions at all costs. It mattered not that one drive-in snack bar served Negroes only on the inside, while its competitor across the street served Negroes only on the outside. Both were committed to making racial distinctions; and in communities where practices and mores had the force of law, the distinction was everything. Such practices were greatly strengthened when, in 1913, the federal government adopted policies that segregated the races in its offices as well as in its eating and rest-room facilities.

By the time of World War I, Negroes and whites in the South and in parts of the North lived in separate worlds, and the apparatus for keeping the worlds separate was elaborate and complex. Negroes were segregated by law in the public schools of the Southern states, while those in the Northern ghettos were sent to predominantly Negro schools, except where their numbers were insufficient. Scores of Negro newspapers sprang up to provide news of Negroes that the white press consistently ignored. Negroes were as unwanted in the white churches as they had been in the late eighteenth century; and Negro churches of virtually every denomination were the answer for a people who had accepted the white man's religion even as the white man rejected his religious fellowship.

Taking note of the fact that they had been omitted from any serious consideration by the white historians, Negroes began in earnest to write the history of their own experiences as Americans. There had been Negro historians before the Civil War, but none of them had challenged the white historians' efforts to relegate Negroes to a separate, degraded world. In 1882, however, George Washington Williams published his *History of the Negro Race in America* in order to "give the world more correct ideas about the colored people." He wrote, he said, not "as a partisan apologist, but from a love for the truth of history."[12] Soon there were other historical works by Negroes describing their progress and their contributions and arguing that they deserved to be received into the full fellowship of American citizens.

It was in these post-Reconstruction years that some of the most vigorous efforts were made to destroy the two worlds of race. The desperate pleas of Negro historians were merely the more articulate attempts of Negroes to gain complete acceptance in American life. Scores of Negro organizations joined in the struggle to gain protection and recognition of their rights and to eliminate the more sordid practices that characterized the treatment of the Negro world by the white world. Unhappily, the small number of whites who were committed to racial equality dwindled in the post-Reconstruction years, while government at every level showed no interest in eliminating racial separatism. It seemed that Negro voices were indeed crying in the wilderness, but they carried on their attempts to be heard. In 1890 Negroes from twenty-one states and the District of Columbia met in Chicago and organized the Afro-American League of the United States. They called for more equitable distribution of school funds, fair and impartial trial for accused Negroes, resistance "by all legal and reasonable means" to mob and lynch law, and enjoyment of the franchise by all qualified voters. When a group of young Negro intellectuals, led by W. E. B. Du Bois, met at Niagara Falls, Ontario, in 1905, they made a similar call as they launched their Niagara Movement.

However eloquent their pleas, Negroes alone could make no successful assault on the two worlds of race. They needed help— a great deal of help. It was the bloody race riots in the early years of the twentieth century that shocked civic minded and socially conscious whites into answering the Negro's pleas for support. Some whites began to take the view that the existence of two societies whose distinction was based solely on race was inimical to the best interests of the entire nation. Soon, they were taking the initiative and in 1909 organized the National Association for the Advancement of Colored People. They assisted the following year in establishing the National Urban League. White attorneys began to stand with Negroes before the United States Supreme Court to challenge the "grandfather clause," local .segregation ordinances, and flagrant miscarriages of justice in which Negroes were the victims. The patterns of attack developed during these years were to become invaluable later. Legal action was soon supplemented by picketing, demonstrating, and boycotting, with telling effect particularly in selected Northern communities.[13]

IV

The two world wars had a profound effect on the status of Negroes in the United States and did much to mount the attack on the two worlds of race. The decade of World War I witnessed a very significant migration of Negroes. They went in large numbers—perhaps a half million—from the rural areas of the South to the towns and cities of the South and North. They were especially attracted to the industrial centers of the North. By the thousands they poured into Pittsburgh, Cleveland, and Chicago. Although many were unable to secure employment, others were successful and achieved a standard of living they could not have imagined only a few years earlier. Northern communities were not altogether friendly and hospitable to the newcomers, but the opportunities for education and the enjoyment of political self-respect were the greatest they had ever seen. Many of them felt that they were entirely justified in their renewed hope that the war would bring about a complete merger of the two worlds of race.

Those who held such high hopes, however, were naive in the extreme. Already the Ku Klux Klan was being revived—this time in the North as well as in the South. Its leaders were determined to develop a broad program to unite "native-born white Christians for concerted action in the preservation of American institutions and the supremacy of the white race." By the time that the war was over, the Klan was in a position to make capital of the racial animosities that had developed during the conflict itself. Racial conflicts had broken out in many places during the war; and before the conference at Versailles was over race riots in the United States had brought about what can accurately be described as the "long, hot summer" of 1919.

If anything, the military operations which aimed to save the world for democracy merely fixed more permanently the racial separation in the United States. Negro soldiers not only constituted entirely separate fighting units in the United States Army, but, once overseas, were assigned to fighting units with the French Army. Negroes who sought service with the United States Marines or the Air Force were rejected, while the Navy relegated them to menial duties. The reaction of many Negroes was bitter, but most of the leaders, including Du Bois, counseled patience and loyalty. They continued to hope that their show of patriotism would win for them a secure place of acceptance as Americans.

Few Negro Americans could have anticipated the wholesale rejection they experienced at the conclusion of World War I. Returning Negro soldiers were lynched by hanging and burning, even while still in their military uniforms. The Klan warned Negroes that they must respect the rights of the white race "in whose country they are permitted to reside." Racial conflicts swept the country, and neither federal nor state governments seemed interested in effective intervention. The worlds of race were growing further apart in the postwar decade. Nothing indicated this more clearly than the growth of the Universal Negro Improvement Association, led by Marcus Garvey. From a mere handful of members at the end of the war, the Garvey movement rapidly became the largest secular Negro group ever organized in the United States. Although few Negroes were interested in settling in Africa—the expressed aim of Garvey—they joined the movement by the hundreds of thousands to indicate their resentment of the racial duality that seemed to them to be the central feature of the American social order.[14]

More realistic and hardheaded were the Negroes who were

more determined than ever to engage in the most desperate fight of their lives to destroy racism in the United States. As the editor of the *Crisis* said in 1919, "We return from fighting. We return fighting. Make way for Democracy! We saved it in France, and by the Great Jehovah, we will save it in the U.S.A., or know the reason why." This was the spirit of what Alain Locke called "The New Negro." He fought the Democratic white primary, made war on the whites who consigned him to the ghetto, attacked racial discrimination in employment, and pressed for legislation to protect his rights. If he was seldom successful during the postwar decade and the depression, he made it quite clear that he was unalterably opposed to the un-American character of the two worlds of race.

Hope for a new assault on racism was kindled by some of the New Deal policies of Franklin D. Roosevelt. As members of the economically disadvantaged group, Negroes benefited from relief and recovery legislation. Most of it, however, recognized the existence of the two worlds of race and accommodated itself to it. Frequently bread lines and soup kitchens were separated on the basis of race. There was segregation in the employment services, while many new agencies recognized and bowed to Jim Crow. Whenever agencies, such as the Farm Security Administration, fought segregation and sought to deal with people on the basis of their needs rather than race they came under the withering fire of the racist critics and seldom escaped alive. Winds of change, however slight, were discernible, and nowhere was this in greater evidence than in the new labor unions. Groups like the Congress of Industrial Organizations, encouraged by the support of the Wagner Labor Relations Act, began to look at manpower resources as a whole and to attack the old racial policies that viewed labor in terms of race.

As World War II approached, Negroes schooled in the experiences of the nineteen-twenties and thirties were unwilling to see the fight against Nazism carried on in the context of an American racist ideology. Some white Americans were likewise uncomfortable in the role of freeing Europe of a racism which still permeated the United States; but it was the Negroes who dramatized American inconsistency by demanding an end to discrimination in employment in defense industries. By threatening to march on Washington in 1941 they forced the President to issue an order forbidding such discrimination. The opposition was loud and strong. Some state governors denounced the order, and some manufacturers skillfully evaded it. But it was a significant step toward the elimination of the two worlds.

During World War II the assault on racism continued. Negroes, more than a million of whom were enlisted in the armed services, bitterly fought discrimination and segregation. The armed services were, for the most part, two quite distinct racial worlds. Some Negro units had white officers, and much of the officer training was desegregated. But it was not until the final months of the war that a deliberate experiment was undertaken to involve Negro and white enlisted men in the same fighting unit. With the success of the experiment and with the warm glow of victory over Nazism as a backdrop, there was greater inclination to recognize the absurdity of maintaining a racially separate military force to protect the freedoms of the country.[15]

During the war there began the greatest migration in the history of Negro Americans. Hundreds of thousands left the South for the industrial centers of the North and West. In those places they met hostility, but they also secured employment in aviation plants, automobile factories, steel mills, and numerous other industries. Their difficulties persisted as they faced problems of housing and adjustment. But they continued to move out of the South in such large numbers that by 1965 one third of the twenty million Negroes in the United States lived in twelve metropolitan centers of the North and West. The ramifications of such large-scale migration were numerous. The concentration of Negroes in communities where they suffered no political disabilities placed in their hands an enormous amount of political power. Consequently, some of them went to the legislatures, to Congress, and to positions on the judiciary. In turn, this won for them political respect as well as legislation that greatly strengthened their position as citizens.

V

Following World War II there was a marked acceleration in the war against the two worlds of race in the United States. In 1944 the Supreme Court ruled against segregation in interstate transportation, and three years later it wrote the final chapter in the war against the Democratic white primary. In 1947 the President's Committee on Civil Rights called for the "elimination of segregation, based on race, color, creed, or national origin, from American life."[16] In the following year President Truman asked Congress to establish a permanent Fair Employment Practices Commission. At the same time he took steps to eliminate segregation in the armed services. These moves on the part of the judicial and executive branches of the federal government by no means destroyed the two worlds of race, but they created a more healthy climate in which the government and others could launch an attack on racial separatism.

The attack was greatly strengthened by the new position of world leadership that the United States assumed at the close of the war. Critics of the United States were quick to point to the inconsistencies of an American position that spoke against racism abroad and countenanced it at home. New nations, brown and black, seemed reluctant to follow the lead of a country that adhered to its policy of maintaining two worlds of race—the one identified with the old colonial ruling powers and the other with the colonies now emerging as independent nations. Responsible leaders in the United States saw the weakness of their position, and some of them made new moves to repair it.

Civic and religious groups, some labor organizations, and many individuals from the white community began to join in the effort to destroy segregation and discrimination in American life. There was no danger, after World War II, that Negroes would ever again stand alone in their fight. The older interracial organizations continued, but they were joined by new ones. In addition to the numerous groups that included racial equality in their over-all programs, there were others that made the creation of one racial world their principal objective. Among them were the Congress of Racial Equality, the Southern Christian Leadership Conference, and the Student Non-Violent Coordinating Committee. Those in existence in the 1950's supported the court action that brought about the decision against segregated schools. The more recent ones have taken the lead in pressing for new legislation and in developing new techniques to be used in the war on segregation.

VI

The most powerful direct force in the maintenance of the two worlds of race has been the state and its political subdivisions. In states and communities where racial separation and discrimination are basic to the way of life, the elected officials invariably pledge themselves to the perpetuation of the duality. Indeed, candidates frequently vie with one another in their effort to occupy the most extreme segregationist position possible on the race question. Appointed officials, including the constabulary and, not infrequently, the teachers and school administrators, become auxiliary guardians of the system of racial separation. In such communities Negroes occupy no policy-making positions, exercise no influence over the determination of policy, and are seldom even on the police force. State and local resources, including tax funds, are at the disposal of those who guard the system of segregation and discrimination; and such funds are used to enforce customs as well as laws and to disseminate information in support of the system.

The white community itself acts as a guardian of the segregated system. Schooled in the specious arguments that assert the supremacy of the white race and fearful that a destruction of the system would be harmful to their own position, they not only "go along" with it but, in many cases, enthusiastically support it. Community sanctions are so powerful, moreover, that the independent citizen who would defy the established order would find himself not only ostracized but, worse, the target of economic and political reprisals.

Within the community many self-appointed guardians of white supremacy have emerged at various times. After the Civil War and after World War I it was the Ku Klux Klan, which has shown surprising strength in recent years. After the desegregation decision of the Supreme Court in 1954 it was the White Citizens' Council, which one Southern editor has called the "uptown Ku Klux Klan." From time to time since 1865, it has been the political demagogue, who has not only made capital by urging his election as a sure way to maintain the system but has also encouraged the less responsible elements of the community to take the law into their own hands.

Violence, so much a part of American history and particularly of Southern history, has been an important factor in maintaining the two worlds of race. Intimidation, terror, lynchings, and riots have, in succession, been the handmaiden of political entities whose officials have been unwilling or unable to put an end to it. Violence drove Negroes from the polls in the 1870's and has kept them away in droves since that time. Lynchings, the spectacular rope and faggot kind or the quiet kind of merely "doing away" with some insubordinate Negro, have served their special purpose in terrorizing whole communities of Negroes. Riots, confined to no section of the country, have demonstrated how explosive the racial situation can be in urban communities burdened with the strain of racial strife.

The heavy hand of history has been a powerful force in the maintenance of a segregated society and, conversely, in the resistance to change. Americans, especially Southerners whose devotion to the past is unmatched by that of any others, have summoned history to support their arguments that age-old practices and institutions cannot be changed overnight, that social practices cannot be changed by legislation. Southerners have argued that desegregation would break down long-established customs and bring instability to a social order that, if left alone, would have no serious racial or social disorders. After all, Southern whites "know" Negroes; and their knowledge has come from many generations of intimate association and observation, they insist.

White Southerners have also summoned history to support them in their resistance to federal legislation designed to secure the civil rights of Negroes. At every level—in local groups, state governments, and in Congress—white Southerners have asserted that federal civil rights legislation is an attempt to turn back the clock to the Reconstruction era, when federal intervention, they claim, imposed a harsh and unjust peace.[17] To make effective their argument, they use such emotion-laden phrases as "military occupation," "Negro rule," and "black-out of honest government." Americans other than Southerners have been frightened by the Southerners' claim that civil rights for Negroes would cause a return to the "evils" of Reconstruction. Insecure in their own knowledge of history, they have accepted the erroneous assertions about the "disaster" of radical rule after the Civil War and the vengeful punishment meted out to the South by the Negro and his white allies. Regardless of the merits of these arguments that seem specious on the face of them—to say nothing of their historical inaccuracy—they have served as effective brakes on the drive to destroy the two worlds of race.

One suspects, however, that racial bigotry has become more expensive in recent years. It is not so easy now as it once was to make political capital out of the race problem, even in the deep South. Local citizens—farmers, laborers, manufacturers—have become a bit weary of the promises of the demagogue that he will preserve the integrity of the races if he is, at the same time, unable to persuade investors to build factories and bring capital to their communities. Some Southerners, dependent on tourists, are not certain that their vaunted racial pride is so dear, if it keeps visitors away and brings depression to their economy. The cities that see themselves bypassed by a prospective manufacturer because of their reputation in the field of race relations might have some sober second thoughts about the importance of maintaining their two worlds. In a word, the economics of segregation and discrimination is forcing, in some quarters, a reconsideration of the problem.

It must be added that the existence of the two worlds of race has created forces that cause some Negroes to seek its perpetuation. Some Negro institutions, the product of a dual society, have vested interests in the perpetuation of that society. And Negroes who fear the destruction of their own institutions by desegregation are encouraged by white racists to fight for their maintenance. Even where Negroes have a desire to maintain their institutions because of their honest commitment to the merits of cultural pluralism, the desire becomes a strident struggle for survival in the context of racist forces that seek with a vengeance to destroy such institutions. The firing of a few hundred Negro school teachers by a zealous, racially-oriented school board forces some second thoughts on the part of the Negroes regarding the merits of desegregation.

VII

The drive to destroy the two worlds of race has reached a new, dramatic, and somewhat explosive stage in recent years. The forces arrayed in behalf of maintaining these two worlds have been subjected to ceaseless and powerful attacks by the increasing numbers committed to the elimination of racism in American life. Through techniques of demonstrating, picketing, sitting-in, and boycotting they have not only harrassed their foes but marshaled their forces. Realizing that another ingredient was needed, they have pressed for new and better laws and the active support of government. At the local and state levels they began to secure legislation in the 1940's to guarantee the civil rights of all, eliminate discrimination in employment, and achieve decent public and private housing for all.

While it is not possible to measure the influence of public opinion in the drive for equality, it can hardly be denied that over the past five or six years public opinion has shown a marked shift toward vigorous support of the civil rights movement. This can be seen in the manner in which the mass-circulation magazines as well as influential newspapers, even in the South, have stepped up their support of specific measures that have as their objective the elimination of at least the worst features of racism. The discussion of the problem of race over radio and television and the use of these media in reporting newsworthy and dramatic events in the world of race undoubtedly have had some impact. If such activities have not brought about the enactment of civil rights legislation, they have doubtless stimulated the public discussion that culminated in such legislation.

The models of city ordinances and state laws and the increased political influence of civil rights advocates stimulated new action on the federal level. Civil rights acts were passed in 1957, 1960, and 1964—after almost complete federal inactivity in this sphere for more than three quarters of a century. Strong leadership on the part of the executive and favorable judicial interpretations of old as well as new laws have made it clear that the war against the two worlds of race now enjoys the sanction of the law and its interpreters. In many respects this constitutes the most significant development in the struggle against racism in the present century.

The reading of American history over the past two centuries impresses one with the fact that ambivalence on the crucial question of equality has persisted almost from the beginning. If the term "equal rights for all" has not always meant what it appeared to mean, the inconsistencies and the paradoxes have become increasingly apparent. This is not to say that the view that "equal rights for some" has disappeared or has even ceased to be a threat to the concept of real equality. It is to say, however, that the voices supporting inequality, while no less strident, have been significantly weakened by the very force of the numbers and elements now seeking to eliminate the two worlds of race.

REFERENCES

1. Benjamin Quarles, *The Negro in the American Revolution* (Chapel Hill, N. C., 1961), pp. 15–18.

2. John Hope Franklin, *From Slavery to Freedom: A History of American Negroes* (New York, 1956), pp. 156–157.

3. Carter G. Woodson, *The Education of the Negro Prior to 1861* (Washington, D. C., 1919), pp. 93–97.

4. P. J. Staudenraus, *The African Colonization Movement, 1816–1865* (New York, 1961), pp. 22–32.

5. John Hope Franklin, *The Militant South, 1800–1861* (Cambridge, Mass., 1956), pp. 83–86.

6. Louis Filler, *The Crusade Against Slavery, 1830–1860* (New York, 1960), pp. 142–145.

7. Leon F. Litwack, *North of Slavery; The Negro in the Free States, 1790–1860* (Chicago, 1961), pp. 216–217.

8. Benjamin Quarles, *The Negro in the Civil War* (Boston, 1953), p. 200.

9. John Hope Franklin, *Reconstruction After the Civil War* (Chicago, 1961), pp. 154–158.

10. Rayford W. Logan, *The Negro in American Life and Thought: The Nadir, 1877–1901* (New York, 1954), pp. 239–274.

11. John Hope Franklin, "History of Racial Segregation in the United States," *Annals of the Academy of Political and Social Science*, Vol. 304 (March 1956), pp. 1–9.

12. George W. Williams, *History of the Negro Race in America from 1619 to 1880* (New York, 1882), p. x.

13. Franklin, *From Slavery to Freedom*, pp. 437–443.

14. Edmund David Cronon, *Black Moses, The Story of Marcus Garvey and the Universal Negro Improvement Association* (Madison, Wis., 1955), pp. 202–206.

15. Lee Nichols, *Breakthrough on the Color Front* (New York, 1954), pp. 221–226.

16. *To Secure These Rights, The Report of the President's Committee on Civil Rights* (New York, 1947), p. 166.

17. John Hope Franklin, "As For Our History," in Charles G. Sellers (ed.), *The Southerner as American* (Chapel Hill, N. C., 1960), pp. 1–18.

II

DIAGNOSTIC FACTORS:
DEMOGRAPHIC, ECONOMIC, AND
FAMILIAL

PHILIP M. HAUSER

Demographic Factors in the Integration of the Negro

THE SIZE, rate of growth, distribution, and composition of the Negro population both influence integration and provide some indications of the extent to which it has been achieved. The precise way in which these demographic factors affect integration, positively or negatively, is not definitely known. Yet, what is known about the process of acculturation, on the one hand, and about population changes, on the other, permits some consideration of their interrelationships and, at least, speculation about the influence of the latter upon the former. This essay is an attempt to summarize the characteristics of the Negro population and to consider how changes in it affect integration.

It is necessary before proceeding with these tasks, however, to define the term "integration." In popular usage the term is employed to encompass a variety of connotations ranging from mere desegregation or admixture of whites and Negroes, as a salt and pepper combination in an audience, to varying degrees of interaction and participation in common life activities. For purposes of this paper integration is viewed as more than mere desegregation; rather, it is seen as social interaction, effective communication, and a sharing in activities that fill one's life. In this sense integration is a social process that may be considered one form of acculturation—social interaction embracing members of diverse racial as well as cultural backgrounds.

Let us review first some highlights in the population history of the Negro in the United States.

Characteristics of the Negro American Population

Total population. When the first Census of Population was

taken in 1790, there were some 3.9 million persons in this country.[1] Of these, 3.2 million were white and 757 thousand were Negro. By that time, Negroes had resided in the colonies for about 175 years as the indentured servants or property of their white slave-owner masters. At the first census, they constituted almost one-fifth (19.3 per cent) of the total population.

Negroes remained about one-fifth of the national total until 1810. From that date to 1930, they became a declining proportion of the population as slave importation ceased and white immigration continued. By 1930, Negroes had decreased to less than one-tenth of the national total (9.7 per cent). Since 1940, the growth rate of the Negro population has exceeded that of the white; thus, by 1960, Negroes constituted slightly above one-tenth (10.6 per cent) of the total population. In fact, their absolute numbers had risen to 4.4 million by the onset of the Civil War, to 8.8 million by the turn of the century, and to 18.9 million by the 18th Decennial Census of Population in 1960.

Components of growth. The growth of the Negro population since 1820 was the result almost entirely of natural increase, that is, excess of births over deaths. Although the Negro birth rate, as the white birth rate, declined between 1850 and 1940, it has consistently been above the level of the white. As measured by the fertility ratio (children under five per 1,000 women twenty to forty-four years old) Negro fertility declined by more than half between 1850 and 1940, while white fertility declined by about one-third.

Between 1940 and 1960, the birth rates of both whites and nonwhites rose with the postwar baby boom. Nonwhite fertility increased by 90 per cent (from a fertility ratio of 418 to 795) while white fertility rose by 88 per cent (from 395 to 742). The great increase in nonwhite birth rates represents an astonishing reversal and occurred, interestingly enough, even while the Negro was becoming rapidly urbanized and metropolitanized as is indicated below. The phenomenal increase in nonwhite fertility is a result of the striking rise in nonwhite urban fertility, largely because of the decrease in childlessness brought about by improved health, including reduction in venereal and debilitating diseases.

For many purposes the best measure of mortality is given by its converse, expectation of life. Negro death rates, as the white, have decreased sharply since the turn of the century. Moreover, throughout the course of this century, because of the improvement in the position of the Negro in the nation, Negro death rates have, from a higher level, come down more sharply than white. In 1900, expectation of life at birth for nonwhites (mainly Negro) was 33.0 years as contrasted with 47.6 years for whites. By 1960, nonwhite life expectancy at birth had increased to 63.6 years, while white increased to 70.6 years. Thus, the difference in life expectation between the nonwhite and white decreased by more than half, from 14.6 years to 7.0 years.

As a result of more rapid decline in mortality and greater increase in fertility in recent decades, Negro natural increase has risen well above the white. Between 1905 and 1910, nonwhite natural increase at a level of 14.7 (excess of births over deaths per 1,000 persons) was not much above the level of white, 13.8. By 1960, nonwhite natural increase, at 22.0, was about two-thirds greater than that of white, at 13.2. The nonwhite rate of population growth in 1960, if sustained, would double the Negro population in a little over thirty years. In contrast, the continuation of the 1960 white rate would require over fifty years before doubling the population.

Some part of the difference in Negro and white natural increase is attributable to the difference in the age structure of the two populations. As will be seen below, the Negro population is appreciably younger than the white, a fact which tends to increase its birth rate and decrease its death rate. Even if this difference is taken into account, however, the nonwhite rate of increase is still over 60 per cent above the white, the nonwhite intrinsic rate being 31.2 in 1960 in contrast with 19.3 for whites.[2]

Age. In 1840, the median age of nonwhites was 17.3 years as compared with 17.9 years for whites. A century later, because of differences in Negro and white fertility, mortality, and immigration, the nonwhite median age was only 25.2 years, compared with 29.5 years for whites. In 1950, nonwhite and white median ages were, respectively, 26.1 and 30.8 years. Because of the baby boom, however, the median age of both the Negro and white populations decreased between 1950 and 1960 to 23.5 and 30.3 years respectively. Another indication that the Negro population is younger than the white is seen in the fact that a greater proportion of their population is under twenty. In 1960, 45.6 per cent of the Negroes, as compared with 39.5 per cent of whites, were under twenty years of age.

A significant aspect of Negro-white differences in age structure, with important implications for integration, is shown by considering differences in the burden of dependency, that is, the difference in the proportion of persons below and above working age in relation to that of persons of working age.

In 1910, Negro and white dependency was approximately the same. The Negro dependency ratio was 105—that is, for each 100 persons of working age (twenty to sixty-four) there were 105 persons either under twenty or sixty-five or over. Of the Negroes of dependent age, 99 were under twenty and 6 were sixty-five or over. The native-white dependency ratio in 1910 was 103, 96 of which were youth and 7 aged. By 1960, however, as a result of the remarkable upsurge in natural increase, the Negro had a considerably greater dependency burden. The Negro dependency ratio reached a level of 107, as contrasted with 90 for native whites. Moreover, Negro dependents were disproportionately young, the youth dependency ratio being 94, compared with 75 for whites. Thus Negro youth dependency in 1960 was at a level 25 per cent above that of white. Aged Negro dependency had increased to 13, but this was still below the level of 15 for whites.

Distribution. In 1790, 91 per cent of the Negroes lived in the South. This regional concentration of Negroes had not changed appreciably by 1910, as recorded in the last census taken before World War I (89 per cent). The first large internal migratory flow of Negroes from the South began during World War I. It was prompted by the combination of need for labor to man the expanding industrial plants of the North, as the United States served as the arsenal for the Allied Powers, and the changing economy of the South which, with the diversification of agriculture and the delayed impact of the industrial revolution, was freeing the Negro from the soil. The flow of Negroes from the South to the North and West continued thereafter, abating somewhat during the depression thirties and accelerating greatly during World War II and its aftermath. In consequence, the proportion of all Negroes living in the North and West almost quadrupled from 1910 to 1960, rising from 11 to 40 per cent.

The regional redistribution of the Negro was achieved primarily, of course, through migration. The internal migratory patterns of Negroes may be analyzed by means of lifetime migration patterns (based on census data on state of residence as compared with state of birth) or of estimates of net migration between censuses. According to the lifetime migration data, in 1910 83 per cent of the nonwhites lived in the state in which they were born, as compared with 77 per cent of the whites. As reported in the Census of 1910,

90 per cent of the native nonwhites lived in the same geographic division in which they were born and 94 per cent in the same region.* Comparable figures for whites were 84 and 90 per cent. Thus, in 1910, on a lifetime basis Negroes were less migratory than whites. However, Negroes had reversed the pattern and had become more migratory than whites by 1960, when only 64 per cent of the native nonwhites resided in the states in which they were born, only 72 per cent in the geographic division, and only 75 per cent in the region. In contrast, comparable figures for native whites were 68, 77, and 83 per cent.

Between 1910 and 1960, the exodus of Negroes from the South accelerated. Between 1910 and 1920, net migration of Negroes out of the South totaled 454,300; between 1920 and 1930, 749,000; between 1930 and 1940, 347,500; between 1940 and 1950, 1,244,700; and between 1950 and 1960, 1,457,000. Six states in the North and West (California, Illinois, Michigan, New York, Ohio, and Pennsylvania) absorbed 72 per cent of all Negro net in-migration between 1910 and 1950. Between 1950 and 1960, the same six states absorbed 68 per cent of all net in-migration of nonwhites.

Negro internal migratory flows effected shifts not only in their regional distribution but, even more important, also in their distribution within urban, rural, and metropolitan areas. In 1910, before large migratory streams of Negroes left the South, 73 per cent of the Negroes in the nation, as compared with 52 per cent of the whites, lived in rural areas, that is, on farms and in areas with fewer than 2,500 inhabitants. By 1960, the distribution of Negroes by urban-rural residence had become completely reversed, with 73 per cent of the Negro population residing in urban areas. Thus, within a period of fifty years, less than a lifetime, the Negro has been transformed from a predominantly rural to a predominantly urban resident. In fact, in 1960, Negroes were more highly urbanized than whites, 70 per cent of whom resided in urban areas.

The great increase in the concentration of Negroes is even more

* The Bureau of the Census classifies the United States into three or four "regions" and nine "geographic divisions." The geographic divisions employed are states grouped as follows: New England, Middle Atlantic, East North Central, West North Central, South Atlantic, East South Central, West South Central, Mountain, and Pacific. The regions are: the North (New England, Middle Atlantic, East North Central, and West North Central); the West (Mountain and Pacific); and the South (South Atlantic, East South Central, and West South Central). For the states in geographic divisions see *Statistical Abstract of the United States, 1964* (Washington, D. C., 1964).

dramatically revealed by analysis of their metropolitanization. In 1910, only 29 per cent of Negroes lived in Standard Metropolitan Statistical Areas (SMSA's). By 1960, the concentration of Negroes in SMSA's had increased to 65 per cent. Between 1920 and 1940, Negroes in SMSA's increased by 65 per cent as compared with 36 per cent for whites; and, between 1940 and 1960, Negroes in metropolitan areas more than doubled, increasing by 109 per cent, as compared with 50 per cent for whites.

Even more striking than the increase of Negroes in metropolitan areas is their concentration in the central cities of these areas. Between 1910 and 1920, the Negro population in central cities of metropolitan areas increased by 40 per cent; between 1920 and 1940, by 83 per cent; and between 1940 and 1960, by 123 per cent. Hence, by 1960, 51 per cent of all Negroes in the United States lived in the central cities of SMSA's. Of all Negroes resident in metropolitan areas, 80 per cent lived in central cities. There was a much higher concentration of Negroes in metropolitan areas and in their central cities in the North and West than in the South. In 1960, of all Negroes in the North 93 per cent were in SMSA's and 79 per cent in the central cities; and in the West 93 per cent in SMSA's and 67 per cent in central cities. In the South, however, 46 per cent of all Negro residents lived in SMSA's and 34 per cent in central cities. Finally, it must be observed that Negroes are disproportionately concentrated in the large SMSA's and especially in their central cities. The twenty-four SMSA's with 1 million or more persons in 1960 contained 38 per cent of the total Negro population, and their central cities, 31 per cent. Comparable figures for whites are 34 and 15 per cent.

Segregation. Negroes, as had white immigrant groups before them, found their ports of entry to cities in the inner slum areas, where they lived in enclaves or ghettos. The process of settlement has been well described both for white ethnic immigrants and the Negro.[3] The residential patterns and initial stages of urban settlement of both groups were characterized by segregation, but there were at least two important differences. First, the Negroes were more highly segregated than white ethnic groups; and, second, Negro segregation has, in general, increased rather than decreased over time.

Duncan and Lieberson, in their analysis of ethnic and racial segregation in Chicago in 1930, report an average index of segregation of 28 for four "old" countries and 41 for six "new" countries.[4]

Thus, it would have been necessary for 28 per cent of the foreign-born whites from earlier immigrations to be moved to match the distribution of native whites and 41 per cent of the foreign-born from more recent immigrations to do the same. In contrast, the index of segregation for Negroes in relation to the various foreign-white stocks varied from levels of 79 to 94. The index of segregation of Negroes in relation to native whites was 85 in 1930. Thus, the segregation of Negroes was much more marked than that of the foreign ethnic groups. In the same study, Duncan and Lieberson showed appreciable declines in the segregation of foreign-born whites relative to native whites between 1930 and 1950. These findings were further corroborated by Lieberson in his study of ten cities from 1930 to 1950.[5] In each of the cities (Boston, Buffalo, Chicago, Cincinnati, Cleveland, Columbus, Philadelphia, Pittsburgh, St. Louis, and Syracuse) segregation for foreign-born whites in relation to native whites decreased during that period. In contrast, Negro segregation in relation to native-white segregation increased in eight of the ten cities and in relation to foreign-white, increased in nine of the ten cities.

The higher level of Negro segregation is further demonstrated by Taeuber and Taeuber in their study of 207 cities in 1960.[6] The average index of Negro segregation for all the cities was 86, with regional variations ranging from an index of 76 in New England to 91 in the South Atlantic states. Moreover, the Taeubers found that the Negro index of segregation increased between 1940 and 1950 in all the eight geographic divisions they examined (New England, Middle Atlantic, East North Central, West North Central, West, South Atlantic, East South Central, West South Central); and, although segregation decreased slightly in the five northern and western divisions between 1950 and 1960, it actually increased in the three southern geographic divisions.

Thus, between 1910 and 1960, the Negro has been redistributed from the South to the North and West, and from rural to urban and metropolitan areas; but within the urban and metropolitan complexes the Negro American has become and has remained much more highly segregated than was true of white immigrants who flocked to the cities before them.

Family. In 1910, only 38 per cent of Negro women between the ages of fifty and fifty-four were living in first marriages with their husband present as contrasted with 59 per cent of the white. Moreover, larger proportions were widowed or divorced—35 and 19 per cent, respectively. By 1940, this differential in marital status had not changed appreciably. Family life must have been, at least temporarily, further disrupted by the large-scale internal migratory flows. In 1960, after fifty years of exodus from the South, less than half (48.6 per cent) of all nonwhite women were married and living with their husbands, as contrasted with almost two-thirds (63.7 per cent) of white women. About 16 per cent of nonwhite women were reported in the Census either as separated, married with their husbands absent, or divorced, in contrast to 6 per cent of the white. About 14 per cent of nonwhite women were widowed as contrasted with 12 per cent of the white.

Family disorganization and unstable family life among Negro Americans is a product of their history and caste status in the United States. During slavery and for at least the first half-century after emancipation, the Negro never had the opportunity to acquire the patterns of sexual behavior and family living which characterized middle-class white society.[7] African family patterns were, of course, destroyed during slavery, when it was virtually impossible to establish any durable form of family organization. Moreover, as a result of the slave traffic, children were necessarily attached to their mother in a more lasting manner than to their father.

This historical tendency toward a matriarchal family structure has been reinforced by the continued inability of the Negro male, because of lack of opportunity and discriminatory practices, to assume the role of provider and protector of his family in accordance with prevailing definitions of the role of husband and father.[8] The Negro male has, in a sense, been the victim of social and economic emasculation which has perpetuated and reinforced the matriarchal Negro family structure created by slavery. Moreover, this pattern has been further bolstered by the fact that the Negro female, in household interaction with middle-class white families of the South as well as the North, has acquired attitudes and norms of behavior which have led her to look down upon any Negro male without similar exposure. The Negro male, condemned largely to illiteracy, rough and dirty work, and limited social and cultural opportunities, could not meet the expectations of the Negro female. Furthermore, the tendency for Negro mothers to raise their children according to standards acquired in their contacts with white households has introduced tensions into relationships of father and child as well as husband and wife.

In view of unstable family life among Negroes, then, it should not be surprising that a smaller proportion of the nonwhite population than of the white lives in primary family groups, 84 per cent as contrasted with 89 per cent. Furthermore, nonwhite children, as contrasted with white, were much less frequently living with both their parents. In 1960, almost one-third (32.2 per cent) of nonwhite children under fourteen, as compared with 8 per cent of white, were being reared in the absence of one or both parents. About four times as large a proportion of nonwhite than white children (19.6 *vs.* 5.5 per cent) were living with their mothers only; and five times as many (10.9 *vs.* 1.8 per cent) were living with neither parent.

Education. In 1910, almost one in every three Negroes ten years old and over in the United States was illiterate (30.4 per cent). Illiteracy among Negroes, therefore, was ten time as great as among native whites(3 per cent). In the rural areas, Negro illiteracy was at a level of over 36 per cent and in urban areas about 18 per cent. Negro illiteracy in the South reached 33 per cent, as contrasted with 10 per cent in the North and 7 per cent in the West. By 1930, the last census in which the literacy question was asked, Negro illiteracy had declined by about half to 16 per cent; but it was still over ten times the level of native whites (1.5 per cent). Illiteracy was still more than twice as high among rural than urban Negroes, and in the South was more than five times as high as in the West and four times as high as in the North.

In 1940, the Bureau of the Census substituted a question on years of school completed for the literacy question. At that date, nonwhite men twenty-five years of age and older had on the average completed only 5.4 years of schooling (median years of schooling) as compared with 8.7 years for whites. Nonwhite adult women had, on the average, completed 6.1 years of schooling, as compared with 8.8 years for white women. By 1960, nonwhite men had attained, on the average, 7.9 years of schooling, as compared with 10.6 years for white men; and nonwhite women 8.5 years as compared with 11.0 years for white women. Thus, between 1940 and 1960 the difference in average educational attainment between nonwhite and white men had decreased from 3.3 to 2.6 years, while the differences between nonwhite and white women decreased slightly from 2.7 and 2.5 years.

More revealing than these measures of average education are the proportions of persons who had reached meaningful levels of schooling. For example, in 1940, 41 per cent of the nonwhite adults had less than five years of schooling and were, therefore, functionally illiterate. This was almost four times the level of white functional illiteracy, at 11 per cent. In 1940, 92 per cent of the nonwhite adults had not completed high school, as compared with 74 per cent of the whites. Only 1.3 per cent of the nonwhites, compared with 4.9 per cent of the whites, had completed college.

By 1960, the proportion of functionally illiterate adult nonwhites had decreased to 23 per cent, but this was still more than three times as great as that of whites, at 7 per cent. Nonwhite adults without a high-school education had dropped to 78 per cent, but the comparable figure for whites had declined to 57 per cent. Nonwhites who had completed a college education had risen to 3.5 per cent, but was still less than half that of whites at 8.1 per cent. Since there is an inverse relationship between age and education (younger persons tend to have higher education) and since the Negro population is younger than the white, the above noted differences in levels of education between whites and nonwhites are understated.

Differences in literacy and education are, of course, produced by differences in school enrollment. In 1910, school enrollment levels for Negro children were well below those for white. Only 59 per cent of the Negro children six to thirteen years old were enrolled in school as compared with 85 per cent of the native white. For youngsters fourteen to fifteen years of age, only 58 per cent of Negroes were in school as compared with 78 per cent of the native whites; for youngsters sixteen to seventeen, 36 per cent of Negroes and 46 per cent of native whites; and among youths eighteen to twenty, the comparable figures for nonwhite and native white were 12 and 17 per cent.

By 1960, Negro school enrollment for children six to thirteen had risen to 93 per cent but was still below white (including foreign born) at 96 per cent. For Negro youngsters fourteen to fifteen, school enrollment had risen to 90 per cent, as compared with 95 per cent for white; for young persons sixteen to seventeen, Negro enrollment was 73 per cent, compared with 82 per cent for white; and for youths eighteen to twenty, Negro enrollment had reached 31 per cent as compared with 37 per cent for white. The improved relative school enrollment of the Negro was one of the consequences of his regional and urban redistribution.

Labor force. The role of the Negro in the economy cannot be understood solely in terms of demography. Study of the composition of the Negro population, however, usually requires some consideration of his economic characteristics. Since participation in the labor force, occupation, and income are vital factors both in influencing the integration of the Negro and in indicating how far the process has gone, they are given brief treatment here.

A larger proportion of the Negro than of the white population has been in the work force over the years. In 1900, 65 per cent of Negroes fourteen years of age and older were workers, as compared with 52 per cent of whites. The high proportion of Negroes was due to the much greater proportion of younger and older persons and of females who were working. This difference between Negro and white patterns of labor-force participation parallels that between the developing regions of the world and the economically advanced areas. With the passage of time, the difference in the work rates of Negroes and whites has diminished. By 1960, 56 per cent of Negroes fourteen years of age and over, as compared with 55 per cent of whites, were in the labor force, and the proportions of younger and older persons and females in the work force had grown much more similar.

Changes in the occupational pattern of Negro workers must be considered in the context of changes in the occupational pattern of the entire nation under the impact of increasing technological development and urbanization. By 1960, the structure of the United States labor force as a whole was completely different from what it was in the first decade of the century. Whereas in 1910 74 per cent of the total work force were engaged in the production of physical goods and only 26 per cent were providing services, by 1960, only 46 per cent were producing goods and 54 per cent were providing services. In 1960, only 6 per cent of the nation's workers were in agricultural pursuits as compared with 38 per cent in 1910; and 42 per cent as compared with 18 per cent were in white-collar work.

In 1910, when the Negro population was still concentrated mainly in the South, Negroes were predominantly agricultural workers in rural areas and unskilled laborers or service workers in urban areas. In 1910, 56 per cent of the Negroes who were gainfully employed, as compared with 33 per cent of all workers, were engaged in agriculture. The next largest category of Negro workers included the 22 per cent who were engaged in domestic and personal service, compared with 10 per cent of all workers. Thus, in 1910, over three-fourths (78 per cent) of all Negro workers were in agriculture or domestic service, as contrasted with 43 per cent of all workers in the nation.

By 1940, the proportion of Negroes in agricultural pursuits had diminished to 41 per cent, but it was still almost twice that of white workers (21 per cent). More than an additional one-fifth of the Negroes in the labor force (21 per cent) were laborers in non-agricultural pursuits, as compared with 7.5 per cent for whites. Hence, in 1940, almost two-thirds of all Negro workers (62 per cent), as contrasted with less than one-third of the white (28 per cent), were in agriculture or unskilled labor. It is noteworthy that, by 1940, the proportion of Negroes in domestic service had shrunk to 2.9 per cent, but twice as many Negroes (12 per cent) as whites were employed in "other services." White-collar workers—those in the professions, clerical and sales work, and proprietary and managerial occupations—accounted for only 9 per cent of all Negro workers, compared with 26 per cent of the white. Craftsmen and operatives accounted for only 17 per cent of all Negro workers, as contrasted with 34 per cent of the white.

By 1960, because of the impact of the war—which greatly accelerated the regional and urban-rural redistribution of the Negro —and the continued changes in the American economy, the occupational pattern of the Negro had greatly changed. In 1960, only 11 per cent of the Negro labor force remained in agriculture and only 8 per cent of the white.

Although unskilled labor in non-agricultural work still accounted for an appreciable proportion of all Negro workers, the Negro had made considerable gains in white-collar work and in skilled crafts. In 1960, 25 per cent of Negro workers, as compared with 20 per cent of white workers, were operatives; 20 per cent, as compared with 6 per cent, were laborers not in agriculture. The proportion of Negroes in craft and allied occupations had more than doubled from 1940 to 1960 to reach a level of 10 per cent, but this was still only half that of the white proportion (21 per cent). Negroes in white-collar occupations had increased to 11 per cent—less than one-third the proportion of whites in white-collar occupations. In fact, the proportion of white workers in white-collar jobs between 1940 and 1960 increased more rapidly than that of Negroes. By 1960, Negroes in domestic service had shrunk to less than 1 per cent, but Negroes in "other services" had increased to 14 per cent, about two and one-half times the level for whites.

All in all, between 1940 and 1960, Negroes made some progress in upgrading their occupational pattern relative to that of whites, but they still lagged far behind. In 1940, the index of dissimilarity for Negro as compared with white workers by broad occupational groupings was 43, and in 1960 it had decreased to 38—that is, in 1940, it would have been necessary to change the occupations of 43 per cent of the Negroes to match the occupational distribution of the whites and, by 1960, this proportion had dropped to 38.

The moderate upgrading in the national Negro occupational pattern is apparent in a longitudinal as well as a cross-sectional analysis, as Nathaniel Hare has shown.[9] A "cohort analysis," the tracing of the same population through successive ages, reveals that the younger cohorts of Negroes are approaching white occupational levels more rapidly than did older cohorts. However, it must be emphasized that an analysis of occupational changes by region and urban-rural residence indicates that the moderate upgrading of the national Negro occupational pattern was primarily the result of his redistribution through internal migration out of the South and into urban and metropolitan areas. Within each region and within urban and metropolitan areas, the Negro continued to work at occupational levels below those of the white.

Since the Negro was employed in farm and unskilled manual work much more frequently than the white, he received much smaller remuneration. Data for comparing the income of whites and nonwhites over a long period of time are not available. In 1939, however, median wage or salary income of nonwhite males fourteen years old and over was only $460 for all workers and $639 for year-round full-time workers.[10] The comparable figures for whites were $1,112 and $1,419. Thus, in 1939 nonwhite wage or salary income for all workers was 41 per cent that of white, and that for year-round full-time workers was 45 per cent of white. In 1960, nonwhite median wage or salary income had risen to $3,075 for all persons with wage or salary income and $3,789 for year-round full-time workers. By 1960, however, comparable white incomes were $5,137 and $5,662. Hence, nonwhite median wage or salary income had risen to 60 per cent of the comparable income of white persons and 67 per cent of that of white year-round full-time workers.

Again, analysis of regional and urban-rural differences indicates that the gains achieved by the Negro were the product of his redistribution within the country. Within each region and urban complex he was still well below the income levels attained by whites and even failed to keep pace with white advances.

Although the lower income of Negroes is largely attributable to their concentration in jobs which require little education or skill, some measure of their lower income stems from discriminatory practices. Herman P. Miller has demonstrated that Negroes do not reach so high a level of employment as do whites with comparable education; and Paul M. Siegel has shown that Negroes earn a lower income than whites with similar jobs.[11] For example, Miller pointed out that in 1960 only 5 per cent of whites, but 16 per cent of non-whites, with high-school education were laborers. Similarly, of Negro high-school graduates only 23 per cent were white-collar workers, whereas this was true of almost twice as large a proportion of whites (41 per cent).

In respect to income, Miller has shown that the Negro with the same education and same occupation as the white receives smaller remuneration. For example, nonwhite high-school graduates get only 60 per cent of the estimated lifetime earnings of white workers. Nonwhite elementary-school graduates earn 64 per cent of the lifetime income of white elementary-school graduates; and Negro college graduates about 50 per cent of comparable whites. Similarly, even when both the Negro's education and occupation are the same as the whites, his earnings are lower. For example, Negro carpenters with an elementary-school education receive only 72 per cent of white earnings; and Negro carpenters with a high-school education get only 76 per cent of the earnings of comparable whites.

Siegel, carrying the analysis further, has actually estimated the monetary cost of being a Negro. The difference between nonwhite and white earnings in 1959 of males twenty-five to sixty-four years old was $2,852 as reported in the Census. Of this difference $1,755, or 62 per cent, is attributable to the differences in the regional, occupational, and educational distribution of whites and nonwhites. Thus, even if nonwhites had achieved the same regional, educational, and occupational distribution as whites, nonwhites would still have earned only $1,097, or 38 per cent below the level of whites. The average cost of being a Negro in the United States in 1960, then, was about $1,000 in earnings. Of considerable significance for integration of the Negro is Siegel's finding that the differences in earnings of whites and nonwhites increase as the educational level increases. The implications of this finding for integration will be discussed below.

Finally, with the national focus on poverty, it is appropriate to consider the position of the Negro in respect to poverty. An analysis by Mollie Orshansky of the Social Security Administration revealed that in 1963 43 per cent of all Negro families had incomes below the "economy level" and 56 per cent below the "low-cost level."[12] In other words, these proportions of Negro families were in the poverty category according to criteria which related income to family size and ability to adhere to "economy" and "low-cost" food plans, respectively. The "low-cost" food plan allows an average of 28 cents per meal per person in a four person family; the "economy" level, an average of 22 cents a meal. In contrast, only 12 per cent of white families had incomes below the "economy level" and 19 per cent below the "low-cost level." Thus, the proportion of poor Negro families by the "economy" criterion was over three and one-half times that of white, and by the "low-cost" criterion, about three times that of white. The plight of the Negro in the South is evident in the fact that 58 per cent of Negro families, as contrasted with 18 per cent of white, were poor at the "economy level"; and 72 per cent of the Negro families, as contrasted with 27 per cent of the white, were poor by the "low cost" criterion. Similarly, poverty was much more common among Negroes than whites who were living alone or as unrelated members of households. Of such Negro individuals, 58 per cent were poor by the "economy level" rating and 62 per cent by the "low-cost level" standard. Comparable figures for unrelated white individuals were 42 per cent and 48 per cent.

Perhaps the most significant impact of poverty on integration lies in its implications for the rearing of children. Of Negro families with one child under eighteen, 33 per cent were poor by the less rigorous standard and 46 per cent by the more rigorous. The proportion of poor Negro families rose to levels of 77 per cent and 88 per cent, respectively, for families with six or more children. In contrast, of white families with one child under eighteen, 10 per cent and 18 per cent, respectively, were poor by these criteria; and the proportion of poor families rose to 35 per cent and 52 per cent for white families with six or more children under eighteen. Of all children under eighteen living in families in the United States, 22 per cent are in families regarded as "poor" by the less rigorous criterion and 31 per cent by the more rigorous.[13] Of all nonwhite children under eighteen, 62 per cent to 76 per cent were in poor families. In contrast, comparable percentages for white children resident in poor families ranged from 15 to 25 per cent.

Moreover, the proportion of children reared in poverty rose as the number of children increased in both white and nonwhite families. But much greater proportions of nonwhite than white children were so handicapped. Of nonwhite children in families with one or two children under eighteen, 39 to 52 per cent were poor, as compared with 9 to 15 per cent for white. Of nonwhite children in families with three or four children, 54 to 68 per cent were living in poverty, compared with 15 to 25 per cent for white. Of nonwhite children in families with five or more children, 81 to 94 per cent were being reared in poverty, as compared with 33 to 48 per cent for white. Probably no other facts link high fertility and poverty so dramatically and point up so vividly the plight of the poor and especially the Negro poor in this country.

Implications for Integration

Although the Negro had lived in this nation for some three centuries by 1910, he had scarcely begun to enter the main stream of American life. Almost nine-tenths of all American Negroes were in the South, where they were living largely in isolation from white society as a segregated, subcultural group steeped in poverty, largely illiterate, and denied participation in the political process. Moreover, about three-fourths of them resided on farms or in places having fewer than 2,500 inhabitants, where even remote contact with white America was limited. In a fundamental sense, then, it may be said that the Negro really did not enter white American society until World War I. Although Negro female household workers did have contact with whites in a restricted manner, the Negro, at present, is in many respects a more recent arrival to the main stream of American life than our most recent mass immigrant white European groups.

The rapid urbanization and metropolitanization of the Negro in the half century following 1910—resulting from technological, political, economic, and social changes—brought the Negro into unprecedented contact with the white society and consequently opened the possibility for widespread integration or assimilation. The emergence of "integration" as a political as well as an economic and social issue must, in large part, be attributed to the migration of the Negro since 1910, from the South to the North and the West, and from rural to urban and metropolitan areas.

Migration and settlement. Hence, a demographic factor, internal migration, may be considered the major factor in opening the door to integration. Once freed from Southern and rural isolation, the Negro gained access to the white community; this paved the way for social interaction and assimilation. Although regional and urban-rural redistribution of the Negro was essential, it could not, by itself, achieve integration. The entrance of the Negro into urban and metropolitan as well as Northern and Western United States paved the way for integration. But the manner of the entrance set up barriers to it. These barriers may be viewed in demographic terms: namely, the magnitude and rate of internal migration and the magnitude and rate of Negro population growth in the North and West and in urban and metropolitan areas.

The volume of Negro in-migration to urban and metropolitan United States, especially under the pressures generated by World War II and postwar developments, literally inundated large sections of the areas of destination. Although American cities had experienced large increments of population during the periods of heavy European immigration, none of the earlier migrations brought in so many persons of one ethnic or racial stock over so short a period of time. Between 1940 and 1960, the Negro population of central cities in metropolitan areas of 1,000,000 or more increased by 4,230,000 persons, or 59.7 per cent of their total population in 1960.

The in-migrant Negro followed the traditional pattern of newcomers by settling into enclaves in sections of the city serving as ports of entry. The greater size of the settlement, however, tended to separate the Negro more sharply from contact with the longer resident white population than had been the case for his white immigrant predecessor. Thus, the size of the Negro ghetto excluded a larger proportion of its inhabitants from physical and, therefore, social contact with non-ghetto whites. Moreover, existing prejudices and categoric reactions augmented the social distance between Negroes and whites, as compared with ghetto and non-ghetto whites.

Thus, it may be argued that the cataclysmic social upheaval occasioned by the two world wars generated both opportunity for and barriers to integration. On the one hand, it removed Negroes from their segregation in the rural South which had precluded meaningful contact with white society and had barred their assimilation into American society. On the other hand, it poured so large a Negro population into the cities, and especially the large cities, over so short a period of time that it made the Negro in-migratory stream relatively unassimilable—economically, socially, and politically. It remains to be seen whether this is a relatively short-term phenomenon or whether, given their huge enclaves in the cities, Negroes have been freed from their segregation and isolation in the rural slum South only to be thrust into a new form of segregation and isolation in the urban slum in the North, West, and South.

Natural increase and growth. It may be anticipated that the Negro population will continue to grow rapidly in the urban and metropolitan areas of the nation even though internal migratory flows of Negroes from the South to other regions diminishes. Large-scale Negro out-migration from the rural South is definitely diminishing as the supply of rural Negroes approaches exhaustion. But Negro urban populations will continue to increase rapidly because natural increase is replacing migration as the chief source of growth. The Negro, like the inhabitant of the developing regions in Asia, Latin America, and Africa, in his new exposure to amenities of twentieth-century living, is experiencing rapidly declining mortality while fertility rates either remain high or, as in urban areas, actually increase. There is some evidence that both the Negro and white birth rates have declined since 1960, but it is too early to appraise the full significance of these declines. In any case, the Negro birth rate is still well above the level of the white.

The continuation of rapid growth will almost certainly serve as a negative factor in the integration or assimilation of the Negro, for it will exacerbate the difficulties faced by the Negro seeking to enter the main stream of white society. There can be little doubt that more moderate growth rates would ease the problems of admixture and of integration. This position is justifiable even though it may be argued that rapidly increasing numbers may hasten the day when the Negro may acquire greater political power with which to attack the problem. But apart from the fact that greatly increased political power is a longer-term matter because of the gap between birth and voting age, law can impose only admixture, and not integration. Moreover, it is possible that the more desegregation or admixture is achieved through legal compulsion rather than free choice, the more integration, that is, assimilation, will be retarded rather than advanced.

This does not mean that there should be an appreciable slow-up in legislative and administrative provisions for desegregation where the alternative of education is hopeless, or nearly so, for indefinite periods as in the Black Belt of the South. It does mean, however, that, wherever possible, every effort should be made to achieve desegregation by voluntary acts based on increased enlightenment. Education as an instrument for desegregation will be discussed in greater detail later.

Continued rapid growth, it may be concluded, will augment rather than decrease the difficulties of integration. There is one aspect of the continued growth of Negro population in some metropolitan areas, however, which may tend to promote integration. Increments in the Negro populations of these areas are increasingly due to natural causes, namely, the excess of birth over deaths, rather than to in-migration. Moreover, as the Taeubers have shown, increasing proportions of these in-migrants are from other urban and metropolitan areas rather than from the rural South.[14] Therefore, they do not bring with them handicaps to integration as did earlier in-migrants from the rural areas of the South. The end of migration from the rural South is producing Negro metropolitan populations increasingly similar to others in the areas to which they have come. From now on, within individual metropolitan areas, the characteristics of future generations of Negro Americans will depend more on the opportunities provided for them where they now reside and less upon the inadequacies of their environments in their areas of origin in the South.

The high birth rate also operates on another level to retard integration and to contribute to the misery of the Negro population. It has been shown that one of the consequences of a high birth rate is a youthful age structure and a high youth dependency ratio. The Negro population, as compared with the white, has an appreciably greater number of dependents to support per person of working age. It is clear that this demographic fact, coupled with the much lower income of the Negro, compounds the difference in per capita expenditure available for rearing and educating Negro and white youngsters. The unfortunate results of this fact may be better appreciated, perhaps, by considering its impact on the Negro child.

High fertility with its consequent large family size handicaps the Negro by limiting the investment the family can make in human resources—that is, in the education and training of the child. Under economic pressure the Negro child, on the one hand, has little incentive to remain in school and, on the other, is often forced to leave even when he desires to obtain an education. Thus, the Negro child tends to be the high-school dropout rather than the high-school graduate. Even if much more is done to remove the Negro family from the bitter consequences of raw poverty, large numbers of children will tend to set limits on the education each child in the Negro community will receive. Certainly the family with two or three children will, for some time to come, be in a better position to support its children through high school than the family with six or more children.

The poverty of the Negro family must rank as the single most important factor preventing the Negro from developing those abilities which could help him to assume both the rights and obligations of being a first-class American citizen. As has been demonstrated above, the large proportion of Negro children now under eighteen cannot possibly be expected to participate fully in the main stream of American life so long as they are steeped in the morass of poverty.

Poverty and high fertility are at present linked in the United States, as in the world as a whole. Largely unrestrained birth rates are found primarily among the poor and uneducated. The better educated and more affluent members of American society have, as a matter of course, access to the knowledge and methods of family planning, while the uneducated and poor, who include the Negro in disproportionate numbers, have no, or inadequate, knowledge about or access to methods of controlling family size. Movements now under way in various parts of the country to provide persons on relief with knowledge and materials for family planning, in accordance with religious scruples, may greatly ameliorate this problem in the coming years. However, much more remains to be done to help the relatively uneducated and impoverished Negro family to restrict its size. Until this is done, many Negro families will be caught in the vicious cycle of poverty, high fertility, inadequate education and skill, and, therefore, continued poverty.

The adverse effect of high fertility on what may be regarded as the quality of the Negro population, that is, its education and skill, apart from its deleterious consequences for each individual, tends to retard mass integration further. As a result of a high birth rate, the Negro population retains characteristics such as inferior occupations, low income, and a style of life precluding association and social interaction with the dominant white society—all of which retard assimilation.

Family disorganization and age structure. The relatively high rate of family disorganization which characterizes the Negro community also hinders integration. As has been shown, in 1960 about one in three Negro children under fourteen, as contrasted with one in twelve white, was in households with one or both parents absent. The Negro child, compared with the white, not only is handicapped by a smaller per capita sum for his rearing but is also more likely to be reared in less favorable family circumstances. The deleterious effects of this situation can only be speculated upon, but it would seem highly probable that being reared in such abnormal family situations must adversely affect the child in a number of ways. To the extent that the result is a maladjusted or deviant child, the prospects for integration, it may be safely concluded, are not enhanced.

Another aspect of Negro family disorganization which must be dealt with is to be found in the historical, economic, and social emasculation of the Negro male. There is a great need for special efforts to enhance the role of the Negro male in the family, to concentrate on providing him with the capabilities of taking on his expected functions, responsibilities, and obligations as husband, father, and provider. Poverty has undoubtedly contributed to the economic and social emasculation of the Negro male, but it is also true that his inferior role contributes to continued Negro poverty. This is only one of the vicious cycles retarding Negro advance which remain to be broken.

The relatively large proportion of young in the Negro population may also vitally affect integration in another way, both positively and negatively. To the extent that younger Negro Americans are acquiring greater education and skills than the older, they are also characterized by higher expectations. The "revolution of rising expectations," to use Harlan Cleveland's felicitous phrase, is manifest among Negro Americans, as it is among the people in the developing regions of the world. The higher expectations and the greater aggressiveness and militancy of the young are important factors in the progressively more vigorous activist programs which characterize the Negro revolt. Whether increased pressure for not only "freedom" but also "equality now" will continue to result in rapid advance or, at some point, produce boomerang effects remains to be seen. In any case, it seems clear that Negro American leadership is becoming increasingly youthful and perhaps, therefore, more militant and activist.

Education and skill. Without question the major factor in the assimilation of the white immigrant groups who came to this country—their "Americanization"—was the school. It was the school and, more specifically, the education and skills it transmitted that enabled each immigrant group in turn to rise from the bottom of the economic, social, and political ladder to limits eventually set only by individual capabilities. Considered in mass, the Negro's major handicap in his efforts to advance in America, apart from his visibility and the categoric prejudicial response which it evokes, is undoubtedly to be found in his limited education and skills.

The data indicate that the education of the Negro is improving. But the process is necessarily slow since it occurs by generation rather than by year. Moreover, because of the ghettoization of the Negro, *de facto* segregation in the schools, and his disadvantaged background, the Negro's achievements in education are, year by year, inferior to those of whites. In consequence, even the Negro high-school and college graduates typically have not attained the level of whites with comparable education. Moreover, the Negro who is more dependent on vocational schools than the white for the acquisition of manual skills, is usually sorely handicapped by the outmoded equipment and curricula of these schools.

Education not only opens the door to better jobs and remuneration but also tends to transform the person's style of life and makes it more compatible with urban living. Education, therefore, has a double effect in facilitating integration. It helps give the Negro access to better residential areas and, simultaneously, it modifies the Negro's way of life to a pattern more consistent and, therefore, less apt to conflict with the white middle-class patterns.

Anything which obstructs the rise in the level of the Negro's education blocks his economic and social mobility. For this reason, it is important to integrate the schools and greatly to improve the quality of education for the Negro child by recognizing his need for compensatory education. Especially vicious is the practice, common in many of the large city public school systems, of promoting virtually all children to the next higher grade without regard to achievement. Few things are more likely to keep the Negro relatively uneducated and unskilled than this benighted "economy" measure. Moreover, there is a great need for revising school curricula in both general and vocational schools so that every child, including the disadvantaged, will receive an education that will enable him to realize his potential abilities. The prevalent high dropout rate is more correctly interpreted as an index of the failure of the schools than of the failure of the child.

As the data indicate, the trend in the school enrollment of the Negro has been upward as Negroes have moved to the North and West and to urban and metropolitan areas. But much remains to be done both to accelerate enrollments among Negro teenagers, especially in the later teenage years, and to provide them with adequate education.

An important factor, other than poverty, in restricting Negro school enrollment and completion of at least a high-school education is to be found in the relative absence of incentive and motivation for acquiring education among Negroes, as compared with white immigrants. This is readily understandable. White immigrants, in the main, came from culturally intact backgrounds which provided incentive and motivation to move ahead. For example, the Poles came with incentive, as embodied in the Polish culture, to acquire property to achieve status. The Jewish immigrant arrived with motivation, as imbedded in his culture, to acquire education. In contrast, the Negro, whose African culture was destroyed during slavery, and whose lot in the United States after slavery scarcely provided him with incentive and motivation for advancement, may in his new metropolitan setting actually possess negative incentives for education. For the Negro is aware that the acquisition of an education by an occasional Negro over the years has not necessarily opened the doors to economic and social advance. An essential element of any program designed to eliminate poverty among Negroes must, therefore, instill in the Negro child the incentive and motivation necessary to take advantage of new and expanding opportunity.

The Negro, as a product of his pathetic share of the American way of life, is, in mass, faced with much greater difficulties in entering the main stream of American life than were foreign-white immigrants. Because of the increased complexity and higher technological level of contemporary society, the Negro's inferior education and skill are a more serious handicap to his upward mobility than was the case with comparable white immigrants. Moreover, the Negro's chronic poverty and style of life at variance with middle-class urban living patterns restrict social contact with whites. These characteristics are reinforced by the prejudicial categoric reaction of whites based on their traditional stereotyped images of the Negro.

In general, it is undeniable that the acquisition of higher education and skills and a style of life more compatible with middle-class white standards would facilitate social contact and interaction. Yet, while upgrading in education, skill, and style of life may be thought of as prerequisites of integration, they are in the case of the Negro, more than in the case of the immigrant, not sufficient in themselves. Evidence indicates that the Negro who has achieved higher education and skill and their correlates in style of life still does not receive commensurate income and entry to white society.

In fact, as Siegel has demonstrated, the higher the Negro's level of education, the greater is the difference between his earnings and that of comparable whites.

Siegel is undoubtedly correct in emphasizing that, in transition at least, the Negro may face more rather than less discrimination. But, it remains true that social contact and interaction with whites increase with advancing education and skills and higher absolute income, despite the greater discrimination or "cost" of being Negro. Higher education will undoubtedly continue to help the Negro, as it did the white immigrant, to break down barriers to assimilation. It is possible, although data are not available to prove this, that the white immigrant may similarly have been more discriminated against in transition as his education and skill increased, even while he was experiencing greater social contact with native whites.

Programs for integration. The implications of the above analysis for policy and programs designed to hasten integration may now be summarized. There are at least two basic sets of factors that retard integration. One is the group of demographic characteristics of the Negro which restrict his participation in the main stream of American life. The second is to be found not in the characteristics of the Negro but in the attitudes and behavior of whites.

The characteristics of the Negro which impede integration include the excessively rapid population growth in urban and metropolitan areas, brought on by high rates of internal migration during the two world wars and now by excessive natural increase. A continuation of this pattern may retard the dispersion of Negro enclaves and thus obstruct social contact and interaction with the white population. Moreover, the high Negro birth rate will tend to retard the upgrading of Negro education and skill by limiting per capita investment in education and training.

In order to break down these demographic barriers to integration it is necessary to decrease Negro birth rates by making available to the Negro community those methods of family planning which are now available to the better educated and more affluent population, for the poor and uneducated should also have the right to determine how many children they will have.

A decrease in the Negro birth rate would simultaneously dampen the rate of Negro population growth, reduce the greater dependency burden that the Negro carries, and permit acceleration in the upgrading of Negro education and skill. It would thus help eliminate poverty, accelerate access to better jobs and earnings, and contribute to the emergence of patterns of living consistent with metropolitanism as a way of life.

Needless to say, a decrease in the birth rate will not automatically produce all these results. It would still be necessary to provide adequate educational and training opportunities at levels and under conditions which would be effective. Current programs designed to improve educational and training opportunities for the "culturally deprived" child are steps in the right direction. But they fall far short, as yet, of providing the education and training necessary to enable every Negro American child to compete in the contemporary, complex economic and social world.

Moreover, such activities must not ignore the Negro adult, and especially the Negro adult male, who may be beyond the age at which it is possible to acquire skills which permit him to make his own way. As an alternative to the dole, serious consideration should be given to the development of intensive labor projects on which such adult Negroes can be usefully employed. In the transition to equal opportunity for the Negro American, it may well be necessary to bear the burden of such programs, despite their low productivity, so that deprived adult Negroes can experience the dignity and income that comes from work, rather than the humiliation and degradation associated with being the recipient of a handout. Opportunity for useful and adequately remunerated work would undoubtedly constitute the major restorative of masculinity and self-respect to the Negro male and, thereby, contribute greatly to the improvement of Negro family structure and organization. It is highly probable that programs of the type suggested would, in the long run, be less expensive than the present combination of inadequate educational and training facilities and wasted human resources resulting from unemployment, welfare and relief, delinquency and crime, and high morbidity and mortality.

Ironically, it may be that the rapid urbanization of the Negro population may lead to the reduction of family disorganization and the restoration of masculinity to the Negro male. But this can come about only if the Negro child is adequately equipped to cope with the urban environment in the coming generation and if, in the transition to equal opportunity, measures are taken to enable the present Negro adult male to fulfill the role which is expected of the male in our society. Unfortunately, not only have no comprehensive programs yet been developed to attain these objectives but, on the contrary, a number of programs exist which tend even further to emasculate the Negro male. Outstanding among them is, of course, the present program of Aid to Families with Dependent Children which, in effect, bolsters the matriarchal family and further denigrates the male. Aid should, of course, be provided to needy mothers and their children but under conditions that would encourage, rather than discourage, the continued presence and participation of the husband and father.

The prevalent pattern of residential segregation constitutes, of course, not only evidence of but a barrier to integration. The massive enclaves of Negro Americans in the central cities of our metropolitan areas are allowing a generation of Negro Americans to be born into a new form of segregation—*de facto* segregation, Northern style, as contrasted with *de jure* segregation, Southern style. Residential segregation produces educational segregation, social segregation, and, to a considerable extent, occupational segregation as well. The Negro is caught in the rigid vise of poverty and residential segregation which imposes isolation from whites and social segregation, which produces educational segregation and inferior education, which restricts occupational and income opportunities, which maintains and reinforces poverty.

For these reasons "open occupancy" has become a crucial element in the push for integration and, without question, will remain a central issue until the Negro is free to choose where he wishes to live. Interestingly enough, the current battle over open occupancy is a battle over symbols rather than reality. It is clear that internal social and economic pressures would prompt Negroes to continue to live in enclaves for some time to come even if there were no barriers to their movement. It must be borne in mind that even the descendents of nineteenth-century immigrants, German, Irish, and Scandinavian, not to mention twentieth-century immigrants and their offspring, still live in voluntary enclaves. There is no reason to believe the situation will be much different for Negroes even when voluntary occupancy becomes a fact. Assimilation and participation in the activities of white society will be achieved only as Negroes become able to avail themselves of the residential opportunities that may open to them and then choose to do so. This will be more difficult for the Negro than for the white immigrant because a fundamental difference will still characterize the Negro who leaves his enclave. Whereas the white who fled his ghetto was also often able simultaneously to flee identification with his ethnic group, the Negro does not have this alternative. He may leave his ghetto but he cannot, except occasionally, manage to escape racial identification.

The second set of factors which impede integration is not to be found in the characteristics of the Negro so much as in the attitudes and practices of whites. The Negro with education and skill and a compatible style of life is still the object of discriminatory practices and is thus prevented from full participation in American society. Such a Negro, having acquired the necessary conditions for greater social interaction, must still await changes in the dominant white society. The whites must be educated in order to break down their outmoded stereotypes of the Negro, to rectify their distorted image of the new emerging Negro, and to allay their fears of the Negro as a competitor and a neighbor.

The need for massive programs to educate whites has not yet been adequately recognized. Just as it is important to think in terms of "compensatory education" for Negroes because of "cultural deprivation" so, also, it is important to think of "corrective education" for whites because of the rudiments of white supremacy and racism and the distorted image of the Negro which are still to be found in large elements of our population. It requires explicit efforts to correct and to supplement present distorted or inadequate textbooks in the schools at all levels. It is necessary to present an accurate picture of the nature of our pluralistic democratic order, an accurate account of the history of the Negro and other minorities in the United States, an appreciation of the cultures and contributions of our diverse ethnic and racial groups, and an understanding of the place of the United States in the world order and the implications of prejudice and discrimination for our role in international affairs.

The proposed program of corrective education for whites must necessarily be on a massive scale. Although much can be achieved through the efforts of individual scholars, teachers, schools, civic, business, industrial, labor, religious, fraternal, and other private organizations, the government—on the federal, state, and local levels—must also be actively involved. Only the government can provide the financial resources to stimulate, initiate, develop, and conduct the corrective educational programs required. Although the schools are the obvious place to begin, it must be recognized that such efforts will affect the next generation more than the present. The mass media can certainly be mobilized to play a much more important role in educating adult whites than they have yet been called upon to do. A saturation program of corrective education for whites is without question as important as compensatory education for Negroes to pave the way for an integrated society.

The United States, at long last, has opened the door to the assimilation of the Negro. There are those that believe the problem of integrating the Negro will continue to be different from that of the white immigrants. That there are significant differences in color and cultural background cannot be denied. But it is a serious mistake to assume that the "color stigma" is different in kind or even in degree from the stigma which accompanied many of our foreign-white immigrant groups. Prejudice toward, and hatred of, the Negro by the most bigoted of our white supremacists is not unlike the attitude of the Pole who spat upon the ground when a "Christ-killer" Jew appeared upon the scene, or the attitude of the primitive fundamentalist Baptist whose hatred of "papists" similarly reached high levels of intensity, or the attitude of the fanatical orthodox Jew toward a prospective Gentile son-in-law. Stigma has been associated with human differences other than those based on color and with equal fervor, righteousness, and fanaticism. There is evidence in the United States as well as in various other parts of the world, that the color difference can be bridged even as religious and other cultural differences have been bridged, through social interaction and consequent acculturation. Elsewhere in this volume the conditions most conducive to such a development are discussed.[15]

Strategies and phasing. In mapping strategies and planning programs for accelerating integration it is essential that there be full awareness of the time dimensions that are necessarily involved. Desegregation or admixture can be relatively simply and quickly achieved, as has been amply demonstrated since World War II. The term "relatively" must be stressed, however, because the desegregation of schools in the South ordered by the United States Supreme Court to take place with "due deliberate speed" has not progressed very far even in the full decade which has elapsed since that historic decision. On the other hand, desegregation of public facilities has been effected more rapidly, and desegregation of the military establishment required merely a military order. Desegregation in all phases of life should, of course, be pushed as rapidly as possible by education and enlightenment and, if necessary, by legal coercion.

Desegregation can be accompanied with little delay by other programs designed to provide full equality of opportunity for the Negro American. Such programs should include provisions for open occupancy, compensatory education and training, and intensive labor projects, if necessary. They should include welfare and aid provisions for those unable to work, programs that are modified to help restore social and economic masculinity to the Negro male and establish normal family structure and living patterns. These types of programs are possible in the intermediate-run and can provide largely an affirmative answer to the Negro's insistence on "now." But the achievement of integration in the sense of acculturation or assimilation is a longer-term affair. The realization of integration in this sense requires generations rather than years or even decades. For integration as acculturation can follow only from social contact and social interaction between the Negro and the white. Integration can be achieved only after desegregation and full equality of opportunity break down present barriers to communication and social intercourse.

In the transition to an integrated society, a delicate balance must be attained and maintained between strategies and tactics of conflict and those of consensus. There are those who believe that only or primarily through incessant conflict and the exercise of power can the Negro achieve his rightful place in the economic, social, and political order. Such tactics, however, even if they were to advance the cause of the Negro in the long run—which is doubtful—would not achieve integration in the sense of acculturation. They would, at best, create a separate and solidified Negro community which, while it may be able to win concessions and better its position, will have also helped to create a separate and solidified white community with which it will have to bargain over an indefinite period.

Another alternative, and a preferable one, is the strategy of maximizing the achievement of consensus, even while being prepared to use other tactics as occasion and circumstances may warrant.[16] Certainly, in theory, the more the relationship between the Negro and white populations is characterized by consensus rather than conflict, and the more social interaction between them is on an interpersonal rather than group basis, the greater will be the likelihood of integration. In any case, whether conflict or consensus be the main strategy, equal status, as distinguished from equal opportunity, cannot be achieved immediately. Against this perspective "freedom now" makes sense; "equality now," however, is pathetic, wishful fantasy.

The test of whether the United States is a democratic and open society for the Negro will depend on at least three different factors: First, it must become evident that desegregation has been achieved. Second, it must be demonstrated that equality of opportunity has been established. Third, it must be shown that integration of the Negro is possible. Individual human beings, Negro and white, must have the freedom to choose whether or not they will continue to live in enclaves or in an admixed and integrated community.

The Negro revolt has, thus far, accelerated efforts toward desegregation and the establishment of equality of opportunity for Negro Americans. It has also undoubtedly accelerated the achievement of integration. It remains to be seen, however, whether the course which the revolt follows will continue to promote integration or whether it will produce a solidified Negro community which, as a conflict group, will help to organize a solidified, and perhaps increasingly resistant, white community. It remains to be seen whether the Negro will have the choice, available to white ethnic groups, of continuing to live in enclaves or of living in an admixed and integrated pattern. It remains to be seen whether the Negro community can follow white ethnic immigrants into an increasingly integrated order or whether it will endure as a separate, even if equal, minority group.

In a fundamental sense integration is an American problem, not a Negro problem. Perhaps this country's major contribution to the history of man lies in her demonstration of the ability to achieve unity out of diversity and to maintain an open pluralistic society in which each person can rise from humble origins to limits set only by his own capabilities. Thus far, this demonstration has applied only to our white ethnic groups. To continue to deny the Negro any of the choices which are available to whites is to threaten the very premises, and to undermine the foundations, of our democratic society.

REFERENCES

1. The population data on the Negro American are drawn from the statistics of the U. S. Bureau of the Census and the National Center for Health Statistics of the U. S. Public Health Service unless otherwise noted. In the interest of economy of space, specific references to sources are avoided. Key references utilized include: U. S. Bureau of the Census, *Historical Statistics of the United States, Colonial Times to 1957* (Washington, D. C.,

1960), and *Statistical Abstract of the United States* (Washington, D. C., annual); Reports of the Decennial Census of Population; Donald J. Bogue, *The Population of the United States* (Glencoe, Ill., 1959); Conrad and Irene Taeuber, *The Changing Population of the United States* (New York, 1958); Irene Taeuber, "The American Negro at Mid-Century," *Population Bulletin,* Population Reference Bureau, Inc., Vol. 14 (November 1958); and U. S. Public Health Service, *Vital Statistics of the United States* (Washington, D. C., annual). Data are sometimes for the "Negro" and sometimes for "nonwhite." Since the Negro makes up 90 per cent of the nonwhite for the United States, the statistics are used interchangeably for the broad analytical purposes of this paper.

2. *Population Index,* Vol. 29 (April 1963), pp. 197–98.

3. Oscar Handlin, *The Uprooted* (Boston, 1951), and *The Newcomers* (Cambridge, Mass., 1959); Otis Dudley Duncan and Beverly Duncan, *The Negro Population of Chicago* (Chicago, 1957).

4. Otis Dudley Duncan and Stanley Lieberson, "Ethnic Segregation and Assimilation," *The American Journal of Sociology,* Vol. 64 (January 1959), pp. 364–74.

5. Stanley Lieberson, *Ethnic Patterns in American Cities* (Glencoe, Ill., 1963).

6. Karl and Alma Taeuber, *Negroes in Cities—Residential Segregation and Neighborhood Change* (Chicago, 1965), Part I (in press).

7. E. Franklin Frazier, *The Negro in the United States* (rev. ed.; New York, 1957).

8. See, for example, Leonard Broom and Norval Glenn, *Transformation of the Negro* (New York, 1964).

9. Nathaniel Hare, "The Changing Occupational Status of the Negro in the United States: An Intracohort Analysis," unpublished Ph.D. dissertation, Department of Sociology, University of Chicago, 1962.

10. "Statement of Herman P. Miller, Special Assistant, Office of the Director, Bureau of the Census," *Hearings Before the Committee on Labor and Public Welfare on Bills Relating to Equal Employment Opportunity,* U. S. Senate, 88th Cong., 1st Sess., July and August 1963.

11. *Ibid.;* see also Paul M. Siegel, "On the Cost of Being a Negro," *Sociological Inquiry,* Vol. 35 (Winter 1965), pp. 41–57.

12. Mollie Orshansky, "Counting the Poor: Another Look at the Poverty Profile," *Social Security Bulletin,* Vol. 28 (January 1965), pp. 3–29.

13. These data derived from Table 8 in *ibid.,* p. 19.

14. Karl and Alma Taeuber, *op. cit.,* Ch. V.

15. See Thomas F. Pettigrew's paper, "Complexity and Change in American Racial Patterns: A Social Psychological View," in this volume.

16. Philip M. Hauser, "Conflict *vs.* Consensus—Woodlawn's Case," *Chicago Sunday Sun-Times, Viewpoint,* December 13, 1964.

RASHI FEIN

An Economic and Social Profile of the Negro American

IN THE author's preface to *An American Dilemma*,[1] Gunnar Myrdal wrote that he was a "stranger" to the American scene and that "Things look different, depending upon 'where you stand.'" It is also true that things look different, depending upon where you look. The profile of the Negro American is a changing profile. What one sees depends on what one looks at, on the period that one examines, and on the comparisons one makes. Our profile will not "look." It will "look different" or "look similar." Without comparisons its significance would be limited.

In this essay I examine a variety of socioeconomic indicators. I do so for various points in time in order to compare the world in which the Negro American lives with the world in which he lived and with the world (both past and present) of the white American. Always we shall compare. For, as indicated, the data have meaning only as they are compared. They may be compared with an American ideal; they may be compared with a potential; they may be compared with the past; but compared they must be. Roosevelt's "one-third of a nation" could be contrasted with the remaining two-thirds and Martin Luther King's dream with a present reality. To understand where the Negro American stands today requires a frame of reference.

The frame of reference, the relevant comparison in drawing an economic and social profile and in understanding the significance of the data that make up the profile, is a comparison between the Negro and other Americans. Such comparisons are given increased dimension when the data examined represent the positions of the two groups at different moments in time. For if we are to understand the attitudes, aspirations, and accomplishments of the Negro American, we need to know not only where he is, but also how he got there, how rapidly conditions have been changing, what has been happening to his relative position. Others may consider whether the most significant influence on the psychology and attitudes of the Negro is where he stands in relation to the white, where he stands in relation to his parents and grandparents, how his status relative to whites compares with the relative status of his parents and grandparents in an earlier period, or a mixture of these that takes account of relative progress as well as relative position. Surely, however, all have some measure of influence.

The frame of reference developed in this essay differs from those most frequently used in analyzing the Negro's progress. It is generally customary either: (1) to compare Negro attainment today with the level of Negro attainment at some earlier time (for example, the Negro maternal mortality rate in 1960 was 98 per 100,000 live births, down from 774 in 1940) or (2) to compare Negro-white differentials today with Negro-white differentials in some earlier period (for example, in 1960 the Negro maternal mortality rate was 3.8 times the white rate while in 1955 it had been 4.0 times).[2] In general, the first type of comparison shows significant improvement—Negroes (just as is true for whites) *are* better off than their grandparents were. But how one assesses one's own situation is, and should be, influenced by how others are faring at the same time. It is true that the second comparison does take account of Negro progress relative to white progress and does attempt to measure where the Negro finds himself in relation to other Americans. It is thus more meaningful than the first comparison. Nevertheless, it is often difficult to interpret. Because white-nonwhite differentials are large and because the rates of change of white and nonwhite indices are different, we sometimes find that the absolute differences between white and nonwhite indicators behave differently than do the ratios of the same indicators. In 1940, for example, the absolute difference between the white and nonwhite infant mortality rate was 31 per 1,000 live births, while in 1962 the difference had declined to 19 per 1,000. Yet in 1940 nonwhite infant mortality was 70 per cent greater than that of whites and in 1962 it was 90 per cent greater. Another example: in 1940 the absolute difference between white and nonwhite maternal mortality was 454 per 100,000 live births while in 1960 the difference had declined to 72. Yet in 1940 nonwhite maternal mortality was 2.4 times that of white and in 1960 it was 3.8 times as great. Sometimes, too, differentials are narrowed because nonwhite indicators are improving (slowly, but improving) while white indica-tors—perhaps pressing against limits of present knowledge—have reached a plateau. The important consideration, however, is that the narrowing differential fails to take account of a frequent and significant phenomenon: the nonwhite is moving up more slowly than the white did when, many years ago, the white stood where the nonwhite now is. That comparison—between speed of move-ment over the same range of experience—is relevant in assessing recent developments and the possibilities for the future.

The measure I introduce is simple yet informative. Where data permit, I calculate a time-lag statistic: how many years earlier did the white American—with the full range of opportunity open to him—attain the particular level (say, of health, education, income) that the Negro—so long denied that opportunity—has reached only today. I ask also whether this gap (in years) is greater or less than at earlier times (that is, was the Negro more years behind in some earlier period). I thus compare the relative speed of movement over the same range of experience. The change in the length of the gap depends upon the relative rates of change of white and Ne-gro indicators over time. The results are disturbing: in a number of cases the time gap has been widening rather than narrowing. To-day the Negro is further behind the white (in years) than he once was.

An illustration may be helpful. Table 1 presents hypothetical data on level of health attainment: the higher the index, the better the health level.

TABLE 1. Hypothetical Health Levels, White and Negro, Selected Years

	1900	1920	1940	1960
1. White	100	200	250	275
2. Negro	—	100	150	200
3. Absolute differential (1-2)	—	100	100	75
4. White-Negro ratio (1÷2)	—	2	1.67	1.375
5. Time gap (years by which Negro progress lags white)	—	20	30	40

The data show a narrowing of differentials in the period 1920-1960 (from 100 down to 75; from a factor of 2 down to 1.375). Yet, whereas the Negro in 1920 was where the white of 1900 had been, that gap of twenty years had widened to forty years by 1960 (in

1960 the Negro was where the white had been in 1920). This occurred because the white had moved from 100 to 200 in two decades, but conditions prevented the Negro from doing so well: in this hypothetical example it takes Negroes four (not two) decades to cover the same terrain. This comparison, the reader will note, focuses on movement over the same range of experience (100 to 200) rather than on movement over the same time period (1920 to 1960). This is its strength, for it helps center attention on the process of growth and on prospects for the near future. In this example it suggests that special efforts will be required if previous growth rates are to be sharply boosted and the time gap narrowed.[3] For if the Negro does only as well as the white once did in moving from an index of 200 to 275, it will take the Negro forty years to achieve equality—even if the white were to make no more progress.

Let me make clear that I do not imply that all groups should be expected to follow the same growth path. Each group—ethnic, racial, religious—in American life has its unique characteristics and is the product of its unique experiences. The "baggage" the Negro brings with him—the traditions, the strengths, the handicaps—is different from that brought by others. Furthermore, the gap (in years) may widen or narrow due to erratic behavior of white indices—unrelated to discrimination against Negroes. Such patterns must be examined carefully. But often the difference in speed of upward movement between Negro and white Americans is—in a broad way—an indication of the effects of present and past differences in opportunity. It is cause for concern.

It is important to recognize that if the Negro in 1965 is where the white was in 1945, this does not mean that the Negro considers himself as well off as the white considered himself twenty years ago. Nor should he. The Negro today is aware that a very substantial majority of the nation has higher income, more education, better health, and so forth than he does. The Negro stands below the median indices for the nation. But this was not true of the white twenty years ago. He did not suffer the psychological disadvantage of being behind—for he was not behind. He was the median American. Thus the situation is vastly different for the Negro who has an income of $3,000 when most other Americans have more, than it was for the white when he had $3,000 income and that was the average for the nation. In a psychological sense—and this molds attitudes toward the problem—the Negro is even further behind than the data show.

The comparison of white-nonwhite differentials is not meant to suggest that every index should be the same for each and every group (or person). America is a land of many tongues and tastes. Different cultures and value systems will reflect themselves in different behavior patterns and thus in socioeconomic indicators. But the indicators selected measure aspects that surely all groups feel are of importance. We all desire lower infant mortality rates, lower unemployment rates, and so forth. Differentials in the particular indicators selected, therefore, tend to reflect differences in equality of opportunity rather than deliberate choices.

In some future year we will surely reach a stage where it will be difficult to judge the significance of differences in white-nonwhite indices (unless we foolishly define white indices as always the desirable standard and incorrectly assume that white middle-class values are the only "proper" values). This difficulty is clear, for example, in regard to occupational structure. Underrepresentation in some occupations can only occur in conjunction with overrepresentation in other occupations. Surely there is nothing undesirable if, as a consequence of group values and traditions, individuals *choose* to enter a particular occupation, thus resulting in group "overrepresentation" in that occupation and "underrepresentation" in some other. Today, however, it is unhappily all too clear that Negro underrepresentation in the professions, for example, is not the result of a desire to move into unskilled labor. The point at issue is that we look forward not to a situation where everyone is identical and the nonwhite is 10 per cent of every occupation, geographic region, and so forth—but to a situation where he could be that (or more) in any given sector if he so desired. Today it is true that all groups are not distributed throughout the occupations as are all other groups (nor are they distributed evenly geographically). It cannot be expected that this will be vastly different tomorrow. Differentials will, therefore, remain. The analytical method we use is not meant to imply that they should not remain (so long as they are a result of free choice and opportunity).

We begin at birth. The child is born. In 1959-61 the Negro male had a life expectancy of 61.5 years at birth. His white counterpart first reached that level in 1931-33, twenty-eight years earlier (and has not dipped below it since 1937-39). In 1959-61 the white male life expectancy at birth was 67.6 years, 6 years more than the nonwhite. But the point is not that Negro life expectancy in years is 91 per cent of white, but that the Negro male child today is where the white was some twenty-two to twenty-eight years earlier. This is the gap of which we speak.

We know more than that. Already in 1921-23 the white had reached a life expectancy level the Negro was not to attain until 1949-51 (thus in 1950 the gap also was twenty-eight years). In 1940 the gap had been twenty-seven years. We have not been making progress in cutting the time gap. It is often easy to forget that the speed of progress is in part dependent on where one starts. The statement, "Since 1900, life expectancy for the total population has increased by more than 20 years; the increase in nonwhite life expectancy, for both males and females, has been about 30 years,"[4] is true. Nevertheless, the following should be noted: in 1900 white male life expectancy at birth was 48.2 years—by 1940, it was 62.8 years—a gain of fifteen years in four decades. But for the Negro, too, a full forty years were needed to progress over the same range: from 47.1 years in 1920 to 61.5 years in 1960. This illustrates the importance of comparing rates of progress over a range that both groups (white and Negro) have experienced—even if they have covered the terrain at different times. The fact that one group made greater progress *over the same chronological time period* than did another may result from the fact that it was in a different range of its (nonlinear)growth curve. If, however, rates of progress are compared over a range common to both groups, we may find—and in this example we do find—that Negro progress was no more rapid than was earlier white progress. This, it is submitted, is surely as relevant for projecting the time dimension of future progress (in the absence of special efforts) as comparisons over the same time period that involve very different ranges.

The significance of the measure should be clear. The Negro covered the same territory from 1920 to 1960 that the white had covered from 1900 to 1940—the same territory in the same length of time. But we would have expected that, given equal opportunity, he would have moved more rapidly. It should be easier for 10 per cent of the population to advance more rapidly (if the other 90 per cent care) than for 90 per cent to advance. Furthermore, the state of scientific knowledge was greater in 1920 than in 1900, greater in 1930 than in 1910, and so on, thus permitting a compression of the time required to make an equal amount of progress. The Negro did not have to wait for the next scientific advance. It had already been made—though he had not fully shared in it. It is here contended that were the Negro to have made his advance only as rapidly as had the white there would be cause for concern (and action). But he was prevented from doing even that well. The often-cited advantages of being late did not accrue to the Negro. The time gap has not been materially shortened in the last four decades.

Also disturbing is the fact that the gap remained the same during the deacde 1950 to 1960. During that period the Negro male added 2.6 years (4.4 per cent) to his life expectancy at birth while the white added only 1.3 years (2.0 per cent). But the Negro moved from 58.9 years to 61.5 years—a very different area of the curve than the white who went from 66.3 to 67.6 years. Gains, perhaps, come easier in the range that the Negro is now covering and that the white had covered at an earlier time. What is important is that it took ten years for the Negro to move from 58.9 to 61.5 years. When the white was covering that range (that is, moving from 58.9 in 1922 to 61.5 in 1932), it also took him ten years. Thus, we are made aware—and later in this essay we will again be reminded—that conditions were less favorable for the Negro during the 1950's than is, perhaps, commonly supposed—certainly than many would like to believe.

The child is born. In 1962 the chances were 87 in 100 that he was born in a hospital. Whites, for whom the chances today are 99 in 100, reached today's Negro rate in 1946—a gap of sixteen years. In 1952 the gap was only eleven years. In 1962 the Negro was where the white had been in 1946; in 1952 the Negro was where the white had been in 1941. Thus it took the Negro ten years (from 1952 to 1962) to do what the white had done in five (from 1941 to 1946)—that is, to increase the percentage of hospital births from 66 to 87. As a consequence the gap has widened. It is true, of course, that hospital birth rates differ considerably in the various regions in which our Negro family may reside—though this is not the case for white families. For Negroes, the percentage distribution of live births in hospitals ranges from a high of 99 per 100 in New England to lows of 64, 81, and 87 in the East South Central, South Atlantic, and West South Central divisions—but the lowest white rate in any division is 97 per 100. Even as late as 1962 the chances were barely 50-50 that a Negro baby born in Mississippi was born in a hospital, but the chances were 99 in 100 for ·white Mississippi-born babies. And for Negro residents of Dallas County and Lowndes County, Alabama, the rates in 1962 were 27 and 9 per 100 (while rates for white residents were 99 and 96 respectively).

The lack of progress in closing the time gap (indeed, its expansion) is all the more remarkable and disturbing since this has occurred in spite of the substantial Negro outmigration from the rural areas and from the South—that is, from areas with lower percentages of hospital births. The fact that the Negro population was becoming more urbanized (now even more urban than the white), and geographically distributed more like the total population, worked in a direction that should cut the gap—but proved insufficient to do so.

In 1960 the chances that the Negro infant would die before reaching its first birthday were 43 per 1,000 live births—double that of a white baby. This rate was achieved by whites two decades earlier, in 1940. The gap is twenty years. In 1950 the Negro had been where the white was only about eleven years earlier (the gap had been seventeen years in 1940 and fifteen years in 1930). Thus, while the infant mortality rate for whites dropped from 100 per 1,000 to 43 per 1,000 in twenty-five years, it took the Negro thirty years to cover the same distance. Progress, as indicated by narrowing and widening of the gap, was uneven. In some decades progress was more rapid, in other decades less rapid. In the decade of the 1930's Negroes covered a range that whites covered in eight years (1915-1923); in the 1940's Negroes covered a range that had taken whites fifteen years, but in the entire decade of the 1950's Negroes made no more progress than whites had made in a tenth of a decade—in one year.

This is the case because infant mortality for the total population (chiefly white) decreased by about 4.3 per cent each year from 1933 to 1949 and by 2.0 per cent from 1950 to 1960. For nonwhites the rate decreased by 4.6 per cent from 1933 to 1949 but only by 1.2 per cent from 1950 to 1956 and in 1960 the rate was what it had been in 1956.[5] Thus in 1960 the rate of nonwhite infant mortality was 1.9 times that of white in 1960, while in 1950 it had been 1.7 times as high.

The gap for the neonatal mortality rate—deaths of infants under twenty-eight days—is about twenty years and also has widened slightly. The Negro mother's chances of dying from complications of pregnancy (maternal mortality rate) are low—only about 10 in 10,000 live births. But whites—with a rate between 2 and 3 per 10,000—had reached a level of 10 in 1948, twelve years earlier. This represents a dramatic reduction in the gap—it was not until 1941-42 that the Negro reached the level that whites had reached in 1915, and Negro progress was rapid in the decade of the 1940's. But again, as with a number of other measures, the gap widened in the decade of the 1950's. In 1950 the gap between white and Negro was only eight years—in 1960 it was eleven years.

The Negro child faces a different world than does today's white baby. So does his family. The mortality rate for his older brother, age twenty, is somewhat over twenty years behind the white mortality rate; the gap for his father is perhaps forty years and for his grandfather exceeds sixty years.[6]

His family faces somewhat different health problems than does the white population. In 1962 the Negro tuberculosis death rate of 11.5 per 100,000 was over twice the white rate of 4.2 (the difference is even greater on an age-adjusted basis), but the gap—as was the case with a number of causes of death, for example, diphtheria and whooping cough—was less than a decade. Other causes of death, such as dysentery and syphilis, exhibited longer lags.

In addition, the Negro family is less frequently covered by hospital or surgical insurance than is its white counterpart. Seventy-four per cent of all whites but only 46 per cent of Negroes were covered by hospital insurance in 1962-63. The Negro coverage rate lags the coverage rate for whites by somewhat more than a decade. Differences in median income account for much of the difference in coverage, but not for all of it. At incomes under $2,000, 38 per cent of whites but only 25 per cent of Negroes were covered, while at incomes between $4,000 and $7,000 coverage was 80 per cent for whites and 66 per cent for nonwhites. The U.S. National Health Survey found that in 1957-59 Negroes on the average had fewer visits per year to physicians (two-thirds the white rate). Their contact with physicians in hospital outpatient clinics far exceeded that of whites (26 per cent of all Negro physician visits were in hospital clinics as compared with only 8 per cent of white visits). During the same time period, in all sections of the United States, whites had double the number of dental visits per person that nonwhites had and, while the number of dental visits for extractions among whites was 1.5 times that among Negroes, the rate for fillings (more of a "luxury" product) was 8 times higher among whites than among Negroes. Finally, in 1958-60 Negroes were less likely to enter hospitals—but likely to stay longer before being discharged.

Many of these differences, as has been pointed out, are largely accounted for by Negro-white income differentials. But, the differences, however they are explained, are substantial. Most Negroes face different health conditions than do most whites.

Thus the Negro male child is born into a world in which (in 1962) his chances of reaching age twenty are about the same as that of a white's reaching thirty-seven. A Negro girl (at birth) has the same chances of attaining age twenty as a white girl has of reaching forty-two. The lags are almost two decades.

We turn to education. The educational attainment of nonwhite adults with whom the child comes in contact is greater than was the attainment of adults whom the 1940 child met. Our child's parents have more education than their parents had. In 1960 the median school years completed by nonwhites twenty-five years old and over was 8.2 years. In 1940 the median number completed by nonwhites then twenty-five years and older was only 5.8 years. Yet already in 1940 white attainment was 8.7 years, a level higher than Negro attainment twenty years later. The gap, therefore, exceeds twenty years. It can be noted, too, that the white median rose from 8.7 in 1940 to 10.9 in 1960 (a rise of 2.2 years) while nonwhite attainment—in spite of the start from a lower base—rose by only 2.4 years (5.8-8.2). The difference, though not great, does represent a reversal of the 1920-1940 experience.[7] Much of the rise in the nonwhite median is explained by the substantial drop in the percentage of Negroes with very little education (in 1940, 71 per cent of persons twenty-five years old and over had completed less than eight years of schooling, but by 1960 this was reduced to 47 per cent; in 1920, 45 per cent of those aged twenty-five to twenty-nine had less than five years of school; by 1940 this was true of only 27 per cent of those aged twenty-five to twenty-nine, and by 1960 it was true of only 7 per cent). Nevertheless, the absolute increase in the percentage of whites completing high school or college was greater than was the increase for nonwhites. In 1960 the percentage of Negroes twenty-five years old and over who had completed college (3.5 per cent) was substantially less than the percentage had been for whites in 1940 (4.9 per cent). Even in 1960 the percentage of Negro male college graduates aged twenty-five to twenty-nine (5.3 per cent) was only equal to the percentage among whites in 1920 and the percentage of high-school graduates in that age group was about the same as among whites in 1940.[8]

Educational attainment is related to future employment possibilities. The demand for educated personnel has increased. It can, therefore, be seen that in a very real sense nonwhites without a college education in 1960 were at a competitive disadvantage vis-à-vis the rest of the labor force as compared with the competitive disadvantage in 1920 for whites with the same educational attainment. Nonwhites with less than a high-school degree in 1960 were similarly at a disadvantage as compared with white non-high-school graduates in 1940. The educational gap—as it would influence employment possibilities—is even greater and more significant than suggested.

Nevertheless, I cannot subscribe to the view that the Negro faces insurmountable problems in entering the world of work. It is said that technological progress is so much more rapid today than in earlier periods—a statement that itself is probably incorrect—that the Negro is falling further and further behind the educational requirements imposed by modern industry. Some conclude, therefore, that earlier minority groups had a considerable advantage over today's Negro. Were there no discrimination in employment, it is doubtful that this would be the case. It is true that educational requirements advance even as the Negro American's educational level advances. Some of the gains that would lead to upgrading are, therefore, "dissipated." But not all the gains are wasted. The rise in educational attainment of younger Negroes, in particular, is very rapid, and the absolute attainment (outside the South) quite high. Earlier minority groups faced a less demanding economy, but also had less educational attainment to offer. It is not clear that on balance, *and abstracting from discrimination,* the situation is significantly *more* disadvantageous to the Negro.

The tasks that lie ahead in the educational sector can, perhaps, be shown by the following data for the fall of 1963: 56 per cent of white five year olds but only 42 per cent of nonwhite children were enrolled in kindergarten; only 7 per cent of the white youngsters aged fourteen to seventeen enrolled in school were still in elementary school, but this was the case with 20 per cent of Negro enrolled youngsters. At ages eighteen and nineteen, 41 per cent of whites and 40 per cent of Negroes were enrolled in school, but only 23 per cent of whites were still in high school (77 per cent were enrolled in college) while this was true of 56 per cent of Negroes (only 44 per cent were enrolled in college). Thus, even when enrollment rates are similar, retardation rates are much higher for Negroes. Detailed data for the 1960 census show the following: in the South, at all ages, the percentage of nonwhites one or more grades behind the modal grade exceeds the retardation rate for white children. By the third grade over 50 per cent of nonwhite children are one or more grades behind the modal grade (grade three). At age fifteen two-thirds of nonwhites enrolled are still not up to the second year of high school (the modal grade for the total population) and almost 40 per cent are still in elementary school. National retardation rates for nonwhites do run somewhat lower than they do in the South, but still remain high.

While data to compare educational attainment as far back through time as we would like are unavailable, a tracing through time can be approximated by comparing persons in various age groups today. In 1964, 16 per cent of Negro males aged twenty to twenty-four had one or more years of college—the same percentage as among white males aged fifty-five to sixty-four, most of whom received their college education thirty-five to forty years ago. Thus, in terms of the percentage with some college education, the young Negro of today is barely attaining what whites who today are fifty-five to sixty-four years old attained when they were young. This represents a gap of over thirty-five years. The gap, though still considerable, is much shorter at lower levels of educational attainment.

Nor is the educational gap between generations always narrowing. As the Bureau of the Census reports, "It thus appears that not only is the nonwhite population more poorly educated than the white population but the net gain of nonwhites at higher levels of education, as calculated from educational differences in the fathers' and sons' generations, has not been as great as for whites."[9] The gap is a generation: in 1962, 10.3 per cent of the fathers of white males aged twenty to sixty-four had some college education (and 25.6 per cent of the sons did) while 10.4 per cent of Negro males aged twenty to sixty-four (the "sons") had some college (and 4.4 per cent of the fathers did). Thus the percentage among white fathers was the same as among Negro sons. A critical question is whether 26 per cent of their *sons* (the sons of today's Negro males aged twenty to sixty-four) will attend college (as is the case for whites who today are aged twenty to sixty-four). College attendance rates will surely accelerate, in part because of the strong positive influence that the level of parents' educational attainment exerts on that of the children. But even if the doors of opportunity open more widely and the 26 per cent rate is achieved, Negroes will be attaining levels that whites attained a generation earlier.

Unfortunately it is impossible to develop an adequate time-lag measure for a number of relevant indices—and certainly impossible to compare the length of lag back through time. The reason is clear. Even today the Negro-white differential is so great and adequate statistics are of such recent vintage that the white was already ahead of today's nonwhite attainment when data were first gathered (or shortly thereafter). In such cases more traditional methods must be used to make comparisons over time. Sometimes these difficulties are compounded by the fact that the data are subject to significant cyclical variation (as is the case, for example, with unemployment rates). If, in those cases, earlier years are cited in which the index for whites equalled today's Negro index, this is not done in order to suggest a time-lag measure. Rather, referring to specific earlier years may help remind the (white) reader of what things were like then. Thus, if one wants to understand what an unemployment rate of 20 per cent represents, it is helpful to be reminded that this was the national rate in 1935.

Let us examine unemployment. Today the Negro faces an unemployment situation unknown to the white for almost two and one-half decades—and the Negro has been facing it for a number of years. What is recession for the white (say, an unemployment rate of 6 per cent) is prosperity for the nonwhite. He last saw an unemployment rate below 7.5 per cent in 1953—a full decade ago. In 1964, when the total unemployment rate for white males twenty years old and over was 3.4 per cent, the nonwhite rate was over twice as high—7.7 per cent. The rate for Negro females aged twenty and over was almost twice as high as for whites, and this was also the case for males and females combined (aged fourteen to nineteen). In 1964—a prosperity year—the Negro confronted an unemployment rate (9.8 per cent) more than 50 per cent higher than the highest rate faced by whites at any time since the great depression. Surely, the Negro must feel wry as he considers the debate about the level of unemployment that shall be considered full employment. His employment rate has not reached the "interim target" of 4.0 per cent a single time in the postwar period.

Let me make it clear that I do not say that the Negro fails to share in upward movements of the economy. He does share in prosperity—just as he is hurt by recessions. There *are* differences between unemployment rates for Negro males of 4.4 per cent in 1953, 13.7 per cent in 1958, and 9.1 per cent in 1964. It is a fact, however, that Negro unemployment rates are higher than white rates at the same moment in time and that the Negro *frequently* faces unemployment rates which—if faced by all workers—would be considered a national scandal. The fact is that the unemployment rate for Negroes in 1964, a year of general prosperity, was over one and one-half times as large as that for whites in *any* of the postwar recessions. Therefore, perhaps, it is appropriate to say that whites fluctuate between prosperity and recession but Negroes fluctuate between depression and great depression.

The difference in over-all white and Negro unemployment rates is not explained entirely by a different age-sex structure. Negro unemployment rates for every age-sex grouping (except for women over fifty-five) are higher—sometimes far higher—than the highest postwar rate for whites in the same age-sex group. We spoke of *fluctuations* between depression and great or deep depression. But for some of the age-sex groups—particularly, but not exclusively, among teen-agers—unemployment rates appear perpetually high: the unemployment rate for male Negroes aged sixteen and seventeen was last below 20 per cent in 1957 (it reached 31 per cent in 1961); it was last below 20 per cent for males aged eighteen and nineteen in 1956; and it was last below 10 per cent for males aged twenty to twenty-four in 1953. In only five of the seventeen years since 1948 has the rate for Negro females aged eighteen and nineteen been below 15 per cent and it has not been below 20 per cent in the last eleven years.

The differential in unemployment rates presents a real and severe problem. It is a problem requiring special attention and strong specific (as well as general) measures. Indeed, it may require relatively stronger action than would have been necessary fifteen years ago. At that time (in 1950) the white unemployment rate was 4.6 per cent and the nonwhite was 8.5 per cent (1.6 times the white). In 1964, with a white rate again at 4.6 per cent, the nonwhite rate was up to 9.8 per cent (2.1 times the white).

And when the Negro is unemployed, it is for a longer period of time. In 1964, nonwhites represented 11 per cent of the labor force and 21 per cent of the unemployed, but they accounted for 23 per cent of those unemployed fifteen weeks or longer and 25 per cent of those unemployed for over half a year. In 1963, 27 per cent of white, but 35 per cent of nonwhite unemployed males were unemployed fifteen weeks or more and 14 per cent of white but 20 per cent of nonwhite unemployed males were unemployed twenty-seven weeks or more. The average duration of unemployment for white males was slightly under fifteen weeks, for nonwhites slightly over nineteen.

Finally, it should be noted that Negroes, when employed, are more likely to be working only part time. In 1963, for example, while 81 per cent of whites at work in nonagricultural industries worked full time, this was true of only 74 per cent of nonwhites. Only 3.1 per cent of whites worked part time for economic reasons —slack work, inability to find full-time work—but this was the case for 9.6 per cent of employed nonwhites. The average number of hours worked by those employed was 8 per cent higher for white males than for nonwhite males.

The Negro faces higher unemployment rates, more frequent periods of unemployment in a given year, longer duration of unemployment, more part-time rather than full-time work—and all this is true even when occupation is held constant. The often-heard comment that the differentials result from the fact that nonwhites have a disadvantageous occupational structure is only partly true. Thus, for example, 6 per cent of white professional and technical workers with work experience in 1962 were unemployed for some time during the year, but this was true of 11 per cent of nonwhites (and while 6 per cent of white male professionals had worked at part-time jobs, 12 per cent of nonwhites had done so). Twelve per cent of white but 18 per cent of nonwhite clerical workers were unemployed in 1962 (and while 25 per cent of the white unemployed clerical workers were unemployed for fifteen or more weeks, this was the case for 38 per cent of the nonwhite unemployed). Thirty-two per cent of white laborers had some unemployment in 1962 but 45 per cent of nonwhites did (and while 50 per cent of whites had two or more spells of unemployment, 69 per cent of nonwhites did).

We have indicated that the unemployment situation is worse for Negroes than for whites even if we correct for occupational structure of the Negro labor force. But it is also true that the unfavorable occupational structure does contribute to the problem. In addition, it affects more than unemployment rates (and income). The sharply different occupational structure among Negroes surely has an impact on the child and narrows his horizons. In 1963—as in earlier years—the white child, for example, had a far greater opportunity to meet white-collar workers than did the Negro child: 47 per cent of whites were so employed, but only 18 per cent of Negroes. While the data are rough, it would appear that already in 1900, when we were still a heavily agricultural country, the percentage of white-collar workers in the white population was 18 per cent—a lag of some sixty years. Similarly, in 1963 about 13 per cent of employed Negroes were laborers (except farm and mine)—the same percentage as in the white population of 1900 (a percentage which for whites had gradually declined to 4 per cent by 1963).

Thus our Negro child grows up in a world in which opportunity seems closed. And surely his aspirations are in part influenced by the achievements of other Negroes. In 1960, when 10 per cent of the male experienced labor force was nonwhite, only 3.5 per cent of male professionals, technical, and kindred workers were nonwhite (and perhaps one-quarter of these were not Negro). Only 1.4 per cent of accountants and auditors were nonwhite, 1.7 per cent of engineers, 1.3 per cent of lawyers and judges, 1.3 per cent of salaried managers, officials, and proprietors, 2.0 per cent of bookkeepers (and 6.8 per cent of clerical and kindred workers), 2.1 per cent of sales workers, and 4.9 per cent of craftsmen, foremen, and kindred workers (all data for males only). But the 10 per cent proportion of the labor force was exceeded in some occupations: 48.4 per cent of private household workers are nonwhite, 26.1 per cent of laborers, and we find large percentages for other occupations at the bottom rungs of the occupational ladder. When a nonwhite child met an employed nonwhite, the chances that he was meeting a janitor were six times as great and the chances that he was meeting an engineer were only one-sixth as great as when a white child met a white employee. There are thirty-one times as many nonwhite male janitors as nonwhite engineers but more white engineers than white janitors. Almost twice as many nonwhite males are janitors as are professional and technical workers, but only one-tenth as many whites are janitors as are professionals. Over four times as many nonwhite males are janitors as are sales workers, but almost seven times as many whites are sales workers as are janitors. And the situation among females, where nonwhites represent 13 per cent of the experienced labor force, is similar: 55 per cent of the private household workers are nonwhite. Surely our Negro child aspires to a higher occupational achievement than nonwhites now have, but how difficult the road ahead appears (and is) when he confronts today's nonwhite occupational distribution.

The difference in educational attainment accounts for much, but not all, of the difference found in occupational structure. In 1962, for example, 20 per cent of nonwhite male high-school graduates were laborers. This was true of only 4 per cent of white male high-school graduates. Even among white males with an elementary education or less, the equivalent percentage was only 9 per cent. Nineteen per cent of nonwhite females with some college were private household workers but this was virtually unknown (1 per cent) among white females who had attended college. It was not even as high as 19 per cent (only 13 per cent) for white females with zero to eight years of elementary school.

The interrelation of the various parts of our description is depressing—the relative disadvantage in one area causes and is caused by disadvantages in another area. Relatively high unemployment and a disadvantageous occupational structure, for example, both contribute to lower incomes for Negroes than for whites. We now examine income patterns. What are our child's chances in that area?

In 1964 the Negro family with income had a median income of $3839—only 56 per cent of that for white families. White families had reached a $3800 income level back in 1951, but the situation is worse than is implied by this thirteen-year gap. Negroes in 1964 purchased commodities at 1964 prices, while whites in 1951 purchased at substantially lower 1951 prices. If we correct for price changes and compare income in dollars with 1964 purchasing power, we find that white income, even as far back as 1947, exceeded present Negro income by, perhaps, 10 to 15 per cent. Census data permit more detailed analysis. Using constant 1959 dollars (dollars with the same purchasing power), we find that in 1960 13.7 per cent of all Negro families had annual total money income of under $1,000 and 32.1 per cent had incomes of under $2,000. Even as long ago as 1947 this was true of only 6.5 per cent and 19.1 per cent of all white families. The lag is found among urban, rural nonfarm, and rural farm families (Table 2).

TABLE 2. Median Annual Money Income and Percentage of Families Below Specified Income Levels, by Residence and Color, 1947 and 1960

(Income levels expressed in dollars with 1959 purchasing power)	Median income	Per Cent of Families	
		Below $1,000	Below $2,000
Urban nonwhite 1960	$3,844	7.0	21.8
Urban white 1947	4,544	3.6	10.8
Rural nonfarm nonwhite 1960	2,000	24.8	50.0
Rural nonfarm white 1947	3,809	6.6	17.0
Rural farm nonwhite 1960	1,155	44.0	77.3
Rural farm white 1947	2,827	16.4	34.9

In 1960 the urban nonwhite caught up to the 1947 level for rural nonfarm whites. The urban white had, of course, achieved this level many years before 1947. To say that in 1960 the *urban* Negro family had the same real money income that the white *rural non-farm* family had in 1947, to say that in 1960 the median Negro family had an income equal to the median white *farm* family is to point up the substantial lag and gap in income.

In 1964 the relative situation was only slightly better: 7.7 per cent of Negro families had incomes below $1,000 (measured in 1964 dollars) but this was true for only 2.7 per cent of whites. Our child had a twenty-two in one hundred chance (unadjusted for differential birth rates by income) of being born to a family with an income below $2,000. A white child would have an eight in one hundred chance. Our child has only a two in one hundred chance of being born in a family with income over $15,000 (eight in one hundred for income of over $10,000). For a white child the chances are seven and twenty-four in one hundred respectively.

If we use a poverty standard—families with incomes under $3,000—the chances in 1963 were forty-three in one hundred that our child was born into a family in poverty (by 1964 the chances were down to thirty-seven in one hundred). It is of course true, as many have pointed out, that the large majority of poor families are white (after all, an even greater majority of all families are white). A program to eliminate poverty cannot, therefore, be successful if it addresses itself only to Negroes. However, the Negro has a far greater chance (almost three times as great) of being in poverty than does the white. Even as late as 1963 the percentage of Negro families in poverty was 50 per cent higher than the white level had been sixteen years earlier in 1947 (measured in 1963 constant dollars). To whom can we ask the Negro to compare himself if he is to have some degree of hope? Apparently only to himself at some earlier period—in 1947 two-thirds of Negro families were poor—but not to the rest of America which already in 1947 was better off than the Negro was in 1963 and which, since 1947, had a decline of 30 per cent in the number of poor families while the number of poor Negro families (in part as a result of the increase in the absolute number of families) *increased* by 2 per cent.

In discussions of income data, the point is often, and validly, made that the worker's educational attainment is an important determinant of income. It is surely small comfort for the Negro to be told that his present low income status is due to his lack of education. Explanations do not assist in making purchases; only money does. Analysis is not a substitute for cash. Perhaps the analysis does make the income determination process a less personal one—things were "determined" at some earlier period, and we are all now acting out our roles. But there is a difficulty with this—even aside from the fact that the Negro's low educational attainment itself is the result of discrimination. The difficulty is that low education does not provide the total explanation for low income. As with a number of variables already discussed, simply being Negro also makes a difference. For in 1963 our Negro child's family had a median income of $4,530 if the family head completed high school. But the white family with the same years of education for the head had an income of $6,997—almost 55 per cent more. Indeed, if the white had but eight years of schooling, his income was $5,454, 20 per cent more than for the Negro high-school graduate. Nor are these unfavorable comparisons isolated cases: The Negro family whose head had some high school earned less than the white with fewer than eight years of schooling; *the Negro who has attended (but not completed) college earns less than the white with only eight years of elementary school,* the Negro college graduate earns but slightly more than does the white high-school graduate. Surely there are differences in the quality of education. In parts of the nation a year of Negro education was not (and is not) equal to a year of white education. Nevertheless, to argue that there is no discrimination in employment and income requires that we argue that the Negro with some college knows no more than does the white with only eight years of elementary school. This is hard to accept. And, surely, the value of an education is less clear when, for those who attended college, Negro male income is only 60 per cent of white male income, but is 68 per cent for those who only completed high school and 73 per cent for those who only attended elementary school. In a survey conducted in February 1963, it was found that 73 per cent of males aged sixteen to twenty-one who had completed less than four years of high school earned $40 a week or more on their first full-time job. This was true for only 41 per cent of nonwhite males. Conversely, 27 per cent of all males, but only 11 per cent of nonwhite males earned more than $60 a week.

It is important to realize the story these data tell. It is true that we cannot correct for quality of education—that the data measure only years of education not amount taught or learned. But even taking this into account, and even taking into account the fact that

Negroes reside disproportionately in the South (a low income region), it is clear that, important as education may be, it does not offer a complete explanation of low Negro incomes. It is a simple fact that the Negro is *qualified* for higher occupational levels and for higher incomes than he attains. The data document a story of discrimination. Some may pessimistically conclude that it is harder to eliminate discrimination than to raise levels of education. I would respond that, painful as is the story the data reveal, there are grounds for optimism. We need not wait until today's and tomorrow's (better educated) youths become adults to increase incomes and raise occupational levels. Discrimination may be harder to combat than poor education—though even this is not certain. But it can be combated *in the short run*. To raise education and reap its rewards must take time—considerable time. But if discrimination accounts for much (though not all) of the income disparity—and I conclude that it does—we can make more rapid, more immediate progress. Perhaps as little as one-third of the total disparity between white and nonwhite incomes is due to less years of education.[10] Corrections for quality of education and geographic distribution of population would lower the proportion that can be accounted for by discrimination. Nevertheless, substantial income increases could result—even with today's educational levels—as a consequence of the elimination of discrimination. Surely we favor better and more education, but we need not wait for the effects of today's better education to take hold a decade hence.

Perhaps the discrimination that exists can be illustrated by comparing 1959 median nonwhite and white earnings for a series of occupations. We also present data for median years of school completed for nonwhites and for the total population in the particular occupation, thus pointing up the fact that differences in income exist even in occupations where high levels of education are not a requisite. Of course, in many of the occupations, experience on the job has had an opportunity to overcome the influence of poor education. Yet, even so, differentials remain.

How low the family's income is will depend, in part, on the region in which the family resides. But the differences between white and nonwhite income are large in all regions. First, income is reduced because, while almost two-thirds of white families are headed by a year-round full-time worker, only one-half of Negro families are so headed. These differences are found in all regions except the West. Furthermore, family income—even if the head is fully employed—is lower for the nonwhite (again in all regions): In the Northeast it is 70 per cent of white, in the North Central 83 per cent, in the South 51 per cent, and in the West 86 per cent. If account is taken of lower full-time employment as well as lower earnings, the percentage that nonwhite family income is of white family income drops significantly to 65, 73, 45, and 76 per cent respectively for the four regions. Clearly, there are large differ-

TABLE 3. Median Income and Median Years of School Completed, Total Population and Nonwhite, by Occupation, 1959

Occupation	Median income		Median years of school completed	
	Nonwhite	Total	Nonwhite	Total
Bakers	$3354	$4633	8.9	9.2
Carpenters	2320	4271	8.1	9.3
Welders and flame-cutters	4454	5116	9.6	9.7
Elevator operators	3122	3487	8.7	8.6
Automobile mechanics	3173	4372	8.9	9.9
Tinsmiths, coppersmiths, and sheet metal workers	4710	5542	11.1	10.8

ences among regions. Equally clearly, the situation is an unhappy one in all regions.

Our Negro child has been born into a family that is substantially poorer than the average white family. In part, this is because the Negro family head has less education than the white, earns less even at the same levels of education, has less chance of year-round full-time employment. All this most of us know. But startling is the fact that there has been very little change in the ratio of non-white family income to white family income over the last decade and a half (there had been extremely rapid progress in the first half of the decade of the 1940's). In 1947 the ratio of nonwhite to white family income was .51 and, though it reached .57 in 1952 (with progress from 1950 to 1952), it had fallen back to .51 in 1958 and stood at .56 in 1964. This was true in spite of the considerable out-migration during the 1950's of Negroes from the South to higher income regions. As has been shown,[11] the ratio of Negro to white income for males fell during the period 1949 to 1959 in every region of the country. Thus, even despite outmigration, the ratio of non-white to white male income in the nation fell in the decade of the 1950's. Progress in reducing the disparity in income ratios has been concentrated in periods of tight labor markets (parts of the

1940's and the early 1950's) but it is unfortunate for all of us and most unfortunate for Negroes that many years have passed since the United States has faced tight labor markets.

What does lower Negro income mean for the living conditions in which our child is raised? We turn to the family's housing. The quality of housing occupied by Negroes is—as we know—markedly inferior to that occupied by whites. Since 1920, when the number of persons per occupied dwelling unit was the same for whites and nonwhites, the rate for whites has declined from 4.3 persons to 3.3 persons per unit in 1960, while the figure for nonwhites has declined only from 4.3 to 4.0. More significant, however, are the figures on the number of persons per room—a crowding measure. In 1960, 14 per cent of nonwhite units had over 1.5 persons per room (down from 23 per cent in 1940), and 28 per cent had more than one person per room (down from 40 per cent in 1940). But comparable 1960 figures for white units were only 2 per cent with more than 1.5 persons per room and 10 per cent with more than one person per room. Already in 1940 the white child was doing his homework under less crowded conditions than our Negro child faced twenty years later. Only 7.5 per cent of white households had more than 1.5 persons per room and only 18 per cent had more than one person per room in 1940—standards considerably better than nonwhites had achieved a full two decades later. The over-crowding statistics result from the fact that in 1960 nonwhite occupied units had fewer rooms (4.2 rooms as contrasted with 4.9 rooms for all units) and larger households (3.2 persons as contrasted with 3.0 persons for all units).

Thus overcrowding is not uncommon in Negro housing. But the situation is made worse by the quality of what is overcrowded. In 1960 30 per cent of housing units occupied by nonwhites lacked bathtubs or showers—a situation true for only 12 per cent of all dwelling units (including vacant ones). Forty-one per cent of nonwhite units had no bathrooms (or had shared ones), but this was the case in only 12 per cent of all dwelling units. Sixty-five per cent of nonwhite housing units had hot and cold piped water inside the structure, but 87 per cent of all units did. A full one-fifth of nonwhite units had no piped water inside the structure, a situation true for only 7 per cent of all units. Finally, while 90 per cent of all units had flush toilets, this was true for only 75 per cent of nonwhite occupied units. In 1960 our family lived in housing that had not reached 1950 U. S. standards on hot and cold water inside the structure or on bathing facilities and had barely reached 1950 standards for toilet facilities.

The Negro thus is more likely to be living in an overcrowded unit that lacks a number of modern facilities. In addition, in 1960 the chances were six times greater (than for whites) that the structure he lived in was dilapidated and two and one-half times greater that it was deteriorating. Seventeen per cent of Negro occupied housing (but only 3 per cent of white) was classified "dilapidated," and 28 per cent of Negro occupied housing was classified "deteriorating" (but this was true for less than 12 per cent of white). Only 55 per cent of Negro housing was "sound," and only 44 per cent was "sound with all plumbing." The odds were heavily against our child. It is true that there are significant regional variations in the percentage of nonwhite units that are "sound with all plumbing": in the South only 31 per cent of housing is so classified, while in the West the figure is 67 per cent. It can be noted, however, that in terms of soundness of housing the best region for nonwhites (the West) is equal to the poorest region for whites (the South). Income —and discriminatory housing practices—thus result in the fact that many Negro families occupy substandard, overcrowded housing that lacks modern conveniences.

The child with whom we began our story thus has shorter life expectancy, lives in less desirable housing, is a member of a family with less education, with a less favorable occupational structure, with more unemployment, and with lower income than the median white baby born at the same time. And the rate of improvement in these indices still leaves the Negro far behind the average for the rest of America.

But, of course, there is no *the* Negro American—as there is no *the* white American. There are many Negro Americans who live in conditions far better than the median Negro American. There are some who live better than the median American. There are many who live in far worse conditions. Geographic location makes an important difference in the indices cited. Our child has a better than even chance of being born in the South where the situation is generally even poorer than is indicated by the national data previously cited. It is a fact that the Negro in the North lives very differently than does the Negro in the South—though not so well as many whites believe or would like to believe. Table 4 illustrates some of these differences. In this table the status of Negroes in Census divisions with extreme highs and lows is shown. For purposes of comparison the median white U. S. averages are also shown.

Though there is significant variation in some of the indicators, in no case is performance in the division with greatest Negro attainment equal to the white median for the entire United States.

TABLE 4.   Range of Values for Selected Indices for Nonwhites in Census Divisions and U.S. Median for Whites*

	Nonwhite		White
	In "Poorest" Division	*In "Best" Division*	*U. S.*
Infant mortality per 1,000 live births (1962)	46.9 (ESC)	30.7 (P)	22.3
Median school years completed (1960)	6.7 (ESC)	10.3 (P)	10.9
Per cent college graduates, of males 25–29 (1960)	3.6 (ESC)	9.8 (P)	15.6
Per cent housing sound with all plumbing (1960)	23.1 (ESC)	70.9 (P)	79.7
Per cent housing with more than one person per room (1960)	46.0 (M)	18.2 (NE)	9.8
Family income (1963)	$2520 (S)	$5417 (W)	$6548
Per cent families with income under $3,000 (1963)	58.4 (S)	19.8 (W)	15.9

* "ESC" stands for the East South Central division; "P" for Pacific; "NE" for New England; "M" for Mountain; "S" for South; and "W" for West.

The significant differences between South and North and between urban and rural areas, combined with the very considerable migration of Negroes from the South to the North and from rural areas to urban areas, help explain much of the improvement over time in many of the indices we have examined. But progress in the future will require upward movement *within* the urban setting since the heaviest rural-urban migration has already taken place. In 1960, 73 per cent of all Negro Americans had urban residences— a higher percentage than was true for whites. South to North migration, it is true, continues. But the situation is far from satisfactory when the national median for Negroes increases relative to whites only as a consequence of population redistribution even as relative declines occur in all regions.

The differentials that exist between the majority of whites and the majority of the Negro minority are great. The lack of opportunity and the previous (and present) discriminatory practices have had their consequences: In many respects the Negro is today living in a world the white has long since left behind. The gains the Negro has made and is making are substantial—all indicators are advancing. The real situation today is better than it once was. Nevertheless, we dare not overestimate the extent of these gains or underestimate the distance still to be covered.

Though the gains are large relative to where an earlier generation of Negroes stood, they are often more limited if the comparison is made of nonwhite indicators relative to those for whites. In such comparisons, (for example, income) we often find that the differential between whites and nonwhites has been widening in recent years. Differentials frequently narrowed in the 1940's but increased again in the latter part of the 1950's. To the economist this underlines the importance of full employment and high-level economic growth in helping to secure advances. Everything is interrelated: Education has an impact on health, and employment on income, and income on education, and so forth. Advances are, therefore, required on a broad front. The generation now growing up will have opportunities opened to them—opportunities to make these advances—that their fathers did not have. But the record of the 1940's and 1950's tells us that these opportunities and the ability to seize them will be greater, the more rapid the growth and expansion of the economy.

Surely, however, the data indicate that the differentials are now so wide and the distance to be covered so great that simply waiting for time to bring improvement is to indulge in unjustified optimism. Many of the nonwhite indicators have not been advancing so rapidly as did the white indicators when they were at comparable levels. It is often taking the Negro longer to move up from "a" to "b" than it took the white. In many cases the narrowing of present differentials results from a redistribution of Negro population—and a "plateauing" of white rates of progress. But "plateauing" could also occur for nonwhites. We cannot be sanguine if we find, for example, that in 1950 the Negro reached levels that the white achieved in 1920 (a gap of thirty years), but that by 1960 he was where the white was in 1925 (a gap of thirty-five years). This kind of advance does not give us confidence concerning the achievement of equality in the not too distant future.

But optimism *is* warranted if concern leads us to take measures directed at the problem. For at no previous time in recent history could measures be so easily taken and progress so readily result.

We have the knowledge, and the means are available. In an economy with a civilian employment upward of 70 million, in an economy generating an additional $40 billion of gross national product annually, there are abundant fruits sufficient for all to feast upon.

And the numbers of persons involved make the problem even easier of solution, for Negroes represent only about 10 per cent of the population (with, perhaps, 5 per cent of the income). The "burden" of special measures, when addressed to 10 per cent but borne by the whole society, is, therefore, not great. This cost—when borne in a growing economy—can be absorbed while everyone advances. Illustrative of this point is that recent rates of economic growth would permit a doubling of nonwhite personal income (perhaps $20 billion) in one year even while—out of growth—white incomes rose.

And, it should be clear that the gains would not accrue solely to the nonwhite. The raising of Negro education, health, productivity, and employment would increase the economy's bounty for all. (The President's Council of Economic Advisers estimates that in time there would be an increase perhaps of as much as $23 billion—measured at today's price levels—in the Gross National Product.)[12] In addition, the indirect benefits to all of advances in education, health, and such in part of the population—while difficult to measure—are significant. Finally, and most importantly, if we remember that the Negro American is not only a Negro but an American, it should be clear that his gains are our gains—gains by all America.

These conclusions do not in themselves suggest how changes in the present situation are to be brought about—how rates of change are to be accelerated. I have already alluded to a number of situations that have policy implications. I summarize them.

I note again that some argue that the external world the Negro faces is vastly different from that faced by other minority groups in the past and that timing has conspired to rob the Negro of his opportunities. He, the argument asserts, is trying to make speedy progress when automation and increased stress on skills make job entrance more difficult and job requirements more demanding. For these reasons, if for no other, the Negro is said to be at a considerable disadvantage compared to other minorities. I agree that the Negro faces a *different* world. However, relative to the Negro American's achievements and accomplishments, it is not clear that, *were there no discrimination*, it would be a harsher world. The economy does place an additional premium on persons with more training—but in 1964 the median number of school years completed by Negroes aged twenty to twenty-four was 12.0 years. This is a far higher educational level than previous generations of Negroes—or previous minority groups—possessed. True it is that technological progress will bring a shift in occupational structure—but this will help unlock opportunities that free the Negro. It is to be preferred to an economic structure that demands less skill but provides less room for upward mobility. In this, as in other areas, expansion, growth, and change are the vital ingredients in Negro advancement. For it is easier to effect advancement for the Negro in a world of change than in a world of rigidity. Free education, expansion of university enrollments, greater concern about poverty, illiteracy, public health, housing codes, economic security—all these surely mean greater opportunity for present and future generations of Negro Americans. The importance of this concern—and commitment—cannot be overemphasized. It is a source of change and of ultimate strength. It is found in many sectors of society, organized and unorganized, public and private. It need not be ephemeral. It is the task of all—perhaps, particularly of the Negro—to keep the fire of concern burning brightly.

Such concern has—and will continue to have—its impact on public and private action—on legislation, on its implementation, and on private (business and non-business) behavior. The catalogue of actions is a long one; it encompasses the daily behavior of individuals and enterprises. What is required is that these actions, that the behavior, be nondiscriminatory, that equality be practiced as well as promised.

The data bear out the fact that a substantial part of America's problem results not only from past but also from present discriminatory behavior, not from objective, quantifiable "shortcomings" of the Negro—for example, less education—but from subjective attitudes of the white. "Men at some times are masters of their fates: The fault, dear Brutus, is not in our stars, But in ourselves, that we are underlings." The fault *is* in *ourselves* (not in the Negro), and we are masters of our fates. We can do much even today without waiting for the educational advancements that bear fruit tomorrow. We can eliminate present discrimination even as we institute programs that help remove the disabilities caused by past discrimination. We can reverse the "slippage" the data reveal.

Elimination of discrimination means a different sharing of the nation's (more abundant) products. I stress that a more equitable division is more easily achieved when the amount of product is growing. This is particularly true if conditions are such that the institution of non-discriminatory programs—and of compensatory, supplemental, and upgrading programs—is advantageous to those undertaking them, that is, if it becomes disadvantageous and expensive to indulge in the "taste" for discrimination and prejudice or to maintain the status quo.

The Negro did advance more rapidly in a rapidly expanding economy (the 1940's) than in an economy not living up to its potential (the latter part of the 1950's). Full employment, tight labor markets, high rates of growth are imperatives. They mean jobs, employer training programs, upgrading of labor, relaxation of undesirable restrictive hiring practices. I contend that the Negro will fare better in a redistribution of the fruits of progress than in a battle with others over the spoils of war.

This strikes close to and is also true for the issue often posed as "preferential treatment." Preferential treatment is not a wholly new concept on the American scene. In a very real sense we have witnessed it for decades—for whites. Separate and *unequal* schools, favoritism in hiring and employment, restrictive housing practices —often these were preferential treatment based on race. Universities have admitted less qualified students who were the sons of alumni, or who played band instruments at football games between groups of (other) preferentially treated students. Government expenditure (and tax) policy has given preference (some desirable— the War on Poverty; some undesirable—tax exemption of interest on state and local bonds). It is clear that preferential treatment can mean many different things and can take many different forms. The fact that it did exist in the past does not in itself mean that it should exist in the future. But it does suggest that it is not something completely new, to be rejected simply because it has not previously been used.

Attitudes to the phrase "preferential treatment" can vary with the policy that it calls to mind. Some may favor compensatory or supplemental educational programs and relaxed admission standards by universities but oppose preferential hiring policies by private employers. Some may favor programs to assist the Negro to attain required levels (via tutorial programs, on-the-job training, retraining, summer educational programs) but oppose preference except through such "compensatory" programs. Some may feel preference means assistance; others may feel it implies lowering of standards. And persons may disagree on the amount of preference to be granted: If assistance, how much? If relaxation of standards, how far? Does preference mean filling a vacancy with a Negro rather than a white when they are equal in all relevant respects, when the Negro is only a little less qualified, when he is substantially less qualified? Does preference mean extra dollars for Negro schools (how many dollars); does it mean extra training and upgrading programs (if so how many)?

Preferential treatment programs can be best discussed and evaluated as specific programs on their individual merits, each with its own costs, each with its own benefits. But all such programs share three things in common: (1) their goal is to speed progress—to leapfrog ahead (and in many areas discontinuities may require large, rapid and dramatic gains rather than an ever so slow but steady movement, for the problems are complex and intertwined and psychology, motivation, and aspiration are part of them); (2) they are more readily accepted when they are designed to upgrade and remove disabilities or deficiencies rather than to "overlook" them; (3) they are more readily accepted when preference for some does not mean retrogression for others. Specific proposals should be evaluated in the light of these considerations. If this is done we may well find disagreement over words translated into agreement over policies.

We paint tomorrow's picture today. Much of the outline was given to us by yesterday's generation, but that rough sketch can be altered and enriched. We—the Negro and the white—are not captives of our yesterdays. Perhaps in years to come such essays will be written not by economists but by economic historians.

REFERENCES

1. Gunnar Myrdal, *An American Dilemma* (New York, 1944), p. xviii.

2. We reject comparisons between the Negro American and other groups living outside the United States. Such comparisons are surely felt to be irrelevant by Negro Americans themselves. The unhappy fact that Negroes are often treated as outsiders in their own land does not makes them insiders in some other. Such comparisons also miss the point that Negro Americans are Americans (and have been so for a long time), and they delimit the American ideal: society has not told Irish Americans, for

example, that their progress is sufficient if their standard of living exceeds that of the rest of the world or that of the Irish in Ireland (what would we tell the American Indian?). The issue, thus, is not whether the 20 million Negro Americans are better off than most of the other 3 billion persons in the rest of the world (they are), but how they compare with the 170 million white Americans.

3. Such time-lag comparisons are valid when we examine data that have strong trends and, at most, relatively small cyclical departures from the trends. Further, "representative" years must be selected (however, as is sometimes done in this paper, a few adjoining years can be averaged to obtain the data for comparison). It should be noted that the measure we introduce cannot be the only yardstick. It adds an important dimension but if relied upon to the exclusion of other measures could, under some circumstances, give misleading results. In the hypothetical example the Negro would be forty years behind the white if in the year 2000 he attained a level of 275. Yet he would have attained equality if the white made no further advances. Clearly the achievement of equality, rather than the forty year lag, would be significant.

4. U. S. Department of Health, Education, and Welfare, *Health, Education, and Welfare Trends,* 1964 Edition, p. 13.

5. U. S. Department of Health, Education, and Welfare, Public Health Service, *Vital Statistics of the Unitel States, 1960,* Volume II, Part A: Mortality, p. 3-3.

6. Data for years prior to 1933 are for the death-registration area only. They are not strictly comparable with data for more recent years. But, in general, the fact that we sometimes compare nonwhite data for years after 1933 with white data prior to 1933 should yield "conservative" results that *understate* the "true" gap. Where both white and nonwhite data are for years after 1933 this problem does not exist.

7. During the 1920-1940 period the differential in average educational level for those aged twenty-five to twenty-nine widened from 3.1 years to 3.7 years; in 1960 it was down to 1.5 years. Data for 1964 are not presented because they are not strictly comparable with 1960 data.

8. Data for 1920 and for persons aged twenty-five to twenty-nine from John K. Folger and Charles B. Nam, "Educational Trends from Census Data," *Demography,* Vol. 1, No. 1 (1964), pp. 247-57.

9. "Educational Change in a Generation, March 1962," *Current Population Reports,* Series P-20, No. 132, p. 4.

10. Derived from data released by the Council of Economic Advisers, "Economic Costs of Racial Discrimination in Employment" (Washington, D. C., September 24, 1962).

11. Alan Batchelder, "Decline in the Relative Income of Negro Men," *Quarterly Journal of Economics,* Vol. 78, No. 4 (November 1964), pp. 525-48.

12. Statement released by the office of the White House Press Secretary, March 25, 1965.

Sources

Data from the following general sources: U. S. Bureau of the Census, *Statistical Abstract of the United States: 1964* (85th edn; Washington, D. C., 1964) and earlier *Abstracts;* U. S. Bureau of the Census, *Historical Statistics of the United States, Colonial Times to 1957* (Washington, D. C., 1960); Donald J. Bogue, *The Population of the United States* (Glencoe, Ill., 1959).

Health data from: U. S. Department of Health, Education, and Welfare, Public Health Service, *Vital Statistics of the United States, 1963,* Vol. I, Natality, Vols. II and III, Mortality (Washington, D. C., 1964) and annual reports for selected years; U. S. Department of Health, Education, and Welfare, *Health, Education, and Welfare Trends,* 1964 edn., Part 1 (Washington, D. C., 1965); U. S. Department of Health, Education, and Welfare, Public Health Service, U. S. National Center for Health Statistics, *Health Insurance Coverage, United States, July 1962-June 1963,* Public Health Service Publication No. 1000—Series 10—No. 11, (Washington, D. C., August 1964); Department of Health, Education, and Welfare, Public Health Service, Division of Public Health Methods, *Health Statistics from the U. S. National Health Survey: Volume of Physician Visits, United States, July 1957-June 1959,* U. S. National Health Survey: Series B—No. 19, (Washington, D. C., August 1960), and *Health Statistics from the U. S. National Health Survey: Dental Care, Volume of Visits, United States, July 1957-June 1959,* U. S. National Health Survey: Series B—No. 15, (Washington, D. C., April 1960), and *Health Statistics from the U. S. National Health Survey: Hospital Discharges and Length of Stay: Short-stay Hospitals, United States, 1958-1960,* U. S. National Health Survey: Series B—No. 32, (Washington, D. C., April 1962).

Education data from: John K. Folger and Charles B. Nam, "Educational Trends from Census Data," *Demography,* Vol. 1, No. 1 (1964), pp. 247-57; U. S. Bureau of the Census, *Current Population Reports: School Enrollment, October 1963,* Series P-20, No. 129 (Washington, D. C., July 24, 1964), and *Current Population Reports: Educational Change in a Generation, March 1962,* Series P-20, No. 132 (Washington, D. C., September 22, 1964); U. S. Bureau of the Census, *U. S. Census of Population: 1960, Subject Reports, School Enrollment,* Final Report PC(2)-5A (Washington, D. C., 1964); U. S. Bureau of the Census, *Population Trends in the United States: 1900 to 1960,* Technical Paper No. 10 (Washington, D. C., 1964); U. S. Bureau of the Census, *Current Population Reports: Educational Attainment, March 1964,* Series P-20, No. 138 (Washington, D. C., May 11, 1965).

Employment, unemployment, and occupation data from: U. S. Department of Labor, *A Report on Manpower Requirements, Resources, Utilization, and Training* (Washington, D. C., March 1965), and reports issued in 1964 and 1963; U. S. Department of Labor, Bureau of Labor Statistics, *Special Labor Force Report,* No. 43, "Labor Force and Employment in 1963," and *Special Labor Force Report,* No. 38, "Work Experience of the Population in 1962"; U. S. Bureau of the Census, *U. S. Census of Population: 1960, Subject Re-*

ports, Occupational Characteristics, Final Report PC(2)-7A, (Washington, D. C., 1963).

Income data from: U. S. Bureau of the Census, *Current Population Reports: Income of Families and Persons in the United States, 1963,* Series P-60 No. 43 (Washington, D. C., September 29, 1964); U. S. ˙Bureau of the Census, *Trends in the Income of Families and Persons in the United States: 1947 to 1960,* Technical Paper No. 8 (Washington, D. C., 1963); Council of Economic Advisers, *Annual Report of the Council of Economic Advisers,* (Washington, D. C., 1964); U. S. Department of Labor, Bureau of Labor Statistics, *Special Labor Force Report,* No. 46, "Out of School Youth, February, 1963"; U. S. Bureau of the Census, *Current Population Reports, Average Family Income up 5 Percent in 1964,* Series P-60, No. 44, (Washington, D. C., May 27, 1965); U. S. Bureau of the Census, *Current Population Reports, Low-Income Families and Unrelated Individuals in the United States: 1963,* Series P-60, No. 45 (Washington, D. C., June 18, 1965).

Housing data from: U. S. Bureau of the Census, U. S. Census of Housing: 1960, Vol. 1, *States and Small Areas, United States Summary,* Final Report HC(1)-1, (Washington, D. C., 1963).

The interested reader will also find useful a variety of U. S. government publications which frequently present white-nonwhite data. The Bureau of the Census, Bureau of Labor Statistics, and Social Security Administration are among the agencies which publish occasional reports and articles of interest.

DANIEL PATRICK MOYNIHAN

Employment, Income, and the Ordeal of the Negro Family

THE CIVIL rights revolution of our time is entering a new phase, and a new crisis. In the first phase, the demands of the Negro American were directed primarily to those rights associated with the idea of Liberty: the right to vote, the right to free speech, the right to free assembly. In the second phase, the movement must turn to the issue of Equality. This dualism, which has always been present in the civil rights movement, simply reflects the dualism of American democracy. From the outset American society has been committed to the twin ideals of Liberty and Equality. These are not the same things. Nor do they appeal to different persons with the same force. The Declaration of Independence began with a proposition about Equality, but the word does not appear in the Constitution until almost a century later. One reason, surely, is that at the time the Constitution was adopted almost one American in five was a slave.

The ideal of Equality, in Robert Harris' words, "is at least coeval with, if not prior to, liberty in the history of Western political thought."[1] But over the years Liberty has enjoyed incomparably the more prestige, especially in the white, Anglo-Saxon, Protestant circles which are still greatly influenced by British attitudes. Equality has been suffered rather than espoused; a scullery dream more than a parlor principle; Sam rather than John Adams; a style of the frontier and the slum; for the longest while Irish rather than English; now increasingly Black rather than White.

As long as Negro demands concentrated on issues of liberty they enjoyed the unquestioned support of the centers of power in American society. Even those who resisted did so in practice, rather than on principle: no one can successfully challenge the principle of liberty in the United States at this time. However, as demands turn toward those associated with equality, this support can only dissipate. Several problems are involved. The first is that of incomprehension. Great portions of the American middle class simply do not understand the nature of the demand for equality. Typically, they assume such demands are met when equal opportunity is provided. Thus Negro Americans have found their staunchest white allies among newer middle-class groups who for varying periods were excluded from the competitions of American life by quotas and other techniques, but who once admitted were quickly successful. But equality, as a fundamental democratic disposition, goes beyond equal opportunity to the issue of equal results. Here middle-class support begins to dissipate, principles are not clear, consensus does not exist.

Given the ethnic group structure of American life, equality for Negro Americans means that they will have open to them the full range of American economic, social, and political life, and that within the pattern of endeavor that they choose, having assessed the comparative advantages of time, place, and cultural endowment, they will have a fully comparable share of the successes, no less than of the small winners and of the outright failures. The test of American society will be whether it can work out arrangements so that this happens more or less naturally for Negro Americans, as it has more or less naturally happened for other groups. The rules are unwritten, but well enough understood. A certain amount of Freemasonry is not only permitted, but necessary. Some concessions are in order from other groups. It is fatal to make an across-the-board assault: highly developed activities are highly resistant to intrusion; the less developed an activity is, the more opportunity it provides for newcomers. More than a generation must pass before the outcome will be clear. It will be uneven, but nonetheless acceptable.

From the very outset, the principal measure of progress toward equality will be that of employment. It is the primary source of individual or group identity. In America what you do is what you are: to do nothing is to be nothing; to do little is to be little. The equations are implacable and blunt, and ruthlessly public.

For the Negro American it is already, and will continue to be, the master problem. It is the measure of white *bona fides*. It is the measure of Negro competence, and also of the competence of American society. Most importantly, the linkage between problems of employment and the range of social pathology that afflicts the Negro community is unmistakable. Employment not only controls the present for the Negro American; but, in a most profound way, it is creating the future as well.

The current situation and recent trends pose a problem of interpretation which may not have been much noticed. It is that in terms of employment and income and occupational status it is quite possible the Negro community is moving in two directions, or rather that two Negro communities are moving in opposite ones. Obviously such a development would be concealed—cancelled out—in aggregate statistics that list all "nonwhites" together. Anyone with eyes to see can observe the emergence of a Negro middle class that is on the whole doing very well. This group has, if anything, rather a preferred position in the job market. A nation catching up with centuries of discrimination has rather sharply raised the demand for a group in short supply. One would be hard put to describe a person with better job opportunities than a newly minted Negro Ph.D. In a wide and expanding range of employment, there would seem to be no question that opportunities for some are rather more equal than for others, and that for the first time in our history the Negro American is the beneficiary of such arrangements. These facts are reflected in the steadily rising level of Negro aspirations and in efforts by the Negro to acquire the education and training that are the *cartes d'identité* of the Great American Middle Class.[2]

At the same time there would also seem to be no question that opportunities for a large mass of Negro workers in the lower ranges of training and education have not been improving, that in many ways the circumstances of these workers relative to the white work force have grown worse. It would appear that this in turn has led to, or been accompanied by, a serious weakening of the Negro social structure, specifically of the Negro family. It could be that this situation has gone on so long that the Negro potential is already impaired; in any event it would hardly seem possible to doubt that if it persists much longer the capacity of the Negro community to make the most of its opportunities will be grievously diminished. Measures that would have worked twenty years ago may not work today, and surely will not work twenty years hence. A crisis of commitment is at hand.

The moral grandeur of the Negro revolution makes it more than normally difficult to speak of these matters; yet it demands that we do so. The plain physical courage which the Negro leaders and their followers have shown in recent years ought at least to summon in the rest of us the moral courage to inquire just how bad things may have become while we were occupied elsewhere. It is probable that such inquiry will be resented by some and misused by others. So be it. The important fact is that it is not likely to cause any great harm if things turn out not to be so bad as they appeared. On the other hand, if present indications are correct, the only hope we have is to state them and face up to them.

I. *Unemployment*

The primary measure of the problem of Negro employment is the rate of unemployment.[3] It is here that the deterioration of the Negro position is most conspicuous. What has happened is that over the past thirty-five years the rate of Negro unemployment, from being rather less than that of whites, has steadily moved to the point where it is now regularly more than twice as great, while, of course, the over-all unemployment rate in the United States has remained higher than that of any other industrial democracy in the world. (As I write, unemployment in Japan is less than one per cent.)

The decennial census shows the steady rise in the ratio.[4]

Unemployment Rates	1930	1940	1950
White	6.6%	14.1%	4.5%
Nonwhite	6.1%	16.9%	7.9%
Ratio, nonwhite to white	.92	1.20	1.76

There is a sense in which this two-to-one ratio has not so much been a situation which has developed among Negroes, as it has been a relation that has long existed for Negroes in certain circumstances and that more and more Negroes have found themselves in those circumstances in recent years.

In 1930, 41 per cent of Negro males were engaged in agriculture where, if incomes were low, so was unemployment. If the South is taken out of the 1930 census data, thereby measuring employment among predominantly urban Negroes, a 1.6 to 1 unemployment ratio appears: white 7.4 per cent, nonwhite 11.5 per cent. By 1940 the two-to-one ratio outside the South had emerged: 14.8 per cent for whites, 29.7 per cent for nonwhites. Since 1930 the proportion of Negroes living in cities has almost doubled. It is now nearly 75 per cent, greater than that of whites. Correspondingly, the two-to-one unemployment ratio has since become general—one of the seemingly fixed ratios of our economy.

The full development of the pattern can be seen in the 1960 census.

White and Nonwhite Unemployment Rates for Males,
Urban and Rural, 1960

	Urban	Rural Nonfarm	Rural Farm
White	4.5	5.9	2.4
Nonwhite	9.3	8.7	3.4

Source: *1960 Census of Population*, Volume 1,
Part 1, Table 194, pp. 1–487 to 1–498.

In order to emphasize that nothing is very clear about the nature of this development, it should be pointed out that while the two-to-one ratio has apparently existed for some time in urban situations, it is not the direct result of *industrial* employment. White and nonwhite unemployment rates in nonfarm industries were about equal in 1930, but the ratio thereafter gradually widened to the familiar two-to-one relationship.

Unemployment Rates in Nonfarm Industries

	1930	1940	1950	1960
White	7.9%	9.3%	NA	4.6%
Nonwhite	8.6%	13.4%	NA	8.3%
Ratio, nonwhite to white	1.09	1.44	NA	1.80

Over the period 1957 to 1964 the economy went from a point of high employment, down into a recession, up, down, and up again into the long, spectacular expansion that began in February 1961 and which by 1964 had brought the over-all unemployment rate almost to 1957 levels. Through all the ups and downs the ratio remained largely unchanged, even, perhaps, growing slightly worse. (See table on p. 750).

It must be emphasized that employment of nonwhites has grown faster than that of whites since 1957, but so has the nonwhite labor force, which rose from 7.3 million in that year to 8.3 million in 1964. Nonwhite unemployment gains have simply not been sufficient to narrow the gap in the unemployment rate. In 1964 nonwhites made up 11 per cent of the civilian labor force, but accounted for 21 per cent of the unemployed and 25 per cent of those jobless for six months or longer. Their unemployment rate of 10 per cent was more than twice that of white workers.

Unemployment Rate of the Civilian Labor Force, by Color:
Annual Averages, 1957–64
(In thousands)

Unemployment Rate	1957	1958	1959	1960	1961	1962	1963	1964
White	3.9	6.1	4.9	5.0	6.0	4.9	5.1	4.6
Nonwhite	8.0	12.6	10.7	10.2	12.5	11.0	10.9	9.8
Ratio of nonwhite to white	2.05	2.07	2.18	2.04	2.08	2.24	2.14	2.13

Source: Bureau of Labor Statistics, U. S. Department of Labor

In terms of emerging patterns, the situation of Negro teenage workers is particularly striking. As recently as 1948 (the first year for which data exist) Negro teenage males had a slightly lower rate of unemployment than did whites—7.6 per cent as against 8.3 per cent. In the years that followed the white rate doubled, but the nonwhite rate quadrupled. In January 1965 the combined unemployment rate for nonwhite teenagers was 29 per cent. Job opportunities for nonwhite teenagers have been notably scarce. The number of nonwhite teenagers employed in 1964 (540,000) remained almost unchanged from seven years earlier, while the number of white teenagers with jobs was rising by 800,000.

The unemployment rate is, of course, a vertical measure—recording the situation at any given moment. The true impact of unemployment in the Negro community can be measured accurately only in horizontal terms—the experience of unemployment over time. Here the facts emerge as something near disastrous. In 1958 only half the nonwhite males who worked at any time during the year worked a full 50 to 52 weeks; in 1963, only 55 per cent. Fewer than a third of the nonwhite women who worked during 1963 had a full year's employment. In some measure these statistics reflect the flexibility of the American work force. White rates, 67 per cent for males and 38 per cent for females during 1963, are also low. At the same time, the degree to which Negroes are forced into this pattern of intermittent employment is unmistakable. In 1964 nonwhites held 10 per cent of the full-time and the voluntary part-time jobs in nonfarm industries, but they accounted for 27 per cent of those working part-time involuntarily for economic reasons. This situation has shown no improvement since 1957. In sum, after an extended period of unprecedented economic growth, the Negro experience in the labor market remains hazardous and intermittent in the extreme.

II. *Occupational Patterns*

In contrast to the experience of unemployment, the occupational patterns of Negro workers have clearly improved over the past three and one-half decades. Slowly they are coming into line with the white work force; but they have a long way to go. The most dramatic and important movement has been out of agriculture. Over one-third of the Negroes were in agriculture in 1930; less than one-tenth in 1960. This movement has been accompanied by migration northward: approximately 70 per cent of the Negro workers were in the South in 1930 and about 50 per cent in 1960.

	1930	1940	1950	1960
Per cent of Nonwhite Civilian Labor Force which is in the South	71.9	72.8	63.0	53.3
Per cent of Experienced Labor Force which is in Agriculture				
White	19.2	16.1	11.4*	6.2
Nonwhite	36.5	30.7	19.5*	9.1

* Based on those employed rather than total labor force.

Employment of nonwhite *farmers and farm managers* has declined substantially over the past decade, falling much more rapidly than employment in that category generally. There were 389,000 nonwhites in this group in 1954, only 145,000 a decade later—a drop of 63 per cent. As a result, the proportion that nonwhite workers represent of total employment in this group fell substantially, declining from 10 per cent in 1954 to 6.3 per cent in 1964. This movement was of course most pronounced in the South. In 1930 nearly half the Southern Negro workers were in agriculture; by 1960, only one-fifth. In short, movement of Negroes out of agriculture to other work in the South was even more marked than their migration to other parts of the country.

It should be noted, however, that the decline of Negro farmers was not matched by a similar decline in Negro *hired farm laborers*. During the decade in which nonwhite farmers and farm managers fell by 63 per cent, nonwhite farm laborers and foremen fell only 14 per cent, from 589,000 to 506,000. As a result, the proportion of nonwhites in this employment category actually rose slightly, from 23.6 per cent in 1954 to 23.8 per cent in 1964. This has been accompanied by increasing rates of unemployment—tenants and sharecroppers, no matter how low their income and living standards, are not so subject as hired farm workers are to unemployment or, possibly, to a decline in social stability.

Unemployment Rates in Agriculture	1930	1940	1950	1960
White	1.3%	4.4%	NA	3.0%
Nonwhite	1.6%	3.9%	NA	7.3%
Ratio, nonwhite to white	1.23	.89	NA	2.43

At the other end of the spectrum, employment of nonwhite *professional and technical workers* has increased sharply over the past decade, growing more rapidly than employment in any other major occupational group. Between 1954 and 1964, employment of nonwhite professional workers increased from 217,000 to 499,000, a growth of 130 per cent. This increase in employment was far more rapid than that for all professional and technical workers in the economy, and, as a result, the proportion that nonwhites represent of all professional workers increased substantially during the decade, rising from 3.9 per cent in 1954 to·5.8 per cent in 1964. The largest part of this increase has occurred since 1961, when the percent nonwhites made up of total employment was still only 4.1.[5]

The rate of increase in employment of nonwhite *clerical workers* was exceeded only by that for professionals during the past decade. The number all but doubled, to a total of 572,000 in 1964, with a corresponding increase in the nonwhite proportion of all clerical workers to 5.4 per cent. A similar movement occurred among nonwhite craftsmen and foremen, whose numbers increased by two-thirds during the decade from 316,000 to 525,000. Their proportion accordingly rose from 3.8 per cent to 5.8 per cent. A perhaps significant ratio is to be seen here. Among professional, clerical, and skilled workers, nonwhites steadily improved their position in the decade following the Korean War, rising to 5.8, 5.4, and 5.8 per cent of the respective groups. From about one-third of their proportionate share, they moved up to about one-half. Each group has now rather more than a half million members. By and large they make up the Negro middle class, for whom things have unmistakably been getting better.

The American work force is classified in eleven broad categories. Among those not so far mentioned, trends in nonwhite employment show few marked changes and some declines. Some are categories Negroes have been trying to escape, and decline can be considered as improvement. Others are those in which the well-paid jobs are for Negro males with limited skills—where stability in the proportion has been to the Negro's disadvantage.

By far the largest group of nonwhite workers are those classified as operatives—the blue-collar workers of the nation's industry. Their number, 1,520,000 in 1964, was almost exactly that of professional, clerical, and skilled workers combined. Their numbers increased very little over the decade, less than 16 per cent.

During that decade there was a long-run decline in manufacturing employment, which has only recently been reversed. Most importantly for the Negro worker, there has been a steady decline or stagnation in manufacturing employment in the Northern and Western cities to which so many of them have been moving. During the period 1960–64, manufacturing employment in the nation increased by 3.0 per cent. However, it decreased by 2.0 per cent in New York, Chicago, Philadelphia, Detroit, Washington, D. C., Los Angeles, Cleveland, St. Louis, Newark, Cincinnati, and Pittsburgh, combined. In New York the drop was 8.2 per cent; in Philadelphia, 3.9 per cent; in Newark, 3.1 per cent; and in Pittsburgh, 4.7 per cent.

There were slightly more than one million nonwhite *private household workers* in 1954, an increase of 13 per cent over the decade. During this period, however, the nonwhite proportion of such workers dropped from 51.4 per cent to 43.6 per cent.

Service workers (except private household workers) provide another large field of employment for nonwhites. Their number grew by one-third during the decade of 1954–64, to a total of 1.4 million, but their proportion of the over-all total declined slightly to 20 per cent. However, an increasing proportion of nonwhite men are employed in service occupations. The proportion rose from 14 per cent in 1959 to 17 per cent in 1963. Those with very much education were leaving service employment, but nonwhite men with little education were moving into it rapidly. From 1959 to 1963 the per cent of nonwhite high-school graduates employed in service occupations declined from 23 to 14. In the same period, the percentage rose for nonwhite men with an elementary education from 11 to 19.

Among *laborers* (except farm and mine) there was an actual decline in nonwhite employment over the same period, the total dropping 4 per cent to 974,000. The nonwhite proportion of the over-all total also declined slightly.

In the South, where half the nonwhite work force is still located, the distribution of employed nonwhite men is even more skewed toward the lower rungs of the occupational ladder. Unskilled labor accounts for 39 per cent of nonwhite male employment in the South, as compared with 19 per cent in the rest of the country. On the other hand, the occupational distribution of white males in the South is not much different from that of all other regions combined.

Negroes fare badly in the category of *sales workers,* for all that their situation may be improving. In 1964 there were 136,000 non-white sales workers, representing 3.1 per cent of the total. This represented an increase of better than 50 per cent in a decade, but subtracting Asians from the total would leave a Negro component of only about 100,000, assuming that Negroes were about the same proportion of nonwhite sales workers in 1964 that they were in 1960. In this area of employment it may be assumed there is a great deal of direct discrimination against Negro workers.

Without question, however, the most conspicuous failure of Negroes to win their way in the world has been in the related field of *managers, officials, and proprietors.* Once again the number of nonwhites in this category increased by nearly half over the decade, but the end result was only 192,000 positions, representing only 2.6 per cent of the total, as contrasted with 2.3 per cent in 1955. Taking away Asians would diminish the number still further, to only about 140,000 Negro positions.

It could well be that Negro Americans are arriving in the nation's cities at a time when opportunities for establishing small businesses are declining, a parallel to the decline in manufacturing jobs, and another example of the problem of the *timing* of the Negro migration. No other immigrant group came upon the scene at a moment of declining employment opportunities. But given the absence of any tradition of Negro entrepreneurship, the scarcity of entrepreneurial opportunity has worked virtually to exclude Negroes from this singularly important echelon of employment. Only 6.5 per cent of nonwhite males with one or more years of college are working in this field, as against 22.7 of whites. In over-all terms, present-day Negroes, as newly arrived migrants in the great urban areas of the nation, present an employment pattern strikingly similar to that of past migrant groups. For example, first- and second-generation Italian immigrants recorded in the 1900 census had almost precisely the occupational pattern of Northern Negroes sixty years later.

The basic question concerning the future employment of Ne-

Occupations of Italians in 1900 Compared with
Northern Negroes in 1960

	Total	Planters, Farmers, Overseers	Professional Services, Trade, and Transportation	Manufacturing and Mechanical	All Others
Italians, 1900	100%	2%	21%	32%	45%
Negroes, North, 1960	100%	*	23%	32%	45%

* Less than 1 per cent

groes is whether the pattern of opportunity is shifting to make it easier or more difficult for them to move into line with the work force in general. We must also question whether or not the existing patterns of employment are affecting the Negro potential for taking advantage of the opportunities which arise in the future.

III. *Income*

The patterns of Negro employment are directly related to those of income. Negro income has risen substantially in recent years, as has employment. But the gap between Negro and white income is not closing; it is widening. And the problems that follow are made more savage by a soaring population.

The principal problem, and the proper focus of public concern, is that of the Negro male worker. His plight does not seem to improve. Income rises. Year-round, full-time workers gained almost $1,000 in the short period from 1957 to 1963. But positions relative to white workers did not improve significantly, nor did the chances of being a year-round, full-time worker.

The family income of nonwhites, relative to that of whites, rose steadily during the 1940's, peaked in the 1950's at about 57 per cent, and has since fallen back. Of late the ratio has remained frozen in a two-to-one proportion reminiscent of the unemployment rates. During the period 1949 to 1959 the ratio of the median income of Negro men to that of white men *declined* in every region of the nation. The ratio went from .75 to .72 in the Northeast, from .50 to .47 in the South, and from .53 to .52 in the country as a whole.[6] From 1959 to 1963 the position of the Negro male appears to have improved somewhat in these terms, but the roughly two-to-one proportion was maintained.

In 1963 the median income of nonwhite males had risen to $2,507, as against $4,816 for whites. However, the Negro position remained precarious in the extreme. Six out of ten nonwhite farmers earned less than $1,000, fewer than one in ten earned over $3,000. Over half the nonwhite males earned less than $3,000. Only 1.2 per cent of nonwhite males earned over $10,000—approximately 70,000 persons in all the United States, of whom as many as 25,000 were probably Chinese or Japanese. The impact of unemployment on nonwhite income is unmistakable. In 1963 those nonwhite men who worked year-round, full-time earned a median income of $4,019 —almost two-thirds the white median of $6,245. However, only 49.7 per cent of nonwhite men with income in 1963 actually worked a full year, as against 60.1 per cent of whites.

In the familiar pattern, income of white and nonwhite workers tends to increase as the amount of education completed rises, but the gain for nonwhite men is much less than for white men. White men who had at least one year of college had a median income in 1963 of $6,829, about 80 per cent more than those who had completed only elementary school. But among nonwhite men with at least one year of college the gain was only about 50 per cent, from $2,740 to $4,070. In fact, the median income of nonwhite men who were high-school graduates ($3,821) was about the same as that for white men who had completed only elementary school ($3,749). The income gap between white and nonwhite men at each additional level in 1963 was not significantly smaller than it had been in 1958.

To the extent that the income gap between the Negro and white world has been closed, it is through the employment of Negro women. While the income gap for men was little changed between 1958 and 1963, it narrowed substantially for women. In 1958, the income of nonwhite women was 59 per cent of white women; by 1963 it had risen to 67 per cent. The gain was concentrated among women with more than a grade-school education, while the income of those having less education decreased slightly. In the longer period from 1949 to 1959, Batchelder reports that Negro women improved their income position relative to white women in each region of the nation, to the point that it was practically equal for all regions other than the South. For example, the ratio rose from .83 to .99 in the Northeast. The low Southern ratio, which rose from .46 to .56, kept the over-all ratio at .60 but the trend of events was clear by 1963 when the income of nonwhite women was two-thirds that of whites.

At the same time that Negro women were closing the income gap, more were working. Between 1950 and 1960 the female proportion of the Negro labor force rose from 35.1 per cent to 40.2 per cent. By 1964, women accounted for 41.3 per cent of the nonwhite labor force. This was a period when women generally were dropping behind men in their earnings. Batchelder calculates that the women-to-men ratio for whites declined from .44 to .35 between 1949 and 1959. The comparable Negro ratio also declined—but by only one-third as much. In the period 1958 to 1963, white women fell further behind white men in income, but nonwhite women improved their position slightly in relation to nonwhite men.[7] Batchelder writes "Something in the labor market permitted Negro, but not white, women to increase their share of the labor force without depressing their incomes relative to men's."[8] Part of this increase was the result of matriarchal strain in Negro family life which would seem to have been reinforced by economic developments of the postwar period. There are still, for example, more Negro women college graduates in the United States than Negro male graduates. The position of these women in relation to their white counterparts has been roughly comparable for some time. But in the short period from 1958 to 1963 the nonwhite women with a year or more of college moved sharply *ahead,* with a median income of $2,904, as against $2,530 for whites. This may be because more of the nonwhite women worked full time, but, in any case, the fact remains that they earned more money. Similarly, between 1958 and 1963 the income of nonwhite women who had a high-school education increased faster than that for white women, and as a result the income gap was narrowed.

This is not the place to describe the health of the Negro. However, it is intertwined with his general economic status. Nonwhites, in all age groups except seventeen to twenty-four, are more often physically disabled, whether measured in terms of days of restricted activity, bed disability days, or days in which work was lost. For fiscal years 1962 and 1963, nonwhite males in the labor force age seventeen and over averaged 13.7 days of restricted activity. Whites averaged 11.2. Generally, a smaller proportion of whites than nonwhites report chronic conditions. However, a higher proportion of nonwhites reported activity limitations resulting from chronic conditions. (Among other things, these results may reflect less use among nonwhites of diagnostic medical services; fewer know they have chronic conditions until the situation is so serious that they cannot work).

While the situation is improving, it is well to keep in mind that the Negro man still has a considerably lower life expectancy than the white man. At the prime working age of thirty, the difference is 5.2 years, with the nonwhite male having a life expectancy of 38.5 years and the white male having 43.7 years remaining.

IV. *The Ordeal of the Negro Family*

The cumulative result of unemployment and low income, and probably also of excessive dependence upon the income of women, has produced an unmistakable crisis in the Negro family, and raises the serious question of whether or not this crisis is beginning to create conditions which tend to reinforce the cycle that produced it in the first instance. The crisis would probably exist in any event, but it becomes acute in the context of the extraordinary rise in Negro population in recent years.

At the time of the founding of the nation, one American in five was a Negro. The proportion declined steadily until it was only one in ten by 1920, where it held until the 1950's when it began to rise. Since 1950 the nonwhite population has grown at a rate of 2.4 per cent per year, compared with 1.7 per cent for the total population. One American in nine is nonwhite today. If the rates of growth between 1950 and 1964 continue, one in eight will be nonwhite by 1972. In 1964 among children under the age of fourteen, 15 per cent were nonwhite. Under one year of age, 16.4 per cent were nonwhite: one in six. Although white and nonwhite fertility rates have declined somewhat since 1959, the nonwhite/white ratio of 1.42 has not narrowed. Between 1950 and 1960 the size of the white family changed very little, while that of nonwhites increased from 4.07 persons to 4.30 persons.

Perhaps most significantly, the gap between what might be called the generation rate between white and nonwhites is particularly wide. Negro women not only have more children, but have them earlier. Thus in 1960, there were 1,247 children ever born per thousand ever-married nonwhite women fifteen to nineteen years of age, as against only 725 for white women, a ratio of 1.7. The effect of this burgeoning population on family life is accentuated by its concentration among the poor. In 1960 nonwhite mothers age thirty-five to thirty-nine with family incomes over $10,000 had 2.9 children; those with less than $2,000 had 5.3. A peculiar, and possibly important phenomenon, which might be termed the Frazier effect, after the distinguished author of *Black Bourgeoisie*, is that Negro upper-class families have fewer children than their white counterparts, while lower-class families have more. In 1960 nonwhite women (married once, husband present) age thirty-five to forty-four married early to undereducated laborers had 4.7 children, as against 3.8 for white women in the same situation. But nonwhite women in that age bracket, married at twenty-two or over to professional or technical workers with a year or more of college, had only 1.9 children, as against 2.4 for whites.

The impact of family size on the life chances of children and the strength of the family can be measured by a number of statistics. The Task Force on Manpower Conservation (1963) studied the nation's young men who failed to pass the Selective Service written test. A passing score on this test indicates the achievement of a seventh- or eighth-grade education. Three out of four of the nonwhite young men failing the test came from families with four or more children. One out of two came from families with six or more children.

A Negro child born to a large family is more likely to be reared in a broken family. Such are the strains of rearing large families with marginal incomes and unemployed fathers. In the urban U. S. in 1960 there were 154,000 one-child nonwhite families headed by married men age twenty to twenty-four with wives present. There were 19,000 such families headed by women separated from their husbands, one-eighth as many as whole families. There were a similar number of such husband-wife families with four or more children, 152,000, but there were 39,000 headed by married women separated from their husbands—one-fourth the number with both husband and wife. Poor families break under the responsibilities imposed by a large number of children. Children from these families become the nation's draft rejectees, because—among other reasons—they have spent a basic learning period in an institution too large for its resources and often with one of the instructors missing.

Poverty is both the cause and the result. In 1963 the median income of nonwhite families was $3,465, about half the $6,548 median of whites. The magnitude of the income gap is illustrated by the fact that incomes were lower in nonwhite families with employed heads than in white families with unemployed heads. What the long trend of the gap will be is not, of course, clear, but from 1960 to 1963 the nonwhite median family income as a per cent of white declined from 55 to 53.

In March 1964 nearly 20 million persons fourteen years and over were living in families with annual incomes under $3,000. Nonwhite persons accounted for a quarter of those living in such families. But nearly half of all nonwhite youths under fourteen are living in families with incomes under $3,000. Nonwhites make up 40 per cent of the children living in such families. Using a flexible scale that relates required family income to family size, the Department of Health, Education and Welfare has estimated that 60 per cent of the Negro children in America today are growing up in poverty-stricken families. In these circumstances the stability of the Negro family, still grievously impaired by the heritage of slavery and segregation, would seem to have been weakened still further.

The fundamental problem is the position of the male. To begin with, the Negro father tends to hold jobs with a minimum either of prestige or income. In 1963, fully one-third of the nonwhite family heads who worked at all had their longest (or only) job in farming, domestic service, or laboring occupations. For these persons, income was well under half that of all families with working heads. In addition to low income and low prestige, the Negro father is burdened with savage rates of unemployment at precisely that moment in his life when family responsibilities are most heavy. The ratio of nonwhite to white unemployment is highest among men between the ages of twenty-five and thirty-four—2.57. This compares with a ratio of 2.17 for all men fourteen and over. The next highest ratio for men was 2.48, at thirty-five to forty-four years of age. In 1963, 29 per cent of nonwhite males in the work force were unemployed at one time or another. Three out of ten nonwhite men who were unemployed in 1963 had three or more periods of unemployment; one-fifth of all unemployed nonwhites were out of work half the year or more.

A measure of the distress of Negro men in their middle years is that they disappear—literally. In 1964 for every 100 white and nonwhite women age thirty to thirty-four years, there were 99.4 white, but only 86.7 nonwhite, men. The Negroes had not died—they begin to reappear after forty—they had simply become invisible. (An interesting question is whether an accurate enumeration of these missing males would not significantly increase current unemployment rates for Negro males.)

It is in the perspective of the underemployment of the Negro father that we must regard the Negro mother as being over-employed. From 1957 to 1964 the civilian labor-force participation rate of nonwhite men dropped from 80.8 per cent to 75.6 per cent. The ratio of nonwhite to white labor-force participation rates *dropped* from .99 to .97. During this period, the civilian labor force participation of nonwhite women *rose* somewhat over-all. It rose particularly in ages twenty to twenty-four, from 46.6 per cent in 1957 to 53.6 per cent in 1964; in ages twenty-five to thirty-four years, from 50.4 per cent in 1957 to 52.8 per cent in 1964; and in ages forty-five to fifty-four where it reached 62.3 per cent in that year. Typically, the nonwhite/white ratio of labor-force participation for women is highest in the middle years, reaching 1.50 for age twenty-five to thirty-four, a stark contrast with the male situation. Strikingly, also, is the fact that the unemployment ratio of nonwhite to white women is *lower* than average in just those middle years when it is highest for nonwhite males. In 1964 it was only 1.73 for women thirty-five to forty-four years of age, compared with 2.48 for men of the same age and 1.96 for all women.

Inevitably, the underemployment of the Negro father has led to the break-up of the Negro family. In 1964, among unemployed white men twenty years and over there were 859,000 married with wife present and only 147,000 of "other marital status" (excluding men never married), the former group being six times the size of the latter. But among nonwhites, for 168,000 unemployed males with wives present, there were 76,000 of "other marital status." Nonwhites made up 34.1 per cent of all unemployed males of "other marital status." These are the men who first lose their jobs and then lose their families.

The first effect is simply that of broken homes. Nearly a quarter of Negro women living in cities who have ever married are divorced, separated, or living apart from their husbands. These rates have been steadily rising and are approaching one-third in, for example, New York City. Almost one-quarter of nonwhite families are headed by a woman, a rate that also continues to rise. At any given moment some 36 per cent of Negro children are living in homes where one or both parents are missing. It is probable that not much more than one-third of Negro youth reach eighteen having lived all their lives with both their parents. The second effect of the deterioration of the position of the Negro male worker has been a sharp increase in welfare dependency among Negro families. It would appear that a majority of Negro youth sooner or later are supported by the Aid to Families of Dependent Children program. In 1961 not quite half of all children receiving AFDC aid were Negro (1,112,106) and half of these were in cities of 250,000 population, where they made up three-quarters of the AFDC recipients. Nonwhites account for almost two-thirds of the increase in AFDC families between 1948 and 1961. The third effect that must be associated with the deteriorating position of the Negro male is the phenomenon Kenneth Clark has described as the tangle of pathology—the complex of interrelated disabilities and disadvantages that feed on each other and seem to make matters steadily worse for the individuals and communities caught up in it.

The cycle begins and ends with the children. A disastrous number begin their lives with no fathers present. Many, in some communities nearly half or more, are illegitimate. In 1963, 24 per cent of all nonwhite births in the nation were illegitimate. Too few live their early years in the presence of a respected and responsible male figure. The mothers, as often as not magnificent women, go to work too soon, if indeed they ever stop. This situation is getting worse, not better. In March 1959, 29.3 per cent of nonwhite women with children under six years of age were in the work force. By March 1964 this proportion had increased to 36.1 per cent! At that moment 56.7 per cent of nonwhite women with children six to seventeen years of age were in the work force—a higher percentage than that of nonwhite women with *no* children under eighteen years of age, which was 50.5 per cent. Although these movements were matched among white women, they clearly have gotten out of proportion among Negroes.

Negro children are going to school in nearly the same proportions as whites in the years from seven to nineteen, when free education is available more or less everywhere in the United States. But after having once closed the gap also in the crucial years on either side of that age span, they have begun to fall back again when education often is not free. In 1953, 18.1 per cent more of the white population than of the nonwhite were in school between the ages of five and six. By 1958 this gap had narrowed to 7.5. By 1963 it had widened again to 13.1. The conclusion must be that Negroes are falling behind once more in terms of the number of students who enter the main grades with advance preparation. Similarly the gap in population enrolled in school age twenty to twenty-four narrowed from 6.5 points in 1953 to 5.4 in 1958, but spread to 8.1 in 1963.

As they go through school, the economic pressures begin to mount. In a survey made in February 1963, half of the white male dropouts, but only one-third of the nonwhite, attributed their leaving school before graduation from high school to school-connected reasons, such as lack of interest in school, poor grades, or difficulties with school authorities. In contrast, more nonwhite males than white gave economic reasons for leaving school.[9]

To be sure, the gap between Negro and white education, however it may fluctuate within a decade, is now very narrow indeed —in formal terms. What has happened in real terms of the quality of education is not clear. Batchelder has suggested that "for the decade of the 1950's that although nonwhites (and surely Negroes too) gained on whites in median years of school completed, in the country as a whole, the average quality of a year of school completed by Negroes living in the North and West was reduced. . . . In educational attainment, quality dilution exceeded quantitative gains for Negroes in the North and West."[10]

Surely there are few developments in the area of employment, where improved education presumedly ought to produce better results, to indicate that the position of the Negro youth entering the labor force at present is improved over the past. Since 1961 the federal government has been engaged in a serious and sustained effort to improve the employment position of the American Negro by breaking down the barriers of discrimination. The President's Committee on Equal Employment has had unprecedented support both within the government and from the business and labor community. Results are slow to come, and the Committee has been loath to proclaim them when they have not existed—one break with the past that does honor to all concerned.

The Committee studies have provided considerable evidence that the position of the Negro worker is certainly not improving much in the normal course of events. Evidence has appeared that in large segments of American industry the number of Negro craftsmen is, if anything, proportionately greater than the number of Negro apprentices. Efforts to increase the number of apprentices have produced steady results, but at a pace and at a level which suggest fashioning a social revolution for twenty million souls one lad at a time.

Nor is it so obvious that middle-class Negroes are finding in ever-more-abundant supply the resources—family, financial, and other—required to pass through the lengthy apprenticeships demanded by the American professions. In 1965 after a decade of splendidly militant legal and political action by the civil rights movement, Clyde Ferguson, Jr., Dean of the Howard Law School, reported that of the 54,265 law students in the entire United States, there were only 543 Negroes.

Obviously, the most pressing question for American social policy is whether the essential first step for resolving the problem of the Negro American is to provide such a measure of full employment of Negro workers that the impact of unemployment on family structure is removed. The assumption would be that only then will the wide and increasing range and level of social services available to the Negro American have their full effect, and only then will there be a Negro population that not only has equal opportunities in the American economy, but is equal to those opportunities.

Cases Opened under AFDC (Excluding Unemployed Parent Segment) Compared with Unemployment Rate of Nonwhite Males

Year	AFDC Cases Opened[1]	Nonwhite Male Unemployment Rate
1964	429,048	9.1
1963	380,985	10.6
1962	370,008	11.0
1961	391,238	12.9
1960	338,730	10.7
1959	329,815	11.5
1958	345,950	13.7
1957	294,032	8.4
1956	261,663	7.3
1955	256,881	8.2
1954	275,054	9.2
1953	222,498	4.4
1952	234,074	4.5
1951	225,957	4.4
1950	291,273	8.9
1949	278,252	8.8
1948	210,193	5.1

[1] Does not include cases opened under program which commenced in some States in 1961 of assistance to children whose fathers are present but unemployed. There were 70,846 such cases opened in 1961, 81,192 in 1962, 80,728 in 1963, and 105,094 in 1964.

Source: AFDC cases opened from HEW; nonwhite male unemployment rates from Department of Labor.

This, of course, is not an inconsiderable assumption. No one knows whether it is justified or not. The relation between economic phenomena, such as employment, and social phenomena, such as family structure, has hardly begun to be traced in the United States. An association between rising economic and social distress in the world of the Negro American can be seen readily enough in data, but proof of a causal relationship is a more complex matter.

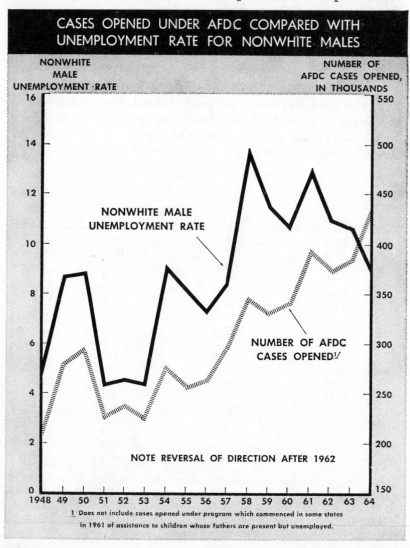

CASES OPENED UNDER AFDC COMPARED WITH UNEMPLOYMENT RATE FOR NONWHITE MALES

NONWHITE MALE UNEMPLOYMENT RATE

NUMBER OF AFDC CASES OPENED, IN THOUSANDS

NONWHITE MALE UNEMPLOYMENT RATE

NUMBER OF AFDC CASES OPENED[1]

NOTE REVERSAL OF DIRECTION AFTER 1962

1948 49 50 51 52 53 54 55 56 57 58 59 60 61 62 63 64

[1] Does not include cases opened under program which commenced in some states in 1961 of assistance to children whose fathers are present but unemployed.

Such is the extent to which science has taught us to be skeptical of what our common senses tell us.[11]

A more sophisticated but not less pressing question is whether the impact of economic disadvantage on the Negro community has gone on so long that genuine structural damage has occurred, so that a reversal in the course of economic events will no longer produce the expected response in social areas. There are several combinations of social and economic data which make it reasonable to ask both of these questions. They prove little, but they suggest a great deal. More importantly, they raise questions researchers should attempt to answer, for many of the answers we are looking for will, in my opinion, be found in the interplay between the economic environment and the social structure.

The relationship between the nonwhite male unemployment rate and the number of *new* AFDC cases opened each year since 1948 (excluding cases under the program begun in some states since 1961 under which fathers may be present but unemployed) is one example. The curves rise and fall together. Between 1948 (when, it will be recalled, the nonwhite unemployment rate first became available) and 1962 they have the remarkable correlation of .91.[12] Between 1955 and 1956, however, the unemployment rate dropped, but the number of new cases went *up* slightly, from 256,881 to 261,663. Unemployment in 1960 was lower than in 1959, but new cases were higher, 338,730 as compared to 329,815. (Note the rising level of new cases.) In 1963 unemployment was down, but new cases were up. In 1964 it went down, but new cases went up again—sharply now, reaching the highest point ever: 429,000.

While the two lines on the chart go hand in hand, the situation is more complex than it first appears. Some of the increase in AFDC cases is the result of white dependency, not Negro. However, almost two-thirds of the increase in the AFDC rolls between 1948 and 1961 is attributable to nonwhite families. While the unemployment rate for nonwhite males is used for comparison, the unemployment rate for all males would show similar changes. Some of the changes in AFDC families among nonwhites are also due to unemployment problems among families headed by females, families broken long ago. At present, these components cannot be isolated completely, and we look to corroboration from additional approaches.

The statistics are available by which we can observe the year-to-year changes in the per cent of nonwhite married women who

Per Cent of Nonwhite Married Women Separated from Husbands and
Unemployment Rates of Nonwhite Males Aged 20 and Over

| Year | Nonwhite Married Women Separated from Their Husbands, March of Each Year | | Unemployment Rate of Nonwhite Males 20 and Over, 9 Months Prior to April 1 of Each Year | |
	Per cent	Deviation from Linear Trend	Per cent	Deviation from Linear Trend
1953	10.6	−2.4	4.1	−2.1
1954	12.7	−0.6	5.6	−1.1
1955	15.1	+1.6	9.3	+2.2
1956	14.2	+0.5	6.8	+0.8
1957	13.1	−0.9	6.8	−1.3
1958	16.0	+1.8	9.8	+1.3
1959	17.6	+3.2	12.3	+3.3
1960	13.8	−0.9	10.2	+0.7
1961	14.3	−0.6	10.7	+0.8
1962	14.9	−0.2	11.2	+0.8
1963	14.6	−0.7	9.8	−1.1
1964	14.8	−0.8	8.6	−2.7

Source: Bureau of Labor Statistics.

are separated from their husbands. The period from 1953 to 1964 was one of generally rising unemployment for Negro men with marked fluctuations corresponding to the rise and fall of the nation's economic activity in this period. This was also a period when the number of broken Negro families was rising, with fluctuations up and down.

The upper half of the chart shows the per cent of nonwhite married women separated from their husbands (as of March of each year) and the unemployment rate (for the nine months preceding separation rate) of nonwhite men twenty years of age and over. The two lines rise and fall together, with both having an upward trend. The bottom half of the chart shows the yearly fluctuations from the trend, and again, the lines rise and fall together. The correlation between the deviations of the two series from their respective trends is .81.

As in the comparison of AFDC cases and unemployment, the strength of the relationship between unemployment and separation is considerably less after 1959 than it was before, at least in the limited period of time we are able to examine it. After 1962, unemployment dropped sharply, but the increase in employment opportunities for Negro men was not accompanied by a decline in broken marriages.

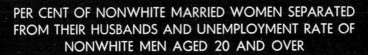

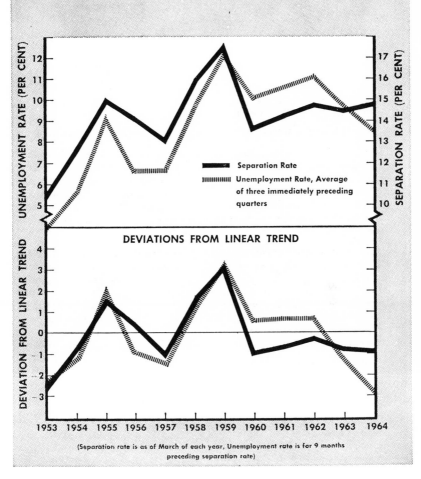

PER CENT OF NONWHITE MARRIED WOMEN SEPARATED FROM THEIR HUSBANDS AND UNEMPLOYMENT RATE OF NONWHITE MEN AGED 20 AND OVER

Separation Rate

Unemployment Rate, Average of three immediately preceding quarters

DEVIATIONS FROM LINEAR TREND

(Separation rate is as of March of each year, Unemployment rate is for 9 months preceding separation rate)

It would be troubling indeed to learn that until several years ago employment opportunity made a great deal of difference in the rate of Negro dependency and family disorganization, but that the situation has so deteriorated that the problem is now feeding on itself—that measures which once would have worked will henceforth not work so well, or work at all.

The important point is not that we do not know whether this is or is not the case. It is rather that until now we have never seriously asked such a question. Obviously an answer, or set of answers, can be had, and public policy can be guided accordingly. Time, not method, is our enemy. In the next six years the nonwhite work force will increase by 20 per cent, about twice the rate of the past decade and the rate for the whites in the coming same six years. The crisis of commitment is at hand.

REFERENCES

1. Robert Harris, *The Quest for Equality* (Baton Rouge, La., 1960), p. 4.

2. In 1964 the number of corporation personnel representatives visiting the campus of Lincoln University in Pennsylvania was twice that of the graduating class. Inasmuch as half the class was going on to graduate school, the representatives of American business outnumbered their potential recruits by four to one. For an excellent survey, see Dorothy K. Newman, "The Negro's Journey to the City," *Monthly Labor Review,* May-June 1965. See also *The New York Times,* May 30, 1965.

3. A statistical note is necessary here. A great deal of data taken to refer to Negroes in fact refers to a larger group, all of whose members are classified as "nonwhite," as opposed to "white." These are the two main categories into which the population is divided in most ongoing statistical series collected by the federal government, as, for example, the employment series. Only in the decennial census is the nonwhite group broken down into subgroups. In 1960 Negroes were 92.1 per cent of all nonwhites. The remaining 7.9 per cent were made up largely of Indians, Japanese, and Chinese. An important fact is that with respect to almost all economic and social data, Chinese and Japanese (who together make up 3.4 per cent of nonwhites) are at the opposite end of the spectrum from Negroes. Japanese and Chinese have twice as large a proportion of their population going to college as do whites; Negroes have a little less than half. Negroes have twice as high a rate of unemployment as do whites; Chinese and Japanese have half. In 1960, 21 per cent of Negro women who had ever married were separated, divorced or had their husband absent for other reasons, as against 7 per cent of Japanese and 6 per cent of Chinese. A consequence of these figures is that statistics for nonwhites generally understate the degree of unemployment among Negroes as well as the extent of family disorganization, and the gap that separates them from the white world. In this study the terms "Negro" and "nonwhite" are not used interchangeably, but rather refer to the smaller or larger group, as the case may be.

4. The 1930 census was taken in the spring of the year before the full effects of the depression were felt. Data are not strictly comparable with those of later years, but ratios are valid.

5. As many as 90,000 of the half-million nonwhite professional workers are *not* Negro. However, about two-thirds of the 90,000 would be Japanese or Chinese.

6. Alan B. Batchelder, "Decline in the Relative Income of Negro Men," *Quarterly Journal of Economics,* Vol. 78 (November 1964), pp. 525–548.

7. Comparisons of income position in 1959 with that of 1949 are based on calculations made by Alan B. Batchelder and reported in "Decline in the Relative Income of Negro Men," *op. cit.,* pp. 531 and 533.

8. *Ibid.,* p. 534.

9. The pinch of poverty is felt early. Negro families can save very little. In 1960–61 Negro families and single consumers living in cities average $23 in savings. White groups saved almost nine times that much.

10. Batchelder, *op. cit.,* p. 538.

11. There have been few attempts to examine the impact of unemployment on the survival of the family. It has been more than a quarter of a century since researchers addressed themselves to such questions in America, and, where investigation occurred, it was of white families, not Negro. An example is *Citizens Without Work* (1940), by Edward Wight Bakke. The most comprehensive analysis of the interrelationships between the ability of the Negro male to perform his expected economic role and the stability of the Negro family is still the work of E. Franklin Frazier. Anthropologists have investigated matrifocal families in search of some universal explanation of why they predominate in some societies. For a recent report, see "A Survey of the Consanguine or Matrifocal Family," by Peter Kunstadter in *American Anthropologist* (February 1963). Kunstadter concludes that the common feature of such societies is a division of labor which results in a physical separation of the male from the family over long periods of time. He reports that several investigators have pointed to the inability of males to fulfill their family economic roles successfully as the predominant feature of matrifocal societies. Kunstadter does not examine Negro American society in any detail which, of course, is quite mixed in this regard. However, the Negro American does not face a problem of a division of labor which results in physical separation. A recent investigation of the differences between white and Negro families with regard to the relative "power" of men and women is that of Robert Blood and Donald Wolfe, *Husbands and Wives: The Dynamics of Married Living* (New York, 1963).

12. A correlation was also computed for the deviations from the linear trends of the two series. With the trend removed, the correlation was .82, thereby ruling out the possibility that a similar but unrelated trend was responsible for the high correlation.

LEE RAINWATER

Crucible of Identity: The Negro Lower-Class Family

But can a people . . . live and develop for over three hundred years by simply reacting? Are American Negroes simply the creation of white men, or have they at least helped create themselves out of what they found around them? Men have made a way of life in caves and upon cliffs, why can not Negroes have made a life upon the horns of the white man's dilemma? . . . American Negro life is, for the Negro who must live it, not only a burden (and not always that) but also a discipline just as any human life which has endured so long is a discipline teaching its own insights into the human conditions, its own strategies of survival. . . .

For even as his life toughens the Negro, even as it brutalizes him, sensitizes him, dulls him, goads him to anger, moves him to irony, sometimes fracturing and sometimes affirming his hopes; even as it shapes his attitude towards family, sex, love, religion; even as it modulates his humor, tempers his joy—it conditions him to deal with his life and with himself. Because it is his life and no mere abstraction in someone's head. He must live it and try consciously to grasp its complexity until he can change it; must live it as he changes it. He is no mere product of his socio-political predicament. He is a product of interaction between his racial predicament, his individual will and the broader American cultural freedom in which he finds his ambiguous existence. Thus he, too, in a limited way, is his own creation.

—*Ralph Ellison*

As LONG as Negroes have been in America, their marital and family patterns have been subjects of curiosity and amusement, moral indignation and self-congratulation, puzzlement and frustration, concern and guilt, on the part of white Americans.[1] As some Negroes have moved into middle-class status, or acquired standards of American common-man respectability, they too have shared these

160

attitudes toward the private behavior of their fellows, sometimes with a moral punitiveness to rival that of whites, but at other times with a hard-headed interest in causes and remedies rather than moral evaluation. Moralism permeated the subject of Negro sexual, marital, and family behavior in the polemics of slavery apologists and abolitionists as much as in the Northern and Southern civil rights controversies of today. Yet, as long as the dialectic of good or bad, guilty or innocent, overshadows a concern with who, why, and what can be, it is unlikely that realistic and effective social planning to correct the clearly desperate situation of poor Negro families can begin.

This paper is concerned with a description and analysis of slum Negro family patterns as these reflect and sustain Negroes' adaptations to the economic, social, and personal situation into which they are born and in which they must live. As such it deals with facts of lower-class life that are usually forgotten or ignored in polite discussion. We have chosen not to ignore these facts in the belief that to do so can lead only to assumptions which would frustrate efforts at social reconstruction, to strategies that are unrealistic in the light of the actual day-to-day reality of slum Negro life. Further, this analysis will deal with family patterns which interfere with the efforts slum Negroes make to attain a stable way of life as working- or middle-class individuals and with the effects such failure in turn has on family life. To be sure, many Negro families live *in* the slum ghetto, but are not *of* its culture (though even they, and particularly their children, can be deeply affected by what happens there). However, it is the individuals who succumb to the distinctive family life style of the slum who experience the greatest weight of deprivation and who have the greatest difficulty responding to the few self-improvement resources that make their way into the ghetto. In short, we propose to explore in depth the family's role in the "tangle of pathology" which characterizes the ghetto.

The social reality in which Negroes have had to make their lives during the 450 years of their existence in the western hemisphere has been one of victimization "in the sense that a system of social relations operates in such a way as to deprive them of a chance to share in the more desirable material and non-material products of a society which is dependent, in part, upon their labor and loyalty." In making this observation, St. Clair Drake goes on to note that Negroes are victimized also because "they do not have the same degree of access which others have to the attributes needed for rising in the general class system—money, education, 'contacts,' and 'know-how.' "[2] The victimization process started with slavery; for 350 years thereafter Negroes worked out as best they could adaptations to the slave status. After emancipation, the cultural mechanisms which Negroes had developed for living the life of victim continued to be serviceable as the victimization process was maintained first under the myths of white supremacy and black inferiority, later by the doctrines of gradualism which covered the fact of no improvement in position, and finally by the modern Northern system of ghettoization and indifference.

When lower-class Negroes use the expression, "Tell it like it is," they signal their intention to strip away pretense, to describe a situation or its participants as they really are, rather than in a polite or euphemistic way. "Telling it like it is" can be used as a harsh, aggressive device, or it can be a healthy attempt to face reality rather than retreat into fantasy. In any case, as he goes about his field work, the participant observer studying a ghetto community learns to listen carefully to any exchange preceded by such an announcement because he knows the speaker is about to express his understanding of how his world operates, of what motivates its members, of how they actually behave.

The first responsibility of the social scientist can be phrased in much the same way: "Tell it like it is." His second responsibility is to try to understand why "it" is that way, and to explore the implications of what and why for more constructive solutions to human problems. Social research on the situation of the Negro American has been informed by four main goals: (1) to describe the disadvantaged position of Negroes, (2) to disprove the racist ideology which sustains the caste system, (3) to demonstrate that responsibility for the disadvantages Negroes suffer lies squarely upon the white caste which derives economic, prestige, and psychic benefits from the operation of the system, and (4) to suggest that in reality whites would be better rather than worse off if the whole jerry-built caste structure were to be dismantled. The successful accomplishment of these *intellectual* goals has been a towering achievement, in which the social scientists of the 1920's, '30's, and '40's can take great pride; that white society has proved so recalcitrant to utilizing this intellectual accomplishment is one of the great tragedies of our time, and provides the stimulus for further social research on "the white problem."

Yet the implicit paradigm of much of the research on Negro

Americans has been an overly simplistic one concentrating on two terms of an argument:

White cupidity————————→Negro suffering.

As an intellectual shorthand, and even more as a civil rights slogan, this simple model is both justified and essential. But, as a guide to greater understanding of the Negro situation as human adaptation to human situations, the paradigm is totally inadequate because it fails to specify fully enough the *process* by which Negroes adapt to their situations as they do, and the limitations one kind of adaptation places on possibilities for subsequent adaptations. A reassessment of previous social research, combined with examination of current social research on Negro ghetto communities, suggests a more complex, but hopefully more veridical, model:

White cupidity
creates
Structural Conditions Highly Inimical to Basic Social Adaptation (low-income availability, poor education, poor services, stigmatization)
to which Negroes adapt
by
Social and Personal Responses which serve to sustain the individual in his punishing world but also generate aggressiveness toward the self and others
which results in
Suffering directly inflicted by Negroes on themselves and on others.

In short, whites, by their greater power, create situations in which Negroes do the dirty work of caste victimization for them.

The white caste maintains a cadre of whites whose special responsibility is to enforce the system in brutal or refined ways (the Klan, the rural sheriff, the metropolitan police, the businessman who specializes in a Negro clientele, the Board of Education). Increasingly, whites recruit to this cadre middle-class Negroes who can soften awareness of victimization by their protective coloration. These special cadres, white and/or Negro, serve the very important function of enforcing caste standards by whatever means seems required, while at the same time concealing from an increasingly "unprejudiced" public the unpleasant facts they would prefer to ignore. The system is quite homologous to the Gestapo and concentration camps of Nazi Germany, though less fatal to its victims.

For their part, Negroes creatively adapt to the system in ways that keep them alive and extract what gratification they can find, but in the process of adaptation they are constrained to behave in ways that inflict a great deal of suffering on those with whom they make their lives, and on themselves. The ghetto Negro is constantly confronted by the immediate necessity to suffer in order to get what he wants of those few things he can have, or to make others suffer, or both—for example, he suffers as exploited student and employee, as drug user, as loser in the competitive game of his peer-group society; he inflicts suffering as disloyal spouse, petty thief, knife- or gun-wielder, petty con man.

It is the central thesis of this paper that the caste-facilitated infliction of suffering by Negroes on other Negroes and on themselves appears most poignantly within the confines of the family, and that the victimization process as it operates in families prepares and toughens its members to function in the ghetto world, at the same time that it seriously interferes with their ability to operate in any other world. This, however, is very different from arguing that "the family is to blame" for the deprived situation ghetto Negroes suffer; rather we are looking at the logical outcome of the operation of the widely ramified and interconnecting caste system. In the end we will argue that only palliative results can be expected from attempts to treat directly the disordered family patterns to be described. Only a change in the original "inputs" of the caste system, the structural conditions inimical to basic social adaptation, can change family forms.

Almost thirty years ago, E. Franklin Frazier foresaw that the fate of the Negro family in the city would be a highly destructive one. His readers would have little reason to be surprised at observations of slum ghetto life today:

. . . As long as the bankrupt system of southern agriculture exists, Negro families will continue to seek a living in the towns and cities. . . . They will crowd the slum areas of southern cities or make their way to northern cities where their families will become disrupted and their poverty will force them to depend upon charity.[3]

The Autonomy of the Slum Ghetto

Just as the deprivations and depredations practiced by white society have had their effect on the personalities and social life of Negroes, so also has the separation from the ongoing social life of the white community had its effect. In a curious way, Negroes have had considerable freedom to fashion their own adaptations within their separate world. The larger society provides them with few resources but also with minimal interference in the Negro community on matters which did not seem to affect white interests. Because Negroes learned early that there were a great many things they could not depend upon whites to provide they developed their own solutions to recurrent human issues. These solutions can often be seen to combine, along with the predominance of elements from white culture, elements that are distinctive to the Negro group. Even more distinctive is the *configuration* which emerges from those elements Negroes share with whites and those which are different.

It is in this sense that we may speak of a Negro subculture, a distinctive *patterning* of existential perspectives, techniques for coping with the problems of social life, views about what is desirable and undesirable in particular situations. This subculture, and particularly that of the lower-class, the slum, Negro, can be seen as his own creation out of the elements available to him in response to (1) the conditions of life set by white society and (2) the selective freedom which that society allows (or must put up with given the pattern of separateness on which it insists).

Out of this kind of "freedom" slum Negroes have built a culture which has some elements of intrinsic value and many more elements that are highly destructive to the people who must live in it. The elements that whites can value they constantly borrow. Negro arts and language have proved so popular that such commentators on American culture as Norman Mailer and Leslie Fiedler have noted processes of Negro-ization of white Americans as a minor theme of the past thirty years.[4] A fairly large proportion of Negroes with national reputations are engaged in the occupation of diffusing to the larger culture these elements of intrinsic value.

On the negative side, this freedom has meant, as social scientists who have studied Negro communities have long commented, that many of the protections offered by white institutions stop at the edge of the Negro ghetto: there are poor police protection and enforcement of civil equities, inadequate schooling and medical service, and more informal indulgences which whites allow Negroes as a small price for feeling superior.

For our purposes, however, the most important thing about the freedom which whites have allowed Negroes within their own world is that it has required them to work out their own ways of making it from day to day, from birth to death. The subculture that Negroes have created may be imperfect but it has been viable for centuries; it behooves both white and Negro leaders and intellectuals to seek to understand it even as they hope to change it.[5]

Negroes have created, again particularly within the lower-class slum group, a range of institutions to structure the tasks of living a victimized life and to minimize the pain it inevitably produces. In the slum ghetto these institutions include prominently those of the social network—the extended kinship system and the "street system" of buddies and broads which tie (although tenuously and unpredictably) the "members" to each other—and the institutions of entertainment (music, dance, folk tales) by which they instruct, explain, and accept themselves. Other institutions function to provide escape from the society of the victimized: the church (Hereafter!) and the civil rights movement (Now!).

The Functional Autonomy of the Negro Family

At the center of the matrix of Negro institutional life lies the family. It is in the family that individuals are trained for participation in the culture and find personal and group identity and continuity. The "freedom" allowed by white society is greatest here, and this freedom has been used to create an institutional variant more distinctive perhaps to the Negro subculture than any other. (Much of the content of Negro art and entertainment derives exactly from the distinctive characteristics of Negro family life.) At each stage in the Negro's experience of American life—slavery, segregation, de facto ghettoization—whites have found it less necessary to interfere in the relations between the sexes and between parents and children than in other areas of the Negro's existence. His adaptations in this area, therefore, have been less constrained by whites than in many other areas.

Now that the larger society is becoming increasingly committed to integrating Negroes into the main stream of American life, however, we can expect increasing constraint (benevolent as it may be) to be placed on the autonomy of the Negro family system.[6] These constraints will be designed to pull Negroes into meaningful integration with the larger society, to give up ways which are inimical to successful performance in the larger society, and to adopt new ways that are functional in that society. The strategic questions of the civil rights movement and of the war on poverty are ones that have to do with how one provides functional equivalents for the existing subculture before the capacity to make a life within its confines is destroyed.

The history of the Negro family has been ably documented by historians and sociologists.[7] In slavery, conjugal and family ties were reluctantly and ambivalently recognized by the slave holders, were often violated by them, but proved necessary to the slave system. This necessity stemmed both from the profitable offspring of slave sexual unions and the necessity for their nurture, and from the fact that the slaves' efforts to sustain patterns of sexual and parental relations mollified the men and women whose labor could not simply be commanded. From nature's promptings, the thinning memories of African heritage, and the example and guilt-ridden permission of the slave holders, slaves constructed a partial family system and sets of relations that generated conjugal and familial sentiments. The slave holder's recognition in advertisements for runaway slaves of marital and family sentiments· as motivations for absconding provides one indication that strong family ties were possible, though perhaps not common, in the slave quarter. The mother-centered family with its emphasis on the primacy of the mother-child relation and only tenuous ties to a man, then, is the legacy of adaptations worked out by Negroes during slavery.

After emancipation this family design often also served well to cope with the social disorganization of Negro life in the late nineteenth century. Matrifocal families, ambivalence about the desirability of marriage, ready acceptance of illegitimacy, all sustained some kind of family life in situations which often made it difficult to maintain a full nuclear family. Yet in the hundred years since emancipation, Negroes in rural areas have been able to maintain full nuclear families almost as well as similarly situated whites. As we will see, it is the move to the city that results in the very high proportion of mother-headed households. In the rural system the man continues to have important functions; it is difficult for a woman to make a crop by herself, or even with the help of other women. In the city, however, the woman can earn wages just as a man can, and she can receive welfare payments more easily than he can. In rural areas, although there may be high illegitimacy rates and high rates of marital disruption, men and women have an interest in getting together; families are headed by a husband-wife pair much more often than in the city. That pair may be much less stable than in the more prosperous segments of Negro and white communities but it is more likely to exist among rural Negroes than among urban ones.

The matrifocal character of the Negro lower-class family in the United States has much in common with Caribbean Negro family patterns; research in both areas has done a great deal to increase our understanding of the Negro situation. However, there are important differences in the family forms of the two areas.[8] The impact of white European family models has been much greater in the United States than in the Caribbean both because of the relative population proportions of white and colored peoples and because equalitarian values in the United States have had a great impact on Negroes even when they have not on whites. The typical Caribbean mating pattern is that women go through several visiting and common-law unions but eventually marry; that is, they marry legally only relatively late in their sexual lives. The Caribbean marriage is the crowning of a sexual and procreative career; it is considered a serious and difficult step.

In the United States, in contrast, Negroes marry at only a slightly lower rate and slightly higher age than whites.[9] Most Negro women marry relatively early in their careers; marriage is not regarded as the same kind of crowning choice and achievement that it is in the Caribbean. For lower-class Negroes in the United States marriage ceremonies are rather informal affairs. In the Caribbean, marriage is regarded as quite costly because of the feasting which goes along with it; ideally it is performed in church.

In the United States, unlike the Caribbean, early marriage confers a kind of permanent respectable status upon a woman which she can use to deny any subsequent accusations of immorality or promiscuity once the marriage is broken and she becomes sexually involved in visiting or common-law relations. The relevant effective status for many Negro women is that of "having been married" rather than "being married"; having the right to be called "Mrs." rather than currently being Mrs. Someone-in-Particular.

For Negro lower-class women, then, first marriage has the same kind of importance as having a first child. Both indicate that the girl has become a woman but neither one that this is the last such activity in which she will engage. It seems very likely that only a minority of Negro women in the urban slum go through their child-rearing years with only one man around the house.

Among the Negro urban poor, then, a great many women have

the experience of heading a family for part of their mature lives, and a great many children spend some part of their formative years in a household without a father-mother pair. From Table 1 we see

TABLE 1

Proportion of Female Heads for Families with Children by Race, Income, and Urban-Rural Categories

	Rural	*Urban*	*Total*
Negroes			
under $3000	18%	47%	36%
$3000 and over	5%	8%	7%
Total	14%	23%	21%
Whites			
under $3000	12%	38%	22%
$3000 and over	2%	4%	3%
Total	4%	7%	6%

Source: U. S. Census: 1960, PC (1) D. U. S. Volume, Table 225; State Volume, Table 140.

that in 1960, forty-seven per cent of the Negro poor urban families with children had a female head. Unfortunately cumulative statistics are hard to come by; but, given this very high level for a cross-sectional sample (and taking into account the fact that the median age of the children in these families is about six years), it seems very likely that as many as two-thirds of Negro urban poor children will not live in families headed by a man and a woman throughout the first eighteen years of their lives.

One of the other distinctive characteristics of Negro families, both poor and not so poor, is the fact that Negro households have a much higher proportion of relatives outside the mother-father-children triangle than is the case with whites. For example, in St. Louis Negro families average 0.8 other relatives per household compared to only 0.4 for white families. In the case of the more prosperous Negro families this is likely to mean that an older relative lives in the home providing baby-sitting services while both the husband and wife work and thus further their climb toward stable working- or middle-class status. In the poor Negro families it is much more likely that the household is headed by an older relative who brings under her wings a daughter and that daughter's children. It is important to note that the three-generation household with the grandmother at the head exists only when there is no husband present. Thus, despite the high proportion of female-headed households in this group and despite the high proportion of households that contain other relatives, we find that almost all married couples in the St. Louis Negro slum community have their own household. In other words, when a couple marries it establishes its own household; when that couple breaks up the mother either maintains that household or moves back to her parents or grandparents.

Finally we should note that Negro slum families have more children than do either white slum families or stable working- and middle-class Negro families. Mobile Negro families limit their fertility sharply in the interest of bringing the advantages of mobility more fully to the few children that they do have. Since the Negro slum family is both more likely to have the father absent and more likely to have more children in the family, the mother has a more demanding task with fewer resources at her disposal. When we examine the patterns of life of the stem family we shall see that even the presence of several mothers does not necessarily lighten the work load for the principal mother in charge.

The Formation and Maintenance of Families

We will outline below the several stages and forms of Negro lower-class family life. At many points these family forms and the interpersonal relations that exist within them will be seen to have characteristics in common with the life styles of white lower-class families.[10] At other points there are differences, or the Negro pattern will be seen to be more sharply divergent from the family life of stable working- and middle-class couples.

It is important to recognize that lower-class Negroes know that their particular family forms are different from those of the rest of the society and that, though they often see these forms as representing the only ways of behaving given their circumstances, they also think of the more stable family forms of the working class as more desirable. That is, lower-class Negroes know what the "normal American family" is supposed to be like, and they consider a stable family-centered way of life superior to the conjugal and familial situations in which they often find themselves. Their conceptions of the good American life include the notion of a father-husband who functions as an adequate provider and interested member of the family, a hard working home-bound mother who is concerned about her children's welfare and her husband's needs, and children who look up to their parents and perform well in school and other outside places to reflect credit on their families. This image of what family life can be like is very real from time to time as lower-class men and women grow up and move through adulthood. Many of them make efforts to establish such families but find it impossible to do so either because of the direct impact of economic disabilities or because they are not able to sustain in their day-to-day lives the ideals which they hold.[11] While these ideals do serve as a meaningful guide to lower-class couples who are mobile out of the group, for a great many others the existence of such ideas about normal family life represents a recurrent source of stress within families as individuals become aware that they are failing to measure up to the ideals, or as others within the family and outside it use the ideals as an aggressive weapon for criticizing each other's performance. It is not at all uncommon for husbands or wives or children to try to hold others in the family to the norms of stable family life while they themselves engage in behaviors which violate these norms. The effect of such criticism in the end is to deepen commitment to the deviant sexual and parental norms of a slum subculture. Unless they are careful, social workers and other professionals exacerbate the tendency to use the norms of "American family life" as weapons by supporting these norms in situations where they are in reality unsupportable, thus aggravating the sense of failing and being failed by others which is chronic for lower-class people.

Going together. The initial steps toward mating and family formation in the Negro slum take place in a context of highly developed boys' and girls' peer groups. Adolescents tend to become deeply involved in their peer-group societies beginning as early as the age of twelve or thirteen and continue to be involved after first pregnancies and first marriages. Boys and girls are heavily committed both to their same sex peer groups and to the activities that those groups carry out. While classical gang activity does not necessarily characterize Negro slum communities everywhere, loosely-knit peer groups do.

The world of the Negro slum is wide open to exploration by adolescent boys and girls: "Negro communities provide a flow of common experience in which young people and their elders share, and out of which delinquent behavior emerges almost imperceptibly."[12] More than is possible in white slum communities, Negro adolescents have an opportunity to interact with adults in various "high life" activities; their behavior more often represents an identification with the behavior of adults than an attempt to set up group standards and activities that differ from those of adults.

Boys and young men participating in the street system of peer-group activity are much caught up in games of furthering and enhancing their status as significant persons. These games are played out in small and large gatherings through various kinds of verbal contests that go under the names of "sounding," "signifying," and "working game." Very much a part of a boy's or man's status in this group is his ability to win women. The man who has several women "up tight," who is successful in "pimping off" women for sexual favors and material benefits, is much admired. In sharp contrast to white lower-class groups, there is little tendency for males to separate girls into "good" and "bad" categories.[13] Observations of groups of Negro youths suggest that girls and women are much more readily referred to as "that bitch" or "that whore" than they are by their names, and this seems to be a universal tendency carrying no connotation that "that bitch" is morally inferior to or different from other women. Thus, all women are essentially the same, all women are legitimate targets, and no girl or woman is expected to be virginal except for reason of lack of opportunity or immaturity. From their participation in the peer group and according to standards legitimated by the total Negro slum culture, Negro boys and young men are propelled in the direction of girls to test their "strength" as seducers. They are mercilessly rated by both their peers and the opposite sex in their ability to "talk" to girls; a young man will go to great lengths to avoid the reputation of having a "weak" line.[14]

The girls share these definitions of the nature of heterosexual relations; they take for granted that almost any male they deal with will try to seduce them and that given sufficient inducement (social not monetary) they may wish to go along with his line. Although girls have a great deal of ambivalence about participating in sexual relations, this ambivalence is minimally moral and has much more to do with a desire not to be taken advantage of or get in trouble. Girls develop defenses against the exploitative orientations of men by devaluing the significance of sexual relations ("he really didn't do anything bad to me"), and as time goes on by developing their own appreciation of the intrinsic rewards of sexual intercourse.

The informal social relations of slum Negroes begin in adolescence to be highly sexualized. Although parents have many qualms about boys and, particularly, girls entering into this system, they seldom feel there is much they can do to prevent their children's sexual involvement. They usually confine themselves to counseling somewhat hopelessly against girls becoming pregnant or boys being forced into situations where they might have to marry a girl they do not want to marry.

Girls are propelled toward boys and men in order to demonstrate their maturity and attractiveness; in the process they are constantly exposed to pressures for seduction, to boys "rapping" to them. An active girl will "go with" quite a number of boys, but she will generally try to restrict the number with whom she has intercourse to the few to whom she is attracted or (as happens not infrequently) to those whose threats of physical violence she cannot avoid. For their part, the boys move rapidly from girl to girl seeking to have intercourse with as many as they can and thus build up their "reps." The activity of seduction is itself highly cathected; there is gratification in simply "talking to" a girl as long as the boy can feel that he has acquitted himself well.

At sixteen Joan Bemias enjoys spending time with three or four very close girl friends. She tells us they follow this routine when the girls want to go out and none of the boys they have been seeing lately is available: "Every time we get ready to go someplace we look through all the telephone numbers of boys we'd have and we call them and talk so sweet to them that they'd come on around. All of them had cars you see. (I: What do you do to keep all these fellows interested?) Well nothing. We don't have to make love with all of them. Let's see, Joe, J. B., Albert, and Paul, out of all of them I've been going out with I've only had sex with four boys, that's all." She goes on to say that she and her girl friends resist boys by being unresponsive to their lines and by breaking off relations with them on the ground that they're going out with other girls. It is also clear from her comments that the girl friends support each other in resisting the boys when they are out together in groups.

Joan has had a relationship with a boy which has lasted six months, but she has managed to hold the frequency of intercourse down to four times. Initially she managed to hold this particular boy off for a month but eventually gave in.

Becoming pregnant. It is clear that the contest elements in relationships between men and women continue even in relationships that become quite steady. Despite the girls' ambivalence about sexual relations and their manifold efforts to reduce its frequency, the operation of chance often eventuates in their becoming pregnant.[15] This was the case with Joan. With this we reach the second stage in the formation of families, that of premarital pregnancy. (We are outlining an ideal-typical sequence and not, of course, implying that all girls in the Negro slum culture become pregnant before they marry but only that a great many of them do.)

Joan was caught despite the fact that she was considerably more sophisticated about contraception than most girls or young women in the group (her mother had both instructed her in contraceptive techniques and constantly warned her to take precautions). No one was particularly surprised at her pregnancy although she, her boy friend, her mother, and others regarded it as unfortunate. For girls in the Negro slum, pregnancy before marriage is expected in much the same way that parents expect their children to catch mumps or chicken pox; if they are lucky it will not happen but if it happens people are not too surprised and everyone knows what to do about it. It was quickly decided that Joan and the baby would stay at home. It seems clear from the preparations that Joan's mother is making that she expects to have the main responsibility for caring for the infant. Joan seems quite indifferent to the baby; she shows little interest in mothering the child although she is not particularly adverse to the idea so long as the baby does not interfere too much with her continued participation in her peer group.

Establishing who the father is under these circumstances seems to be important and confers a kind of legitimacy on the birth; not to know who one's father is, on the other hand, seems the ultimate in illegitimacy. Actually Joan had a choice in the imputation of fatherhood; she chose J.B. because he is older than she, and because she may marry him if he can get a divorce from his wife. She could have chosen Paul (with whom she had also had intercourse at about the time she became pregnant), but she would have done this reluctantly since Paul is a year younger than she and somehow this does not seem fitting.

In general, when a girl becomes pregnant while still living at home it seems taken for granted that she will continue to live there and that her parents will take a major responsibility for rearing the children. Since there are usually siblings who can help out and even siblings who will be playmates for the child, the addition of a third generation to the household does not seem to place a great stress on relationships within the family. It seems common for the first pregnancy to have a liberating influence on the mother once the child is born in that she becomes socially and sexually more active than she was before. She no longer has to be concerned with preserving her status as a single girl. Since her mother is usually willing to take care of the child for a few years, the unwed mother has an opportunity to go out with girl friends and with men and thus become more deeply involved in the peer-group society of her culture. As she has more children and perhaps marries she will find it necessary to settle down and spend more time around the house fulfilling the functions of a mother herself.

It would seem that for girls pregnancy is the real measure of maturity, the dividing line between adolescence and womanhood. Perhaps because of this, as well as because of the ready resources for child care, girls in the Negro slum community show much less concern about pregnancy than do girls in the white lower-class community and are less motivated to marry the fathers of their children. When a girl becomes pregnant the question of marriage certainly arises and is considered, but the girl often decides that she would rather not marry the man either because she does not want to settle down yet or because she does not think he would make a good husband.

It is in the easy attitudes toward premarital pregnancy that the matrifocal character of the Negro lower-class family appears most clearly. In order to have and raise a family it is simply not necessary, though it may be desirable, to have a man around the house. While the AFDC program may make it easier to maintain such attitudes in the urban situation, this pattern existed long before the program was initiated and continues in families where support comes from other sources.

Finally it should be noted that fathering a child similarly confers maturity on boys and young men although perhaps it is less salient for them. If the boy has any interest in the girl he will tend to feel that the fact that he has impregnated her gives him an additional claim on her. He will be stricter in seeking to enforce his exclusive rights over her (though not exclusive loyalty to her). This exclusive right does not mean that he expects to marry her but only that there is a new and special bond between them. If the girl is not willing to accept such claims she may find it necessary to break off the relationship rather than tolerate the man's jealousy. Since others in the peer group have a vested interest in not allowing a couple to be too loyal to each other they go out of their way to question and challenge each partner about the loyalty of the other, thus contributing to the deterioration of the relationship. This same kind of questioning and challenging continues if the couple marries and represents one source of the instability of the marital relationship.

Getting married. As noted earlier, despite the high degree of premarital sexual activity and the rather high proportion of pre-marital pregnancies, most lower-class Negro men and women eventually do marry and stay together for a shorter or longer period of time. Marriage is an intimidating prospect and is approached ambivalently by both parties. For the girl it means giving up a familiar and comfortable home that, unlike some other lower-class subcultures, places few real restrictions on her behavior. (While marriage can appear to be an escape from interpersonal difficulties at home, these difficulties seldom seem to revolve around effective restrictions placed on her behavior by her parents.) The girl also has good reason to be suspicious of the likelihood that men will be able to perform stably in the role of husband and provider; she is reluctant to be tied down by a man who will not prove to be worth it.

From the man's point of view the fickleness of women makes marriage problematic. It is one thing to have a girl friend step out on you, but it is quite another to have a wife do so. Whereas pre-marital sexual relations and fatherhood carry almost no connotation of responsibility for the welfare of the partner, marriage is supposed to mean that a man behaves more responsibly, becoming a provider for his wife and children even though he may not be expected to give up all the gratifications of participation in the street system.

For all of these reasons both boys and girls tend to have rather negative views of marriage as well as a low expectation that marriage will prove a stable and gratifying existence. When marriage does take place it tends to represent a tentative commitment on the part of both parties with a strong tendency to seek greater commitment on the part of the partner than on one's own part. Marriage is regarded as a fragile arrangement held together primarily by affectional ties rather than instrumental concerns.

In general, as in white lower-class groups, the decision to marry seems to be taken rather impulsively.[16] Since everyone knows that sooner or later he will get married, in spite of the fact that he may not be sanguine about the prospect, Negro lower-class men and women are alert for clues that the time has arrived. The time may arrive because of a pregnancy in a steady relationship that seems gratifying to both partners, or as a way of getting out of what seems to be an awkward situation, or as a self-indulgence during periods when a boy and a girl are feeling very sorry for themselves. Thus, one girl tells us that when she marries her husband will cook all of her meals for her and she will not have any housework; another girl says that when she marries it will be to a man who has plenty of money and will have to take her out often and really show her a good time.

Boys see in marriage the possibility of regular sexual intercourse without having to fight for it, or a girl safe from venereal disease, or a relationship to a nurturant figure who will fulfill the functions of a mother. For boys, marriage can also be a way of asserting their independence from the peer group if its demands become burdensome. In this case the young man seeks to have the best of both worlds.[17]

Marriage as a way out of an unpleasant situation can be seen in the case of one of our informants, Janet Cowan:

Janet has been going with two men, one of them married and the other single. The married man's wife took exception to their relationship and killed her husband. Within a week Janet and her single boy friend, Howard, were married. One way out of the turmoil the murder of her married boy friend stimulated (they lived in the same building) was to choose marriage as a way of "settling down." However, after marrying the new couple seemed to have little idea how to set themselves up as a family. Janet was reluctant to leave her parents' home because her parents cared for her two illegitimate children. Howard was unemployed and therefore unacceptable in his parent-in-law's home, nor were his own parents willing to have his wife move in with them. Howard was also reluctant to give up another girl friend in another part of town. Although both he and his wife maintained that it was all right for a couple to step out on each other so long as the other partner did not know about it, they were both jealous if they suspected anything of this kind. In the end they gave up on the idea of marriage and went their separate ways.

In general, then, the movement toward marriage is an uncertain and tentative one. Once the couple does settle down together in a household of their own, they have the problem of working out a mutually acceptable organization of rights and duties, expectations and performances, that will meet their needs.

Husband-wife relations. Characteristic of both the Negro and white lower class is a high degree of conjugal role segregation.[18] That is, husbands and wives tend to think of themselves as having very separate kinds of functioning in the instrumental organization of family life, and also as pursuing recreational and outside interests separately. The husband is expected to be a provider; he resists assuming functions around the home so long as he feels he is doing his proper job of bringing home a pay check. He feels he has the right to indulge himself in little ways if he is successful at this task. The wife is expected to care for the home and children and make her husband feel welcome and comfortable. Much that is distinctive to Negro family life stems from the fact that husbands often are not stable providers. Even when a particular man is, his wife's conception of men in general is such that she is pessimistic about the likelihood that he will continue to do well in this area. A great many Negro wives work to supplement the family income. When this is so the separate incomes earned by husband and wife tend to be treated not as "family" income but as the individual property of the two persons involved. If their wives work, husbands are likely to feel that they are entitled to retain a larger share of the income they provide; the wives, in turn, feel that the husbands have no right to benefit from the purchases they make out of their own money. There is, then, "my money" and "your money." In this situation the husband may come to feel that the wife should support the children out of her income and that he can retain all of his income for himself.

While white lower-class wives often are very much intimidated by their husbands, Negro lower-class wives come to feel that they have a right to give as good as they get. If the husband indulges himself, they have the right to indulge themselves. If the husband steps out on his wife, she has the right to step out on him. The commitment of husbands and wives to each other seems often a highly instrumental one after the "honeymoon" period. Many wives feel they owe the husband nothing once he fails to perform his provider role. If the husband is unemployed the wife increasingly refuses to perform her usual duties for him. For example one woman, after mentioning that her husband had cooked four eggs for himself, commented, "I cook for him when he's working but right now he's unemployed; he can cook for himself." It is important, however, to understand that the man's status in the home depends not so much on whether he is working as on whether he brings money into the home. Thus, in several of the families we have studied in which the husband receives disability payments his status is as well-recognized as in families in which the husband is working.[19]

Because of the high degree of conjugal role segregation, both white and Negro lower-class families tend to be matrifocal in comparison to middle-class families. They are matrifocal in the sense that the wife makes most of the decisions that keep the family going and has the greatest sense of responsibility to the family. In white as well as in Negro lower-class families women tend to look to their female relatives for support and counsel, and to treat their husbands as essentially uninterested in the day-to-day problems of family living.[20] In the Negro lower-class family these tendencies are all considerably exaggerated so that the matrifocality is much clearer than in white lower-class families.

The fact that both sexes in the Negro slum culture have equal right to the various satisfactions of life (earning an income, sex, drinking, and peer-group activity which conflicts with family responsibilities) means that there is less pretense to patriarchal authority in the Negro than in the white lower class. Since men find the overt debasement of their status very threatening, the Negro family is much more vulnerable to disruption when men are temporarily unable to perform their provider roles. Also, when men are unemployed the temptations for them to engage in street adventures which repercuss on the marital relationship are much greater. This fact is well-recognized by Negro lower-class wives; they often seem as concerned about what their unemployed husbands will do instead of working as they are about the fact that the husband is no longer bringing money into the home.

It is tempting to cope with the likelihood of disloyalty by denying the usual norms of fidelity, by maintaining instead that extra-marital affairs are acceptable as long as they do not interfere with family functioning. Quite a few informants tell us this, but we have yet to observe a situation in which a couple maintains a stable relationship under these circumstances without a great deal of conflict. Thus one woman in her forties who has been married for many years and has four children first outlined this deviant norm and then illustrated how it did not work out:

My husband and I, we go out alone and sometimes stay all night. But when I get back my husband doesn't ask me a thing and I don't ask him anything. . . . A couple of years ago I suspected he was going out on me. One day I came home and my daughter was here. I told her to tell me when he left the house. I went into the bedroom and got into bed and then I heard him come in. He left in about ten minutes and my daughter came in and told me he was gone. I got out of bed and put on my clothes and started following him. Soon I saw him walking with a young girl and I began walking after them. They were just laughing and joking right out loud right on the sidewalk. He was carrying a large package of hers. I walked up behind them until I was about a yard from them. I had a large dirk which I opened and had decided to take one long slash across the both of them. Just when I decided to swing at them I lost my balance—I have a bad hip. Anyway, I didn't cut them because I lost my balance. Then I called his name and he turned around and stared at me. He didn't move at all. He was shaking all over. That girl just ran away from us. He still had her package so the next day she called on the telephone and said she wanted to come pick it up. My husband washed his face, brushed his teeth, took out his false tooth and started scrubbing it and put on a clean shirt and everything, just for her. We went downstairs together and gave her the package and she left.

So you see my husband does run around on me and it seems like he does it a lot. The thing about it is he's just getting too old to be pulling that kind of stuff. If a young man does it then that's not so bad—but an old man, he just looks foolish. One of these days he'll catch me but I'll just tell him, "Buddy you owe me one," and that'll be all there is to it. He hasn't caught me yet though.

In this case, as in others, the wife is not able to leave well enough alone; her jealousy forces her to a confrontation. Actually seeing her husband with another woman stimulates her to violence.

With couples who have managed to stay married for a good many years, these peccadillos are tolerable although they generate a great deal of conflict in the marital relationship. At earlier ages the partners are likely to be both prouder and less innured to the hopelessness of maintaining stable relationships; outside involvements are therefore much more likely to be disruptive of the marriage.

Marital breakup. The precipitating causes of marital disruption seem to fall mainly into economic or sexual categories. As noted, the husband has little credit with his wife to tide him over periods of unemployment. Wives seem very willing to withdraw commitment from husbands who are not bringing money into the house. They take the point of view that he has no right to take up space around the house, to use its facilities, or to demand loyalty from her. Even where the wife is not inclined to press these claims, the husband tends to be touchy because he knows that such definitions are usual in his group, and he may, therefore, prove difficult for even a well-meaning wife to deal with. As noted above, if husbands do not work they tend to play around. Since they continue to maintain some contact with their peer groups, whenever they have time on their hands they move back into the world of the street system and are likely to get involved in activities which pose a threat to their family relationships.

Drink is a great enemy of the lower-class housewife, both white and Negro. Lower-class wives fear their husband's drinking because it costs money, because the husband may become violent and take out his frustrations on his wife, and because drinking may lead to sexual involvements with other women.[21]

The combination of economic problems and sexual difficulties can be seen in the case of the following couple in their early twenties:

When the field worker first came to know them, the Wilsons seemed to be working hard to establish a stable family life. The couple had been married about three years and had a two-year-old son. Their apartment was very sparsely furnished but also very clean. Within six weeks the couple had acquired several rooms of inexpensive furniture and obviously had gone to a great deal of effort to make a liveable home. Husband and wife worked on different shifts so that the husband could take care of the child while the wife worked. They looked forward to saving enough money to move out of the housing project into a more desirable neighborhood. Six weeks later, however, the husband had lost his job. He and his wife were in great conflict. She made him feel unwelcome at home and he strongly suspected her of going out with other men. A short time later they had separated. It is impossible to disentangle the various factors involved in this separation into a sequence of cause and effect, but we can see something of the impact of the total complex.

First Mr. Wilson loses his job: "I went to work one day and the man told me that I would have to work until 1:00. I asked him if there would be any extra pay for working overtime and he said no. I asked him why and he said, 'If you don't like it you can kiss my ass.' He said that to me. I said, 'Why do I have to do all that?' He said, 'Because I said so.' I wanted to jam (fight) him but I said to myself I don't want to be that ignorant, I don't want to be as ignorant as he is, so I just cut out and left. Later his father called me (it was a family firm) and asked why I left and I told him. He said, 'If you don't want to go along with my son then you're fired.' I said O.K. They had another Negro man come in to help me part time before they fired me. I think they were trying to have him work full time because he worked for them before. He has seven kids and he takes their shit."

The field worker observed that things were not as hard as they could be because his wife had a job, to which he replied, "Yeah, I know, that's just where the trouble is. My wife has become independent since she began working. If I don't get a job pretty soon I'll go crazy. We have a lot of little arguments about nothing since she got so independent." He went on to say that his wife had become a completely different person recently; she was hard to talk to because she felt that now that she was working and he was not there was nothing that he could tell her. On her last pay day his wife did not return home for three days; when she did she had only seven cents left from her pay check. He said that he loved his wife very much and had begged her to quit fooling around. He is pretty sure that she is having an affair with the man with whom she rides to work. To make matters worse his wife's sister counsels her that she does not have to stay home with him as long as he is out of work. Finally the wife moved most of their furniture out of the apartment so that he came home to find an empty apartment. He moved back to his parents' home (also in the housing project).

One interesting effect of this experience was the radical change in the husband's attitudes toward race relations. When he and his wife were doing well together and had hopes of moving up in the world he was quite critical of Negroes; "Our people are not ready for integration in many cases because they really don't know how to act. You figure if our people don't want to be bothered with whites then why in hell should the white man want to be bothered with them. There are some of us who are ready; there are others who aren't quite ready yet so I don't see why they're doing all of this hollering." A scarce eight months later he addressed white people as he spoke for two hours into a tape recorder, "If we're willing to be with you, why aren't you willing to be with us? Do our color make us look dirty and low down and cheap? Or do you know the real meaning of 'nigger'? Anyone can be a nigger, white, colored, orange or any other color. It's something that you labeled us with. You put us away like you put a can away on the shelf with a label on it. The can is marked 'Poison: stay away from it.' You want us to help build your country but you don't want us to live in it. . . . You give me respect; I'll give you respect. If you threaten to take my life, I'll take yours and believe me I know how to take a life. We do believe that man was put here to live together as human beings; not one that's superior and the one that's a dog, but as human beings. And if you don't want to live this way then you become the dog and we'll become the human beings. There's too much corruption, too much hate, too much one individual trying to step on another. If we don't get together in a hurry we will destroy each other." It was clear from what the respondent said that he had been much influenced by Black Muslim philosophy, yet again and again in his comments one can see the displacement into a public, race relations dialogue of the sense of rage, frustration and victimization that he had experienced in his ill-fated marriage.[22]

Finally, it should be noted that migration plays a part in marital disruption. Sometimes marriages do not break up in the dramatic way described above but rather simply become increasingly unsatisfactory to one or both partners. In such a situation the temptation to move to another city, from South to North, or North to West, is great. Several wives told us that their first marriages were broken when they moved with their children to the North and their husbands stayed behind.

"After we couldn't get along I left the farm and came here and stayed away three or four days. I didn't come here to stay. I came to visit but I liked it and so I said, 'I'm gonna leave!' He said, 'I'll be glad if you do.' Well, maybe he didn't mean it but I thought he did. . . . I miss him sometimes, you know. I think about him I guess. But just in a small way. That's what I can't understand about life sometimes; you know—how people can go on like that and still break up and meet somebody else. Why couldn't—oh, I don't know!"

The gains and losses in marriage and in the post-marital state often seem quite comparable. Once they have had the experience of marriage, many women in the Negro slum culture see little to recommend it in the future, important as the first marriage may have been in establishing their maturity and respectability.

The house of mothers. As we have seen, perhaps a majority of mothers in the Negro slum community spend at least part of their mature life as mothers heading a family. The Negro mother may be a working mother or she may be an AFDC mother, but in either case she has the problems of maintaining a household, socializing her children, and achieving for herself some sense of membership in relations with other women and with men. As is apparent from the earlier discussion, she often receives her training in how to run such a household by observing her own mother manage without a husband. Similarly she often learns how to run a three-generation household because she herself brought a third generation into her home with her first, premarital, pregnancy.

Because men are not expected to be much help around the house, having to be head of the household is not particularly intimidating to the Negro mother if she can feel some security about income. She knows it is a hard, hopeless, and often thankless task, but she also knows that it is possible. The maternal household in the slum is generally run with a minimum of organization. The children quickly learn to fend for themselves, to go to the store, to make small purchases, to bring change home, to watch after themselves when the mother has to be out of the home, to amuse themselves, to set their own schedules of sleeping, eating, and going to school. Housekeeping practices may be poor, furniture takes a terrific beating from the children, and emergencies constantly arise. The Negro mother in this situation copes by not setting too high standards for herself, by letting things take their course. Life is most difficult when there are babies and preschool children around because then the mother is confined to the home. If she is a grandmother and the children are her daughter's, she is often confined since it is taken as a matter of course that the mother has the right to continue her outside activities and that the grandmother has the duty to be responsible for the child.

In this culture there is little of the sense of the awesome responsibility of caring for children that is characteristic of the working and middle class. There is not the deep psychological involvement with babies which has been observed with the working-class mother.[23] The baby's needs are cared for on a catch-as-catch-can basis. If there are other children around and they happen to like babies, the baby can be over-stimulated; if this is not the case, the baby is left alone a good deal of the time. As quickly as he can move around he learns to fend for himself.

The three-generation maternal household is a busy place. In contrast to working- and middle-class homes it tends to be open to the world, with many non-family members coming in and out at all times as the children are visited by friends, the teenagers by their boy friends and girl friends, the mother by her friends and perhaps an occasional boy friend, and the grandmother by fewer friends but still by an occasional boy friend.

The openness of the household is, among other things, a reflection of the mother's sense of impotence in the face of the street system. Negro lower-class mothers often indicate that they try very hard to keep their young children at home and away from the streets; they often seem to make the children virtual prisoners in the home. As the children grow and go to school they inevitably do become involved in peer-group activities. The mother gradually gives up, feeling that once the child is lost to this pernicious outside world there is little she can do to continue to control him and direct his development. She will try to limit the types of activities that go on in the home and to restrict the kinds of friends that her children can bring into the home, but even this she must give up as time goes on, as the children become older and less attentive to her direction.

The grandmothers in their late forties, fifties, and sixties tend increasingly to stay at home. The home becomes a kind of court at which other family members gather and to which they bring their friends for sociability, and as a by-product provide amusement and entertainment for the mother. A grandmother may provide a home for her daughters, their children, and sometimes their children's children, and yet receive very little in a material way from them; but one of the things she does receive is a sense of human involvement, a sense that although life may have passed her by she is not completely isolated from it.

The lack of control that mothers have over much that goes on in their households is most dramatically apparent in the fact that their older children seem to have the right to come home at any time once they have moved and to stay in the home without contributing to its maintenance. Though the mother may be resentful about being taken advantage of, she does not feel she can turn her children

away. For example, sixty-five-year-old Mrs. Washington plays host-
ess for weeks or months at a time to her forty-year-old daughter and
her small children, and to her twenty-three-year-old granddaughter
and her children. When these daughters come home with their
families the grandmother is expected to take care of the young
children and must argue with her daughter and granddaughter to
receive contributions to the daily household ration of food and
liquor. Or, a twenty-year-old son comes home from the Air Force
and feels he has the right to live at home without working and to
run up an eighty-dollar long-distance telephone bill.

Even aged parents living alone in small apartments sometimes
acknowledge such obligations to their children or grandchildren.
Again, the only clear return they receive for their hospitality is the
reduction of isolation that comes from having people around and
interesting activity going on. When in the Washington home the
daughter and granddaughter and their children move in with the
grandmother, or when they come to visit for shorter periods of time,
the occasion has a party atmosphere. The women sit around talking
and reminiscing. Though boy friends may be present, they take little
part; instead they sit passively, enjoying the stories and drinking
along with the women. It would seem that in this kind of party
activity the women are defined as the stars. Grandmother, daughter,
and granddaughter in turn take the center of the stage telling a
story from the family's past, talking about a particularly interesting
night out on the town or just making some general observation
about life. In the course of these events a good deal of liquor is
consumed. In such a household as this little attention is paid to the
children since the competition by adults for attention is stiff.

Boy friends, not husbands. It is with an understanding of the
problems of isolation which older mothers have that we can obtain
the best insight into the role and function of boy friends in the
maternal household. The older mothers, surrounded by their own
children and grandchildren, are not able to move freely in the
outside world, to participate in the high life which they enjoyed
when younger and more foot-loose. They are disillusioned with marriage as providing any more secure economic base than they can
achieve on their own. They see marriage as involving just another
responsibility without a concomitant reward—"It's the greatest
thing in the world to come home in the afternoon and not have some
curly headed twot in the house yellin' at me and askin' me where
supper is, where I've been, what I've been doin', and who I've been

seein'." In this situation the woman is tempted to form relationships with men that are not so demanding as marriage but still provide companionship and an opportunity for occasional sexual gratification.

There seem to be two kinds of boy friends. Some boy friends "pimp" off mothers; they extract payment in food or money for their companionship. This leads to the custom sometimes called "Mother's Day," the tenth of the month when the AFDC checks come.[24] On this day one can observe an influx of men into the neighborhood, and much partying. But there is another kind of boy friend, perhaps more numerous than the first, who instead of being paid for his services pays for the right to be a pseudo family member. He may be the father of one of the woman's children and for this reason makes a steady contribution to the family's support, or he may simply be a man whose company the mother enjoys and who makes reasonable gifts to the family for the time he spends with them (and perhaps implicitly for the sexual favors he receives). While the boy friend does not assume fatherly authority within the family, he often is known and liked by the children. The older children appreciate the meaningfulness of their mother's relationship with him—one girl said of her mother's boy friend:

"We don't none of us (the children) want her to marry again. It's all right if she wants to live by herself and have a boy friend. It's not because we're afraid we're going to have some more sisters and brothers, which it wouldn't make us much difference, but I think she be too old."

Even when the boy friend contributes ten or twenty dollars a month to the family he is in a certain sense getting a bargain. If he is a well-accepted boy friend he spends considerable time around the house, has a chance to relax in an atmosphere less competitive than that of his peer group, is fed and cared for by the woman, yet has no responsibilities which he cannot renounce when he wishes. When women have stable relationships of this kind with boy friends they often consider marrying them but are reluctant to take such a step. Even the well-liked boy friend has some shortcomings—one woman said of her boy friend:

"Well he works; I know that. He seems to be a nice person, kind hearted. He believes in survival for me and my family. He don't much mind sharing with my youngsters. If I ask him for a helping hand he don't seem to mind that. The only part I dislike is his drinking."

The woman in this situation has worked out a reasonably stable adaptation to the problems of her life; she is fearful of upsetting this adaptation by marrying again. It seems easier to take the "sweet" part of the relationship with a man without the complexities that marriage might involve.

It is in the light of this pattern of women living in families and men living by themselves in rooming houses, odd rooms, here and there, that we can understand Daniel Patrick Moynihan's observation that during their mature years men simply disappear; that is, that census data show a very high sex ratio of women to men.[25] In St. Louis, starting at the age range twenty to twenty-four there are only seventy-two men for every one hundred women. This ratio does not climb to ninety until the age range fifty to fifty-four. Men often do not have real homes; they move about from one household where they have kinship or sexual ties to another; they live in flop houses and rooming houses; they spend time in institutions. They are not household members in the only "homes" that they have— the homes of their mothers and of their girl friends.

It is in this kind of world that boys and girls in the Negro slum community learn their sex roles. It is not just, or even mainly, that fathers are often absent but that the male role models around boys are ones which emphasize expressive, affectional techniques for making one's way in the world. The female role models available to girls emphasize an exaggerated self-sufficiency (from the point of view of the middle class) and the danger of allowing oneself to be dependent on men for anything that is crucial. By the time she is mature, the woman learns that she is most secure when she herself manages the family affairs and when she dominates her men. The man learns that he exposes himself to the least risk of failure when he does not assume a husband's and father's responsibilities but instead counts on his ability to court women and to ingratiate himself with them.

Identity Processes in the Family

Up to this point we have been examining the sequential development of family stages in the Negro slum community, paying only incidental attention to the psychological responses family members make to these social forms and not concerning ourselves with the effect the family forms have on the psychosocial development of the children who grow up in them. Now we want to examine the effect that growing up in this kind of a system has in terms of socialization and personality development.

Household groups function for cultures in carrying out the initial phases of socialization and personality formation. It is in the family that the child learns the most primitive categories of existence and experience, and that he develops his most deeply held beliefs about the world and about himself.[26] From the child's point of view, the household *is* the world; his experiences as he moves out of it into the larger world are always interpreted in terms of his particular experience within the home. The painful experiences which a child in the Negro slum culture has are, therefore, interpreted as in some sense a reflection of this family world. The impact of the system of victimization is transmitted through the family; the child cannot be expected to have the sophistication an outside observer has for seeing exactly where the villains are. From the child's point of view, if he is hungry it is his parents' fault; if he experiences frustrations in the streets or in the school it is his parents' fault; if that world seems incomprehensible to him it is his parents' fault; if people are aggressive or destructive toward each other it is his parents' fault, not that of a system of race relations. In another culture this might not be the case; if a subculture could exist which provided comfort and security within its limited world and the individual experienced frustration only when he moved out into the larger society, the family might not be thought so much to blame. The effect of the caste system, however, is to bring home through a chain of cause and effect all of the victimization processes, and to bring them home in such a way that it is often very difficult even for adults in the system to see the connection between the pain they feel at the moment and the structured patterns of the caste system.

Let us take as a central question that of identity formation within the Negro slum family. We are concerned with the question of who the individual believes himself to be and to be becoming. For Erikson, identity means a sense of continuity and social sameness which bridges what the individual *"was* as a child and what he is *about to become* and also reconciles his *conception of himself* and his community's recognition of him." Thus identity is a "self-realization coupled with a mutual recognition."[27] In the early childhood years identity is family-bound since the child's identity is his identity *vis-à-vis* other members of the family. Later he incorporates into his sense of who he is and is becoming his experiences outside the family, but always influenced by the interpretations and evaluations of those experiences that the family gives. As the child tries on identities, *announces* them, the family sits as judge of his pretensions. Family members are both the most important judges and the most critical ones, since who he is allowed to become affects them in their own identity strivings more crucially than it affects anyone else. The child seeks a sense of valid identity, a sense of being a particular person with a satisfactory degree of congruence between who he feels he is, who he announces himself to be, and where he feels his society places him.[28] He is uncomfortable when he experiences disjunction between his own needs and the kinds of needs legitimated by those around him, or when he feels a disjunction between his sense of himself and the image of himself that others play back to him.[29]

"Tell it like it is." When families become involved in important quarrels the psychosocial underpinnings of family life are laid bare. One such quarrel in a family we have been studying brings together in one place many of the themes that seem to dominate identity problems in Negro slum culture. The incident illustrates in a particularly forceful and dramatic way family processes which our field work, and some other contemporary studies of slum family life, suggests unfold more subtly in a great many families at the lower-class level. The family involved, the Johnsons, is certainly not the most disorganized one we have studied; in some respects their way of life represents a realistic adaptation to the hard living of a family nineteen years on AFDC with a monthly income of $202 for nine people. The two oldest daughters, Mary Jane (eighteen years old) and Esther (sixteen) are pregnant; Mary Jane has one illegitimate child. The adolescent sons, Bob and Richard, are much involved in the social and sexual activities of their peer group. The three other children, ranging in age from twelve to fourteen, are apparently also moving into this kind of peer-group society.

When the argument started Bob and Esther were alone in the apartment with Mary Jane's baby. Esther took exception to Bob's playing with the baby because she had been left in charge; the argument quickly progressed to a fight in which Bob cuffed Esther around, and she tried to cut him with a knife. The police were called and subdued Bob with their nightsticks. At this point the rest of the family and the field worker arrived. As the argument continued, these themes relevant to the analysis which follows appeared:

1) The sisters said that Bob was not their brother (he is a half-brother to Esther, and Mary Jane's full brother). Indeed, they said their mother "didn't have no husband. These kids don't even know who their daddies are." The mother defended herself by saying that she had one legal husband, and one common-law husband, no more.

2) The sisters said that their fathers had never done anything for

them, nor had their mother. She retorted that she had raised them "to the age of womanhood" and now would care for their babies.

3) Esther continued to threaten to cut Bob if she got a chance (a month later they fought again, and she did cut Bob, who required twenty-one stitches).

4) The sisters accused their mother of favoring their lazy brothers and asked her to put them out of the house. She retorted that the girls were as lazy, that they made no contribution to maintaining the household, could not get their boy friends to marry them or support their children, that all the support came from her AFDC check. Mary Jane retorted that "the baby has a check of her own."

5) The girls threatened to leave the house if their mother refused to put their brothers out. They said they could force their boy friends to support them by taking them to court, and Esther threatened to cut her boy friend's throat if he did not co-operate.

6) Mrs. Johnson said the girls could leave if they wished but that she would keep their babies; "I'll not have it, not knowing who's taking care of them."

7) When her thirteen-year-old sister laughed at all of this, Esther told her not to laugh because she, too, would be pregnant within a year.

8) When Bob laughed, Esther attacked him and his brother by saying that both were not man enough to make babies, as she and her sister had been able to do.

9) As the field worker left, Mrs. Johnson sought his sympathy. "You see, Joe, how hard it is for me to bring up a family. . . . They sit around and talk to me like I'm some kind of a dog and not their mother."

10) Finally, it is important to note for the analysis which follows that the following labels—"black-assed," "black bastard," "bitch," and other profane terms—were liberally used by Esther and Mary Jane, and rather less liberally by their mother, to refer to each other, to the girls' boy friends, to Bob, and to the thirteen-year-old daughter.

Several of the themes outlined previously appear forcefully in the course of this argument. In the last year and a half the mother has become a grandmother and expects shortly to add two more grandchildren to her household. She takes it for granted that it is her responsibility to care for the grandchildren and that she has the right to decide what will be done with the children since her own daughters are not fully responsible. She makes this very clear to them when they threaten to move out, a threat which they do not really wish to make good nor could they if they wished to.

However, only as an act of will is Mrs. Johnson able to make this a family. She must constantly cope with the tendency of her adolescent children to disrupt the family group and to deny that they are in fact a family—"He ain't no brother of mine"; "The baby has a check of her own." Though we do not know exactly what processes communicate these facts to the children it is clear that in growing up they have learned to regard themselves as not fully part of a solidary collectivity. During the quarrel this message was reinforced for the twelve-, thirteen-, and fourteen-year-old daughters by the four-way argument among their older sisters, older brother, and their mother.

The argument represents vicious unmasking of the individual members' pretenses to being competent individuals.[30] The efforts of the two girls to present themselves as masters of their own fate are unmasked by the mother. The girls in turn unmask the pretensions of the mother and of their two brothers. When the thirteen-year-old daughter expresses some amusement they turn on her, telling her that it won't be long before she too becomes pregnant. Each member of the family in turn is told that he can expect to be no more than a victim of his world, but that this is somehow inevitably his own fault.

In this argument masculinity is consistently demeaned. Bob has no right to play with his niece, the boys are not really masculine because at fifteen and sixteen years they have yet to father children, their own fathers were no goods who failed to do anything for their family. These notions probably come originally from the mother, who enjoys recounting the story of having her common-law husband imprisoned for nonsupport, but this comes back to haunt her as her daughters accuse her of being no better than they in ability to force support and nurturance from a man. In contrast, the girls came off somewhat better than the boys, although they must accept the label of stupid girls because they have similarly failed and inconveniently become pregnant in the first place. At least they can and have had children and therefore have some meaningful connection with the ongoing substance of life. There is something important and dramatic in which they participate, while the boys, despite their sexual activity, "can't get no babies."

In most societies, as children grow and are formed by their elders into suitable members of the society they gain increasingly a sense of competence and ability to master the behavioral environment their particular world presents. But in Negro slum culture growing up involves an ever-increasing appreciation of one's shortcomings, of the impossibility of finding a self-sufficient and gratifying way of living.[31] It is in the family first and most devastatingly that one learns these lessons. As the child's sense of frustration builds he too can strike out and unmask the pretensions of others. The result is a peculiar strength and a pervasive weakness. The strength involves the ability to tolerate and defend against degrading verbal and physical aggressions from others and not to give up completely. The weakness involves the inability to embark hopefully on any course of action that might make things better, particularly action which involves cooperating and trusting attitudes toward others. Family members become potential enemies to each other, as the frequency of observing the police being called in to settle family quarrels brings home all too dramatically.

The conceptions parents have of their children are such that they are constantly alert as the child matures to evidence that he is as bad as everyone else. That is, in lower-class culture human nature is conceived of as essentially bad, destructive, immoral.[32] This is the nature of things. Therefore any one child must be inherently bad unless his parents are very lucky indeed. If the mother can keep the child insulated from the outside world, she feels she may be able to prevent his inherent badness from coming out. She feels that once he is let out into the larger world the badness will come to the fore since that is his nature. This means that in the identity development of the child he is constantly exposed to identity labeling by his parents as a bad person. Since as he grows up he does not experience his world as particularly gratifying, it is very easy for him to conclude that this lack of gratification is due to the fact that something is wrong with him. This, in turn, can readily be assimilated to the definitions of being a bad person offered him by those with whom he lives.[33] In this way the Negro slum child learns his culture's conception of being-in-the-world, a conception that emphasizes inherent evil in a chaotic, hostile, destructive world.

Blackness. To a certain extent these same processes operate in white lower-class groups, but added for the Negro is the reality of blackness. "Black-assed" is not an empty pejorative adjective. In the Negro slum culture several distinctive appellations are used to refer to oneself and others. One involves the terms, "black" or "nigger." Black is generally a negative way of naming, but nigger can be either negative or positive, depending upon the context. It is important to note that, at least in the urban North, the initial development of racial identity in these terms has very little directly to do with relations with whites. A child experiences these identity placements in the context of the family and in the neighborhood peer group; he probably very seldom hears the same terms used by whites (unlike the situation in the South). In this way, one of the effects of ghettoization is to mask the ultimate enemy so that the understanding of the fact of victimization by a caste system comes as a late acquisition laid over conceptions of self and of other Negroes derived from intimate, and to the child often traumatic, experience within the ghetto community. If, in addition, the child attends a ghetto school where his Negro teachers either overtly or by implication reinforce his community's negative conceptions of what it means to be black, then the child has little opportunity to develop a more realistic image of himself and other Negroes as being damaged by whites and not by themselves. In such a situation, an intelligent man like Mr. Wilson (quoted on pages 181-182) can say with all sincerity that he does not feel most Negroes are ready for integration—only under the experience of certain kinds of intense personal threat coupled with exposure to an ideology that places the responsibility on whites did he begin to see through the direct evidence of his daily experience.

To those living in the heart of a ghetto, black comes to mean not just "stay back," but also membership in a community of persons who think poorly of each other, who attack and manipulate each other, who give each other small comfort in a desperate world. Black comes to stand for a sense of identity as no better than these destructive others. The individual feels that he must embrace an unattractive self in order to function at all.

We can hypothesize that in those families that manage to avoid the destructive identity imputations of "black" and that manage to maintain solidarity against such assaults from the world around, it is possible for children to grow up with a sense of both Negro and personal identity that allows them to socialize themselves in an anticipatory way for participation in the larger society.[34] This broader sense of identity, however, will remain a brittle one as long as the individual is vulnerable to attack from within the Negro community as "nothing but a nigger like everybody else" or from the white community as "just a nigger." We can hypothesize further that the vicious unmasking of essential identity as black described above is least likely to occur within families where the parents have some stable sense of security, and where they therefore have less need to protect themselves by disavowing responsibility for their children's behavior and denying the children their patrimony as products of a particular family rather than of an immoral nature and an evil community.

In sum, we are suggesting that Negro slum children as they

grow up in their families and in their neighborhoods are exposed to a set of experiences—and a rhetoric which conceptualizes them —that brings home to the child an understanding of his essence as a weak and debased person who can expect only partial gratification of his needs, and who must seek even this level of gratification by less than straight-forward means.

Strategies for living. In every society complex processes of socialization inculcate in their members strategies for gratifying the needs with which they are born and those which the society itself generates. Inextricably linked to these strategies, both cause and effect of them, are the existential propositions which members of a culture entertain about the nature of their world and of effective action within the world as it is defined for them. In most of American society two grand strategies seem to attract the allegiance of its members and guide their day-to-day actions. I have called these strategies those of *the good life* and of *career success.*[35] A good life strategy involves efforts to get along with others and not to rock the boat, a comfortable familism grounded on a stable work career for husbands in which they perform adequately at the modest jobs that enable them to be good providers. The strategy of career success is the choice of ambitious men and women who see life as providing opportunities to move from a lower to a higher status, to "accomplish something," to achieve greater than ordinary material well-being, prestige, and social recognition. Both of these strategies are predicated on the assumption that the world is inherently rewarding if one behaves properly and does his part. The rewards of the world may come easily or only at the cost of great effort, but at least they are there.

In the white and particularly in the Negro slum worlds little in the experience that individuals have as they grow up sustains a belief in a rewarding world. The strategies that seem appropriate are not those of a good, family-based life or of a career, but rather *strategies for survival.*

Much of what has been said above can be summarized as encouraging three kinds of survival strategies. One is the strategy of the *expressive life style* which I have described elsewhere as an effort to make yourself interesting and attractive to others so that you are better able to manipulate their behavior along lines that will provide some immediate gratification.[36] Negro slum culture provides many examples of techniques for seduction, of persuading others to give you what you want in situations where you have very little that is tangible to offer in return. In order to get what you want you learn to "work game," a strategy which requires a high development of a certain kind of verbal facility, a sophisticated manipulation of promise and interim reward. When the expressive strategy fails or when it is unavailable there is, of course, the great temptation to adopt a *violent strategy* in which you force others to give you what you need once you fail to win it by verbal and other symbolic means.[37] Finally, and increasingly as members of the Negro slum culture grow older, there is the *depressive strategy* in which goals are increasingly constricted to the bare necessities for survival (not as a social being but simply as an organism).[38] This is the strategy of "I don't bother anybody and I hope nobody's gonna bother me; I'm simply going through the motions to keep body (but not soul) together." Most lower-class people follow mixed strategies, as Walter Miller has observed, alternating among the excitement of the expressive style, the desperation of the violent style, and the deadness of the depressed style.[39] Some members of the Negro slum world experiment from time to time with mixed strategies that also incorporate the stable working-class model of the good American life, but this latter strategy is exceedingly vulnerable to the threats of unemployment or a less than adequate pay check, on the one hand, and the seduction and violence of the slum world around them, on the other.

Remedies. Finally, it is clear that we, no less than the inhabitants of the ghetto, are not masters of their fate because we are not masters of our own total society. Despite the battles with poverty on many fronts we can find little evidence to sustain our hope of winning the war given current programs and strategies.

The question of strategy is particularly crucial when one moves from an examination of destructive cultural and interaction patterns in Negro families to the question of how these families might achieve a more stable and gratifying life. It is tempting to see the family as the main villain of the piece, and to seek to develop programs which attack directly this family pathology. Should we not have extensive programs of family therapy, family counseling, family-life education, and the like? Is this not the prerequisite to enabling slum Negro families to take advantage of other opportunities? Yet, how pale such efforts seem compared to the deep-seated problems of self-image and family process described above. Can an army of social workers undo the damage of three hundred years by talking and listening without massive changes in the social and economic situations of the families with whom they are to deal? And, if such changes take place, will the social-worker army be needed?

If we are right that present Negro family patterns have been created as adaptations to a particular socioeconomic situation, it would make more sense to change that socioeconomic situation and then depend upon the people involved to make new adaptations as time goes on. If Negro providers have steady jobs and decent incomes, if Negro children have some realistic expectation of moving toward such a goal, if slum Negroes come to feel that they have the chance to affect their own futures and to receive respect from those around them, then (and only then) the destructive patterns described are likely to change. The change, though slow and uneven from individual to individual, will in a certain sense be automatic because it will represent an adaptation to changed socioeconomic circumstances which have direct and highly valued implications for the person.

It is possible to think of three kinds of extra-family change that are required if family patterns are to change; these are outlined below as pairs of current deprivations and needed remedies:

Deprivation effect of caste vicitimization	*Needed remedy*
I. Poverty	Employment income for men; income maintenance for mothers
II. Trained incapacity to function in a bureaucratized and industrialized world	Meaningful education of the next generation
III. Powerlessness and stigmatization	Organizational participation for aggressive pursuit of Negroes' self-interest
	Strong sanctions against callous or indifferent service to slum Negroes
	Pride in group identity, Negro *and* American

Unless the major effort is to provide these kinds of remedies, there is a very real danger that programs to "better the structure of the Negro family" by direct intervention will serve the unintended functions of distracting the country from the pressing needs for socioeconomic reform and providing an alibi for the failure to embark on the basic institutional changes that are needed to do anything about abolishing both white and Negro poverty. It would be sad, indeed, if, after the Negro revolt brought to national prominence the continuing problem of poverty, our expertise about Negro slum culture served to deflect the national impulse into symptom-treatment rather than basic reform. If that happens, social scientists will have served those they study poorly indeed.

Let us consider each of the needed remedies in terms of its probable impact on the family. First, the problem of poverty: employed men are less likely to leave their families than are unemployed men, and when they do stay they are more likely to have the respect of their wives and children. A program whose sole effect would be to employ at reasonable wages slum men for work using the skills they now have would do more than any other possible program to stabilize slum family life. But the wages must be high enough to enable the man to maintain his self-respect as a provider, and stable enough to make it worthwhile to change the nature of his adaptation to his world (no one-year emergency programs will do). Once men learn that work pays off it would be possible to recruit men for part-time retraining for more highly skilled jobs, but the initial emphasis must be on the provision of full-time, permanent unskilled jobs. Obviously it will be easier to do this in the context of full employment and a tight labor market.[40]

For at least a generation, however, there will continue to be a large number of female-headed households. Given the demands of socializing a new generation for non-slum living, it is probably uneconomical to encourage mothers to work. Rather, income maintenance programs must be increased to realistic levels, and mothers must be recognized as doing socially useful work for which they are paid rather than as "feeding at the public trough." The bureaucratic morass which currently hampers flexible strategies of combining employment income and welfare payments to make ends meet must also be modified if young workers are not to be pushed prematurely out of the home.

Education has the second priority. (It is second only because without stable family income arrangements the school system must work against the tremendous resistance of competing life-style adaptations to poverty and economic insecurity.) As Kenneth Clark has argued so effectively, slum schools now function more to stultify and discourage slum children than to stimulate and train them. The capacity of educators to alibi their lack of commitment to their charges is protean. The making of a different kind of generation must be taken by educators as a stimulating and worthwhile challenge. Once the goal has been accepted they must be given the resources with which to achieve it and the flexibility necessary to experiment with different approaches to accomplish the goal. Education must be broadly conceived to include much more than classroom work, and probably more than a nine-months schedule.[41]

If slum children can come to see the schools as representing a really likely avenue of escape from their difficult situation (even before adolescence they know it is the only *possible* escape) then their commitment to school activities will feed back into their families in a positive way. The parents will feel proud rather than ashamed, and they will feel less need to damn the child as a way to avoid blaming themselves for his failure. The sense of positive family identity will be enriched as the child becomes an attractive object, an ego resource, to his parents. Because he himself feels more competent, he will see them as less depriving and weak. If children's greater commitment to school begins to reduce their involvement in destructive or aimless peer-group activities this too will repercuss positively on the family situation since parents will worry less about their children's involvement in an immoral outside world, and be less inclined to deal with them in harsh, rejecting, or indifferent ways.

Cross-cutting the deprivations of poverty and trained incapacity is the fact of powerlessness and stigmatization. Slum people know that they have little ability to protect themselves and to force recognition of their abstract rights. They know that they are looked down on and scape-goated. They are always vulnerable to the slights, insults, and indifference of the white and Negro functionaries with whom they deal—policemen, social workers, school teachers, landlords, employers, retailers, janitors. To come into contact with others carries the constant danger of moral attack and insult.[42] If processes of status degradation within families are to be interrupted, then they must be interrupted on the outside first.

One way out of the situation of impotence and dammed-up in-group aggression is the organization of meaningful protest against the larger society. Such protest can and will take many forms, not always so neat and rational as the outsider might hope. But, coupled with, and supporting, current programs of economic and educational change, involvement of slum Negroes in organizational activity can do a great deal to build a sense of pride and potency. While only a very small minority of slum Negroes can be expected to participate personally in such movements, the vicarious involvement of the majority can have important effects on their sense of self-respect and worth.

Some of the needed changes probably can be made from the top, by decision in Washington, with minimal effective organization within the slum; but others can come only in response to aggressive pressure on the part of the victims themselves. This is probably particularly true of the entrenched tendency of service personnel to enhance their own sense of self and to indulge their middle-class *ressentiment* by stigmatizing and exploiting those they serve. Only effective protest can change endemic patterns of police harassment and brutality, or teachers' indifference and insults, or butchers' heavy thumbs, or indifferent street cleaning and garbage disposal. And the goal of the protest must be to make this kind of insult to the humanity of the slum-dweller too expensive for the perpetrator to afford; it must cost him election defeats, suspensions without pay, job dismissals, license revocations, fines, and the like.

To the extent that the slum dweller avoids stigmatization in the outside world, he will feel more fully a person within the family and better able to function constructively within it since he will not be tempted to make up deficits in self-esteem in ways that are destructive of family solidarity. The "me" of personal identity and the multiple "we" of family, Negro, and American identity are all inextricably linked; a healthier experience of identity in any one sector will repercuss on all the others.

REFERENCES

1. This paper is based in part on research supported by a grant from the National Institutes of Mental Health, Grant No. MH-09189, "Social and Community Problems in Public Housing Areas." Many of the ideas presented stem from discussion with the senior members of the Pruitt-Igoe research staff—Alvin W. Gouldner, David J. Pittman, and Jules Henry—and with the research associates and assistants on the project. I have made particular use of ideas developed in discussions with Boone Hammond, Joyce Ladner, Robert Simpson, David Schulz, and William Yancey. I also wish to acknowledge helpful suggestions and criticisms by Catherine Chilman, Gerald Handel, and Marc J. Swartz. Although this paper is not a formal report of the Pruitt-Igoe research, all of the illustrations of family behavior given in the text are drawn from interviews and observations that are part of that study. The study deals with the residents of the Pruitt-Igoe housing projects in St. Louis. Some 10,000 people live in these

projects which comprise forty-three eleven-story buildings near the downtown area of St. Louis. Over half of the households have female heads, and for over half of the households the principal income comes from public assistance of one kind or another. The research has been in the field for a little over two years. It is a broad community study which thus far has relied principally on methods of participant observation and open-ended interviewing. Data on families come from repeated interviews and observations with a small group of families. The field workers are identified as graduate students at Washington University who have no connection with the housing authority or other officials, but are simply interested in learning about how families in the project live. This very intensive study of families yields a wealth of information (over 10,000 pages of interview and observation reports) which obviously cannot be analyzed within the limits of one article. In this article I have limited myself to outlining a typical family stage sequence and discussing some of the psychosocial implications of growing up in families characterized by this sequence. In addition, I have tried to limit myself to findings which other literature on Negro family life suggests are not limited to the residents of the housing projects we are studying.

2. St. Clair Drake, "The Social and Economic Status of the Negro in the United States," *The Negro American* (Boston, 1966), p. 4.

3. E. Franklin Frazier, *The Negro Family in the United States* (Chicago, 1939), p. 487.

4. Norman Mailer, "The White Negro" (City Light Books, San Francisco, Calif., 1957); and Leslie Fiedler, *Waiting For The End* (New York, 1964), pp. 118-137.

5. See Alvin W. Gouldner, "Reciprocity and Autonomy in Functional Theory," in Llewellyn Gross (ed.), *Symposium of Sociological Theory* (Evanston, Ill., 1958), for a discussion of functional autonomy and dependence of structural elements in social systems. We are suggesting here that lower-class groups have a relatively high degree of functional autonomy *vis à vis* the total social system because that system does little to meet their needs. In general the fewer the rewards a society offers members of a particular group in the society, the more autonomous will that group prove to be with reference to the norms of the society. Only by constructing an elaborate repressive machinery, as in concentration camps, can the effect be otherwise.

6. For example, the lead sentence in a *St. Louis Post Dispatch* article of July 20, 1965, begins "A White House study group is laying the ground work for an attempt to better the structure of the Negro family."

7. See Kenneth Stampp, *The Peculiar Institution* (New York, 1956); John Hope Franklin, *From Slavery to Freedom* (New York, 1956); Frank Tannenbaum, *Slave and Citizen* (New York, 1946); E. Franklin Frazier, *op. cit.;* and Melville J. Herskovits, *The Myth of the Negro Past* (New York, 1941).

8. See Raymond T. Smith, *The Negro Family in British Guiana* (New York, 1956); J. Mayone Stycos and Kurt W. Back, *The Control of Human Fertility in Jamaica* (Ithaca, N. Y., 1964); F. M. Henriques, *Family and Colour in Jamaica* (London, 1953); Judith Blake, *Family Structure in Jamaica* (Glencoe, Ill., 1961); and Raymond T. Smith, "Culture and Social Structure in The Caribbean," *Comparative Studies in Society and History,* Vol. VI (The Hague, The Netherlands, October 1963), pp. 24-46. For a broader comparative discussion of the matrifocal family see Peter Kunstadter, "A Survey of the Consanguine or Matrifocal Family," *American Anthropologist,* Vol. 65, No. 1 (February 1963), pp. 56-66; and Ruth M. Boyer, "The Matrifocal Family Among the Mescalero: Additional Data," *American Anthropologist,* Vol. 66, No. 3 (June 1964), pp. 593-602.

9. Paul C. Glick, *American Families* (New York, 1957), pp. 133 ff.

10. For discussions of white lower-class families, see Lee Rainwater, Richard P. Coleman, and Gerald Handel, *Workingman's Wife* (New York, 1959); Lee Rainwater, *Family Design* (Chicago, 1964); Herbert Gans, *The Urban Villagers* (New York, 1962); Albert K. Cohen and Harold M. Hodges, "Characteristics of the Lower-Blue-Collar-Class," *Social Problems,* Vol. 10, No. 4 (Spring 1963), pp. 303-334; S. M. Miller, "The American Lower Classes: A Typological Approach," in Arthur B. Shostak and William Gomberg, *Blue Collar World* (Englewood Cliffs, N. J., 1964); and Mirra Komarovsky, *Blue Collar Marriage* (New York, 1964). Discussions of Negro slum life can be found in St. Clair Drake and Horace R. Cayton, *Black Metropolis* (New York, 1962), and Kenneth B. Clark, *Dark Ghetto* (New York, 1965); and of Negro community life in small-town and rural settings in Allison Davis, Burleigh B. Gardner, and Mary Gardner, *Deep South* (Chicago, 1944), and Hylan Lewis, *Blackways of Kent* (Chapel Hill, N. C., 1955).

11. For general discussions of the extent to which lower-class people hold the values of the larger society, see Albert K. Cohen, *Delinquent Boys* (New York, 1955); Hyman Rodman, "The Lower Class Value Stretch," *Social Forces,* Vol. 42, No. 2 (December 1963), pp. 205 ff; and William L. Yancey, "The Culture of Poverty: Not So Much Parsimony," unpublished manuscript, Social Science Institute, Washington University.

12. James F. Short, Jr., and Fred L. Strodtbeck, *Group Process and Gang Delinquency* (Chicago, 1965), p. 114. Chapter V (pages 102-115) of this book contains a very useful discussion of differences between white and Negro lower-class communities.

13. Discussions of white lower-class attitudes toward sex may be found in Arnold W. Green, "The Cult of Personality and Sexual Relations," *Psychiatry,* Vol. 4 (1941), pp. 343-348; William F. Whyte, "A Slum Sex Code," *American Journal of Sociology,* Vol. 49, No. 1 (July 1943), pp. 24-31; and Lee Rainwater, "Marital Sexuality in Four Cultures of Poverty," *Journal of Marriage and the Family,* Vol. 26, No. 4 (November 1964), pp. 457-466.

14. See Boone Hammond, "The Contest System: A Survival Technique," Master's Honors paper, Washington University, 1965. See also Ira L. Reiss, "Premarital Sexual Permissiveness Among Negroes and Whites," *American Sociological Review*, Vol. 29, No. 5 (October 1964), pp. 688-698.

15. See the discussion of aleatory processes leading to premarital fatherhood in Short and Strodtbeck, *op. cit.*, pp. 44-45.

16. Rainwater, *And the Poor Get Children, op. cit.*, pp. 61-63. See also, Carlfred B. Broderick, "Social Heterosexual Development Among Urban Negroes and Whites," *Journal of Marriage and the Family*, Vol. 27 (May 1965), pp. 200-212. Broderick finds that although white boys and girls, and Negro girls become more interested in marriage as they get older, Negro boys become *less* interested in late adolescence than they were as preadolescents.

17. Walter Miller, "The Corner Gang Boys Get Married," *Trans-action*, Vol. 1, No. 1 (November 1963), pp. 10-12.

18. Rainwater, *Family Design, op. cit.*, pp. 28-60.

19. Yancey, *op. cit.* The effects of unemployment on the family have been discussed by E. Wright Bakke, *Citizens Without Work* (New Haven, Conn., 1940); Mirra Komarovsky, *The Unemployed Man and His Family* (New York, 1960); and Earl L. Koos, *Families in Trouble* (New York, 1946). What seems distinctive to the Negro slum culture is the short time lapse between the husband's loss of a job and his wife's considering him superfluous.

20. See particularly Komarovsky's discussion of "barriers to marital communications" (Chapter 7) and "confidants outside of marriage" (Chapter 9), in *Blue Collar Marriage, op. cit.*

21. Rainwater, *Family Design, op. cit.*, pp. 305-308.

22. For a discussion of the relationship between Black Nationalist ideology and the Negro struggle to achieve a sense of valid personal identity, see Howard Brotz, *The Black Jews of Harlem* (New York, 1963), and E. U. Essien-Udom, *Black Nationalism: A Search for Identity in America* (Chicago, 1962).

23. Rainwater, Coleman, and Handel, *op. cit.*, pp. 88-102.

24. Cf. Michael Schwartz and George Henderson, "The Culture of Unemployment: Some Notes on Negro Children," in Schostak and Gomborg, *op. cit.*

25. Daniel Patrick Moynihan, "Employment, Income, and the Ordeal of the Negro Family," *The Negro American* (Boston, 1966), pp. 149–50.

26. Talcott Parsons concludes his discussion of child socialization, the development of an "internalized family system" and internalized role differentiation by observing, "The internalization of the family collectivity as an object and its values should not be lost sight of. This is crucial with

respect to . . . the assumption of representative roles outside the family on behalf of it. Here it is the child's family membership which is decisive, and thus his acting in a role in terms of its values for 'such as he.' " Talcott Parsons and Robert F. Bales, *Family, Socialization and Interaction Process* (Glencoe, Ill., 1955), p. 113.

27. Erik H. Erikson, "Identity and the Life Cycle," *Psychological Issues*, Vol. 1, No. 1 (1959).

28. For discussion of the dynamics of the individual's *announcements* and the society's *placements* in the formation of identity, see Gregory Stone, "Appearance and the Self," in Arnold Rose, *Human Behavior in Social Process* (Boston, 1962), pp. 86-118.

29. The importance of identity for social behavior is discussed in detail in Ward Goodenough, *Cooperation and Change* (New York, 1963), pp. 176-251, and in Lee Rainwater, "Work and Identity in the Lower Class," in Sam H. Warner, Jr., *Planning for the Quality of Urban Life* (Cambridge, Mass., forthcoming). The images of self and of other family members is a crucial variable in Hess and Handel's psychosocial analysis of family life; see Robert D. Hess and Gerald Handel, *Family Worlds* (Chicago, 1959), especially pp. 6-11.

30. See the discussion of "masking" and "unmasking" in relation to disorganization and re-equilibration in families by John P. Spiegel, "The Resolution of Role Conflict within the Family," in Norman W. Bell and Ezra F. Vogel, *A Modern Introduction to the Family* (Glencoe, Ill., 1960), pp. 375-377.

31. See the discussion of self-identity and self-esteem in Thomas F. Pettigrew, *A Profile of the Negro American* (Princeton, N. J., 1964), pp. 6-11.

32. Rainwater, Coleman, and Handel, *op. cit.,* pp. 44-51. See also the discussion of the greater level of "anomie" and mistrust among lower-class people in Ephriam Mizruchi, *Success and Opportunity* (New York, 1954). Unpublished research by the author indicates that for one urban lower-class sample (Chicago) Negroes scored about 50 per cent higher on Srole's anomie scale than did comparable whites.

33. For a discussion of the child's propensity from a very early age for speculation and developing explanations, see William V. Silverberg, *Childhood Experience and Personal Destiny* (New York, 1953), pp. 81 ff.

34. See Ralph Ellison's autobiographical descriptions of growing up in Oklahoma City in his *Shadow and Act* (New York, 1964). The quotations at the beginning of this article are taken from pages 315 and 112 of this book.

35. Rainwater, "Work and Identity in the Lower Class," *op. cit.*

36. *Ibid.*

37. Short and Strodtbeck see violent behavior in juvenile gangs as a kind of last resort strategy in situations where the actor feels he has no other choice. See Short and Strodtbeck, *op. cit.,* pp. 248-264.

38. Wiltse speaks of a "pseudo depression syndrome" as characteristic of many AFDC mothers. Kermit T. Wiltse, "Orthopsychiatric Programs for Socially Deprived Groups," *American Journal of Orthopsychiatry,* Vol. 33, No. 5 (October 1963), pp. 806-813.

39. Walter B. Miller, "Lower Class Culture as a Generating Milieu of Gang Delinquency," *Journal of Social Issues,* Vol. 14, No. 3 (1958), pp. 5-19.

40. This line of argument concerning the employment problems of Negroes, and poverty war strategy more generally, is developed with great cogency by James Tobin, "On Improving the Economic Status of the Negro," *Dædalus* (Fall 1965), and previously by Gunnar Myrdal, in his *Challenge to Affluence* (New York, 1963), and Orville R. Gursslin and Jack L. Roach, in their "Some Issues in Training the Employed," *Social Problems,* Vol. 12, No. 1 (Summer 1964), pp. 68-77.

41. See Chapter 6 (pages 111-153) of Kenneth Clark, *op. cit.,* for a discussion of the destructive effects of ghetto schools on their students.

42. See the discussion of "moral danger" in Lee Rainwater, "Fear and the House-as-Haven in the Lower Class," *Journal of the American Institute of Planners,* February 1966 (in press).

ADELAIDE CROMWELL HILL
AND FREDERICK S. JAFFE

Negro Fertility and Family Size Preferences: Implications for Programming of Health and Social Services

The subtlest and most pervasive of all influences are those which create and maintain the repertory of stereotypes. We are told about the world before we see it. We imagine most things before we experience them. And those preconceptions, unless education has made us acutely aware, govern deeply the whole process of perception. . . . There is another reason, besides economy of effort, why we so often hold to our stereotypes when we might pursue a more disinterested vision. The systems of stereotypes may be the core of our personal tradition, the defenses of our position in society. . . . Any disturbance of the stereotypes seems like an attack upon the foundation of the universe. It is an attack upon the foundations of our universe, and, where big things are at stake, we do not readily admit that there is any distinction between our universe and the universe. A world which turns out to be one in which those we honor are unworthy, and those we despise are noble, is nerve-racking. There is anarchy if our order of precedence is not the only possible one. For if the meek should inherit the earth, if the first should be the last, if those who are without sin alone may cast a stone, if to Caesar you render only the things that are Caesar's, then the foundations of self-respect would be shaken for those who have arranged their lives as if these maxims were not true . . . .
—*Walter Lippmann,* Public Opinion

SEVERAL YEARS ago, Cornell sociologist J. Mayone Stycos evaluated fertility control efforts in developing nations and found that a principal obstacle to acceleration of programs is rooted, not simply in objective conditions, but in the *subjective explanations* which the élite and ruling classes of most countries offer for the high fertility of lower-class groups. He identified a complex of related attitudes summed up in the expression, "procreation is the poor man's recreation." These attitudes have three major components: (1) lower-class parents do not *care* how many children they have; or (2) they *want* many children; and (3) they have an *unusually active sex drive* uninhibited by a sense of morality or social responsibility, which derives from their basic "nature," variously defined as primitive, child-like, animal-like, amoral, and/or immoral. Stycos found that, although the evidence in the developing countries at that time (and since reinforced substantially) contradicted each of these postulates, the social policies advocated by the élites followed from their own unfounded preconceptions. Thus they placed less emphasis on measures aimed at modifying economic and social conditions (including the availability of family planning services). Rather, they advocated confronting high fertility among the lower classes primarily by "more direct" measures such as "teaching 'self-control,' reducing sexual frequency by state-provided avenues of sublimation, and the reduction of illegitimacy by legal, religious and social pressures." He concluded that "the initial and perhaps major hurdle" which must be surmounted for the expansion of fertility control in the developing countries is the attitude of their élite ruling classes.[1]

Stycos' model of upper-class stereotypes blocking the development of sound policies and programs is focused on experience with fertility control efforts, but has considerable relevance for a broader range of problems in both the developing countries and the United States. It offers an especially useful insight in the current discussion of the problems of impoverished Negro families stimulated by the Department of Labor study, *The Negro Family: The Case for National Action,* because (1) these problems are most frequently defined precisely in terms of the different fertility behavior of the Negro poor and (2) upper-class biases about lower-class fertility (which Stycos found to be universal in all societies) are in this case reinforced and augmented by racial biases as well.

The basic facts outlining the trend of white-nonwhite fertility changes since World War II are hardly in dispute. The postwar baby boom was the result of increased levels of fertility among all Americans, but was more pronounced among Negro families. Nonwhite fertility increased very rapidly in the late 1940's and continued at quite high levels until 1957, when it began to decline along a path parallel to the decline in white fertility. In the last several years, in fact, there has been a somewhat larger absolute decline in nonwhite fertility rates than in white rates. Nevertheless, in 1963 nonwhite fertility was still 40 per cent higher than white—144.8 births per thousand women aged fifteen to forty-four compared to 103.7.[2]

Through painful experience, demographers have learned to avoid offering simplistic explanations for complex changes over time in fertility behavior. Investigators are currently attempting to elucidate both the causes of the baby boom itself and the widening of fertility differentials by color, which is especially puzzling because it occurred at a time when the nonwhite population was becoming increasingly urbanized, achieving higher educational levels, and improving on some socio-economic indices. These are changes, of course, which in many societies have, in the long run, been associated with declining fertility levels.

To some observers, however, the postwar widening of the fertility gap is "proof" of nothing more or less than an all-pervasive pathology among impoverished Negroes—a pathology which has become internalized, is self-perpetuating, and has produced in "zoological tenements" of the urban ghetto a state of "biological anarchy."[3] Such a conclusion generates "remedies" quite similar to those which Stycos found were advocated by élites in developing nations: more efficacious exhortation of the poor to be more responsible, coupled with a variety of pressures, not excluding punitive and coercive measures (such as compulsory sterilization of mothers of out-of-wedlock children) which have thus far been regarded by most Americans as impermissible.

In the United States, as in the developing countries, the available evidence contradicts the essential premises of this kind of instant demography. A *detailed* examination of recent nonwhite fertility behavior reveals a far different picture—one of considerable underlying (but for the most part thwarted) aspiration for family limitation and upward mobility. It is our view that this is of the highest significance for structuring sound—and humane—programs in a variety of problem areas for those Negro families which are disadvantaged and economically deprived. In this paper, we shall attempt a closer look at nonwhite fertility, summarize research findings on the family size preferences of impoverished Negroes, and assess the fertility and family planning practices of Negro parents in the context of the actual medical services which have been available to them. From this analysis, hopefully, will emerge some implications for both short- and long-term programming of major health and social services to meet the needs of impoverished Negro families.

A Closer Look at Fertility Behavior

Negro families in the United States are not divided simply into a group of relatively successful middle-class families, on the one hand, and a large, undifferentiated group of impoverished and disorganized families on the other. There is a growing group of well-to-do Negroes at the top and a wide variety of types of middle-class families within the Negro community. There are also significant socioeconomic sub-groups among low-income Negro families, as among all families, such as a stable blue-collar working class. Even in a slum, a great diversity of family structure is found.[4]

If likes are to be compared with likes, therefore, it is essential that differential fertility be analyzed among comparable groups. Thorough studies of postwar trends in white-nonwhite fertility reveal that, when various measures of socioeconomic status are held constant, white-nonwhite differences in fertility are either reduced very significantly, eliminated entirely, or, in some cases, even reversed. In Chicago in 1950, "almost all of the difference between white and nonwhite total fertility could be accounted for by differences in socio-economic status."[5] For the nation as a whole in the same year, when fertility rates were compared by educational status, the same result was found.[6] Ten years later, the 1960 census showed that nonwhites with four years of high-school education have about the same number of children as whites with the same amount of education, while those with four years of college have fewer than comparable whites. When fertility is compared by occupational status and income, there is still a gap between white and nonwhite rates. However, the gap is narrowed considerably in the occupation and income categories above the most impoverished level; for example, while nonwhite mothers aged forty-five to forty-nine with incomes below $2,000 have one-third more children than comparable whites, in the income brackets above $3,000 the difference is cut in half.[7]

These analyses strongly suggest that continuing high fertility is more a consequence of the Negro's disproportionately low socioeconomic status than of any other factor. This conclusion is reinforced when one unique variable—Southern farm background with its particular blend of rural and regional influences—is independently traced. Current higher fertility levels among nonwhites are the result partly of the *unusually* high fertility of the minority of nonwhite couples who presently live in the rural South and partly of the *moderately* high fertility of the many nonwhite couples who were born on Southern farms and have since emigrated. "When we come to nonwhite couples with *no* previous southern farm residence, we find average past and expected numbers of births that do not differ significantly from those of white couples. *In other words, by the time nonwhite couples are one generation or more removed from the rural South, their fertility is very much like that of the white population.*"[8] This finding[9] of the 1960 Growth of American Families study is especially significant in light of the fact that Negroes who are one generation or more removed from the rural South are still subject to continuing discrimination in employment, income, housing, education, and health services which does not affect their white counterparts;[10] as St. Clair Drake has so aptly put it, they continue to be victims of "a system of social relations [which] operates in such a way as to deprive them of a chance to share in the more desirable material and non-material products of . . . society [and which deprives them of] the same degree of access which others have to the attributes needed for rising in the general class system."[11]

In addition to the general improvements in economic and social conditions which sparked the overall postwar baby boom, the medical advances of the last several decades appear to have substantially affected the nonwhite rate of population growth in a manner not too different from the way in which sharp reductions in mortality rates have been the prime cause of the population explosion in developing countries. The medical advances which increased significantly the childbearing and infant survival potential of nonwhites include the greater proportion of nonwhite deliveries occurring in hospitals, an increase from approximately 18 per cent of births in 1935 to 89 per cent in 1964; the rapid fall in the incidence of diseases which often caused sterility; and the general decrease in maternal, neonatal, and fetal mortality since 1935.[12] The immediate effect of an increase in childbearing potential among a population "which is not widely employing sophisticated methods of birth control" is a very rapid increase in birth rates.[13]

Finally, much of the fertility differential is explained by a higher proportion of larger families among nonwhites. Fifth order births or higher totalled nearly one-third of all nonwhite births—almost twice the proportion for white women.[14] (However, since 1960, nonwhite rates for fifth and higher order births have declined more rapidly than white rates for similar birth orders.) The significance of this finding is indicated by Mollie Orshansky's observation that "the larger the family, the greater the poverty hazard for children. . . . Of the 15 million children being reared in poverty, 6½ million or 43 per cent were growing up in a home with at least 5 youngsters under age 18. Indeed the poverty rate among families rose sharply from 12 per cent when there was one child in the home to 49 per cent when there were 6 or more children. . . . *The poverty rate for all families with 5 or 6 children is three and a half times as high as for families with 1 or 2 children.*"[15]

Since 1957, both white and nonwhite fertility has declined, but there has been a slightly larger drop in nonwhite rates; between 1959 and 1963 there was a decrease of 11.2 births per thousand nonwhite women aged fifteen to forty-four compared to 10.2 per thousand white women.[16]

The Question of Illegitimacy

Detailed examination of white-nonwhite fertility trends also requires something better than mechanical repetition of the *registered* rates of out-of-wedlock births by color, which are often seized upon to support the image of widespread pathology, rampant sexuality, and galloping family disintegration among Negroes. Apart from the fact that even these registered rates are almost never analyzed by socioeconomic status (which would help to compare likes with likes), it is clear that knowledgeable population scholars have serious doubts of their validity. The expert committee convened by the National Center for Health Statistics and the Census Bureau to scrutinize all aspects of the collection and interpretation of fertility data points out that the published rates are certainly incomplete because some out-of-wedlock births are not registered as such; the committee concludes ruefully that *"the most that can be said* about the illegitimacy figures is that they indicate the minimum extent of illegitimacy."[17] Clearly the opportunity for underregistration and misstatement of legitimacy status is more available to whites than to nonwhites, if only because of the disproportionately greater reliance of nonwhites on public and charity hospitals where concealment is extremely difficult.

There has been one systematic study thus far which attempts to illuminate the extent of white-nonwhite differences in *out-of-wedlock conceptions* (an index that might be more indicative than *registered illegitimate births* of the actual state of differential unmarried sexual activity unprotected by contraception). In this careful study linking marriage certificates and birth records in Detroit, coupled with a mail survey, the ratio found in 1960 was one out-of-wedlock *conception* among whites to three among nonwhites, as compared to a ratio of one to eight for registered illegitimate *births*. The study also showed that while most pregnant whites married *before* the birth of the child, a substantial proportion of nonwhite "illegitimate" children are legitimized *after* birth by subsequent marriage of the natural parents. The investigator concluded that "the dramatic difference between white and nonwhite illegitimate births, then, is as much or more a function of fewer marital resolutions before the birth of the child [among nonwhites] as it is a function of higher illegitimate conceptions." In other words, precipitous marriages among whites and illegitimate births among nonwhites are largely different adjustments to the same underlying trend of rising out-of-wedlock conceptions.[18]

It should be pointed out that even this striking reduction in the color differential does not fully correct the impression given by the illegitimacy statistics, since this study does not take into account the considerably higher proportion of whites who resort to illegal abortion when they become pregnant out of wedlock,[19] nor does it estimate illegitimate births to women *remaining* single which are registered as legitimate. It seems reasonable that if adequate data on differential utilization of abortion and concealment were combined with the findings of this study on forced marriages, the differential between white and nonwhite rates of out-of-wedlock *conceptions* would be reduced even further or might well become negligible, even without controlling for socioeconomic status.

This is not to dismiss the fact that a significant proportion of Negro children are born in a status branded illegitimate, nor to deny the serious social consequences which result. It suggests, however, that formation of sound policies aimed at equalizing the outcomes of out-of-wedlock conceptions can be based only on an honest confrontation of the total reality and not merely a fragment. Despite the vast expressed concern over the increasing incidence of illegitimacy, there is little demand for comprehensive studies which would illuminate the central operative factors: the extent of unmarried sexual activity among different socioeconomic groups, the true incidence of out-of-wedlock pregnancy, and the different adjustments (for example, abortion, concealment, forced marriage, illegitimate birth, adoption) to out-of-wedlock pregnancy. There is in fact considerable resistance to confronting the limited knowledge we do have, as can be seen in the opposition to extending publicly financed family planning services even to unmarried *mothers*, which would help somewhat to equalize access to contraceptive guidance between the unmarried poor and non-poor.

Indeed, perhaps nothing better illustrates élitist and class-biased attitudes, such as Stycos found in the developing countries, than our society's differential treatment of the issues of sexual morality and illegitimacy. Almost without exception, and whatever the author's point of view, books, magazine and newspaper articles, and television shows about sexual morality and/or immorality are concerned with what are regarded as lowered sexual standards in a middle- or upper-class setting (*Sex on Campus, Sex in Suburbia, Sex and the Single Girl, Sex in the Office,* and so on). It is the *changed nature* of the sexual activity itself which is criticised, approved, or explained, and the psychodynamic impact of this change on "relationships" of boy to girl, man to woman, husband to wife. It is striking that the question of illegitimacy is almost never raised in this setting since it is presumed (sometimes wrongly) that middle-class couples have access to effective contraception and, if they slip, to competent abortion. (A report by a distinguished group of psychiatrists on *Sex and the College Student* discusses, matter-of-factly, not merely the availability of contraception—"many college students view contraceptive information as a right that is due them" —but also the resort to abortion either at the hands of illegal practitioners or on dubious legal grounds or in a foreign country where the operation is legal. Apparently these alternatives, and precipitous marriage, dispose of most campus pregnancies since, the report states, "the few unmarried pregnant college women who decide to carry their babies to term usually then give them up for adoption."[20])

In the context of lower-class (and usually nonwhite) behavior, on the other hand, illegitimacy is *always* discussed; it is *never* seen as a different adjustment to the same sexual revolution which has changed the attitudes and practices of all Americans in the last forty years, but rather is presumed to be the outcome of a historic, unchanged, and unchanging lower-class promiscuity that can only be dealt with moralistically and punitively. Deluged by this veritable flood of double-standard literature (Freud and interpersonal relationships for the upper class, Calvin and judgmentalism for the lower), James Baldwin has been led to comment: "White people seem to ask us, if they ask us anything, 'Come into my nightmare with me; be like me; have abortions instead of illegitimate children'."[21] To our knowledge, no one has yet responded to the policy implications of his observation.

Family Size Preferences

It is clear from the data that socioeconomic and educational status, and particularly the influence of fertility patterns of the rural South,. continue to play a decisive role in shaping nonwhite fertility trends. Several investigators[22] suggest that the gap in white-non-white fertility will be narrowed as general socioeconomic conditions improve, as more Negroes move from the rural South, and as higher educational levels are achieved by nonwhites. These conclusions are reinforced by the findings of the 1960 Growth of American Families study which provides, for the first time, a nationwide view of the family size preferences of nonwhite parents. The study demonstrates that nonwhite wives want *fewer* children than white wives. The average number wanted by nonwhite respondents was 2.9, compared to 3.3 by the white wives. (Only the small number of non-white wives currently living on Southern farms expressed a desire for more children than their white counterparts; for the South as a whole, both groups wanted an average of 3.0). Furthermore, 46 per cent of nonwhites said they wanted no more than two children, compared to 29 per cent of whites.[23]

These findings are based on a national sample survey of married women of childbearing age now living with their husbands, but they are confirmed by numerous local studies which investigated family size preferences without regard to formal or present marital status: In Chicago, twice as many nonwhites as whites said they wanted only two children,[24] and 90 per cent of a group of AFDC mothers of out-of-wedlock children said they did not want to have the child;[25] in Florida, 70 per cent of a predominantly Negro group of public-health maternity patients said they wanted to have no more children;[26] in New Orleans, 56 per cent of a sample of very low-income Negroes said they wanted no more than three children, 94 per cent said they thought family planning services should be made available to the medically indigent, and 75 per cent of those between fifteen and thirty-four expressed a desire for more information themselves.[27] Confirmation is also provided by the Greenleigh study of poverty in Detroit, which surveyed 2,081 low-income, largely Negro households to identify the services the impoverished families required to ameliorate poverty. The survey showed that family planning services ranked sixth in a listing of twenty-eight needed services, outranked only by such obvious needs as financial assistance, job training, help with children's school problems, and day-care facilities.[28]

Response to Family Planning Services

The above studies, though demonstrating that impoverished Negro parents almost uniformly express a strong desire for effective family limitation, may perhaps be viewed with skepticism because they represent mere verbal expression. They are, however, confirmed by the response of impoverished Negro parents in those communities where family planning services are made available to them with dignity, energy, and skill. Privately organized Planned Parenthood centers in some 120 communities are still the main birth-control clinics available to low-income families in the U.S.; among the 282,000 patients served by these centers in 1964, the largest single ethnic group—47 per cent—was Negro. The birth-control program initiated by the District of Columbia Health Department is described as "one of the most popular programs that we have."[29] In two hospital clinics operated by the University of Buffalo Medical School for low-income patients, 88 per cent of the patients are nonwhite—a significantly higher proportion than in the hospitals' other medical services.[30] Similar findings are reported from North Carolina,[31] Grady Hospital in Atlanta, Georgia, and in the fourteen birth-control clinics located in New York City's municipal hospitals which have experienced a remarkable increase of more than 150 per cent in new patients seen during the last year alone.[32] In a hospital-centered maternity care project in Augusta, Georgia, a nurse tells of the response of patients to the offer of contraception: "Almost everyone who is told about it wants it."[33] In Chicago, nonwhite birth rates dropped 22 per cent in the last five years—an "extraordinary" decline —as a result of an intensive program of birth-control service and education; the differential between white and nonwhite fertility has declined by one fourth.[34]

Perhaps the most significant finding to date is contained in a recently published study from the Chicago Planned Parenthood clinic of more than 14,000 low-income patients on oral contraception; 83 per cent of the patients were nonwhite, nearly half had not completed high school, one out of six were welfare recipients. Between 70 and 83 per cent of the patients (72 to 84 per cent of non-white patients) continued to take the pills regularly thirty months after they came to the clinic.[35] This is an astonishingly high retention rate for *any* procedure requiring continuous self-administration of medication, and is testimony to the readiness of the poor generally, and particularly the Negro poor, to respond to well-conceived, energetically-delivered voluntary programs employing modern contraceptive methods.

The operative consideration here lies in the combination of proper conception and energetic delivery of the service.[36] The most successful demonstration programs have, to one degree or another, been considerably different from the kind of medical care which impoverished Negroes normally receive. Instead of compelling patients to sit for hours on end in dingy waiting rooms, appointments are often scheduled (as in private practice) and efforts are made to offer a bright and cheerful atmosphere. Many clinics are located in the heart of impoverished neighborhoods, not halfway across town, and sessions may be scheduled at night or other unusual times to fit patients' needs. Staff members are urged to refrain from imposing their attitudes and values upon patients, and non-professional workers have been employed to interpret to potential patients how family planning can help them to realize *their* desires about family size. Baby-sitting services are sometimes provided. Fees are adjusted to what the patient can afford. And, perhaps most significant, clinics are not segregated by color.

Medical Care for the Negro Poor

Through these and other fairly simple innovations, efforts have been made in the best clinics to approach the atmosphere of mutual respect and understanding which governs private medical practice, and impoverished Negro parents have responded. But they have not often been given the opportunity. While most Americans of higher income are easily able to secure competent and sympathetic guidance in fertility control from their private physicians, if they desire it, the Negro poor have to depend very heavily on charity or tax-supported medical facilities which for the most part still do not make family planning services available.

This denial is but one aspect of what Commissioner Alonzo S. Yerby has vividly described as "a two class system of health care" that gives the poor medical services which are piecemeal, inadequate, underfinanced, uncoordinated, and offered without compassion or concern for the dignity of the individual.[37] But the Negro poor do not share equally even in this inferior system of medical care, though there is ample evidence that their health needs are greatest. Citing current rates of perinatal mortality as an example, Yerby demonstrates that "in terms of health, there is a special disadvantage to being a Negro in the United States which transcends being poor."[38]

The net effect of this double discrimination is to discourage impoverished Negroes from seeking preventive and diagnostic medical care, and to confine their care to those emergency and chronic conditions which make medical services absolutely necessary.[39] Among those who do get some medical care, one out of three visits to a physician among Negroes occurs in a hospital outpatient clinic, compared to one out of ten among whites.[40] Even this understates the extent of the deprivation in regard to family planning services, since Negroes rely more heavily on public or charity medical facilities during the childbearing period when the subject of family planning normally comes up. Data from the National Center for Health Statistics shows that in 1963–4, 48.6 per cent of nonwhite hospitalizations for delivery were in government institutions, compared to 23.7 per cent of white hospitalizations.[41] In New York City between 1955 and 1959, 82 per cent of married nonwhites delivered their babies in municipal hospitals or on ward services of voluntary hospitals, compared with 14.5 per cent of whites.[42] In Washington, D.C. in 1961, 75 per cent of nonwhite births were staff cases.[43] In 1961, 57 per cent of Negro live births in California occurred in county hospitals, compared to 13 per cent of white.[44] The 1961 report of the Obstetrical Statistical Cooperative, based on 66,000 discharges at approximately twenty hospitals in New York, New Haven, Hartford, Philadelphia, San Francisco, Baltimore, and other cities, showed that nearly 94 per cent of nonwhite deliveries were on ward service, compared to 35 per cent of whites.[45]

These figures make clear that the vast majority of nonwhite mothers do not have ready access to a private physician during the childbearing period. They help explain the findings of the 1960 GAF study that, despite their expressed interest in family limitation, only 59 per cent of nonwhite couples had used *some* method of fertility control, compared to 81 per cent of whites, and that nonwhites relied much more on methods which are relatively low in effectiveness (douche, jelly, and vaginal suppositories) and do not require "medical advice which is generally less available to nonwhite than to white wives."[46] The 1960 study, of course, was conducted before the introduction of oral pills and intrauterine devices which, in the clinical reports noted above, have proved to be particularly acceptable to low-income couples generally[47]—but which require competent medical guidance and prescription.

Thus the denial of birth-control services to the Negro poor is an integral part of the denial of adequate medical services in general and during the child-bearing period in particular—a discrimination which has contributed to the continuation of doubled and quadrupled rates of infant and maternal mortality for nonwhites as compared to whites. Furthermore, the higher rate of nonwhite fertility, caused in part by unequal access to adequate fertility control services, in turn tends to keep these mortality rates high, since maternal and infant mortality and morbidity increase significantly with increasing parity and with shorter intervals between births.[48]

Implications for Programs for the Disadvantaged Negro Family

These, then, are some of the main features of the current Negro fertility picture. Fertility levels among Negroes are substantially higher than whites, reflecting the disproportionately low socioeconomic status of the Negro community and particularly the influence of Southern farm background. Negro parents in all socioeconomic groups (except the few now living on Southern farms) express a consistent desire for smaller families than do whites. In those few communities where skillful and sympathetic birth control services have been made available to impoverished Negroes, the response has been considerable. Adequate instruction in fertility control, however, is still beyond the reach of the poor because tax-supported and charity medical agencies do not yet generally offer these services. The Planned Parenthood Federation of America estimates that there are some five million American women in impoverished families—about one-fourth Negro—who are in their child-bearing years, fertile, and not pregnant or seeking a pregnancy at any given time, and who thus may be considered the minimum patient load for subsidized contraceptive services in the United States. Approximately 500,000 of these women are estimated to receive contraceptive services either from Planned Parenthood Centers or public agencies, leaving 4.5 million women not now being served.[49]

What are the implications of these related findings for programming of health and social services?

First, it seems clear that voluntary family planning services must be made available to impoverished Americans generally, including the Negro poor, in order to give them a genuine opportunity to carry out *their* desires in regard to family size. The implementation of comprehensive family planning services should result, fairly rapidly, in fewer unwanted conceptions and, over a longer term, in reduced rates of maternal and infant mortality and morbidity. Many observers believe that there would also be significant social consequences, such as a decrease in desertion and divorce, as more couples learn that it is possible to control at least part of their life circumstances.[50]

Family planning is not a panacea for all the problems of poverty and dependency, nor is it a substitute for massive social programs to enable impoverished Negroes to obtain jobs, increase income levels, enlarge educational opportunities, and otherwise improve their living conditions. But the reduction of poverty and dependency will be slowed significantly, no matter how comprehensive these programs, unless the poor, white and nonwhite, are also able to have only the number of children they want. In the spectrum of urgently needed programs, family planning is one which is achievable relatively quickly and easily: With modern methods, we have sufficient knowledge and technology; it is a relatively simple and inexpensive aspect of medical care; the number of patients to be served is quite limited; and, most important, the poor have shown considerable readiness to respond to this service.[51] It is not necessary to remold basic attitudes or develop new aspirations among many impoverished Negroes, but to provide the means of realizing aspirations they already have.

This does not mean that *any* kind of program will work automatically. If the program is proffered with racist overtones, if it is coupled with constant threats to sterilize unmarried mothers on welfare, if it is presented as a punitive means of reducing relief costs, and if the mere request for birth control is taken as *prima facie* evidence that there's a "man in the house," thus jeopardizing the woman's eligibility for public assistance, the response is likely to be negligible. Moreover, this kind of program gives credence to those groups in the Negro community who reject family planning as an effort by the white majority to reduce Negro power. In spite of these vocal attacks by some individuals and nationalist organizations, it is significant that militant Negro political figures have given outstanding leadership during the last several years in campaigns to modify restrictive laws or liberalize public policies on birth control in such states as New York, Illinois, Michigan, Maryland, and Wisconsin.

A second implication of this analysis is that the extension of birth-control services will require a very considerable expansion in the maternity care services—and in the full spectrum of health services—which are available to the Negro poor. This expansion must involve both the development of additional facilities and considerable improvements in the quality and comprehensiveness of the services provided, and in the arrangements for their organization and delivery. In other words, it will require significant movement toward ending the "two class system," certainly as far as maternity care is concerned.

The Modernization Process

Expansion of family planning services and improvements in maternity care would directly affect fertility itself. We believe, however, that there are less obvious underlying implications for a much wider range of services. Here it may be useful to draw on the understanding, which is emerging among students of population problems in the developing countries, of the "basic unity of the modernization process."[52] This concept, which means that economic and social development on the one side and declining fertility on the other are integrally related parts of the same process of modernization, may be of use in understanding the full significance of the expressed desires of the Negro poor for effective family limitation. For the concept is based upon the premise that social, cultural and psychological readiness for fertility control does not and cannot take place unless it is a part of social, cultural, and psychological readiness for general economic and social development. In simple terms, the readiness of parents for family planning reveals a desire to insure a better life for the children—a theme which is repeated continually in interviews among parents in all countries and ethnic groups who express an interest in fertility control. Thus the readiness of the Negro poor for family limitation confirms Hylan Lewis' finding that "a major aspiration of low-income parents for their children is to see that their children do better in life—especially in jobs, education and family behavior—than they have been able to do themselves."[53]

That impoverished Negroes have profound hopes for their children's futures ought to be obvious in the light of the civil rights revolution. Yet in most health, social, and educational services, it is often maintained that the poor and the Negro poor are "unmotivated" to take advantage of services which they need and would benefit by. It is our view that the expressed and demonstrated readiness of the Negro poor for fertility control is but one aspect of a readiness for a wide variety of measures aimed at improving mobility, and suggests that the response will be considerable to genuine services which are properly organized and delivered.[54] The task is to use our intelligence, imagination, and affluence to restructure existing service systems—health, welfare, education, and so forth—in order to fulfill these hopes and not thwart them.

Far from revealing disintegration and unrelieved pathology, current trends in Negro fertility attitudes and behavior suggest a substantial reservoir of aspiration and indeed of strength on which positive service programs for impoverished Negro families can be based. In this country, as in the developing nations, such programs can be developed only with a genuine understanding of real human beings in the real world, and not with élitist stereotypes which, in the United States too, appear to be "the initial and perhaps major hurdle" to be surmounted.

The authors wish to acknowledge with gratitude the suggestions and criticisms of Arthur A. Campbell, National Center for Health Statistics; Lisbeth Bamberger, Office of Economic Opportunity; Bruce Jessup, M.D., Department of Health, Education, and Welfare; Lincoln Day, Yale University; and the following staff members of Planned Parenthood Federation; Steven Polgar; Mrs. Naomi Thomas Gray; Mrs. Jeannie Rosoff; and Richard Lincoln.

References

1. J. M. Stycos, "Obstacles to Programs of Population Control—Facts and Fancies," *Marriage and Family Living*, Vol. 25, No. 1 (February 1963).

2. A. S. Lunde, "White-Nonwhite Fertility Differentials in the United States," *Health, Education and Welfare Indicators*, September 1965.

3. T. H. White, *The Making of the President 1964* (New York, 1965), pp. 221–242.

4. Cf. H. Lewis, "Child Rearing Among Low-Income Families," reprinted in L. A. Ferman *et al.* (ed.), *Poverty in America* (Ann Arbor, Mich., 1965);

and "The Family: Resources for Change," Agenda Paper prepared for Planning Session for the White House Conference "To Fulfill These Rights," November 1965.

5. E. M. Kitagawa and P. M. Hauser, "Trends in Differential Fertility and Mortality in a Metropolis—Chicago," in E. W. Burgess and D. Bogue (eds.), *Contributions to Urban Sociology* (Chicago, 1964), pp. 74–75.

6. A. and E. Lee, "The Future Fertility of the American Negro," *Social Forces*, Vol. 37, No. 3 (March 1959), p. 229.

7. Lunde, *op. cit.*, p. 28.

8. A. A. Campbell, "Fertility and Family Planning Among Nonwhite Married Couples in the United States," *Eugenics Quarterly* Vol. 12, No. 3 (September 1965), pp. 126, 131. Emphasis added.

9. The 1960 census confirms the findings of sample surveys which show that the excess of nonwhite over white fertility is concentrated in the South. While all ever-married nonwhite women aged eighteen to thirty-nine, regardless of socioeconomic status, living outside the South had only 11 per cent more children than white women, the differential in the South was 42 per cent, ranging from 34 per cent in southern urban areas to 64 per cent on southern farms. *1960 Census PC (1)-1D, Table 249.*

10. It would be interesting to study comparable segments of the major immigrant groups—for example, Irish, Italians, Northern Europeans, Eastern Europeans, and Jews, who came from rural backgrounds—to determine how long it took these groups to approximate the childbearing patterns of urban America, and which groups achieved this adaptation within one generation after arriving in the United States.

11. St. Clair Drake, "The Social and Economic Status of the Negro in the United States," *The Negro American* (Boston: Houghton Mifflin, 1966), p. 4.

12. Cf. especially R. Farley, "Recent Changes in Negro Fertility," paper presented at Population Association of America, April 1965. The relative difference between white and nonwhite rates of maternal, neonatal and fetal mortality has in fact increased since 1950, but nonwhite rates were in absolute terms so high in the mid-30's that the decline was significant enough to enhance nonwhite childbearing potential; for example nonwhite maternal mortality declined from 875.8 per 100,000 live births in 1935–39 to 98.1 in 1963.

13. Farley, *op. cit.*

14. Lunde, *op. cit.*, p. 31.

15. M. Orshansky, "Who's Who Among the Poor: A Demographic View of Poverty," *Social Security Bulletin* (July 1965), pp. 14–15, emphasis added.

16. *Vital Statistics of the United States, 1963*, Volume I, "Natality," Table 1-2, pp. 1–4.

17. National Center for Health Statistics, *Fertility Measurement: A Report of the United States National Committee on Vital and Health Statistics* (September 1965), p. 8, emphasis added.

18. W. F. Pratt, "Premarital Pregnancy in a Metropolitan Community," paper presented at Population Association of America, April 1965. Since nonwhites have repeated out-of-wedlock births more often than whites, the published rates of illegitimate *births* give a misleading impression of the numbers of *women* involved. When repeaters are taken into account, the color differential is reduced even further: Pratt found that in Detroit the proportion of nonwhite *women* ever experiencing illegitimate conception is only about twice as high as among whites.

19. P. H. Gebhard et al., *Pregnancy, Birth and Abortion* (New York, 1958).

20. Group for the Advancement of Psychiatry, *Sex and the College Student* (New York, 1965), pp. 43–55.

21. *Life*, May 24, 1963.

22. Lunde, *op. cit.*; Lee and Lee, *op. cit.*; Farley, *op. cit.*

23. P. K. Whelpton, A. A. Campbell and J. Patterson, *Fertility and Family Planning in the United States* (Princeton, N. J., 1966).

24. A. O. Blair, "A Comparison of Negro and White Fertility Attitudes," Master's Thesis submitted at University of Chicago, 1963.

25. Greenleigh Associates, *Facts, Fallacies and Future*, 1960.

26. R. L. Browning and L. L. Parks, "Childbearing Aspirations of Public Health Maternity Patients," *American Journal of Public Health*, Vol. 54 (November 1964), p. 1831.

27. J. D. Beasley, M.D., C. L. Harter and A. Fischer, "Attitudes and Knowledge Relevant to Family Planning Among New Orleans Negro Females," paper presented at American Public Health Association, October 1965.

28. Greenleigh Associates, *Home Interview Study of Low-Income Households in Detroit, Michigan*, 1965.

29. M. Grant, M.D., Testimony, *Hearings on District of Columbia Appropriations for 1966—H.R. 6453*, Subcommittee of Committee on Appropriations, U.S. Senate, 1965, p. 590.

30. J. Lippes, M.D. and C. L. Randall, M.D., "Participation of Area Hospitals in Family Planning," in S. Polgar and W. Cowles (eds.), Public Health Programs in Family Planning, a supplement to *American Journal of Public Health*, January 1966.

31. E. Corkey, M.D. "A Family Planning Program for the Low-Income Family," *Marriage and the Family*, Vol. 26, No. 4 (November 1964).

32. A. S. Yerby, M.D., personal communication.

33. K. Close, "Giving Babies a Healthy Start in Life," *Children*, Vol. 12, No. 5 (September-October 1965), p. 181.

34. D. Bogue, *West Side Fertility Report*, Community and Family Study Center, University of Chicago (in press).

35. R. Frank, M.D., and C. Tietze, M.D., "Acceptance of an oral contraceptive program in a large metropolitan area," *American Journal of Obstetrics and Gynecology*, Vol. 93 (September 1, 1965), p. 122. The difference between 70 per cent and 83 per cent is explained by assignment of the small number of patients lost to follow-up, with the lower figure representing the minimum number of continuing users and the larger the maximum.

36. Cf. N. T. Gray, *Recruiting Low-Income Families for Family Life Education Programs*, Child Study Association, 1965, and J. S. Martin, M.D., "The Implementation of Family Planning: Experiences In an Urban Community," paper presented at District V, American College of Obstetricians and Gynecologists, Cleveland, October 30, 1965.

37. A. S. Yerby, M.D., "The Disadvantaged and Health Care," paper presented at White House Conference on Health, November 3, 1965, and "The Problems of Medical Care for Indigent Populations," *American Journal of Public Health*, Vol. 55, (August 1965), p. 1212. Cf also M. A. Glasser, "Extension of Public Welfare Medical Care: Issues of Social Policy," *Social Work* (October 1965); L. H. Berry, M.D., "Disadvantaged Populations," paper presented at White House Conference on Health, November 3, 1965; and A. Yankauer, "Maternal and Child Health Problems," *The Annals* (September 1964).

38. "The Disadvantaged and Health Care," *op. cit.*

39. W. Cowles and S. Polgar, "Health and Communication in a Negro Census Tract," *Social Forces*, Vol. 10, No. 3 (Winter, 1963).

40. National Center for Health Statistics, *Volume of Physician Visits by Place of Visit and Type of Service—U.S. July 1963-June 1964*, June 1965, p. 8.

41. P. S. Lawrence, personal communication (special tabulation of data from National Center for Health Statistics).

42. J. Pakter *et al.*, "Out of Wedlock Births in New York City, No. 1—Sociologic Aspects," *American Journal of Public Health*, Vol. 51, No. 5 (May 1961).

43. E. Oppenheimer, "Population Changes and Perinatal Mortality," *American Journal of Public Health*, Vol. 51, No. 2 (January 1961).

44. State of California, Department of Public Health Birth Records.

45. Obstetrical Statistical Cooperative, *1961 Combined Report*.

46. Campbell, *op. cit.*, p. 129.

47. Workers in Planned Parenthood centers credit the doubling of patient loads in the last five years to the much greater acceptability of the new methods among low-income couples. For a discussion of the importance of type of contraceptive method in understanding family planning behavior of the poor, see S. Polgar, "The Impact of New Contraceptive Methods in Impoverished Neighborhoods of New York," paper presented at Population Association of America, April 1965.

48. These relationships were demonstrated in classic studies by such investigators as Jacob Yerushalmy in the early '40's. The extensive recent literature has been summarized in F. S. Jaffe and S. Polgar, "Medical Indications for Fertility Control," Planned Parenthood Federation of America, 1964 (mimeographed).

49. F. S. Jaffe, "Financing Family Planning Services," *American Journal of Public Health* (in press).

50. Without attempting to state a causal relationship for which adequate studies have not been done, Orshanky (*op. cit.*, p. 16) comments on the interaction between high fertility and family breakdown: "What cannot be said is how often the poverty itself may have antedated and even contributed to the family dissolution. Age for age, mothers without a husband present have borne more children than women still living with a husband. Knowing that it is often the worker with low earnings potential who has the larger family, one can only wonder about the possible relation between too many children, too little family income and the breakup of a marriage." See also Lewis, "The Family: Resources for Change," *op. cit.*, p. 7.

51. Cf. F. S. Jaffe, "Family Planning, Public Policy and Intervention Strategy," *Journal of Social Issues* (in press).

52. I. Taeuber, "Future Population Trends," paper presented at United Nations World Population Conference, September 1965.

53. "The Family: Resources for Change," *op. cit.*, p. 18.

54. The potentially strategic role of medical agencies is suggested by Greenleigh (*Home Interview Study, op. cit.*, p. 10) and by Dean Julius Richmond who observes: "Health personnel with an interest and competence in dealing with the social problems of their patients, and operating in a setting providing personalized, dignified care, may find they have a unique entree to helping families to deal with their social and psychological problems." ("Infants and Children," paper presented at White House Conference on Health, November 3, 1965).

III

DIAGNOSTIC FACTORS:
PERSONALITY, IDENTITY, AND
ATTITUDES

ERIK H. ERIKSON

The Concept of Identity in Race Relations: Notes and Queries

Introductory Remark

THE FOLLOWING notes represent an expansion of the remarks on the concept of identity which I was asked to make in November 1964 at the meeting of the committee gathered to plan the issues of *Dædalus* devoted to the Negro American. Shortly after that meeting, I undertook a trip abroad in order to interview the surviving witnesses and to study the remaining documents of what seemed, when the study was first planned, a long-past episode in a faraway country, namely, one of Gandhi's nonviolent campaigns. I am now returning to my fragmentary contribution to this symposium for the very reason that the concept or at least the term identity seems not only to have pervaded the literature on the Negro revolution in this country, but also to have come to represent in India (and in other countries) something in the psychological core of the revolution of the colored races and nations who seek inner as well as outer emancipation from colonial rule and from the remnants of colonial patterns of thought. When, for example, Nehru said (as I have been told) that "Gandhi gave India an identity," he obviously put the term into the center of that development of a nonviolent technique, both religious and political, by which Gandhi strove to enhance a unique unity among Indians while insisting on their complete autonomy within the British Empire. But what did Nehru mean?

R. P. Warren, in his *Who Speaks for the Negro?* reacts to the first (but by no means last) mention of the word by one of his informants with the exclamation:

I seize the word *identity*. It is a key word. You hear it over and over again. On this word will focus, around this word will coagulate, a dozen issues, shifting, shading into each other. Alienated from the world to which he is born and from the country of which he is a citizen, yet surrounded by the successful values of that world, and country, how can the Negro define himself?[1]

Usually, the term is used without explanation as if it were obvious what it means; and, indeed, faddish as the word has become, it has also come to mean to many something both profound and unfathomable.

Social scientists sometimes attempt to make it more concrete. However, if they do not quickly equate it with the strangely pat question "Who am I?" they make such words as "identity crisis," "self-identity," or "sexual identity" fit whatever they are investigating. For the sake of logical or experimental maneuverability (and in order to keep in good academic company) they try to treat these terms as matters of social roles, personal traits, or conscious self-images, shunning the less manageable and the less obscure (and often more sinister) implications of the concept. Its use has, in fact, become so indiscriminate that the other day a German reviewer (of a new edition of my first book in which I first used the term in the context of psychoanalytic ego theory) called the concept the pet subject of the *amerikanische Popularpsychologie*. As we might say in American popular psychology: that does it. I return to the subject because (in spite of slogan-like misuse and lip service) it does seem to speak to the condition of many serious observers at this juncture of history. I will try to explain some of its dimensions and relate them to what can only be approximate illustrations from race-relations. I will claim no further status for this effort than "notes and queries"[2] within a symposium, that is, in a context in which what will be referred to here as a *revolution of awareness* can be seen against the background of what Gandhi called the "four-fold ruin" wrought by political and economic as well as cultural and spiritual degradation; for surely, power, or at least the power to choose, is vitally related to identity. In this context, I shall emphasize rather than minimize the alternatives and controversies, the ambiguities and ambivalences concerning various aspects of the identity issue.

I. *Individual and Communal*

At a time when the term identity refers, more often than not, to a more or less desperate quest, or even (as in the case of the Negro American) to something mostly negative or absent ("invisible," "inaudible," "unnamed"), it may be well to introduce the subject with quotations from two men who asserted strongly what identity feels like when you become aware of it. My two witnesses are the bearded and patriarchal founding fathers of the kind of psychology on which this writer's thinking on identity is based. As a *subjective sense* of an *invigorating sameness* and *continuity,* what I would call a sense of identity seems to me best described by William James in a letter to his wife. "A man's character," he wrote, "is discernible in the mental or moral attitude in which, when it came upon him, he felt himself most deeply and intensely active and alive. At such moments there is a voice inside which speaks and says: '*This* is the real me!' " Such experience always includes

"an element of active tension, of holding my own, as it were, and trusting outward things to perform their part so as to make it a full harmony, but without any *guaranty* that they will. Make it a guaranty—and the attitude immediately becomes to my consciousness stagnant and stingless. Take away the guaranty, and I feel (provided I .am *uberhaupt* in vigorous condition) a sort of deep enthusiastic bliss, of bitter willingness to do and suffer anything . . . and which, although it is a mere mood or emotion to which I can give no form in words, authenticates itself to me as the deepest principle of all active and theoretic determination which I possess. . . ."[3]

James uses the word "character," but I am taking the liberty of claiming that he describes what today we would call a sense of identity, and that he does so in a way which can in principle be experienced by any man. To him it is both mental and moral (the last a word also often swallowed up by ours); and he experiences it as something that "comes upon you" as a re-cognition, almost as a surprise rather than as something strenuously "quested" after. It is an active tension (rather than a paralyzing question)—a tension which, furthermore, must create a challenge "without guaranty" rather than one dissipated in a clamor for certainty. But let us remember in passing that James was in his thirties when he wrote this, that he had faced and articulated an "identity crisis" of honest and desperate depth, and that he became *the* Psychologist-Philosopher of American Pragmatism only after having attempted to integrate other cultural, philosophic, and professional identity elements.[4]

One can study in James' life history the emergence of a "self-made" identity in a new and expansive civilization. But for a statement of that unity of *personal and cultural* identity which is rooted in an ancient people's fate we turn to Sigmund Freud. In an address to the Society of B'nai B'rith in Vienna in 1926 he said:

> What bound me to Jewry was (I am ashamed to admit) neither faith nor national pride, for I have always been an unbeliever and was brought up without any religion though not without a respect for what are called the "ethical" standards of human civilization.
>
> Whenever I felt an inclination to national enthusiasm I strove to suppress it as being harmful and wrong, alarmed by the warning examples of the peoples among whom we Jews live. But plenty of other things remained over to make the attraction of Jewry and Jews irresistible—many obscure emotional forces, which were the more powerful the less they could be expressed in words, as well as a clear consciousness of inner identity, the safe privacy of a common mental construction. And beyond this there was a perception that it was to my Jewish nature alone that I owed two characteristics that had become indispensable to me in the difficult course of my life. Because I was a Jew I found myself free from many prejudices which restricted others in the use of their intellect; and as a Jew I was prepared to join the Opposition and to do without agreement with the "compact majority."[5]

No translation ever does justice to the grandiose choice of words in Freud's German original. "Obscure emotional forces" are *"dunkle Gefuehlsmaechte"*; the "safe privacy of a common mental construction" is *"die Heimlichkeit der inneren Konstruktion"*—not just "mental," then, and certainly not "private," but a deep communality known only to those who share in it.

This quotation takes on new meaning in the context for which this is written, for *this* "consciousness of inner identity" includes a sense of bitter pride preserved by a dispersed and often despised people throughout a long history of alternating persecution and re-establishment. It is anchored in a particular (here intellectual) gift which had victoriously emerged from the suppression of other opportunities. At the same time, it should not be overlooked (for we will need to refer back to it later) that this *positive identity* is seen against the background of a *negative* counterpart in all "the peoples among whom we Jews live," namely, "prejudices which restrict others in the use of their intellect." Identity here is one aspect of the struggle for ethnic survival: one person's or group's identity may be relative to another's; and identity awareness may have to do with matters of an *inner emancipation* from a more dominant identity, such as the "compact majority." An exquisite triumph is suggested in the claim that the same historical development which restricted the prejudiced in the free use of their intellect made those discriminated against freer and sturdier in intellectual matters.

These two statements (and the life-histories behind them) serve to establish a first dimension of identity which immediately helps to explain why it is so tenacious and yet so hard to grasp: for here we deal with something which can be experienced as "identical" *in the core of the individual* and yet also identical *in the core of a communal culture,* and which is, in fact, the identity of those two identities.

But we can also see that this is a matter of *growth,* both personal and communal. For a mature psychosocial identity presupposes a community of people whose traditional values become significant to the growing person even as his growth and his gifts assume relevance for them. Mere "roles" which can be "played" interchangeably are not sufficient; only an integration of roles which foster individual vitality within a vital trend in the existing or developing social order can support identities. (We may speak, then, of a *complementarity* of an *inner synthesis* in the individual and of *role integration* in his group.)

In all their poetic spontaneity these two statements prove to be the product of trained minds and therefore exemplify the main dimensions of a positive sense of identity almost systematically: from here one could proceed in a number of directions. But since these utterances are taken not from theoretical works, but from special communications (a letter to his wife from a man who married late; an address to his "brothers" by an observer long isolated in his field), it would seem most fitting now to quote corresponding voices among Negroes. But the mere contemplation of the task reveals two difficulties. The corresponding statements of Negro authors are couched in terms so negative that they at first suggest an absence of identity or the prevalence of what we will call *negative* identity elements. From Du Bois' famous passage (quoted in Myrdal's introduction to *Dark Ghetto*)[6] on the *inaudible* Negro, we would be led to Baldwin's and Ellison's very titles suggesting *invisibility, namelessness, facelessness.* But I would not approach these themes as a mere plaintive expression of the Negro American's sense of "nobody-ness," a social role which, God knows, was his heritage. Rather, I would tend to interpret the desperate and yet determined pre-occupation with invisibility on the part of these creative men as a demand to be heard and seen, recognized and faced as *individuals with a choice* rather than as men marked by what is all too superficially visible, namely, their color (and by the stereotypes which go with it). In a haunting way they defend an existing but in some ways voiceless identity against the stereotypes which hide it. They are involved in a battle to reconquer for their people, but first of all (as writers must) for themselves, what Vann Woodward calls a "surrendered identity." I like this term because it does not assume total absence as many contemporary writings do, something to be searched for and found, to be granted or given, to be created or fabricated, but something to be liberated. This will be emphasized in this paper because I consider it to be an actuality, and thus the only bridge from past to future.

I almost quoted Ellison as saying that his writing was indeed an attempt to transcend "as the blues transcended the painful conditions with which they deal." But I stopped myself; and now I have quoted him to show up a second difficulty. Except for extraordinary moments of lucidity, all self-images and images of otherness (and, yes, even the blues) change their connotation kaleidoscopically before our eyes and in our discussions; and no writer of today can escape this. To have something to hold on to, we all use stereotypes temporarily endowed with ideological connotations which are a measure of Negro or white distance from the thoughtless accommodation to the postslavery period from which we are all emerging. What before was a more unconscious mixture of guilt and fear on the white side, and a mixture of hate and fear on the other, is now being replaced by the more conscious and yet not always more practical sentiments of remorse and mistrust. We have, at the moment, no choice but to live with those stereotypes and these affects: confrontation will disprove some of them, history dissolve others. In the meantime, it may be helpful to bring some concepts to bear on this problem so that the kaleidoscope may reveal patterns as well as bewildering changes.

II. *Conscious and Unconscious*

A "sense of identity" obviously has conscious aspects, such as the experience of an increased unity of the physical and mental, moral and sensual selves, and of a oneness in the way one experiences oneself and the way others seem to experience us. But this process *can* also be visible to others, for he who "knows where he is going and who is going with him" demonstrates an unmistakable, if not always easily definable, unity and radiance of appearance, physiognomic as well as postural. And yet, just when a person, to all appearances, seems to "find himself," he can also be said to be "losing himself" in new tasks and affiliations. He transcends identity-consciousness; and this is surely so in the early days of any revolution and was so in the case of the young of the Negro revolution who found themselves and, in fact, found their generation in the very decision to lose themselves (as well as all guaranty) in the intensity of the struggle. Here identity-consciousness is absorbed in actuality. There are vivid and moving descriptions of this state (none more so than in Howard Zinn's account of the early days of SNCC).[7] Afterwards, no doubt, these at first anonymous heroes faced redoubled self-consciousness, a kind of double-take on the stage of history. Conversely, Negroes who must now prove themselves in the sober light of a more integrated day cannot escape a self-consciousness which is apt to interfere with the happiness of finding or losing oneself: there are and there will be the martyrs of self-chosen or accidentally aggravated identity-consciousness, who must sacrifice the innocent unity of living to a revolutionary awareness.

But the core of that inner unification called identity is at best (as we psychoanalysts would say) *pre-conscious,* that is, accessible only to musings at moments of special awareness or to the revelatory experiences of intuitive writers. Mostly it is *unconscious* and even repressed, and hereby related to all those unconscious conflicts to which only psychoanalysis has found a methodical access. Thus the concept not only is difficult to work with; it also arouses deep-seated "resistances," which must be pointed out not in the hope of doing away with them (for they are an intricate and insurmountable part of the problem of human awareness), but in order to get acquainted with a shadow which will always follow us.

"Resistance" is a term from psychoanalytic treatment proper. There it indicates a "technical" problem met with in the therapeutic attempt to induce an individual to recognize the nature (or sometimes the very fact) of his illness, to describe his thoughts freely, and to accept the interpretations given to him. But the term has also been used in a wider sense in order to characterize a general resistance to psychoanalytic insights or, indeed, to "psychic reality" itself. However, the widespread acceptance of psychoanalysis (or of what Freud is understood to have said or is reported to have said) and the freer commission of sexual and verbal acts, the omission of which is now considered to be a symptom of repression, have not done away with a more fundamental aspect of "resistance," for it concerns the relation of man's awareness to his need for a free will, and thus something in the core of man's identity. This resistance can come to awareness in vague discomfort, often the more gnawing as it contradicts our professed interest in enlightenment:

1. If unconscious determinants should, indeed, prove operative in our very sense of self and in the very pathos of our values, does this not carry the matter of determination to a point where free will and moral choice would seem to be illusory?

2. If a man's individual identity is said to be linked to communal identities, are we not faced with another crypto-Marxism which makes man's very sense of destiny a blind function of the dialectics of history?

3. And if such unconscious determinants could, indeed, be demonstrated, is such awareness good for us?

Philosophers, no doubt, have answers to these questions, which recur in the reactions of the best-trained students when faced somewhat more systematically with insights which they otherwise devour eagerly in a non-systematic mixture of paperbacks.[8] But it must be clear that nobody can escape these questions which are really only part of a wider trend in the scrutiny of human motivation ranging from Darwin's discovery of our evolutionary animal ancestry and Marx's uncovery of class-bound behavior, to Freud's systematic exploration of the unconscious. The preoccupation with identity, therefore, may be seen not only as a symptom of "alienation," but also as a corrective trend in psychosocial evolution. It may be for this reason that revolutionary writers and writers from national and ethnic minority groups (like the Irish expatriots or our Negro and Jewish writers) have become the artistic spokesmen and prophets of identity confusion. Artistic creation, as pointed out, goes beyond complaint and exposure; it includes the moral decision that a certain painful identity-consciousness may have to be tolerated in order to provide the conscience of man with a critique of conditions, with the insight and with the conceptions necessary to heal himself of what most deeply divides and threatens him, namely, his division into what we will call *pseudo-species*.

In this new literature, pre-conscious processes are faced and unconscious ones symbolized in a way which often resembles the process of psycho-analysis; but the "case" is transcended by human revolt, the inner realignment by intense contact with historical actuality. And, in the end, are these writers not proclaiming also an essential superiority of identity-in-torment over those identities which feel as safe and remote as a suburban home?

What is at stake here is nothing less than the realization of the fact and the obligation of man's specieshood. Great religious leaders have attempted to break through the resistances against this awareness, but their churches have tended to join rather than shun the development which we have in mind here, namely, man's deep-seated conviction that some providence has made his tribe and race or class, caste, or religion "naturally" superior to others. This seems to be part of a psychosocial evolution by which he has developed into *pseudo-species*. This fact is, of course, rooted in tribal psychology and based on all the evolutionary changes which brought about man. Among these is his prolonged childhood during which the newborn, "naturally" born to be the most "generalist" animal of all and adaptable to widely differing environments, becomes specialized as a member of a human group with its complex interplay of an "inner world" and an ethological environment. He becomes indoctrinated, then, with the conviction that his "species" alone was planned by an all-wise deity, created in a special cosmic event, and appointed by history to guard the only genuine version of humanity under the leadership of elect élites and leaders. "Pseudo" suggests pseudologia, a form of lying with at least transitory conviction; and, indeed, man's very progress has swept him along in a combination of developments in which it seems hard to bring to bear what rationality and humanity he can muster against illusions and prejudices no longer deserving of the name mythology. I mean, of course, that dangerous combination of technological specialization (including weaponry), moral righteousness, and what we may call the *territoriality of identity*, all of which make *hominem hominis lupum* far exceeding anything typical for wolves among wolves. For man is not only apt to lose all sense of species, but also to turn on another subgroup with a ferocity generally alien to the "social" animal world and, of course, with an increasing sophistication in all three—lethal weaponry, moral hypocrisy, and identity-panic. Sophistication, in fact, seems to escalate the problem just at the time when (and this would seem to be no coincidence) a more universal, a more inclusive human identity seems forcefully suggested by the very need for survival. National-socialist Germany is the most flagrant and all too recent manifestation of the murderous mass-pseudologia which can befall a modern nation.

While we all carry with us trends and tendencies which anchor our identities in some pseudo-species, we also feel in our bones that the Second World War has robbed such self-indulgence of all innocence, and that any threat of a third one would lead man's adaptative genius to its own defeat. But those who see what the "compact majority" continues to deny and to dissimulate must also attempt to understand that for man to realize his specieshood and to exchange a wider identity for his pseudo-species, means not only the creation of a new and shared technological universe, but also the out-growing of prejudices which have been essential to all (or almost all) identities in the past. For each *positive identity* is also defined by *negative* images (as we saw even in Freud's reference to the intellectual components of his identity), and we must now discuss the unpleasant fact that our god-given identities often live off the degradation of others.

III. *Positive and Negative*

As I restudied Freud's address, I remember a remark made recently by a warm-hearted and influential American Jew: "Some instinctive sense tells every Jewish mother that she must make her child study, that his intelligence is his pass to the future. Why does a Negro mother not care? Why does she not have the same instinctive sense?" This was a rhetorical question, of course; he wanted to know which of many possible answers I would give first. I suggested that, given American Negro history, the equivalent "instinctive sense" may have told the majority of Negro mothers to keep their children, and especially the gifted and the questioning ones, away from futile and dangerous competition, that is, for survival's sake to keep them in their place even if that place is defined by an indifferent and hateful "compact majority."

That the man said "mothers" immediately marks one of the problems we face in approaching Negro identity. The Jewish mothers he had in mind would expect to be backed up by their husbands or, in fact, to act in their behalf; the Negro mothers would not. Negro mothers are apt to cultivate the "surrendered identity" forced on Negro men for generations. This, so the literature would suggest, has reduced the Negro to a reflection of the "negative" recognition which surrounded him like an endless recess of distorting mirrors. How his positive identity has been undermined systematically—first under the unspeakable system of slavery in North America and then by the system of enslavement perpetuated in the rural South and the urban North—has been extensively, carefully, and devastatingly documented.

Here the concept of a negative identity may help to clarify three related complications:

1. Every person's psychosocial identity contains a hierarchy of positive *and* negative elements, the latter resulting from the fact that the growing human being, throughout his childhood, is presented with evil prototypes as well as with ideal ones (by reward and punishment, by parental example, and by the community's typology as revealed in wit and gossip, in tale and story). These are, of course, culturally related: in the background which gives prominence to intellectual achievement, some such negative roles as the Schlemihl will not be wanting. The human being, in fact, is warned *not* to become what he often had no intention of becoming so that he can learn to anticipate what he must avoid. Thus, the positive identity (far from being a static constellation of traits or roles) is always in conflict with that past which is to be lived down and by that potential future which is to be prevented.

2. The individual belonging to an oppressed and exploited minority, which is aware of the dominant cultural ideals but prevented from emulating them, is apt to fuse the negative images held up to him by the dominant majority with his own negative identity. The reasons for this exploitability (and temptation to exploit) lie in man's very evolution and development as pseudo-species. There is ample evidence of "inferiority" feelings and of morbid self-hate in all minority groups; and, no doubt, the righteously and fiendishly efficient way in which the Negro slave in America was forced into and kept in conditions preventing in most the incentive for independent ambition now continues to exert itself as a widespread and deep-seated inhibition to utilize equality even where it is "granted." Again, the literature abounds in descriptions of how the Negro, instead, found escape into musical or spiritual worlds or expressed his rebellion in compromises of behavior now viewed as mocking caricatures, such as obstinate meekness, exaggerated childlikeness, or superficial submissiveness. And yet, is "the Negro" not often all too summarily and all too exclusively discussed in such a way that his negative identity is defined *only* in terms of his defensive adjustments to the dominant white majority? Do we (and can we) know enough about the relationship of positive and negative elements *within* the Negro personality and *within* the Negro community? This alone would reveal how negative is negative and how positive, positive.

3. As yet least understood, however, is the fact that the oppressor has a vested interest in the negative identity of the oppressed because that negative identity is a projection of his own unconscious negative identity—a projection which, up to a point, makes him feel superior but also, in a brittle way, whole. The discussion of the pseudo-species may have clarified some of this. But a number of questions remain. One comes to wonder, for example, about the ways in which a majority, suddenly aware of a vital split in itself over the fact that it has caused a near-fatal split in a minority, may, in its sudden zeal to regain its moral position and to face the facts squarely, inadvertently tend to *confirm* the minority's negative image of itself and this in the very act of dwelling exclusively and even self-indulgently upon the majority's sins. A clinician may be forgiven for questioning the curative values of an excessive dose of moral zeal. I find, for example, even the designation "culturally deprived" somewhat ironic (although I admire much of the work done under this banner) because I am especially aware of the fact that the middle-class culture, of which the slum children are deprived, deprives some of the white children of experiences which might prevent much neurotic maladjustment. There is, in fact, an exquisite poetic justice in the historical fact that many white young people who feel deeply deprived *because* of their family's "culture" find an identity and a solidarity in living and working with those who are said to be deprived for lack of such culture. Such confrontation may lead to new mutual insights; and I have not, in my lifetime, heard anything approaching the immediacy of common human experience revealed in stories from today's South (and from yesterday's India).

In this connection we may also ask a question concerning the measurements used in diagnosing the Negro American's condition; and diagnosis, it must be remembered, defines the prognosis, and this not least because it contributes to the patient's self-awareness and attitude toward his suffering.

Our fellow panelist Thomas Pettigrew, in his admirable compilation *A Profile of the Negro American,* employs identity terms only in passing. He offers a wealth of solid and all the more shocking evidence of the disuse of the Negro American's intelligence and of the disorganization of his family life. If I choose from the examples reported by Pettigrew one of the most questionable and even amusing, it is in order to clarify the place of single testable *traits* in the whole *configuration* of an individual's development and of his people's history.

Pettigrew, following Burton and Whiting, discusses the problem that

[Boys] from fatherless homes must painfully achieve a *masculine self-image* late in their childhood after having established an original self-image on the basis of the only parental model they have had—their mother. Several studies point to the applicability of this *sex-identity problem* to lower-class Negro males.

He reports that

Two objective test assessments of widely different groups—Alabama jail prisoners and Wisconsin working-class veterans with tuberculosis—found that Negro males scored higher than white males on a *measure of femininity*. . . . This measure is a part of the Minnesota Multiphasic Inventory (MMPI), a well-known psychological instrument that requires the respondent to judge the applicability to himself of over five hundred simple statements. Thus, Negroes in these samples generally agreed more often with such "feminine" choices as, "*I would like to be a singer*" and "*I think that I feel more intensely* than most people do."[9]

Pettigrew wisely puts "feminine" in quotation marks. We will assume that the M.M.P.I. is an "objective test assessment for widely different groups" including Alabama jail prisoners and patients on a tubercular ward, and that incidental test blemishes in the end all come-out-in-the-wash of statistics so that the over-all conclusions may point to significant differences between Negroes and whites and between indices of femininity and of masculinity. That such assessment singles out as "feminine" the wish to be a singer and "feeling more intensely than most people do," may be a negligible detail. And yet, this detail suggests that the choice of test items and the generalizations drawn from them may say at least as much about the test and the testers as about the subjects tested. To "want to be a singer" or "to feel intensely" seems to be something only a man with feminine traits would acknowledge in that majority of respondents on whom the test was first developed and standardized. But why, one wonders, should a lower-class Negro locked up in jail or in a tuberculosis ward not admit to a wish to be a man like Paul Robeson or Harry Belafonte, and also that he feels more intensely (if, indeed, he knows what this means) than the chilly business-like whites around him? To be a singer and to feel intensely may be facets of a masculine ideal gladly admitted if you grew up in Alabama (or, for that matter, in Napoli), whereas it would be a blemish to be denied in a majority having adjusted to other masculine ideals. In fact, in Alabama and in Naples an emphasis on artistic self-expression and intense feeling may be close to the core of your positive identity—so close that the loss or devaluation of such emphasis by way of "integration" may make you a drifter on the murky sea of adjustable "roles." In the case of the compact white majority, the denial of "intense feelings" may, in turn, be part of a white identity problem which contributes to the prejudiced rejection of the Negro's potential or periodical intensity. Tests harboring similar distinctions may be offering "objective" evidence of racial differences, but may also be symptomatic of them. If this is totally overlooked, and this is my main point, the test will only emphasize, and the tester will only report, and the reader of the report (white or Negro) will only perceive the distance between the Negro's "disintegrated" self-imagery and what is assumed to be the white's "integrated" one.

As Pettigrew (in another connection) says starkly, putting himself in the shoes of a Negro child to be tested:

> . . .After all, an intelligence test is a middle-class white man's instrument; it is a device whites use to prove their capacities and get ahead in the white world. Achieving a high test score does not have the same meaning for a lower-status Negro child, and it may even carry a definite connotation of personal threat. In this sense, scoring low on intelligence measures may for some talented Negro children be a rational response to perceived danger[10]

The whole *test-event* thus itself underlies a certain historical and social relativity to be clarified in each case in terms of the actual identity configuration. By the same token, it is by no means certain that the individual undergoing such a procedure will be the same person when he escapes the predicament of the test procedure and joins, say, his peers on the playground or on a street corner. Thus, a "profile" of the Negro American made up of different methods under different conditions may offer decisively different configurations of "traits." This does not make one procedure wrong and the other right, but it makes both (and more) essential in the establishment of criteria for an existing identity configuration. On the other hand, it is all too often taken for granted that the *investigator* (and his identity conflicts) invisibly blends into his method even when he is a representative of a highly (and maybe defensively) verbal subgroup of whites and is perceived as such by subjects who are near-illiterate or come from an illiterate background.

In this connection, I would like to refer to Kenneth Clark's moving characterization of the sexual life of the "marginal young people in the ghetto." As a responsible father-figure, he knows he must not condone what he nevertheless must also defend against deadly stereotypes.

Illegitimacy in the ghetto cannot be understood or dealt with in terms of punitive hostility, as in the suggestion that unwed mothers be denied welfare if illegitimacy is repeated. Such approaches obscure, with empty and at times hypocritical moralizing, the desperate yearning of the young for acceptance and identity, the need to be meaningful to someone else even for a moment without implication of a pledge of undying fealty and foreverness. . . .To expose oneself further to the chances of failure in a sustained and faithful relationship is too large to risk. The *intrinsic value* of the relationship is the only value because there can be no other.[11]

This places a legal or moral item into its "actual" context—a context which always also reveals something about those who would judge and stereotype rather than understand: for is not the *intrinsic value of the relationship* exactly that item (hard to define, hard to test, and legally irrelevant) which may be lost in some more fortunate youths who suffer under a bewildering and driving pluralism of values?[12]

IV. *Past and Future*

Turning now to the new young Negroes: "My God," a Negro woman student exclaimed the other day in a small meeting, "what am I supposed to be integrated *out of?* I laugh like my grandmother—and I would rather die than not laugh like that." There was a silence in which you could hear the stereotypes click; for even laughter had now joined those aspects of Negro culture and Negro personality which have become suspect as the marks of submission and fatalism, delusion and escape. But the young girl did not give in with some such mechanical apology as "by which I do not mean, of course . . ." and the silence was pregnant with that immediacy of joint experience which characterizes moments when an identity conflict becomes palpable. It was followed by laughter —embarrassed, amused, defiant.

To me, the young woman had expressed one of the anxieties attending a rapid reconstitution of identity elements: "supposed to" reflects a sense of losing the active, the choosing role which is of the essence in a sense of identity as a continuity of the living past and the anticipated future. I have indicated that single items of behavior or imagery can change their quality within new identity configurations; and yet these same indices once represented an integration as well as an integrity of Negro life—"such as it was," to be sure, but the only existing inner integration for which the Negro is now "supposed to" exchange an unsure outer integration. Desegregation, compensation, balance, re-conciliation—do they all sometimes seem to save the Negro at the cost of an absorption which he is not sure will leave much of himself left? Thus the "revolution" poses an "identity crisis" in more than one way; the Negro writer's "complicated assertions and denials of identity" (to use Ellison's words) have simpler antecedents, not less tragic for their simplicity.

For identity development has its time, or rather two kinds of time: a *developmental stage* in the life of the individual, and a *period* in history. There is, then, also a complementarity of life-history and history. Unless provoked prematurely and disastrously (and the biographies of sensitive Negro writers as well as direct observations of Negro children attest to such tragic prematurity) psychosocial identity is not feasible before the beginning, even as it is not dispensable after the end of *adolescence,* when the body, now fully grown, grows together into an individual appearance; when sexuality, matured, seeks partners in sensual play and, sooner or later, in parenthood; when the mind, fully developed, can begin to envisage a career for the individual within a historical perspective—all idiosyncratic developments which must fuse with each other in a new sense of sameness and continuity. But the increasing irreversibility of all choices (whether all too open or foreclosed) leads to what we call the *identity crisis* which here does not mean a *fatal turn* but rather (as in drama and in medicine) an *inescapable turning point* for better *or* for worse. "Better" here means a confluence of the constructive energies of individual and society, which contributed to physical grace, sexual spontaneity, mental alertness, emotional directness, and social "actualness." "Worse" means prolonged *identity confusion* in the young individual. Here it must be emphasized—for this is the point at which the psychosexual theories of psychoanalysis fuse with the psychosocial ones—that identity formation is decisive for the integration of sexuality (whether the cultural trend is toward repression or expression) and for the constructive use of aggression. But the crisis of youth is also the crisis of a generation and of the ideological soundness of its society. (There is also a complementarity of identity and ideology). The crisis is least marked and least "noisy" in that segment of youth which in a given era is able to invest its fidelity[13] in an ideological trend associated with a new technical and economic expansion, (such as mercantilism, colonialism, industrialization). For here new types and roles of competence emerge. Today this includes the young people in all countries and in all classes who can fit into and take active charge of technical and scientific development, learning thereby to identify with a lifestyle of testing, inventing, and producing. Youth which is eager for such experience but unable to find access to it will feel estranged from society, upset in its sexuality, and unable to apply its aggression constructively. It may be that today much of Negro Youth as well as an artistic-humanistic section of White Youth feel disadvantaged and, therefore, come to develop a certain solidarity in regard to "the crisis" or "the revolution": for young people in privileged middle-class homes as well as in underprivileged Negro homes may miss that sameness and continuity throughout development which makes a grandmother's warmth and a fervent aspiration part of an identical world. One may go further and say that this whole segment of American youth is attempting to develop its own ideology and its own rites of confirmation by following the official call to the external frontiers of the American way of life (Peace Corps), by going to the internal ones (deep South), or by attempting in colleges (California) to fill an obvious void in the traditional balance of the American way of life—a void caused by a dearth of that realism, solidarity, and ideology which welds together a functioning radical opposition.

We will come back to this point. Here we may suggest that identity also contains a complementarity of past and future both in the individual and in society: it links the actuality of a living past with that of a promising future. This formulation excludes, I hope, any romanticizing of the past or any salesmanship in the creation of future "postures."

In regard to "the revolution" and its gains, one can only postulate that the unblinking realism and ruthless de-masking of much of the present literature supports a new sense of toughness in the "face of reality." It fits this spirit that Pettigrew's "Profile," for example, fails to list such at any rate untestable items as (in alphabetical order) companionability, humor, motherhood, music, sensuality, spirituality, sports, and so forth. They all are suspect, I know, as traits of an accommodation romanticized by whites. But this makes presently available "profiles" really the correction of caricatures, rather than attempts at even a sketch of a portrait. But can a new or renewed identity emerge from corrected caricatures? One thinks of all those who are unable to derive identity gains from the "acceptance of reality" at its worst (as the writers do and the researchers) and to whom a debunking of all older configurations *may* become a further *confirmation*[14] of worthlessness and helplessness.

It is in this context also that I must question the fact that in many an index the Negro father appears *only* under the heading of "absence." Again, the relationship between family disintegration, father-absence, and all kinds of social and psychiatric pathology is overwhelming. "Father absence" does belong in every index and in the agenda of national concern. But as the *only* item related to fatherhood *or* motherhood does it not do grave injustice to the presence of many, many mothers, and at least some of the fathers? Whatever the historical, sociological, or legal interpretation of the Negro mother's (and grandmother's) saving presence in the whole half-circle of plantation culture from Venezuela through the Caribbean into our South, is it an item to be omitted from the agenda of the traditional Negro identity? Can Negro culture afford to have the "strong mother" stereotyped as a liability? For a person's (and a people's) identity begins in the rituals of infancy, when mothers make it clear with many pre-literate means that to be born is good and that a child (let the bad world call it colored or list it as illegitimate) is deserving of warmth. As I pointed out in the *Dædalus* issue on Youth, these mothers have put an indelible mark on "Negro Culture" and what they accomplished should be one of the proudest chapters in cultural history.

The systematic exploitation of the Negro male as a domestic animal and the denial to him of the status of responsible fatherhood are, on the other hand, two of the most shameful chapters in the history of this Christian nation. For an imbalance of mother-and-father presence is never good, and becomes increasingly bad as the child grows older; for then the trust in the world established in infancy may be all the more disappointed. Under urban and industrial conditions it may, indeed, become the gravest factor in personality disorganization. But, again, the "disorganization" of the Negro family must not be measured solely by its distance from the white or Negro middle-class family with its one-family housing and legal and religious legitimizations. Disintegration must be measured and understood also as a distortion of the *traditional* if often unofficial *Negro family pattern*. The traditional wisdom of the mothers will be needed as will the help of the Negro men who (in spite of such circumstances) actually did become fathers in the full sense.

In the meantime, the problem of the function of both parents, each strong in his or her way, and both benignly present in the home when needed most is a problem facing the family in any industrial society on a universal scale. The whole great society must develop ways to provide equality of opportunity in employment and yet also differential ways of permitting mothers and fathers to attend to their duties toward their children. The maternal-paternal dimension may well also serve to clarify the fact that each stage of development needs its own optimum environment, and that to find a balance between maternal and paternal strength means to assign to each a period of dominance in the children's life. The mother's period is the earliest and, therefore, the most basic. There is a deep relation between the first "identity" experienced in the early sensual and sensory exchanges with the mother(s)—the first re-cognition—and that final integration in adolescence when all earlier identifications are assembled and the young person meets his society and his historical era.

V. *Total and Whole*

In his book *Who Speaks for the Negro?* R. P. Warren records another exclamation by a young woman student:

. . .The auditorium had been packed—mostly Negroes, but with a scattering of white people. A young girl with pale skin, dressed like any coed anywhere, in the clothes for a public occasion, is on the rostrum. She is leaning forward a little on her high heels, speaking with a peculiar vibrance in a strange irregular rhythm, out of some inner excitement, some furious, taut élan, saying: "—and I tell you I have discovered a great truth. I have discovered a great joy. I have discovered that I am black. I am black! You out there—oh, yes, you may have black faces, but your hearts are white, your minds are white, you have been whitewashed!"

Warren reports a white woman's reaction to this outburst and surmises that if this woman

at that moment heard any words in her head, they were most likely the echo of the words of Malcolm X: "White devils!" And if she saw any face, it must have been the long face of Malcolm X grinning with sardonic certitude.

I think we understand this fear. She has witnessed what I will call a "totalistic" re-arrangement of images which is, indeed, basic to some of the ideological movements of modern history. By totalism I mean an inner regrouping of imagery, almost a *negative conversion*, by which erstwhile negative identity elements become totally dominant, making out of erstwhile positive elements a combination to be excluded totally.[15] This, however, can happen in a transitory way in many young people of all colors and classes who rebel and join, wander off or isolate themselves; it can subside with the developmental storm or lead to an unexpected commitment. Depending on historical and social conditions, the process has its malignant potentials, as exemplified in "confirmed" pervert-delinquent or bizarre-extremist states of mind and forms of behavior.

The chill which this process can give us in its political implications refers back to our sense of historical shock when post-Versailles German youth, once so sensitive to foreign critique, but then on the rebound from a love of Kultur which promised no realistic identity, fell for the Nazi transvaluation of civilized values. The transitory Nazi identity, based on a *totalism* marked by the radical *exclusion* of foreign otherness, failed to integrate historically given identity elements, reaching instead for a pseudologic perversion of history. Obviously both radical segregationism, in its recourse to an adjusted Bible, and Black Muslimism are the counterparts of such a phenomenon in this country. In the person of Malcolm X the *specific rage* which is aroused wherever identity development loses the promise of a traditionally assured wholeness, was demonstrated theatrically. Such latent rage (by no means always unjustified) is easily exploited by fanatic and psychopathic leaders: it can explode in the arbitrary destructiveness of mobs; and it can in a more repressed form serve the efficient violence of organized machines of destruction. Yet, the Black Muslims, too, were able to call on some of the best potentials of the individuals who felt "included."

This country as a whole, however, is not hospitable to such totalistic turns, and the inability or, indeed, unwillingness of youth in revolt to come to systematic ideological conclusions is in itself an important historical fact. The temporary degeneration of the Free Speech Movement in California into a revolt of dirty words was probably representative of the intrusion of an impotent totalism into a promising radicalism. This reluctance to be regimented in the service of a political ideology, however, can make the latent violence in our disadvantaged youth that much more destructive to personal unity and, sporadically, to "law and order." But note also, that the rate of crime and of delinquency in some Southern counties was reported to have dropped sharply when the Negro population became involved in social protest.

The alternative to an exclusive totalism is the wholeness of a *more inclusive identity*. This leads to another question: If the Negro American wants to "find" that wider identity which will permit him to be self-certain as a Negro (or a descendant of Negroes) *and* integrated as an American, what joint *historical actuality* can he count on? For we must know that when all the *objective realities* are classified and investigated, and all the studies assessed, the question remains: what are the *historical actualities* with which we can work?

Returning once more to the individual, I can now register a certain impatience with the faddish equation of the term identity with the question "Who am I?" This question nobody would ask himself except in a more or less transient morbid state, in a creative self-confrontation, or in an adolescent state sometimes combining both; wherefore on occasion I find myself asking a student who claims that he is in an "identity-crisis," whether he is complaining or boasting. For most, the pertinent question really is "What do I want to make of myself—and—what do I have to work with?" Here, the awareness of inner motivations is, at best, useful in keeping the future from being swamped by infantile wishes and adolescent defenses. Beyond that, only a restored or better trained sense of historical actuality can lead to a deployment of those energies which both activate and are activated by potential developments. How potential developments become historical fact is demonstrated by the way in which "culturally deprived" Negro children meet a sudden historical demand with surprising dignity and fortitude. In an unpublished manuscript, Robert Coles, who has made significant contributions to this problem, presents psychiatric data which (according to our theories) would have predicted for a lone Negro boy an inevitable and excusable failure in his task of personifying (with one other child) the desegregation of a whole school. But he did stand up to it unforgettably—and he is on his way.

In all parts of the world the struggle now is for anticipatory and *more inclusive identities*: what has been a driving force in revolutions and reformations, in the founding of churches and in the building of empires has become a contemporaneous world-wide competition. Revolutionary doctrines promise the new identity of peasant-and-worker to the youth of countries which must overcome their tribal, feudal, or colonial past; new nations attempt to absorb regions; new markets, nations; and world space is extended to include outer space as the proper locale for a universal technological identity.

At this point, we are beyond the question (and Gandhi did much to teach this to the British) of how a remorseful or scared colonialist may dispense corrective welfare in order to appease the need for a wider identity. The problem is rather how he includes himself in the wider pattern. For a more inclusive identity is a development by which two groups who previously had come to depend on each other's negative identities (by living in a traditional situation of mutual enmity or in a symbiotic accommodation to one-sided exploitation) join their identities in such a way that new potentials are activated in both.

VI. *Exclusive and Inclusive*

What wider identities are competing for the Negro American's commitment? Some, it seems, are too wide to be "actual," some too narrow. As too wide I would characterize the identity of a "human being" bestowed, according to a strange modern habit of a latter-day humanistic narcissism, by humans to humans (patients, women, Negroes, and so on). While this at times represents genuine transcendence of the pseudo-species mentality, it often also implies that the speaker, having undergone some revelatory hardships, is in a position to grant membership in humanity to others. But it also tends to take all specificity out of "human" relations; for man meets man always in categories (be they adult and child, man and woman, employer and employee, leader and follower, majority and minority) and "human inter-relations" can truly be only the expression of divided function and the concrete overcoming of the specific ambivalence inherent in them. I would not be surprised to find that our Negro colleagues and friends often sense a residue of species-wide colonialism in our vague humanity. In contrast, the concrete work on the achievement of minimum rights for the *Negro American citizen* has created moments of the most intense sharing of the human condition.

Probably the most inclusive and the most absorbing identity potential in the world today is that of *technical skill*. This is what Lenin meant when he advocated that first of all the mushik be put on a tractor. True, he meant: as a preparation for the identity of a class-conscious proletarian. But it has come to mean more today, namely, the participation in an area of activity and experience which (for better or for worse) verifies modern man as a worker and planner. It is one thing to exclude oneself from such verification because one has proven oneself gifted in other respects and able to draw on the traditional verification provided by Humanism or the Enlightenment—at least sufficiently so that alienation from the present, too, adds up to some reasonably comfortable "human identity." It is quite another to be excluded from it by literacy requirements which prevent the proof that one is mechanically gifted or the use of the gift after such proof is given. Israel, a small country with a genius for renewing identities, has shown (for example, in the use of its army as an educational institution) that illiteracy can be corrected in the process of putting people where they feel they are needed and are needed.

The *"African identity"* is a strong contender for a wider identity, as Harold Isaacs has shown. It offers a highly actual setting for the solidarity of black skin color, and probably also provides the American Negro with an equivalent of what all other Americans could boast about or disavow: an (if ever so remote) homeland. However, the American Negro's mode of separation from Africa robbed him of the identity element *"immigrant."* There seems to be a question also whether to Africans a Negro American is more black or more American, and whether the Negro American, in actual contacts with Africans, wants to be more American or more Negro. The Black Muslims, at any rate, seem to have called themselves at first Asiatics, to emphasize the wider mystical unity of Muslimism.

The great *middle class* as the provider of an identity of consumers (for whom, indeed, Pettigrew's prescription of "dollars and dignity" seems to be most fitting) has been discussed in its limitations by many, but by none more eloquently than by the President in his Howard University speech. The middle-class identity (a class pre-occupied with matters of real estate and of consumption, of status and of posture) will include more and more of the highly gifted and the fortunate, but, if it does not yield to the wider identity of the Negro American, it obviously creates new barriers between these few and the mass of Negroes, whose distance from white competition is thereby only increased. "Work and dignity" may be a more apt slogan, provided that work dignifies by providing a "living" dollar as well as a challenge to competence, for without both "opportunity" is slavery perpetuated.

But here as everywhere the question of the Negro American's identity imperceptibly shades into the question of what *the* American wants to make of himself in the technology of the future. In this sense, the greatest gain all around (and one now to be consolidated) may be what the doctors at Howard University have discussed as *pro-social action* on the part of Negroes. I mean the fact that their protest, pervaded by nonviolent spirit and yet clearly defying local law and custom, has been accepted by much of the nation as American, and that the President himself would echo the slogan "we shall overcome," thus helping to align "pro-social" action with American action. The judiciary and legislative levels, too, have attempted to absorb "the revolution" on a grand scale. But absorption can be defensive and merely adjustive, or it can be adaptive and creative; this must as yet be seen.

In the meantime, the success of pro-social action should not altogether obscure an *anti-social* identity element relevantly recounted in the autobiographies of Negro Americans. I mean the tragic sacrifice of youth designated as delinquent and criminal. They, no doubt, often defended whatever identity elements were available to them by revolting in the only way open to them—a way of vicious danger, and yet often of self-respect and solidarity. Like the outcast heroes of the American frontier, some anti-social types among the Negroes are not expendable from the history of their people—not yet.

Our genuinely humanist youth, however, will continue to extend a *religious identity element* into race-relations: for future over-all issues of identity will include the balance within man of technological strivings and ethical and ultimate concerns. I believe (but you must not tell them for they suspect such words) that the emergence of those youths who stepped from utter anonymity right into our national affairs does contain a new and *wider religious element* embracing nothing less than the promise of a mankind freer of the attitudes of a pseudo-species: that utopia of universality proclaimed as the most worthy goal by all world religions and yet always entombed in new empires of dogma which turned into or allied themselves with new pseudo-species. The churches, too, have come to the insight that earthly prejudices—fanatical or outspoken, hiding in indifference, or latent and repressed—feed into that deadly combination which now makes man "the lethal factor" in the universe, for as pointed out it ties limitless technical ambition (including the supremacy of weapons of annihilation) and the hypocrisy of outworn moralistic dogma to the territoriality of mutually exclusive identities. The counter force, *nonviolence,* may always be a compelling and creative actuality only at critical moments, and only for "the salt of the earth." But Gandhi took the first steps toward a world-wide application to politics of principles once purely religious.

As far as the world-wide frontier of *post-colonial* and *colored identities* is concerned, it is hard to predict their fate in the clash of new national interests in Africa and Asia. As of now, however, one cannot ignore the possible implications of American action in Viet-nam for a world-wide identification of colored people with the naked heroism of the Vietcong revolutionaries. The very demand that North Vietnam give in (and even if it were nearly on her own terms) to a super-organized assault by a superfluity of lethal weapons may simply be too reminiscent of the function of firepower in colonial expansion in general; of police power in particular; and of a certain (implicitly contemptuous) attitude which assumes that "natives" will give in to pressures to which the master-races would consider themselves impervious (*vide* the British in the Blitz). It must be obvious that differences of opinion in this country in re-gard to American military involvement in Asia are not merely a mat-ter of the faulty reading of facts or of lack of moral stamina on one side or the other, but also of a massive identity conflict. Intrinsic to the dominant political-technological nucleus of an American identity is the expectation that such power as can now be unleashed can be used to advantage in limited employment, and has built-in safe-guards against an unthinkable conflagration. But there will be urgent voices abroad and sincere protest at home expressing the per-plexity of those who perceive only one active moral frontier of equal-ity and of peace extending from the center of the daily life of America to the peripheries of its foreign concerns. Here the Negro American shares the fate of a new and wider American dilemma.

I have now listed a few of the emerging "wider" identity ele-ments in order to introduce queries which other members of the symposium are better equipped to answer. Such listing can only lead to one tentative impression, namely, that none of these alterna-tives offers to the American Negro a nucleus for a total realignment, and that all of them must find their place in a new constellation, the nucleus of which is already clearly suggested by the two words Negro and American.

Concluding Remark

As used in the foregoing, the term identity has betrayed its clinical origin in the study of individual disturbances and of social ills. But even where applied to the assessment of a social problem it remains clinical in methodology, that is, it can be used only to focus the thinking of a "staff." For the consideration of identity problems calls for the "taking of history," the localization and the diagnostic assessment of disintegration, the testing of intact resources, the approximate prognosis, and the weighing of possible action—each based on specialties of approach and often of temperament. In addition to all this, a certain intuitive insight based on experience *and* on conviction is indispensable in the assessment of *verifiable reality* and of *modifiable actuality*. On the way some theory may help; but a concept should be retained only as long as it brings some preliminary order into otherwise baffling phenomena.[16]

REFERENCES

1. Robert Penn Warren, *Who Speaks for the Negro?* (New York, 1965), p. 17.

2. These notes are a counterpart to the "Memorandum on Identity and Negro Youth," *Journal of Social Issues*, Vol. 20, No. 4 (October 1964).

3. Henry James (ed.), *The Letters of William James*, Vol. I (Boston, 1920), p. 199.

4. See my introduction to G. B. Blaine and C. C. McArthur (eds.), *Emotional Problems of the Student* (New York, 1961).

5. Sigmund Freud, "Address to the Society of B'nai B'rith," in *The Standard Edition* (London, 1959), p. 273.

6. Kenneth B. Clark, *Dark Ghetto* (New York, 1965).

7. Howard Zinn, *SNCC, The New Abolitionists* (Boston, 1964).

8. Not all doubt or discomfort regarding the conception of identity is to be seen as "resistance" by any means. Powerful methodological quandaries are inescapable. I would also share the reluctance to accept psychosocial identity as "all there is" to human identity. Psychosocial phenomena, however, are part of that engagement in a period of the life cycle and in a given historical era without which an unfolding of human potentials (including an eventual transcendence) seems unthinkable.

9. Thomas F. Pettigrew, *A Profile of the Negro American* (Princeton, N. J., 1964), p. 19. (Italics added.)

10. *Ibid.*, p. 115.

11. Kenneth B. Clark, *op. cit.*, p. 73. (Italics added.)

12. Under the tense conditions of a sudden awareness of facts long suppressed and distorted, new stereotypes are apt to enter the imagery of the most thoughtful. In *Crisis in Black and White,* C. E. Silberman discusses S. M. Elkin's basic book *Slavery* and, half-quoting and half-editorializing, uses the stereotype "childlike" as a common denominator of Negro personality and the transient regressions of inmates in concentration camps. Along with truly childish qualities, such as silliness, we find fawning, servile, dishonest, mendacious, egotistic, and thievish activities all summed up under "this childlike behavior." (p. 76). Here childlike replaces childish or regressed, as feminine often replaces effeminate, which is both misleading and destructive of the image of the genuine article.

13. See Erik H. Erikson, "Youth: Fidelity and Diversity," *Youth: Change and Challenge* (New York, 1963), pp. 1-23.

14. Erik H. Erikson and Kai T. Erikson, "The Confirmation of the Delinquent," in Hendrik M. Ruitenbeek (ed.), *The Condition of Modern Man in Society* (New York, 1962).

15. See Robert J. Lifton, *Thought Reform and the Psychology of Totalism* (New York, 1961).

16. Attempts at transverting clinical concepts into quantifiable items subject to experimental verification are always undertaken at the risk of the experimenter.

ROBERT COLES

"It's the Same, but It's Different"

SALLY, ONE of the Negro children I knew in New Orleans, drew heavily upon her grandmother's spirit when confronted with the hate and violence of mobs and the forced, pointed loneliness brought on by the boycott of "her" desegregated school. The little girl had been born in northern Louisiana, and in her grandmother's farmhouse—unlike many of those nearby, a rather solid building. Her grandparents were, in fact, relatively prosperous and substantial people in their community, having acquired title to their land, added to it, cultivated it wisely and assiduously, and eventually invested its profits in a neighborhood store. (*Their* parents had been sharecroppers, their grandparents, slaves.) Running the store was now the grandmother's business; her husband still cared for his farm, though with considerable help from several of his sons. Sally's mother had wanted to stay in that small town. It was her husband who took his wife and two small children to New Orleans. He wanted a job of his own, away from farm work and running errands at the family store. Sally was four at the time, and disliked leaving her grandmother. Still, she saw her regularly, for her parents continued to make weekend trips to the country.

Like the other three girls selected, Sally (and her parents) had no idea that she would face exposure to mobs as the price for entering a once all-white elementary school. Her parents had submitted her application because many of their neighbors were doing likewise. Having arrived only recently in New Orleans, they had assumed that its attitudes were not those of the state's rural areas. So much else was different in New Orleans—its buildings that anyone could enter, its streetcars where anyone could sit anywhere, its sidewalks where Negroes could walk on the "inside" without interruption instead of retiring to the road at the approach of a white person, its stores serving *all* customers by proper turn—that school desegregation seemed another miracle to be accepted quickly as part of living in the city.

Sally and her parents were eventually to realize they were fated to challenge their city rather than quietly enjoy some of its advantages. There came a point in my observations of how they managed such a fate when I was puzzled at their continuing calm in the midst of danger. I frankly wondered—at first to myself, then aloud to them—why they did not gather themselves together and leave. Sally's grandmother (during the worst of the ordeal, she had moved to be with her embattled children) gave the following explanation: "If we run away, we'll fool ourselves; you can't run away from being a colored man. It don't make any difference where you go—you has the same problem, one way or another." I asked her whether she thought those problems in any way comparable to those faced by white people—for example those few white families who were resisting the mob's will, defying its boycott to keep their children at school with Sally. "Yes," she replied firmly, "we is all the same under God, so we has the same problems; but colored folk has special ones, too. It's the same being colored as white, but it's different being colored, too." Then she repeated the words, nodding her agreement with them, "It's the same, but it's different."

It may seem a bit obvious and simple-minded to insist upon putting the Negro's problems in the context of those shared by all of us as human beings; moreover, it hardly seems surprising to learn that the Negro has problems that are all his own. Still, I think research into what it means to be a Negro will sooner or later meet up with the methodological hazards involved in abstracting people on racial grounds (on religious, social, economic, or geographical ones as well) and then talking about "their" feeling (in contrast to any individual's or, for that matter, those found in *all* individuals). I do not think either Sally, her parents, or her grandmother established any new record of courage and endurance in the face of threats. In many ways the crowds were angrier at the few white parents who defied them by keeping their children in school. Each family—confronting similar daily odds—stood fast for its own reasons, even as they all had some purposes in common. We lose when we dwell exclusively on either the private or the shared experience or intention.

What interested me about the remarks of Sally's grandmother was that she gave me an essentially matter-of-fact explanation for her steadfastness: there was simply no alternative. A Negro cannot flee danger, try though he might. Danger is everywhere, a never-ending consequence of his social and economic condition. Danger is written into history with his blood, into everyday customs by laws, into living itself by the size of his wages, the nature of his neighborhood. In contrast, every white parent I knew fell back upon another kind of reason for his actions. One father was a minister; he called upon his religious faith. Another parent was especially devoted to the education of her children; she could not stand idle while a school was destroyed, her children untaught. One family had only recently come to New Orleans; they did not "believe" in segregation—and they were stubborn and plucky enough to want to stand up for their beliefs, or, in this case, the absence of them. (Of course, I met a few others who put their ideals more positively; they were very much "for" integration; yet they were also "for" the safety of their children, enough so that they yielded to the prevailing storm and sought out other schools for their children).

What all these white families revealed together was a willingness to "choose" danger in the pursuit of an ideal or goal. Each one of them would mention the possibility open to them of rejecting a role in school desegregation. One father mentioned travel, just as Sally's grandmother did: "When I saw those people acting that way, I became ashamed of this city. We even talked of moving away, to Texas or California; but then we thought we just couldn't rest easy, running away." Each one of them rejected flight from the mobs, or indifference to them. Many others, very much like them, could rationalize their disinterest in desegregation, or defend their unwillingness to oppose segregationist street violence, by pointing to the fact that even the police—let alone the majority of the white parents in the school district—were disinclined to disperse the mob.

I do not think that situation in New Orleans was unlike the general situation in our country, as it confronts Negro and white people. The stakes may usually be less grim, less distinctly defined, less dangerously at issue; but the Negro has his skin to help him establish the nature of his problems and his beliefs, while white people must grapple for other mainstays of self-awareness or faith. Nor am I merely being ironic here. I have come to see that children who grow up and experience the Negro's lot in our society—no matter how various its expressions—achieve at least some measure of self-definition. It may be insufficient, it may lead to ruin, yet it cannot be seen only as a burden. To quote again from Sally's grandmother:

"We may not have anything; but at least we know why." She was telling me about the whites of her region, whose ability to look down upon her did little to elevate their material or spiritual welfare. Oppressors, they knew little about the reasons for their own impoverishment.

What can be said about how Sally feels being a Negro, about how her grandmother feels, or any of the other children, the other adults I have met and come to know? All that has been said about the meaning of skin color to Negro children[1] surely holds for Sally— and has always held for her parents and grandparents. Sally at six could tell me rather openly that she wished she were white. I have seen Negro children her age who denied and concealed similar wishes with great vehemence—that they, in fact, had such wishes was all too clear from their drawings, games, and "innocent" or "unintended" remarks.

Still, as we grow, or live, we all want occasionally to be what we are not, or cannot really ever become. What must be done is to establish the relevance, the importance of Sally's fantasies about her skin for the rest of her life. To do so requires placing discrete psychological events (and the observations made by psychiatrists of those events) in the context of the general growth and development of the child, including, of course, the influences of society upon how he is reared and taught to regard himself.

For instance, fairly quickly after my encounter with Negro children I could see in drawing after drawing their sensitivity to the colors black and brown—and, conversely, to white, yellow, and orange. Their sketches revealed their sense of fear of white people, their sense of lack at not having white skin, their sense of foreboding at what the future held for them as Negroes. One child drew himself small and mutilated in contrast to white children; another pictured himself so noticeably larger and stronger that one had to wonder why. (When I did, I heard the following reply: "Well, you have to be big if you're not going to get killed.") Then there were children who never wanted to draw themselves or anyone else as Negro; or those who had no idea how to sketch their white classmates except by making them a lighter shade of brown.

Perhaps more interesting than such evidence of color-consciousness in children of five or six are the lessons associated with such awareness. Again and again when a Negro child wants to show in a drawing how crippled he may feel—or others may be—the arms he sketches suffer, while the legs seem quite intact, appropriately depicted, and often enough in motion. My wife first noticed this, and eventually mentioned it to one of the little Negro girls we knew best. She told us directly that "legs mean more than hands, so I gives them more attention. . . . If you can run, you're O. K., but if you take something you get in trouble." She smiled nervously and in embarrassment when I asked her what she had in mind "taking." She eventually told me that she had recently been punished for taking some candy from a dime-store counter. A saleslady had witnessed the deed, and strenuously reprimanded the girl and her mother. I discovered later that she had scolded the girl more for being Negro than an incipient thief. Since girls often want to steal at six, and many do, we must ask whether Negro children face special challenges in the course of learning the ordinary do's and don'ts of this world, let alone those special restrictions obviously associated with their position in our society.

My clinical impression—slowly consolidated over these past years of working with Negro children—is that most of the "usual" problems and struggles of growing up find an additional dimension in the racial context. In a very real sense being Negro serves to organize and render coherent many of the experiences, warnings, punishments, and prohibitions that Negro children face. The feelings of inferiority or worthlessness they acquire, the longing to be white they harbor and conceal, the anger at what they find to be their relatively confined and moneyless condition, these do not fully account for the range of emotions in many Negro children as they come to terms with the "meaning" of their skin color. Sally's grandmother said more concisely what I am struggling to say: "They can scream at our Sally, but she knows why, and she's not surprised. She knows that even when they stop screaming, she'll have whispers, and after them the stares. It'll be with her for life. . . . We tell our children that, so by the time they have children, they'll know how to prepare them. . . . It takes a lot of preparing before you can let a child loose in a white world. If you're black in Louisiana it's like cloudy weather; you just don't see the sun much."

The "preparation" for such a climate of living begins in the first year of life. At birth the shade of the child's skin may be very important to his parents—so important that it determines in large measure how he is accepted, particularly in the many Negro marriages which bring together a range of genes which, when combined, offer the possibility of almost *any* color. What is often said about color-consciousness in Negroes (their legendary pursuit of skin bleaches and hair-straightening lotions) must be seen in its relentless effect upon the life of the mind, upon babies, and upon child-rearing. A Negro sociologist—involved in, rather than studying, the sit-in movement—insisted to me that "when a Negro child is shown to his mother and father, the first thing they look at is his color, and then they check for fingers and toes." I thought such a remark extreme indeed, until two years later when I made a point of asking many parents I knew what they thought of it—and found them unashamedly in agreement.

As infants become children, they begin to form some idea of how they look, and how their appearance compares with that of others. They watch television, accompany their mothers to the local market or stores downtown. They play on the street and ride in cars which move through cities or small towns. They hear talk, at the table or in Sunday school, or from other children while playing. By the time they enter school, at five or six, to "begin" to learn, they have already learned some lessons of self-respect (or its absence) quite well.

I have been continually astonished to discover just how intricately children come to examine the social system, the political and economic facts of life in our society. I had always imagined myself rather sensible and untouched by those romantic nineteenth-century notions of childhood "innocence." As a child psychiatrist I had even committed myself to a professional life based on the faith that young children see and feel what is happening in their family life—and if properly heard will tell much of it to the doctor, whether by words, in games, or with crayons. Yet I had never quite realized that children so quickly learn to estimate who can vote, or who has the money to frequent this kind of restaurant or that kind of theater, or what groups of people contribute to our police force—and why. Children, after all, have other matters on their minds—and so do many adults.

I do not think Negro children are, by definition, budding sociologists or political scientists, but I have been struck by how specifically aware they become of those forces in our society which, reciprocally, are specifically sensitive to *them*. They remark upon the scarcity of colored faces on television, and I have heard them cheer the sight of a Negro on that screen. In the South they ask their parents why few if any policemen or bus drivers are colored. In the ghettos of the North they soon enough come to regard the Negro policeman or bus driver as specially privileged—as indeed he is, with his steady pay, with his uniform that calls for respect and signifies authority—and perhaps as an enemy in the inevitable clash with "whitey."

"The first thing a colored mother has to do when her kids get old enough to leave the house and play in the street is teach them about the white man and what he expects. I've done it with seven kids, and I've got two more to go; and then I hope I'll be through." She was talking about her earnest desire to "be done with" bringing children into the world, but she had slipped into a recital of how Negro mothers must be loyal to the segregationist customs of Southern towns. Still, she preferred them to the North; and so did her son, a youth I had watched defy sheriffs (and his mother's early admonitions) in Alabama and Mississippi for several years. "In the North," her son added, "I'd have learned the same thing, only it's worse, because there a mother can't just lay it on the line. It takes time for the boy to get the full pitch, and realize it's really the same show, just a little dressed-up; and until he makes that discovery, he's liable to be confused. The thing we're not down here is confused."

The Negro child growing up is thus likely to be quite rigidly and fearfully certain about what he may do, where he may go, and who he eventually will be. In the desegregated schools of the South, where Southern whites have had a fresh opportunity and reason to watch Negro children closely, teachers have been especially impressed by what one of them called the "worldliness" of the colored child. She did not mean the jaded, tough indifference of the delinquent—perhaps a later stage of "development." She simply was referring to the shrewd, calculating awareness in children who have been taught—worried about, screamed at, slapped, and flogged in the process—the rules of the game as they apply to Negroes. She had come to realize that growing up as a Negro child had its special coherence and orderliness as well as its chaos. The children she was teaching were lonely, isolated, and afraid—a few of them in a large, only recently desegregated white elementary school in Tennessee —but they also knew exactly what they feared, and exactly how to be as safe as possible in the face of what they feared.

For that matter, it is not simply that Negro children learn the bounds of their fate, the limits of the kinds of work allowed to them, the extent of their future disfranchisement, the confines of their social freedom, the edge of the residential elbowroom permitted them, the margin of free play, whim, or sport available to them now or within their grasp when they are grown. They learn how to make use of such knowledge, and in so doing gain quite gradually and informally an abiding, often tough sense of what is about them in the world, and what must be in them to survive. In the words of Sally's grandmother, "Sally can get through those mobs; she was born to, and one way or another she'll have to do it for the rest of her life."

So it is not all disorder and terror for these children. As they grow older, go to school, think of a life for themselves, they can envision a life which is quiet, pleasant, and uneventful for long stretches of time, or at least as much so as for any "other" children. That is, the Negro child will play and frolic, eat and sleep like all other children; and, though this may seem no great discovery, it is essential that it be mentioned in a discussion which necessarily singles out special pains or hazards for analysis. Sometimes when I read descriptions of "what it is like to be a Negro" I have to turn away in disbelief: the children I have been working with—in sharecropper cabins and migrant camps as well as in cities—simply do not resemble the ones portrayed. Perhaps it is impossible in *any* description to do justice to the continuity and contradiction of life, but we can at least try by qualifying our assumptions, by acknowledging that they do not encompass the entire range of human experience.

"It's like being two people: when I'm around here I'm just me; when I leave and go to school or go downtown, I'm just another person." A high-school student in Atlanta is speaking, a Negro youth who is trying to integrate those two facets of his personality as well as himself into a white school. Yet, not even his sharp, clear-cut statement can account for the range of sensibilities which develop in Negro children as a result of their race's history and present condition.

As in all matters of human behavior each Negro child or adult I have met has developed or is developing his or her own style of dealing with what is essentially a social experience that becomes for the individual a series of psychological ones capable of giving "significant" structure or form to a life. Some of the styles are well established in folklore and in the daily expectations of both whites and Negroes: subservience, calculated humiliation, sly ingratiation, self-mockery; or, changing the tone somewhat, aloof indifference, suspicious withdrawal, sullen passivity, or grim, reluctant compliance. Again, in areas of diminished repression, where outright submission has been replaced by the possibility of social and racial dis-engagement or "co-existence," one sees impatience, or ill-tempered, measured distrust; indeed, in evidence is everything from irritability and barely concealed resentment to an almost numbing hatred and fury.

What most Negro children of ten or twelve have learned is a tendency, stimulated by the white man's presence or appearance, for one or (more likely) a mixture of several of these or other adaptive modes of dealing with him. The choice, of course, depends on the private life of the child, his general development of personality —there are reasons other than racial ones for being prone to good-humored supplication or to anger, despair, resignation, sulkiness, insensibility, or inertia. The manner of adjustment also varies, as I mentioned, by region and by class or occupation, too.

Even though Negroes in general grow to be especially sensitive to—and on their guard with—whites, the quality and quantity of experience, hence of feeling, between Negroes and whites is not all of a kind. Some Negroes are constantly in contact with whites: taking care of their homes, waiting on them, carrying out their orders in offices and stores, or working along side them, even of late giving them orders or directions. Others live in the shadow of the white world, but really have very little direct encounter with white individuals. "They touches on us, but we don't much see them, to tell the truth." The wife of a sharecropper, she worked the land of a white farmer, lived in his house, saw him or his deputies drive by; yet, her actual, person-to-person meetings with white people were few. She and her family carried on their daily lives with that mixture of freedom and restraint characteristic of poor rural folk. Though their "inheritance" as Negroes—their social and cultural traditions—set a different atmosphere for them than, say, white sharecroppers or small farmers in the same county, the similarities of living in that county are by far more striking. Negroes tend to discount the importance of "legal" marriage, are often much more open and relaxed about breast-feeding or toilet training, and tend to keep less orderly households. On the other hand, white parents tend to be more attentive to their children as they become of school age, their individual preferences indulged where reasonable or possible. However, what both races share are similar routines, similar worlds with which they must contend. These common experiences fashion a common attitude toward education, food, clothing, and other people in contrast to those of one's own family.[2]

In the ghettos, or the all-Negro middle-class areas of our cities, a somewhat similar pattern holds, of random association with whites in the midst of an ordinarily exclusive relationship with one's own people. Naturally, class differences obtain, it being one thing to try to imitate the white middle-class world (and to have the means to do it) and quite another to live the uncertain, hand-to-mouth existence characteristic of any slum. Yet, in Atlanta, where there is a Negro residential district of matchless elegance (that is, if the standards are all other Negro districts, but only *some* white ones), the experience of crossing into contiguous white areas demands its recognition, a recognition not unlike that in the Negro who leaves the same city's ample slums on a shopping trip or to look for a job downtown.

The word "caste" only partially explains such shared feelings, which persist in the North regardless of class, even among those Negroes—their number is obviously increasing now—who live predominantly in the white world. For that matter, in the psychotherapeutic or psychoanalytic relationship—where presumably troubled *individuals* are consulting *doctors*—psychiatrists have commented on certain general problems which arise out of the difference between the patient's skin color and the doctor's.[3] Regardless of their particular symptoms, Negroes and whites in the psychiatric office have a special problem to face, not necessarily difficult, by no means insurmountable, but nonetheless real and rather commonly present. There is a likelihood of more distrust, more fearful hesitation, than is usually the case; and the mind of both the Negro and white person—whether doctor or patient—will find it difficult to refrain from noticing and responding to the various symbolic and emotional meanings of color.[4] They are, after all, part of our entire culture, and certainly significant in the childhood and adulthood of Negroes in America.

When I lived in Mississippi I had a home in a small town. For a long time I was not interested in the civil rights issue: there was none in the state at that time. The people I knew were intelligent and kindly—all of them white, middle-class people who were born in the state, brought up from their first days by Negro "mammies." I recall their weekly trips to "nigger town"—they were adults now, and there was laundry to take there, or a favorite servant's birthday to remember. After I became interested in how young Negroes lived and got along with whites, I went with a doctor and his wife one day to the colored section of our town. They had always ignored laundromats, would not think of buying a washing machine; Louisa had been washing and ironing their sheets and shirts for years. Louisa and her mother had taken care of the doctor's wife when she was a child: "She fed me as a baby. I was the first baby she cared for; she learned from her mother how to do it—I don't remember much of it; I just remember Louisa smiling and helping me choose a dress to wear for a party at school, and maybe a game or two she played with us." Later that day this very sensitive woman told me of an experience she *did* remember, and quite clearly: "I think I was seven or eight, and I went with my mother to a five-and-dime store. It was one of those old ones; I can still see the counters, and the fans going. They hung in rows from the ceilings. . . . Anyway, we were walking down the aisle, and I bumped right into a nigra woman. I said, 'Excuse me, ma'am,' and right in front of her my mother told me never to use 'ma'am' with the colored. It was O. K. to say 'excuse me,' because that showed I was a well-mannered girl; but 'ma'am' was different. . . . I had trouble making sense of that, and I asked my mother her reasons for being so against using 'ma'am' with the nigra. She tried to tell me that it was the way we did things in the world, but it never made sense to me. . . . I think what *did* make sense to me was that I had to obey my mother's wish. Then you grow older, and you stop trying to make sense of things like that. You just know that there are things you can do, and things you can't, and that's it. My brother once tried to get my parents to explain to him why he had to wear a tie one place, and not another. It was the same thing. My daddy just said, 'Jimmie, that's the way it is, and that's the way we have to do it.'"

I have been listening to and recording conversations with individuals like this lady for several years since that day, and find it a rare occasion—even among poor whites—when similar memories are not mentioned. The confused and tortured intimacy of white and Negro people in the South has been described by writer after writer.[5] Yet to be confronted by it comes as a challenge to anyone interested in just how the human mind deals with the inconsistencies and contradictions of social existence. That woman today—in spite of her ordinary civility and even graciousness—is grimly opposed to any change in the way Negroes and whites get along with one another. She feels that others, "outsiders," are imposing strange and unsettling demands upon her. The strangeness of her own childhood, of her own relationship to Negroes as a child, no longer troubles her. Yes, there are memories, and if she is not pressed, not questioned with any intent to argue or even interpret but simply to learn, she will reveal them to herself as well as her listener. All in all, though, her present anger at Negroes and her long-standing sense of them as beyond the bounds of her politesse combine to exact a price: she cannot really feel comfortable with some of the best moments in her own childhood; she must work hard at denying them in order to keep her present attitudes properly charged and effective in her daily life. There is no romantic indulgence in Faulkner's descriptions of the passion that fuels the hate of white Southerners for Negroes, particularly of those white yoemen hard-pressed by hunger, self-doubt, personal loneliness, and social lawlessness, whether in relation to other Southerners or (as even well-to-do Southerners often feel) in relation to their countrymen in other regions.

If the white man must often deny his early, increasingly confusing friendliness with Negroes, the Negro has little choice but to come to terms with his early, equally confusing awe, envy, and hate of whites, and his friendliness with them. "Keep your fear of the white man, I has to tell it to every child all the time until they knows it for themselves." I asked this poor, uneducated wife of a former sharecropper whether her children had *only* fear of whites. She shook her head. "They be jealous of them. Sometimes they might want to see how they live; so my husband drives them over and picks me up from work." (She worked as a maid in a comfortable Atlanta suburb, and her daughter was now at school with children who lived in that suburb.) "I told her, we can have all the rights they have, but you can't feel easy with them so fast. . . . I just make sure my kids know to be afraid."

The "ma'am" that the white child learns to drop the Negro child learns to say—say fearfully, say anxiously, say reluctantly, say eagerly, say out of habit, say with conviction, say and mean, or say with reservations that surely include a wide range of bitterness and resentment. Doubtless the experience of a Negro growing up in Boston is different from that of a Negro in the Black Belt of Alabama, but I think the common need persists everywhere in America for Negro youth to gauge their relationships to white people warily. While the white man loses part of his own life history, his own kindness or goodwill when he isolates his present self from his past feelings, the Negro loses part of his own life history, his natural self-protective assertiveness, his confidence with others and ease about himself, when he learns to separate his past experience of surprised indignation from his present sense of what the world expects and will demand. Just as we can compare white people by how easily they submit the occasions or psychological moments in their "private" lives to the judgment of social and cultural imperatives, so I should imagine Negroes differ in their willingness to deny and surrender themselves in order to curry the favor of the white man.

I have been astonished at how clearly Negro parents put the matter before their children. As I was preparing to write this paper, my wife reminded me of an interview—neither one of us is likely ever to forget it—with the parents of one of the sit-in students we know best. He is one of seven children, and the only one to show his kind of tough defiance of the laws and customs of his native Alabama. Why he? No psychiatrist should fail to remind himself that any schemes he has devised to comprehend some portion—it can only be some—of man's behavior have yet to explain such questions as why one person does a given deed or develops in a particular way, while another whose life and problems seem remarkably similar reacts quite differently. Ours is still a heavily retrospective rather than a predictive kind of knowledge. Lawrence's mother and father were struggling with a similar order of perplexity, with the problems of *their* knowledge. They were, after all, the young man's parents; why should they not be able to review his life, contrast it with that of their other children, and arrive at an explanation for Lawrence's singular courage and willfulness? Yet, it was hard for them to do so.

Listening to the taped interview once again, I saw that dreary row of houses on the unpaved streets of Gadsden, Alabama—the colored sections of Southern towns always seem to begin with unpaved streets. Though we were in the South, the December day was chilly; the house was drafty, and warmed by one of those gas burners that often enough explode. If you sit near them you sweat; if you move only a few feet away, the flame might as well be extinguished. I had asked why Lawrence was the one child in that home (his father is a frequently unemployed handyman, his mother a domestic) to take a stand against the Alabama State Highway Patrol in order that he and others like him might register to vote. "To tell the truth, I don't know," was the way his mother began her reply. Her husband was more equivocal: "I don't either, but I think it's because he's just stubborn, and he hasn't lost it like you do when you gets older." Now his mother's mind had been set in motion: "That's right. Lawrence always knew what he wanted, so he's just gone and stood up for it. Of course, I think all of us want the same thing he does. It's just in his nature to go after it more than others will." I wanted to know how that quality had taken root only in Lawrence, but they had no explanation. They did have some comments—and perhaps all the explanation there could be: "Lawrence does what he believes is right," his father said proudly, "but it's in the air these days for us to stand up and be counted. . . .Mind you, I'm not taking anything away from the boy, but I think all our children feel the same on being treated better. It's his age. The younger ones can't do anything because they're not yet grown; and the older ones, they've just had their dreams die." His wife took up that theme immediately; "You get older and get a family, and that's the end. But don't you think Lawrence is alone! Every colored child in America wants what he does. I'm his mother, and I'm proud of him; but I has to say the truth."

She clearly feared that what little distinction had come her family's way might dissolve in the face of a truth she had to acknowledge. Her husband, a second beer well in him, said what was to be the last word on the subject: "Anything Lawrence has done, we all want to do. He had a chance to do it, but all the kids were with him every inch. . . . I'll bet every colored boy in America has the same dream Lawrence has. Maybe only a few of them can do anything about it, but we all has the same dream." I think he is right; yet men have a number of dreams in them and some of them work at odds with others. Lawrence's determination—in the face of extreme danger—has simply not been matched by others, even those of his age. A common heritage and condition do not ensure either bravery or cowardice.

One of the most thoughtful and careful investigators of how Negroes endure their lot in American society has asked in one of his papers:[6] "Why do not all Negro men become schizophrenic?" The very fact that such a question can be formulated suggests at once some of the problems facing both Negroes and social scientists. We do not know for certain the cause (or causes) of schizophrenia; but we do feel that consistently disorganized, brittle, tense, fearful parents in some way influence its development in their children. It does not seem fatuous, therefore, to inquire why *all* Negro men are not schizophrenic. A number of observers, from several disciplines,[7] have remarked upon the serious psychological problems facing large numbers of Negroes who live impoverished lives, in a social and cultural climate which commonly rejects them, and in families often enough unstable, disturbed, and split apart.

Of course, it is obvious that millions of Negroes survive such special strains—if not handily, then at least with no crippling mental disease. As a matter of fact, what is puzzling to those of us who have worked with the more penniless, "backward," rural Negroes is our continuing sense of the remarkable sturdiness and poise in many of them. Many others, of course, are tired, apathetic, almost lifeless; though even people in this latter group show a striking capacity to come alive when exposed to the momentum of social and political change.

About a year ago a group of us—lawyers, educators, doctors—were asked by some students active in the civil rights movement to interview about thirty of the men, women, and children with whom they lived and for whom (and many others, too) they struggled to organize voter registration efforts, freedom schools, or health-education clinics. One after another we heard those fellow-citizens recite the terrible facts of their lives as Negroes in the deep South. We heard those facts, but we also observed the remarkable self-possession of the witnesses, the composure which accompanied their testimony. We felt their considerable vitality and robust humor. There were also moments of resignation and gloom, but such emotions did not appear overwhelming. For a while none of us seemed to get the point of the rather ironic scene: people, asked to tell of the abuse by a social system still unprepared to grant them even elementary dignity, were indeed testifying to such conditions of existence, yet they were also unwittingly offering—by their appearance, spirit, and manner of expression—a confusing example of how astonishingly well a brutal world can be resisted. One of us remarked that he wished *his* children had the vigor, wit, and spontaneity of the children from Mississippi. Another one of us expressed admiration not only for the courage shown by these people, but for their gentle, wry wisdom, their delightful, charming presence. It was no mere condescension at work among us: we were genuinely bewildered by the challenge of reconciling the facts of persecution with the "results" of persecution—this gathering of impressive human beings. I think it fair to mention what one of us said, a bit exasperated by the dilemma: "We can't say that Mississippi destroys the Negroes' self-respect when we see people who have more of it than many of us do. Maybe we need more of Mississippi in Northern suburbs."

It is no easy job dealing with such problems, but trying to do so can help make us skeptical of some of the rhetoric that sees only wicked, pale-faced sheriffs and irreparably damaged, brutalized colored people. Indeed, one of the most demanding tasks facing social scientists today is that of learning how individual members of an aggrieved class of people succeed in achieving a measure of order and survival.

In recent years I have found myself continually puzzled by the capacity of sharecroppers or migratory workers, the very poorest of our poor, and politically the most defenseless of our outcasts, to maintain for themselves and their children a striking quality of stubborn, willful endurance that is not only grim (I was expecting, even looking for that) but often enough resilient, light-hearted, and exceedingly canny. Now, to be droll, flexible, quick-witted, and sensible is to possess virtues presumably nourished in "civilized" societies. To be confronted with the degrading, humiliating poverty of Negro migrant farmers or sharecroppers is to wonder how humanity can even minimally maintain itself under such circumstances; the discovery of any refinements of mind or heart seems utterly surprising and unaccountable.

In the slums we can always—I think wrongly—fall back on our schools or general climate of city life to explain an alert, capable boy, or else summon those handy "genes." Conversely, the widespread violence and delinquency in the cities are attributed to the poor housing, the bad education, the joblessness in the ghettos. Among millions of Negroes in the South, still in rural or semi-rural situations, equivalent explanations do not hold. Many of the children are quite capable and impressive, with only dismal schools and few other "advantages" to be had; moreover, there are farming communities in the Black Belt which combine extreme hardship for Negroes with a relatively small incidence of crime among them. (Violence toward whites is out of the question, but in some of these areas there is little violence among Negroes, too.)

I find such observations unsettling. They lead us away from some of the prevalent "conclusions" of our time: that prejudice, segregation, and extreme poverty corrode the stamina of people and make them self-destructive or inert; that a move from the terror in rural Mississippi to the earnest climate of progress in civil rights which characterizes many Northern cities is altogether desirable and beneficial for Negroes; that improving the lot of Negroes is an urgent problem lest millions of them succumb to, or perpetuate, the personal and public chaos that is so predominantly theirs.

I agree with those conclusions. However, I also think we must go more carefully into the problems such conclusions attempt to describe and embrace. When we had finished hearing those "witnesses" from Mississippi, we had no desire to defend the way Negroes live there. We made our sincere, public statements of dismay and horror. The evidence, the information of our informants substantiated every word of ours. Still, we also had evidence that there is more to the Negro's life in Mississippi (I would add, in all America) than terror and submission to terror, or poverty and its corrosive effects upon human beings. To abstract the cheerless, hand-to-mouth existence of people may well be desirable in order to expose it and put an end to it. To understand the complicated manner in which individuals come to terms with their world, and even use its vicissitudes to fashion their necessarily sturdy survival, requires a moment—I'm not recommending a long spell of it—of suspended outrage, of condemnation withheld.

I have only my impressions to "prove it" (and I don't think any "proper," statistically valid evidence can as yet be marshaled on matters like this) but I feel that the privation, the domination and oppression of the Negro in this country have been all of a special kind. It is futile to compare it to the intermittent excessess of colonial powers, or to the sadistic regressions to bestiality characteristic of totalitarian regimes; for that matter, I am not sure there isn't a real difference between the way persecuted minorities once lived with their oppressors in the various European countries and the way Negroes and whites have lived in the South. Likewise, the caste systems in Asia are not quite like ours. Despite our flaws, we claim ourselves a democracy, and have almost torn ourselves apart for a century working to justify the assertion. In addition to holding the Negro first a slave, then isolated legally and socially, we have also lived side-by-side with him, blended our blood and skin with his, shared our homes and names with him, entrusted our children to him, and in the South, scene of his longest and most dismal affliction, nevertheless and coincidentally joined him in poverty and suffering, given him food and clothing and even affection. It may not be very easy these days to consider the kindness and warmth over the generations of many white Southerners toward Negroes[8] as anything but condescension, or a peculiar refinement of an exploitative social and economic system. Nevertheless, for many years such living habits, and particularly the emotional climate that accompanied them, have constituted a very definite psychological inheritance for millions of Negro people—setting standards for their behavior, giving form to their individual feelings. I don't know where else in the world, when else in history, two groups of people have had quite so wide a range of relationships—spread over time, involving all the complicated and often conflicting social, economic, political, and psychological influences at play in our nation, our South.

When I first started interviewing Negro children and their parents my chief concern was with the hard life they faced, the special stresses they met when seeking entrance into a society often only grudgingly willing to greet and welcome them. My chief task—as I saw it for a long time—was to document carefully and precisely the specific psychiatric toll such personal hardship, such social repudiation exacted from these individuals.

Though in no way do I deny what Kardiner and Ovesey[9] have called the "mark of oppression" (in fact, I have ample evidence to add further confirmation of just how cruel, enfeebling, and unsettling a brand it can be), it remains equally true that alongside suffering I have encountered resilience and an incredible capacity for survival. To travel about with migrant workers, to stop with them as they visit their sharecropper brothers or cousins, is to realize how tenaciously and sternly they persist, as well as how unequipped they are for our white, middle-class world. Moreover, I will risk being called anything from a fool to a sentimental apologist for a dying order by insisting upon the fun, good times, and frolic I daily saw in these people. Of course, they have downcast and sour moments, too—often brought on by the presence of white people. Yet, as one man reminded me, "We can always forget them when they're gone, and most of the time they're just not here to bother us —we know they're always on our back, but it's when they get in front of us and try tripping us up that we get upset." I watched his angry petulance, his artful self-abasement with the white foreman on the farm he helped cultivate; I also saw how very pleasant and even sprightly he could be at home with his wife and children. "We has it rough, but we knows how to live with it, and we learned it so long ago it's second nature; so most of the time it's not so bad; tell the truth, it's only once in a while things get bad . . . so long as you keeps your wits and doesn't ask for but your rights." Even in segregated, impoverished rural areas there are "rights" in the sense that the social system is not erratic, chaotic, or inconsistent with its own (if peculiar and arbitrary) traditions.

I have, for instance, seen migrant farmers cut a farmer to the quick, refuse to appear on his land, because he has gone "too far," screamed too loudly at a worker. Sheriffs can use electric prods and shout to a pitch of frenzy at Negroes demonstrating for the right to vote, but they will often hardly so much as raise their voices with other Negroes "going about their business," even if they are annoyed at, or critical of, how badly or ineffectively that business is being done.

In general, I have been trying to indicate that I find the task of talking about "the Negro" difficult indeed, the more so because of how many individual Negro men, women, and children I know. Even their common suffering, a suffering that has cursed all Americans since the beginning of this country and has yet to be ended, fails to bind them together sufficiently to cause them to lose their individuality, a fact that may be sad for zealous social scientists but is ultimately hopeful for America.

There is, there must be, a certain danger in talking about millions of people as a group, whether we talk about their "negritude" or their chronicle of hurts and wants. Sometimes I feel I have gathered a mass of impressions about how Negroes, in contrast, say, to middle-class whites, live, think, and feel. Still, the heart and soul of their existence, and the spirit which informs their lives, probably are as terribly various and stubbornly resistant to generalizations as those we call "ours."

I *do* know that there is a concrete *reality* in being an American Negro; that millions of people are tied down to it; that some of them are driven mad by it; that others are frightfully torn by its prospects; that the spectacle of what its consequences have been for this nation is not yet completed; that in its grip people have faltered, cowered, and pretended; that from its grip people have fled and battled their way; and that, finally, the worst and best in mankind have emerged.

Today any person or people is lucky to escape some kind of categorical approximation. The Negro, surely, has not suffered alone on *that* account. Nor has his meaning for white people been left uncatalogued. I hear talk about his childlike behavior in the face of a culture that so regards him. I hear that he is a symbol of this or that to nervous, sexually troubled whites; or that he is himself foolishly, childishly wanton and bold, or fearfully thwarted and stunted. I hear that he has his special black soul, mysterious and wonderful, defying description—the very attempt to describe it being a characteristic of the white soul.

Who can limit by any list of attributes the nature of any person, the possibilities in any group of people? We cannot forsake our informed attempts to do just that, particularly in the case of those kept so long outside us while so deeply and sacrificially within us. I would only hope that some day soon the Negro will achieve an order of freedom that will make our descriptions and categories no longer so relevant—indeed, not only out of date, but out of order. It may not now be impertinent for a psychiatrist to talk about *"the* problems" of *"the* Negro," but I surely hope it soon will be.

Until that time comes, we shall all doubtless have to live dangerously: attempts to probe the truth of individual lives will be no more exempt from partisan pressures of one sort or another than are the efforts of others—historians, political scientists, novelists, or poets.

In this regard I recall a sleepless night I spent last summer (1964) in Mississippi. It wasn't the police and their scrupulously attentive hostility that kept us up; we—some college students, a lawyer, and I—were sharing our views and experiences with one another in one of those Freedom Houses that bore witness, among other things, to the fact that a flimsy shack can almost instantly achieve enormous dignity. The students were Negro and white, from the North and the South; and I think I am being quite fair when I say that we argued, most of them setting themselves against the lawyer and me.

At first I thought the discussion reflected the modest generational gap between youths in their early twenties and young professional men who, in fact, had slipped into the cautions and restraints of middle age, whatever their physical shape and the capacity of their minds to scorn the decade or more that separated them from their fellow workers in the cause of civil rights. I was trying to make a case for how torn-up many Southern whites felt. They countered with a reminder of the centuries of brutality and exploitation that had gone into making the neighborhood we all inhabited at that very moment. I said that such facts could live side-by-side with one another. They said no, that in a time of critical change, when the outcome by no means was settled, any emphasis upon the quandary of white people could lead only to suspension of the social and political momentum necessary for the achievement of the Negro's ordinary civil rights, let alone his long-term needs for more money and power. Besides, they *did* feel competitive about the matter of suffering—how *could* I compare the hurt of the oppressor with that of the oppressed, the long and unremittingly oppressed, at that?

Talk of oppression brought us no nearer to one another. I mentioned their admiration for our various hosts in the town, their genuine respect for the strong-willed and courageous people we daily met that summer. Some of what they were saying about the oppression of the Negro was hard to reconcile with the truth, the daily presence of such people. They acknowledged their *own* trouble with such a paradox, but they insisted that they tended to forget it, or explain it as a result of the necessary encounter of the "best"— the most spirited and least damaged—of the Negro people with the civil rights movement. What about the numberless apathetic, forlorn Negroes in Mississippi or Harlem? And, anyway, why did I bear down so heavily on survival, even survival with dignity against grim odds, as if it were some virtue rather than a terrible, albeit ironic, fact of human existence?

I replied that my job was to bear down on anything that came my way about human beings and their psychological adjustment. I had no idea how "correct" I was, but I had an obligation to take account of anything that regularly—or, for that matter, irregularly— cropped up in the talks I was having with people. One student reminded me of the work of Elkins and of Kardiner's studies.[10] How did I reconcile *them* with my ideas—and, anyway, how systematic *were* my studies?

We spent a good hour on the problem of methodology in the social sciences. Were my impressions "valid"?[11] In brief, as Robert Penn Warren was later to put it so very shrewdly: who *does* speak for the Negro?[12] One Negro from Mississippi, the son of one of our hosts in the town, said that "Negroes don't have it so bad they can't recover mighty fast, if we only get a chance to." I thought that about said what I was trying to emphasize: there has been unspeakable brutality, but also survival, extreme resilience, inspiration, improvisation, and an originality—of words and phrases, of music and voice, of manners and outlook. I suppose that I would call it a "culture" or a "subculture"; another age, with more felicity, might refer to a particular kind of sensibility. Does persecution—as the Negro has experienced it in America—absolutely preclude such a development? We debated that question for a time, and we all agreed that the answer was no, that there was indeed every reason to emphasize the quite real and quite available sources of strength and imagination both in individual Negro families and in many Negro communities. We agreed that slavery had been a progressive kind of Hell, as Elkins has shown historically, and that oppression did indeed leave its mark, as Kardiner and Ovesey have documented; but at the same time we all acknowledge that many Negroes were surviving well enough—and even so well as to warrant making *that* clear, too.

All of this means—I said it then, and have repeated it elsewhere and often—that the dignity of the Negro is not served *either* by seeing only his exploitation or by turning his condition into yet another excuse for fake envy, based on romanticized celebrations of what in point of fact was disastrous suffering. A Negro girl in Little Rock told me once: "Some ways it's not bad at all, but other ways it's worse than anything can be." The point is that people can be frightfully damaged; yet their lives unfold in a promising fashion, so that they are ready for such actual promises as the present civil rights movement hopes to realize. Why such an observation should be anything but a cliché puzzles me. On the other hand, we have all grown up in this century with a keen appreciation for wrongdoing and minds gone astray. We are, perhaps, less comfortable comprehending the sources of strength and purpose in "ordinary" people under such circumstances. Some people are jolted at the very notion of inquiry into the development of stamina and vitality in human beings—as if every sign of competence, excellence, or honor had to be derived from some ruinous, senseless urge.

The last matter we explored—it was near dawn—involved the advisability, the political propriety, of any public discussion that emphasizes the positive elements in Negro life. By now we were less in disagreement. Two Northern Negroes felt not only that Southern rural life had its supports, but that the Negro experience in some parts of the ghetto was worth looking at, too: "Where did Baldwin get his strength? Where did I? Sometimes I wonder. I don't know, but it's in me, that's the truth." Still, we all agreed, there were those who would misunderstand—segregationists in order to justify tyranny, and others because they would feel cheated of clear-cut rhetoric and consequently mistake an attempt to see the widest range of possibilities in people as a resort to moral indifference.

There was a time when I would airily dismiss such "strategic" talk as out of the question: truth must be sought and stated. I have come to realize that in what Erik Erikson has nicely called "ongoing history"[13] the remarks of this observer or that one can have their own modest contribution (or harm) to make—and, therefore, must be very carefully spelled out. We all agreed that our very presence in Mississippi spoke for itself, said what we felt about the justice there. We all agreed that we should do work in the North, too, even if we had already done so. We also agreed that we could not expect others to take our deeds for granted, that anything we said might be used in any way convenient by anyone so disposed. "It's hard to make myself known," I once was told by a Negro mother. She has all of us for company.

After years in the South I am now back in Boston; and still the elusive truth compounds itself and makes conclusive judgments and far-reaching generalizations tempting (why not give in to them?) but most often unbearable (why, indeed, give in to them when they ring hollow?). I know already, from my present work in the Northern ghetto, that Southern life is not Northern life, that Southern Negroes see things differently, feel differently than Northern Negroes do—as is the case with whites, too. Even that regional distinction is another reminder that differences afflict and grace the colored man, making him as defiantly various as the rest of us. Indeed, as I go from home to home in Boston's Roxbury slum I can hear Sally's grandmother talking: it *is* the same as with Negro families I knew in the South, but it's different up North, too.

"Where are we going?" I have heard tough, battle-weary sit-in students shout at midnight planning sessions in Mississippi or Alabama. They are asking the question in its broadest sense. Sometimes they will ask it of a particular person—ask him where he is going—when they want to pin him down, have his specific thought in the most explicit, concrete form. I can imagine being asked that question by those students, and replying in a flash, "with you." I hope I would also have the honesty and respect for them that would enable me to add: "but sometimes by myself." The duty to work with others for a kinder, more honorable society carries with it the obligation to stand apart as an individual. Such responsibilities will always generate their countervailing forces, their consequent tensions, or will do so until anarchy or totalitarianism resolves the matter one way or the other.

As a matter of fact, there is no way of escaping it: the Negro's struggle for his life and limb, for his rights, for his own worth and excellence, reminds any of us who care to be reminded that all of us share this struggle and will always need one another's example and help in coming to terms with it.

REFERENCES

1. See Mary Ellen Goodman, *Race Awareness in Young Children* (Cambridge, Mass., 1952). K. B. Clark and M. Clark, "The Development of Consciousness of Self and the Emergence of Racial Identification in Negro Preschool Children," *Journal of Social Psychology,* Vol. 10, No. 4 (November 1939), pp. 591-599. K. B. Clark and M. Clark, "Skin Color as a Factor in Racial Identification of Negro Preschool Children," *Journal of Social Psychology,* Vol. 11, No. 1. (February 1940), pp. 159-169. K. B. and M. Clark, "Emotional Factors in Racial Identification and Preference in Negro Children," *Journal of Negro Education,* Vol. 19 (1950), pp. 341-350. Eugene B. Brody, "Color and Identity Conflict in Young Boys," *Psychiatry,* Vol. 26, No. 2 (May 1963), pp. 188-201. Eugene B. Brody, "Color and Identity Conflict in Young Boys, II," *Archives of General Psychiatry,* Vol. 10 (April 1964), pp. 354-360. R. Coles, "Southern Children Under Desegregation," *American Journal of Psychiatry,* Vol. 120, No. 4 (October 1963), pp. 332-344. R. Coles, "Racial Conflict and a Child's Question," *Journal of Nervous and Mental Disease,* Vol. 140, No. 2 (February 1965), pp. 162-170.

2. I tried to illustrate the development of such attitudes among the rural poor in "The Lives of Migrant Farmers," read at the annual meeting of American Psychiatric Association, May 1965.

3. For example, H. R. St. Claire, "Psychiatric Interview Experiences with Negroes," *American Journal of Psychiatry,* Vol. 108, No. 2 (August 1951), pp. 113-119; Viola W. Bernard, "Psychoanalysis and Members of Minority Groups," *Journal of the American Psychoanalytic Association,* Vol. 1, No. 2 (April 1953), pp. 256-267; Walter A. Adams, "The Negro Patient in Psychiatric Treatment," *American Journal of Orthopsychiatry,* Vol. 20, No. 2 (April 1950), pp. 305-310.

4. See Harold R. Isaacs, *The New World of Negro Americans* (New York, 1963), pp. 62–96, for an excellent discussion, with references, of the symbolic meaning of color to Negroes. See also A. Kardiner and L. Ovesey, *The Mark of Oppression* (New York, 1951). An interesting paper on this subject is Janet Kennedy's "Problems Posed in the Analysis of Negro Patients," *Psychiatry,* Vol. 15, No. 3 (August 1952), pp. 313–327.

5. Lillian Smith, *Killers of the Dream* (New York, 1949); W. J. Cash, *Mind of the South* (New York, 1941); C. Vann Woodward, *The Strange Career of Jim Crow* (New York, 1955). Southern writers like Faulkner, Eudora Welty, Shirley Ann Grau, and Flannery O'Connor constantly return to the

themes of savage hate and sly or desperate love between whites and Negroes. William Taylor's *Cavalier and Yankee* (New York, 1961) illustrates how the racial problem similarly touched and influenced writers in earlier times.

6. Eugene B. Brody, "Social Conflict and Schizophrenic Behavior in Young Adult Negro Males," *Psychiatry*, Vol. 24, No. 4 (November 1961), pp. 337–346.

7. For example, Allison Davis and John Dollard, *The Children of Bondage* (Washington, D. C., 1940); Gunner Myrdal, *An American Dilemma* (New York, 1944 and 1962); Kenneth B. Clark, *Prejudice and Your Child* (Boston, 1955); Marie Jahoda, *Race Relations and Mental Health* (Paris, 1960); Group for the Advancement of Psychiatry, "Psychiatric Aspects of Desegregation," Report No. 37, 1957; Kardiner and Ovesey, *op. cit.*

8. John Dollard, in *Caste and Class in a Southern Town* (Garden City, N. Y., 1957), gives a close analysis to the roots of such emotions. Less analytical than descriptive and autobiographical are such books as Hodding Carter's *Southern Legacy* (Baton Rouge, La., 1950); or William A. Percy's *Lanterns on the Levee* (New York, 1959).

9. Kardiner and Ovesey, *op. cit.*

10. Stanley M. Elkins, *Slavery* (Chicago, 1959); Kardiner and Ovesey, *op. cit.*

11. I have elsewhere described both the value and hazards of clinical fieldwork in social psychiatry. Whatever "validity" my impressions have rests on five years of extensive and intensive interviews with Negro and white Southerners under the various conditions and stresses of desegregation. By no means have I cursorily spoken with children and adults. In two score cases I have known them for four years, and followed them closely (once or twice a week) for at least two of those years. As a child psychiatrist, I have spent my fair share of time on my hands and knees with the younger children, trying to learn their vision of the world, their feelings about themselves and others through their games and frolic, their drawings and paintings. In this regard, see the sections on "method" in the two papers mentioned in footnote one. See, also, R. Coles, "Social Struggle and Weariness," *Psychiatry*, Vol. 27, No. 4 (November 1964), pp. 305–315; "Observation or Participation: The Problem of Psychiatric Research in Social Issues," read at District Assembly of American Psychiatric Association, Philadelphia, November 1964, in print, *Journal of Nervous and Mental Disease*, 1965; "A Matter of Territory," *Journal of Social Issues*, Vol. 20, No. 4 (October 1964), pp. 43–53. For more general and speculative discussion see R. Coles, "Children and Racial Demonstrations," *American Scholar*, Vol. 34, No. 1 (Winter 1964–65), pp. 78–92; "The South That Is Man's Destiny," *Massachusetts Review*, Vol. 6, No. 2 (Winter 1965), pp. 257–269; "Serpents and Doves: Non-Violent Youth in the South" in Erik H. Erikson (ed.), *Youth: Change and Challenge* (New York, 1963); and "Private Problems and Public Evil: Psychiatry and Segregation," *Yale Review*, Vol. 14, No. 4 (Summer 1965), pp. 513–531.

12. Robert Penn Warren, *Who Speaks for the Negro?* (New York, 1965).

13. See Erik H. Erikson's essay "Psychological Reality and Historial Actuality" in *Insight and Responsibility* (New York, 1964). See, also, his paper "Psychoanalysis and Ongoing History—Problems of Identity, Hate and Non-Violence," read at Annual Meeting of the American Psychiatric Association, May 1965.

G. FRANKLIN EDWARDS

Community and Class Realities: The Ordeal of Change

ONE OF the paradoxes of American life is that though the Negro is an old-line American he is not yet fully American. His presence in this country antedates that of most immigrant groups, but his career and community life are greatly different from those of immigrants from northern and southern Europe. In terms of the basic socialization processes and the community contexts in which they occur, differences between the Negro and these immigrant groups, including the most recent large-scale arrivals, the Puerto Ricans, are apparent.

Immigrant groups from Europe have followed a somewhat typical process as they moved into the main stream of American life. Most members of these groups entered the work force at the bottom of the economic ladder, as small farmers and as unskilled, semiskilled, and service workers. They lived initially among fellow immigrants in small village communities or in poorer city neighborhoods in which communal institutions helped cushion the cultural shock induced by the differences between life in their countries of origin and life in the United States. Family, church, the foreign language press, and mutual aid organizations helped in the adjustment process. Members of the second and succeeding generations acquired increasing amounts of education and the skills necessary to take advantage of available opportunities; eventually the Americanization process was fairly complete. By and large, members of these groups have assimilated American values and today experience little physical and cultural isolation based upon ethnicity. Although individual members of these groups continue to experience discrimination in the areas of admission to educational institutions, job promotions in industry, and acceptance into voluntary associations, a consciousness of group rejection does not exist. In those instances where strong in-group community life exists, it is owing more to the persistence of group cohesion than to restraints from without.

In contrast to the pattern of immigrant groups, the Negro has remained socially and morally isolated from the American society. At no time in the almost three and a half centuries of his history in this country has he been "counted in." His caste-like position is owing more to restraints from without than to any centripetal force serving to keep him separated from other groups. He has lived, according to E. Franklin Frazier's characterization, as "a nation within a nation."[1] Robin Williams recently has referred to the general Negro community as "a world in the shadow,"[2] and James Silver, in describing an extreme instance of a local community's exclusion of Negroes, has referred to the "closed society."[3]

One basic difference between the Negro and these immigrant groups is that the former served for nearly two centuries as slaves. Although succeeding generations of Negroes acquired increased amounts of education after the Emancipation, access to opportunities commensurate with formal training often was denied because of color. The failure to learn certain basic skills to qualify for jobs in the world of work placed serious limitations upon the horizontal and social mobility experienced by members of the group. As a matter of fact, the social mobility of Negroes up to the present has been determined more by conditions within the Negro community than by those of the broader society. The number and distribution of Negroes within the professions, for example, have been related more directly to the needs of the Negro community for certain types of services than to the demands of the broader society.[4] It is for this reason that clergymen and teachers, functionaries required by the segregated Negro community, have represented at least one-half of all Negro professional persons at any given period.

The segregation of Negroes from the main stream of American life has produced institutional patterns and behavior which have a bearing upon contemporary efforts to eliminate inequalities between the two major racial groups. The behaviors are expressed as deviations of Negroes from many normative patterns of American life and suggest something of the magnitude of the differentials which must be dealt with if reconciliation, rather than further alienation, is to be achieved.

The contrasts in background experiences between the Negro and immigrant groups raise the fundamental question of whether, given the promise of recent changes, the Negro will now be integrated into American society in much the same manner as have these other groups. Any strict analogy between the future course of the Negro's relationsip to American society and the processes which occurred in the experiences of immigrant groups, however, is subject to serious limitations and error.

The long history of oppression has profoundly affected the Negro's self-esteem. The fears, suspicions and feelings of inadequacy generated in the Negro by his subordinate status are not duplicated in the experiences of immigrant groups. Moreover, color and other physical traits distinguish the Negro sharply from other groups in the society. In the past these characteristics were taken as physical stigmata which reinforced negative attitudes toward the Negro. Sharp physical differences were not present to complicate the relationships of immigrants to American society, although differences in this regard can be observed between the northern Europeans, on the one hand, and southern Europeans and Orientals, on the other.

The attitudes of the Negro toward himself are merely reciprocals of the attitudes of other groups toward him. There always have been serious reservations on the part of American whites regarding the Negro's capacity to live on a basis of equality with other Americans. Such reservations about the potentialities of immigrant groups for assimilation were not held in the same serious way.

Finally, it should be observed that significant advancement in the status of the Negro comes at a time when economic conditions are quite different from those faced by immigrant groups. The great influx of immigrants came at a time when there was a market for agricultural labor and unskilled work and mobility through these avenues was still possible. The Negro today has been displaced from the farm and must now compete for work in an urban market which requires a somewhat higher degree of education and technical skill than was the case a half century ago. Given the present educational and occupational inadequacies of a large segment of the Negro population, the task of overcoming these deficiencies is formidable.

While it is clear that further changes in the status of the Negro will occur in the years ahead, moving the Negro nearer to equality with other Americans, the processes by which this will be achieved are certain to be difficult and tortuous. The remainder of this essay is an elaboration of this viewpoint.

Foremost among the indicators of the social isolation of Negroes is the Negro ghetto. It represents at once the restrictions placed upon the living space of the Negro minority and, as Kenneth Clark recently has pointed out, a way of life with a peculiar institutional patterning and psychological consequences.[5] Unlike most immigrant ghettos, which show a tendency to break up, the Negro ghetto, especially in Northern cities, has become more dense.

Karl Taeuber and Alma Taeuber, on the basis of an examination of segregation indices in 109 American cities from 1940 to 1960, note that in 83 of the 109 cities the segregation index was higher in 1950 than in 1940. Between 1950 and 1960, only 45 of these cities showed an increase. But it was observed that cities with already high levels of segregation were prominent among those with increases. A most significant observation is that in recent years Southern cities have had the highest increases in the physical segregation of Negroes, and the South now has the highest index of any region.[6] This is important inasmuch as in earlier periods Negroes were less segregated in the older Southern cities than in cities located in other regions.[7]

The concentration of Negroes in the central cities of our metropolitan areas and within the inlying cores of these central cities is too well documented to warrant elaboration here. Our concern is with the fact that the areas inhabited by Negroes are inferior in terms of housing quality, recreational facilities, schools, and general welfare services, and that all of these deficiencies contribute to crime, delinquency, school dropouts, dependency, broken families, excessive deaths, and other conditions which represent the "pathology of the ghetto." The pathology is most evident in housing. In 1960, for example, 44 per cent of all dwelling units occupied by Negroes were substandard. Though nonwhites occupied only 10 per cent of all dwelling units, they occupied 27 per cent of those classed as substandard. Thirteen per cent of nonwhites lived in units which were seriously overcrowded, and there was an increase of 85,000 such units occupied by Negroes between 1950 and 1960.[8]

Efforts to break up the ghetto, and hence to ameliorate the pathological conditions generated by it, have not been productive. Attempts by Negroes to leave the ghetto run afoul of a most formidable network of relationships involving brokers, builders, bankers, realtors, and citizens' organizations serving to restrict Negroes to certain neighborhoods.[9] There is, indeed, a vast profit to be made from slum housing, and this accounts for much of the behavior of some realtors. One study demonstrates that a slum landlord receives fifteen dollars more monthly if a substandard unit is rented to a Negro family than if the same unit were rented to a white family.[10]

Myths regarding neighborhood deterioration following Negro occupancy persist, despite empirical studies which expose their fallacious character.

By and large, our urban renewal programs, designed to revitalize the older, more dilapidated areas of our cities, have not succeeded in providing better accommodations in the renewal areas for most Negroes, the majority of the displacees. They have succeeded very largely in having Negroes move into public housing and blighted areas. While in many instances the physical accommodations to which displaced populations moved represent an improvement over their former dwellings,[11] segregation has not been lessened. In our metropolitan centers, for example, despite recent efforts to build small, scattered public housing units, most projects constructed under this program have been large in size and have contributed to segregation as they became either nearly all-white or nearly all-Negro.

It is clear that the Negro ghetto, unlike other ghettos, has had great external pressure to keep it "hemmed in." While some of the greater concentration of Negroes in the older areas of our cities stems from income differentials between Negroes and whites, the Taeubers, using data for the city of Chicago, found that income differentials accounted for only 14 per cent of the observed racial segregation in housing in 1950 and 12 per cent in 1960.[12] They further observed that "on every measure—the Puerto Rican population [of Chicago] is less well off—it is less educated, of lower income, more crowded, less likely to be homeowners, less well housed, and lives in older buildings, yet the index of residential segregation for Puerto Ricans is sixty-seven as compared to eighty-two for Negroes.[13] There is now considerable evidence, also, that after two generations of strong community solidarity Chinese and Japanese communities in our cities show a considerable dispersion.[14]

Although in recent years some moderation of the tight housing market has occurred within the central city—thus permitting Negroes to obtain housing left by the whites who moved to the suburbs—the proportion of the suburban population which is Negro has declined steadily since 1900. Negroes have become increasingly locked in the central city, giving rise to the observation that there is a white noose around our central cities. In 1960, Negroes were less than 5 per cent of the population of metropolitan areas outside central cities, but they made up 17 per cent of the central city population of these areas.[15]

There is some hope that Executive Order 11063, issued by President Kennedy on November 20, 1962, banning discrimination in housing insured by agencies of the federal government, will have a salutary effect in reducing the degree of concentration and segregation of the Negro population. But skeptics point out that the Order does not cover all home-mortgage insuring agencies of the federal government, the Home Loan Bank Board constituting an important exception, and in recent years a smaller proportion of new construction has been built with federal insurance. Most importantly, the Order is not retroactive, leaving unaffected the housing stock existing at the time of its issuance.

Access by Negroes to much of the newly constructed housing must depend upon the supplementation of the national Order against discrimination by state and local ordinances having the same objective. In recent years there has been an increase in the number of such ordinances. By and large, however, the basic approach of local communities is conciliation of disputes, and much depends upon the vigor with which these local ordinances are enforced if they are to have any significant effect in countering discrimination and reducing segregation.

But significant moderation of Negro concentration and segregation depends upon more than laws against discrimination, however important these may be. The attitudes of both Negroes and whites toward integrated community life are important determinants of the extent to which deconcentration will occur, given enforcement of even the most severe sanctions against discrimination. There is abundant evidence, as mentioned earlier, that myths exist regarding the lowering of housing values and the maintenance of community patterns following invasion by Negroes, and many whites are inclined to move, so that in time complete succession, or turnover of neighborhoods from white to Negro, occurs. On the other hand, there is some resistance on the part of Negroes to moving into areas, especially the suburbs, where few Negroes live. This is particularly characteristic of families with children who must attend school and are dependent on neighbors for play and other social experiences. The well-founded fear of rejection by white neighbors leads to a foregoing of economic advantages which purchases in white areas represent or, in the case of suburban purchases, of a style of living consistent with one's social and economic level. Though numerous white liberal groups, mainly in suburban communities, have organized to encourage Negroes to purchase homes in their neighborhoods, they are often disappointed with the responses to their sincerest solicitations. The centripetal forces tying Negroes to the Negro community are the products of fear and isolated living and are likely to discourage any large exodus of Negroes to suburban communities in the immediate future. Doubtless open-occupancy patterns will result in a significantly larger number of Negroes residing in mixed areas at some future period, but the pattern of increase is likely to be exponential rather than linear.

This continued physical separation of the major racial groups has an impact upon social relationships between them. It limits the number of intimate contacts and the possibilities for understanding which grow out of association. Robin Williams, on the basis of an examination of the patterns of interracial contact in a large number of communities, concludes that the presence of a Negro subcommunity limits Negro interaction with whites, and barriers to communication between the two groups lead to inadequate understanding and to a perception of the other group as hostile.[16] Duncan and Lieberson make the same point in a somewhat different way when they state that segregation is inversely related to assimilation.[17]

The growing awareness of the limitations of life in the ghetto, as a result of the influence of mass media, increased physical mobility, and better education, has played a vital part in precipitating the "Negro Revolution." The mass demonstrations for equality of treatment in places of public accommodations, for access to better quality schools, for equal employment opportunities and voting rights are thought of as efforts by Negroes to achieve first-class citizenship. In another sense, they are efforts to overcome the barriers which have isolated Negroes from aspects of American life.

The difficulty of overcoming the problems created by the physical fact of the ghetto is indicated by attempts to improve the quality of education of schools in slum areas. In our large metropolitan cities, because of the segregation in housing and the traditional neighborhood concept of school attendance, a disproportionate number of schools, particularly at the elementary level, becomes predominantly Negro or predominantly white, with the Negro schools being inferior. Opposing theories for dealing with this situation, generally regarded as undesirable, have generated serious community conflicts. There are those who feel that the efforts should be concentrated upon improving the quality of education in these depressed areas by larger allocations for plant improvement, remedial work, new curricula, and better trained teachers. Other students of the problem contend that substantial improvement of slum schools cannot be achieved until such schools lose their predominantly Negro or predominantly white character. It becomes necessary in the thinking of the protagonists of this latter view to develop methods for overcoming racial imbalances in the schools. While a variety of techniques have been proposed, each has generated rather serious opposition. It is patent that this problem, one of the serious concerns of the leaders of the Negro Revolution largely because it is tied to segregation in housing, will not be easily solved.

As mentioned previously, the ghetto has not only restricted the interaction of Negroes with other members of the society, and hence symbolized the isolation under which Negroes have lived; but it has also been a primary force in the generation and persistence of atypical institutional patterns which are viewed as dysfunctional in any effort at reconciliation. Doubtless the foremost of these institutions is the Negro family which, because of historical circumstances connected with slavery and the isolated conditions under which Negroes have lived in both urban and rural areas, is characterized by rather significant variations from the dominant American family pattern. It is not so much the differences *per se,* or any mere deviation of Negro family characteristics from those of white middle-class families, but the variations in structural and interactional features known to be desirable in family living which become causes of concern.

The most salient feature of Negro family life which captures the attention of those concerned with integration of Negroes into American life is the degree of disorganization represented by structural breakdown. In only three-quarters of all Negro families, as compared with approximately nine-tenths of all white families, were both spouses present. One Negro family in five (21 per cent) was headed by a female and 5 per cent had only the male head present. Thus one Negro family in four, as compared with one white family in ten, was headed by a single parent. This differential in the percentage of families headed by one parent accounts in part for the fact that in 1960 only one-third of Negro children under eighteen years of age, as compared with one in ten white children of comparable age, lived in families in which only one parent was present.

The assumption underlying the desirability of family unity—the presence of both spouses—is that on balance the economic, social, and affectual roles may be best discharged when both mates are present in the home. Divorce, desertion, and separation follow the generation and expression of tensions which, even before rupture occurs, reduce the effectiveness with which the mates can discharge the duties and obligations of family life, as well as deny the satisfactions derived from the intimate sharing of experiences and attainment of goals. In essence, the organized and unified family becomes at once a matrix for the personal satisfaction of the marital partners and for the protection, proper socialization, and well-being of their children. This is not to deny that the basic goals of family life, regarding child-rearing and other functions, may not be achieved by the single-parent family. Given the complexities of modern urban life and the established normative values around which the modern family is organized, however, the discharge of family functions may best be achieved when the family is unified.

In analyzing the statistics on the Negro family one becomes aware that the instability of the Negro family unit is greater than is represented by statistics on the percentages of males and females enumerated as widowed or divorced. In 1960, 15 per cent of all Negro males and 20 per cent of all Negro females, though enumerated by the Census as married, were living apart from their mates. The percentage of Negro males separated from their mates is four times as large as the comparable percentage for white males, and for Negro females four and one-half times as large as for white females.

The instability of Negro family life is explained only in part by the historical conditioning of attitudes toward family life, beginning with slavery, when strong family ties were not encouraged and Negroes, as Elkins has suggested, were made dependent upon whites.[18] The phenomenon arises also from forces of contemporary American life which place limits upon the possibility of successful family organization. These are reflected in the statistics on characteristics of the heads of Negro families.

As reported by the last Census, approximately one-half, 48.5 per cent, of the heads of nonwhite (mainly Negro) families had not finished elementary school. Even in urban areas where access to educational opportunities is somewhat greater and school-attendance laws somewhat better enforced than in rural farm and nonfarm areas, two out of five nonwhite family heads failed to reach the last year of elementary school. Of nonwhite heads living in rural nonfarm and rural farm areas, 70 and 80 per cent, respectively, had failed to attain this level of schooling.[19] The low level of educational achievement for such a large proportion of nonwhite family heads has obvious implications for the cultural life to which the Negro child is exposed in the home and doubtless for the type of motivation the child receives for achievement in school. It also is related to the labor-force participation and income of nonwhites.

In an economy in which automation is rapidly introducing changes in the demand for certain types of labor, the heads of nonwhite families were disproportionately represented in those occupational categories in which fewer workers are required and monetary returns are small. Only 13 per cent of all nonwhite family heads, as compared with 40 per cent of white heads, were in professional, managerial, and clerical occupations for which labor demands are increasing. One in five white heads, but only one in ten among nonwhite, was a skilled worker. Thus, one in four nonwhite heads, as compared with three in five white, were white-collar and skilled workers.[20] The heavier identification with semiskilled and unskilled work accounts in part for the nonwhite employment rate being twice as large as the comparable rate of whites and for greater underemployment among nonwhites.

The type of job and both underemployment and unemployment influence the relatively low income of nonwhite family heads. The median nonwhite family income of $3,465 in 1963 was only approximately 53 per cent of the white family income of $6,548. More than two-fifths of all nonwhite families (41 per cent) earned less than $3,000 in 1963, which placed them at the poverty level, and only one in twenty earned $10,000 or more in the same year.[21] It is significant to note, in line with our previous discussion regarding the desirability of family closure—both parents in the home—that in 1959 families in which both husband and wife were present in the home had a median income of $3,633 as compared with a median of $1,734 for families having a female head.[22]

The problems of the Negro family, then, in terms of its instability and the associated phenomena of crime, delinquency, school dropouts, high morbidity and mortality are related to a complex of interwoven factors, of which level of educational attainment and income are important components. The President of the United States, in a historic speech at Howard University in June 1965, pointed to the complexity of the problem by stating that the provision of jobs, decent homes, welfare and social programs, care of the sick, and understanding attitudes are only partial answers to the conditions of the Negro family.[23] "The breakdown of the Negro family," he stated, "is related to centuries of oppression and persecution of the Negro man. It flows from long years of degradation and discrimination which have attacked his dignity and assaulted his ability to produce for his family."[24] The President added that though we know much about Negro family life, other answers are still to be found. For this reason he indicated he would call a White House Conference in the fall to explore the problem further.

A definitive study by Hylan Lewis of child-rearing practices among low-income Negro families in the District of Columbia reveals that there is, indeed, still much to be learned about the operating dynamics and underlying causes of disorganization among such units.[25] What often is accepted as knowledge about these families is in fact mythology. It is noted, in the first instance, that these families are not homogeneous as regards their organization, functioning, and ambitions for their children. In many of them considerable strength is to be noted, but the exigencies of daily living often deny the achievement of the parents' most ambitious plans. Though parents set training and discipline goals for their children, these are often undermined by influences beyond their power, and the actual control over their children may be lost as early as the fifth or sixth year.

Investigation reveals that many of these parents, particularly the mothers, are warm, human, and concerned individuals who, despite deprivation and trouble, are persistent in their desires to have their children become respectable and productive citizens and in their willingness to sacrifice for them. The picture contrasts with the common belief that in an overwhelming majority of low-income families parents reject their children and are hostile to them.

Lewis' study raises questions regarding assigned reasons for alleged male irresponsibility toward family obligations and the degree of family concern with pregnancy out of wedlock and illegitimate births. There does appear to be a greater degree of concern by the male regarding his responsibilities and by family members regarding the sexual behavior of their offspring than is commonly recognized. What in fact emerges is that the behavior of these lower-income families is a practical response to untoward circumstances which undermine the well-intentioned, but often unattainable, goals of these units.

The major problems of the Negro family are experienced in urban areas where more than 70 per cent of such families now live.

There has been a heavy migration during the past twenty-five years from farms and small towns to large metropolitan areas. The limited extent to which many of these families can cope with the demands of urban life, given the low educational level and obsolescent skills of the adults, raises serious questions for the American society as well as for the families themselves. The War on Poverty, youth opportunity programs, medicare and other changes in our social security program are certain to exercise some influences in ameliorating existing conditions. But the deep-seated nature of many of those conditions and the personality damage they have produced, as expressed in feelings of powerlessness, hopelessness, and forms of anti-social conduct, give rise to the prediction that no easy solution to problems of the Negro family may be found. This is especially true of those "hard core" or multi-problem families in many of which at least two generations have been dependent on public assistance programs. Present efforts to focus upon the young, as evidenced in Project Head Start and programs for youth, on the assumption that this population is most amenable to change, are based upon sound theory. There remains, however, the complex problem of improving the skills and enhancing the self-esteem of the adult members whose personalities are crystallized and whose levels of expectation have been shaped under an entirely different set of conditions. What is apparent is that the problems of the Negro family are intimately tied to those of the larger community.

The elimination of many of these difficulties depends upon a commitment to invest a great deal more of our resources in improving educational and social services, including more effective family limitation programs. What is indicated is that by opening the opportunity structure and providing both formal and informal education on a more extensive scale through diverse programs, key figures in many Negro problem families will be enabled over time to develop self-esteem and a "rational" approach to urban life, which many students regard as indispensable for successful adjustment to the urban environment. This can hardly occur as long as the present constraints and limitations continue to operate against a large segment of the Negro population or, to put it differently, as long as the isolation of the Negro is continued.

The difficulty of changing existing patterns is evident in a number of current efforts. The Manpower Retraining Program, for example, has encountered difficulty in working with enrollees with less than an eighth-grade education, which would exclude large numbers of Negro males from successful participation. Of all projects started under the Manpower Development and Retraining Act in 1963, 3 per cent of the enrollees had less than eight years of schooling, while 36 per cent had between eight and eleven years. Fifty-one per cent were high-school graduates, and another 10 per cent had gone beyond the high-school level.[26] Educational levels must be raised considerably before some of the disadvantaged can benefit from available training opportunities.

The problems of developing motivation, rather than supplying specific job skills, appear to be even harder to overcome. Charles Silberman, among others, has pointed out that the effort to eliminate poverty must involve the poor in action programs if the motivation to improve their lot is to be realized. Recent controversies over involvement of the poor in strikes, boycotts, and pickets and the use of other techniques to dramatize their condition and counteract feelings of apathy and cynicism have been sharply criticized by local citizens, especially those in the power structure.[27]

Finally, the bold program advanced by Whitney Young, Executive Director of the National Urban League, calling for a "Marshall Plan" for Negroes as a means of upgrading the competency and well-being of the Negro family, encounters serious opposition.[28] The charge of preferential treatment is raised, and this runs counter to the ideology of equal treatment. What is more important is that the practical operation of such a program would encounter difficulty from institutionalized patterns. To request preferential treatment for Negroes in apprentice programs and preferential hiring after completion of training, for example, cross-cuts seniority and other established principles of union organization and practice.

All of the above are mere illustrations of the complications involved in any effort to strengthen the Negro family in particular and to upgrade Negro life in general. They should serve to introduce some caution into the thinking of those sanguine persons who are persuaded that broad-scale and rapid changes are likely to occur in a short period of time. (The position taken here is not an apology for the gradualist position regarding race relations changes. It is, indeed, understandable that civil rights groups must inveigh continuously against the gradualist perspective as a matter of strategy. Our concern is with traditional and countervailing influences which have the effect of slowing the pace at which change might occur.)

The disabilities of the Negro family discussed in the preceding paragraphs are most characteristic of low-income units. Not all Negro families are affected by inadequate income, education, and employment opportunities, and many of them do not lack strong family traditions. There is a considerable differentiation within the Negro community in terms of status groups and social classes.

E. Franklin Frazier observed that as late as World War I the Negro middle class was composed "principally of teachers, doctors, preachers, trusted persons in personal service, government employees, and a few business men."[29] He stated further that:

This group was distinguished from the rest of the Negro population not so much by economic factors as by social factors. Family affiliation and education to a less degree were as important as income. Moreover, while it exhibited many middle-class features such as its emphasis on morality, it also possessed characteristics of an upper class or aristocracy.[30]

The urbanization of the Negro population, beginning with World War I and continuing to the present, resulted in the formation of large ghettos in Northern and Southern cities and provided the condition for greater occupational differentiation within the Negro community. The differentiation was more pronounced in Northern communities where Negroes had a substantially greater opportunity to enter clerical and technical occupations than was true in Southern cities, and where the large population base provided economic support for a sizeable corps of professional functionaries. Education and income became more important than social distinctions in determining class membership.

The Negro middle class today includes a still relatively small, but expanding, number of persons. If occupation is used as a criterion for determining membership and those in professional and technical, clerical, sales, and skilled occupations are included, only approximately 26 per cent of all nonwhite workers belong to the middle class. White workers in these above-mentioned categories represent 64 per cent of all whites in the labor force.[31] The contrast between the two occupational structures is further indicated by the fact that the percentage of white workers, taken as a proportion of all white workers, is twice as large as the comparable percentage of nonwhite workers in professional and kindred occupations, and in clerical and skilled work; four times as large in managerial occupations; and three times as large in the sales category.

In none of the specific occupational categories associated with the middle class did nonwhite male workers achieve parity with white males in median income. The nearest approximation to parity in 1959 was in clerical and kindred occupations in which the non-white male median earnings of $4,072 was approximately 85 per cent of the white male median of $4,785. In none of the other categories did nonwhite male workers receive so much as 70 per cent of the median income of white males in the category.[32]

The expansion of the Negro middle class has been most marked by accretion of persons in professional, technical, clerical, and sales occupations. This expansion by approximately 300,000 persons since 1940 has been influenced in part by government policy which prohibits those business firms holding contracts with the federal government from discriminating against workers on the basis of race, religion, creed, or national origin. In engineering, architecture, and the natural sciences, occupations oriented to the wider world of work rather than to the Negro community, the increases among Negroes, though small in absolute numbers, have been rather dramatic. Between 1950 and 1960, there was a three-fold increase in the number of Negro engineers. The number of Negro architects increased by 72 per cent, and the number of natural scientists by 77 per cent.[33] This expansion comes at the end of a half century in which Negroes could hardly expect to earn a living in these fields and thus were not encouraged to prepare for entering them.

The number of Negroes in medicine, dentistry, and law, whose services traditionally have been oriented to the Negro community, has begun to increase rather significantly. During the 1950's, physicians increased by 14 per cent, dentists by 31 per cent, and lawyers by 43 per cent.[34] More substantial fellowship and scholarship aid, ability to pay for professional education, as well as the opening of the segregated professional schools in the Southern states, have contributed to this result.

It is not only the increase in number of these professionals which deserves attention; the improved opportunities for advanced training and learning experiences are also of importance. On the basis of increased opportunities for internships and residency training, the number of Negro physicians who became diplomates of medical specialty boards increased from 92 in 1947 to 377 in 1959.[35] Negro physicians, lawyers, and dentists are admitted today to membership in local societies of national professional organizations in larger numbers and enjoy the privileges these societies provide for continued professional growth.

It should be remembered, however, that these gains, while significant in terms of what has occurred in Negro life heretofore, are relatively small. The ratios of the actual to expected numbers of Negroes in middle-class occupations, as measured by the total labor force distribution, are extremely small.[36]

The differences between Negro and white community life cannot be measured solely by variations in income, occupation, education, and other objective indicators. In assessing the differences, it is important to recognize that the Negro class structure and institutions have emerged in response to segregation and represent adjustments to the isolation under which Negroes have lived. The meaning of relationships within the community and the values placed upon them must be considered.

Frazier has observed, for example, that in the absence of a true upper class based upon old family ties and wealth, the Negro middle class simulates the behavior of the white upper class without possessing the fundamental bases upon which such behavior rests.[37] Moreover, segregation has provided a monopoly for many Negroes in business and the professions and has introduced, in many cases, differential standards of performance. This has important consequences for any consideration of desegregation, for those who enjoy a vested interest in the segregated community are not likely to welcome competition from the broader community. The Negro church represents an extreme instance of vested interest in the Negro community and, at the same time, is the most important institution giving expression to the Negro masses. For this reason no degree of acceptance of Negroes by white churches is likely to bring about the dissolution of Negro churches.[38]

The Negro community doubtless will be the source of social life of Negroes for some time into the future. Sororities, fraternities, clubs, and other organizations will continue to serve a meaningful function. The acceptance by whites of Negroes as fellow workers often bears little relationship to their willingness to share social experiences with them outside the plant or office or to have them as neighbors.

The importance of the Negro community as a source of social life is indicated by the fact that, though the majority of the members of a Negro professional society felt that its members should identify with the local chapter of the national organization representing the profession when the opportunity became available, one-quarter had some reservation about joining and another 5 per cent were opposed to joining. The underlying reasons for reservations to becoming members of the formerly white organization were that, though Negroes may be accepted as professional colleagues, they would not be treated as social equals and that opportunities for leadership roles would be lost if the Negro association were dissolved.[39] What is patently indicated is that most members thought they should have the *right* to membership in the local chapter of the national organization, but they should retain their own association for social and professional reasons.

Despite the effort to conserve the conceived advantages of the Negro community, the larger social forces are introducing changes. Already the small Negro entrepreneurial group is threatened by these forces. Speaking to a group of Negro businessmen in Detroit, the Assistant Secretary of Commerce for Economic Affairs referred to the disappearance of the monopoly Negroes formerly held in certain businesses.[40] The impact of desegregation is being felt, he said, in the Negro market, for, as the income of Negro consumers expands, white businessmen become more conscious of the Negro's purchasing power. To this end they have added a cadre of professional Negro salesmen to their payrolls for the specific purpose of developing the Negro market. The success of this undertaking is indicated by the fact that many of the employed Negroes have risen to top executive posts in these organizations. Moreover, Negroes have begun to buy in increasing amounts from shopping centers serving the Negro community and have begun to patronize places of public accommodations other than those traditionally operated by Negroes. This change in consumer behavior represents a steady and gradual erosion of the position of the Negro businessman. The cruelest blow of all, the Assistant Secretary stated, is that "the large life insurance companies serving the market at large are bidding away Negro life insurance salesmen at an increasing rate."[41] These and other changes are certain to influence the structure of the Negro community.

The Ordeal of Change

From observing current developments in race relations and the operation of the larger social forces in our society, it is evident that several basic conditions operate to influence the pattern and pace at which change is occurring. These provide some insight into what may be expected in the future in regard to the general status of the Negro minority; they document the theory of slow and gradual change for some time to come in most areas and somewhat more rapid change in others.

A first consideration, not prominently mentioned heretofore, is the opposition to change by segments of the white community. Beginning with the school desegregation decision, there has been a mobilization of white community efforts to prevent the attainment of desegregation in many aspects of community life. This opposition has taken a variety of forms: the closing of schools, violence visited upon Negroes, intimidation of Negroes and threats to their job security, the rise of some hate groups—such as Citizens' Councils and Night Riders—and the strengthening of others—such as the Ku Klux Klan—the resurrection of racial ideologies having the purpose of establishing the inferiority of the Negro, and a variety of other techniques designed to slow the desegregation process.[42]

What is important in this connection is that many of the organizations connected with the opposition have had the support, if not the leadership, of prominent persons in the power structure; many governors, mayors, legislators, and prominent businessmen have all given support to the resistance efforts, owing to political and economic expediency, if not to personal sentiment. Moreover, persons with some claim to scientific respectability in the academic community have contributed to the questioning of whether differentials between Negroes and whites stem from the former's disadvantaged community life or from the Negro's innate biological inferiority.[43]

There is no doubt that these forces have served to slow the process of desegregation. As late as December 1964, only 2 per cent of Negro pupils in eleven Southern states formerly having segregated school systems were attending schools with whites. If the six Border states where desegregation did not encounter the same serious opposition as in the other eleven states are included in the count, only 11 per cent of Negro pupils attend schools having a mixed population.[44] This has led to one student's referring to developments in this area as "ten years of prelude," suggesting that the pace may be somewhat more rapid in the future.[45]

There does appear to be a lessening of the opposition in many areas as a result of several important factors. These include self-interest on the part of prominent businessmen, many of whom have spoken out against violence and have used their influence otherwise. The passage of important legislation within the past year—the

Civil Rights Act of 1964 and the Voting Rights Act of 1965—are certain to have an influence in softening open resistance. But doubtless resistance to change will continue in subtle ways, perhaps under a blanket of legitimacy, as in the instance of the large-scale discharge of Negro teachers in Southern states in recent months following the necessity of having to comply with the Commissioner of Education's "Statement of Policies" for enforcement of Title VI of the Civil Rights Act, by which Southern school systems are expected to make a substantial start toward complete desegregation by September 1965 and to complete the process by the fall of 1967.

A second important force affecting change is inherent in the nature of the phenomenon itself, especially the contribution made by the accumulated disabilities of the Negro family, and in individuals in terms of inadequate education, job skills, housing, patterns of dependency, and low self-esteem. The advancement toward a more equalitarian society depends upon how fully these disabilities can be overcome or eliminated. Any analysis must consider the generational problem, for the extent to which the education and job skills of many adult family heads—those over forty-five, for example—can be improved is problematic.

A stronger basis of hope rests with the generation which begins school under improved educational conditions and whose levels of aspiration will be shaped by a social context which varies considerably from that of the past half century, and may be expected to vary even more in the future. But even under the most favorable circumstances, the improvement of educational qualifications of Negroes to a position of parity with those of whites, an essential factor for job equality, may not be easily achieved. One prominent sociologist on the basis of statistical calculations concluded:

Whatever the future may hold with respect to the on-coming cohorts of young Negroes, the performance to date, together with the postulate that educational attainment is a "background" characteristic [for employment], enables us to make a most important prediction: the disparity between white and nonwhite levels of education attainment in the general population can hardly disappear in less than three-quarters of a century. Even if Negroes in their teens were to begin immediately to match the educational attainment of white children, with this equalization persisting indefinitely, we shall have to wait fifty years for the last of the cohorts manifesting race differentials to reach retirement age.[46]

The achievement of educational and occupational equality is

far more difficult to attain than equal treatment in public accommodations. Many civil rights leaders recognize this and, now that the public accommodations struggle has been successful, consider that the movement has entered a new and much tougher phase.

A third force affecting change is the attitudes held by certain Negroes who either have a vested interest in segregation or are generally fearful of the deleterious consequences desegregation will bring. This has been discussed in an earlier section, and only a further example will be furnished here. As early as 1954 Negro teachers in South Carolina registered great fear over the possible untoward effects of desegregation of the public school system on their professional status as teachers. The chief fears expressed concerned the large amount of possible job displacement, new ways to evade the granting of equality in pay, employment, and benefits, greater demands for professional preparation, and the employment of fewer couples in the school system. Though most of these teachers were ideologically committed to desegregation, their fears regarding their jobs and community relationships with whites suggest that many of them, of necessity, were ambivalent toward desegregation.[47]

It is not likely that these attitudes strongly counteract tendencies to change. Their significance lies more in the manifest desire of Negroes to maintain social distance from whites in community relations as a result of their perception of the adverse use of power by whites.

The most significant influence in determining the pattern and pace of race relations changes is the federal government. The early court decisions, particularly in the area of public accommodations, orders by the executive, and recent legislation by the Congress have had salutary effects in altering disability-producing conditions. With more rigorous enforcement, they are likely to have an even more important influence in the future. The Civil Rights Act of 1964 provides a wedge for undermining, or at least neutralizing, much of the support for denying the constitutional rights of Negroes. The sanctions provided in Title VI of the Act, relating to nondiscrimination in federally assisted programs, is certain to produce a high measure of compliance. Under the Voting Rights Act of 1965, it is expected that between 50 and 70 per cent of eligible Negro voters in the five Deep South states (Alabama, Georgia, Louisiana, Mississippi, and South Carolina) will be registered to vote by the time of the 1966 elections.[48] This result, along with the greater political consciousness of Negroes throughout the country, is certain to improve the power position of the group and result in the election of large numbers of Negroes to public office.[49]

The change in the position of the government in respect to the status of Negroes results from the altered position of this country in world affairs since the end of World War II and to a substantial shift in public opinion regarding the position of the Negro during that period. It is important, therefore, to view contemporary changes as a part of broader social movements toward improved welfare for the disadvantaged within the country and in the world. These broad forces tend to override resistances, but they are subject to challenges and counter pressures. If viewed in this broad perspective, it is clear that more significant changes which will bring the Negro greater opportunities for participation in our society lie ahead. When, in fact, basic equalities will be achieved cannot be predicted.

REFERENCES

1. E. Franklin Frazier, *Black Bourgeoisie* (New York, 1957), p. 15.

2. Robin M. Williams, Jr., *Strangers Next Door* (New York, 1964), p. 252.

3. James W. Silver, *Mississippi: The Closed Society* (New York, 1963), p. 164.

4. G. Franklin Edwards, *The Negro Professional Class* (Chicago, 1959), pp. 23-26.

5. Kenneth Clark, *Dark Ghetto* (New York, 1965), pp. 63-80.

6. Karl Taeuber and Alma Taeuber, *Negroes in Cities* (Chicago, 1965), pp. 37-43.

7. *Ibid.*, pp. 43-53.

8. *Our Nonwhite Population and its Housing: The Changes between 1950 and 1960*, Office of the Administrator, Housing and Home Finance Agency (Washington, D. C., 1963), pp. 13, 15.

9. A discussion of the supports for housing segregation is given in the Report of the Commission on Race and Housing, *Where Shall We Live?* (Berkeley, Calif., 1958), pp. 22-34.

10. Beverly Duncan and Philip Hauser, *Housing a Metropolis* (Chicago, 1960), p. 208.

11. Statistics on improvements in the quality of housing received by relocated families is given in *The Housing of Relocated Families*, Office of the Administrator, Housing and Home Finance Agency (Washington, D. C., 1965).

12. Karl Taeuber and Alma Taeuber, "Recent Trends in Race and Ethnic

Segregation in Chicago," *Proceedings of the Social Statistics Section, American Statistical Association* (Washington, D. C., 1962), p. 14.

13. *Ibid.*, p. 13.

14. *Where Shall We Live?, op. cit.*, p. 248.

15. U. S. Bureau of the Census, *U. S. Census of Population: 1960.* Selected Area Reports, Standard Metropolitan Areas, Final Report PC(3)-ID (Washington, D. C., 1963), Table 1.

16. Robin M. Williams, Jr., *op. cit.*, p. 248.

17. Otis Dudley Duncan and Stanley Lieberson, "Ethnic Segregation and Assimilation," *American Journal of Sociology*, Vol. 64 (January 1959), p. 370.

18. Stanley Elkins, *Slavery* (Chicago, 1959), pp. 115-133.

19. The statistics in this section are taken from G. Franklin Edwards, "Marriage and Family Life Among Negroes," *The Journal of Negro Education*, Vol. 32 (Fall 1963), pp. 451-465.

20. *Ibid.*, p. 463.

21. Current Population Reports, "Income of Families and Persons in the United States: 1963," Series P-60, No. 43 (Washington, D. C., 1964), Table 1, p. 21.

22. *U. S. Census of Population: 1960, U. S. Summary*, Detailed Characteristics, Final Report PC(1)-ID (Washington, D. C., 1963), Tables 224 and 225, pp. 594-603.

23. *The Howard University Magazine*, Vol. 7, No. 4 (July 1965), p. 7.

24. *Ibid.*

25. Lewis' study, conducted over a period of five years, is now being prepared for publication. The references in this paper were taken from various reports which the investigator made available to the writer.

26. *Manpower Report of the President* (Washington, D. C., 1964), Table F-3, p. 253.

27. Charles E. Silberman, *Crisis in Black and White* (New York, 1964), pp. 309 ff.

28. Whitney Young, Jr., *To Be Equal* (New York, 1964), pp. 22-33.

29. E. Franklin Frazier, "The New Negro," in *The New Negro Thirty Years Afterward* (Washington, D. C., 1955), p. 26.

30. *Ibid.*

31. Computed from U. S. Bureau of the Census *U. S. Census of Population: 1960, U. S. Summary*, Detailed Characteristics, Final Report PC (1)-ID, Table 208.

32. *Ibid.*

33. Computed from *U. S. Census of Population: 1940*, Vol. II, *Characteristics of the Population*, Part 1, *U. S. Summary*, Table 128, p. 278; and *U. S.*

Census of Population: 1960, Vol. I, *Characteristics of the Population,* Part 1, *U. S. Summary,* Table 205, p. 544.

34. *Ibid.*

35. From data supplied the writer by W. Montague Cobb, M. D., editor of the *Journal of the National Medical Association.*

36. Ratios for many of these occupations are supplied in Leonard Broom and Norval Glenn, *Transformation of the Negro American* (New York, 1965), Table 5, pp. 112-113.

37. This is the thesis of E. Franklin Frazier, *Black Bourgeoisie* (Chicago, 1957). See, especially, pp. 195-212. See, also, Frazier, "Human, All too Human," *Survey Graphic:* twelfth Calling America Number (January 1947), pp. 74-75, 99-100.

38. E. Franklin Frazier, "Desegregation as a Social Process," in Arnold Rose (ed.), *Human Behavior and Social Processes* (Boston, 1962), p. 619.

39. Martha Coffee, "A Study of a Professional Association and Racial Integration," unpublished Master's Thesis, Department of Sociology, Howard University, Washington, D. C., 1953.

40. "Desegregation and the Negro Middle Class," remarks of Dr. Andrew F. Brimmer, Assistant Secretary of Commerce for Economic Affairs, Detroit, Michigan, July 16, 1965.

41. *Ibid.,* p. 8.

42. A good discussion of these hate groups is given in James W. Vander Zanden, *Race Relations in Transition: The Segregation Crisis in the South* (New York, 1965), pp. 25-54. See, also, Arnold Forster and Benjamin Epstein, *Report on the Ku Klux Klan* (New York, 1965).

43. See the following: Wesley C. George, *The Biology of the Race Problem* (A report prepared by commission of the Governor of Alabama, 1962); and Dwight J. Ingle, "Racial Differences and the Future," *Science,* Vol. 146 (October 16, 1964), pp. 375-379.

44. Figures from *Southern School News,* Vol. 11 (December 1964), p. 1.

45. Benjamin Muse, *Ten Years of Prelude: The Story of Integration Since the Supreme Court's 1954 Decision* (New York, 1964).

46. Otis Dudley Duncan, "Population Trends, Mobility and Social Change," a paper prepared for the Seminar on Dimensions of American Society, Committee on Social Studies, American Association of Colleges for Teacher Education, p. 52. (Quoted with the permission of the author.)

47. Hurley Doddy and G. Franklin Edwards, "Apprehension of Negro Teachers Concerning Desegregation in South Carolina," *Journal of Negro Education,* Vol. 24 (Winter 1955), Table 1, pp. 30-31.

48. *The Washington Post,* September 6, 1965, p. 1.

49. For a list of the growing number of Negro office holders, see Harold F. Gosnell and Robert E. Martin, "The Negro as Voter and Office Holder," *Journal of Negro Education,* Vol. 32 (Fall 1963), pp. 415-425.

PAUL B. SHEATSLEY

White Attitudes Toward the Negro

ANY ATTEMPT to describe white attitudes toward Negroes in the 1870's or the 1890's, or immediately before or after World War I, must necessarily rely on impressionistic or anecdotal evidence, or on secondary studies of contemporary newspapers, letters, diaries, and similar materials. Only since the advent of public opinion research in the mid-nineteen thirties has it been possible to address a series of standard questions to representative samples of the general population by means of personal interviews, and to cross-tabulate the results by such factors as age, sex, race, and geographical region.

It tells much about white attitudes toward the Negro that, during the seven years from 1935 to 1942, only four questions bearing even indirectly on the subject seem to have been asked by the national public opinion polls of that time.[1] Three of these questions, dealing with opinions about the "lynching bill" then before Congress in 1937, are practically irrelevant because the results simply show that most Americans thought people should not be lynched and the question itself said nothing about race. The fourth question was asked in 1939 and reveals that two-thirds of the American public approved of Mrs. Franklin D. Roosevelt's resignation from the Daughters of the American Revolution in protest against the refusal of that organization to permit a "well-known Negro singer" to give a concert in a D.A.R. hall. The polls, for obvious reasons, tend to ask their questions about the issues that are hot, and it is clear that, during the decade preceding World War II, race relations did not qualify on this basis. Negroes had their place, and it was a rare American white who became exercised over this fact of life.

Today, of course, the situation is entirely different. Since mid-summer 1963, the question of race relations has been consistently cited by Americans as "the most important problem facing the United States," except when it has been temporarily displaced by some international crisis such as Vietnam.[2] As in 1935–42, public opinion polls have responded to the times, but today they are doing so by asking every question they can think of which will reveal more clearly the white American's response to the Negro protest movement. The results of these polls are widely publicized, but quite often are contradictory and confusing. A recent Gallup report, for example, tells us that "Today, white Americans seem more sympathetic to Negro rights than they have ever been";[3] a recent Harris report, on the other hand, warns that "At least for now, the dominant mood of white America is to put a brake on the pace of civil rights progress."[4] Actually, surveys such as these tell us much more than the quotations suggest, and one poll does not differ from others so much as it differs from itself, depending upon the questions asked. Hardly any white Americans have attitudes toward Negroes which are clearly thought out and rigidly maintained; and even those who do may have sudden qualms when they read about racial murders in the South or Negro violence on Northern streets. The problem is one of interpreting what the polls and surveys tell us so we can understand what it all means.

Proper interpretation of survey data requires some baseline or norm against which a particular finding can be evaluated. While it is of interest to know, for instance, that "eight in ten white Americans said they would not move" if a Negro family moved next door, or that 41 per cent feel that the pace of civil rights progress is too fast,[5] the numbers have little meaning unless we can anchor them somehow. One means of anchoring is to compare findings over the course of time. The figures take on added significance if we can determine whether they are increasing or decreasing in response to events. A second means is to compare subgroup differences (for example, North *vs.* South, the well-educated *vs.* those with little formal education) against the national norm. We propose to examine past and current survey findings with a view to clarifying and interpreting their meaning. In the course of this examination we shall rely mainly, though not exclusively, on data gathered by the National Opinion Research Center of the University of Chicago. The NORC data are particularly suitable for two reasons. First, the earliest national survey of white attitudes toward Negroes was conducted by NORC on behalf of the Office of War Information in 1942, and a number of the same questions have been periodically repeated in subsequent surveys. Second, in December 1963, NORC devoted an entire interview schedule to questions on race relations, administered to a national sample of white Americans. The possibilities of fruitful analysis of such a study are more promising than the examination of scattered poll results from a great number of separate surveys.

Twenty-Year Trends on School Integration[6]

Chart I shows for each of three years—1942, 1956, and 1963—

CHART I
Per Cent Who Say White Students and Negro Students
Should Go to the Same Schools

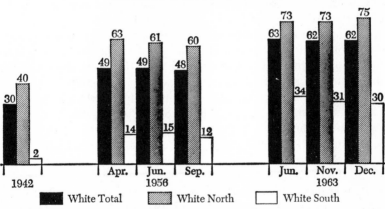

(This is an adaptation of a chart which appeared in an article by H. H. Hyman and P. B. Sheatsley, "Attitudes Toward Desegregation," *Scientific American,* Vol. 211, July 1964).

the proportion of American whites who expressed approval of integration when asked the question, "Do you think white students and Negro students should go to the same schools or to separate schools?"[7] The most striking message of the chart is the revolutionary change in white attitudes, both North and South,[8] which has taken place on this explosive issue in less than a generation. In 1942, not one American white in three approved of integrated schools. Even in the North, majority sentiment was strongly opposed, while in the South only two whites in one hundred could be found to support the proposition. By 1956, two years after the historic Supreme Court decision which abolished the "separate but equal" doctrine, white attitudes had shifted markedly. Nationwide, support for integration was now characteristic of about half the white population, while in the North it had clearly become the majority view. In the South, where only one white person in fifty had favored integration fourteen years earlier, the proportion by 1956 had risen to approximately one in seven.

The continuation of the trend from 1956 to 1963 is especially noteworthy, since the years between were marked by agitation and occasional violence which might easily have led one to suspect a reversal of attitudes and a white revulsion against integration. Desegregation of Southern schools in accordance with the Supreme Court decision had sparked physical conflict not only in Little Rock in 1957 but in dozens of smaller communities during these years. The start of the "sit-in" movement in 1960, the freedom rides of 1961, the Oxford riots of 1962 might well have hardened white attitudes and halted the trend toward acceptance of integration. But repetition of the same question to three different national samples in 1963 showed that this massive trend was still intact. By that year, almost two-thirds of all American whites expressed approval of integrated schools; among white persons in the North, the proportion was close to three in four. And in the South, which was then bearing the brunt of the Negro protest movement, sentiment for integration had climbed even faster, so that almost a third of all white Southerners agreed that white students and Negro students should attend the same schools.

The strength of the long-term trend was further attested by its immunity to short-run events. In both 1956 and 1963, it was possible to ask the question on three separate surveys at different times of the year, and it is evident that all three surveys in each year produced essentially identical results.[9] One would not necessarily have expected such short-term stability. Though largely forgotten now, there appeared between the June and September 1956 surveys the first banner headlines of racial conflict as the long slow task of Southern school desegregation began in Clay, Kentucky, Clinton, Tennessee, and other small towns in border states across the country. Between June and November 1963, there occurred the march on Washington and the September school openings, while between the November and December surveys there intervened the shocking assassination of President Kennedy in a Southern metropolis. But even so dramatic an event, with all its implications for the civil rights movement, failed to disturb, in either North or South, the attitudes which had been expressed a month earlier.

The figures shown on the chart for the South represent, of course, a geographical composite of Deep South states like Mississippi and Alabama, border states such as West Virginia and Kentucky, and southwestern states such as Arkansas and Oklahoma. We shall indicate certain regional differences later. It is possible, however, to sort the Southern respondents to the 1963 surveys into three groups, according to the amount of school integration in their communities. When this is done, it is found that a solid majority of Southern whites (58 per cent), in those few places where there had been (as of 1963) considerable integration of schools, declared that they approved of school integration. In Southern communities which had accepted only some token desegregation, 38 per cent approved; while in the hard-core segregationist communities, only 28 per cent were in favor of integration. Though the sample sizes are small, particularly in the desegregated areas, the correlation is clear: Where integration exists in the South, more whites support it.[10]

It is dangerous to try to unravel cause and effect from mere statistical correlation, yet a close analysis of the data indicates that official action to desegregate Southern schools did not wait for majority opinion to demand it, but rather preceded a change in community attitudes. In the 1956 surveys, only 31 per cent of Southern whites in those few areas which had begun at least token desegregation expressed approval of integrated schools. Clearly there was no public demand for integration in those areas then. Furthermore, by 1963 the integrated areas included not only those communities which had pioneered in integration in 1956, but also many additional communities where anti-integration sentiment had in 1956 been even stronger. Yet by 1963 the majority of Southern whites in such communities had accepted the integration of their schools. It may be noted that even in the most segregationist parts of the South, approval of integration has continued to climb. In 1956, only 4 per cent of Southern whites residing in segregated school areas approved of integration, but by 1963 the proportion in communities which had not by then introduced even token integration—the essential "hard-core" areas—had nevertheless risen to 28 per cent.

Trends on Other Racial Issues

School integration is one of the most basic and explosive of the civil rights issues, and it has provided perhaps the most apt illustration of the dramatic shift in white attitudes over the past two decades. Additional evidence from the same surveys is available, however, to show that the increasing accommodation of whites to equal rights has not been restricted to the schools, but extends to other spheres as well. Table 1 shows the trends in attitudes with re-

TABLE 1. Per Cent Who Approve Residential and Public Transportation Integration in 1942, 1956, June and December, 1963

		Surveys in		
Approval of . . .	*1942*	*1956*	*June 1963*	*Dec. 1963*
Residential Integration				
National white total	35	51	61	64
Northern whites only	42	58	68	70
Southern whites only	12	38	44	51
Public Transportation Integration				
National white total	44	60	79	78
Northern whites only	57	73	89	88
Southern whites only	4	27	52	51

spect to residential integration and the integration of public transportation. The three later surveys used exactly the same questions that were employed in 1942. These were: "If a Negro with the same income and education as you have moved into your block, would it make any difference to you?"[11] and "Generally speaking, do you think there should be separate sections for Negroes on streetcars and buses?" Nationwide, in 1942 only 35 per cent of American whites would not have objected to a Negro neighbor of their own social class; by 1963 almost two out of three would accept such a neighbor. Nationwide, in 1942 fewer than half of all American whites approved of integrated transportation facilities; by 1963 almost four out of five had adopted this view. The changes are especially dramatic among Southern whites, for in 1942 only one out of eight of them would have accepted a Negro neighbor and but one in twenty-five the idea of sharing transportation facilities on an integrated basis. By the end of 1963, both forms of integration had achieved majority approval.

Though not shown in the data thus far presented, it should be noted that throughout this twenty-one-year period the proportion of persons having "No opinion" on any of these questions rarely exceeded 3 or 4 per cent. This finding is in sharp contrast to the public's answers on most other national issues, where it is common to find upwards of 10 per cent expressing ignorance or indecision. The fact that almost everybody has been aware of the civil rights issue and has had an opinion on it during all this time has implications for the significance of the trends we have observed. There have been no masses of apathetic or undecided people, swayed this way and that by events, and drifting from segregationist to doubtful, from doubtful to integrationist, and perhaps back again. Rather, support for civil rights today comes from a younger generation that, during the last two decades, has come of age and has replaced an older, more segregationist generation in our population; and from former segregationists whose senses and consciences have been touched by the Negro protest, or who have simply changed their opinions as segregation appears increasingly to be a lost cause.

On four occasions, starting in July 1957, the Gallup Poll has asked the question: "Do you think the day will ever come in the South when whites and Negroes will be going to the same schools, eating in the same restaurants, and generally sharing the same public accommodations?" In 1957 and 1958, only a small majority of white people answered "Yes" to that question; in 1961, the proportion had grown to three-fourths, and by 1963, to five-sixths. Conversely, the proportion who answered "No" (or "Never") had dropped by 1963 to 13 per cent. As the Civil Rights Act of 1964 hastens the day when whites and Negroes actually are sharing the same restaurants and public accommodations and as the pace of Southern school desegregation quickens, it is difficult to foresee any reversal in the massive trends we have shown.

An important shift in white beliefs on one further issue helps explain the trends we have observed and underlines the solid base on which they rest. In 1942, a national sample of whites was asked, "In general, do you think that Negroes are as intelligent as white people—that is, can they learn things just as well if they are given the same education and training?" At that time only about half the Northern whites and one Southern white in five answered "Yes." Today, four-fifths of the white population in the North and a substantial majority in the South (57 per cent) believe that Negroes are as intelligent as white people. The implications of this revolutionary change in attitudes toward Negro educability are far-reaching. It has undermined one of the most stubborn arguments formerly offered by whites for segregated schools and has made the case for segregation much more difficult to defend.

Subgroup Differences in White Attitudes Toward the Negro

THE NORC survey of December 1963 asked a national sample of white persons a broad range of questions designed to measure their attitudes toward Negroes and toward the civil rights movement. From this range of questions it was possible to form a Guttman scale of pro-integration attitudes based upon the eight items shown in Table 2.[12] The properties of a Guttman scale are such that if a

TABLE 2.   Guttman Scale of Pro-Integration Sentiments

Item	Per Cent Giving Pro-Integration Response (December 1963)
1. "Do you think Negroes should have as good a chance as white people to get any kind of job, or do you think white people should have the first chance at any kind of job?" ("As good a chance.")	82
2. "Generally speaking, do you think there should be separate sections for Negroes in street cars and buses?" ("No.")	77
3. "Do you think Negroes should have the right to use the same parks, restaurants and hotels as white people?" ("Yes.")	71
4. "Do you think white students and Negro students should go to the same schools, or to separate schools?" ("Same schools.")	63
5. "How strongly would you object if a member of your family wanted to bring a Negro friend home to dinner?" ("Not at all.")	49
6. "White people have a right to keep Negroes out of their neighborhoods if they want to, and Negroes should respect that right." ("Disagree slightly" or "Disagree strongly.")	44
7. "Do you think there should be laws against marriages between Negroes and whites?" ("No.")	36
8. "Negroes shouldn't push themselves where they're not wanted." ("Disagree slightly" or "Disagree strongly.")	27

person rejects one item on the scale, the chances are at least nine in ten that he will also reject all items below it. Thus, those who reject the top item—equal job rights for Negroes—are highly unlikely to endorse any of the other items on the scale and may be considered extreme segregationists. At the other end of the scale, the 27 per cent who disagree with the proposition that "Negroes shouldn't push themselves where they're not wanted" are extremely likely to take a pro-integrationist position on all seven of the other items.

It may be seen that each of the top four items—equal job rights and integration of transportation facilities, public accommodations, and schools—has the support of at least 63 per cent of the white population. (It helps in interpreting the magnitude of public opinion poll percentages to remember that Lyndon Johnson polled only 62 per cent of the popular vote in his "landslide" election over Barry Goldwater. Americans are seldom unanimous about anything, and majorities as high as 80 per cent on any serious issue are extremely rare.) Opinions are more evenly divided on social mixing and residential integration (Items 5 and 6), while the great majority of whites take a firm stand against racial intermarriage and aggressive integrationist activity (Items 7 and 8).[13]

The Pro-Integration Scale provides a convenient measure of integrationist sentiment, since it is possible to assign each individual in the survey a score ranging from 0 to 8, depending upon the number of pro-integration responses he gave. From there it is a small step to compute mean (average) scores for various population groups to determine the locus of pro- and anti-civil rights attitudes. A simple calculation reveals that the mean score for all white Americans is 4.29, which indicates that the average white person accepts the first four propositions and would dislike but would not totally reject the idea of a family member bringing a Negro friend home to dinner. Table 3 shows the distribution of the mean scores among the more relevant subgroups of the white population.

Not surprisingly, the greatest differences are regional. The differences between Northern whites and Southern whites, even when such factors as age, sex, and educational level are controlled, are almost always greater than the differences between various population groups within the same region. Northern whites *in toto*, for example, have a scale score of 4.97. (The average white Northerner endorses integrated schools and would scarcely object if a Negro guest were brought home to dinner.) Southern whites, in contrast, show a scale score of 2.54. (The average white Southerner accepts equal job opportunities and integrated transportation facilities, but he is doubtful about parks, restaurants, and hotels, and he still draws the line at school integration.) But within the two broad geographical regions, interesting differences are nevertheless observable. (See Table 3-A.) In the North, pro-

TABLE 3. Mean Scores on Pro-Integration Scale
(White Population, U.S.A., December 1963)

	North	South			North	South
TOTAL	4.97	2.54				

	North	South
A. *By Region:*		
New England	5.03	—
Middle Atlantic	5.47	—
East North Central	4.61	—
West North Central	4.37	—
South Atlantic	—	2.53
East South Central	—	1.89
West South Central	—	2.70
Mountain	4.33	—
Pacific	5.43	—
B. *By Population Size:*		
10 largest M.A.'s	5.33	a
All other M.A.'s	4.97	2.65
Urban counties	5.04	1.36
Rural counties	4.23	2.70
C. *By Number of Negroes in Public Schools:*		
No Negroes	4.62	2.29
A few Negroes	5.01	2.80
Considerable number	5.49	a
D. *By Prior Residence:*		
Formerly lived in South	4.80	—
Never lived in South	5.05	—
Formerly lived in North	—	3.22
Never lived in North	—	1.97
E. *By Sex:*		
Male	4.91	2.57
Female	5.03	2.51

	North	South
F. *By Age Group:*		
Under 25	5.70	2.76
25–44	5.34	2.86
45–64	4.71	2.33
65–up	4.07	2.10
G. *By Religion:*		
Protestant	4.75	2.38
Catholic	5.18	3.41
Jewish	6.44	a
H. *By Strength of Religious Belief:*		
Very strong	5.00	2.34
Strong	5.15	2.86
Moderate	4.87	2.53
Not strong	4.30	2.37
I. *By Educational Level:*		
8 years or less	3.88	1.70
9–12 years (H.S.)	5.01	2.71
Attended college	5.96	3.54
J. *By Family Income:*		
Under $5,000	4.36	2.20
$5,000–7,499	5.24	2.75
$7,500–9,999	5.26	2.78
$10,000 or over	5.56	3.41
K. *By Occupation:*		
Professional	6.08	4.32
Proprietors, managers	5.09	2.79
Clerical, sales	4.96	2.98
Skilled	4.90	2.04
Semi-skilled	4.77	1.63
Unskilled	4.73	1.82
Farm	3.86	2.87

a Insufficient cases to justify reliable answers.

integration sentiment is strongest on the East and West coasts, weakest in the Midwest. Specifically, the highest scores are found in the Middle Atlantic region (New York, New Jersey, Pennsylvania) and in the three Pacific states. New England is somewhat lower, but still higher than the East North Central area (Ohio, Indiana, Illinois, Michigan, Wisconsin), which in turn is higher than the less urbanized states of the plains area comprising the West North Central region, and the Mountain region. Geographical variation appears also in the South, where Southwestern states (Arkansas, Louisiana, Texas, Oklahoma) have the highest pro-integration score, closely followed by the South Atlantic region (stretching from Delaware and Maryland through Virginia and the Carolinas to Georgia and Florida). Lowest of all is the East South Central region, which includes Kentucky and Tennessee, but also Mississippi and Alabama. Yet even in the latter region (where many whites score "0" on the scale), the average white person has just about accepted two of the eight pro-integration statements.

As of December 1963, the highest scale scores were found in the ten largest metropolitan areas, all but one of which (Washington, D. C.) are in the North (3-B). However, the date of the survey preceded the summer riots in some of these Northern cities in 1964 and the increased protests against job discrimination and *de facto* school segregation that have occurred in New York, Chicago, Boston, Cleveland, and other Northern metropolises during the last year or two. Whether and to what extent these more recent events may have increased or reduced pro-integrationist attitudes in the large Northern cities is not known. It will be noted that, in both North and South, the more Negroes are integrated into the public schools, the higher the scores on the Pro-Integration Scale (3-C). There are too few Southern respondents living in areas where the schools are "considerably" integrated to justify presentation of the figure, but it is still higher than that for areas in which only a "few Negroes" attend the schools. The general finding confirms our earlier analysis of the trend data.

Turning from community variables, such as region, population size, and degree of school integration, to individual characteristics, perhaps one of the most significant findings is that shown in Part D of the table. Northerners who formerly lived in the South (and these may be either Southern migrants or Northerners who spent some time in the South) are only slightly less pro-integrationist than their neighbors who have never been exposed to Southern life. In contrast, Southerners who have previously resided in the North differ greatly from their co-regionalists who have known nothing but Southern life. The net effect of migration from one of the regions to the other seems to be a strengthening of the cause of integration. Ex-Southerners who move to the North appear generally to conform to Northern attitudes, while ex-Northerners who move to the South (and Southerners who have been temporarily exposed to Northern living) tend to reject the more extreme segregationist views of the life-long Southerner.

Men and women differ little in their scores on this Pro-Integration Scale, but age differences are more marked and are of considerable interest (3-E,F). In both North and South, the older age groups are clearly the more segregationist. The forty-five to sixty-four group has lower scores than the twenty-five to forty-four, while those sixty-five or older have the lowest scores of all. The same finding was observed in the 1956 NORC studies, and suggests that part of the long-term trend in white attitudes is due to the passing of an elderly less tolerant generation and their replacement in the population by younger adults who are more likely to accept racial integration. But we note a singular inversion of the relationship between age and pro-integration sentiment among the two youngest age groups in the South. Unexpectedly, the very youngest Southern adults (aged twenty-one to twenty-four) have lower Pro-Integration Scale scores than the twenty-five to forty-four year old group. The same result occurred in the June 1963 survey but not in the 1956 studies. We have suggested elsewhere[14] that the current group of young white adults in the South have grown up and received their schooling and formed their attitudes during the stormy years which followed the 1954 Supreme Court decision outlawing segregated schools. It is they who have been most immediately exposed to the crises and dislocations brought to the South by the Negro protest movement. Perhaps the surprise is that these Southern white youths today are nonetheless more pro-integrationist than are their parents and grandparents who are over the age of forty-five.

Among Northern whites, Catholics are slightly more integrationist than Protestants, and Jews much more so (3-G). In the South, Catholics are among the most liberal of all the groups shown in the table, scoring well above the Southern norm. All persons interviewed were asked not only their religious preference, but also "How strongly do you feel about your religious beliefs?" The respective scale scores are shown in Part H of Table 3. The pattern, clearly in the South and to some extent in the North, is for the middle groups ("strongly" and "moderately") to have the higher Pro-Integration scores, while both extreme groups are lower. One might speculate that persons who feel strongly or even moderately about their religious beliefs are more likely to see all men as equal in the sight of God and to regard segregation (or at least some aspects of segregation) as immoral, while those who hold only nominal religious beliefs or none at all might lack this moral imperative. The fact that those who are "very strongly" religious score lower than expected on the scale, and especially low in the South, suggests that such persons may derive support for their segregationist views from certain passages of the Bible often quoted by fundamentalist preachers.

Occupation, educational level, and family income are highly intercorrelated and are often combined to provide a single measure of socioeconomic status. Presented independently, as they are in Table 3 (I,J,K), they all point in the same direction, with quite remarkable consistency. The inescapable conclusion is that the higher a person's socioeconomic status, as measured by these three characteristics, the higher his score on the Pro-Integration Scale. The differences by educational level are remarkably strong and have been duplicated in all earlier NORC studies. Education is correlated with age, of course, so that much of the differences by age which we noted earlier simply reflects the higher educational level attained by younger adults, as compared with their parents and grandparents. This is not to say that education, or any other single factor, is all-important. It may be observed that the Southern white who attended college nevertheless has a lower scale score than the Northern white with eight years of schooling or less. Yet, as higher proportions of the nation's youth go on to college, as higher proportions enter white-collar and professional rather than farm or production employment, and as (and if) family income levels continue to rise, we may reasonably expect the long-term trend in white attitudes toward acceptance of racial integration not only to continue but even to accelerate.

Views of the Civil Rights Movement

We have described the changing attitudes of white Americans over a twenty-year period and have examined what might be called the epidemiology of anti-Negro prejudice as it existed at the end of 1963. We have seen which subgroups of white persons manifest the greatest support for and the greatest resistance to integration. We have also indicated, by means of the Pro-Integration Scale, some of the components of these attitudes—the forms of Negro equality which are acceptable to various groups of whites and the kinds at which they draw the line. As stated earlier, however, the Pro-Integration Scale utilized only eight of a much larger number of questions about Negro-white relations. It will be instructive now to observe how Northern whites and Southern whites and persons of varying degrees of prejudice regard the Negro protest movement in general as well as in some of its ramifications. The first two columns of Table 4 compare the opinions of Northern whites and Southern whites, without regard to their Pro-Integration Scale scores. The next four columns compare the opinions of four groups, ranging in scale scores from High Segregationist to High Integrationist, without regard to their place of residence.

We see first (Table 4-A) that the main goals of the civil rights movement are similarly perceived by all white Americans—North and South, integrationist and segregationist. Three-quarters or more of all of these groups believe that most Negroes feel strongly about equal job opportunities and the right to vote. It is probably no coincidence that job equality and the vote are the very things which a representative sample of Negroes themselves have said are "most important to work for," and are also the Negro demands which white Americans are most willing to accept.[15] Almost as many whites, in December 1963, perceived that Negroes feel strongly about equal access to parks, hotels, restaurants, and other public accommodations. The right to send their children to white schools was believed to be very important to Negroes by the majority of Northern whites, but by only about a third of the Southerners. Similarly, more Northern than Southern whites believe Negroes feel strongly about residential integration. These differences probably reflect the actualities of the civil rights struggle in the two regions. In many cities throughout the North, Negroes have made plain their demands for better housing and an end to *de facto* school segregation, while demonstrations in the South have focused more often on voting rights, employment, and public accommodations. Recognition of what it is that the Negro wants is distorted remarkably little by the white person's own attitudes toward integration. The overwhelming majority of even the most highly segregationist group do not deny that the Negro feels strongly about job

TABLE 4. White Attitudes Toward Negro Protest Movement in North and South, and by Scores on Pro-Integration Scale, December 1963

			Pro-Integration Scale Scores			
			0–2 (High Seg.)	3–4 (Mod. Seg.)	5–6 (Mod. Int.)	7–8 (High Int.)
Per Cent Who Say:	*North*	*South*				
A. Most Negroes feel strongly about						
The right to vote...........	80%	77%	79%	76%	84%	79%
Right to hold same jobs as white people.............	84	81	76	84	85	89
Right to use same parks, hotels, restaurants.........	84	80	67	82	83	90
Right to send children to same schools as whites.....	63	35	45	51	59	66
Right to live in white neighborhoods............	45	33	42	39	42	44
Right to marry white people.	10	8	13	9	7	10
Having a separate area of U. S. set aside for Negroes.......	5	3	7	6	4	2
B. The Negro protest movement has been generally violent rather than peaceful................	47%	63%	78%	50%	47%	30%
C. Demonstrations have hurt rather than helped the Negro cause....	43%	60%	71%	52%	45%	24%
D. Generally disapprove of actions Negroes have taken to obtain civil rights..................	59%	78%	89%	73%	62%	33%
E. Negro groups are asking for too much....................	37%	55%	74%	45%	31%	16%
F. "Others" are really behind the Negro protest movement.......	39%	52%	56%	46%	43%	24%
Communists are behind it......	21	27	30	26	22	12
G. Problem of Negro rights should be left to states rather than federal government...........	34%	59%	57%	45%	36%	24%
H. Negro-white relations will always be a problem for U. S..........	42%	49%	61%	52%	36%	26%
*I. Self or family have been affected favorably by integration................	4%	1%	—%	2%	4%	7%
Have been affected unfavorably	9	11	16	14	4	3
Have not been affected........	87	83	82	83	91	87
J. Are around Negroes:						
Almost every day...........	29%	39%	33%	28%	31%	35%
Less often than that........	45	52	45	47	46	51
Never around Negroes.......	26	9	22	25	23	14

* Percentages do not always add to 100 per cent. Omitted are a small group who answered vaguely or irrelevantly.

equality and the right to vote; nor, as the percentage figures indicate, do they delude themselves that Negroes feel strongly about their right to marry white people or that they really want to have their own separate state.

The items shown on Lines B-F of Table 4, on the other hand, all refer to Negro actions in the civil rights struggle, rather than to Negro goals, and here we find sharp cleavages between North and South and between persons with low and high Pro-Integration scores. The majority of Southern whites, and even larger proportions of the highly segregationist group, perceive the Negro protest movement as having been generally violent rather than generally peaceful; they think that demonstrations and other direct action by Negroes have hurt their cause rather than helped it; they themselves disapprove of "the actions Negroes have taken to get the things they want"; they say Negroes are asking for "too much," rather than "too little" or "just about what they should"; and they believe that, not the Negro people, but "some other person or group" is "really behind the recent Negro actions." A substantial majority of Northern whites also say they generally disapprove of Negro actions in the struggle, but on none of the other of these items (B-F) can a majority be mustered in the North. Persons who score high on the Pro-Integration Scale are even more sympathetic to the Negro protest movement and overwhelmingly reject all of these opinions. Differences are also found on Lines G-H, which reflect a larger view of Negro-white relations. Segregationists, for example, tend to believe that "the question of Negro rights is more a problem that individual states should solve," and Southerners, whatever their attitudes toward integration, are even more likely to hold this view. The great majority of integrationists and of Northerners, on the other hand, see Negro rights as "a problem that the federal government should solve." Similarly, segregationists are much more pessimistic about the future, the majority of them believing that "Negro-white relations will always be a problem for the United States"; but the great majority of integrationists believe that "a solution will eventually be worked out."

Part I of Table 4 is of considerable interest and importance. The percentages are based on replies to the open-ended question, "In what ways have you or any members of your family been affected by integration?" The question came toward the end of the interview, after extended discussion of the civil rights movement, and interviewers were instructed to probe for any ways at all in which the respondent or any members of his family had been personally affected. Somewhat surprisingly, 86 per cent of American whites said they had not been affected at all, and the proportion differed very little from North to South, or according to attitudes toward integration. As shown on Line J, large numbers of American whites have had little or no exposure to the opposite race; one-fourth of Northern whites say they are "never around Negroes" and only 29 per cent are around them almost every day. On the other hand, it was clear from the verbatim replies that a substantial proportion of the unaffected had actually experienced integration and accepted it quite casually: "No, I just go my way and they don't bother me." "Not at all. My boy goes to school with them but he never mentions any problems." "None, my husband works with some colored fellows and they get along fine." About one white person in ten said he had been affected unfavorably by integration. The behavior of Negro children in school, an influx of Negroes into the neighborhood, or unpleasant contacts with Negroes in public places were each mentioned by 2 or 3 per cent of the white public. Only 1 per cent referred to unfavorable effects of job integration. Three per cent of all whites reported favorable effects of integration, explaining that the Negroes had not turned out to be so bad after all or that they enjoyed excellent relations. The ratio of unfavorable to favorable effects was 11-to-1 in the South, but only 2.5-to-1 in the North. Among those with pro-integrationist attitudes, favorable effects were mentioned more often than unfavorable

Since December 1963

We are aware that many readers will question the relevance of public opinion poll findings from December 1963 to the situation today. After all, the year 1964 alone saw the nomination of Barry Goldwater, the Presidential election campaign, general elections in every state, Congressional passage of a comprehensive Civil Rights Act, Negro rioting in several Northern cities, the murder of three civil rights workers in Mississippi—to mention only some of the most striking events which might have affected the attitudes we have described. And the pace of the civil rights movement in 1965 has shown no signs of slackening. We urge such readers, however, to regain their perspective by looking again at the twenty-year trend shown in Chart 1, and especially at the absence of short-run change over the three separate surveys conducted in 1956 and

1963, when racial tensions were also high. It cannot be doubted that people do respond to short-run events and often have very strong opinions about them. But all the evidence we know of indicates that attitudes toward the basic issues included in the Pro-Integration Scale—such as school and residential integration, social mixing, the use by Negroes of public accommodations—are not subject to sudden and dramatic shifts. If all the events in the months and years preceding December 1963 did not halt the rising trend toward acceptance of integration, it may be doubted that more recent events have produced any major change in the attitudes we have examined.

Indeed, the 1964 Presidential election itself provided a very important test of civil rights sentiment in the United States, for there, "in the privacy of the voting booth," the widely heralded "white backlash" failed to materialize in the North, while President Johnson carried the South in spite of his forthright stand on civil rights for Negroes. The result could hardly be construed as other than a rejection by the American people of the views of those who would try to stem the progress of the Negro protest movement. Yet, both the Gallup Poll and the Harris Survey, during 1964 and 1965, reported seeming inconsistencies in the attitudes of the white public. Each has found, just as we saw in the 1963 NORC study, that whites generally disapprove of direct action by Negroes and would welcome relief from racial tensions. Thus, Harris reported (August 17, 1964) that "Fully 87 per cent of the American people feel that the recent riots in New York, Rochester and Jersey City have hurt the Negro cause," and (May 17, 1965) that there existed an ". . . apparent uneasiness of the American people over the current pace of civil rights progress. Six months ago, the public tended to feel that steady and sound progress was being registered. After recent events, the number who feel things are moving 'too fast' has risen rather sharply." (The increase was from 32 per cent in November to 41 per cent in May, shortly after the events in Selma, Alabama.) Only six days earlier (May 11, 1965) Gallup had also warned that "Criticism of integration speed has grown among Northern whites. . . . The number who believe the Johnson Administration is pushing integration 'too fast' has grown considerably over the last few weeks." Gallup had also been reporting such results as (June 7, 1964) "Eight in ten say demonstrations more likely to hurt than to help Negro. . . . Opposition among both races has grown," and (November 12, 1964) "Six in ten favor a gradual approach" to enforcement of the new Civil Rights Law rather than "strict enforcement right from the beginning." In that same release, Gallup reported that 73 per cent of his sample "think Negroes should stop demonstrating, now that they have made their point."

But both of these polling agencies have also reported a steady support for civil rights measures. Harris found a large and increasing majority for the 1964 Civil Rights bill between November 1963 and April 1964, with 70 per cent of the public favoring it by the latter date. Both polls reported public approval of the 1965 voting rights bill, though their figures differed considerably. Gallup (April 14, 1965) found 76 per cent in favor, Harris (May 10, 1965) only 53 per cent, the difference apparently tracing to a reference in the Harris question that "opponents feel this is an invasion of the rights of states to control their own elections." The Gallup question made no mention of states' rights. Gallup also found (March 19, 1965) that 56 per cent of the public believe that people who cannot read or write should nevertheless have the right to vote and that 63 per cent disagree with the proposition that only persons who have had at least five years of schooling should be allowed to vote.

Opportunity to apply a more rigorous test of the hypothesis that the long-term trends are still intact finally occurred in June 1965, when NORC was able to append a few of the 1942-1963 questions to a current national survey. It was not possible to ask all of the items included in the December 1963 survey, but the measures which were obtained strongly confirmed the inexorability of the trend. The proportion of white Americans who favor school integration rose from 62 per cent to 67 per cent during this eighteen-month period, and the proportion who would not object to a Negro neighbor of the same social class rose from 64 per cent to 68 per cent. Increases again are recorded in both North and South, with the change in the South especially noteworthy. The proportion of Southern whites who favor integrated schools rose from 30 per cent at the end of 1963 to 36 per cent in mid-1965. Again, it was found that exposure to integration fosters pro-integrationist attitudes. Of Southern whites whose children had attended school with Negroes, a substantial majority (59 per cent) said that Negroes and whites should attend the same school; of Southern whites whose children had not attended school with Negroes, only 29 per cent held that view.

There will, of course, be those who now ask, "But what about Los Angeles? Surely that violence must have produced a white revulsion against civil rights"—but if the past is any guide, the answer can be predicted with considerable assurance. Certainly large majorities of American whites, and especially the dwindling ranks of segregationists, will say that the Los Angeles rioting has "hurt the Negro's cause," that "they have made their point," and that nothing is settled by violence, but not even Los Angeles will halt the massive attitudinal changes we have demonstrated over the last generation. Furthermore, it should be noted that the rioting in Watts took scarcely anyone by surprise. The June 1965 NORC survey asked, "As you probably recall, there were race riots in several Northern cities last summer. The way it looks now, do you expect that this summer there will be many race riots around the country, some, hardly any, or none at all?" Only 2 per cent said they expected no Negro rioting during the summer, and almost a quarter of the white population expected many riots. Thus, the unprecedentedly high level of support expressed for integration in this survey actually seems to have discounted Los Angeles in advance. With the full expectation of at least some riots in Northern cities, American whites nevertheless (or perhaps for that reason?) actually increased their support of integration.

A recent (but pre-Los Angeles) Gallup Poll release confirms the remarkable change in white Southern attitudes between 1963 and 1965. In May 1963, Gallup asked a representative sample of white parents, "Would you yourself have any objection to sending your children to a school where a few of the children are colored?" and 61 per cent of those in the South said, "Yes, I would object." When he repeated the same question two years later, the proportion of Southern parents who would object had dropped abruptly to 37 per cent. Similar, though less dramatic, changes were found in the attitudes of Northern parents. The millennium has scarcely arrived. Gallup went on to ask whether the parents would object to sending their children to a school where half, and then where more than half, of the children were colored. A majority of white parents in the North and almost four out of five of those in the South said they would object to the latter situation.

Certainly there is no evidence that the majority of American whites eagerly look forward to integration. Most are more comfortable in a segregated society, and they would prefer that the demonstrators slow down or go away while things are worked out more gradually. But most of them know also that racial discrimination is morally wrong and recognize the legitimacy of the Negro protest. Our survey data persuasively argue that where there is little or no protest against segregation and discrimination, or where these have the sanction of law, racial attitudes conform to the existing situation. But when attention is kept focused on racial injustice and when acts of discrimination become contrary to the law of the land, racial attitudes change. Conversely, there is no persuasive evidence thus far that either demonstrations and other forms of direct action, or legal sanctions applied by government, create a backlash effect and foster segregationist sentiment. On the contrary, they may simply demonstrate, ever more conclusively, that it is more costly to oppose integration than to bring it about. The mass of white Americans have shown in many ways that they do not want a racist government and that they will not follow racist leaders. Rather, they are engaged in the painful task of adjusting to an integrated society. It will not be easy for most, but one cannot at this late date doubt the basic commitment. In their hearts they know that the American Negro is right.

REFERENCES

1. Hadley Cantril, *Public Opinion, 1935-1946* (Princeton, N. J., 1951). This volume is a compendium of published poll results during the first dozen years of systematic opinion research. All twenty-seven questions listed under "Negroes" are dated 1942 or later; thirty-two of thirty-three questions listed under "U.S. Race Relations" are dated 1942 or later. The three questions on lynching referred to below were found under "Crime and Criminals."

2. Gallup Poll releases, July 21, 1963, October 2, 1963, *et passim.* The question, "What do you regard as the most vital issue before the American people today?" was first asked in September 1935 (the answer was "Unemployment") and has been repeated by the Gallup Poll at regular intervals, with slight changes of wording, since that time. "Racial problems" was not mentioned frequently enough to receive a separate code until 1944-1945.

3. "America's Mood Today," *Look,* June 29, 1965.

4. Harris Survey news release, May 17, 1965.

5. *Look* and Harris survey, *op. cit.*

6. Much of the material in this section has previously been presented in Herbert H. Hyman and Paul B. Sheatsley, "Attitudes Toward Desegregation," *Scientific American*, Vol. 211 (July 1964), pp. 16-23.

7. The question was asked also in 1944 and 1946. Results for those years, while consistent with the trend, are not shown for reasons of space. Absence of financial support precluded asking the question on any other occasions, so we cannot conclude that the trend lines are uniformly smooth.

8. "South" refers to the South Atlantic, East South Central, and West South Central regions, as defined by the Bureau of the Census. "North" refers to the rest of the country, except Alaska and Hawaii, where no interviews were conducted.

9. Sample sizes ranged from 1,250 to 1,500. The minor changes from one 1956 or 1963 survey to another are well within the range of normal sampling error.

10. The same holds true for the North. Northern whites living in segregated school areas were 65 per cent for integration, but in areas where there had been considerable integration, 83 per cent favored the policy.

11. In the 1956 and 1963 surveys, a special category was added for the response, "Yes, I would welcome it," and persons giving this reply were combined with the "No Difference" group.

12. We are indebted to Donald J. Treiman of the NORC staff for construction of this scale.

13. The latter item is admittedly loaded, since it is perfectly reasonable to take the position that nobody—white or Negro—should push himself where he isn't wanted. The item does have the advantage, however, of defining a minimum estimate of pro-integrationist sentiment in the country, since anyone who disagrees with it is hardly likely to be unsympathetic to any aspect of the civil rights movement.

14. *Scientific American, op. cit.*

15. Negro data from unpublished NORC survey, May 1963. In the survey under discussion, 79 per cent of the white public agreed that "It should be made easier than it is now for Negroes to vote in the South."

THOMAS F. PETTIGREW

Complexity and Change in American Racial Patterns: A Social Psychological View

MR. FAWKS is a white American who feels he "knows" Negroes. He works in a desegregated aircraft plant in Marietta, Georgia, lives a few hundred yards from "the colored part of town," and sends his children to a school that recently received its first Negro pupil. Yet Mr. Fawks knows only three of his Negro co-workers and none of his Negro neighbors by name, and he dares not socialize with them. His professed knowledge comes, then, almost entirely from racist folklore, from which he exempts his Negro co-workers on the grounds they are "different."

Mr. Seemes is another white American who feels he understands the racial scene. Although he knew no Negroes as a boy and none lives within miles of his suburban Connecticut town today, he has made friends with two Negroes in his New York office. They were hired a few years ago when the company became "an equal opportunity employer" because of its many federal contracts. Mr. Seemes genuinely likes his co-workers, though he seldom has social contacts with them after office hours. Consequently, he has decided that "the whole problem is really a matter of social class."

Likewise, Mr. Brown is a Negro American who has great hopes for the future of American race relations. He recently graduated from an all-Negro high school in Durham, North Carolina, and now finds himself one of the first Negroes hired in a previously all-white Southern-based insurance company. His pastor recommended him to the firm, and he started only a few months ago in an entirely Negro section of the city. But his employers urge him to develop new white business, and he has selected as likely prospects faculty liberals of nearby Duke University.

By contrast, Mr. Davis is a Negro American who has given up

hope that any racial change will ever improve his personal lot. Born on a Southern farm, he moved with his mother to Harlem while still young. And there he has remained—deep within the ghetto. Mr. Davis has repeated contact with whites in only three roles—as employers, landlords, and merchants. These formal and invariably financial relations with whites combine with ghetto folklore to convince him that "the man" is never going to allow significant racial alterations.

The American racial scene has always been highly complex, defying facile generalizations by its variety and inconsistency. And, as these four cases and millions like them reveal, the current period of rapid change acts to heighten this complexity. It is appropriate, then, to explore this complexity and its implications for the nation's future racial patterns.

I. The Complexity of American Racial Patterns

Racial roles. One useful way to conceptualize American racial patterns is to describe them in role-theory terms.[1] Discriminatory encounters between whites and Negroes require that both parties "play the game." The white must act out the role of the "superior"; by direct action or subtle cue, he must convey the expectation that he will be treated with deference. For his part, the Negro must, if traditional norms are to be obeyed, act out the role of the "inferior"; he must play the social role of "Negro." And should he refuse to play the game, he would be judged by many whites as "not knowing his place," and harsh sanctions could follow.[2]

The socially stigmatized role of "Negro" is the critical feature of having dark skin in the United States. At the personality level, such enforced role adoption divides each individual Negro both from other human beings and from himself. Of course, all social roles, necessary as they are, hinder to some extent forthright, uninhibited social interaction. An employer and employee, for example, may never begin to understand each other as complete human beings unless they break through the formality and constraints of their role relationships. Likewise, whites and Negroes can never communicate as equals unless they break through the role barriers. As long as racial roles are maintained, both parties find it difficult to perceive the humanity behind the facade. Many whites who are by no means racists confuse the role of "Negro" with the people who must play this role. "That's just the way Negroes are," goes the phrase. Conversely, many Negroes confuse the role of "white man" with whites. "Whites are just like that, they are born thinking they should be boss."

Intimately associated with this impairment of human relatedness is an impairment of the individual's acceptance and understanding of himself. Both whites and Negroes can confuse their own roles as being an essential part of themselves. Whites can easily flatter themselves into believing that they are in fact "superior"; after all, does not the deferent behavior of the role-playing Negro confirm this "superiority"? And Negroes in turn often accept much of the mythology; for does not the imperious behavior of the role-playing white confirm this "inferiority"?

These ideas are supported by a large body of social psychological research. This research convincingly demonstrates the power of role playing to change deeply-held attitudes, values, and even self-conceptions.[3] Moreover, these remarkable changes have been rendered experimentally by temporary role adoptions of an exceedingly trivial nature when compared to the life-long role of "Negro." Imagine, then, the depth of the effects of having to play a role which has such vast personal and social significance that it affects virtually all realms of daily living. In short, racial roles have profound and direct psychological as well as behavioral effects upon their adopters.

In broadest outline, this role relationship of "superior" white and "inferior" Negro has, historically, structured racial interaction in America. But it is a basic theme around which there is a great range of variations, for racial patterns systematically vary according to specific situation, institution, socio-economic class, and region.

Variation by situation. Mr. Fawks, the white aircraft worker in Georgia, has never thought his interracial neighborhood was strange and accepts the desegregation of the plant in which he works, yet he objects strenuously to public school desegregation. "I never went to no school with colored people," he grumbles, "and I never thought I'd see my kids doing it." There is nothing uniquely Southern about Mr. Fawks' selective reaction to racial patterns. Mr. Seemes approves of the interracial character of his work situation, but he entertains serious doubts about interracial neighborhoods. "I've heard Negroes' moving into an area lowers property values," he explains, "and most of my Connecticut neighbors are dead against it—so I don't think it's a good idea."

These inconsistencies by situation and institution are commonplace. For example, in Panama there is a divided street, one side of which is in the United States Canal Zone and the other side in Panama. For many years, the facilities on the Canal Zone side were tightly segregated by race, while no segregation was practiced on the Panamanian side.[4] Yet customers conducting their business managed to adjust their behavior easily as they crossed first to one side of the street and then to the other. Similarly, in the coal mining county of McDowell, West Virginia, Negro and white miners at one time followed a traditional pattern of desegregation below the ground and almost complete segregation above the ground.[5] Obviously, the Canal Zone residents did not shift their racial views each time they crossed and recrossed the business street. Nor did the West Virginian miners change their racial attitudes each time they went below the ground and came above it. Attitudes and behavior need not always be congruent; particular situations can structure how most people behave in spite of the attitudes they may harbor.

Social scientists were first alerted to this by a 1934 study of verbal versus actual discrimination.[6] A Chinese couple traveled widely over the United States, stopping at 250 sleeping and eating establishments. They were refused service only once. Later, the same places received inquiries by mail as to whether or not they served "members of the Chinese race." About half did not reply; of those which did, over 90 per cent announced they did not accommodate Chinese guests. A control sample of comparable, unvisited establishments yielded similar results.

This phenomenon was repeated in eleven restaurants in a northeastern suburban community.[7] Three women, two white and one Negro, went to the establishments, encountered no difficulty, and in each received exemplary service. Two weeks later, requests were sent to the restaurants for reservations for a similar group. Ten of the letters went unanswered, and follow-up phone calls met great resistance. Control calls for all-white parties led to ten reservations. It is more difficult to reject another human being face to face than through impersonal letters and phone calls.

The power of specific situational norms to shape racial patterns of behavior is dramatized by the difficulties which arise when there are no such norms. One ingenious project studied New York State facilities unaccustomed to Negro patronage.[8] Negro researchers would enter a tavern, seek service, and later record their experiences, while white researchers would observe the same situation and record their impressions for comparison. Typically the first reaction of waitresses and bartenders was to turn to the owner or others in authority for guidance. When this was unavailable, the slightest behavioral cue from anyone in the situation was utilized as a gauge of what was expected of them. And if there were no such cues, confusion often continued until somehow the threatening situation had been structured.

Variation by institution. Comparable observations have been recorded for inconsistent racial patterns across different societal institutions. Consider a neighborhood of white steel workers in the Chicago area.[9] These men were all members of the same thoroughly desegregated union and worked in desegregated plants. In fact, Negroes held elected positions as shop stewards, executive board members, and vice-president of the union and shared with whites the same locker rooms, lunch rooms, showers, and toilets in both the union hall and the plants. Only 12 per cent of the 151 whites who were studied evidenced "low acceptance" of Negroes in this work situation; and the deeper the involvement in union activities, the greater was the white acceptance of Negroes as co-workers. But neighborhood acceptance was a vastly different matter. Bolstered by a neighborhood organization which opposed desegregation, 86 per cent of the white steel workers rejected the idea of allowing Negroes to live near them, with those men most involved in the collective existence of the neighborhood evincing the most adamant opposition. The effects of harmonious interracial patterns in employment did not extend to housing. No relationship existed between acceptance of Negroes as fellow workers and acceptance of them as neighbors.

The social psychological key to understanding this process is the operation of the organizations in each of the realms. Most of the steel workers conform to what is expected of them, even when these expectations counter one another. Thus, their inconsistency is more apparent than real; it appears conflicting to the outside observer, but to the person involved such behavior is perfectly reasonable. In other words, the steel worker is living by the norms of the groups to which he refers his behavior—his *reference groups*.[10] And these reference-group norms often act in modern American society to produce what appear to be inconsistent racial patterns and to restrict the generalization of contact-induced attitude change from one institution to another.

Once again we encounter the distinction between expressed attitudes and actual behavior. A 1951 investigation of almost a thousand Texas manufacturers found that their attitudes toward Negroes and their actual practice for hiring Negroes were not related.[11] And a 1953 study of thirty discriminatory fraternities at the University of Michigan noted that the members were more willing to accept Jewish than Negro students as "brothers," though they were more intensely anti-Semitic than anti-Negro in their attitudes.[12]

Thus, in order to comprehend some of the complexity of American racial patterns, it becomes necessary to examine separately some of the major institutions of American society. Other papers in this volume provide racial analyses in depth of many of these institutions. It is sufficient here to sketch the principal trends, although even these generalizations run the risk of becoming quickly outdated.

The family remains the most racially homogeneous institution in American life. Indeed, twenty states still have explicitly anti-miscegenation laws, although the constitutionality of these statutes is currently up for review in Virginia and Oklahoma.[13] Rates of racial intermarriage in states where the practice is both legal and recorded—California, Hawaii, Michigan, and Nebraska—remain very low save for Hawaii and appear to have increased only slightly in recent years.[14] And white American attitudes on the subject have shifted very little during this era of racial change. A 1963 *Newsweek* poll found 90 per cent of a representative sample of the nation's whites objected to their "own teen-age daughter dating a Negro."[15] A more striking finding of this same poll concerns whites who had experienced previous social contact with Negroes. While this contact group was overwhelmingly accepting of Negroes in other institutional realms, 80 per cent objected to their teen-age daughter dating a Negro and 70 per cent objected to a close friend or relative marrying a Negro.[16]

Opinion is divided, however, about anti-miscegenation laws. Gallup shows that 48 per cent of white Americans approve and 46 per cent disapprove of such statutes.[17] A large regional difference exists on the question: 72 per cent of white Southerners, compared with only 42 per cent of white Northerners and Westerners, favor anti-miscegenation legislation. Thus, legal alterations in this realm seem possible in the near future, but interracial marriages are not likely to become commonplace until the special Negro stigma is eliminated.

Organized religion is also an extensively segregated institution. The vast majority of Negroes who maintain religious ties are Protestant, and more than 90 per cent of Negro Protestants belong to all-Negro denominations.[18] Among those relatively few Negroes who are members of predominantly white denominations, a large majority attend racially separate churches within these denominations. Moreover, church-sponsored facilities—hospitals, colleges, welfare agencies—are often more segregated, if possible, than the churches.[19] Consequently, the organized church has not been a conspicuous source of interracial contact in the United States, although protest groups such as the Catholic Interracial Council and the Episcopal Society for Cultural and Racial Unity may signal a significant change in this respect for the future.

Racial patterns in education are now in considerable flux. While public education from primary to college levels was separate in the South until recently, the pattern has been somewhat more varied in the North. Pre-World War II Negro ghettos in Northern cities were neither so dense nor so large as today; thus biracial education at the primary and secondary levels was quite common. This explains why many middle-aged white and Negro Northerners today recall that they knew members of the other race best during their early school days. This Northern pattern did not, however, extend into college. Among the few Negro Northerners who managed to go onto higher education, the great majority enrolled either in all-Negro colleges in the South or similar institutions in the North —some private (for example, Lincoln University in Pennsylvania and Wilberforce University in Ohio) and some public (such as Cheyney State College in Pennsylvania).

The present educational picture is more complex. Southern public education is no longer tightly segregated. The first eleven years after the 1954 Supreme Court ruling against *de jure* segregation of public schools have witnessed slow, but fundamental, alterations. By the fall of 1964, 43 per cent of biracial Southern school districts had begun at least token desegregation programs that placed one out of every nine Negro Southern school children in schools with white Southerners.[20] A disproportionate share of this progress, however, has occurred in the border South. While 93 per cent of biracial school districts in the border South had desegregated, only 27 per cent of the ex-Confederate South had done so; and while three out of every five border-state Negro children attended biracial schools, only one in forty-seven did so in the ex-Confederate

South. Yet there are unmistakable signs that this pace is quickening. The annual average number of newly-desegregated school districts in the South has recently increased three-fold, with the threatened cut-off of federal educational funds under Title VI of the 1964 Civil Rights Act proving an effective stimulant. Thus, if the first decade after the 1954 Supreme Court desegregation ruling can be termed a slow-paced era of judicial orders, then the second decade after the ruling promises to be a somewhat faster-paced Civil Rights Act era.[21]

Ironically, however, as *de jure* segregation of schools decreases, *de facto* segregation is rapidly increasing. The ever-growing Negro ghettos in major cities throughout the United States combine with the neighborhood-school principle to establish an entrenched pattern of racially-separate education. The problem is particularly serious at the locally-based elementary level. Even in Boston, where in 1960 only 9 per cent of the population was nonwhite, there are seventeen elementary and two junior high schools with 90 per cent or more Negro pupils.[22] The *de facto* school segregation controversy is presently raging in the North and West and will soon erupt in the nominally "desegregated" cities of the South, and its judicial and legislative status is only now taking shape.[23] But for present purposes, it must be emphasized that this expansion of urban ghettos and the development of *de facto* segregated education have meant that Negroes growing up in these areas have generally had far *less* equal-status contact with whites in their formative years than had Negroes of earlier generations.

Since family, religious, and educational institutions provide only limited interracial contact, encounters on the job between Negro and white Americans assume special importance. Negro employment has been upgraded slightly in recent years, though the pace has hardly been breath-taking. For example, if the rate of nonwhite gains between 1950 and 1960 continued, nonwhites would not attain equal proportional representation nationally among clerical workers until 1992, among skilled workers until 2005, among professionals until 2017, among sales workers until 2114, and among business managers and proprietors until 2730![24] Nor are these data merely a result of Southern discrimination. In metropolitan Boston, for example, a continuation of the nonwhite rate of change in employment in the 1950's would mean nonwhite Bostonians would not be proportionately represented among clerical and skilled workers until the late 1980's, among professionals until the early 1990's, and among business managers and sales workers until the twenty-second and twenty-third centuries respectively.[25]

Alert and rigorous enforcement of the 1964 Civil Rights Act, particularly Title VII's provisions for ending discrimination in employment, will be required for basic structural change in this critical area. And the need for such basic change is obvious: the low ratio in the median income of Negro and white workers has remained substantially the same since 1951; technological innovations are disproportionately displacing Negroes from their jobs; except for a few major unions (teamsters, meatpackers, and the steel and automotive workers, for example), Negroes are still essentially excluded from organized labor in key industries (such as the building trades and textiles); employment services and apprenticeship and vocational training programs still typically discriminate against Negroes; and unemployment rates among riot-age Negro youth are almost twice those of white youth and rise as high as 60 and 70 per cent in certain ghetto areas.[26] But if Title VII is forcefully applied and if the Job Corps and other relevant aspects of the "War on Poverty" can achieve major structural alterations, economic institutions could well become the major source for some years of equal-status interracial contact in American society.

This conclusion is bolstered by the increasingly apparent fact that residential patterns are not going to provide widespread opportunities for Negro and white contact in the foreseeable future. It is a paradox of racial change over the past generation that as desegregation proceeds in other realms, housing becomes more racially separate. Residential segregation, state the Taeubers, "has increased steadily over past decades until it has reached universally high levels in cities throughout the United States, despite significant advances in the socio-economic status of Negroes."[27] Federal programs of urban renewal and public housing have often augmented this trend, and the late President Kennedy's executive order against housing discrimination has proven severely limited. Neither state housing anti-discrimination statutes nor the 500-or-so private Fair Housing Practices Committees has made substantial progress. In general, both state laws and citizens' committees apply a case-by-case approach, relying upon individual complaints or contacts; yet the problem has such deep roots—ranging from property tax laws to land-use planning—that only direct confrontation of these fundamental issues and the housing industry as a whole offers any hope for sweeping improvement in this realm.[28]

Variation by socio-economic class. Mention of housing segregation raises an interesting socio-economic class phenomenon. Higher-status whites generally give more support to racial desegregation than lower-status whites, but this tendency does not seem to hold for attitudes toward interracial housing. Thus, a 1956 national survey noted that 61 per cent of college-educated whites approved of school desegregation, compared with 51 per cent of the high-school-educated and 36 per cent of the grammar-school-educated; and 72 per cent of the college-educated approved of the desegregation of public transportation, compared with 64 per cent of the high-school-educated and 46 per cent of the grammar-school-educated; but virtually no difference appeared among the three groups in response to the query— "If a Negro with the same income and education as you moved into your block, would it make any difference to you?"[29]

Other research suggests that this special reluctance of upper-status whites to support housing desegregation is maintained despite the fact they often realize that these beliefs are in direct conflict with their own religious and national ideals.[30] Part of this phenomenon is explained by the fact that housing desegregation directly affects them in a way other changes typically do not. In addition, there is a tendency for many middle-class white Americans to assume that their own values are typically different from those of Negroes—even when the survey question specifies a Negro neighbor with the same income and education.

This is not to imply that white Americans make no distinction among Negroes of different social classes. Indeed, Westie has shown that the willingness of whites to associate with Negroes is a direct function of both the social status of the respondent and that of the particular Negro being judged.[31] That is, the higher the status of the white, the greater is his willingness to interact with Negroes and the greater the tendency for him to make a differentiation between, say, a Negro doctor and a Negro machine operator. Lower-status whites are more rejecting of Negroes in general and less prepared to distinguish between Negroes of different social standings.

Interestingly, Westie repeated this research with Negroes, measuring their social distance attitudes toward whites, and obtained essentially the same findings.[32] Higher-status Negroes are far more willing than other Negroes to interact with whites and draw sharper differentiations between whites of various occupations. Another set of studies investigated the stereotypes of whites as a group held by Negroes of varying social classes in the North and South.[33] In general, the same over-all stereotype emerged for all classes in both regions: whites tend to be seen as "ambitious, sticking together, businesslike, deceitful and tricky, feeling superior, keeping the Negro down, underestimating the Negro's ability, judging Negroes by the worst type, and not caring to be among Negroes." Yet higher-status Negroes, particularly those in the North, are considerably more favorable in their image of whites than other Negroes.

Variation by Region. The relatively more favorable view of whites held by upper-status Negro Northerners is largely a function of their much greater opportunity for equal-status contact with whites. Though still relatively small in number, this group is especially significant for the future—as Northern migration and middle-class expansion continue among Negroes. Thus, it is of interest to look in the following table at the reported interracial experiences of a representative sample of 250 middle-income Negro housewives residing in Roxbury, the Negro ghetto of Boston.[34]

These women typically knew whites well as children—though this is not the case for their children growing up in the ghetto. It appears the husband's work situation is the family's principal contact with whites, with mutual visiting with white work associates almost reaching the level of all such contacts with whites. An additional contact comes through professional family services—such as the family doctor and dentist. But less than one in four of the women reports membership in a church which substantial numbers of whites attend.

Such interracial contacts, of course, are severely restricted for low-income Negroes in both the North and South. They are less likely to have known whites as children; they are more likely to work in laboring and semi-skilled jobs with other lower-status Negroes as associates and whites only as supervisors and employers; they are not likely to have a family doctor or dentist, but to depend upon the impersonal services of public hospitals and clinics; and they seldom belong to a church with white members.

Middle-income Negro Southerners are also more constrained than similarly-situated Negro Bostonians. Segregation sealed them off in ghettos with longer histories and more developed Negro infrastructures than Northern ghettos. Consequently, they, too, are less likely than their Northern counterparts to have known whites as children, to work and visit with whites, to have white physi-

Interracial Contacts of
Middle-Income Negroes of Boston*

Source of Contact	Percentage Reporting
As a child:	
played with white children	86.0
lived in racially-mixed neighborhood	75.0
attended integrated school	67.5
Today:	
family very friendly with white people	83.1
white people visit home at least once a month	43.8
visit white people at their home at least once a month	39.9
husband works with white people	93.2
white work associates visit home at least once a month	37.6
visit white work associates at their home at least once a month	34.8
family doctor is white	56.0
family dentist is white	40.4
member of a church which is: virtually all white	0.0
mostly white	15.0
roughly equal	8.4
mostly Negro	10.3
virtually all Negro	66.4

*Source: H. F. Freeman, Helen H. Hughes, T. F. Pettigrew, and L. G. Watts, *The Middle-Income Negro: Stake and Status in the Ghetto.* Manuscript in preparation. The sample consisted of 250 Negro housewives whose families resided in the ghetto and had a total family income of not less than $5,200 annually; the percentages exclude the few cases which did not answer the query or did not belong to a church, and so forth.

cians and dentists, and to belong to interracial church congregations. Yet here the racial patterns are rapidly changing. While the revolution of the past few years has not significantly altered the lives of most lower-status Negroes, the lives of higher-status Negro Southerners are undeniably affected. The desegregation of public golf courses, expensive restaurants, and the Atlanta opera and the new opportunities for skilled Negroes with federal contractors have not meant much yet to the poor and unskilled, but such changes have pried open the ghetto's lid for those in the middle class who want to take advantage of them. In a few years, middle-income Negroes in the urban South may report interracial patterns, especially those revolving around employment, quite similar to those cited for Boston.

Mention of Southern racial change raises other interesting regional differences. Negroes are not strangers or interlopers on the Southern scene, as they are often perceived in the North. White and Negro Southerners are both products of the same subculture. They share a common history and a common religion, while white and Negro Northerners frequently share neither. These advantages have tempted Southern liberals, Negro and white, to speculate about the possibility that the South will take the giant step from formal desegregation to informal integration with greater ease and alacrity than the North. The writer has at times shared this dream with his Southern compatriots, though the present adoption by the urban South of strict residential segregation makes it appear that the South, too, will have to work through a difficult period of *de facto* segregation similar to that of the present-day North.[35]

Nevertheless, these cultural and religious bonds between Negro and white Southerners are an important element in the explanation for the present difference in "moods" between Negro communities in the South and North. To risk oversimplification, this difference seems to involve hope and despair. Negroes in the South, including most lower-status Negro Southerners, still "believe," still have faith that the revolution is bringing "freedom." Despite governors like Barnett and Wallace, despite police brutality and wanton murders, Negro Southerners are rewarded in this belief by seeing *de jure* segregation crumble. In sharp contrast, Negro Northerners, particularly the lower-status residents of the bowels of the Harlems and South Sides, either have lost or are losing such hope for the future. A brooding and desperate despair develops from failing to see the Mayor Wagners and the School Superintendent Willises even nudged by protests against *de facto* segregation. And, progress stifled, despair spills over into rioting. This regional difference is made blatant by the response of a hardened Harlemite to a young Negro Southerner visiting New York. "Baby," he jeered, "down South you're just fighting to get where we are now—and we can tell you that once you get here it's just a solid blank wall."[36]

This dramatic regional difference in Negro "mood" is borne out by national survey data. Gallup reports that between 1963 and 1965 the proportion of Negro Southerners who said that they feel they are treated "not very well" or "badly" declined from roughly 90 to 70 per cent, while virtually no change was noted among Negro Northerners.[37] Another important ingredient in this regional difference lies in the distinction between aspirations and attainment. Social motivation is more directly determined by *relative,* rather than absolute, deprivation.[38] Negro Southerners have aspired to far less than Negro Northerners, and hence have perceived greater reinforcement from smaller racial advances. But this situation will obviously not last much longer. As the Negro American revolution proceeds, aspirations will tend to rise faster than actual gains. Moreover, as *de jure* segregation fuses into *de facto* segregation, gains are certain to come less rapidly and dramatically. Will the Negro Southerner continue even then "to believe"? The answer obviously depends largely upon the response of the urban South, a response that has not been encouraging so far.

II. *Change in American Racial Patterns*

Contact and change. Many well-meaning Americans have expressed the opinion that if only Negroes and whites could experience more contact with each other the nation's racial difficulties would solve themselves. Unfortunately, the case is not so simple. Africans and Europeans have more contact in the Republic of South Africa than anywhere else on the African continent, and Negro and white Americans have more contact in the South than in any other region of the nation; yet neither of these areas is conspicuous for its interracial harmony. It appears almost as if contact between the two peoples exacerbates, rather than relieves, intergroup hostility; but this conclusion would be just as hasty and fallacious as the naive assumption that contact invariably lessens prejudice.

Increasing interaction, whether it be of groups or individuals, intensifies and magnifies the processes already underway. Hence, more interracial contact can lead either to greater prejudice and rejection or to greater respect and acceptance, depending upon the situation in which it occurs. The basic issue, then, concerns the types of situations in which contact leads to distrust and those in which it leads to trust.

Gordon Allport, in his review of the relevant research, concludes that four characteristics of the contact situation are of utmost importance.[39] Prejudice is lessened when the two groups: (1) possess equal status, (2) seek common goals, (3) are cooperatively dependent upon each other, and (4) interact with the positive support of authorities, laws, or custom.

If groups are of widely different social status, contact between them may do little more than reinforce old and hostile stereotypes.

In the typical Southern situation of interracial contact, most Negroes encountered by white Southerners are servants and other low-status service workers. Many whites eventually conclude that these are the types of jobs best suited for Negroes, that somehow this is the Negro's "proper place." To be sure, there are Negro professionals in the South, but, as noted above, segregation has forced them to stay deep within the Negro ghetto where whites rarely meet them. The segregationist who boasts that he "really knows Negroes" is usually referring to his casual encounters with Negroes of lower status. This is a principal reason that the plentiful Negro-white patterns of contact in the South have not led to more interracial understanding.

As previously mentioned, many whites are convinced that Negroes do not share their interests and values, a belief which compounds racial prejudice with assumed value conflict. *Equal-status* contact attacks this problem in two ways. First, people of equal status are more likely than others to possess congruent outlooks and beliefs simply by virtue of their common positions in society. Second, equal-status situations provide the optimal setting in which this congruence can be mutually perceived.

When groups work together toward *common goals,* further opportunities are presented for developing and discovering similarities of interests and values. The reduction of prejudice through contact generally requires an active, focused effort, not simply intermingling for its own sake. Athletic teams furnish a pertinent example. In striving to win, interracial teams not only create an equal-status contact situation but one in which Negro and white team members cannot achieve their common goal of winning without the assistance of each other. Under such conditions, race loses importance.

Not only must groups seek common goals, but the attainment of these goals must be a *mutually dependent* effort involving no competition along strictly racial lines. For instance, if the San Francisco Giants were an all-white baseball team and the Los Angeles Dodgers were all Negro, they could probably play indefinitely and not become more racially tolerant. Though equal-status and common goal conditions would prevail, the lines of competition would make race relevant. Fortunately, professional athletic teams are interracial and provide a notable case of successful desegregation. But the lesson is clear. The contact situations which lead to interracial harmony must involve cooperative interdependence.

The final factor concerns the auspices of the contact. If the situation has *explicit social sanction,* interracial contact is more readily accepted and leads to more positive effects. Though the situation may be a bit awkward at first, the support of authorities helps make it seem "right." Failure of local authorities, law, and custom to bolster even minimal desegregation in much of the South is a chief reason for the failure of many white Southerners to respect federal court orders.

Research literature abounds with examples of these contact principles in operation. One study found that white merchant marines tended to hold racial attitudes in direct relation to how many voyages they had taken with equal-status Negro seamen—the more desegregated voyages, the more positive their attitudes.[40] Another investigation noted that white Philadelphia policemen who had personally worked with Negro colleagues were far more favorable toward the desegregation of their force than other white policemen.[41] A third study of white government workers, veterans, and students found that those who had known Negro professionals were far less prejudiced toward Negroes than those who had known only unskilled Negroes.[42]

Evidence appears even in times of crisis. While Negro and white mobs raged during the Detroit race riot of 1943, integrated co-workers, university students, and neighbors of long standing peacefully carried on their lives side-by-side.[43] Mention of neighborhood integration introduces the most solid research evidence available. Repeated studies have found that integrated living in public housing developments which meet all four of Allport's contact criteria sharply reduces the racial prejudice among both Negro and white neighbors.[44] And these same studies demonstrate that living in segregated, but otherwise identical, housing developments structures interracial contact in such a way that, if anything, racial bitterness is enhanced. Additional data derive from the desegregation of the Armed Forces.[45] Once again, conditions involving equal status, cooperative striving toward common goals, and authority support led directly to the reduction of racial prejudice among both Negro and white servicemen. As a Negro officer in Korea candidly phrased it: "After a while you start thinking of whites as people."

One important qualification attends attitude change through interracial contact: At least in the initial stages, the change is often limited to the specific situation involved. Recall the steel workers whose experiences in a fully integrated union had not noticeably influenced their views on interracial housing. These limitations of the effects of even optimal contact are a result of the depth and complexity with which segregation has snarled the vital fabric of American life. Untying one knot does not prove that a solution has been found, but as desegregation proceeds there should be increasing generalization from one situation to another.

The law and change. Within this perspective, a reappraisal can be made of the old saw—"Laws cannot change the hearts and minds of men." A case in point is the 1945 anti-discrimination employment legislation enacted by New York State. This law led to the initial hiring of Negroes as sales clerks in New York City department stores. Two investigators conducted separate tests of the effects of this law-induced desegregation. One study of white sales personnel revealed that those who had experienced the new equal-status job contact with Negroes held more favorable attitudes toward interracial interaction in the work situation.[46] Once again, however, the initial effects of this contact did not extend beyond the immediate situation; equal-status clerks were not more accepting of Negroes in eating and residential situations. The other investigation questioned customers.[47] Their responses showed widespread acceptance of this legally-required racial change. They were concerned largely with shopping conveniently and efficiently; many hesitated to challenge the firm *fait accompli* established by the law; and for many the new pattern was consistent with their belief in the American creed of equal opportunity for all.[48]

Contrary to the old adage, then, laws *can* change the hearts and minds of men. They do so through a vital intermediate step. Laws first act to modify behavior, and this modified behavior in turn changes the participants' attitudes. Notice that this is precisely the opposite sequence commonly believed to be the most effective method of social change. When people are convinced to be less prejudiced through informational and good-will campaigns, conventional reasoning asserts, then they will discriminate less. To be sure, this sequence is sometimes effective, but the preponderance of social psychological evidence attests to the greater efficacy of the opposite approach. Behaving differently is more often the precursor to thinking differently.

The celebrated annual rituals of brotherhood week, brotherhood dinners, and brotherhood awards illustrate the point. While they remind participants of their religious and national ideals and strengthen the already convinced, these events appear of limited value in convincing the unconvinced. The basic problem with such observances is that they do not require participants to change their behavior. The interracial contact is brief and artificial, and the emphasis is placed on exhortation and influencing attitudes directly. A vast body of psychological data indicates that prejudiced individuals in such situations will avoid the message altogether, deny its relevance for themselves, or find ways of twisting its meaning.[49] In addition, ritualistic exhortations for brotherhood may often serve an unanticipated negative function. By attending the annual dinner and paying the tax-deductible $50 or $100 per plate, many individuals of considerable influence regularly relieve their guilt. Having gone through the motions of supporting "equality for all," participants are psychologically released to go on discriminating as before.

Anti-discrimination laws can also be tuned out by prejudiced individuals and used as conscience salves by the guilty. Frequently, the laws remain unenforced except on a case-by-case basis which fails to attack the structural pattern supporting discrimination. But if properly enforced and pattern-directed, such legislation offers a potential means for achieving behavioral change not possessed by exhortation. Several reasons for this are apparent. There is, of course, the threat of punishment and unfavorable publicity for recalcitrants. But more important is the "off-the-hook" function such laws provide. Thus, the department stores in New York City may each have been afraid to hire Negro sales personnel as long as there were no assurances their competitors would follow suit. But the anti-discrimination law, applied to all stores, furnished this needed assurance. And the legally-established *fait accompli,* unlike exhortations for tolerance, generates its own acceptance.[50] The improvement it achieves is a year-round process, a constant, institutionalized reminder that racial harmony is the sanctioned norm. Finally, the new behavior required by the law psychologically commits the individual, for when a person has behaved publicly in a new manner and has been rewarded for doing so he is likely to become personally committed to the racial change.[51]

A microcosmic case in point. The fundamental principles underlying racial attitude change are dramatically highlighted by an ingenious field study conducted in Oklahoma.[52] Twenty young boys, of homogeneous backgrounds but previously unacquainted with one another, attended an experimental summer camp. From the start, the boys were divided into two groups—"The Rattlers" and "The Eagles." The first stage of the experiment was designed to develop high *espirit de corps* within each of the groups. Separated from each other, the Rattlers and Eagles engaged in a variety of satisfying experiences, and each group soon evidenced the pride and sense of "we-ness" characteristic of strong in-group solidarity.

The second stage brought the groups face-to-face in a series of grimly competitive tasks—tugs-of-war, baseball and football games, and tent pitching. In all of these contact situations, only one group could win and the other had to lose. The inevitable intergroup animosity soon appeared. Derogatory songs and slogans were composed; destructive raids on "the enemy's" cabin began; negative stereotypes developed; and even preferences for group segregation were voiced. Competitive contact had wreaked its usual havoc.

The experiment's third stage tried to mend the damage. "The brotherhood dinner" approach came first. The boys met in such non-competitive situations as eating good food in the same room, shooting off fireworks, and attending a movie together—all of them involving passive conduct without common goals or group interdependence. And, understandably, intergroup friction did not abate; in fact, the boys employed these unfocused events as opportunities for further vilification of their hated rivals. Next, the investigators introduced carefully contrived problems that required the cooperation of both groups for their solution. Fixing together the damaged water tank that supplied the whole camp, raising the funds to show a favorite movie, and other functionally dependent behavior achieved a striking decrement in intergroup hostility. While at the close of the competitive second stage over half of the characteristics assigned by the boys to their group rivals were sharply unfavorable, over two-thirds of such judgments were favorable at the close of the interdependent third stage. Moreover, the percentage of friendship choices across group lines multiplied fourfold.

One final result of this intriguing investigation replicates the limited nature of the attitude change initially induced even under optimal contact conditions. The first interdependent encounters of the two camp groups by no means removed all of the bad feeling between the Rattlers and the Eagles. But as these socially-sanctioned confrontations continued, the prejudice-reducing power of this type of contact accumulated. This suggests that, as the desegregation process proceeds, it may well receive increasingly greater support and have increasingly greater effects upon the participants, both Negro and white.

The growth of institutional protections. The Rattlers and the

Eagles demonstrate a basic principle undergirding the changing of America's racial patterns: namely, effective efforts must attack the patterns directly. It is not enough to be concerned with the reduction of anti-Negro prejudice. Indeed, the very changes that eliminate social barriers to Negro progress structure new situations which in turn alter individual attitudes to the greatest possible extent. Allport's four situational criteria for lessening prejudice are virtually impossible to achieve without prior elimination of racial discrimination.

At the broadest level, the elimination of discrimination requires the development of institutional protections for minorities. Other papers in this volume describe in detail many of these institutional protections in the political, legal, and economic realms.[53] Suffice it to add that these protections often appear in forms not ostensibly related to minorities and come in a variety of ways. For example, changes in municipal property tax laws and minimum wage coverage are desperately needed by many Negroes—and whites. Property tax structures tend to foster and perpetuate slum housing in many cities. Slum landlords are encouraged to allow property to deteriorate in the ghetto by tax incentives and by the lack of enforcement of building and sanitation codes. Likewise, the concentration of Negroes in service work not covered by minimum wage legislation feeds ghetto disorganization. The meager income from such work makes it nearly impossible for a man to support a family and thus swells the ranks of broken homes.

American institutional protections for minorities have evolved in a variety of ways. Sometimes they emerge dramatically, as in the enactment of the 1964 Civil Rights Act; more often they come quietly and without national attention, as in the acceptance of minorities into previously discriminatory professions and college social fraternities.[54] But generally these protections have been won, at least in large part, through pressure exerted by the minorities themselves. Of course, most groups of Americans are numerical minorities, but a combination of minorities easily forms a majority. Indeed, the largest political party in the nation is a delicately-balanced coalition of minorities, including among others the predominant share of the country's Negroes, Jews, and Roman Catholics. And this party has managed to win seven of the last nine presidential elections in part because of its achievements in establishing precisely the type of institutional protections under discussion. Given the momentum of this trend and the growing expectations of practically all of the nation's minorities, there is good reason to expect that the evolution of institutional protections will continue.

Success vs. *test strategies of change.* The United States government is not the only sponsor of institutional protections, but it has become by far the chief agent of planned change in Negro-white relations. And frequently a "success *vs.* test" strategy conflict confronts government officials in this and other areas.

Consider an official with a reasonably tight budget, a limited staff, and a broad legislative mandate for immediate action. He could be an official of the Office of Education charged with enforcing Title VI of the 1964 Civil Rights Act and preparing to cut off federal funds from a variety of school districts which refuse to comply with the non-discriminatory provisions of the Act. Or he could be an official administering the Manpower Retraining Act or the Job Corps and preparing to select the Negroes and whites for the program out of the vast pool of people who need and desire such training. In each of these situations the organizers must decide where to focus the limited resources. Should the principal effort be directed at those cases which are most likely to change easily and thus will demonstrate that the program is a *"success"*— the so-called "skimming-off-the-cream" approach? Should it be directed at those cases least likely to change easily and thus provide a rigorous *test* of the program? Or should it be directed primarily at cases of medium difficulty, or at some combination of these possibilities?

Frequently, civil rights specialists have criticized federal programs for following the path of least resistance and tackling only the easy cases. Yet a reasonable argument can be made for this approach: why not change those who obviously can be changed? Indeed, this policy yields more conspicuous gain per dollar spent than any other strategy—a not irrelevant consideration. Consequently, it has appeal for political purposes and for the career aspirations of those administrators involved in directing the program. In addition, a show of early success safeguards the program's continuance, making it theoretically possible for a later attack on the core of the problem from a stronger posture. And it can establish a *fait accompli* effect that enhances the program's image as one that is making progress.

But maximizing early success has its obvious drawbacks as a strategy for planned change. If the Office of Education followed this approach, it would reward the most belligerent and recalcitrant school districts practicing racial discrimination by exempting them from the initial stages of the enforcement of Title VI. Likewise, in the job training programs, this process would differentially operate against the enrollment of Negroes because the ghetto floor of deprivation is qualitatively and quantitatively below that of disadvantaged whites. Fundamentally, then, the dangers of the early success approach are that it may squander a major chance for basic and needed change and ease consciences while only scratching the problem's surface.

These weaknesses point up the advantages of the counterstrategy—the need to put change programs to the full *test* by concentrating upon the most difficult cases. In enforcing Title VI, this test strategy would require the use of virtually all resources for school districts in Alabama, Mississippi, Louisiana, northern Florida, and southwest Georgia; in the Manpower Retraining and Job Corps programs, it would necessitate accepting only the hard-core unemployed. Consequently, the most debilitated segments of the Negro ghetto would be far more likely to be included in significant numbers. In addition to affording a real test of the program, such a strategy provides a genuine attempt at initiating the basic institutional alterations needed before truly society-wide solutions are possible.

But basic institutional alterations are generally politically dangerous; and there is a greater chance of short-run failure with the test strategy. Moreover, greater expenditures of public funds for less conspicuous success will generally be involved, for the cost per person effectively prepared for the labor market in, say, the Manpower Retraining program would necessarily be greater if the hard-core unemployed comprised the principal clientele. Thus, the test strategy seriously jeopardizes the continuation of the whole program on several counts.

The striking complementary nature of the advantages and disadvantages of these rival strategies suggests the usefulness of a third possibility. A dual strategy might involve a judicious mixture of both the success and test strategies, employed simultaneously, taking as many of the easiest and hardest cases as resources allow while omitting the middle-range. The political need for early success can be met largely with the easier cases, while the more difficult allow head-on grappling with the most recalcitrant and early experience with the fundamental issues of the problem at its worst.

The most effective methods for the easy cases will almost undoubtedly not be the same as those for the difficult cases. Nor has modern social science any "bag of tricks" or even well-tested techniques for such tasks as training the most seriously disadvantaged young people now being enrolled in the Job Corps. A successful attack on the effects of racism and poverty must have an evolving strategy, it must learn as it unfolds; and it probably cannot operate in this fashion if it does not have, on the one hand, easy instances for reasons of publicity, politics, and the program's future and, on the other hand, difficult instances from which to learn how to shape the program in the future.

III. *Future American Racial Patterns*

The Negro-American stigma. At first glance, the plight of Negroes trapped in urban ghettos recalls the immigrant ghettos of previous generations. Both moved from near-peasant status to form the lower classes of large metropolitan centers. But here the analogy abruptly breaks down. As Talcott Parsons ably demonstrates in this volume, the Negro American poses a sharply different problem of inclusion into America's "societal community" than immigrant Americans.

The immigrant-Negro analogy is exceedingly misleading. It provokes the often heard query: "What's so special about Negroes? We Irish (or Italians or Jews) made it on our own—why all this fuss over the Negro's problems?" In addition to its debatable accuracy concerning how immigrants were absorbed into American society, such a question overlooks all that is unique about the Negro case from slavery to current times. In particular, the analogy obscures the principal social psychological problem of American race relations—the persistent fact that there is in American society a special and debilitating *stigma* placed upon Negro status.

The concept of "stigma" is here used in its social psychological sense: that is, stigma signifies a handicap which disqualifies an entire class of persons from full social acceptance.[55] It need *not* be a permanent handicap, and the concept should not be confused with certain popular usages of the term as a lasting physical mark or blemish. The Negro stigma revolves largely around the presumption of primitive inferiority.[56] And manifestations of the stigma include the white American attitudes toward interracial marriage cited earlier and the expected subservient role of "Negro." The special stigma becomes apparent when the Negro's societal position is compared with that of other deprived groups. Negro Texans, for example, have a median of two years more education than Texans of Mexican descent, yet their median family income falls well below even that of the culturally-handicapped Spanish Americans. Nor is this stigma a matter of mere color and visibility; compare the Negro American's place in American society with that of Japanese and Chinese Americans.

Outgroup stigmata often take one of two contrasting forms. One type is rooted in super-ego concerns, with the outgroup stereotyped as shrewd, mercenary, pushy, ambitious, sly, and clannish. The other type is rooted in id concerns, with the outgroup stereotyped as superstitious, lazy, happy-go-lucky, ignorant, dirty, irresponsible, and sexually uninhibited. The psychoanalytic interpretation of these distinctive stereotypes is straight-forward. Outgroups serve in part as alter-egos for the bigot; intergroup animosities are seen as projections of the bigot's own unacceptable inner impulses onto a minority group. In the United States, the prejudiced person thus personifies his own super-ego sins of ambition, deceit, and egotism in the Jew and his own id sins of the flesh in the Negro.[57]

This psychoanalytic distinction between super-ego and id stereotypes is applicable to a variety of cross-cultural situations. Thus, outgroups assigned a super-ego stigma are usually merchants who are not native to an area, middle-men caught between the landed and the laboring classes as were the European Jews in the Middle Ages.[58] Nor are the people who invoke the super-ego stereotype unaware of this similarity, for the Chinese merchants of Malaysia and Indonesia are often called the "Jews of Asia" and the Muslim Indian merchants of East and South Africa, the "Jews of Africa." Likewise, the id stigma is invoked in many parts of the world for groups that are usually found on the bottom of the social structure; in Europe, Gypsies and Southern Italians are often the targets.[59] Yet the Negro American inherits the id stigma with special force. Not only is he typically confronted by class barriers at the bottom of the social structure, but he is also confronted by caste barriers as the degrading legacy of three centuries of slavery and segregation.[60]

This id stigma branded upon the Negro American is only now beginning to recede. Compared with the results of a study in the early 1930's, a follow-up study of Princeton University undergraduates in 1950 found that the Negro stereotype, like other stereotypes, had lost some of its salience. The percentage of students regarding the Negro American as "superstitious" had declined from 84 to 41 per cent, as "lazy" from 75 to 31 per cent, as "happy-go-lucky" from 38 to 17 per cent, and as "ignorant" from 38 to 24 per cent.[61] Evidence of a similar trend for the entire adult population comes from repeated surveys of the National Opinion Research Center asking: "In general, do you think Negroes are as intelligent as white people—that is, can they learn just as well if they are given the same education and training?" The percentage among the white respondents answering "yes" in 1942 was only 42, by 1946 this figure had risen to 52, by 1956 it had climbed to 77, and in 1963 it still remained at 77.[62] Even among white Southerners, 59 per cent said "yes" to the query by 1963.

For striking evidence of how this shift is reflected in the mass media, one need only compare contemporary materials with the early issues of *Life Magazine*.[63] While occasionally portraying Negroes neutrally or as "credits to their race," *Life* in the late 1930's overwhelmingly presented Negroes as either musical, primitive, amusing, or religious, or as violent and criminal; occupationally, they were pictured as either servants, athletes, or entertainers, or as unemployed. Pictures included a Negro choir at a graveside funeral, an all-Negro chain gang, and Negro W.P.A. workers beating a drum "in tribal fashion" at a W.P.A. circus. Dialect was common: to the question of who was Father Divine's father, "Mrs. Mayfield cackled, 'Lawd chile, that been so long ago, I done fergit.'" Descriptions of Negroes dancing included such terms as "barbaric," "jungle," and "native gusto." Today the mass media would not consider such material.

This is not to imply that the id stigma of Negroes has faded completely from view. A 1963 national survey of white Americans revealed that 68 per cent still believe that Negroes "laugh a lot," 66 per cent that they lack ambition, 60 per cent that they "smell different," 55 per cent that they "have looser morals," 46 per cent that they "keep untidy homes," and 41 per cent that they "want to live off the handout."[64] Nevertheless, the id stigma is slowly receding. The upgrading of the Negro labor force and the improvement of mass media racial content combine with the assertive resourcefulness of the Negro revolution to spell the gradual abolition of the centuries-old stigma. It will recede from view, as John Turner notes, in direct relation to how dysfunctional it becomes for American society, but this process will undoubtedly require a number of generations before the most entrenched aspects of the stigma are eradicated.

Future interracial patterns. Erasure of the Negro stigma will in large part be a function of changing interracial patterns. And the current Negro-American revolution guarantees that there will be changes in these patterns; but it is equally certain that these alterations will come unevenly.

Racial patterns in 1984, to select a fateful year, will differ most from those of today in the employment realm and least in the areas of housing and family. Employment contact—most of it meeting Allport's criteria for reducing intergroup animosity—will expand rapidly in the future, leaving by the 1980's only pockets of the economic sector (for example, automobile executives) which lack at least token Negro representation. Nevertheless, these occupational gains will be limited by the capacity of public education and such intervention programs of the federal government as the Job Corps and the pre-school "Head Start" effort to upgrade Negro skills.[65] This educational factor may well prove to be a severe limitation. Here the importance of *de facto* segregation of schools looms large, for Negroes cannot be expected to work in interracial situations at high standards if they have overwhelmingly been trained in uniracial schools with low standards. The racial balancing of schools, however, may well be a slow process at best in the future; and it will probably require state and federal legislative initiatives as opposed to judicial action against *de jure* school segregation. At any rate, public education will provide steadily increasing opportunities in the higher grades for interracial contact that meets Allport's criteria; but these opportunities will not increase so rapidly as employment and may deter the racial integration of the American labor force.

The whole issue of *de facto* segregation in schools, churches, and other neighborhood-based institutions revolves around residential segregation. Interracial housing trends of recent years portend a future generation resembling the one just past—that is, a period of rapid racial change in other realms with housing integration sharply lagging behind. Some of the barriers to interracial housing are structural. Further progress is inseparably intertwined with such larger issues as the total supply of low-cost housing, property tax laws, and land-use planning. These are not issues for which picketing, sit-ins, and other protest techniques are ideally suited. Some of the barriers are less subtle and are erected by fierce white resistance. Racial discrimination in housing is usually blatant, entrenched, and pervasive throughout the nation and the class structure. It is not only fueled by status and financial fears as well as bigotry, but is encouraged by much of the real-estate industry.

In addition to white resistance, the lack of Negro insistence is a critical barrier to the alteration of housing patterns. Segregation has led to large and concentrated Negro ghettos in a great majority of America's cities; and each of these ghettos has developed institutions and a community life in many ways distinct from and independent of the wider community. These deeply-rooted Negro communities present formidable barriers to an eventual integrated society. As Franklin Frazier often pointed out, separate community life causes many Negroes to develop a vested interest in segregation.[66] Thus, Negro professionals and businessmen enjoy a captive market within the walls of a tight ghetto, but they must meet extensive competition in a desegregated society. Likewise, the all-Negro church and other all-Negro institutions naturally thrive best in a racially segregated society. Consequently, there is every reason to expect that even when residential discrimination essentially ends and Negroes as a group are prosperous enough to afford a wide range of housing, there will be binding ghetto ties that restrain many Negroes from moving to interracial areas.

Research on Boston's middle-income Negroes found that only a small fraction of these families have seriously considered living in the predominantly white suburbs.[67] Despite the fact that they are now in the direct path of urban renewal, that suburban housing is available in their income range, that suburban Fair Housing Practices Committees seek and welcome them, that they are upset over the ghetto's inferior and racially imbalanced schools, and that the few Negroes who have moved to the suburbs around Boston have typically adjusted quite well,[68] only 9 families of 250 (less than 4 per cent) moved to interracial areas during a critical ten-month period. For that matter, less than 20 per cent of these prosperous Negro Bostonians have made any realistic effort to investigate suburban housing. In short, most of these people have their stake and status in the ghetto and are not sufficiently motivated to leave it.

Yet some change, even in housing patterns, can be expected during the next generation. Such change will definitely be selective, however, unless massive federal intervention in housing occurs along lines far different from the usually ghetto-tightening efforts of the past. There may well be somewhat more federally sponsored interracial contact at the low-cost housing level. But in general only the prospering middle-class Negroes in the urban North will be able to purchase or rent the type of housing that will be available in interracial areas on the private market. This will be true for two reasons. First, those predominantly white communities with the range of housing most suited to Negro middle-income needs (about $12,000 to $20,000) are typically more resistant to Negro occupancy than those with housing far beyond the resources of even middle-income Negroes (roughly $30,000 and up). Second, a number of studies agree that those relatively few Negroes who are particularly anxious to move to the suburbs not only earn a higher income than most other Negroes, but also are typically Northern-born, well-educated, young, and light-skinned.[69]

The selective nature of this housing trend will give many white Americans living in the "better" residential districts the strong impression that considerable change is underway. After all, their suburban neighborhoods are likely to shift from having no Negro residents whatsoever to one Negro family or even an "invasion" of two or three Negro families. This will mean that token integration patterns in suburban churches and schools are likely to become the rule, while the ghettos of the central cities grow ever larger.[70]

"The other Negro America." The Negro ghetto seems destined to remain a part of the American scene for years to come, though it may evolve over time from a racial prison into an ethnic area of choice. In a few places, this evolution is already beginning, but the choice to live in or out of the ghetto is confined to high-status Negroes. Indeed, a distinction between lower- and higher-status Negroes has had to be drawn continually throughout this paper. Those Negroes less scarred by past deprivations are in a position to take advantage of current racial change, and it is to these people that fingers point when "racial progress" of recent years is proudly cited. These are the Negro Americans who by 1984 will be not just desegregated but truly integrated into "the affluent society."

Progress for "the affluent Negro America" is, of course, not unimportant. Successful middle-class Negroes offer needed achievement models for the Negro community; they can effectively obliterate racial barriers by being "the first of the race" in previously all-white situations; they help eliminate the Negro stigma by providing a constant contradiction between class and caste; and they furnish the great majority of protest leaders. But middle-class Negroes are only a minority of the group.

To borrow from Michael Harrington, there is "the other Negro America." Now constituting perhaps two-thirds of all Negroes,[71] this other Negro America has not as yet been significantly touched by present racial adjustments. Nor has it had any increased contact with white Americans in recent years; rather, it slips further and further into the depths of "the dark ghetto" and its own desperate despair. Its hopes were raised in the 1950's;[72] but now it cannot even rationalize personal failure entirely in racial terms, for *Ebony* bulges each month with evidence that "the affluent Negro America" is making rapid strides.

No realistic assessment of American racial patterns in 1965 can ignore "the other Negro America." Progress for those who are already prosperous is important, but is hardly sufficient. The future of race relations in the United States will depend ultimately on the nation's ability and willingness to penetrate the veneer of success and alter the lives of this "other Negro America" in a truly meaningful fashion.

REFERENCES

1. An extended application of role theory to American race relations is provided in: T. F. Pettigrew, *A Profile of The Negro American* (Princeton, N. J., 1964).

2. The terror such a subordinate role can have for a white person, inexperienced in its subtleties, is revealed in John Griffin, *Black Like Me* (Boston, 1961).

3. Pettigrew, *op. cit.*

4. J. Biesanz and L. M. Smith, "Race Relations of Panama and the Canal Zone," *American Journal of Sociology*, Vol. 57 (July 1951), pp. 7-14.

5. R. D. Minard, "Race Relations in the Pocahontas Coal Field," *Journal of Social Issues*, Vol. 8, No. 1 (1952), pp. 29-44.

6. R. T. LaPiere, "Attitudes versus Actions," *Social Forces*, Vol. 13 (December 1934), pp. 230-237.

7. B. Kutner, Caroll Wilkins, and Penny R. Yarrow, "Verbal Attitudes and Overt Behavior Involving Racial Prejudice," *Journal of Abnormal and Social Psychology*, Vol. 47 (July 1952), pp. 649-652.

8. M. L. Kohn and R. M. Williams, Jr., "Situational Patterning in Intergroup Relations," *American Sociological Review*, Vol. 21 (April 1956), pp. 164-174.

9. J. D. Lohman and D. C. Reitzes, "Note on Race Relations in Mass Society," *American Journal of Sociology*, Vol. 58 (November 1952), pp. 240-246; J. D. Lohman and D. C. Reitzes, "Deliberately Organized Groups and Racial Behavior," *American Sociological Review*, Vol. 19 (June 1954), pp.

342-344; and D. C. Reitzes, "The Role of Organizational Structures: Union versus Neighborhood in a Tension Situation," *Journal of Social Issues*, Vol. 9, No. 1 (1953), pp. 37-44.

10. Note that a "reference group" is not the same as a membership group. People may or may not be members of their reference groups. What is critical is that the reference group supplies standards which an individual may use to guide his own behavior and with which he may compare his own position in life. See H. H. Hyman, "The Psychology of Status," *Archives of Psychology*, Vol. 38, No. 269 (June 1942), pp. 5-94; H. H. Kelley, "Two Functions of Reference Groups," in G. E. Swanson, T. M. Newcomb, and E. L. Hartley (eds.), *Readings in Social Psychology* (Rev. edn., New York, 1952), pp. 410-414; and R. K. Merton and Alice S. Kitt, "Contributions to a Theory of Reference Group Behavior," in R. K. Merton and P. F. Lazarsfeld (eds.), *Studies in the Scope and Method of "The American Soldier"* (Glencoe, Ill., 1950).

11. H. A. Bullock, "Racial Attitudes and the Employment of Negroes," *American Journal of Sociology*, Vol. 56 (March 1951), pp. 448-457.

12. A. Kapos, "Some Individual and Group Determinants of Fraternity Attitudes Toward the Admission of Members of Certain Minority Groups," Unpublished doctoral dissertation, University of Michigan, 1953.

13. The twenty states include the eleven ex-Confederate states, five border states (Delaware, Missouri, Oklahoma, Kentucky, and West Virginia), plus Idaho, Indiana, Utah, and Wyoming. A dozen others have stricken similar statutes from their books in recent years. Utah and Wyoming still have what must be the most all-inclusive anti-miscegenation laws of all. Among other provisions, their statutes forbid Negroes and Malayians to marry—though it is not known if any Malayians even live in these states. G. E. Simpson and J. M. Yinger, *Racial and Cultural Minorities* (3rd edn.; New York, 1965), pp. 375-376.

14. David M. Heer, "Recent Trends in Negro-White Marriages in the United States," *American Journal of Sociology*, in press.

15. William Brink and Louis Harris, *The Negro Revolution in America* (New York, 1964), p. 148. The comparable percentages for just white Southerners are 97 and 91 objecting.

16. *Ibid.*

17. George Gallup, "Public Split on Banning of Interracial Marriages," American Institute of Public Opinion release of March 9, 1965.

18. Simpson and Yinger, *op. cit.*, p. 401.

19. T. F. Pettigrew, "Our Caste-Ridden Protestant Campuses," *Christianity and Crisis*, Vol. 21 (May 29, 1961), pp. 88-91; and T. F. Pettigrew, "Wherein the Church Has Failed in Race," *Religious Education*, Vol. 59 (January-February 1964), pp. 64-73.

20. *Southern School News*, Vol. 11, No. 6 (December 1964), p. 1.

21. T. F. Pettigrew, "Continuing Barriers to Desegregated Education in the South," *Sociology of Education*, Vol. 38 (Winter 1965), pp. 99-111.

22. Massachusetts State Advisory Committee to the U. S. Commission on Civil Rights, *Report on Racial Imbalance in the Boston Public Schools*, January 1965, p. 49.

23. See Arnold Rose, *De Facto Segregation* (New York, 1964); and T. F. Pettigrew, "De Facto Segregation, Southern Style," *Integrated Education*, Vol. 1, No. 5 (October-November 1963), pp. 15-18.

24. N. D. Glenn, "Some Changes in the Relative Status of American Non-Whites, 1940 to 1960," *Phylon*, Vol. 24 (Summer 1963), pp. 109-122.

25. T. F. Pettigrew, "Metropolitan Boston's Race Problem in Perspective," in *Social Structure and Human Problems in the Boston Metropolitan Area* (Cambridge, Mass., 1965), pp. 33-51.

26. Herbert Hill, "Racial Inequality in Employment: The Patterns of Discrimination," *The Annals of the American Academy of Political and Social Science*, Vol. 357 (January 1965), pp. 30-47; and S. A. Levitan, *Youth Employment Act* (Kalamazoo, Mich., 1963).

27. K. E. Taeuber and Alma F. Taeuber, "Is the Negro an Immigrant Group?" *Integrated Education*, Vol. 1, No. 3 (June 1963), pp. 25-28. The Taeubers note, however, that growth in the size of a city's Negro population does not necessarily lead to increased indices of residential separation by race.

28. Leon Mayhew, "Law and Equal Opportunity: Anti-Discrimination Law in Massachusetts," unpublished doctoral dissertation, Harvard University, 1964.

29. H. H. Hyman and P. B. Sheatsley, "Attitudes Toward Desegregation," *Scientific American*, Vol. 195 (December 1956), pp. 35-39.

30. R. W. Friedrichs, "Christians and Residential Exclusion: An Empirical Study of a Northern Dilemma," *Journal of Social Issues*, Vol. 15, No. 4 (October 1959), pp. 14-23.

31. Frank R. Westie, "Negro-White Status Differentials and Social Distance," *American Sociological Review*, Vol. 17 (October 1952), pp. 550-558.

32. Frank R. Westie and David H. Howard, "Social Status Differentials and the Race Attitudes of Negroes," *American Sociological Review*, Vol. 19 (October 1954), pp. 584-591.

33. T. C. Cothran, "Negro Conceptions of White People," *American Journal of Sociology*, Vol. 56 (March 1951), pp. 458-467; and P. A. McDaniel and N. Babchuk, "Negro Conceptions of White People in a Northeastern City," *Phylon*, Vol. 21 (Spring 1960), pp. 7-19.

34. Howard F. Freeman, Helen H. Hughes, T. F. Pettigrew, and Lewis G. Watts, *The Middle-Income Negro: Stake and Status in the Ghetto* (manuscript now in preparation).

35. Pettigrew, "De Facto Segregation, Southern Style," *op. cit.;* and Pettigrew, "Continuing Barriers to Desegregated Education in the South," *op. cit.*

36. Nat Hentoff, personal communication. For a vivid and penetrating analysis of this Northern ghetto mood, see K. B. Clark, *Dark Ghetto* (New York, 1965).

37. George Gallup, "Negroes, Whites Disagree on Treatment of Former," American Institute of Public Opinion, May 4, 1965.

38. Pettigrew, *Profile of the Negro American, op. cit.*, Ch. 8.

39. G. W. Allport, *The Nature of Prejudice* (Cambridge, Mass., 1954), Ch. 16.

40. I. N. Brophy, "The Luxury of Anti-Negro Prejudice," *Public Opinion Quarterly,* Vol. 9 (Winter 1945-46), pp. 456-466. One possible explanation for the results of this study and others cited below is that the people who were the least prejudiced to begin with sought out interracial contact. Most of these studies, however, rule out the operation of this self-selection factor.

41. W. M. Kephart, *Racial Factors and Urban Law Enforcement* (Philadelphia, 1957), pp. 188-189.

42. Barbara MacKenzie, "The Importance of Contact in Determining Attitudes Toward Negroes," *Journal of Abnormal and Social Psychology,* Vol. 43 (October 1948), pp. 417-441.

43. A. M. Lee and N. D. Humphrey, *Race Riot* (New York, 1943), pp. 97, 130, 140.

44. M. Deutsch and Mary Collins, *Interracial Housing: A Psychological Evaluation of a Social Experiment* (Minneapolis, Minn., 1951); Marie Jahoda and Patricia West, "Race Relations in Public Housing," *Journal of Social Issues,* Vol. 7, Nos. 1 and 2 (1951), pp. 132-139; D. M. Wilner, Rosabelle Walkley, and S. W. Cook, *Human Relations in Interracial Housing: A Study of the Contact Hypothesis* (Minneapolis, Minn., 1955); and E. Works, "The Prejudice-Interaction Hypothesis from the Point of View of the Negro Minority Group," *American Journal of Sociology,* Vol. 67 (July 1961), pp. 47-52.

45. S. A. Stouffer, E. A. Suchman, L. C. DeVinney, Shirley A. Star, and R. M. Williams, Jr., *Studies in Social Psychology in World War II,* Vol. 1, *The American Soldier: Adjustment During Army Life* (Princeton, N. J., 1949), Ch. 10.

46. J. Harding and R. Hogrefe, "Attitudes of White Department Store Employees Toward Negro Co-Workers," *Journal of Social Issues,* Vol. 8, No. 1, (1952), pp. 18-28.

47. G. Saenger and Emily Gilbert, "Customer Reactions to the Integration of Negro Sales Personnel," *International Journal of Opinion and Attitude Research,* Vol. 4 (Spring 1950), pp. 57-76.

48. Prohibition provides an interesting contrast at this point. It apparently

failed largely because it was neither rigorously enforced nor, despite its moral overtones for some Protestants, did it articulate with national traditions or ease the consciences of many Americans.

49. Eunice Cooper and Marie Jahoda, "The Evasion of Propaganda: How Prejudiced People Respond to Anti-Prejudice Propaganda," *Journal of Psychology*, Vol. 23 (January 1947), pp. 15-25; and H. H. Hyman and P. B. Sheatsley, "Some Reasons Why Information Campaigns Fail," *Public Opinion Quarterly*, Vol. 11 (Fall 1947), pp. 413-423.

50. For an interesting political example of this phenomenon, see: H. Cantril (ed.), *Gauging Public Opinion* (Princeton, N. J., 1944), pp. 226-230.

51. W. A. Scott, "Attitude Change Through Reward of Verbal Behavior," *Journal of Abnormal and Social Psychology*, Vol. 55 (July 1957), pp. 72-75; and W. A. Scott, "Attitude Change by Response Reinforcement: Replication and Extension," *Sociometry*, Vol. 22 (December 1959), pp. 328-335.

52. M. Sherif, D. J. Harvey, B. J. White, W. R. Hood, and Carolyn Sherif, *Intergroup Conflict and Cooperation: The Robbers Cave Experiment* (Norman, Okla., 1961).

53. In particular, see James Tobin's discussion in this volume of lowering the unemployment rate—a prime example of an "economic protection" in the sense it is used in this paper.

54. An excellent recent example of a "quiet protection" with extensive consequences involved the announcement of the Federal Government banning local United Fund solicitations of government employees at work unless all agencies receiving the United Fund aid were free of discrimination. The effects were immediate. Agencies eager to remain in their Funds—such as the Y.M.C.A. of Richmond, Virginia—began pronouncing new policies of non-discrimination.

55. E. Goffman, *Stigma: Notes on the Management of Spoiled Identity*. (Englewood Cliffs, N. J., 1963).

56. See Talcott Parson's paper in this volume.

57. Bruno Bettelheim and Morris Janowitz, *Social Change and Prejudice* (New York, 1964); and T. W. Adorno, Else Frenkel-Brunswik, D. J. Levinson, and R. N. Sanford, *The Authoritarian Personality* (New York, 1950).

58. The super-ego outgroup pattern also typically involves a middle-man minority which is separatist in an expanding nationalist state which emphasizes unity. Thus, the Huguenots of England and Ireland were not separatist, nor was India when it received the Parsis an expanding nationalist state—and neither the Huguenots nor the Parsis triggered the super-ego pattern. S. Stryker, "Social Structure and Prejudice," *Social Problems*, Vol. 6 (Spring 1959), pp. 340-354.

59. Direct parallels between the American stereotype of the Negro and the Northern Italian stereotype of the Southern Italian are demonstrated in M. W. Battacchi, *Meridioanli e Settentrionali nella Struttura del Pregiudizio*

Ethnico in Italia [Southerners and Northerners in the Structure of Ethnic Prejudice in Italy] (Bologna, Italia, 1959).

60. Moreover, as Tannenbaum has pointed out, modern slavery differed from earlier forms of the institution by being totally identified with one specific group. Before it had been a condition anyone might suffer, and so it was regarded as a misfortune. But when the slave status came to be occupied solely by Negroes, the question naturally arose: *Why the Negro?* Modern racism was called upon to supply an answer; and the stigma of slavery attached to the Negro took an especially lasting form. See Frank Tannenbaum, *Slave and Citizen: The Negro in the Americas* (New York, 1947), p. 110.

61. D. Katz and K. W. Braly, "Racial Stereotypes of 100 College Students," *Journal of Abnormal and Social Psychology*, Vol. 28 (October-November 1933), pp. 280-290; and G. M. Gilbert, "Stereotype Persistence and Change Among College Students," *Journal of Abnormal and Social Psychology*, Vol. 46 (April 1951), pp. 245-254.

62. H. H. Hyman and P. B. Sheatsley, "Attitudes Toward Desegregation," *op. cit.;* and "Attitudes Toward Desegregation," *Scientific American*, Vol. 211 (July 1964), pp. 16-23.

63. I am indebted to Patricia Pajonas, research assistant in the Harvard University Laboratory of Social Relations, for her analysis of all racial material appearing in thirty-four issues of *Life* sampled from November 1936 to March 1938.

64. Brink and Harris, *op. cit.,* pp. 140-141.

65. Rashi Fein points out that the children in the Head-Start pre-school program of 1965 will be only twenty-two years old by 1984.

66. E. F. Frazier, "The Negro Middle Class and Desegregation," *Social Problems*, Vol. 4 (April 1957), pp. 291-301.

67. Freeman, *et al., op. cit.;* and L. G. Watts, H. E. Freeman, Helen Hughes, Robert Morris, and T. F. Pettigrew, *The Middle-Income Negro Family Faces Urban Renewal* (Boston, Mass., 1965).

68. Helen Hughes and L. G. Watts, "Portrait of the Self-Integrator," *Journal of Social Issues*, Vol. 20 (1964), pp. 103-115.

69. Freeman, *et al., op. cit.;* Watts, *et al., op. cit.;* Morton Rubin, "The Negro Wish to Move: The Boston Case," *Journal of Social Issues*, Vol. 15 (October 1959), pp. 4-13; and Robert Johnson, "Negro Reactions to Minority Group Status," in M. L. Barron (ed.), *American Minorities* (New York, 1957), pp. 192-212.

70. This dual pattern of suburban tokenism and central city segregation suggests one important and largely untapped source of future interracial contact. This would entail programs where the suburbs pitch in to help the

central city through the acceptance of a specified number of inner-city Negro children in their schools, the acceptance of low-cost public housing, and so forth.

71. Obviously, the particular figure chosen varies with the particular definition chosen.
72. Pettigrew, *Profile of the Negro American, op. cit.,* pp. 184-185.

IV

SECTORS OF THE SOCIETY IN PROCESS OF CHANGE

PAUL A. FREUND

The Civil Rights Movement and
the Frontiers of Law

> *And the end men looked for cometh not,*
> *And a path is there where no man sought.*
> *So hath it fallen here.*
>
> —*Euripides*

THE IRONIES of the civil rights movement in the courts began with the first case to reach the Supreme Court under the 14th Amendment. The *Slaughterhouse Cases,*[1] decided in 1873, did not involve racial discrimination at all, but a challenge to a commercial monopoly created by the Reconstruction government in Louisiana, and the newly adopted guarantees of due process, equal protection, and privileges and immunities of national citizenship were invoked on behalf of the complainants by John A. Campbell, who had resigned from the Court at the outbreak of the war to become a cabinet officer in the Confederacy. Although the effort to convert the 14th Amendment into a bulwark for free business enterprise did not succeed in that case, the ideas implanted there soon came to fruition, and for more than half a century the Civil War Amendments served mainly as a check on experimental economic legislation. Today, when a revived civil rights movement has recaptured the Amendments, they are used to overcome legislation that has been long entrenched.

The ironies, however, persist. The movement has produced, for example, a development in the law of defamation that can be as much an embarrassment as a boon. The New York *Times* published a political advertisement, signed by a group of civil rights leaders, attacking the methods of law enforcement employed in Montgomery, Alabama. Certain factual statements in the message were inaccurate in what may fairly be called minor details. The police commissioner, who had not been named in the advertisement, sued to recover actual and punitive damages for libel, and was awarded a verdict for half a million dollars, which was upheld by the highest court of the state. When the case reached the Supreme Court in Washington, on petition of the *Times*, the judgment was assailed as an abridgement of freedom of the press, as in practical effect it surely was. The Court might have upset the judgment in any one of a number of ways, all of them breaking new ground as a matter of constitutional law. The Court might have held that a newspaper is not liable for the contents of a paid advertisement; or that there was no evidence of damage to the reputation of the commissioner; or that punitive damages are improper in this political context because they are too reminiscent of discredited concepts of seditious libel; or that the state court had applied too impossibly severe a standard for the defense of truth. Choosing to reject all these grounds, which would have placed the case in a fairly narrow compass, the Court decided that the defamation of a public official is not actionable, in view of the overriding interest in free political debate, unless the statement is published maliciously, that is, with knowledge of its falsity or with reckless disregard of its truth or untruth.[2]

The decision was a victory for freedom of critical dissent and, in its context, for the untrammeled publicizing of civil rights violations. But since the law is principled, it can cut in both directions. The decision has already been applied to immunize a group of Birchites who falsely charged a liberal state representative with communist membership.

The frontiers of the law have been pushed back by the civil rights movement in many sectors that are far broader than the interests of the movement itself. One of the most exigent needs of the legal system is the provision of legal services, both advice and representation, for those of moderate means. Plans of group representation (aside from legal aid societies) have run afoul of the canons of legal ethics as well as state laws forbidding barratry, canons and rules based on several interlocking policies: the avoidance of conflicts of interest between the group and a member; maintenance of a personal lawyer-client relationship; and the prevention of the fomenting of litigation. When the NAACP in Virginia set up a panel of lawyers to represent potential litigants in desegregation cases, the state courts enjoined the execution of the plan. On review in the Supreme Court, the plan was held to be constitutionally protected, as a form of speech and association on matters appropriate for political expression.[3] Litigation to secure desegregation is itself, the Court said, a mode of political expression, and the feared abuses of group representation, with a lay intermediary, were too attenuated in this instance to prevail against the constitutional claim.

The momentum of the decision was sufficient to carry it to other fields of legal representation. The Brotherhood of Railroad Trainmen maintained a panel of lawyers to whom members were referred for services in connection with personal injury claims. The plan had been disapproved in several states. Virginia again took action, and again the Supreme Court reversed.[4] The organized bar of almost every state joined in a petition for rehearing, but the Court stood firm. To be sure, the association for political expression was highly attenuated here, but, having erected that scaffolding for the NAACP, the Court was now able to make the ascent without it. The American Bar Association is now in the process of revising its canons of professional ethics, as a result of the revolt led by the NAACP.

Another anachronism in the law has been the relationship between landlord and tenant. The obligations of the tenant to pay rent and the landlord to make repairs have generally been treated as independent duties; rent is regarded more as an incident of feudal tenure than as one term of an interdependent contract; the tenant's remedy is to move out if the premises are uninhabitable (an unrealistic recourse for many tenement dwellers) or to sue the landlord (also unrealistic because slow and expensive). The rent strike in Harlem proved to be more than a phase of the civil rights movement. It led to long-overdue legislation in New York whereby if a landlord is in default a tenant may withhold the rent or place it in escrow and have it applied by court order to the making of needed repairs.[5] So does the law move from status to contract.

If a local government enacted a zoning ordinance on racial lines, the act would clearly be unconstitutional, as a denial by the state of equal protection of the laws. It was long assumed that property owners, however, could accomplish the same end by private neighborhood covenant, since the act was not attributable to the state. The Supreme Court nevertheless held that when a state court undertook to enforce such a covenant against a willing seller and buyer, the state was sufficiently responsible to bring the 14th Amendment into play and make the enforcement of the covenant void.[6] The bounds of this decision are a matter of considerable uncertainty, but the generating principle must surely carry it beyond its immediate facts. Analytically it is arguable that the principle would, for example, invalidate any enforcement of a national fraternity's restrictive by-laws against a local chapter willing to admit members without racial or religious bias. How much further will the identification of private covenant and public act be carried? Since a government may not prescribe religious affiliation, is it unconstitutional for a court to enforce a trust agreement under which a beneficiary is to receive income only so long as she remains within the faith, or does not marry outside of it? Questions such as this, raising the whole problem of the line between the private and public sectors of choice and responsibility, will suggest that the civil rights movement is transforming much more in the law than relations between the races.

On a more philosophical level the movement has compelled us to think more insistently about two central questions in the legal order: what is the meaning of equality, and what is the basis for the duty of obedience to law.

Is there room in morals and in law for color preference, or is color blindness the only legitimate standard? That "the Constitution is color-blind" sufficed for a long time as a liberal principle. Drawn from Justice Harlan's dissenting opinion in *Plessy v. Ferguson*[7] in 1896 (he presumably drew it from a brief amicus by Albion Tourgeé, the novelist-lawyer, in that case), the maxim has come to seem too constricting to contain the newer aspirations of civil rights leaders. The problem has been largely avoided, and happily so, by programs that are general in scope while benefiting most the Negroes, if they have been the preponderant victims of the injustices against which the programs are levelled. Measures to relieve poverty, to reform bail practices in the criminal law, to provide counsel for the indigent, to safeguard the interests of suspected persons in the process of arrest and thereafter in the station house —all of these have obvious relevance to the civil rights movement but do not stir issues of preferential treatment on color lines. These general measures, in their impact on racial problems, are the counterparts of the racial programs already discussed that have made a generalized impact on the legal system.

Suppose, however, that the question of preference is raised without evasion. To characterize a preference as compensatory is hardly a satisfying answer to all the complexities. If in a community there has been a history of discrimination in private employment, and the government now orders that Negroes be given a preference in jobs, the compensatory feature is crude at best. On the side of the employers, the preferential rule may be applied without regard to the record of the particular establishment, and regardless of the guilt or innocence of white applicants who may be passed over. On the side of the preferred job-seekers, compensation is given not on the basis of rectifying individual victimization in the past, but on the basis of group identity, which rather begs the question—the question, that is, whether persons should be treated as individuals and not members of a race, even when they (or others) have in the past been mistreated as members of a race.

But the concept of compensation does suggest some possible differentiations or gradations in the problem of preference. Where the government itself was responsible for discrimination in the past, there is a better case for its reverse preference now. So too where the preference is, so to speak, transitional, by way of preparing the members of the group to be treated as individuals. And it is the easier to justify a preference the less positive the harm to others; easier to justify additional attention in schooling than a competitive preference in the job market. Moreover, there is an ethical sense in which discrimination in favor of a minority is not to be equated with discrimination against it. Compare a scholarship fund carrying a preference for descendants of Timothy Murphy with one carrying a preference for all others. Most of us would feel more comfortable about the first than the second. If this is a sound moral judgment, it is relevant to the judgment of the law as well, for equal protection of the law is at bottom the embodiment of a moral standard.

The moral and legal issues raised by civil disobedience are no easier than those of equality. Here too the difficulties have largely been bypassed. For one thing, the prosecutor's discretion can be used to forego legal proceedings. When the civil rights leaders in Boston called a one-day school boycott, they may have been in violation of the law, but there was no serious threat of prosecution. More often a collision course with the law has been averted by judicial decisions that taxed the resources of judicial statecraft.[8] Prosecutions of sit-in demonstrators for disturbing the peace were ordered to be dismissed on the ground that there was no evidence to support that charge. When the charge was framed as trespass, it fared no better, for other reasons. The trespass statute was not to be interpreted to cover sit-ins, lest the defendants suffer from inadequate legal warning; or the proprietor's rule of segregation was not wholly his but was to be ascribed to an unconstitutional city ordinance; or even without an ordinance the mayor's warning to sit-in demonstrators was taken as governmental responsibility for the private policy of segregation. Finally, the whole residue of sit-in cases involving restaurants and the like was held to have abated by reason of the enactment of the federal public accommodations law.[9] If a criminal statute is repealed, the ordinary rule is that pending prosecutions for prior violations do not lapse; but when national prohibition was repealed by the 21st Amendment, the consequence was otherwise: all pending cases were ordered dismissed because the fundamental turnabout in public policy made it incongruous to proceed with prosecutions. The public accommodations law was deemed by the Supreme Court to come within the category of the repeal of prohibition, marking as it did a thorough repudiation of past practices.

Despite these avoidances, the problem of the law's treatment of civil disobedience is not stilled. From one point of view the issue may seem to be unreal, for civil disobedience presupposes a liability to suffer punishment; it is this deliberate exposure, together with the ethical claims of the cause, that gives an essential moral quality to the act of disobedience. Nevertheless the act of disobedience is designed ultimately to change the law, to convert new vision into revision, and it is open to the law to make its revision in the very case at hand. And the suffering of punishment remains as a risk.

Two factors are pertinent in any assessment of the moral and legal quality of a given exercise of protest through disobedience. For one thing, the availability of redress through the normal channels of a lawsuit militates strongly against the instrument of disobedience for its own sake and not as a step toward litigation. "Availability" means more than theoretical access to the corrective processes of the law; it means that these are in fact kept open in good faith without obstruction or reprisal. Secondly, the degree of opportunity to participate in the political process is an element of real significance. If indeed the foundation of the duty to obey the law is the recognition of a symbolic covenant, a social compact, then the denial of a right of participation is a breach of the covenant which may help to justify a measured non-performance on the other side. The principle of the covenant, ethically and politically fruitful from the Old Testament to the *Mayflower* compact and modern constitutionalism, is built on the idea of reciprocity as in some sense the basis of justice. Magna Carta itself embodied this idea of reciprocity in a suggestive way, providing in Article 61 that in the event of a breach by the Crown, the barons, through a committee, would have license to distrain on Crown property. A measured response, that is, in the form of what would otherwise have been illegal and presumptuous behavior, not outright rebellion, was conceived to be a fitting sanction in case of infidelity by the government. Systematic and arbitrary denials of basic civil rights, notably the right to vote and to exercise political authority without discrimination (including appointment to office, to the police force and the probation service), may serve to take a similar measured response out of the category of simple illegality, at least to the point where the discretionary dispensing power may be used—in the decision whether to prosecute, whether to suspend sentence, and whether to pardon.

The civil rights movement, finally, has raised anew the question whether the law is an appropriate means of reforming ingrained human attitudes. Of course the vindication of civil rights through legislation and decisions does not have for its purpose the eradication of prejudice; its aim is the correction of overt discrimination. But if prejudice cannot be affected by law and is bound to manifest itself in discrimination, is the legal effort worth the cost? If the question is asked whether law can change our human nature, the answer may well be: No, but our human nature can change us with the help of law.

There is a tension between one's moral attitudes and one's practices which constantly seeks harmonization by bringing the one into closer conformity with the other. This psychological phenomenon, observed in a variety of contexts, gives some promise that enforced changes in behavior will in fact affect inward dispositions. Against this proposition there is frequently adduced the unhappy example of prohibition. Actually this counterexample is wanting in real persuasive force, for the reason that prohibition lacked a deep moral base in the feelings of most people, a base deep enough to produce an anxious tension in the experience of nonconformity, and surely the process of law enforcement was calculated to produce cynicism rather than inner disequilibrium. The prevailing sentiment was undoubtedly Ring Lardner's: "Anyhow, prohibition is better than no liquor at all."

The spiritual atmosphere of the civil rights movement is a very different thing. For the very reason that it makes its appeal to professed ideals of great intensity, the effort to come to terms with it is a potentially transforming experience. On balance it is a hopeful sign that our problem is in truth an American dilemma.

REFERENCES

1. 16 Wall. 36.

2. N.Y. Times v. Sullivan, 376 U.S. 254 (1964).

3. NAACP v. Button, 371 U.S. 415 (1963).

4. Brotherhood of Railroad Trainmen v. Virginia, 377 U.S. 1 (1964).

5. N.Y. Laws 1965 chs. 909, 911.

6. Shelley v. Kraemer, 334 U.S. 1 (1948).

7. 163 U.S. 537 (1896).

8. E.g., Garner v. Louisiana, 368 U.S. 157 (1961); Taylor v. Louisiana, 370 U.S. 154 (1962); Bouie v. City of Columbia, 378 U.S. 347 (1964); Robinson v. Florida, 378 U.S. 153 (1964), Cox v. Louisiana, 379 U.S. 536 (1965).

9. Hamm v. City of Rock Hill, 379 U.S. 306 (1964).

HAROLD C. FLEMING

The Federal Executive and Civil Rights: 1961-1965

WHEN John F. Kennedy assumed the Presidency, the prospects for orderly progress in civil rights were far from bright. Years of inaction during the preceding administration were yielding a predictable harvest of discontent. The civil rights movement was both accelerating and assuming new and more demanding forms. The strategy of almost exclusive reliance on court action, brilliantly led by the legal staff of the National Association for the Advancement of Colored People, was giving way to techniques of mass protest and nonviolent direct action. Vying for preeminence in the increasingly militant struggle were such organizations as the Congress of Racial Equality, the Southern Christian Leadership Conference, and the Student Nonviolent Coordinating Committee. Crisis was no longer the occasional and accidental byproduct of court-directed change, but the continuing and conscious result of planned confrontation between opponents and defenders of the existing racial order.

Nevertheless, civil rights advocates generally viewed the prospects under the Kennedy administration with high expectation—excessively high, perhaps, under the circumstances. The explanation is two-fold. First, there was the mere fact that the White House was being occupied by a young President who promised a vigorous and innovative administration. The "moral leadership" of the White House, absence of which had been so long and bitterly decried by civil rights spokesmen, was seen as an imminent reality. A second factor was Kennedy's behavior in the campaign, which won him the acclaim of Negro citizens and their overwhelming support at the polls. His telephone call to Mrs. Martin Luther King, Jr., expressing concern for her jailed husband, and Robert Kennedy's intercession to effect King's release convinced the great majority of Negroes that Kennedy would be a bold and effective champion of their cause.

The fact that Negro support was an indispensable factor in his election strengthened this conviction.

There were other, countervailing factors, however, in Kennedy's initial calculations of his administration's approach to civil rights. His victory had been an exceedingly narrow one, dependent on Southern electoral votes, among others. A loss of Democratic seats in Congress had left him with a perilously thin margin of potential support for his legislative program. An array of critical international problems laid immediate and heavy claim on him. Prudence dictated a course that would yield as much progress in civil rights as possible without alienating essential Congressional allies, thwarting his hopes for a broader national consensus and diverting an excessive amount of his time, attention, and prestige from foreign affairs and other pressing matters.

The broad outlines of Kennedy's strategy for achieving this balance soon became evident—at least by inference—and may be summed up as follows:

1. No new legislation would be sought; instead, expanded use of executive action would be emphasized. This was foreshadowed by Kennedy's statement during the campaign when asked about his plans for civil rights legislation. "First," he replied, "there is a good deal that can be done by the Executive branch without legislation. For example, the President could sign an executive order ending discrimination in housing tomorrow. Second, the President could compel all companies which do business with the Government, and after all that is nearly every American company, to practice open, fair hiring of personnel without regard to race, creed, or color. . . . In addition, the Department of Justice can pursue the right to vote with far more vigor. . . . So I would say that the greater opportunity is in the Executive branch without Congressional action."

2. Executive action would be taken mainly in those areas where federal authority is most complete and undisputed, as in federally connected employment, in contrast to areas of sensitive federal-state relationships, as in federal assistance programs. Sanctions would be imposed as a last resort after all efforts at persuasion and conciliation had failed.

3. The President's personal influence and prestige would be drawn upon sparingly. Attorney General Robert F. Kennedy would be the acknowledged strategist and leader of the administration's civil rights activities. As the President's brother, he could speak and act with unusual authority, thus supplying by deputation some of

the moral leadership that normally only the President could exert.

4. First priority would be assigned to securing the right to vote, through negotiation and litigation by an invigorated Civil Rights Division of the Department of Justice.

The pressure of Negro militancy and a series of critical episodes in the South led to major alterations in this approach, beginning in the summer of 1961. Nevertheless, it was possible to speak meaningfully of a federal civil rights strategy, however rudimentary, for the first time in living memory. For when John F. Kennedy entered the White House in 1961, he inherited no comprehensive program in this field, only a legacy of piecemeal legislation and executive actions.

Franklin D. Roosevelt had instituted new social and economic programs unrelated to civil rights but beneficial to low-income groups, in which Negroes were conspicuous. While he avoided the confrontation with Southern Congressmen that would have resulted from advocacy of civil rights legislation, he was persuaded by the pressure of Negro leadership to issue an executive order creating a Fair Employment Practices Committee.

Harry S. Truman was unable to preserve the fledgling FEPC, which was killed by Congressional action in 1946. As a substitute, he established the more limited Committee on Government Contract Compliance charged with promoting equal employment opportunity among firms doing business with the federal government. He also put new emphasis on nondiscrimination in the government's own employment practices. More important, he signed an unprecedented executive order requiring integration and equality of treatment in the Armed Forces. He adopted as his own the bold recommendations of his Committee on Civil Rights for anti-lynching, anti-poll tax, and fair employment laws, waging an aggressive campaign for their enactment by Congress. His legislative efforts were foredoomed, but through them he demonstrated for the first time that a Democrat could be elected President without the support of the segregationist South, and he set a precedent for legislative proposals that were to be enacted some years later.

Throughout the Roosevelt and Truman administrations, the United States Supreme Court handed down a series of decisions validating the Negro's constitutional claims to equality under the law. In steady·progression, it upheld the right of Negroes to travel unsegregated on interstate carriers, to register and vote in the Southern Democratic primaries, and to enroll in publicly supported institutions of higher education. The culmination of this judicial revolution came in 1954, when the Supreme Court repudiated the long-standing "separate but equal" doctrine and held that racially segregated public schools were unconstitutional. Although much civil rights litigation was yet to come, the 1954 decision left no doubt that all forms of state-supported segregation and discrimination would ultimately be prohibited.

The urgency of the civil rights issue had been mounting steadily since the outset of World War II. The historic 1954 decision soon catapulted it to the top of the nation's domestic concerns. The demands and expectations of Negroes began to take on a new and increasing militancy, while the traditional South of the old Confederacy stiffened its defenses against racial change. An era of national crisis was at hand.

It is ironic that as the storm began to gather, the Presidency was assumed by a man whose personal and political philosophy was antipathetic to strong leadership, particularly on such an issue as civil rights. Throughout his eight years as chief executive, Dwight D. Eisenhower reiterated his essentially *laissez-faire* views on civil rights. He held that this was an issue to be resolved at the local level and at an evolutionary pace, that laws in this field were of dubious value, that alteration of "the hearts and minds of men" was a precondition of change, that local intervention by the federal government was to be assiduously avoided. He also declined to throw the moral weight of his office into the balance, repeatedly refusing to express his personal view of the Supreme Court's school decision on the ground that such an expression would be improper. More than once, in fact, his statements seemed to imply reservations about the wisdom of the decision and the pace of even such modest change as it had generated.

Despite the generally low priority accorded civil rights during the Eisenhower administration, some noteworthy executive actions were taken. The Contract Compliance Committee established by Truman was continued under the chairmanship of Vice President Nixon. It did little to improve the economic status of the Negro, however, since it relied mainly on broad programs of public relations rather than systematic review and enforcement of nondiscrimination requirements. A second committee, severely limited in staff and resources, was created to promote equal employment opportunity within the federal government. President Eisenhower also carried forward the integration of the Armed Forces begun by Truman. He gave effective leadership in the desegregation of public accommodations and schools in the District of Columbia. Although his own role in the matter was at best ambiguous, his administration at the initiative of Attorneys General Herbert Brownell and William Rogers proposed the first successful civil rights legislation since Reconstruction—the Civil Rights Act of 1957 and its sequel in 1960, both dealing primarily with voting rights.

Eisenhower's most important civil rights action—one in which he was pressed to a drastic reversal of his non-interventionist philosophy—was the dispatch of federal troops to Little Rock in September 1957. The hands-off posture of the administration, coupled with the President's public assurance that he could imagine no circumstance that would prompt him to send federal troops into the South, evidently encouraged Arkansas' Governor Orval Faubus to believe that he could successfully thwart a federal court order admitting nine Negro pupils to a Little Rock high school. In any case, Faubus's defiance and the rioting that followed posed a supreme test of the enforceability of federal court orders. If Eisenhower was indecisive until the eleventh hour of the Little Rock crisis, once the issue was inescapably drawn he acted with resolution. Order was restored and the court ruling enforced by one thousand men of the 101st Airborne Infantry Division. An irrevocable precedent was set for use of federal military power when necessary to quell active resistance to the orders of a federal court.

These, then, were the major precedents for federal action in the civil rights field as of January 1961: two statutes concerned primarily with voting discrimination, executive orders providing essentially educational programs for nondiscrimination in federally connected employment, a presidential ban on segregation and discrimination in the Armed Forces, and the use of U. S. troops to enforce federal court orders in the face of civil disturbances. Among these were some of the essential components of an effective federal effort, but many vital elements were lacking and most of the existing ones were too weak or too limited to achieve their purpose.

The evolution of federal executive action in civil rights during the succeeding five years is treated here in three broad categories—administrative action and executive orders, law enforcement, and presidential leadership and legislative proposals. Needless to say, the following treatment of each of these areas is necessarily both abbreviated and highly selective.

Administrative Action and Executive Orders

Administrative machinery. If executive action on civil rights was to have high priority in the incoming administration, it was necessary to create new mechanisms for planning and direction of the augmented effort. The first step in this direction was the appointment of a special assistant for civil rights on the White House staff. This position was filled for only one year, by Harris Wofford, Jr., a lawyer with extensive knowledge of civil rights. When he resigned to take another post in the government, the position was discontinued. Subsequently, civil rights was one of a number of responsibilities handled by Lee White, Assistant Special Counsel (now Special Counsel) to the President. Civil rights groups periodically urged that one or more full-time specialists in this field be added to the White House staff, but this step was not taken. The White House did, however, draw on the staff services of the U.S. Commission on Civil Rights, and early in 1965 President Johnson created a new body to oversee civil rights activities.

During Wofford's tenure, two new groups were constituted to deal with racial problems. One was a small *ad hoc* committee that met frequently and informally to discuss ongoing programs and propose solutions for the emergencies of the moment. The second was a larger and more formal body, the Subcabinet Committee on Civil Rights, composed of senior departmental and agency staff members with assigned responsibility for equal employment opportunity and other civil rights functions. William L. Taylor, a staff member (now staff director) of the Civil Rights Commission, served as secretary of the Subcabinet Committee.

For a time, the initial arrangement proved serviceable; the *ad hoc* committee assisted Wofford in the many tactical and administrative problems on which he advised the President and his chief lieutenants and the Subcabinet Committee provided a forum for orderly discussion and communication of policy that affected all or a number of agencies. Later, however, the *ad hoc* group gradually fell into disuse, its role being assumed to some extent by staff members of the Civil Rights Commission. Major questions of policy and executive action to meet large-scale crises were dealt with, as they had been from the start, by the Attorney General and his assistants, especially Assistant Attorney General Burke Marshall of the Civil Rights Division.

Although the Subcabinet Committee still exists today, its meetings have grown less frequent and its importance has declined. As more and more agencies developed civil rights concerns, it became too big for efficient discussion, and the issues became too varied to permit a common focus. By 1964 it existed more on paper than in fact.

From 1961 through 1964, the Civil Rights Commission operated on more than one level. In keeping with its statutory mandate of 1957, it studied and held hearings on "denial of equal protection of the laws" in general and federal laws and policies affecting equal protection in particular. Beginning in 1959, it issued a series of memorable reports and recommendations to the President and Congress. Many of the recommendations were ultimately implemented by legislative and executive action and others no doubt will be in the future.

As an independent, bipartisan agency, however, the Commission was not really considered an arm of the administration. In fact, there was a certain amount of periodic disagreement and tension between the Commission, on one hand, and the Justice Department and the White House, on the other. Two publicized examples were the frustration of the Commission's desire to hold public hearings in Mississippi, because of the Attorney General's objections, and the President's rebuff of a Commission recommendation in April 1963 that federal grants-in-aid to Mississippi be withheld. On an informal level, however, the Commission staff gave indispensable advice and assistance to overworked White House aides.

Passage of the Civil Rights Act of 1964 created many new civil rights functions within the Executive Department. Title VI alone, which requires nondiscriminatory use of federal funds, affects the administrative operation of dozens of agencies and some 190 programs of federal assistance. With new agencies superimposed on old ones, new functions overlapping existing ones, and responsibilities widely diffused, the danger of confusion and duplication was obvious. Until consolidation of functions and agencies could be achieved, rigorous coordination was urgently required.

To meet this impelling need, President Johnson, early in 1965, appointed the Council on Equal Opportunity, composed of Cabinet officers and heads of agencies with major civil rights responsibilites. Vice President Hubert H. Humphrey was designated chairman and given authority to appoint staff, require reports from agencies and departments, and appoint working groups to fashion coordinated plans and procedures. Named as its executive secretary was Wiley

A. Branton, the first Negro graduate of the University of Arkansas Law School, who represented the plaintiff school children of Little Rock and later headed the Voter Education Project. Neither the Council nor its chairman had operational responsibility—that remains with the agencies and the President.

The new mechanism was too short-lived, however, to permit much judgment of its potential effectiveness. In September 1965 the Vice President submitted and the President approved a proposed reorganization of federal civil rights functions under which the President's Council was subsequently abolished and the Vice President was relieved of his specific civil rights assignments. The President explained this action by saying that he intended to give civil rights activities more centralized and forceful direction by putting full responsibility where authority lay—with the appropriate department heads. Under the new dispensation, the Attorney General became the unquestioned chief of federal civil rights programs. Assuming no Congressional veto, he was to take over the Community Relations Service from the Department of Commerce. He was given explicit responsibility for strategy as well as for legal implementation of voting rights; Wiley Branton was named his special assistant for this and perhaps other civil rights assignments.

Continuing coordination across agency and department lines, limited mainly to Title VI responsibilities, was also assigned to the Attorney General. In civil rights quarters, this development was viewed with some skepticism, not altogether unjustified, about the wisdom of delegating the coordinating authority to the departmental level. The question which remains to be answered is whether or not this arrangement can adequately bring the President's authority to bear on the ramified civil rights responsibilities of the Executive Branch.

One thing seems clear: The times are no longer congenial to tentative and makeshift approaches to planning and coordination of administrative action on civil rights. The momentum of the civil rights movement is formidable. It is no longer enough for the national government to respond to pressure and crisis; it must initiate preventive and affirmative action. To redirect the vast administrative structure of the federal establishment toward this end—against the weight of inertia, a multitude of countervailing pressures, and residual prejudice among administrators themselves—will require a determined effort.

Administrative innovation. The sensitivity of the Kennedy-Johnson administration to questions of racial equality may be publicly dated from January 20, 1961, when John F. Kennedy noted the absence of Negroes among Coast Guard marchers in the inaugural parade. His subsequent inquiry launched the Coast Guard Academy on a large-scale talent search for Negro candidates. This same sensitivity led to the appointment of scores of Negroes to high-level federal posts. Among the most prominent were Thurgood Marshall as an appointee to the Second Circuit Court of Appeals and later to be the Solicitor General of the United States, Robert C. Weaver as head of the Housing and Home Finance Agency, George L-P Weaver as Assistant Secretary of Labor, Carl T. Rowan as, successively, Deputy Assistant Secretary of State, Ambassador to Finland, and head of the U. S. Information Agency, Lisle Carter as Deputy Assistant Secretary of the Department of Health, Education, and Welfare.

There were other examples of affirmative use of executive powers. Normal administrative processes were by-passed to permit distribution of surplus food to Negro victims of economic reprisals in Fayette and Heywood Counties, Tennessee. Cabinet officers and other high-ranking federal officials were ordered to avoid segregated meetings and facilities. Federal financing of language institutes at Southern colleges was conditioned on nondiscrimination. Later, an energetic and partly successful effort was made to end segregation of off-base schools serving children of military personnel. The existence of these and other problems of discrimination against servicemen caused the President to appoint a Committee on Equal Opportunity in the Armed Forces, a panel of outstanding citizens which delivered a series of wise and forceful recommendations. The President also issued several executive orders against discrimination, two of which are discussed later.

Yet these and other steps that might be cited did not constitute the comprehensive sort of executive action that President Kennedy had seemed to promise and that many negroes had hoped for. With the notable exception of some areas for which the Justice Department had peculiar responsibility, the executive thrust in civil rights was blunted by political judgments, not the least of which concerned the reactions of powerful Southern Congressmen.

Harris Wofford, in a speech of impressive candor delivered in the spring of 1961, described the process to his fellow civil rights advocates in these terms:

❋

I do not mean that the new avenue of executive action will be easy. This course has plenty of contradictions and it will not . . . resolve the built-in political contradictions. The need for the enactment of vital measures for the general welfare . . . may still at any given moment have to be weighed against other actions to advance civil rights. Since these social measures have the most direct impact on our racial minorities, so many of whom are at the bottom of our economic ladder, the weighing process is sometimes painful. You may on occasion disagree with the result of the weighing of priorities. But for your disagreement to be effective you will need to look at the process through a political lens that takes into account the major contradictions shaping this problem.

The results of the weighing process were frequently disappointing to the organizations supporting civil rights. Several of them—the Leadership Conference on Civil Rights, the Southern Regional Council, the National Urban League, and the National Association of Intergroup Relations Officials—submitted to the President detailed recommendations for a campaign of executive action against discrimination. Many of their proposals, including the most important, were not adopted until the Civil Rights Act of 1964 gave them statutory authority.

Chief among these were recommendations that the massive sums of federal aid dispensed to states and localities carry the obligation of equal treatment. With few exceptions, such as those mentioned above, the administration steadfastly rejected such a course. Even in programs supported almost entirely by federal funds, such as the existing federal public housing and the National Guard, segregation was not prohibited. The Justice Department did engage in court action challenging the constitutionality of segregation in federally aided hospitals and impacted school districts, but the slow processes of litigation were eventually overrun by Congressional action in 1964.

The "weighing of priorities" caused the executive hand to falter in other areas of civil rights. Perhaps the most serious examples occurred when the traditional influence of U. S. Senators on the selection of federal judges led President Kennedy to name several ardent segregationists to Southern district courts. As a consequence, not only civil rights workers but the Department of Justice as well have been seriously hampered in securing court orders that would protect and advance civil rights in the Deep South. The predicament in which President Kennedy found himself and the alternatives available to him have been well summed up by Professor Alexander Bickel of the Yale Law School:

*

Justice Department officials say that, of course, the President would not appoint a man who, he had reason to believe, would fail to do his duty; which one may cheerfully grant, whatever it may mean. And they say further that Senators from the state concerned have a virtual veto over appointments to the district courts, and that the choice is therefore not among various possible appointments, but between a semi-permanent vacancy and the one man who can be confirmed. Vacancies are serious, no doubt. However, the Chief Justice of the United States has ample and frequently exercised power to assign judges from other districts, including retired judges, to districts where there is a vacancy. . . . This is a usable counter-pressure to the Senatorial veto. And the South is not devoid of men who will do their judicial duty in an ampler sense than merely by not committing impeachable acts or refusing to follow unavoidable precedents from higher courts. President Eisenhower found a goodly number of them, as did even President Truman, whose judicial appointments are not his greatest claim to enduring renown. And so, to be sure, has President Kennedy—with, however, what appear to be some rather glaring exceptions.

President Johnson has not entirely escaped the difficulties posed by this dilemma. In June 1965, his appointment of former Mississippi Governor James P. Coleman, a "moderate" segregationist, to the Fifth Circuit Court of Appeals drew the fire of some civil rights groups.

The Executive Order on Housing. President Kennedy's campaign promise to ban discrimination in federally aided housing by "a stroke of the pen" was not acted on until almost two years after he took office. This delay is commonly said to have been the result of his apprehension that such an order would depress new construction and antagonize Southern congressmen whose support was desperately needed for the Foreign Trade Bill and other legislation. If so, these fears were exaggerated. Executive Order 11063, finally issued on November 20, 1962, was something of an anti-climax. Neither at that time nor since has it had any measurable adverse effect on the housing industry. And no revolt against the administration broke out in the halls of Congress.

Admittedly the order was narrow in coverage and, partly as a consequence, has been administered in gingerly fashion. It applied only to new housing (after November 20, 1962) owned or operated by the federal government, built on urban renewal land, or financed with loans made or guaranteed by the government. It did not apply to any existing housing, even federal public housing. Nor did it apply to conventionally financed housing. The order did contain a "good offices" provision, Section 102, under which the housing agencies were directed to take "appropriate action permitted by law, including the institution of appropriate litigation, if required, to promote the abandonment of discriminatory practices with respect to residential property and related facilities heretofore provided with Federal financial assistance . . ." With a few exceptions in the realm of persuasion, mostly ineffective, this approach to desegregation of existing housing has not been used. Not a single law suit has been filed to implement it. The net effect of the order was to bring under the nondiscrimination requirement less than 20 per cent of new housing starts annually. When the turnover of existing units is considered, this is only a small fraction of the housing market in a given year.

Legal doubts as well as political calculations figured in these limitations. Fair housing advocates had urged—as they still do—that the order cover housing financed by Savings and Loan Associations and commercial banks whose deposits are insured by the federal government. Some lawyers, inside and outside the government, maintained that such provisions would exceed presidential authority, or come imprudently close to doing so. Others argued to the contrary.

This disagreement is still unresolved. But it has become painfully clear that Executive Order 11063 in its present form is too limited in coverage to have any significant impact on the prevailing pattern of residential segregation. The very fact that the order affects only a portion of the market, putting it at a potential disadvantage with respect to the rest, militates against a vigorous enforcement program. It also places those leaders and developers who comply in danger of unfair competition. Analogous arguments were used effectively by the administration in advocating passage of the public accommodations title of the Civil Rights Act; they are no less applicable to the field of housing.

The President's Committee on Equal Opportunity in Housing, headed by former Governor David Lawrence of Pennsylvania, has repeatedly recommended that the President extend the coverage of the housing order, as have the Mortgage Bankers Association and various other spokesmen for lenders, builders, and realtors, as well as civil rights groups. If constitutional or other doubts restrain the President from doing so, it is likely that in time circumstances will force him to ask for Congressional enactment of a fair housing law, however inexpedient that might seem at the moment.*

---

* This prophecy was in fact fulfilled by the President in his State of the Union message of January 12, 1966.

The Executive Order on Employment. Kennedy's earliest and most promising executive action was the issuance in April 1961 of Executive Order 10925 on equal opportunity in federal and federally connected employment. (It was supplemented in 1963 by Executive Order 11114 regulating employment in federally assisted construction.) The order greatly strengthened standards of compliance and methods of enforcement applying to contractors and federal agencies. It also established, under the chairmanship of then Vice President Lyndon B. Johnson, a committee of public and private members with broad powers of regulation and review of the agencies' programs. Civil rights spokesmen greeted the order as impressive evidence that, in Mr. Johnson's words, "we mean business." Administrators of federal programs affected by the directive also saw the action as an indication of strong presidential concern, conferring high priority on the employment effort.

As a result, the objectives of the Order were pursued with far more energy than had ever before been manifested. The military departments, which administer the greatest dollar volume of federal contracts, employed a number of fair employment specialists to assist their contract management personnel in enforcing the nondiscrimination requirements. The federal agencies stepped up their efforts at recruiting and upgrading Negroes and other minorities. In each case, the stated goal was not merely passive nondiscrimination but "affirmative action"—generally construed to mean concern for the identification, training, and motivation of present and potential minority employees. The sharp rate of increase in the number of complaints filed after 1961 was no doubt indicative of the greater air of seriousness with which the equal employment program was carried on.

Despite this more energetic performance, the implementation of Executive Order 10925 has fallen below expectation. This is attributable in part to unavoidable problems. The government's contractual relationships—and hence the Order—afforded little jurisdiction over labor unions. Moreover, the employment effort coincided with the growth of automation and the resulting decline in the less skilled blue-collar jobs. Because of inadequate education and training, there was a limited supply of qualified Negro applicants for jobs requiring a substantial degree of technical skill. Not all of the shortcomings of the program could be explained by immutable economic and social forces, however; some resulted from the way in which the program was administered.

The great virtue of Executive Order 10925 was that it provided, for the first time, the basis for effective use of the federal government's formidable contractual power, systematically and across the board, to enforce standards of equal employment in thousands of American corporations. To achieve this result, two things were needed: steady insistence on the employers' obligation through the channels of contract management, including the use of sanctions when necessary, and strong and continuing backing for this approach from high officials in the administration. Voluntary action going beyond the requirements of the Order could be a desirable adjunct, as long as it was kept wholly distinct from, and secondary to, the contractual obligation.

Unfortunately, these administrative conditions were not fully maintained. The sense of high priority and presidential interest initially communicated to the contracting agencies soon diminished. From the beginning, the Committee was beset by internal dissension over the balance to be struck between persuasion, education, and promotion of voluntary action, on the one hand, and systematic compliance and enforcement efforts, on the other. Some Committee members and civil rights leaders were critical of the "Plans for Progress" program, under which many of the largest contractors signed agreements to advance equal employment opportunity by voluntary means; this emphasis on "voluntarism," it was argued, could only weaken the approach to firm and uniform application of compliance procedures to all contractors, large and small. Defenders of the program, whose views prevailed, maintained that the two approaches were not incompatible but supplementary.

This controversy later subsided, and today few of its former critics would deny the usefulness of the Plans for Progress program as it has developed. It is undeniable, however, that the enforcement provisions of the order have gone virtually unused. The ultimate sanction—contract termination—has never been applied, no hearings have been held, and only a few companies have been put on the list of ineligibles for future contracts pending improved performance. Statistics published by the Committee indicate some welcome, if relatively slight, gains by both Federal agencies and contractors.* But the over-all figures tend to obscure the fact that gains have been quite uneven, the accomplishments of some of the larger

* By 1964 the Committee was able to report that since 1961 Negroes had increased from 12.9 to 13.2 per cent of all federal employees; and that in 103 Plans for Progress companies the comparable increase was from 5.1 to 5.7 per cent.

and better performing employers compensating for little or no progress on the part of many others.

It should be added that the government employment effort has reflected less dilution of priority and aggressiveness, although gains in the Deep South have been slow and token at best. As recently as April 1965 LeRoy Collins, then director of the Community Relations Service, declared: "Equality of opportunity in employment is a hard-and-fast policy of the Federal Government—at the top, but it is not yet very visible out in the Selmas [Alabama]."

The civil rights reorganization announced by President Johnson in September 1965 basically altered administrative responsibility for these programs. The President's Committee on Equal Employment Opportunity was disbanded. Supervisory responsibility for the contractor employment program was placed in the Department of Labor. The Civil Service Commission was charged with overseeing equal employment within the federal establishment itself. These changes were consistent with the President's stated policy of fixing civil rights responsibilities in the mainline agencies, rather than in specially created bodies within the executive office of the President. Whether or not the critics of this approach are right in questioning its effectiveness will take some time to determine.

A new chapter in the equal employment effort was opened with the passage of the Civil Rights Act of 1964. Title VII of the Act, based on the federal power to regulate interstate commerce, will ultimately require non-discriminatory employment practices of most companies with twenty-five or more employees. It provided for an Equal Employment Opportunity Commission to administer the program, with jurisdiction beginning in July 1965. At this writing the Commission, chaired by Franklin D. Roosevelt, Jr., has been operational too short a time for any serious appraisal of its effectiveness. State fair-employment programs dependent on complaints—as is the new federal program—have not been notably successful. The federal Commission suffers the added handicap of having no enforcement powers of its own. Until such time as this legislative shortcoming is remedied, the hope for an effective program must rest on three existing bases. The first is the authority of the Commissioners themselves to initiate complaints. The second is the power of the Attorney General to bring suit when a "pattern or practice" of discrimination is discovered. The third is the prospect of a vigorous, affirmative approach through education, persuasion, and technical assistance.

Enforcing the Law

The Kennedy Administration was less than four months old when Attorney General Robert F. Kennedy, in a notable speech at the University of Georgia, sounded the keynote of the Justice Department: "I say to you today that if the orders of the court are circumvented, the Department of Justice will act. We will not stand by or be aloof. We will move. . . . We will not make or interpret the laws. We shall enforce them—vigorously, without regional bias or political slant."

These were bold words. And they were put to the test almost immediately. The day before the Attorney General made his Georgia speech, an interracial team of CORE members boarded a south-bound bus in Washington, D. C., and began what was to become known as the "Freedom Ride." Their object was to test the integration of waiting-room facilities for interstate travelers, long required by court interpretations but ignored in many parts of the South. The trip was uneventful until one bus arrived in Anniston, Alabama, where it was set upon and burned by pro-segregation extremists. A second bus was mobbed in Birmingham and its passengers brutally beaten, while local policemen remained strangely absent until the damage was done.

From this point on, the Justice Department became a veritable command post. The Attorney General bombarded Alabama Governor John Patterson with persistent but unanswered telephone calls. He finally dispatched an emissary who extracted from the Governor an assurance that a new group of Freedom Riders headed for Montgomery would have state protection. More mob violence occurred in Montgomery, however, with only belated intervention by the police. The Attorney General promptly sent a force of 600 deputy marshals and other federal officers to the scene, narrowly averting further violence.

The recalcitrant South thus learned that the Kennedy administration would not shrink from the use of force if necessary to preserve explicit federal guarantees. But the most important result of the Freedom Rides was the Justice Department's skillful engineering of a long overdue administrative remedy. The Attorney General and his aides persuaded the independent Interstate Commerce Commission to issue in record time new regulations prohibiting segregation in interstate bus and rail terminals. They also moved through negotiation and litigation to effect the desegregation of air terminals, more difficult to reach through regulation.

By the end of 1961, the administration had weathered with credit its first major crisis in federal-state relations. But other challenges were soon to come.

In September 1962, state resistance and civil disorder greeted the court-ordered admission of the first Negro to the University of Mississippi. The episode began when the administration sought assurances from Governor Ross Barnett that he would protect the Negro student, James Meredith, and would maintain order. It ended with massive rioting, resulting in two deaths and many injuries, and with federal intervention in the form of deputy marshals and, later, federalized national guardsmen. It can be persuasively argued that much of the violence might have been prevented if the Governor's assurances (which were not fulfilled) had been given less credence, or if there had not been an unaccountable delay in the arrival of the troops. But these criticisms do not detract from the commitment and resourcefulness displayed by Robert Kennedy and then Deputy Attorney General Nicholas DeB. Katzenbach, the determination of President Kennedy, and the courage of the federal officers who withstood the attacks of the mobs without arms. The heroism of James Meredith was, of course, an indispensable factor.

The experience gained in Alabama in 1961 and Mississippi in 1962 was put to effective use in subsequent law enforcement crises —for example, in 1963 when Alabama Governor George Wallace threatened to bar admission of Negro students to the University of Alabama and, more recently, in the spring of 1965 when Wallace refused to provide protection for the Reverend Martin Luther King, Jr., and his followers on their march from Selma to Montgomery.

Any dispassionate analysis must credit the Kennedy and Johnson Administrations with an impressive performance in the enforcement of federal court orders. But the civil rights movement of the 1960's is not inclined toward dispassionate analysis. Americans have been terrorized, beaten, gassed, unfairly arrested and prosecuted, bombed, and on occasion killed in attempts to exercise constitutionally protected rights. Sometimes state and local police have been the perpetrators of these brutalities, sometimes they have been acquiescent bystanders. Yet federal police actions have been confined to a few large-scale disturbances after federal court orders have been secured.

The Justice Department has with some success sought to enjoin economic reprisals against Negroes involved in the civil rights movement. It has turned to the overburdened and slow-moving federal courts to counter misuse of state criminal procedures. It has occasionally attempted prosecutions under Sections 241 and 242, Title 18, U. S. Code, a Reconstruction statute aimed at conspiracies and official acts intended to deprive individuals of their civil rights. But the old statute is a weak instrument, and Southern juries, albeit federally impaneled, are loath to hand down indictments and convictions in such cases. As a result, abuses of civil rights workers and those they seek to help have usually gone unpunished.

In the view of a growing number of Americans—particularly the younger and more militant civil rights workers—this is both intolerable and indefensible. They reject the Justice Department's contention that the federal government has no legitimate means of providing police protection or of taking preventive action against possible violence. Burke Marshall has written lucidly of these conflicting views. In the Spring of 1964, he summed up the federal dilemma as follows:

Those who say that civil rights issues cut into the fabric of federalism are correct. They cut most deeply where police power is involved, for the police as well as for those in conflict with the police. There would be vast problems in any attempts at federal control of the administration of justice, even through the moderate method of federal court injunctions. Yet vast problems have been created already by police indifference to Negro rights in the South, and they will grow if the trend is not turned. The loss of faith in law—the usefulness of federal law and the unfairness of local law—is gaining very rapidly among Negro and white civil rights workers. The consequences in the future cannot be foreseen.

Within a year after that was written, a new crisis produced new consequences. Police brutality and Ku Klux Klan violence (including two murders) directed against demonstrators in Selma, Alabama, created a wave of national indignation and prompted President Johnson to ask for legislation to curb vigilante extremists. At this writing, the precise content of the prospective legislation has not been announced. But it is unlikely that it will go far enough to resolve the problem posed by Mr. Marshall. Only a dramatic change for the better in the hard-core South can silence the chorus of demands for a radical revision of federal-state relations in the administration of justice.

The right to vote. Both President Kennedy and his brother the Attorney General made it amply clear from the start that they regarded voting as the "master right" through which a basic settlement of the civil rights problem could be achieved. Although the Civil Rights Acts of 1957 and 1960 had granted the Attorney General the authority to initiate voting suits, only six such cases had been filed under President Eisenhower, and those mainly in the waning months of his administration.

Beginning early in 1961, the invigorated Civil Rights Division of the Justice Department launched an unremitting campaign to enforce the neglected voting rights laws. First Assistant John Doar (who was later to succeed Marshall) and other lawyers of the Division took to the county seats and backroads of the South to compile the evidence of discrimination. There was a sharp upsurge in the number of voting suits initiated, from the original six to a total of fifty-eight through 1963, and scores of new investigations were undertaken.

But fear, ignorance, and apathy were also obstacles to Negro political participation. Robert Kennedy and Burke Marshall correctly perceived that Negro registration would not advance rapidly by federal action alone. Accordingly, they urged civil rights organizations to expend more effort in this direction. This advice was received coolly, even with suspicion and resentment. It was seen, along with the Attorney General's call for a "cooling-off" period during the inflamed summer of 1961, as an attempt to divert the Negro protest from direct action that was embarrassing to the administration. Yet only a few months later, the major civil rights groups did join in a cooperative Voter Education Project, sponsored by the Southern Regional Council with the aid of foundation funds. At the end of two and a half years of operation, VEP reported that Negro voters in the South had increased by an estimated 688,800.

Notwithstanding these accelerated governmental and private efforts, it soon became apparent that Negro registration was growing at a hopelessly slow pace. The Justice Department's suits had produced some impressive breakthroughs in such Black Belt counties as Macon, Bullock, Montgomery, and Jefferson counties in Alabama and Washington, Bienville, and Jackson parishes in Louisiana. But generally progress was frustrated by the repressive climate of the rural South and the interminable delays of litigation. As Marshall has written:

The federal government has demonstrated a seeming inability to make significant advances, in seven years' time, since the 1957 law, in making the right to vote real for Negroes in Mississippi, large parts of Alabama and Louisiana, and in scattered counties in other states . . . Does this mean that this basic problem is beyond solution and the simple right beyond realization?

*

The experience of the Justice Department to date would not justify this conclusion . . . The harder question is whether the tempo of the civil rights movement has not quickened to such a degree that there is not enough time left . . . The only tangible result in the near future will be a mass of litigation in the federal courts which will take months or years to resolve. And that in itself will be divisive between Negroes and whites, between state and federal governments, with racial issues continuing to be a prime political factor in any election.

It was recognition of these problems that led President Kennedy to end his moratorium on requested civil rights legislation. In January 1962, he asked Congress for a supplementary voting rights law that would make six years of schooling *prima facie* evidence of literacy. His appeal went unheeded, as did the administration's 1963 proposal for federal voting referees in counties where fewer than 15 per cent of the eligible Negroes were registered. A relatively weak voting rights provision was included in the 1964 Civil Rights Act. But it remained for President Johnson in 1965 to persuade a more receptive Congress to pass a measure commensurate to the problem. The 1965 Act empowered the Justice Department to send federal examiners to counties where low registration indicates persistent discrimination—principally in the Deep South.

The lawyers of the Civil Rights Division have worked untiringly from 1961 on to overcome voting discrimination against Negroes. That so much time and effort went to waste because of inadequate legal tools is an incalculable loss to the nation. Now, the debate has shifted to the strategy of implementation—how widely and vigorously the Attorney General should apply the enforcement mechanism of the new 1965 Act. As 1966 began, the trend was toward increasing use of these new powers.

School desegregation. Following the Supreme Court's 1954 decision, desegregation of Southern school systems proceeded at a glacial pace. As late as mid-1963, the Attorney General reported that some 2,000 school districts were still operating dual school systems. At the outset of the Kennedy administration, the Justice Department set out to try to hasten the process. The Attorney General and his staff sought to promote peaceful and voluntary compliance through quiet discussions with scores of state and local officials, politicians, educators, and civic leaders. They also stayed in close touch with communities where court-ordered desegregation might be met by official interference or mob violence.

The most conspicuous new approach, however, was in the area

of litigation. In the spring of 1961, the Justice Department entered four Louisiana school cases as a friend of the court—the first such government initiative taken for the purpose of advancing desegregation. But not all federal judges were amenable to government participation. In heavily Negro Prince Edward County, Virginia, the public schools had been closed in 1959 to avoid compliance with a desegregation ruling. The seemingly endless battle of litigation was still dragging on in 1961, with no visible hope of resolution. Meanwhile, the county's Negro children went uneducated, while whites attended a private academy funded by state tuition grants. The Justice Department sought to enter the case as a friend of the court but was refused by the district judge. When 1963 brought the prospect of a fifth school-less year for the Negro children, Robert Kennedy acted. Quietly, he and his staff, working with the U. S. Office of Education, mustered private support for a full program of instruction to be carried out in public school buildings for all who wished to attend. With endorsement from prominent Virginians, including the Governor, free schooling again became available to more than 1500 Negro youngsters and the few whites who elected to join them. A year later, the tangle of litigation was at last unwound, and public schools were again operating in Prince Edward County.

Despite the Justice Department's best efforts, executive action clearly was not enough. Belatedly, the Civil Rights Act of 1964 gave the Attorney General authority to initiate school desegregation suits; even more important, perhaps, it supplemented the too-deliberate speed of the courts with the threat that the federal government would withhold funds from segregated school districts. These measures, at last, provided a realistic hope that the Supreme Court's 1954 decision would be translated into fact. Thus far, however, the pace of change has been disappointingly slow when measured against the magnitude of the problem. At the beginning of the 1965–66 school year, the number of Southern Negro pupils still in segregated classrooms was variously estimated at 92.5 to 94.8 per cent of the total. Civil rights groups were united in demanding that the Office of Education hold Southern school systems to more exacting standards.

Presidential Leadership and Legislative Proposals

As we have seen, President Kennedy's original plan of approach to civil rights barely survived intact through the first year of his term. Reliance on executive action was producing only modest results; pressure for civil rights legislation was mounting; the administration had had to meet a major federal-state crisis in curbing disorder in Alabama; and despite strenuous efforts voting discrimination had yielded little ground. That matters were not worse was due in no small part to the able men on the administration's first civil rights team: White and Wofford of the White House staff, Marshall, Katzenbach, and John Siegenthaler of the Department of Justice, Berl Bernhard of the Civil Rights Commission, John Feild of the employment committee, Louis Martin of the Democratic National Committee, and others who worked with them. But it was Robert Kennedy who spared the President most. His forthright public role enabled the President to reserve his personal influence without creating doubt about his position.

At various times in the first eighteen months, the President referred to civil rights in messages and news conferences, making plain his concern for the racial problem and his conviction that it was first and foremost a moral issue. But it was not until September of 1962 that he made his first major statement to the nation on a civil rights emergency. Nationally telecast, it was essentially an appeal to the students of "Ole Miss" to accept the enrollment of James Meredith without disorder. Ironically, as it was being delivered, the rioting broke out on the Oxford, Mississippi, campus.

In February of 1963 the President again addressed himself exclusively to civil rights—this time in a message to Congress requesting a more far-reaching civil rights bill. On two previous occasions the administration had been identified with proposed legislation. The first identification, in 1961, was the result of an erroneous news report describing the Clark-Celler Bill as administration sponsored; a frigid White House denial administered the death sentence to this proposal. The second identification, bona fide but equally ill-fated, was the 1962 bill establishing a sixth-grade presumption of literacy. Not only did Congress refuse to pass the bill—partly, it seems, out of a belief that the President's advocacy was less than whole-hearted—but civil rights spokesmen were sharply critical of it as being unacceptably weak.

In his February 1963 message the President sought to overcome both liabilities—the first by unmistakably committing his personal prestige, the second by proposing a more comprehensive though still moderate "package." It included provisions intended to expedite voting litigation, establish a presumption of literacy, prohibit dual standards of voter qualification, provide for the appointment of temporary voting referees while a federal suit was in progress, afford technical and financial assistance to desegregating school districts, and extend the life and broaden the functions of the Civil Rights Commission.

Civil rights leaders were by no means satisfied that these proposals went far enough, but their objections shortly became moot. The crisis which erupted in Birmingham, Alabama, in April marked an historic turning point in the nation's perception of the civil rights issue and in the administration's approach to it. For weeks Negroes marched and demonstrated in the Alabama city, beset by savage police dogs, fire hoses, and massive arrests. An uneasy truce was finally achieved, mainly as a result of Burke Marshall's patient negotiations. But the Birmingham excesses and other atrocities, including the murder of the NAACP's Medgar Evers in Jackson, Mississippi, shocked the nation and triggered a chain reaction of angry protests in hundreds of cities, north and south. In the ten weeks following the Birmingham truce, the Justice Department counted a nationwide total of 758 racial demonstrations.

In response to the national upheaval, President Kennedy discarded the caution that had characterized his previous public statements and legislative approaches to civil rights. On June 11, he made an urgent address to the nation on television, and on June 19 he directed a second civil rights message to Congress.

"The events in Birmingham and elsewhere," he declared, "have so increased the cries for equality that no city or state or legislative body can prudently choose to ignore them. . . . [The] result of continued Federal legislative inaction will be continued, if not increased, racial strife—causing the leadership of both sides to pass from the hands of reasonable and responsible men to the purveyors of hate and violence."

He then proposed a number of legislative provisions to supplement those advocated in his February message. Among them were the prohibition of discrimination in a wide variety of public accommodations, authority for the Attorney General to initiate school desegregation suits, the creation of a Community Relations Service to conciliate racial disputes, and a requirement of nondiscrimination in programs financed or assisted by the federal government. This was an impressive set of proposals, stronger by far than could have been realistically expected only a few months earlier.

But the momentum of the civil rights movement was such that

even the President's stepped-up proposals were not considered strong enough. The racial turmoil of the "long, hot summer," culminating in the massive though peaceful march on Washington in August, generated pressure inside and outside Congress for a strengthened civil rights bill. The Leadership Conference on Civil Rights, which included representatives from the major organizations supporting the bill, carried on an energetic lobby in Congress. The constituent groups—labor, religion, and civil rights—activated their members across the country. The churches, in particular, became for the first time an effective pressure group, whose influence was powerfully felt in the Capitol.

By the time the bill had assumed substantially final form in October, it had in fact been strengthened in several respects. The principal addition, inclusion of which had initially been opposed by the administration, was a fair employment practices title. The President had endorsed the principle of an FEPC, but he had not submitted it among his specific proposals, prudently advocating instead certain measures to enlarge existing programs for full and fair employment. He and his advisers feared that inclusion of so controversial a provision would doom the bill to defeat at the hands of a conservative coalition. That it did not is hardly conclusive evidence of faulty administration judgment, although this was the view commonly held by civil rights advocates; for between June 1963 and July 1964, when the bill was finally passed, developments on the civil rights front and in the Presidency itself had significantly altered the bounds of possibility.

What is indisputably clear is that by the time of his assassination in November 1963 President Kennedy had moved from a position of cautious and sparing use of his personal influence for civil rights to a posture of leadership that was bold and unreserved. Undoubtedly his sense of history, no less than his personal values, convinced him that the issue was of such national gravity that it must transcend normal political considerations.

He recognized, too, that governmental action, though indispensable, was not sufficient in itself to procure a final solution of the civil rights problem. Accordingly, he threw his personal influence and the prestige of his office into a large-scale effort to enlist private leadership in the struggle. He convened a series of White House meetings, at which he urged action on governors, mayors, businessmen, lawyers, and leaders of labor, religion, education, and women's groups. Within a forty-day period, there were twenty-one such meetings, attended by some 1700 persons. Among the tangible results were the formation of the Lawyers' Committee for Civil Rights under Law, the Women's Committee for Civil Rights, and a community relations program of the United States Conference of Mayors. Moreover, much of the voluntary desegregation that occurred in the ensuing months, particularly in public accommodations, was unquestionably facilitated by the President's appeals for local action.

Those who feared that President Johnson would retreat from his predecessor's advanced position on civil rights were in for a gratifying surprise. In his first address to Congress after taking office, he put the drive for full civil rights first among the legacies of the slain President that he was determined to carry on. He pressed successfully for the passage of the Civil Rights Act of 1964. And when the first racial crisis of his own administration erupted in Alabama in 1965, his utterances and actions were resolute—though barely swift enough for impatient civil rights leaders and outraged citizens generally. His statements on civil rights to Congress and the nation at that time were the strongest and most impassioned words on this subject yet heard from an American President. He all but demanded of a predominantly friendly Congress that it pass without delay a new voting rights act that would put registration machinery under federal control in the most recalcitrant Southern states.

In these actions, and in others yet to come, President Johnson has advantages that were denied his predecessor: He is President by virtue of a landslide vote; he is supported by a civil rights revolution that will not be ignored; he can point to his own Southern origins; and he can build on the precedents established by painful trial and error during the Kennedy years when public sentiment was less favorable. He is obviously determined not only to use but to improve on these advantages.

It is a fact of our time, however, that the specter of inequality, so long quiescent, now outruns all attempts to exorcise it. Lyndon Johnson will not have to struggle with the same aspects of the civil rights problem that vexed John Kennedy. There is an almost complete array of federal tools with which to root out the rank discriminations that still abound in the South. The challenge is to use them rapidly and efficiently enough to spare the nation more destructive racial turmoil and division. It will not be easy to translate federal law and policy into daily practice in the tradition-bound towns and hamlets where Southerners regard Washington with uncomprehending anger.

Nor is the struggle confined to the South; it has long since spread to the cities of the North and West, with their bitter, congested ghettos. The basic conditions affecting Negroes there—wretched housing, poor schools, unemployment, hopefulness, resentment, alienation—will not yield to simple fiats. Their solution will require an enormous mobilization of leadership, money, and national will. The federal remedies thus far provided or in sight—the anti-poverty program, aid to education, urban and housing reforms—are promising but relatively trifling beginnings. Much larger public investments, acceptance of inconvenience and dislocations in political and economic power must precede any major victories over inequality in the big urban areas.

Above all, federal law and policy must undergo a profound shift in interpretation—from the present prohibition of overt discrimination to a new, affirmative commitment to the goal of desegregation. Patterns of segregation are now so firmly fixed in our society that they can never be undone merely by granting minority citizens the individual right to complain of provable acts of discrimination directed personally at them. Vast urban patterns of housing, schooling, employment, and public services must be reshaped if equal opportunity is to be realized not merely in principle but in fact.

There is every prospect that the United States will never again want for presidential leadership and federal action on behalf of civil rights as traditionally defined. But in the next decade the federal executive, like the nation as a whole, will have to cope with human rights problems of a complexity not yet fully perceived.

No one has stated this challenge more eloquently than President Johnson himself. Speaking at the Howard University commencement in June 1965, he declared:

But freedom is not enough. You do not wipe away the scars of centuries by saying: Now you are free to go where you want, do as you desire, and choose the leaders you please.

You do not take a person who, for years, has been hobbled by chains and liberate him, bring him up to the starting line of a race and then say, "you are free to compete with all the others," and still justly believe that you have been completely fair.

Thus it is not enough just to open the gates of opportunity. All our citizens must have the ability to walk through those gates.

This is the next and more profound stage of the battle for civil rights. We seek not just freedom but opportunity—not just legal equity but human ability—not just equality as a right and a theory, but equality as a fact and as a result.

There is every prospect that the United States will never again want for presidential leadership and federal action on behalf of civil rights as traditionally defined. But in the next decade the federal executive, like the nation as a whole, will have to cope with human rights problems of a complexity not yet fully perceived.

Conclusion

What lessons can be drawn from the federal civil rights experience of the past five years? The major one, to which others are corollary, is as important as it is obvious: The federal executive tends to innovate forcefully and effectively only in response to an evident sense of national urgency. No administration, however wisely or humanely led, is likely to initiate far-reaching action in the face of public indifference, to say nothing of hostility. The quality of federal civil rights performance, then, depends directly on the ability of Negro Americans to dramatize their cause in such a way that it enlists the support of other influential segments of the society. Obvious though it may be, this conclusion has been explicitly rejected by some of the militant Negro leadership and it is often ignored in practice by others of both races.

The high hopes for executive action in civil rights that marked the beginning of the Kennedy administration were only spottily realized. They were vindicated most fully in the federal response to crisis—as at the University of Mississippi in 1962. They were fulfilled more prosaically and less completely in the internal management of the federal establishment itself, as in government appointments and employment. But, despite much committed effort, affirmative achievements in the areas of general employment, education, housing, and day-to-day administration of justice were few and far between. On the infrequent occasions when noteworthy gains were made in these areas it was usually because federal officials could point to widespread evidence of minority discontent. Not until this discontent and the brutal methods used to contain it won the sympathy of millions of Americans did Congress provide meaningful weapons with which to wage a large-scale attack on discrimination.

The Civil Rights Act of 1964 was more than a simple Congressional response to national emergency and moral crisis. It was also a recognition that the civil rights forces had assembled a coalition which any practical politician could respect. Not only the civil rights groups but organized labor and religion as well were at least momentarily united in a crusade that commanded the allegiance of a majority of Americans. The churches mobilized unprecedented support in localities where civil rights had not previously been of much concern to voters. A continuing coalition of this kind will be sorely needed in the days to come. It will be essential in insuring effective implementation of the laws and executive orders already on the books, and in strengthening and supplementing them as needed. Above all, it will be a prerequisite of an effective federal attack on the social disorders of the cities which so drastically penalize Negroes and other minorities.

Preoccupation with urban pathologies, acute as these are, should not obscure the fact that civil rights *per se* are still far from full achievement. New federal laws and the programs they have created are not self-executing. They rely for the most part on complaints to trigger the enforcement mechanism. Experience clearly indicates that it is difficult to bring to light a substantial number of valid complaints. The victims of discrimination are often persons of limited education and little confidence in their ability to win redress through appeals to a large and complicated bureaucracy. It will take all the resources the civil rights organizations and like-minded groups can muster to see that federal civil rights processes are activated as the law provides and then are truly responsive to need. Sympathetic government administrators could wish nothing more, for they are the first to recognize that without outside prodding their ability to move forcefully against discrimination is seriously weakened.

Housing discrimination is a case in point. In this field lack of vigorous pressure by the civil rights coalition, coupled with widespread public resistance to the prospect of housing integration, has resulted in a minimal federal effort, lower in priority than any other civil rights program. This, in an area of American life where federal influence and federal obligation, because of past delinquencies, are enormous. A broadening of the housing order or even passage of a fair housing act would not provide any wholesale remedy for the housing problems of Negroes. But they would permit a significant beginning in an area where segregation has its deepest roots and is least challenged.

It is a commonplace to say that racial inequities are the nation's most pressing domestic problem and that nothing short of massive intervention by the national government can meet it adequately. But, this having been said, it remains to create the conditions of

It is a commonplace to say that racial inequities are the nation's most pressing domestic problem and that nothing short of massive intervention by the national government can meet it adequately. But, this having been said, it remains to create the conditions of effective governmental action. The principle of federal responsibility in civil rights has been solidly established. Now, more systematic effort must be directed to producing the kind of interplay between public and private forces that will make this principle a working reality.

BIBLIOGRAPHY

Bickel, Alexander M., "Civil Rights: The Kennedy Record," *The New Republic,* December 15, 1962.

Fleming, Harold C., "Civil Rights," *Britannica Book of the Year* (Chicago, 1962, 1963, 1964).

Fuller, Helen, *Year of Trial: Kennedy's Crucial Decisions* (New York, 1962).

Golden, Harry, *Mr. Kennedy and the Negroes* (Cleveland, Ohio, 1964).

Leadership Conference on Civil Rights, *Federally Supported Discrimination* (New York, 1961).

Lewis, Anthony, and *The New York Times, Portrait of a Decade: The Second American Revolution* (New York, 1964).

Marshall, Burke, *Federalism and Civil Rights* (New York, 1964).

Muse, Benjamin, *Ten Years of Prelude: The Story of Integration Since the Supreme Court's 1954 Decision* (New York, 1964).

National Association of Intergroup Relations Officials, *Executive Responsibility in Intergroup Relations* (Washington, D. C., 1961).

National Urban League, *The Time Is Now* (New York, 1961).

"Notre Dame Conference on Congressional Civil Rights Legislation," *Notre Dame Lawyer,* June 1963.

The Potomac Institute, *The Federal Role in Equal Housing Opportunity* (Washington, D. C., 1964).

————, *The Federal Dollar and Nondiscrimination: A Guide to Community Action under Title VI of the Civil Rights Act of 1964* (Washington, D. C., 1965).

Southern Regional Council, *The Federal Executive and Civil Rights* (Atlanta, Ga., 1961).

————, *Executive Support of Civil Rights* (Atlanta, Ga., 1962).

Sullivan, Donald Francis, *The Civil Rights Programs of the Kennedy Administration: A Political Analysis,* Unpublished Dissertation, University of Oklahoma, 1964.

HAROLD C. FLEMING

U. S. Commission on Civil Rights, Reports for 1959, 1961 (5 vols.), 1963 (Washington, D. C., 1959, 1961, 1963).

U. S. President's Committee on Equal Employment Opportunity, *Report to the President* (Washington, D. C., 1963).

U. S. President's Committee on Equal Opportunity in The Armed Forces, *Equality of Treatment and Opportunity for Negro Military Personnel Stationed within the United States* (Washington, D. C., 1963).

JOSEPH H. FICHTER

American Religion and the Negro

THE ROLE of organized religion in the current Negro freedom movement is symbolized by the leadership of Martin Luther King, who is
primarily concerned neither with an appointment to a "white pulpit" nor with the dissolution of Negro church denominations. In
other words, neither the mixing of the races nor the mixing of the
religions is the main objective of any churchman's participation in
the movement for Negro rights. What is important is "freedom
now" for both races, and "equality now" for all citizens, regardless
of racial and religious affiliation. A free society can be pluralistic by
the choice and decision of its citizens, but a pluralistic society can
be free only if its major institutions support freedom for all.

Better than any other institution, organized religion ought to understand the terms of the struggle for racial freedom and equality.
Religious-minded people ought to grasp more readily than others
such concepts as reparation for wrong-doing, reconciliation of the
estranged, resolution for improvement, commitment to values, firm
purpose of amendment, fellowship and brotherhood, love and justice. The slogan of the rights movement, "freedom now," had great
significance to the ancient Jews in bondage, to the early Christians
in pagan Rome, to the Catholics in the English persecutions, to the
Huguenots in the French persecutions. If the historical analogy between religious liberty and racial liberty is so close, one wonders
why the churches delayed so long before entering the civil rights
movement. But now that the commitment has been made and the
struggle has been joined, one may speculate about further and
fuller religious influence and participation in the movement.

Organized religion has certainly contributed to the moral awakening of Americans to the race problem, and the young generation
of people now in the pulpits and pews of American churches and

synagogues gives assurance that this will continue. These people do not accept the old caricature of religion as merely a personal and private affair. They have repudiated the peculiar notion that the race question is a political and legal matter, not a religious and moral concern. The "proper scope" of religious activity has been widened by them; we now frequently hear about the relevance of religion to modern life, to the crowded city, to business practices, to political organizations, to educational systems, and to racial and other minority problems.

Changes in religious activities are uneven, as they are in all institutionalized areas of society. There are major trends and minor counter-trends, but the main direction of religious influence in this regard is clear and ineluctable. There is criticism of white clergymen who have few Negroes in their own congregations, but who go South to engage in sit-ins at restaurants and to picket voting registrars. There is criticism of church leaders who use their moral influence more often for the desegregation of non-church institutions than they do for the desegregation of their own organizations. It is said, on the one hand, that "the present movement to do away with segregation as an ultimate ideal has stemmed mainly from the churches,"[1] and, on the other hand, that "as long as churches remain segregated through subtle techniques, they give moral sanction to segregation in other areas of social life."[2]

It has often been said, and by religious people themselves, that Sunday morning at church is the most segregated time in America; and it probably offers little consolation to insist that Saturday night at the country club is an even more segregated time. We do not expect the country club to set standards of moral principle and practice, but we do await guidance from the church in both respects. The church cannot afford to wait for the Congress, the President, and the Supreme Court to provide its moral standards and values. Yet, as Liston Pope has remarked, the church has "lagged behind the Supreme Court as the conscience of the nation on questions of race."[3]

White religionists have found this disconcerting, and Negro religionists have considered it a demonstration of white insincerity. As Embree wrote more than thirty years ago, "Segregation in Christian churches is an embarrassment. In a religion whose central teaching is brotherly love and the golden rule, preachers have to do a great deal of rationalizing as they expound their own gospel."[4] We are not limiting the present discussion to the extent to which the churches have remained internally conservative and segregated or have become internally progressive and integrated. We are interested also in the moral impact which the church has had on the larger society, the extent to which church people have promoted external, non-denominational integration and reconciliation of the races. Whatever their previous conservative stance has been, the churches have now become "spearheads of reform."[5]

The ways in which churches approach the problem of desegregation vary according to region and are the result both of the voluntary nature of church membership and of local cultural patterns. Thus, in the Southern states, where local customs—and often legal intimidation—prevent the races from associating voluntarily even in the churches, those interested in racial justice become involved in non-church desegregation, as of public facilities, schools, buses, libraries, parks, and voting. In the North and West, however, where Negroes and whites can associate more freely than in the South, the churches tend to promote the desegregation of their own congregations as well as of public and civic institutions.

I

What have the churches in America done about their own internal pattern of racial segregation? It must be said in all fairness that in the second half of the last century segregated patterns in religion came as a *consequence* of community practice and legislation.[6] In this sense, the church bowed to the culture instead of resisting and reforming it. The seeds of separation had been sown even before the Civil War, when large Southern Protestant denominations declared their independence. In the ensuing decades the separation of the Negro Protestant bodies came about either by expulsion from the white denominations or by the Negroes' own withdrawal to independent churches.

Negro religion in America is by definition segregated religion, but it embraces a wide range of structures, patterns, and attitudes. At one end are the completely separatist religious cults, the best known of which is now the Black Muslim Movement, which repudiates Christian and Caucasian civilization and turns to Asiatic culture and the religion of Islam.[7] An earlier Negro nationalist cult, now declining in influence, is the Moorish Temple of Science in America, which also repudiates the white man, his religion, and his culture.[8] These groups extoll the black man as superior to the white and scoff at the notion of reconciliation or integration with white Christians. One of the most spectacular anti-white movements was Marcus Garvey's Universal Mutual Improvement Association, which was both political and religious. It did not turn to Asia and Islam, but glorified Negritude with its black Christ and black God. It disparaged white culture and wanted to return to Africa for the fulfillment of a pure religion and a higher civilization.[9] The memory of Garvey as the "lost savior" of the race lingers among Negroes, and some of his former adherents are seeking the new savior among the Black Muslims.

These black religious and nationalist movements, because they are antagonistic to whites and fight against cultural assimilation, are opposed by most Negro leaders and feared by some whites. They speak boldly of the need for Negro courage and physical resistance to white discrimination and injustice. They are the most vocal protest of despair and frustration over the white man's failure to practice the ideals of Christianity and the principles of democracy in relation to American Negroes. They serve to dramatize the Negro's plight in America, and, while proclaiming the advantages of withdrawal from white America, they are also serving the latent function of arousing white America to the need for interracial justice and integration.[10]

The black nationalist groups make a direct appeal to the racial pride of the most disadvantaged Negroes and are effective in reforming the moral behavior of their members. They are puritanical in their rules on sexual behavior, smoking, drinking, dancing, and work habits. While repudiating Christianity they are emulating the Christian, Puritan, bourgeois way of life. The numerous Holiness sects also have great influence on the behavior of the lower classes of urban Negroes. These people seek personal sanctification and a sinless way of life. Their preachers concentrate on other-worldly sermons and the futility of worldly and material comforts, possessions, and status. They are seldom concerned about social justice, integration, and the civil rights movement. Instead of demanding separatism, as the Black Muslims do, they seem to accept it apathetically as a worldly evil, and for this they are chided by American Negro leadership.[11]

The positive segregation of the black nationalists and the negative segregation of the Holiness sects both are functions of their differing religious ideologies, and they both make their appeal to the poorest class of Negroes. The great majority of American Negroes belong to the large Protestant denominations, but they are also in a segregated church system. This must be said of the Baptist denomination, to which six out of ten Negro church members belong.[12] It must also be said of the Methodist denomination, which has the second largest Negro membership and which was reorganized in 1939 into five white geographical jurisdictions and one Negro Central Jurisdiction, embracing all Negro congregations regardless of their location.[13]

From the point of view of ultimate socio-religious integration, the large separate Negro Protestant churches present a double rationalization. The first is that their white fellow Protestants, especially in the Southeast, are not "ready" for integration and that if congregational integration were now to take place the Negro members would again be relegated to the fringes of church participation. The second is that Negroes have freer expression within their own congregations, enjoy a common meeting place and center of communication; they can discuss and promote the elimination of Negro disabilities. "The Negro church remains one of the few areas in which the Negro can retain his identity as an individual and yet have a vehicle for self-expression and the exercise of his own abilities."[14]

It can be argued that the *felix culpa* of the Negro Protestant denominations is that they have been a training ground for the most successful integrationist leaders. We must remember that Nat Turner, leader of the slave revolt in 1831, was a preacher, and many Negro political leaders during Reconstruction were recruited from the pulpit.[15] It was only when the Negro preacher advised patience and forbearance among his congregation that he came to earn "considerable good will among the whites," and religion was "assumed to be a force for good in all respects and, particularly, in race relations."[16] As Charles Johnson wrote a quarter of a century ago, "the indifference of the Negro church to current social issues and its emphasis on the values of a future life lent indirect but vital support to the race patterns."[17]

The relatively recent emergence of Negro preachers as outspoken proponents of civil rights has been accompanied by a loss of this "white good will." The burnings and bombings of Negro churches in the South by white racists clearly demonstrate that religion is no longer "good" for conservation of racial segregation. The anomaly, therefore, is that the segregated Negro Protestant church has been the most effective instrument in breaking down non-church segregation. If these people had been absorbed into the white Protestant denominations they may well have lost their leadership to whites, and would probably have lost the sense of solidarity that now characterizes their program of desegregation.[18]

Whatever the ambiguous position of the Negro clergy may have been before the 1950's, whether they had been a hindrance or a help to integration, whether they had been leaders or followers in the upsurge of Negro protest, there can be no doubt that they have contributed both techniques and ideology to the current civil rights movement.[19] They evolved a moral philosophy of non-violence, which draws upon the teachings of Ghandi and also presents a powerful example of Christian virtue. This effective weapon of passive resistance, Christian patience and love, must not be confused with the escapist philosophy that is still found among the Negro Holiness sects and is condemned by all prominent Negro leaders in the country.[20]

To what extent have the white Protestant denominations "cleaned their own house" of racial discrimination? At the national level every major Protestant Church body has gone on record in favor of desegregating its own congregations. Although preserving the Negro Central Jurisdiction, seventy-four Methodist bishops joined in a 1960 declaration on race relations, saying: "To discriminate against a person solely on the basis of his race is both unfair and un-Christian. There must be no place in the Methodist Church for racial discrimination or enforced segregation."[21]

The Baptists probably have a wider separation than do any of the other large denominations. The National Baptist Convention, USA, and the National Baptist Convention of America are the two largest Negro religious bodies in the country. Among the whites, the Southern Baptists differ quite sharply from the American Baptist Convention, for they continue to maintain and defend a formalized policy against internal integration. There is a similar problem of disagreement between the United Presbyterian Church and the Presbyterian Church of the United States, the latter being made up of Southern adherents who are reluctant to change segregated patterns.[22] The Protestant Episcopal Church does not have a "Southern Branch," and most of its bishops and lay leaders have spoken out clearly for racial unity, but some of its Southern officials have taken exception to this stand.[23]

The religious denomination is not the only social organization in which national and regional policies clash with local customs.

The urban church congregation includes people who live mainly in racially separated residential areas. There have been genuine efforts to achieve desegregation in local Protestant churches, but these still tend to be exceptions to the pattern.[24] Despite all efforts to the contrary, the membership of a congregation does change when the population of the neighborhood shifts. For example, one Methodist congregation in Los Angeles deliberately planned total integration, but "rather than racial inclusiveness, what the church really achieved was a relatively trouble-free transition from a Caucasian to a Negro membership."[25] The experience of this congregation is probably a paradigm for local urban churches elsewhere. "There were Negroes in the community long before there were Negroes in this church. Negroes did not come to worship until the Caucasians had largely left. The Caucasian exodus accelerated when Negroes did begin to come in significant numbers. The implication would seem to be clear: for the most part these Caucasian churchmen did not wish to live alongside or worship God together with Negro churchmen. A further implication is that for the most part Negro churchmen return this particular compliment of their white brethren."[26]

There are several reasons that white Protestantism, even with the best will of its ministers and leading lay people, has not succeeded widely in integrating its churches: (a) Protestant denominations lack the coercive influence of ecclesiastical authority at the higher levels and therefore allow each local congregation to determine its own course of action and its own moral rationalization for not acting to desegregate. (b) The different local congregations do not take a united position on the race issue.[27] (c) The Protestant principle of face-to-face primary groupings and close fellowship is difficult to institute in the religious context when it does not exist between the races in other community activities. (d) Protestant congregations are often willing to pay the high cost of moving their church to another location in order to remain segregated.[28]

Except for a few places in Maryland, Kentucky, and Louisiana, the Roman Catholic Church has been almost exclusively a white church in America. It has had relatively little influence in the Southeastern states, where the majority of Negroes lived, and even with its high rate of urban conversions it can probably still claim only about five per cent of the Negro population. Although the Catholic Church followed local patterns in providing separate facilities for Negroes, there have always been Negroes who attended

Mass in white parishes and whites who attended Mass in Negro parishes. Myrdal pointed out that, in the South, "the Roman Catholic Church is the only one where Negroes are allowed to attend white churches," and he says later that because the Church includes persons from all classes in the same congregation "there is a relatively greater feeling of equality among Catholic laymen."[29]

The Catholic Church in America is not subdivided into regional or racial denominations, and it is thus in a strategic position to implement internal integration. Even in those places where segregated parishes and schools are still maintained—as in some Southern dioceses—the Negroes, priests, and others involved in them are under the jurisdiction of the same bishop and chancery office as are their neighboring white Catholics. The continuation of separate Negro parishes remains the major obstacle to complete Catholic racial integration. On it depend separate parochial schools, parents' clubs, local organizations such as the Holy Name Society, the Sodality, Altar and Rosary societies, choirs, acolytes, youth clubs, study groups, and so forth.[30] Catholic colleges and universities, and in some instances high schools, which are under the authority of diocesan officials and religious orders, are generally desegregated. Practically all seminaries, as well as novitiates and houses of study for religious Sisters, have by this time opened their doors to Negro candidates. There are, however, still a few segregated Catholic hospitals in the Southeastern states.

Like the leaders of the Protestant churches, the bishops of the Catholic Church, individually and collectively, have condemned racism. The Popes have spoken on the subject as early as the sixteenth century. Bishop Waters of Raleigh, North Carolina, was the first of the Southern prelates to integrate the Churches of his diocese; and Archbishop Rummel, through the Catholic Committee of the South, preached about the immorality of segregation. Perhaps the most effective churchman in this regard was the late Father LaFarge, who founded the Catholic interracial Councils in various cities.[31]

It is probably true that the hierarchal structure of the Catholic Church, with its emphasis on episcopal authority in the realm of faith and morals, has an advantage in imposing integration "from above."[32] The threat of excommunication, though seldom employed, is also an effective instrument.[33] Perhaps of more importance is the fact that the typical urban parish tends to be a large, secondary association in which most parishioners are not expected to have the close social bonds of fellowship that one finds in Protestant congregations. In spite of the recent liturgical drive for communal awareness, the typical Catholic still tends to focus his attention on the altar more than on his fellow parishioners.[34]

In spite of the common religious commitment to the moral value of interracial brotherhood, there is an important difference between the *gemeinschaftlich* and the *gesellschaftlich* structure of a church congregation. This is roughly similar to the associational type of industrial labor union, which has indeed had greater success in assimilating Negro workers than has the more close-knit, primary, exclusive type of craft union. The "higher law" principle of human relations should be operative in both types, but internal, local, structural integration can be better achieved where there is more stress on the worship of God and less on the fellowship of human beings.

II

The ability of a religious denomination or local congregation to integrate its own membership is not the same as its capacity to influence race relations in the surrounding community. In this instance it appears that success in creating cooperation across racial lines, as it has been across creedal lines, is greatest when the moral issues are clearest and when the personal contacts are informal. There is a lesson here in the ecumenical experiences of the last decade. Ancient concepts of better or worse, of inferior or superior, had to be put aside. Respect for the dignity and worth of individuals of another religious persuasion underlay the whole approach to ecumenism. Taking the larger picture of the American society, we may ask in what ways religious bodies have affected the structure of race relations outside their own organizations. First, it must be mentioned that some of the most virulent propagandists for the preservation of racial segregation are fundamentalist preachers, that some Southern ministers have been members of the Ku Klux Klan, and that clergymen sometimes lend respectability to White Citizens' Councils by offering a prayer at their meetings.[35] These are, of course, a small and diminishing minority when compared to the vast number of American clergymen who stand in opposition to racial discrimination.

Since the end of the Second World War there has been an enormous increase in religious preachment about better race relations.

One of the most widely publicized examples of this was "An Appeal to the Conscience of the American People," adopted at the close of the National Conference on Religion and Race in Chicago in 1963, in which more than seventy organizations representing the major religious denominations participated.[36] This appeal sought a reign of justice, love, courage, and prayer in the area of American race relations; and the closing plenary session accepted sixty-two practical program suggestions dealing with almost every conceivable aspect of the racial situation.[37] Subsequently, local councils on religion and race have been established throughout the country, including the deep South.

The day is long past when the pulpit was used to expound theological and Biblical arguments in favor of racial segregation. Only the racist extremists are attempting to revive these discredited arguments.[38] In fact, a flood of arguments favoring racial integration has come from the main religious representatives of the National Council of Churches, the National Catholic Welfare Conference, and the Synagogue Council of America. Perhaps no group has been so energetic in promoting the religious basis for civil rights and racial integration as the Anti-Defamation League of B'nai B'rith. Since there are very few Negro Jews, the temples and synagogues are not faced with the problem of integrating their congregations, but Jewish leaders have been very active in promoting better race relations.[39]

The great practical impact of the moral pronouncements of religious leaders about racial integration stems in part from the fact that they are so completely in accord with the democratic values of the American culture. Religious and political motivations are mutually supportive—the politician can use scripture to confirm constitutional arguments, and the religious spokesman can use the principles of democracy to confirm the need for brotherhood under God.[40] From a sociological point of view, one may debate, and perhaps never settle, whether in American society religion simply reflects the culture or whether cultural patterns are largely the consequence of religious values. The case of the Southeastern region must be considered in this regard since in the matter of racial beliefs and practices the regional differences are greater than the differences among the major religious denominations.

Compared to other sections of the nation, the Southeast was least influenced by the rational and religious reforms of the last century and by the social gospel movement at the beginning of this century.[41] In his most recent book, James Dabbs charges white Southern Protestants with failure. "The South tried to live, on the one hand, by a highly social culture, on the other by a highly individualistic religion. The culture did not support the religion, the religion did not support the culture."[42] In spite of its high rate of church affiliation and attendance at religious services, the white Southeast is still generally reluctant to accept the modern American and religious interpretation of civil rights and race relations.

In spite of Will Herberg's protestation that an American "culture religion" is developing and President Johnson's assertions that race relations constitute a "national problem," the issue is joined in the Southeastern states, and Negro Protestant clergymen now provide the most effective influence there. It is somewhat surprising, then, to find that the Negro clergy is under attack for refusing to participate in the civil rights struggle,[43] or to read that "neither religious ideology nor religious leaders were in any important way responsible for the increased restiveness and mood of protest among Negroes during the mid-1950's."[44] Negro ministers, and especially Martin Luther King, must be given credit for their role in developing the non-violent techniques of protest.

The significant contribution of Negro preachers and Negro churches toward the elimination of racial discrimination has sometimes been misunderstood. In his small, posthumous book, E. Franklin Frazier wrote that the Negro church was "the most important cultural institution created by Negroes," but that it was also "the most important institutional barrier to integration and the assimilation of Negroes." He speaks also of the few Negro individuals who have been "able to escape from the stifling domination of the church."[45] In his review of this book, Horace Cayton remarks that "Frazier did not live to witness the fervor of the continuing Negro rebellion and the position of leadership which the church and churchmen are taking in it. Perhaps, if he had, his final judgment on the importance and resilience of the Negro church might have been tempered."[46]

If religious organizations were not segregated, probably no other form of American organization would be segregated, and there would be no need for a springboard like the Negro churches from which an attack could be mounted against other forms of institutional segregation and discrimination. It seems true to say that, on the American scene, racial integration is resisted most in groups where the membership is voluntary, where the organizational status is private (that is, non-governmental), and where the relationships are personal and primary. These characteristics are present, at least conceptually, in the typical religious congregation, which is deliberately exempted from anti-segregation legislation and from official public pressure.

They are present too in the Negro church, and it seems symptomatic of their interpretation of different types of institutions that Negroes are more interested in integrating schools (70 per cent) than in going to church with whites (52 per cent).[47] Furthermore, the segregated congregation is a concomitant—if not always a consequence—of other social phenomena. For example, the cultural taboo against interracial marriage and the hard facts of residential segregation work against the kind of association that is ideally expected among members of the same religious congregation. The existence of integrated religious organizations would be a demonstration that these factors had been minimized, and that non-church types of segregation had decreased.

The organized church, the "most important Negro cultural institution," has provided continued protest against all forms of racial injustice and discrimination. The most famous slave insurrections were led by Negro preachers, Gabriel Prosser in 1800, Denmark Vesey in 1822, Nat Turner in 1831. Speaking from a historical perspective, Liston Pope has said that "the mounting spirit of revolt among Negroes, often robed in biblical teachings on release from bondage, revealed most especially in insurrections and revolts in the period between 1800 and 1831, was also related to the creation of separate Negro denominations."[48]

Anyone who has been observing developments on the racial front since the 1955 Montgomery bus boycott need not be reminded that "Negro ministers constitute the largest segment of the leadership class." Obviously, as Thompson points out, the clergy must spend most of his time on pastoral duties. This is their primary professional function. Nevertheless, "there are a few prominent Negro ministers who can always be found in the vanguard of the Negro's march toward full participation in community affairs. These ministers are generally well-trained, articulate and courageous. Their churches are made available for mass meetings, forums, and other types of programs designed to acquaint the Negro masses with major social issues facing them."[49]

It must be remembered, too, that white clergymen, Christian and Jewish, also have a primary obligation to pastoral duties and that one cannot expect the majority of them to be involved mainly in action programs for civil rights. Anyone who has participated in Southern demonstrations, marches, and other civil rights programs has heard the cry of white segregationists that preachers should stay in their pulpits and not "meddle" in these affairs. In fact, the three bishops of Alabama, Catholic, Episcopal, and Methodist, said as much about non-Southern clergymen (and Sisters) who participated in the Selma-Montgomery demonstrations of 1965. They felt that these "outsiders" should stay home and "clean up their own backyard."

It may be argued that neither churches nor churchmen should be "used" as an instrument to promote "extraneous" purposes. Major institutions, economic, political, and educational, are said to function well in the American culture because the means they employ are focused exclusively on definite objectives. This is only relatively true, however, because all cultural institutions intermesh in daily life and affect each other's means and ends—a fact which is becoming increasingly evident. Only those who argue for "complete" separation of the religious and political institutions, Church and State, continue to be blind to the fact that neither can divorce itself "completely" from the other.

The Negro clergyman typically does not "mind his own business" in the restricted sense of remaining apart from the large social problems of his people, while the white clergyman, priest, or rabbi, in his segregated church or synagogue, often stays aloof from the larger social problems of the day. This contrast is sharpened when we realize that racial segregation has been forced upon Negro churches, has been instituted and perpetuated by white churches.[50] It requires a special effort by white clergymen to look outside their own groups and to recognize the areas of discrimination and injustice in the larger community. The importance of the Protestant "witness" as a servant church to the society has been the theme of the writing of Gibson Winter and Peter Berger in recent years.[51]

If white clergymen maintain a personal, individual philosophy of religious behavior, they are likely to withdraw completely from the area of civic behavior or even, as some have done, oppose their colleagues who are socially concerned. If they are aware of the social problems of their communities, they may limit themselves to the level of preaching and prayer or may operate at the level of action and involvement. Since the end of the Second World War there has been a continuous increase in the number of ministers, priests, and rabbis who preach and pray about race relations, and an even more rapid growth in the number who have involved themselves in action programs.

Clergymen were instrumental in changing California's laws on miscegenation and in desegregating their own high schools, colleges, and seminaries; they participated in the Freedom Rides, in demonstrations and sit-ins all over the South, in the march on Washington, and in the march on Montgomery. The sympathy marches that occurred all over the country following the murder of Reverend James Reeb and of Mrs. Viola Liuzzo were often promoted and always participated in by clergymen. The reluctance and reticence noted by Thomas Pettigrew among the ministers of Little Rock have since been far outbalanced by the vocal and physical presence of clergymen in the struggle for racial justice.[52]

When discussing the march on Washington in 1963, James Reston felt that moral reaction would have to precede political reaction. "This whole movement for equality in American life will have to return to first principles before it will 'overcome' anything."[53] This is the familiar argument, used by moralists and clergymen and by some psychologists, that there must be a "change of heart" and reformed attitudes among the people before we can expect law and customs to improve. There is no doubt that genuine spiritual conversion has a marked effect on the external behavior of the convert; thus the more converts there are to love and brotherhood, the more quickly will America rid itself of racial discrimination.

The march on Washington in 1963 was indeed followed by continued interest and action by organized religious bodies, and was followed also by the Civil Rights Law of 1964. One cannot prove a causal sequence here—the political action perhaps would have occurred without the intervening religious action. A clearer sequence is seen in the active religious leadership of the march on Montgomery in 1965, which was followed immediately by President Johnson's proposal for a voting rights law.[54] In this instance there can be no doubt that the "call to conscience" made by the moral and religious leaders of America led to practical results.

The involvement of organized religion in the race problems of Americia has sharpened the recognition of the logical connection between prayer, study, and personal virtue, on the one hand, and action, cooperation, and social virtue, on the other. These are mutually reinforcing elements in the whole complex approach to a better human relationship between the races. College students concerned with religion have shifted "from study-involvement to involvement-study," as Paul Zietlow has remarked.[55] They started the sit-ins in 1960, initiated demonstrations in Birmingham, Jackson, Greensboro, Nashville, and other places in 1963, and participated in marches wherever they have occurred. A National Student Leadership Conference on Religion and Race also had ecumenical overtones in the cooperation of the B'nai B'rith Hillel Foundations, National Club Foundation, National Federation of Catholic College Students, and the National Student Christian Federation.

While trying to ameliorate present conditions of discrimination, Negroes are probably more interested today in the removal of unjust external racial practices than they are in the growth of love and kindness in the hearts of prejudiced people. There is ample evidence that white attitudes toward racial integration have improved in accompaniment to the legal and actual removal of racial barriers.[56] This has occurred even though we cannot make a universal application of this principle. "It is certainly true," wrote Gordon Allport in 1964, "that prejudiced attitudes do not always lead to prejudiced behavior. It is equally true that a person with equalitarian attitudes may engage in unjust discrimination, especially if he lives in South Africa or in Mississippi."[57]

III

Cultural change has affected religious people and religious institutions, as it has other areas of American life, and it has been so rapid that any precise forecast of combined religious and racial trends would be senseless. Who could have foreseen the effective impact of religious people and organizations on Washington officialdom before the 1960's? To go back further, who could have foreseen that the conservative religious forces which influenced Southern state legislatures even to the extent of textbook censorship, which urged the Congress to pass the Volstead Act, which intervened so strongly in the 1928 presidential campaign, would now have lost most of their influence?

Organized religion has had, and should have, a conservative and preservative role in the larger society, but in too many instances this role seems to function in a negative and reactionary fashion. What has come to the fore in the civil rights movement is the prophetic, creative, and positive role of religion, which has long been recognized almost exclusively in the area of personal piety and family morality. That the church has also a positive social function in the larger society has not always been clearly understood, perhaps because the society is much more morally complex than the individual human being. To be against sin, personal and social, is only one aspect of genuine religiosity. To be for virtue, personal and social, is a morally inalienable imperative of the church and its members.

Change and development have not led to an abandonment of the "old time" religion, or of the eternal truths, as some rigid racists would claim. We have not diluted or repudiated genuine religious truths, principles, and values. We have reviewed them in light of new knowledge about psychological and sociological phenomena. This creative social revolution, which churchmen now sponsor so vigorously, implies an expansion and fulfillment of divine precepts of behavior which we have always struggled to understand in an imperfect and human way.

Why are churchmen so deeply involved in the civil rights movement, and why are they impelled to continue this mission to the larger society? The principal motivation must always be that this is the right and moral thing to do. Store owners and factory managers may say that improved race relations are good for the economy. Mayors and governors may say that the racial solution must be found for the sake of peace and order in the community. National leaders may worry about the "world image" of American democracy that must offset Communist rivalries and meet the expectations of emerging nations. The religionist can certainly approve all of these reasons, but his most impelling motive is that the virtues of love and justice demand the removal of racism and all of its discriminatory effects and practices.

Aside from interim strategies and long-range programs, which may require the technical knowledge of social scientists more than the theological knowledge of churchmen, the church has had its greatest effect in the current drive for Negro freedom precisely because Americans are willing to listen to the moral argument. Whatever one may think of Myrdal's analysis of the American race problem, it is significant that he recognized the moral dilemma of the white man's conscience. As James Weldon Johnson has said, the solution of the race problem involves the salvation of the white man's soul and of the black man's body.[58] If the ordinary American has an uneasy conscience about the American record on race relations, he ought to be able to turn to his religion, the "keeper" of his conscience, for the grace and strength to do the right thing.

The much-discussed "failure" of church members and clergymen, of organized Protestants, Catholics, and Jews, has been so widely publicized that it has evoked wide-spread contrition. The current movement toward rectification of this failure and toward positive implementation of moral principles is basically a religious movement. It is probably true to say that the postwar American experience of race relations has been a major catalyst for both the organizational and doctrinal perspectives of American religion. The self-analysis that has been forced upon religious-minded individuals, and upon the religious bodies to which they belong, has certainly clarified the American moral dilemma of race. Quite aside from these speculative considerations, this test of America's religious ideology has resulted in pragmatic decisions to reconstitute congregational membership; it has resulted, perhaps more significantly, in the deliberate moral impact of religious leaders on the extra-church institutions of the American culture.

REFERENCES

1. Anson Phelps Stokes *et al.*, *Negro Status and Race Relations in the United States* (New York, 1948), p. 50.

2. David Moberg, *The Church as a Social Institution* (Englewood Cliffs, N. J., 1962), p. 453.

3. Liston Pope, *The Kingdom Beyond Caste* (New York, 1957), p. 105.

4. Edwin R. Embree, *Brown America* (New York, 1931), pp. 208–209.

5. It is Myrdal's theory that the Church changes with the community. "Few Christian Churches have ever been, whether in America or elsewhere, the spearheads of reform." Gunnar Myrdal, *An American Dilemma* (New York, 1944), p. 877.

6. C. Vann Woodward, *The Strange Career of Jim Crow* (New York, 1955), has demonstrated that formal segregation of the races is a much more recent phenomenon than many people realized, especially in the Southeast.

7. See C. Eric Lincoln, *The Black Muslims in America* (Boston, 1961); and E. U. Essien-Udom, *Black Nationalism* (Chicago, 1962).

8. C. Eric Lincoln, *op. cit.*, p. 53.

9. Edmund D. Cronon, *Black Moses: The Story of Marcus Garvey and the Universal Negro Improvement Association* (Madison, Wis., 1955).

10. For an analysis of various Negro religious cults, see Arthur H. Fauset, *Black Gods of the Metropolis* (Philadelphia, 1954).

11. See the views of Benton Johnson, "Do Holiness Sects Socialize in Dominant Values?" *Social Forces,* Vol. 39 (May 1961), pp. 309–316. James Baldwin came out of this kind of religious environment. He has repudiated this philosophy, but has not embraced the ideology of the Black Muslims.

12. See Frank S. Loescher, *The Protestant Church and the Negro: A Pattern of Segregation* (New York, 1948).

13. Dwight W. Culver, *Negro Segregation in the Methodist Church* (New Haven, Conn., 1953).

14. Lyle E. Schaller, *Planning for Protestantism in Urban America* (New York, 1965), p. 188.

15. Myrdal, *op. cit.*, p. 861.

16. *Ibid.*, p. 862.

17. Charles S. Johnson, *Growing Up in the Black Belt* (Washington, D. C., 1941), pp. 135–136. See also the more recent analysis of Joseph R. Washington, "Are American Negro Churches Christian?" *Theology Today* (April 1963), pp. 76–86.

18. See Martin Luther King, *Stride Toward Freedom* (New York, 1958). "The non-violent movement in America has come not from secular forces but from the heart of the Negro church. This movement has done a great deal to revitalize the Negro church and to give its message a relevant and authentic ring." King, p. 165, in Mathew Ahmann (ed.), *Race: Challenge to Religion* (Chicago, 1963).

19. Norval Glenn, "Negro Religion and Negro Status in the United States," in Louis Schneider (ed.), *Religion, Culture and Society* (New York, 1964), pp. 623–638, argues as though the Negro preachers were only reluctantly drawn into the civil rights struggle. "The middle-class ministers of the city could hardly have avoided involvement in the boycott: King and several of the others organized and led it." (p. 633) Yet, nearly half (47 per cent) of the Negroes told the *Newsweek* poll that their ministers are "helping a lot." See William Brink and Louis Harris, *The Negro Revolution in America* (New York, 1963), Ch. 6, "The Role of the Negro Church," and the tables on pp. 220–223.

20. See James W. Vander Zanden, "The Non-Violent Resistance Movement Against Segregation," *American Journal of Sociology,* Vol. 68 (March 1963), pp. 544–550.

21. Reported in *The New York Times,* April 28, 1960. For the attitudes of Southern Methodist laymen on racial segregation, see Stotts and Deats, *Methodism and Society: Guidelines for Strategy* (Nashville, Tenn., 1959), Vol. 4, Appendix A.

22. See David M. Reimers, "The Race Problem and Presbyterian Union,"

Church History (June 1962), pp. 203–215; and also John L. Bell, "The Presbyterian Church and the Negro in North Carolina," *North Carolina Historical Review* (January 1963), pp. 15–36.

23. See the summary on the Protestant Churches by W. Seward Salisbury, *Religion in American Culture* (Homewood, Ill., 1964), pp. 472–475. See also the penetrating analysis by Thomas F. Pettigrew, "Wherein the Church Has Failed in Race," *Religious Education*, Vol. 59, No. 1 (January-February 1964), pp. 64–73; and Walter B. Posey, "The Protestant Episcopal Church; An American Adaptation," *Journal of Southern History* (February 1959), pp. 3–30.

24. For examples at the local church level see Robert W. Root, *Progress Against Prejudice* (New York, 1957).

25. Reported by Grover C. Bagby in Galen R. Weaver (ed.), *Religion's Role in Racial Crisis* (New York, 1964), p. 16.

26. *Ibid.*, p. 16; see also the research report by Henry Clark, "Churchmen and Residential Desegregation," *Review of Religious Research*, Vol. 5, No. 3 (Spring 1964), pp. 157–164.

27. The difficulty of getting inter-denominational consensus on the race question seems to reflect the lack of moral and doctrinal consensus among the Protestant denominations. See Kyle Haselden, *The Racial Problem in Christian Perspective* (New York, 1964).

28. These reasons are discussed by Lyle E. Schaller, *op. cit.*, pp. 187–190. He considers residential segregation an "excuse," but not a reason for the perpetuation of racial segregation in churches. See also the earlier article by Samuel S. Hill, "Southern Protestantism and Racial Integration," *Religion in Life*, Vol. 33, No. 3 (Summer 1964), pp. 421–429, where he discusses similar "factors" as operative in the South.

29. Myrdal, *op. cit.*, pp. 870, 1411. In the *Newsweek* poll, more Negroes (58 per cent) think that "Catholic priests" are helpful to the cause than say this about "white churches" (24 per cent). Brink and Harris, *op. cit.*, pp. 133, 233.

30. Joseph H. Fichter, "The Catholic South and Race," *Religious Education*, Vol. 59, No. 1 (January-February 1964), pp. 30–33; also Joseph H. Fichter and George L. Maddox, "Religion in the South, Old and New," in John McKinney and Edgar Thompson (eds.), *The South in Continuity and Change* (Durham, N. C., 1965).

31. John LaFarge, "Caste in the Church: The Roman Catholic Experience," *Survey Graphic*, Vol. 36 (January 1947), pp. 61 ff., 104–106; also *The Catholic Viewpoint on Race Relations* (Garden City, N. Y., 1960).

32. Liston Pope, *op. cit.*, p. 140, feels that this is "in line with the findings of social scientists in the last few years as the most effective means of achieving desegregation and the diminution of prejudice."

33. The excommunication of three Louisiana Catholics by Archbishop Rummel

did not seem to diminish their racist activities in the White Citizens' Council, although it probably acted as a deterrent to others.

34. The difference between "objective and subjective worship" of Catholicism and Protestantism was analyzed by James B. Pratt, *The Religious Consciousness* (New York, 1920), pp. 290–309, reprinted in Schneider, *op. cit.*, pp. 143–156. The way in which this applies to race relations among Catholics is indicated by Elizabeth M. Eddy, "Student Perspectives on the Southern Church," *Phylon*, Vol. 25, No. 4 (Winter 1964), pp. 369–381.

35. There seems to be a "pattern" in clergymen's attitudes. "The small-sect minister is typically segregationist and vocal, whereas the denomination minister is typically integrationist and silent." Ernest Q. Campbell, "Moral Discomfort and Racial Segregation—An Examination of the Myrdal Hypothesis," *Social Forces* (March 1961), p. 229.

36. Mathew Ahmann (ed.), *Race, Challenge to Religion* (Chicago, 1963), pp. 171–173, contains the original essays of the prominent speakers at the Conference.

37. Galen R. Weaver (ed.), *Religion's Role in Racial Conflict* (New York, 1963), Ch. 7, "Programmatic Recommendations."

38. The propaganda of the White Citizens' Councils in several Southeastern States abounds with these "Biblical proofs" that God was the First Segregationist, and with charges that integrationists, especially white clergymen, are the dupes of atheistic Communism. What Negroes think of Communism is shown in the fact that about the same minority (6 per cent) approve of the Black Muslim movement as believe (5 per cent) the Communist claim of no discrimination under their system. Brink and Harris, *op. cit.*, pp. 201, 225.

39. See, for example, the speeches of Rabbi Morris Adler, Dr. Julius Mark, and Dr. Abraham J. Heschel, in Mathew Ahmann (ed.), *op. cit.*, at the National Conference on Race and Religion.

40. For a few examples of this trend see William S. Nelson (ed.), *The Christian Way in Race Relations* (New York, 1948); Will Campbell, *Race and Renewal of the Church* (Philadelphia, 1962); and Benjamin E. Mays, *Seeking to be a Christian in Race Relations* (New York, n.d.).

41. See Kenneth K. Bailey, *Southern White Protestantism in the Twentieth Century* (New York, 1964); also James Sellers, *The South and Christian Ethics* (New York, 1962); and Robert M. Miller, *American Protestantism and Social Issues,* (Chapel Hill, N. C., 1958).

42. James McBride Dabbs, *Who Speaks for the South?* (New York, 1965). That the Southerner, even in his religion, is not just another American, was also held by W. J. Cash, *The Mind of the South* (1940), C. Vann Woodward, *The Burden of Southern History* (1960), and Francis B. Simkins, *The Everlasting South* (1963). Others have seen the Southerner as American, for example, Harry Ashmore, *An Epitaph for Dixie* (1957), Charles Sellers, *The Southerner as American* (1960), Thomas D. Clark,

The Emerging South (1961), and Howard Zinn, *The Southern Mystique* (1964).

43. This is the contention of Simeon Booker, *Black Man's America* (Englewood Cliffs, N. J., 1964).

44. See Norval Glenn, *op. cit.*, p. 632; also James W. Vander Zanden, "The Non-Violent Resistance Movement against Segregation," *American Journal of Sociology*, Vol. 68 (March 1963), pp. 544–550.

45. E. Franklin Frazier, *The Negro Church in America* (New York, 1963), pp. 70, 86.

46. Horace Cayton, "E. Franklin Frazier: A Tribute and a Review," *Review of Religious Research*, Vol. 5, No. 3 (Spring 1964), pp. 137–142 (p. 141).

47. Brink and Harris, *op. cit.*, pp. 223, 236.

48. Liston Pope, "The Negro and Religion in America," *Review of Religious Research*, Vol. 5, No. 3 (Spring 1964), pp. 142–152 (p. 144). He adds that "the Negro ministry is on the ascendancy in the eyes of all Americans." (p. 147). In the same issue of the *Review*, Walter Muelder, "Recruitment of Negroes for Theological Studies," pp. 152–156, says that "the ministry, once the chief outlet for Negro ambition, is declining significantly in relative importance among professionals. It should be noted that Negro enrollments in medicine and law have also been dropping." (p. 155).

49. Daniel C. Thompson, *The Negro Leadership Class* (Englewood Cliffs, N. J., 1963), p. 36.

50. The oft-repeated expression of white Southerners that "Negroes prefer to be by themselves" has validity only if it means that they prefer this to unjust and discriminatory treatment in churches, schools, parks, buses, restaurants, and elsewhere.

51. See Gibson Winter, *The Suburban Captivity of the Churches* (New York, 1962) and *The New Creation as Metropolis* (1963); and Peter Berger, *The Noise of Solemn Assemblies* (1961) and *The Precarious Vision* (1963).

52. Ernest Q. Campbell and Thomas Pettigrew, *Christians in Racial Crisis* (Washington, D. C., 1959), and their article, "Racial and Moral Crisis: The Role of Little Rock Ministers," *American Journal of Sociology*, Vol. 64 (March 1959), pp. 509–516.

53. James Reston, "The Churches, the Synagogues, and the March on Washington," *Religious Education*, Vol. 59, No. 1 (January-February 1964), pp. 5 ff., reprinted from *The New York Times*, August 30, 1963.

54. It may be argued that the shocking brutality, official and unofficial, of the die-hard segregationists in Alabama was the main galvanizing force for reform.

55. Carl P. Zietlow, "Race, Students, and Non-Violence," *Religious Education*, Vol. 59, No. 1 (January-February 1964), pp. 116–120.

56. See the study done for *Newsweek* by William Brink and Louis Harris, *The Negro Revolution in America* (New York, 1964); also the changes noted by Herbert Hyman and Paul Sheatsley, "How Whites View Negroes, 1942–1963," *New York Herald Tribune,* November 19, 1963; and "Attitudes Toward Desegregation—Seven Years Later," *Scientific American,* Vol. 211, No. 1 (July 1964).

57. Gordon W. Allport, "Prejudice: Is it Societal or Personal?" *Religious Education,* Vol. 59, No. 1 (January-February 1964), pp. 20–29.

58. James Weldon Johnson, *Along This Way* (New York, 1933), p. 318, quoted by Myrdal, *op. cit.,* p. 43.

JAMES Q. WILSON

The Negro in Politics

PERHAPS THE best way to understand the political position of the
American Negro today is to compare what some Negroes are asking of politics with what politics seems capable of providing. I mean
here politics in the narrower sense—the competitive struggle for
elective office and deliberate attempts to influence the substance of
government decisions—and not, in the broadest sense, as any activity by which conflict over goals is carried on. Although something is sacrificed by limiting the definition (rent strikes, boycotts,
and sit-ins may have consequences for office-holders and legislation), the sacrifice is necessary if we are to understand what is
meant by the statement that the civil rights movement, and Negro
protest generally, ought to become a *political* movement. Bayard
Rustin, in a recent issue of *Commentary*, has put the argument in
its most succinct and lucid form in an article significantly entitled,
"From Protest to Politics: The Future of the Civil Rights Movement."[1] Briefly, Rustin argues that the problems of the Negro cannot be solved by granting him even the fullest civil rights, for it is
his fundamental social and economic conditions, more than his legal
privileges, which must be changed. Such changes, in the magni-
tudes necessary, require radical—indeed, revolutionary—programs
in education, housing, and income redistribution; these programs,
in turn, will be attained only by an organized radical political coalition of Negroes, trade unions, church groups, and white liberals.

Those who remember the political currents of the 1930's may
smile wanly at the call today for a Negro-labor alliance. When the
call was issued thirty years ago, few responded. In the South, the
Negro was almost entirely disfranchised; in the North, he was po-

423

litically unorganized except by a few (largely Republican) big-city machines. Everywhere, Negroes—including the miniscule leadership class—were effectively excluded from almost all the institutions of American life. Negroes had nothing and attempted little. It was probably fortunate for A. Phillip Randolph that he was not required to deliver on his threat of a massive march on Washington in 1941. In their most charitable mood, even the more radical trade union leaders saw Negroes as a group which could produce (perhaps worthy) demands but not votes or money or influence; less generously, they viewed Negroes as scabs and strike-breakers.

Apparently, enough has changed since to suggest that a reappraisal may be in order. The Negro electorate has grown greatly in both North and South. It is estimated (no one knows) that as many as six million Negroes were registered in 1964, about a third of whom were in the South. In most of the large cities where these voters are to be found, there is no political machine; in the typical case, leadership is competitive, uncontrolled, sometimes demagogic but just as often responsible, and to an increasing extent aggressive. A massive and impressive march on Washington has occurred. The proliferation and vigor of civil rights organizations suggest that expectations are rising more rapidly than achievements; the national leaders of these groups have become *the* spokesmen of the American Negro, virtually eclipsing elective officials. Among these men, all shades of radical (as well as moderate) opinion can be found, accompanied, as one might expect, by a passionate concern for distinguishing subtle (and sometimes vague) sectarian differences. And in 1964, the Negroes gave President Johnson an unprecedented 94 per cent of their vote (according to an estimate by the Gallup Poll). Perhaps these changes are sufficient to make the Negroes ready for an effective and liberal coalition.

While there is little doubt that Negro voters will continue to exert a liberalizing influence on American politics, the possibility of a stable, organized liberal—to say nothing of radical—coalition is, I believe, slight. Furthermore, attempts to fashion one may be dangerous unless it is a very loose and *ad hoc* arrangement. The Negro is already a partner in a set of tacit, though unorganized, coalitions; they are probably the only viable ones but they are certainly not radical ones. To break existing alliances, tenuous though they are, in favor of a new alliance which may be impossible of realization may be a costly experiment. This is particularly true in the South; it is to a lesser extent true in the North.

I. *The Negro Voter in the South*

A useful oversimplification is that, in the South, the enemy of the Negro is the lower- and lower-middle-class, particularly rural, white, and the ally of the Negro is the upper-middle-class, particularly urban, white. Since Reconstruction, the Bourbons and the Populists have engaged in intermittent political warfare; occasionally the Negro has been used—particularly in the last two decades of the nineteenth century—as an ally of one white class against the other, while at other times—particularly in the first half of the twentieth century—he has been disfranchised in order to prevent him from being allied with either class. The political suppression of the Negro did not, as C. Vann Woodward makes clear, occur immediately after the withdrawal of Union troops but only after the white community, divided along class lines, discovered that the competitive wooing of Negro votes created a politically unstable situation best resolved by eliminating the Negro vote—and thus the Republican party—and bringing the white majority into the dominant Democratic party.[2]

But the Negro is no longer disfranchised, except in Black Belt counties; probably one-third of the potential Negro vote has been registered, and more gains can be anticipated. Negroes of voting age constitute one-fifth of the adult population of the eleven Southern states but less than one-twelfth of the registered Southern voters. If another 570,000 Negroes can be added to registration rolls now estimated to contain nearly two million Negroes, half the potential Negro voters will be eligible. In those areas where the Negro vote is already significant, the politics of a "Second Reconstruction" seem to be emerging—with the important difference that the Negro may no longer be disfranchised if competition for his vote proves unsettling.

Negroes, when they vote, can cause a startling change in the style, if not the substance, of Southern politics. Segregationists will have to choose between abandoning race-baiting as a political tactic or getting out of politics. (The prospect of large numbers of politicians quitting politics—especially in the South, where politicians are shrewd and politics is a way of life—seems, to say the least, remote.) And politicians who are by nature inclined to entertain sympathetically legitimate Negro demands will be encouraged to entertain them publicly. For example, Rep. Charles L. Weltner, Democrat of Georgia, voted against the 1964 Civil Rights Act when it first came before the House in February, 1964. By July, however, when the bill came back from the conference committee for final passage, he had changed his mind and voted in favor of it. It does not detract from the moral quality of Weltner's bold action to note that between the two crucial votes the governor of Georgia signed into law a bill to redistrict the state's congressional seats in a manner that substantially increased the proportion of enfranchised Negroes and decreased the proportion of lower-middle-class whites in Weltner's district.[3]

In the past, at least, neither political party could take the Southern Negro vote for granted. A majority of their votes twice went to Dwight Eisenhower and frequently were cast for Republican candidates in such cities as Atlanta and Louisville. In 1960, many—though not all—Southern Negro precincts voted for President Kennedy; in 1964, almost all of them supported President Johnson.

The independence—which, to the politician, can mean only uncertainty—of the Southern Negro vote has various causes. One, of course, is that the Southern Democratic party has so conspicuously been the enemy, its candidates in all but a few cases outbidding each other in defending segregation. Another is that the issue confronting the Southern Negro in many elections is clear and dramatic: which white candidate scores lowest on the segregation scale, this being, for the Negro, the only important scale. Unstable politics is here the result of single-issue politics. A third reason is that potential Negro political leaders, being largely excluded from an active role in both the majority party and the increasingly "lily-white" Republican minority party, have not been co-opted by the system. Negro politicians, without permanent organizational commitments to white leaders, have been free to deliver Negro votes to whichever candidate or party seemed most attractive in each election. Where the Negro leader was corrupt, he delivered the vote in exchange for tangible considerations;[4] where honest, in exchange for intangible concessions.[5] Negro politics in the South has yet to be professionalized, and thus the distinction—commonplace in the North—between the (usually moderate) party hierarchy and the (often militant) civic and "race" leadership has not become widespread.

To say that the Southern Negro political leadership is unprofessional does not mean that it is either unskillful or unsuccessful. In those cities or counties where the Negro voter is neither terrorized nor apathetic, he is capable of voting with almost incredible unanimity and precision, at least for the most visible offices. When

Ivan Allen, Jr., ran against Lester Maddox in 1961 for mayor of Atlanta, Negro precinct 7-D gave Allen 2,003 votes, or 99.9 per cent of the total, and Maddox 4 votes. Since there were five white voters living in the precinct, it is quite likely that Allen got *all* of the Negro votes—an almost unbelievable feat of organization and communication, especially when one recalls that Allen was a wealthy white businessman who was scarcely an all-out integrationist.[6] The single-issue politics of the South has produced a form of political behavior among Negroes and whites which is highly rationalistic and extraordinarily sophisticated.[7] Voters become exceptionally sensitive to almost imperceptible differences in the positions candidates take, publicly or privately, on "The Issue" and go to considerable lengths to conceal group preferences lest premature revelation prove counterproductive.

In the South, more than anywhere else, a deliberate balance of power politics may be practiced in which viable coalitions may be formed. The most important and most successful example of this is what might be called the Atlanta Coalition. Formed in the 1950's by Mayor (now "Mayor Emeritus") William B. Hartsfield and continued by Mayor Ivan Allen, Jr., it is, stripped to its essentials, a tacit alliance between upper-middle-class whites and Negroes against lower-middle-class whites. In even blunter terms, the Bourbons and the Negroes have voted together to exclude the rednecks from power in the city. There are, of course, strains in the alliance. The more militant Negroes are restless with the leadership of the Atlanta Negro Voters' League and with what they regard as the insufficient progress in race relations under Hartsfield and Allen. White businessmen, in turn, often feel the mayor has gone too far, as when Allen testified before Congress in favor of the elimination of segregation in public accommodations. Furthermore, it is not clear that every Southern city could put together such a coalition even if it wanted to do so. Some cities have lost their Bourbons to the suburbs (Atlanta carefully annexes all upper-income suburbs and avoids annexing any working-class suburbs) while others have a business leadership that is composed of small shopkeepers rather than a commercial and industrial élite concerned with establishing the city as a great regional center.[8] And in some cities, such as New Orleans, the Negroes themselves have been unable to create a stable and effective political organization representative of all elements of the community.[9]

Whatever the limitations or difficulties, however, there can be little doubt that the natural ally of the Southern Negro, for the foreseeable future, is the cosmopolitan white bourgeoisie.[10] In part, this reflects self-interest: race conflict is bad for business, destructive of property, and productive of unfavorable national publicity. In part, it reflects an enlarged conception of the common interest: Negroes have a moral right to vote, to be free from arbitrary arrest, and to be protected from official abuse, even if century-old prejudices require that the Negro not live next door to whites. The issues now being pressed by the Negro in the South make the most fundamental claims of elementary justice; when the claims of simple justice are reinforced by self-interest, the potential for effective action is great. But this white ally has little interest in a massive redistribution of income, the nationalization of political authority, or the reordering of society.

In the Black Belt, where Negroes outnumber whites, such alliances are hard to create. In Mississippi, there seem to be no allies whatsoever. It is precisely in such areas that a more radical Negro politics is emerging, though it is still so apocalyptic in its vision and unrealistic in its methods that it can point to little progress. The Freedom Democratic party won a great victory at the Democratic National Convention in Atlantic City, but the radical leadership which now appears to influence it not only rejected that convention's seating compromise but seems intent on rejecting all compromises with what, to it, is an essentially corrupt and hypocritical society. Given the massive, unyielding, and violent nature of white resistance to Negro demands in many Black Belt counties, it is not hard to understand some of the attitudes of the increasingly radical Negro political leadership. Early and measured accommodation to Negro political demands has, in many Southern cities, led to the emergence of relatively moderate Negro leaders and of a Negro strategy emphasizing limited objectives. But the Black Belt has not, except in a few cases, made concessions—in part because Negroes there are in the majority and in part because such largely rural or small-town areas lack a white upper class of sufficient size and strength to challenge white extremists.

There are some Black Belt counties where Negroes can and do vote, but ironically the gains that have accrued to them from politics in these areas are less than the gains from politics in areas where Negroes are a minority but where social and economic conditions are more favorable to political organization, articulation of demands, and bargaining over changes in the welfare or status of Negroes. Where Negro voting has occurred in the Black Belt, it has meant (in general) the cessation of police abuse and administrative discrimination, the appointment of Negroes to certain government positions, and higher expenditures on public facilities in Negro neighborhoods.[11] It has rarely meant general integration of schools or public accommodations or new public works programs to improve Negro living conditions. The financial resources and community tolerance for such efforts simply do not exist. White voters do not even approve such projects for themselves. By contrast, in some of the highly urbanized areas where Negroes vote but are in a distinct minority, a combination of factors—the availability of tax resources, a well-organized white political structure with which bargains can be struck, and a large and self-sufficient Negro leadership class—makes it easier to translate votes into substantive gains.

All this suggests that the substantive, rather than psychological, consequences of Negro voting in Black Belt counties are not likely to be so great as the diehard white resistance might imply. The resistance itself, however, should it continue for long, may change this significantly. When the social, economic, and political demands of a group are linked with a protracted and bitter struggle for the franchise, the members of that group are more likely to acquire a permanent sense of political identity and a more intense commitment to the goals of the group than would be the case if substantive goals were asserted long after the franchise had been won. (One of the reasons—there are many—that no socialist or labor party developed among American workers may be that their major economic demands were made long after the franchise had been acquired without a struggle.)[12] The campaign for the vote now developing among Southern Negroes is likely to have profound effects on subsequent Negro political organization and tactics, for the campaign can generate morale, a sense of unity (the vote is a wholly instrumental objective that permits otherwise competing leaders to submerge their differences), and an independence from traditional party loyalties.

Discussion, in such states as Mississippi, of the possibility of a Negro political party suggests one alternative—in my judgment, a disastrous one—to the pattern of coalition politics now being practiced outside the Black Belt. For the Negro vote to be (potentially) the marginal vote, it is not enough that it be an uncommitted vote. Since Negroes in every Southern state are a minority (although in some states a very large one), it is also necessary that the white vote be divided. In such states as Georgia and North Carolina, the Negro vote can be the marginal vote—both because white votes are divided along party or factional lines and because the Negro vote is not an automatic expression of traditional party loyalties. Within the Black Belt, not only must the franchise be won for the Negro, but some way must be found of dividing the white vote. This is not the case in Mississippi, where in a clear choice Barry Goldwater defeated Lyndon Johnson by winning an incredible 87 per cent of the vote. In the table below, the present and potential Negro vote is shown for each Southern state. In the first column is the percentage of registered voters who, in 1964, were estimated (by the Voter Education Project) to be Negro; in the second column is the percentage of all voting-age persons who in 1960 were Negro. If *all* adults, Negro and white, voted, this last figure would be the "Negro vote." If every Negro in Mississippi had voted in 1964, Goldwater would still have won; in other states, the Negro's need for allies is even greater.

The Southern Negro Vote, Present and Potential

State	Percentage of all registered voters who are Negro (April, 1964)	Percentage of all voting-age persons who are Negro (1960)
Alabama	5.7%	26.2%
Arkansas	7.7	18.5
Florida	7.8	15.2
Georgia	9.9	25.4
Louisiana	9.0	28.5
Mississippi	2.4	36.0
North Carolina	9.7	21.5
South Carolina	10.5	30.6
Tennessee	10.1	15.0
Texas	6.8	11.7
Virginia	5.2	18.9
THE SOUTH	7.7	20.0

Dividing the white vote will not be easy under the best of circumstances, but it is not likely to be easier if Negro political strategists either elect to form a separate party or emphasize objectives which draw closer the white cosmopolitan élite and white lower-middle-class extremists. Continued Negro pressure, with federal assistance, for the franchise and for the observance of constitutional and legislative guarantees will ultimately divide the opposition;

broadening Negro demands at this time to include more radical objectives may unite it. This may be an expression of the willingness on the part of the bourgeoisie to support demands for *liberty* (the franchise, legal justice, and equal access to public facilities) but to oppose demands for *equality* (the elimination of intergroup differences in income, occupation, and place of residence). Negro-white coalitions in the South, where they exist at all, are by and large libertarian rather than egalitarian in purpose.

The history of one such coalition—or rather sequence of coalitions—is illuminating. Described by Donald Matthews and James Prothro in their forthcoming book on Southern Negro politics, the events took place in a city which the authors call "Urbania."[13] A thriving commercial center in the Piedmont region, the city has a cosmopolitan white business élite as well as a strong Negro middle-class and a unionized industrial labor force. As early as 1935, a Negro political organization was formed (at a meeting held at the Negro Tennis Club!); by the 1940's, a coalition of Negroes with white liberals and union leaders had been formed that was strong enough to capture the county Democratic organization. The alliance, never a firm one, was successful as long as it had limited political objectives. After the 1954 Supreme Court school desegregation decision, however, strains developed. Because of the defection of white workers, the coalition lost control of the party by 1958; nonetheless —and this may be suggestive of the emerging pattern of Southern politics—the mayor remained sympathetic to the Negro demands and he and other city officials worked openly, before and after the tense months of the 1963-1964 protest demonstrations, to integrate public facilities and private businesses. This policy of accommodation apparently was in part the result of the attitude of the white business élite, part (but not all) of which was sufficiently cosmopolitan to favor whatever degree of integration was necessary to avoid a "bad business climate" or unfavorable national repercussions. It was not, on the other hand, in favor of the liberal economic policies of the early labor-Negro coalition. In Urbania, the Negroes found unionized white workers the appropriate allies when political power was the object; when progress on certain libertarian issues (here, school desegregation) was at stake, the labor alliance collapsed and the support of white businessmen became important.

Coalition politics is important not only because of the need for allies, but also because of the problem of motivating Negro voters. As a result of their low socio-economic position, getting Negroes to register and vote even after all administrative barriers have collapsed can be very difficult. (In 1959, Southern urban Negroes had a median income less than *half* that of Southern urban whites.) Surprisingly high voter participation can be obtained, however, when the contest is important *and the Negro vote may decide the outcome*. In the Allen-Maddox election in Atlanta, for example, 80 per cent of the registered voters in nine predominantly Negro precincts turned out to vote; by comparison, only 69 per cent of the registered voters in ten predominantly lower-income white precincts voted.[14] (Negroes participate less than whites in elections for offices less visible than mayor; they also register in slightly smaller proportions.) Although there is no direct evidence on this, it seems likely that the remarkably high Negro voter turnout in cities like Atlanta might be much lower if the candidate supported by Negroes had no chance of winning—as would be the case if he did not have the backing of a substantial block of white voters.

II. *The Negro Voter in the North*

It is in the North that politics as conventionally practiced seems less relevant to the needs of the Negro. This may appear paradoxical, given the great importance attached to the Northern urban Negro vote in influencing contests for President, governor, and senator. It is of course true that the Negro is concentrated in areas of high strategic significance for state-wide or national political candidates. The Negro vote for President Kennedy was, in several Northern industrial states, greater than the margin by which Kennedy carried those states. The same, however, can be said for the Jewish vote, the Catholic vote, and the labor vote. With so many apparently marginal votes cast, a President might be forgiven if he allowed himself to be paralyzed by the competing demands of their spokesmen. (For some time it appeared that President Kennedy was in exactly this position, but he responded to Negro protests which began in the spring of 1963 with a vigorous affirmation of the moral rights of Negroes—becoming not only the first President to have said this, but perhaps the first to have believed it.) In Congress, the Negro vote is likely to have a much greater long-run effect in the South than in the North. Over *half* of all Southern congressional districts in 1963 had a population that was one-fifth or more Negro. In the North and West, by contrast, fewer than one-twelfth of the districts had so high a proportion of Negroes.

Furthermore, the civil rights legislation so far enacted has been directed primarily at remedying discrimination against the Negro in the South—in voting, public accommodations, and the like. To the extent that Negro political influence in the North contributed to the passage of these bills, it was influence wielded on behalf of Southern Negroes and as part of a much larger liberal coalition in which religious organizations played an exceptionally important role.[15] Further legislative progress on behalf of Southern Negroes is still possible; the question, however, is what progress can be made on behalf of Northern Negroes and what political tactics should be used.

The utility of politics to the Northern Negro is limited for a variety of reasons. First, his traditional party loyalties are strong and thus his vote, particularly in general elections, is less likely to be uncertain. There are some obvious exceptions to this pattern, of course. In cities such as Boston, where party organization is almost nonexistent and where an attractive Negro candidate can be found in the Republican party, Negroes will cross party lines in very large numbers. (Edward Brooke, the Negro Republican Attorney General of Massachusetts, carried Negro precincts by margins of ten to one at the same time that Democrat Lyndon Johnson was carrying these precincts by margins of fifty to one.) In most of the largest Northern cities, however, the only question surrounding the Negro vote in partisan elections is its size rather than its direction.

Second, the major issues confronting the mass of Northern Negroes are economic and cultural rather than political or legal. Rustin is entirely correct in saying that "at issue, after all, is not *civil rights*, strictly speaking, but social and economic conditions."[16] The paradox is two-fold. On the one hand, American political institutions provide no way for the organized political pressure of a particular disadvantaged group to reshape in any fundamental sense social and economic conditions. Whereas the identity and political obligations of a sheriff or a governor can profoundly affect the lives of Negroes in the South by determining whether or how they will be intimidated or harassed, the election of a public official in the North rarely has any direct or obvious consequences for the average Negro voter. (It is *because* it makes so little difference, of course, that Northern party leaders have found it relatively easy to instill traditional party commitments in Negroes. A simple decision rule—such as "vote Democratic"—is more economical, for both the party and the voter, than the kind of elaborate and subtle group interest calculations that occur where, as in the South, the outcome *is* important.)

That is not to say that it makes no difference which party or faction controls the White House or Congress. The probability of there being certain kinds of redistributionist and welfare programs enacted does depend on election outcomes, but not in a way that makes it possible for any particular voting bloc to hold any particular public official responsible for such programs. Such considerations ought to be borne in mind when one evaluates assertions about the "alienation" of the urban voter, particularly the low-income Negro. That politics seems irrelevant to their daily preoccupations is not necessarily an expression of neurotic withdrawal or separateness but may well be the rational conclusion of a reasonably well-informed citizen.

The other paradoxical element is that, when major programs *are* launched to deal with basic social and economic conditions, they are likely to be the product of a political coalition in which the persons whose lives are to be changed play a relatively small role. The recent federal programs to deal with delinquency, poverty, and housing were assembled by bureaucrats, professors, and White House politicians. The most dramatic of these—the "war on poverty" —did not come about, as Daniel Patrick Moynihan makes clear, as the result of any great upsurge of popular demand.[17] Nor were these programs aimed explicitly at the "Negro problem." Indeed, it might have been much harder to get them adopted if they had been defined as "Negro programs." (In fact, some of these programs—particularly the antipoverty program—were in part intended by many of their supporters, probably including the President, to dampen the civil rights "revolution" by improving the material condition of Negroes.) At the local level, public expenditures for the benefit of the poor are often authorized in local referenda elections in which the civic leadership as well as a substantial portion of the votes comes from upper-class whites who join with lower-class Negroes to secure the adoption of measures which, if they were national rather than local matters, these whites would oppose.[18] Rich suburbanites will favor free medical care for the indigent if the issue is stated in terms of building a new county hospital and is voted on locally but not if the issue is called "socialized medicine" and is voted on in Washington.

All this suggests that the Negro is in need not of a single grand alliance, but of many different and often conflicting alliances which take into account the different bases of support available for different kinds of issues. Nationally, organized labor may support civil rights and income-transfer measures but locally it is often likely to support (at least tacitly) segregated housing and economy in government. Religious groups are very effective when the issue is voting rights; they are much less effective in dealing with economic questions where simple morality is not at issue. Upper-class businessmen may support Negro voting claims in Southern cities and Negro oriented public works programs in Northern cities, but nationally they will oppose large-scale income redistribution. A grand Negro-liberal coalition, if achieved, may so rationalize these inconsistent positions as to deliver the leadership of would-be allies into the hands of those elements who are least in favor of (or least effective on behalf of) Negro causes. Nowhere are these problems better seen than in the relationship between Negro and white workers in our major industrial cities.

While it may be true that Negroes and whites have a common interest in ending unemployment, improving housing and education, and resisting technological displacement, a stable and enduring alliance to attain these objectives will not be easily achieved. The only major political mechanism by which poor whites and Negroes have in the past been brought into alliance—the big-city machine—is collapsing; except for a few large industrial unions, no substitute has yet appeared.

Only Philadelphia and Chicago, of the larger Northern cities, have strong city-wide machines (that is, political parties based on the distribution of material rewards). In these areas, Negro and white political leaders are paid to work together, albeit for very limited objectives; Negro and white voters, in turn, are induced by door-to-door persuasion to vote together, particularly in primaries.[19] Such organizations cannot endure much longer, for the resources at their command are diminishing. When they collapse, Negro political leadership will fall into the hands of men who can find effective substitutes for organization: personal charisma and bellicose militancy (such as that of Adam Clayton Powell in New York or Cecil Moore in Philadelphia), expertise in factional manipulation and strategic alliances (such as that of J. Raymond Jones in New York), or successful appeals to middle-class white voters and white political leaders (such as that of Edward Brooke in Massachusetts or Augustus Hawkins in Los Angeles).[20] Yet to emerge, but certain to come, are Negro political leaders who will obtain their major support from the more militant civil rights organizations. In only a very few cases does there seem to be much likelihood of organized political coalition between white and Negro workers similar to that found from time to time in Detroit. The United Auto Workers, and to a lesser extent the United Steel Workers, have, through the political action of integrated locals, elected carefully balanced tickets of Negro and white politicians.

Even under UAW leadership, the Negro-white workers' coalition has been subject to tensions. The most important of these has been the necessity of emphasizing economic objectives that do not require social reorganization (such as integrated housing) close to home. The UAW cannot deliver votes of white workers for liberal mayors or those of Negro workers for conservative mayors without great difficulty. Furthermore, the coalition was created in a period of rising demand for workers; how it will function when Negroes and whites are competing for a decreasing number of jobs remains to be seen. (The fact that the locals are integrated and that an elaborate code of seniority rules has been devised may help reduce what might otherwise be a starkly racial conflict over jobs.) Finally, no one should allow himself the comfort of believing that President Johnson's massive victory over Barry Goldwater disproves the existence of strong anti-Negro sentiments among many white Northern Democratic voters. At most it suggests that, faced with a complex political decision involving issues of foreign relations, economic policy, and welfare programs as well as civil rights, the white worker decided that peace and security were, under the circumstances, more important than registering a protest against Negro claims.

The area in which this latent conflict between Negro claims and white resistance is most likely to erupt is that of public safety and administration of criminal justice. It is one of the few issues (schools are another) in the North over which a clear political contest can be waged. The police are highly sensitive to the explicit and implicit directives of local elective officials; unlike economic issues, a political victory here can have direct and immediate—although perhaps not drastic—consequences for Negroes. The white concern over "violence in the streets" and unchecked criminality is not (as critics of Goldwater charged) simply a rhetorical mask for opposition to civil rights demonstrations or even for anti-Negro sentiment (though it involves a significant element of this). Polls taken by both parties during the campaign suggest that Johnson was never able to meet this issue effectively; perhaps a majority of voters thought Goldwater was best able to handle this problem.[21] For the Negroes, the issue of "police brutality" and police corruption is probably the single most effective appeal for the mobilization of mass Negro protest activity, particularly among rank-and-file lower-income Negroes. Many middle-class Negroes will, of course, admit privately that they, too, would like to see the police check criminal behavior among lower-class Negroes, but it is becoming increasingly difficult for them to say this publicly.

What is remarkable is that so few candidates for mayor or governor are openly exploiting white fears of crime, particularly Negro crime. In part this is because too many of them must face Negro voters who would immediately interpret such views as anti-Negro prejudice even if, in fact, prejudice had nothing to do with it. And in part this is because there is a deep and general distrust of the police among upper-middle-class whites, particularly white liberals, such that it is often better politics to be "anti-cop" than "anti-Negro." On this issue, even more than on the issue of income redistribution, the natural Northern ally of the Negro is the white liberal.

It is, of course, fashionable today to attack the "white liberal" as hypocritical on civil rights issues. After all, he is likely to live in a "lily-white" suburb, attend a "lily-white" church, and perhaps teach in a university with no Negroes on its faculty. And the white liberal, in the eyes of Negro radicals, makes the fatal error of believing that meaningful change can be accomplished within the present political, social, and economic system. By accepting the system, he accepts the necessity of compromise, and compromise is seen as both morally wrong and practically unworkable.

All this misses the point, which is that the white liberal is, in the North, one of the Negro's *only* significant allies in a situation in which allies are essential. He is not and cannot be an all-purpose ally, however. The upper-class business or professional man is a more useful ally in the South where, by halting and nervous steps, his support is being mobilized to achieve voting rights and end police abuse; he is also a more useful ally in the North when the issue is legitimating a local public welfare program. The principal value of the white liberal, on the other hand, is to supply the votes and the political pressures (increasingly mobilized through religious organizations) that make it almost suicidal for an important Northern politician openly to court anti-Negro sentiment.

The alliance, however, is as much tacit as explicit. If Negroes increasingly distrust liberals (because they are both ideologically suspect and rivals for power), liberals have had difficulty finding Negroes who have both a genuine mass following and a commitment to what the liberals regard as appropriate means and ends. The hoped-for alliance in Manhattan between liberal Democratic reform clubs and Harlem political leaders has not materialized to any degree.[22] The most popular Negro leader in Philadelphia, Cecil Moore, is regarded with incredulous disdain by white liberals. Negro machine politicians, such as William Dawson of Chicago, are rejected by both those middle-class Negroes and those middle-class whites whose commitment to social change exceeds their faith in the Democratic party leadership.[23] Negroes, such as Edward Brooke, whom white liberals find attractive are usually prevented by their position (that is, being responsive to a largely white constituency) from being in the visible forefront of civil rights campaigns. The cause of most of this unrequited love is that the Negro has come of age politically at a time when not only machines are collapsing, but the whole lower-class style of politics—the politics of friendships, trades, patronage, and neighborhood localism—is falling into disrepute. Negroes are expected to climb a political ladder which, as a result of several decades of successful reform efforts, is now missing most of its rungs. For whites, vaulting to the top is easy—television is one way; converting an established business or civic reputation into appointive and elective office is another. But the Negro community lacks the business and civic infrastructure which is necessary to convert private success into public office. Enough money has yet to be earned by enough Negroes to produce a significant precipitate of Negro civic statesmen.

Negroes know this and therefore are demanding that economic differences between Negroes and whites be eliminated. If the white liberal reformer is to be allowed to abolish the system by which political and economic progress was once made, then he must (many Negroes argue) replace it with something better. The Negro demand for economic equality is no longer, as Nathan Glazer points out, simply a demand for equal opportunity; it is a demand for equality of economic *results*.[24] American politics has for long been accustomed to dealing with ethnic demands for recognition, power, and opportunity; it has never had to face a serious demand for equal economic shares. Thus, in the North as well as the South the principal race issue may become a conflict between liberty and equality. This may be the issue which will distinguish the white liberal from the white radical: the former will work for liberty and equal opportunity, the latter for equal shares. This distinction adds yet another complication to the uneasy liberal-Negro alliance.

If the alliance is hard to sustain today, it will be subject to even greater strains in the future. The Northern Negro community, lacking a single clear objective and a well-organized and unified leadership, will continue to be volatile. Protest demonstrations will reveal less discipline than those in the South, and the likelihood of violence will be greater. The church simply does not have the importance to the Northern Negro that it does to the Southern, nor are the targets in the North so visible as those in the South. The Negro riots of the summers of 1964 and 1965 in Harlem, Rochester, Chicago, Brooklyn, Los Angeles, and elsewhere were not in any obvious sense "race" riots (that is, riots of Negroes against whites in protest against claimed injustices) or the outgrowth of civil rights demonstrations. But whatever their cause (simple hooliganism was an important element), their lesson for genuine civil rights demonstrations is clear: there is always a potential for violence, particularly when the demonstration is as much against indifference as against injustice.

That the movement is badly organized, understaffed, and threatened by violence does not mean it is ineffective. As other sources of power decline in strength, the power of the civil rights organizations increases. It is not yet possible for them to *elect* candidates, even in all-Negro districts, to many significant offices, but it is entirely possible for them to *prevent* someone else from being elected, even in heavily white districts. In most Northern cities, there are now a small number of Negro civil rights leaders whose reputation is such that their concerted opposition to a Negro candidate would prevent his election. They are often strong enough to hurt the chances of white candidates by casting on them (rightly or wrongly) an "anti-civil-rights" label which will be the kiss of death for white liberal (and even not-so-liberal) voters. As one Negro leader in Boston, a hopelessly unorganized city, told me recently, "We are entering a new political era of guerrilla warfare in which the lack of organization and discipline will not be nearly so important as the possibility of well-placed sniping at the enemy."

Competition to get the pro-civil-rights label (or, more accurately, to avoid getting the anti-civil-rights label) will become more intense. The 1964 presidential campaign may well have facilitated this process by involving Negroes in unprecedented numbers both as voters and as campaigners. The intense opposition to Goldwater resulted in Negroes registering as Democrats in overwhelming proportions in both North and South. The Democratic National Committee mobilized ministers, barbers, beauticians, and other strategically placed Negroes as volunteer campaigners. Nationally known civil rights leaders, particularly Martin Luther King, toured the country giving ostensibly "nonpartisan" speeches, urging Negroes to vote but not telling them whom to vote for (that was hardly necessary). Only time will tell what effect Goldwater will have on Negro political loyalties (particularly in the South, where they have been in doubt) and on the number and style of Negro political activists. It is possible, though far from certain, that 1964 will have fixed Negro political loyalties in the same way that Al Smith in 1928 and Franklin D. Roosevelt in 1936 fixed white loyalties and will bring into politics a new cadre of Negro leaders just as 1952 and 1956 brought in new white cadres. Regardless of whom the Republicans nominate, the Democrats will be running against Goldwater for the next twenty years.

Apart from building fires under politicians, there remains the question of what Negro (or Negro-white liberal) politics can accomplish. Simply electing more Negroes to public office will make some difference, for politics depends as much as anything on communication. Groups not in a position to know in time cannot act in time; protest as a strategy is better suited to *blocking* change than to initiating it, and this requires a good intelligence network. There are already an estimated 280 Negroes holding elective office, including 6 congressmen and 90 state legislators.[19] And as Negroes rise in seniority in various legislative systems, they will acquire power with which to bargain. (For better or worse, Representative Adam Clayton Powell, as chairman of the House Committee on Education and Labor, is an astute bargainer perfectly prepared to trade a concession on a bill favoring organized labor for a consession by labor on a matter of interest to Negroes.) Furthermore, the greater and more direct involvement of the federal government in the affairs of cities and metropolitan areas under circumstances which require that federal authorities not visibly deny the precept of equal justice for all means that Negroes, through injunctive procedures as well as political pressure, will be able to compel changes in the administration of local programs in schools, housing, and the like as a precondition to receiving the growing volume of federal aid.[20]

In those areas where elective officials administer and are directly responsible for programs affecting the lives of Negroes, Negro voting strength will, of course, be important. One such area is the administration of justice. In the South, the impact of Negro enfranchisement on these practices could be revolutionary; even in the North, Negro political power can significantly constrain mayors and police chiefs. (The mayor of Detroit, Jerome Cavanaugh, attracted widespread—and possibly decisive—Negro electoral support because of Negro discontent with Detroit police practices under the previous administration; immediately upon assuming office, Cavanaugh replaced the police commissioner and supported efforts to alter police behavior in Negro neighborhoods.) Education is another area where elected officials can sometimes be held accountable to the voters. But here the Negro voter faces a paradox: in cities (such as New York) where Negroes are sufficiently numerous to be taken seriously by politicians, they are also so numerous as to make a solution to the problems of racial imbalance or low standards in the public schools very hard to find. Where (as in Boston) Negroes are sufficiently few in number to make solutions possible (at least in principle), they are also so few as to be a relatively inconsequential political force.

Negroes, in short, will increasingly be able to play marginalist politics. But this approach rarely produces wholesale or fundamental changes in the life chances of large numbers of people. Some Negro (and white) leaders, recognizing the limitations of conventional politics, are suggesting new forms of organization. One of these is the power-oriented neighborhood association, exemplified by The Woodlawn Organization (TWO) in Chicago.[21] Such groups mobilize Negroes (or lower-income voters generally) by defining and dramatizing adverse local conditions which are the result of the indifference or hostility of outside forces, such as the city administration or nonresident white businessmen. Relying on indigenous leadership, the organization mounts a neighborhood protest against the outside "enemies"; by blocking proposed changes or by effectively challenging current programs, the group acquires the power to bargain with outsiders, especially city politicians and administrators. Demands are made and enforced concerning the appropriate kinds and levels of city services to be provided in the area.

The key to this strategy is the effort to build an indigenous political organization which is not part of the city-wide political apparatus and thus is not subject to its constraints. The plan is to fill the vacuum created by the decay of the ward organization of city-wide machines by substituting a nonpartisan but power-oriented civic association which seeks to provide collective rather than divisible benefits (such as patronage) for its members and followers. Since it trades in general rather than individual benefits, the civic association must find new ways to motivate its members; it does so by relying on a combative ideology. There are at least two major problems with this strategy, however. First, the resources with which to sustain such an organization are very scarce. It obviously cannot rely on government or business support (although the recent history of New York's Mobilization for Youth, patterned in many ways on the TWO model, suggests that at least in the immediate future it may be possible to use government funds—such as federal antipoverty or antidelinquency money—to launch organizations aimed at challenging government policies). Foundation and philanthropic support is available (TWO was begun in this way), but such support depends on the programs of the action groups being consistent with what middle-class white liberals who operate foundations will tolerate. In short, it depends on a Negro-liberal white alliance.

The second problem is that it may prove difficult to generalize such a strategy. Building a coalition of several neighborhood combat organizations necessitates finding the terms on which groups with essentially local interests can work together. This is difficult even for a traditional political party which can control patronage and nominations for office. A nonpartisan neighborhood association, on the other hand, which attempts to maximize benefits for its area often must do so at the expense of other areas; this potentially competitive situation may make collaboration difficult. A coalition might, of course, be formed out of a common allegiance to a candidate for major political office, but this means accepting the constraints (principally, moderation) that inevitably accompany electoral contest.

III. *The Negro Voter in the Future*

In short, the possibility for an effective radical Negro political strategy seems remote and the effort to achieve it costly. In the South, the potential supporters of at least current Negro objectives are the members of the commercial and industrial élite. Although they are everywhere slow to emerge and in some places wholly absent, there is at present no reasonable alternative. Atlanta is an example of both the strengths and weaknesses of such an alliance; even there, of course, it rests on a delicate population equilibrium which could be upset should either the Negroes become too numerous or the upper-class whites too few. What will happen after federal intervention has opened the ballot box to Negroes in the Black Belt counties remains to be seen. There are very few precedents from which one might infer predictions about political behavior when Negroes are in the majority in a city or county and vote. (In Washington, D. C., Negroes are the voting majority, but there are few issues of substance to decide.) There are some Southern communities which are over 50 per cent Negro and in which many (though not all) Negroes vote. Little is known about them except that, while the franchise has ended harassment by public officials and law enforcement officers, it has not revolutionized the living conditions of the Negroes. Perhaps the safest prediction is that the vote will have very different effects in different places. In some communities, patronage-based Negro political machines will emerge; in others, non-ideological Negro-white alliances will develop; in still others, militant and even radical Negro movements will appear (particularly, perhaps, in parts of Mississippi where the young cadres of SNCC and the Freedom Democratic party have begun to instill a radical ideology, though not yet to build a serious organization). In general, the type of Negro political organization which emerges will depend crucially on the type of white political organization already in existence.

In the North, the Negro, facing goals more complex and less clearly moral than those faced in the South, will continue to require white liberal, business, and union support for slow progress toward programs productive of income, education, and wider opportunities. The urban vote already greatly influences the presidential election; how much more it will influence state and congressional elections now that reapportionment is upon us is uncertain. It will clearly be on state legislatures that the Supreme Court's edict will fall most heavily. Congress is not likely to be revolutionized; indeed, there is some evidence that an absolutely equal apportionment system might *strengthen* the "conservative" vote.[28] In any case, the role of Congress is more the product of our localistic political structure than of the apportionment system, and this is not likely to change significantly for a very long time.

Negro-labor alliances will still be possible, but like all such alliances in American politics they will be *ad hoc*, imperfectly organized, and difficult to sustain. From the point of view of the Negro, one of the chief advantages of the American political system is surely that the "undemocratic" convention and caucus system by which political parties are governed makes possible *leadership* coalitions that, while not based on a perfect fusion of interests and aims, are not without influence in the choice of candidates and even the outcome of elections. Indeed, to the extent political parties are made internally more "democratic"—by abolishing conventions in favor of primaries, by reforming the governance of local political organizations, and by flooding the deliberations of party leaders with the merciless light of publicity—these coalitions may become more difficult to assemble and sustain, for an informed rank and file requires leaders who emphasize rather than compromise the very great differences which now separate, for example, white and Negro working-class voters.

The fact that many different alliances must be maintained will not only call for a high degree of tactical flexibility; it will probably also mean that the civil rights movement will remain divided and even at war with itself. The divisions among Negro leaders are the result not simply of personal rivalry or organized ideology, but of the effort to adapt a movement to the necessity of simultaneously occupying incompatible positions in order to draw strength from others.

The various white partners in these alliances will themselves be changed by civil rights activity. The nonpolitical strategies developed by the Negro for gaining bargaining power—the sit-in, the protest march, and passive resistance—have already been adopted by whites concerned with everything from American foreign policy to university administration.[29] Physically obstructing the operation of an organization—often illegally—has, in the 1960's, become a commonplace method for attempting to change the behavior of that organization. This "spill-over" of civil rights tactics into other areas of social conflict has probably been one of the most important consequences of increased Negro militancy.

Because of the structure of American politics as well as the nature of the Negro community, Negro politics will accomplish only limited objectives. This does not mean that Negroes will be content with those accomplishments or resigned to that political style. If Negroes do not make radical gains, radical sentiments may grow. How these sentiments will find expression is perhaps the most perplexing and troubling question of all.

REFERENCES

1. *Commentary* (February 1965), pp. 25–31.

2. C. Vann Woodward, *The Strange Career of Jim Crow* (New York, 1957), pp. 38–47, 60–68.

3. Rep. Weltner voted against final passage of HR 7152 on February 10, 1964. On February 17, the United States Supreme Court ordered redistricting in Georgia (Wesberry v. Sanders, 376 U. S. 1 [1964]). The Georgia Senate, anticipating the ruling, had already passed a redistricting bill on February 12; the House followed suit on February 21. The governor signed the bill into law on March 10; it divided Weltner's old district into two new districts—Weltner's (the Fifth), consisting of Fulton County (Atlanta); the other (the Fourth) consisting of suburban DeKalb County. As a result of this change, the percentage of Weltner's district which was Negro rose from 26.5 to 33.3. Weltner voted for House acceptance of the Senate-amended Civil Rights Act in July. An interesting analysis of Weltner's relationship to the Negro vote is M. Kent Jennings and L. Harmon Zeigler, "A Moderate's Victory in a Southern Congressional District," *Public Opinion Quarterly*, Vol. 28 (Winter 1964), pp. 595–603.

4. Alfred B. Clubok, John M. Degrove, and Charles D. Farris, "The Manipulated Negro Vote; Some Pre-Conditions and Consequences," *Journal of Politics*, Vol. 26 (February 1964), pp. 112–129. This is not confined to the South. In 1964, certain Negro precincts in Harrisburg, Pennsylvania, voted for Senator Goldwater while Northern Negroes elsewhere were voting ten-to-one for President Johnson. One can only speculate on the ways by which that extraordinary result was achieved.

5. Cf. H. Douglas Price, *The Negro and Southern Politics: A Chapter of Florida History* (New York, 1957); Bradbury Seasholes and Frederic N. Cleaveland, "Negro Political Participation in Two Piedmont Crescent Cities," in F. Stuart Chapin and Shirley F. Weiss (eds.), *Urban Growth Dynamics* (New York, 1962), pp. 265–270; Henry Holloway, "The Negro and the Vote: The Case of Texas," *Journal of Politics*, Vol. 23 (August 1961), pp. 526–556. These Negro voters' leagues are effective only if they operate within the consensual framework of the Negro community. Price (on page 72) notes that a "league endorsement of a wrong candidate in a contest where a clear difference in attitude toward the Negro exists does not swing many Negro votes; rather it raises the question, 'who sold out?' " Holloway (on pages 539–540) observes that "Negro leaders don't have the power to deliver a bloc vote at will. . . . The Negro voter has his own fairly constant voting propensies which leaders disregard at risk to themselves."

6. Jack Walker, "Negro Voting in Atlanta: 1953–1961," *Phylon*, Vol. 24 (Winter 1963), pp. 379–387.

7. Negro voting in many Southern cities is an empirical case of the rationality model suggested in Anthony Downs, *An Economic Theory of Democracy* (New York, 1957).

8. The Atlanta Coalition is described in Edward C. Banfield, "Atlanta: Strange Bedfellows," in *Big City Politics* (New York, forthcoming).

9. Daniel C. Thompson, *The Negro Leadership Class* (Englewood Cliffs, N. J., 1963), pp. 112–114.

10. Survey data on the importance of education (and class position) for the racial attitudes of Southern whites can be found in Herbert B. Hyman and Paul B. Sheatsley, "Attitudes Toward Desegregation," *Scientific American* (July 1964), pp. 16–23, and Melvin M. Tumin, *Desegregation* (Princeton, N. J., 1958). But Matthews and Prothro, using ecological correlations, show that the level of education among Southern whites must be very high before it affects Negro voter registration rates. Donald R. Matthews and James W. Prothro, "Social and Economic Factors and Negro Voter Registration in the South," *American Political Science Review*, Vol. 57 (March 1963), pp. 36–38.

11. United States Commission on Civil Rights, *1961 Report* (Book 1, Part 3).

12. Seymour Martin Lipset, *Political Man* (Garden City, N. Y., 1960), pp. 84–85.

13. Donald R. Matthews and James W. Prothro, *Negro Political Participation in the South* (New York, forthcoming).

14. Walker, *op. cit.*, p. 384.

15. The importance of political factors other than the Negro vote in obtaining civil rights legislation is illustrated by the state adoption of "open occupancy" laws barring discrimination in the private housing market. The first states to pass such laws were typically states with a very small Negro population. See James Q. Wilson, "The Negro in American Politics" in John P. Davis (ed.), *American Negro Reference Book* (New York, forthcoming).

16. *Commentary* (February 1965), p. 26.

17. Daniel Patrick Moynihan, "Three Problems," an address given before the Conference on Poverty in America at the University of California at Berkeley, February 26–28, 1965 (mimeo).

18. James Q. Wilson and Edward C. Banfield, "Public-Regardingness as a Value Premise in Voting," *American Political Science Review*, Vol. 58 (December 1964), pp. 876–887.

19. James Q. Wilson, *Negro Politics* (New York, 1960), Chs. ii, iii, iv; and James Reichley, *The Art of Government: Reform and Organization Politics in Philadelphia* (New York, 1959).

20. Edward C. Banfield and James Q. Wilson, *City Politics* (Cambridge, Mass., 1963), chap. xx, discusses alternative Negro political styles.

21. See *Election '64*, a report of the Ripon Society (Cambridge, Mass., 1965), p. 29.

22. James Q. Wilson, *The Amateur Democrat* (Chicago, 1962), Ch. ix, discusses reform-Negro relations.

23. In Chicago, certain white and Negro civil rights groups ran a Negro candidate (A. A. Rayner, Jr.) against Rep. William L. Dawson in the 1962 Democratic primary. Dawson won, easily carrying the lower-income Negro precincts but losing (by as much as two-to-one) many middle-class Negro precincts. The Dawson organization is very strong among lower-income Negroes, particularly those in public housing projects.

24. Nathan Glazer, "Negroes and Jews: The New Challenge to Pluralism," *Commentary* (December 1964), p. 34.

25. *The New York Times,* December 23, 1964, quoting the Democratic National Committee.

26. Title VI of the Civil Rights Act of 1964 will facilitate challenges.

27. Charles Silberman, *The Crisis in Black and White* (New York, 1964), Ch. x, describes TWO.

28. Andrew Hacker, *Congressional Districting* (Washington, D. C., 1963), pp. 87–91.

29. Recently, internes protesting the pay policies of a California county hospital practiced a "heal-in." They flooded the hospital with patients, many not in need of hospitalization, in order to overload the organization and thus acquire bargaining power vis-à-vis the administration.

A *Photographic Essay*
by BRUCE DAVIDSON

with an Introduction
by A. D. Trottenberg

The Negro American is not a "reformist" book designed to shock the reader into a state of guilt and horror about the plight of the Negro in America. It does bring to bear the expertise of a group of scholars and of others who have long studied this social problem of staggering complexity.

The editors of this volume recognized that some qualities such as tenderness, bitterness, and dignity in the face of great adversity form a substantial portion of this exacting examination. They found in the photographs of Bruce Davidson an opportunity to illustrate for the reader those human dimensions that cannot be fully described in the text.

James Agee and Walker Evans first produced this kind of strong written-visual statement in *Let Us Now Praise Famous Men,* an extraordinary documentation of the tenant farmer in the deep South. In his preface James Agee wrote about the photography of Walker Evans:

The photographs are not illustrative. They and the text are coequal, mutually independent, and fully collaborative. By their fewness, and by the impotence of the reader's eye, this will be misunderstood by most of the minority which does not wholly ignore it. In the interests, however, of the history and future of photography, that risk seems irrelevant and this flat statement necessary.

Documentary photography in America has a long and effective history. In the 1870's Gardner, Jackson, and O'Sullivan accompanied the great government expeditions to the West, and their remarkable photographs were influential in the determination of federal land and park policy. The photographs of Jacob Riis and Lewis W. Hine, taken at the turn of the century, stirred strong public reaction with their visual record of slum conditions, child labor, and immigrant misfortune. In 1935 the Farm Security Administration began, under the direction of Roy A. Stryker, a seven-year photographic examination of rural and small-town life in America. Such photographers as Dorothea Lange, Ben Shahn, Arthur Rothstein, Russell Lee, Carl Mydans, and others showed the public the wretchedness of the dust bowl and the Depression, the despair of the migrant farm worker and the unemployed.

The photographs in this volume require no captions. While they are not literally related to the text, neither are they disparate fragments shot simply to demonstrate the desolation of Harlem or the brutal truth of Selma. In order of appearance they are designed to present a constantly moving but coherent visual statement. They appear in four distinct groups of eight photographs each.

We are first introduced to Negro Americans by studying their faces, gestures, posture. Here are bitterness, defiance, resignation expressed in the simplest visual terms: the hand of a father on a child's head, the fixed defiant glare of an octogenarian.

The next group of photographs is concerned with the conditions under which the Negro American lives. Here the photograph of the decrepit one-room schoolhouse describes eloquently the doctrine of separate but equal facilities. The elderly Negro woman hopelessly struggling with legal forms under the sullen supervision of the sheriff shows clearly the sickness of "white supremacy."

In the third group of photographs we see how the Negro American earns his living. Manual work and menial occupation predominate, but so does the innate dignity of the people involved. We sense something new happening, however, in the photograph of the brisk young executive with dispatch case in hand.

The protest movement in all its forms is the subject of the last group of photographs. The progression from the recently won integrated lunch counter to the complex organization of the Selma-to-Montgomery march and the Washington civil rights rally is shown here as a unified thrust that can no longer be denied. The strength of the movement is expressed in the bold visual forms of the arrested, the defiant and the determined single Negro, as well as in the massing of thousands before the Washington Monument.

A. D. TROTTENBERG

MILLER GRO. MKT.
PHONE
DRINK
Coca-Cola
IN BOTTLES
HALL ST. WASHATE
STOP
4 WAY
COIN
OPERATED
WASHERS

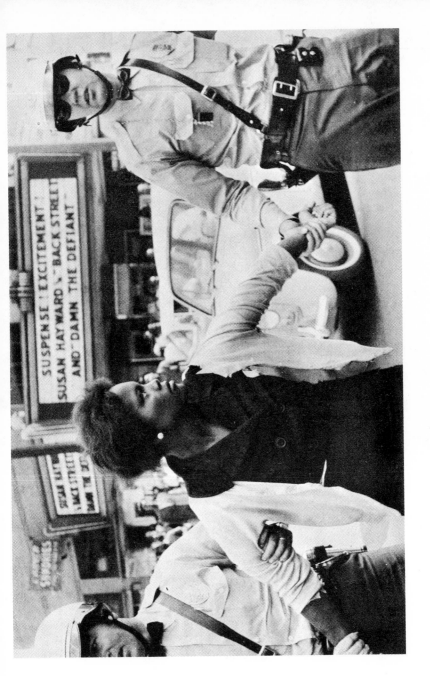

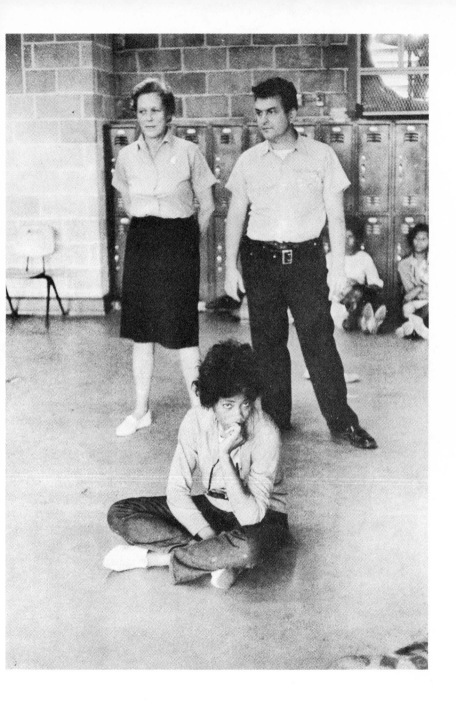

V

FIELDS AND PROPOSALS
FOR POLICY

JAMES TOBIN

On Improving the Economic Status of the Negro

I START from the presumption that the integration of Negroes into the American society and economy can be accomplished within existing political and economic institutions. I understand the impatience of those who think otherwise, but I see nothing incompatible between our peculiar mixture of private enterprise and government, on the one hand, and the liberation and integration of the Negro, on the other. Indeed the present position of the Negro is an aberration from the principles of our society, rather than a requirement of its functioning. Therefore, my suggestions are directed to the aim of mobilizing existing powers of government to bring Negroes into full participation in the main stream of American economic life.

The economic plight of individuals, Negroes and whites alike, can always be attributed to specific handicaps and circumstances: discrimination, immobility, lack of education and experience, ill health, weak motivation, poor neighborhood, large family size, burdensome family responsibilities. Such diagnoses suggest a host of specific remedies, some in the domain of civil rights, others in the war on poverty. Important as these remedies are, there is a danger that the diagnoses are myopic. They explain why certain individuals rather than others suffer from the economic maladies of the time. They do not explain why the over-all incidence of the maladies varies dramatically from time to time—for example, why personal attributes which seemed to doom a man to unemployment in 1932 or even in 1954 or 1961 did not so handicap him in 1944 or 1951 or 1956.

Public health measures to improve the environment are often more productive in conquering disease than a succession of individual treatments. Malaria was conquered by oiling and draining swamps, not by quinine. The analogy holds for economic maladies.

Unless the global incidence of these misfortunes can be diminished, every individual problem successfully solved will be replaced by a similar problem somewhere else. That is why an economist is led to emphasize the importance of the over-all economic climate.

Over the decades, general economic progress has been the major factor in the gradual conquest of poverty. Recently some observers, J. K. Galbraith and Michael Harrington most eloquently, have contended that this process no longer operates. The economy may prosper and labor may become steadily more productive as in the past, but "the other America" will be stranded. Prosperity and progress have already eliminated almost all the easy cases of poverty, leaving a hard core beyond the reach of national economic trends. There may be something to the "backwash" thesis as far as whites are concerned.[1] But it definitely does not apply to Negroes. Too many of them are poor. It cannot be true that half of a race of twenty million human beings are victims of specific disabilities which insulate them from the national economic climate. It cannot be true, and it is not. Locke Anderson has shown that the pace of Negro economic progress is peculiarly sensitive to general economic growth. He estimates that if nationwide per capita personal income is stationary, nonwhite median family income falls by .5 per cent per year, while if national per capita income grows 5 per cent, nonwhite income grows nearly 7.5 per cent.[2]

National prosperity and economic growth are still powerful engines for improving the economic status of Negroes. They are not doing enough and they are not doing it fast enough. There is ample room for a focused attack on the specific sources of Negro poverty. But a favorable over-all economic climate is a necessary condition for the global success—as distinguished from success in individual cases—of specific efforts to remedy the handicaps associated with Negro poverty.

The Importance of a Tight Labor Market

But isn't the present over-all economic climate favorable? Isn't the economy enjoying an upswing of unprecedented length, setting new records almost every month in production, employment, profits, and income? Yes, but expansion and new records should be routine in an economy with growing population, capital equipment, and productivity. The fact is that the economy has not operated with reasonably full utilization of its manpower and plant capacity since

1957. Even now, after four and one-half years of uninterrupted expansion, the economy has not regained the ground lost in the recessions of 1958 and 1960. The current expansion has whittled away at unemployment, reducing it from 6.5 to 7 per cent to 4.5 to 5 per cent. It has diminished idle plant capacity correspondingly. The rest of the gains since 1960 in employment, production, and income have just offset the normal growth of population, capacity, and productivity.

The magnitude of America's poverty problem already reflects the failure of the economy in the second postwar decade to match its performance in the first.[3] Had the 1947-56 rate of growth of median family income been maintained since 1957, and had unemployment been steadily limited to 4 per cent, it is estimated that the fraction of the population with poverty incomes in 1963 would have been 16.6 per cent instead of 18.5 per cent.[4] The educational qualifications of the labor force have continued to improve. The principle of racial equality, in employment as in other activities, has gained ground both in law and in the national conscience. If, despite all this, dropouts, inequalities in educational attainment, and discrimination in employment seem more serious today rather than less, the reason is that the over-all economic climate has not been favorable after all.

The most important dimension of the overall economic climate is the tightness of the labor market. In a tight labor market unemployment is low and short in duration, and job vacancies are plentiful. People who stand at the end of the hiring line and the top of the layoff list have the most to gain from a tight labor market. It is not proves in a tight labor market and declines in a slack market. Unsurprising that the position of Negroes relative to that of whites imemployment itself is only one way in which a slack labor market hurts Negroes and other disadvantaged groups, and the gains from reduction in unemployment are by no means confined to the employment of persons counted as unemployed.[5] A tight labor market means not just jobs, but better jobs, longer hours, higher wages. Because of the heavy demands for labor during the second world war and its economic aftermath, Negroes made dramatic relative gains between 1940 and 1950. Unfortunately this momentum has not been maintained, and the blame falls largely on the weakness of labor markets since 1957.[6]

The shortage of jobs has hit Negro men particularly hard and thus has contributed mightily to the ordeal of the Negro family,

JAMES TOBIN

which is in turn the cumulative source of so many other social disorders.[7] The unemployment rate of Negro men is more sensitive than that of Negro women to the national rate. Since 1949 Negro women have gained in median income relative to white women, but Negro men have lost ground to white males.[8] In a society which stresses breadwinning as the expected role of the mature male and occupational achievement as his proper goal, failure to find and to keep work is devastating to the man's self-respect and family status. Matriarchy is in any case a strong tradition in Negro society, and the man's role is further downgraded when the family must and can depend on the woman for its livelihood. It is very important to increase the proportion of Negro children who grow up in stable families with two parents. Without a strong labor market it will be extremely difficult to do so.

Unemployment. It is well known that Negro unemployment rates are multiples of the general unemployment rate. This fact reflects both the lesser skills, seniority, and experience of Negroes and employers' discrimination against Negroes. These conditions are a deplorable reflection on American society, but as long as they exist Negroes suffer much more than others from a general increase in unemployment and gain much more from a general reduction. A rule of thumb is that changes in the nonwhite unemployment rate are twice those in the white rate. The rule works both ways. Nonwhite unemployment went from 4.1 per cent in 1953, a tight labor market year, to 12.5 per cent in 1961, while the white rate rose from 2.3 per cent to 6 per cent. Since then, the Negro rate has declined by 2.4 per cent, the white rate by 1.2.

Even the Negro teenage unemployment rate shows some sensitivity to general economic conditions. Recession increased it from 15 per cent in 1955-56 to 25 per cent in 1958. It decreased to 22 per cent in 1960 but rose to 28 per cent in 1963; since then it has declined somewhat. Teenage unemployment is abnormally high now, relative to that of other age groups, because the wave of postwar babies is coming into the labor market. Most of them, especially the Negroes, are crowding the end of the hiring line. But their prospects for getting jobs are no less dependent on general labor market conditions.

Part-time work. Persons who are involuntarily forced to work part time instead of full time are not counted as unemployed, but their number goes up and down with the unemployment rate. Just as Negroes bear a disproportionate share of unemployment, they bear more than their share of involuntary part-time unemployment.[9] A tight labor market will not only employ more Negroes; it will also give more of those who are employed full-time jobs. In both respects, it will reduce disparities between whites and Negroes.

Labor-force participation. In a tight market, of which a low unemployment rate is a barometer, the labor force itself is larger. Job opportunities draw into the labor force individuals who, simply because the prospects were dim, did not previously regard themselves as seeking work and were therefore not enumerated as unemployed. For the economy as a whole, it appears that an expansion of job opportunities enough to reduce unemployment by one worker will bring another worker into the labor force.

This phenomenon is important for many Negro families. Statistically, their poverty now appears to be due more often to the lack of a breadwinner in the labor force than to unemployment.[10] But in a tight labor market many members of these families, including families now on public assistance, would be drawn into employment. Labor-force participation rates are roughly 2 per cent lower for nonwhite men than for white men, and the disparity increases in years of slack labor markets.[11] The story is different for women. Negro women have always been in the labor force to a much greater extent than white women. A real improvement in the economic status of Negro men and in the stability of Negro families would probably lead to a reduction in labor-force participation by Negro women. But for teenagers, participation rates for Negroes are not so high as for whites; and for women twenty to twenty-four they are about the same. These relatively low rates are undoubtedly due less to voluntary choice than to the same lack of job opportunities that produces phenomenally high unemployment rates for young Negro women.

Duration of unemployment. In a tight labor market, such unemployment as does exist is likely to be of short duration. Short-term unemployment is less damaging to the economic welfare of the unemployed. More will have earned and fewer will have exhausted private and public unemployment benefits. In 1953 when the over-all unemployment rate was 2.9 per cent, only 4 per cent of the unemployed were out of work for longer than twenty-six weeks and only 11 per cent for longer than fifteen weeks. In contrast, the unemployment rate in 1961 was 6.7 per cent; and of the unemployed in that year, 17 per cent were out of work for longer than twenty-six weeks and 32 per cent for longer than fifteen weeks. Between the first quarter of 1964 and the first quarter of 1965, over-all unemployment fell 11 per cent, while unemployment extending beyond half a year was lowered by 22 per cent.

As Rashi Fein points out elsewhere in this volume, one more dimension of society's inequity to the Negro is that an unemployed Negro is more likely to stay unemployed than an unemployed white. But his figures also show that Negroes share in the reduction of long-term unemployment accompanying economic expansion.

Migration from agriculture. A tight labor market draws the sur-plus rural population to higher paying non-agricultural jobs. South-ern Negroes are a large part of this surplus rural population. Migra-tion is the only hope for improving their lot, or their children's. In spite of the vast migration of past decades, there are still about 775,000 Negroes, 11 per cent of the Negro labor force of the coun-try, who depend on the land for their living and that of their fami-lies.[12] Almost a half million live in the South, and almost all of them are poor.

Migration from agriculture and from the South is the Negroes' historic path toward economic improvement and equality. It is a smooth path for Negroes and for the urban communities to which they move only if there is a strong demand for labor in towns and cities North and South. In the 1940's the number of Negro farmers and farm laborers in the nation fell by 450,000 and one and a half million Negroes (net) left the South. This was the great dec-ade of Negro economic advance. In the 1950's the same occupa-tional and geographical migration continued undiminished. The movement to higher-income occupations and locations should have raised the relative economic status of Negroes. But in the 1950's Negroes were moving into increasingly weak job markets. Too often disguised unemployment in the countryside was simply trans-formed into enumerated unemployment, and rural poverty into urban poverty.[13]

Quality of jobs. In a slack labor market, employers can pick and choose, both in recruiting and in promoting. They exaggerate the skill, education, and experience requirements of their jobs. They use diplomas, or color, or personal histories as convenient screening devices. In a tight market, they are forced to be realistic, to tailor job specifications to the available supply, and to give on-the-job training. They recruit and train applicants whom they would other-wise screen out, and they upgrade employees whom they would in slack times consign to low-wage, low-skill, and part-time jobs.

Wartime and other experience shows that job requirements are adjustable and that men and women are trainable. It is only in slack times that people worry about a mismatch between supposedly rigid occupational requirements and supposedly unchangeable qualifications of the labor force. As already noted, the relative status of Negroes improves in a tight labor market not only in respect to unemployment, but also in respect to wages and occupations.

Cyclical fluctuation. Sustaining a high demand for labor is important. The in-and-out status of the Negro in the business cycle damages his long-term position because periodic unemployment robs him of experience and seniority.

Restrictive practices. A slack labor market probably accentuates the discriminatory and protectionist proclivities of certain crafts and unions. When jobs are scarce, opening the door to Negroes is a real threat. Of course prosperity will not automatically dissolve the barriers, but it will make it more difficult to oppose efforts to do so.

I conclude that the single most important step the nation could take to improve the economic position of the Negro is to operate the economy steadily at a low rate of unemployment. We cannot expect to restore the labor market conditions of the second world war, and we do not need to. In the years 1951-1953, unemployment was roughly 3 per cent, teenage unemployment around 7 per cent, Negro unemployment about 4.5 per cent, long term unemployment negligible. In the years 1955-57, general unemployment was roughly 4 per cent, and the other measures correspondingly higher. Four per cent is the official target of the Kennedy-Johnson administration. It has not been achieved since 1957. Reaching and maintaining 4 per cent would be a tremendous improvement over the performance of the last eight years. But we should not stop there; the society and the Negro can benefit immensely from tightening the labor market still further, to 3.5 or 3 per cent unemployment. The administration itself has never defined 4 per cent as anything other than an "interim" target.

Why Don't We Have a Tight Labor Market?

We know how to operate the economy so that there is a tight labor market. By fiscal and monetary measures the federal government can control aggregate spending in the economy. The government could choose to control it so that unemployment *averaged* 3.5 or 3 per cent instead of remaining over 4.5 per cent except at occasional business cycle peaks. Moreover, recent experience here and abroad shows that we can probably narrow the amplitude of fluctuations around whatever average we select as a target.

Some observers have cynically concluded that a society like ours can achieve full employment only in wartime. But aside from conscription into the armed services, government action creates jobs in wartime by exactly the same mechanism as in peacetime—the government spends more money and stimulates private firms and citizens to spend more too. It is the *amount* of spending, not its purpose, that does the trick. Public or private spending to go to the moon, build schools, or conquer poverty can be just as effective in reducing unemployment as spending to build airplanes and submarines —if there is enough of it. There may be more political constraints and ideological inhibitions in peacetime, but the same techniques of economic policy are available if we want badly enough to use them. The two main reasons we do not take this relatively simple way out are two obsessive fears, inflation and balance of payments deficits.

Running the economy with a tight labor market would mean a somewhat faster upward creep in the price level. The disadvantages of this are, in my view, exaggerated and are scarcely commensurable with the real economic and social gains of higher output and employment. Moreover, there are ways of protecting "widows and orphans" against erosion in the purchasing power of their savings. But fear of inflation is strong both in the U.S. financial establishment and in the public at large. The vast comfortable white middle class who are never touched by unemployment prefer to safeguard the purchasing power of their life insurance and pension rights than to expand opportunities for the disadvantaged and unemployed.

The fear of inflation would operate anyway, but it is accentuated by U.S. difficulties with its international balance of payments. These difficulties have seriously constrained and hampered U.S. fiscal and monetary policy in recent years. Any rise in prices might enlarge the deficit. An aggressively expansionary monetary policy, lowering interest rates, might push money out of the country.

In the final analysis what we fear is that we might not be able to defend the parity of the dollar with gold, that is, to sell gold at thirty-five dollars an ounce to any government that wants to buy. So great is the gold mystique that this objective has come to occupy a niche in the hierarchy of U.S. goals second only to the military defense of the country, and not always to that. It is not fanciful to link the plight of Negro teenagers in Harlem to the monetary whims of General de Gaulle. But it is only our own attachment to "the dollar" as an abstraction which makes us cringe before the European appetite for gold.

This topic is too charged with technical complexities, real and imagined, and with confused emotions to be discussed adequately here. I will confine myself to three points. First, the United States is the last country in the world which needs to hold back its own economy to balance its international accounts. To let the tail wag the dog is not in the interests of the rest of the world, so much of which depends on us for trade and capital, any more than in our own.

Second, forces are at work to restore balance to American international accounts—the increased competitiveness of our exports and the income from the large investments our firms and citizens have made overseas since the war. Meanwhile we can finance deficits by gold reserves and lines of credit at the International Monetary Fund and at foreign central banks. Ultimately we have one foolproof line of defense—letting the dollar depreciate relative to foreign currencies. The world would not end. The sun would rise the next day. American products would be more competitive in world markets. Neither God nor the Constitution fixed the gold value of the dollar. The U.S. would not be the first country to let its currency depreciate. Nor would it be the first time for the U.S.— not until we stopped "saving" the dollar and the gold standard in 1933 did our recovery from the Great Depression begin.

Third, those who oppose taking such risks argue that the dollar today occupies a unique position as international money, that the world as a whole has an interest, which we cannot ignore, in the stability of the gold value of the dollar. If so, we can reasonably ask the rest of the world, especially our European friends, to share the burdens which guaranteeing this stability imposes upon us.

This has been an excursion into general economic policy. But the connection between gold and the plight of the Negro is no less real for being subtle. We are paying much too high a social price for avoiding creeping inflation and for protecting our gold stock and "the dollar." But it will not be easy to alter these national priorities. The interests of the unemployed, the poor, and the Negroes are under-represented in the comfortable consensus which supports and confines current policy.

Another approach, which can be pursued simultaneously, is to diminish the conflicts among these competing objectives, in particular to reduce the degree of inflation associated with low levels of unemployment. This can be done in two ways. One way is to improve the mobility of labor and other resources to occupations, locations, and industries where bottlenecks would otherwise lead to wage and price increases. This is where many specific programs, such as the training and retraining of manpower and policies to improve the technical functioning of labor markets, come into their own.

A second task is to break down the barriers to competition which now restrict the entry of labor and enterprise into certain occupations and industries. These lead to wage- and price-increasing bottlenecks even when resources are not really short. Many barriers are created by public policy itself, in response to the vested interests concerned. Many reflect concentration of economic power in unions and in industry. These barriers represent another way in which the advantaged and the employed purchase their standards of living and their security at the expense of unprivileged minorities.

In the best of circumstances, structural reforms of these kinds will be slow and gradual. They will encounter determined economic and political resistance from special interests which are powerful in Congress and state legislatures. Moreover, Congressmen and legislators represent places rather than people and are likely to oppose, not facilitate, the increased geographical mobility which is required. It is no accident that our manpower programs do not include relocation allowances.

Increasing the Earning Capacity of Negroes

Given the proper over-all economic climate, in particular a steadily tight labor market, the Negro's economic condition can be expected to improve, indeed to improve dramatically. But not fast enough. Not as fast as his aspirations or as the aspirations he has taught the rest of us to have for him. What else can be done? This question is being answered in detail by experts elsewhere in this volume. I shall confine myself to a few comments and suggestions that occur to a general economist.

Even in a tight labor market, the Negro's relative status will suffer both from current discrimination and from his lower earning capacity, the result of inferior acquired skill. In a real sense both factors reflect discrimination, since the Negro's handicaps in earning capacity are the residue of decades of discrimination in education and employment. Nevertheless for both analysis and policy it is useful to distinguish the two.

Discrimination means that the Negro is denied access to certain markets where he might sell his labor, and to certain markets where he might purchase goods and services. Elementary application of "supply and demand" makes it clear that these restrictions are bound to result in his selling his labor for less and buying his livelihood for more than if these barriers did not exist. If Negro women can be clerks only in certain stores, those storekeepers will not need to pay them so much as they pay whites. If Negroes can live only in certain houses, the prices and rents they have to pay will be high for the quality of accommodation provided.

Successful elimination of discrimination is not only important in itself but will also have substantial economic benefits. Since residential segregation is the key to so much else and so difficult to eliminate by legal fiat alone, the power of the purse should be unstintingly used. I see no reason that the expenditure of funds for this purpose should be confined to new construction. Why not establish private or semi-public revolving funds to purchase, for resale or rental on a desegregated basis, strategically located existing structures as they become available?

The effects of past discrimination will take much longer to eradicate. The sins against the fathers are visited on the children. They are deprived of the intellectual and social capital which in our society is supposed to be transmitted in the family and the home. We have only begun to realize how difficult it is to make up for this deprivation by formal schooling, even when we try. And we have only begun to try, after accepting all too long the notion that schools should acquiesce in, even re-enforce, inequalities in home backgrounds rather than overcome them.

Upgrading the earning capacity of Negroes will be difficult, but the economic effects are easy to analyze. Economists have long held that the way to reduce disparities in earned incomes is to eliminate disparities in earning capacities. If college-trained people earn more money than those who left school after eight years, the remedy is to send a larger proportion of young people to college. If machine operators earn more than ditchdiggers, the remedy is to give more people the capacity and opportunity to be machine operators. These changes in relative supplies reduce the disparity both by competing down the pay in the favored line of work and by raising the pay in the less remunerative line. When there are only a few people left in the population whose capacities are confined to garbage-collecting, it will be a high-paid calling. The same is true of domestic service and all kinds of menial work.

This classical economic strategy will be hampered if discrimination, union barriers, and the like stand in the way. It will not help to increase the supply of Negro plumbers if the local unions and contractors will not let them join. But experience also shows that barriers give way more easily when the pressures of unsatisfied demand and supply pile up.

It should therefore be the task of educational and manpower policy to engineer over the next two decades a massive change in the relative supplies of people of different educational and professional attainments and degrees of skill and training. It must be a more rapid change than has occurred in the past two decades, because that has not been fast enough to alter income differentials. We should try particularly to increase supplies in those fields where salaries and wages are already high and rising. In this process we should be very skeptical of self-serving arguments and calculations —that an increase in supply in this or that profession would be bound to reduce quality, or that there are some mechanical relations of "need" to population or to Gross National Product that cannot be exceeded.

Such a policy would be appropriate to the "war on poverty" even if there were no racial problem. Indeed, our objective is to raise the earning capacities of low-income whites as well as of Negroes. But Negroes have the most to gain, and even those who because of age or irreversible environmental handicaps must inevitably be left behind will benefit by reduction in the number of whites and other Negroes who are competing with them.

Assuring Living Standards in the Absence of Earning Capacity

The reduction of inequality in earning capacity is the fundamental solution, and in a sense anything else is stopgap. Some stopgaps are useless and even counter-productive. People who lack the capacity to earn a decent living need to be helped, but they will not be helped by minimum wage laws, trade union wage pressures, or other devices which seek to compel employers to pay them more than their work is worth. The more likely outcome of such regulations is that the intended beneficiaries are not employed at all.

A far better approach is to supplement earnings from the public fisc. But assistance can and should be given in a way that does not force the recipients out of the labor force or give them incentive to withdraw. Our present system of welfare payments does just that, causing needless waste and demoralization. This application of the means test is bad economics as well as bad sociology. It is almost as if our present programs of public assistance had been consciously contrived to perpetuate the conditions they are supposed to alleviate.

These programs apply a strict means test. The amount of assistance is an estimate of minimal needs, less the resources of the family from earnings. The purpose of the means test seems innocuous enough. It is to avoid wasting taxpayers' money on people who do not really need help. But another way to describe the means test is to note that it taxes earnings at a rate of 100 per cent. A person on public assistance cannot add to his family's standard of living by working. Of course, the means test provides a certain incentive to work in order to get off public assistance altogether. But in many cases, especially where there is only one adult to provide for and take care of several children, the adult simply does not have enough time and earning opportunities to get by without financial help. He, or more likely she, is essentially forced to be both idle and on a dole. The means test also involves limitations on property holdings which deprive anyone who is or expects to be on public assistance of incentive to save.

In a society which prizes incentives for work and thrift, these are surprising regulations. They deny the country useful productive services, but that economic loss is minor in the present context. They deprive individuals and families both of work experience which could teach them skills, habits, and self-discipline of future value and of the self-respect and satisfaction which comes from improving their own lot by their own efforts.

Public assistance encourages the disintegration of the family, the key to so many of the economic and social problems of the American Negro. The main assistance program, Aid for Dependent Children, is not available if there is an able-bodied employed male in the house. In most states it is not available if there is an able-bodied man in the house, even if he is not working. All too often it is necessary for the father to leave his children so that they can eat. It is bad enough to provide incentives for idleness but even worse to legislate incentives for desertion.[14]

The bureaucratic surveillance and guidance to which recipients of public assistance are subject undermine both their self-respect and their capacity to manage their own affairs. In the administration of assistance there is much concern to detect "cheating" against the means tests and to ensure approved prudent use of the public's money. Case loads are frequently too great and administrative regulations too confining to permit the talents of social workers to treat the roots rather than the symptoms of the social maladies of their clients. The time of the clients is considered a free good, and much of it must be spent in seeking or awaiting the attention of the officials on whom their livelihood depends.

The defects of present categorical assistance programs could be, in my opinion, greatly reduced by adopting a system of basic income allowances, integrated with and administered in conjunction with the federal income tax. In a sense the proposal is to make the income tax symmetrical. At present the federal government takes a share of family income in excess of a certain amount (for example, a married couple with three children pays no tax unless their income exceeds $3700). The proposal is that the Treasury pay any family who falls below a certain income a fraction of the shortfall. The idea has sometimes been called a negative income tax.

The payment would be a matter of right, like an income tax refund. Individuals expecting to be entitled to payments from the government during the year could receive them in periodic installments by making a declaration of expected income and expected tax withholdings. But there would be a final settlement between the individual and the government based on a "tax" return after the year was over, just as there is now for taxpayers on April 15.

A family with no other income at all would receive a basic allowance scaled to the number of persons in the family. For a concrete example, take the basic allowance to be $400 per year per person. It might be desirable and equitable, however, to reduce the additional basic allowance for children after, say, the fourth. Once sufficient effort is being made to disseminate birth control knowledge and technique, the scale of allowances by family size certainly should provide some disincentive to the creation of large families.

A family's allowance would be reduced by a certain fraction of every dollar of other income it received. For a concrete example, take this fraction to be one third. This means that the family has considerable incentive to earn income, because its total income including allowances will be increased by two-thirds of whatever it earns. In contrast, the means test connected with present public assistance is a 100 per cent "tax" on earnings. With a one-third "tax" a family will be on the receiving end of the allowance and income tax system until its regular income equals three times its basic allowance.[15]

Families above this "break-even" point would be taxpayers. But the less well-off among them would pay less taxes than they do now. The first dollars of income in excess of this break-even point would be taxed at the same rate as below, one-third in the example. At some income level, the tax liability so computed would be the same as the tax under the present income tax law. From that point up, the present law would take over; taxpayers with incomes above this point would not be affected by the plan.

The best way to summarize the proposal is to give a concrete graphical illustration. On the horizontal axis of Figure 1 is measured family income from wages and salaries, interest, dividends, rents, and so forth—"adjusted gross income" for the Internal Revenue Service. On the vertical axis is measured the corresponding "disposable income," that is, income after federal taxes and allowances. If the family neither paid taxes nor received allowance, disposable income would be equal to family income; in the diagram this equality would be shown by the 45° line from the origin. Disposable income above this 45° line means the family receives allowances; disposable income below this line means the family pays taxes. The broken line OAB describes the present income tax law for a married couple with three children, allowing the standard deductions. The line CD is the revision which the proposed allowance system would make for incomes below $7963. For incomes above $7963, the old tax schedule applies.

Beneficiaries under Federal Old Age Survivors and Disability Insurance would not be eligible for the new allowances. Congress should make sure that minimum benefits under OASDI are at least as high as the allowances. Some government payments, especially those for categorical public assistance, would eventually be replaced by basic allowances. Others, like unemployment insurance and veterans' pensions, are intended to be rights earned by past services regardless of current need. It would therefore be wrong to withhold allowances from the beneficiaries of these payments, but it would be reasonable to count them as income in determining the size of allowances, even though they are not subject to tax.

Although the numbers used above are illustrative, they are in-

Figure 1
Illustration of Proposed Income Allowance Plan
(Married couple with three children)

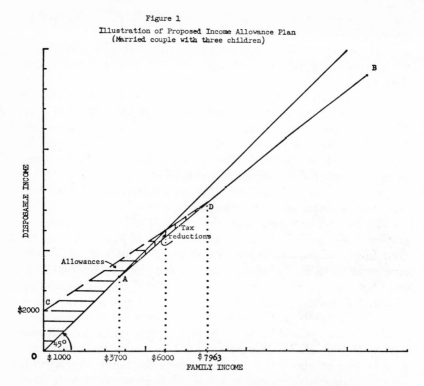

dicative of what is needed for an effective program. It would be expensive for the federal budget, involving an expenditure of perhaps fifteen billion dollars a year. Partially offsetting this budgetary cost are the savings in public assistance, on which governments now spend five and six-tenths billion dollars a year, of which three and two-tenths billion are federal funds. In addition, savings are possible in a host of other income maintenance programs, notably in agriculture.

The program is expensive, but it need not be introduced all at once. The size of allowances can be gradually increased as room in the budget becomes available. This is likely to happen fairly rapidly. First of all, there is room right now. The budget, and the budget deficit, can and should be larger in order to create a tight labor market. Second, the normal growth of the economy increases federal revenues from existing tax rates by some six to seven billion dollars a year. This is a drag on the economy, threatening stagnation and rising unemployment unless it is matched by a similar rise in federal spending or avoided by cutting taxes. With defense spending stable or declining, there is room both for increases in civilian spending, as in the war on poverty, and for further tax cuts. Indeed, periodic tax reduction is official administration policy, and President Johnson agrees that the next turn belongs to low-income families. Gradually building an allowance system into the federal income tax would be the best way to lower the net yield of the tax—fairer and more far-reaching than further cuts in tax rates.

I referred to programs which make up for lack of earning capacity as stopgaps, but that is not entirely fair. Poverty itself saps earning capacity. The welfare way of life, on the edge of subsistence, does not provide motivation or useful work experience either to parents or to children. A better system, one which enables people to retain their self-respect and initiative, would in itself help to break the vicious circle.

The proposed allowance system is of course not the only thing which needs to be done. Without attempting to be exhaustive, I shall mention three other measures for the assistance of families without adequate earning capacity.

It hardly needs emphasizing that the large size of Negro families or non-families is one of the principal causes of Negro poverty. There are too many mouths to feed per breadwinner, and frequently the care of children keeps the mother, the only possible breadwinner, at home. A program of day care and pre-school education for children five and under could meet several objectives at once—enriching the experience of the children and freeing the mother for training or for work.

The quality of the medical care of Negroes is a disgrace in itself and contributes to their other economic handicaps.[16] Even so the financing of the care of "the medically indigent" is inadequate and chaotic. Sooner or later we will extend the principle of Medicare to citizens under sixty-five. Why not sooner?

As mentioned above, much Negro poverty in the South reflects the inability of Negroes to make a livelihood in agriculture. As far as the traditional cash crop, cotton, is concerned, mechanization and the competition of larger-scale units in the Southwest are undermining the plantation and share-cropping system of the Southeast. The Negro subsistence farmer has too little land, equipment, and know-how to make a decent income. Current government agricultural programs, expensive as they are to the taxpayer, do very little to help the sharecropper or subsistence farmer. Our whole agricultural policy needs to be recast, to give income support to people rather than price support to crops and to take people off the land rather than to take land out of cultivation. The effects on the social system of the South may be revolutionary, but they can only be salutary. Obviously there will be a tremendous burden on educational and training facilities to fit people for urban and industrial life. And I must emphasize again that substantial migration from agriculture is only possible, without disaster in the cities, in a booming economy with a tight labor market.

Conclusion

By far the most powerful factor determining the economic status of Negroes is the over-all state of the U.S. economy. A vigorously expanding economy with a steadily tight labor market will rapidly raise the position of the Negro, both absolutely and relatively. Favored by such a climate, the host of specific measures to eliminate discrimination, improve education and training, provide housing, and strengthen the family can yield substantial additional results. In a less beneficent economic climate, where jobs are short rather than men, the wars against racial inequality and poverty will be uphill battles, and some highly touted weapons may turn out to be dangerously futile.

The forces of the market place, the incentives of private self-interest, the pressures of supply and demand—these can be powerful allies or stubborn opponents. Properly harnessed, they quietly and impersonally accomplish objectives which may elude detailed legislation and administration. To harness them to the cause of the American Negro is entirely possible. It requires simply that the federal government dedicate its fiscal and monetary policies more wholeheartedly and singlemindedly to achieving and maintaining genuinely full employment. The obstacles are not technical or economic. One obstacle is a general lack of understanding that unemployment and related evils are remediable by national fiscal and monetary measures. The other is the high priority now given to competing financial objectives.

In this area, as in others, the administration has disarmed its conservative opposition by meeting it halfway, and no influential political voices challenge the tacit compromise from the "Left." Negro rights movements have so far taken no interest in national fiscal and monetary policy. No doubt gold, the federal budget, and the actions of the Federal Reserve System seem remote from the day-to-day firing line of the movements. Direct local actions to redress specific grievances and to battle visible enemies are absorbing and dramatic. They have concrete observable results. But the use of national political influence on behalf of the goals of the Employment Act of 1946 is equally important. It would fill a political vacuum, and its potential long-run pay-off is very high.

The goal of racial equality suggests that the federal government should provide more stimulus to the economy. Fortunately, it also suggests constructive ways to give the stimulus. We can kill two birds with one stone. The economy needs additional spending in general; the wars on poverty and racial inequality need additional spending of particular kinds. The needed spending falls into two categories: government programs to diminish economic inequalities by building up the earning capacities of the poor and their children, and humane public assistance to citizens who temporarily or permanently lack the capacity to earn a decent living for themselves and their families. In both categories the nation, its conscience aroused by the plight of the Negro, has the chance to make reforms which will benefit the whole society.

REFERENCES

1. As Locke Anderson shows, one would expect advances in median income to run into diminishing returns in reducing the number of people below some fixed poverty-level income. W. H. Locke Anderson, "Trickling Down: The Relationship between Economic Growth and the Extent of Poverty Among American Families," *Quarterly Journal of Economics,* Vol. 78 (November 1964), pp. 511-524. However, for the economy as a whole, estimates by Lowell Galloway suggest that advances in median income still result in a substantial reduction in the fraction of the population below poverty-level incomes. "The Foundation of the War on Poverty," *American Economic Review,* Vol. 55 (March 1965), pp. 122-131.

2. Anderson, *op. cit.,* Table IV, p. 522.

3. This point, and others made in this section, have been eloquently argued by Harry G. Johnson, "Unemployment and Poverty," unpublished paper presented at West Virginia University Conference on Poverty Amidst Affluence, May 5, 1965.

4. Galloway, *op. cit.* Galloway used the definitions of poverty originally suggested by the Council of Economic Advisers in its 1964 Economic Report, that is: incomes below $3000 a year for families and below $1500 a year

for single individuals. The Social Security Administration has refined these measures to take better account of family size and of income in kind available to farmers. Mollie Orshansky, "Counting the Poor: Another Look at the Poverty Profile, *Social Security Bulletin*, Vol. 28 (January 1965), pp. 3-29. These refinements change the composition of the "poor" but affect very little their total number; it is doubtful they would alter Galloway's results.

5. Galloway, *op. cit.*, shows that postwar experience suggests that, other things equal, every point by which unemployment is diminished lowers the national incidence of poverty by .5 per cent of itself. And this does not include the effects of the accompanying increase in median family income, which would be of the order of 3 per cent and reduce the poverty fraction another 1.8 per cent.

6. For lack of comparable nationwide income data, the only way to gauge the progress of Negroes relative to whites over long periods of time is to compare their distributions among occupations. A measure of the occupational position of a group can be constructed from decennial Census data by weighting the proportions of the group in each occupation by the average income of the occupation. The ratio of this measure for Negroes to the same measure for whites is an index of the relative occupational position of Negroes. Such calculations were originally made by Gary Becker, *The Economics of Discrimination* (Chicago, 1957). They have recently been refined and brought up to date by Dale Hiestand, *Economic Growth and Employment Opportunities for Minorities,* (New York, 1964), p. 53. Hiestand's results are as follows:

Occupational position of Negroes relative to whites:

	1910	1920	1930	1940	1950	1960
Male	78.0	78.1	78.2	77.5	81.4	82.1
Female	78.0	71.3	74.8	76.8	81.6	84.3

The figures show that Negro men lost ground in the Great Depression, that they gained sharply in the nineteen forties, and that their progress almost ceased in the nineteen fifties. Negro women show a rising secular trend since the nineteen twenties, but their gains too were greater in the tight labor markets of the nineteen forties than in the nineteen thirties or nineteen fifties.

Several cautions should be borne in mind in interpreting these figures: (1) Much of the relative occupational progress of Negroes is due to massive migration from agriculture to occupations of much higher average income. When the over-all relative index nevertheless does not move, as in the nineteen fifties, the position of Negroes in non-agricultural occupations has declined. (2) Since the figures include unemployed as well as employed persons and Negroes are more sensitive to unemployment, the occupational index understates their progress when unemployment declined (1940-50) and overstates it when unemployment rose (1930-40 and 1950-60). (3)

Within any Census occupational category, Negroes earn less than whites. So the absolute level of the index overstates the Negro's relative position. Moreover, this overstatement is probably greater in Census years of relatively slack labor markets, like 1940 and 1960, than in other years.

The finding that labor market conditions arrested the progress of Negro men is confirmed by income and unemployment data analyzed by Alan B. Batchelder, "Decline in the Relative Income of Negro Men," *Quarterly Journal of Economics,* Vol. 78 (November 1964), pp. 525-548.

7. This is emphasized by Daniel Patrick Moynihan in his contribution to this volume.

8. Differences between Negro men and women with respect to unemployment and income progress are reported and analyzed by Alan Batchelder, *op. cit.*

9. Figures are given in other papers in this volume: see, for example, the essays by Rashi Fein and Daniel Patrick Moynihan.

10. In 34 per cent of poor Negro families, the head is not in the labor force; in 6 per cent, the head is unemployed. These figures relate to the Social Security Administration's "economy-level" poverty index. Mollie Orshansky, *op. cit.*

11. See *Manpower Report of the President,* March 1964, Table A-3, p. 197.

12. Hiestand, *op. cit.,* Table I, pp. 7-9.

13. Batchelder, *op. cit.,* shows that the incomes of Negro men declined relative to those of white men in every region of the country. For the country as a whole, nevertheless, the median income of Negro men stayed close to half that of white men. The reason is that migration from the South, where the Negro-white income ratio is particularly low, just offset the declines in the regional ratios.

14. The official Advisory Council on Public Assistance recommended in 1960 that children be aided even if there are two parents or relatives *in loco parentis* in their household, but Congress has ignored this proposal. *Public Assistance: A Report of the Findings and Recommendations of the Advisory Council on Public Assistance,* Department of Health, Education, and Welfare, January 1960. The Advisory Council also wrestled somewhat inconclusively with the problem of the means test and suggested that states be allowed to experiment with dropping or modifying it for five years. This suggestion too has been ignored.

15. Adjusting the size of a government benefit to the amount of other income is not without precedent. Recipients of Old Age Survivors and Disability Insurance benefits under the age of seventy-two lose one dollar of benefits and only one dollar for every two dollars of earned income above $1200 but below $1700 a year.

16. See the statistics summarized by Rashi Fein elsewhere in this volume.

ROBERT A. DENTLER

Barriers to Northern School Desegregation

The Current Scene

NORTHERN PUBLIC schools, from kindergarten to the graduate level, have been racially segregated on an extensive scale since the Reconstruction. Statistics have been collected by communities and states only since the Brown decision in 1954, but these show that *hundreds* of elementary and secondary schools in the Northeast and the Midwest have student bodies composed of more than 90 per cent Negroes.

The racial census released by the New York Education Department in 1962 is typical. Twenty elementary schools outside of New York City had over 90 per cent Negro pupils; forty-six had more than 50 per cent. A total of 103 was 31 per cent or more Negro.[1] And this was true in a state in which the proportion of Negroes within the total population of all but a few communities is less than 15 per cent!

In the largest survey of school segregation in the North to date,[2] 200 public school systems were studied. These were in towns spread across nineteen states, which included 75 per cent of the Negro population in the North. Some 1,141 schools were listed as having nonwhite enrollments of 60 per cent or more. About 60 per cent of these segregated schools were clustered in six of the larger cities: New York City, Chicago, Philadelphia, Detroit, Cleveland, and Los Angeles. Most of the others were located in other large central cities or in neighboring suburbs. School segregation is thus so pronounced in certain cities in the North that if public schools are placed on a scale from all white pupils to all Negro, the great majority of them will cluster at the far extremes. Mixed student bodies are very uncommon.

However, as the New Jersey Supreme Court noted in June 1965, a public school need not be all or even 80 per cent Negro in order

472

to be racially segregated. A school is racially segregated if the ratio of Negro to white students is substantially in excess of the ratio common to the community as a whole.[3] This definition applies to a school that is 50 per cent Negro in a community where Negroes comprise 20 per cent of the total population. It also includes a school that is 95 per cent white in the same community.

Minority segregated public schools in the North tend quite uniformly to have poorer facilities, less qualified staff, and inferior programs of instruction than majority segregated schools.[4] Even when differences in facilities are eliminated, minority segregation impedes both teaching and learning. Attendance at a minority segregated public school tends to reinforce the damage already experienced by children maturing in a milieu drenched with discriminatory stimuli. Indeed, attendance at a racially segregated public school is probably harmful whether the segregation is minority or majority. The isolation experienced by students in all-white schools stimulates ignorance, fear, and prejudice, just as it confirms the self-belief in inferiority among students in all-Negro schools.[5]

Protests were lodged by Negro groups against school segregation in the North on many occasions between 1917 and 1954. But the Brown decision brought awareness among educational decision-makers to a new focal point.[6] Only in the last decade have the gravity and scope of the problem been identified, solutions advanced, and resistance to change mobilized.

We are presently in the eye of a Northern storm of community conflict. The issue has been joined; it has become a one-sided question with but one set of social facts, all of which indicate that Negro racial segregation in schools is bad, and most that white segregation is bad, too. It has become a matter which *must* be dealt with if racial and cultural cleavages are to be resolved and if social inclusiveness within cultural pluralism is to be achieved. Moreover, the elimination of school segregation has, like all serious modern social problems, become an issue illuminated by an awareness of attendant *costs:* If school desegregation is to be achieved, public education, its political context, and its fiscal support must be changed too, in ways that are demanding, even harsh.

The pace of racial integration in Northern schools has been equivalent to that of integration in Southern schools, although the Southern pace quickened enormously with the incentive of federal aid in 1965. Most cities and suburbs in the six Northern states with a Negro population of 5 per cent or more contain at least one minority segregated school. Five to ten of these have been eliminated each year since 1960, while new ones crop up to replace them as populations redistribute. If no new rate of change develops, the North will exhibit deep and extensive racial segregation in its urban schools as late as the middle of the next century.

The Smaller Communities

There is little point in talking about Northern school segregation as a uniform condition. More than two-thirds of all the racially segregated public schools in the North are located in ten of the largest cities. There, population density, the hardening of ghetto boundaries, the class structure, and political organization, all militate powerfully against school desegregation. These must be distinguished from the hundreds of smaller urban communities where desegregation is not only as desirable but more feasible.

The communities in the North where school desegregation has been agreed upon and sometimes implemented effectively are all smaller cities and suburbs. Berkeley, California, is one.[7] There, the Board of Education authorized a citizens' committee to recommend approaches to the problem of segregation as early as 1958. The committee was established after pressure from the Berkeley chapter of the NAACP. It made several good suggestions, none of which was implemented effectively, however, for several years.

But in 1962, the Berkeley Superintendent, responding to pressure from CORE and to growing convictions about the educational undesirability of school segregation, secured his board's authorization of another citizens' committee. This group worked for nearly a year. It defined de facto school segregation as extant in any public school whose white to nonwhite ratio "varies significantly from the same ratio of the District as a whole." With this yardstick, the committee found that three elementary schools, one junior high school, and the high school were not segregated, while sixteen schools were.

The committee asserted that this condition was bad, blamed it on the concept of neighborhood schools and on housing patterns, and proposed ten programs for its elimination. These included redistricting, pairing of some schools, open enrollment, a program of curricular improvement, and the strengthening of services and facilities. Some of these potentially transformative proposals were implemented, including positive, fairly radical changes in the composition of junior high schools. Indicative of the mood of the community is the fact that, in 1964, two members of the Berkeley school board were re-elected in a recall election.

White Plains, New York, offers a comparable illustration and, as an Eastern community, is more relevant to the problem of Northern school segregation than is Berkeley.[8] The Board of Education and the Superintendent of Schools in White Plains were aware of "racial imbalance" in their system as early as 1961; they had instituted special services in the one elementary school which was roughly two-thirds Negro, and they had made a few minor adjustments as early as 1962. Beyond a concern with compensatory education and related services, however, there was little professional readiness to define school segregation as salient.

Two forces converged to change this. The Negro leadership of White Plains and the officers of the New York State Education Department in Albany exerted persuasive pressure. The leadership threatened political action, and the state officials offered assistance, advice, and a flow of information showing how school segregation (always referred to in communications as "racial imbalance") impaired public education. The Superintendent and his Board then began carefully planned but prompt, unanimous action to desegregate. They acted during 1964, the same year in which the Superintendent became convinced that "racial imbalance" was a blight on the level of professional performance of his administration and teaching staff. Had this redefinition not occurred, it is unlikely that change would have taken place.

Other small cities have desegregated their public schools during the last five years in response to similar political and educational administrative pressures, or for different yet functionally equivalent reasons. Englewood, New Jersey, and New Rochelle, New York, for example, desegregated under court orders. Other towns have desegregated for essentially social reasons, such as population change, special real-estate conditions, or cultural values. Greenburgh, New York, is a case in point. There, in one of four districts, school integration began early and has become a source of social pride.

From participation in several school desegregation programs in smaller Northern communities, I would speculate that there are some rather uniform conditions under which desegregation becomes *possible* politically and educationally. Negroes must protest in a visible, unequivocal manner. This protest must resonate positively with some segment of the white population which already commands the attention of local schoolmen or board members.

Of equal importance is a clear, sufficiently intense stimulus from state or other extra-local authorities. Little change has occurred in Pennsylvania and Illinois, where many smaller cities maintain segregated schools because of weak state educational agencies. It also seems plain from case experiences that a community must be free from a very highly *stratified* class structure grounded substantially in religious or racial groupings. The prospect of too severe a change in the foundations of the local structure of social rewards is relatively certain to prevent school desegregation.

Illustrating Barriers in Smaller Cities

We can best depict these conditions and connect them with impediments to change within the school systems themselves through details from a case study of a smaller city on the Northeastern seaboard which moved to the edge of school integration but then drew back and renewed its efforts to preserve its historic ghetto. We shall call the community "Little City."

Interviews documented the belief that the *status quo* system of race relations persists in Little City, that the system is old and durable, and that most Negroes as well as whites in the community subscribe to and reinforce it, in spite of its disadvantages.

This *status quo* is common to hundreds of established, thriving Northern communities. Under it, Negroes are tolerated by whites and there is cooperation as long as the minorities accept the confines of what is a partial caste system. Whites assume that Negroes "prefer" to live in the Bilbo Area Ghetto (although a few families are sprinkled elsewhere in other low-income blocks). They also presume that Negroes will share unequally in the resources and services of the community, but that few Little City Negroes will ever aspire to upper-level occupational positions. They will instead aspire toward, and then be employed in, service and lower semiskilled jobs.

There are, in other words, *niches* for Negroes in the residential, resource, and job structures of the community. The value of the *niches* to Negroes is dual. They supply more opportunities than are available in some other localities, and they are equal to those available to a small proportion of low-income whites within Little City. Historically, the *status quo* has been maintained because Negroes have fared better in Little City than they have reason to expect they might fare elsewhere. In exchange, they have maintained polite civil relations.

This pattern has been challenged in Little City within the last few years. Nearly all Little City parents are aware of this challenge. A majority, regardless of race, try to suppress this awareness by attributing it to the work of CORE or other "outside trouble-makers." The attempt fails, however, for the same parents have internalized the message from the nation at large that a fundamental change in race relations is taking place.

All of the imagery of school segregation among parents concentrates upon the Bilbo Street School and neighborhood, in spite of the zoning change and the fraction of Negroes located in other neighborhoods. Generally, most parents think of Bilbo as having a sound enough physical plant and as *equal* to all other Little City schools in quality of services. Some combine the two ideas and think of the Bilbo School as slightly superior to some other schools. A few Bilbo parents and a smaller minority of others say openly that the Bilbo School staff is inferior and, more significantly, that Negro children are less well educated than whites within the Bilbo School. Most Little City parents favor current school zones and desire *no change* in the future. They view the neighborhood schools as the best of all possible arrangements; they believe that revising the neighborhood concept would reduce Negro progress and produce added evils such as traffic hazards.

A few parents advance the idea that minor additional zoning changes and some "open enrollment" would be appropriate for Little City. About 20 per cent of the tax paying parents *favor* more change than this. Another 20 per cent would resist greater change with vigor, particularly if the concept of the neighborhood school, upon which the residential structure of the town is grounded, were altered drastically.

White parents in Little City, in the main, do not know what would be gained through school desegregation. In view of the saturation coverage of this question through the mass media, this suggests that they do not want to know. Most parents emphasize that Little City neighborhood schools at present all offer the same quality of education, that they use the same books and teach the same subjects. As one white father commented, "What difference would it make if 'they' sat next to a white child? How will they learn more that way?"

A majority of Little City parents believe, according to one of them, that "There is no racial problem in Little City. Whatever trouble has developed has come from four or five hotheads who have turned this supposed problem into a political football." A Negro mother confirmed this interpretation: "I grew up in Little City and I have several children in school here and the schools give equal opportunity for all." A Negro couple followed this remark with the statement: "There is no racial issue here at all. If some people feel that there is, they are wrong or mistaken."

It is therefore not surprising that most parents see *no need* to search for desegregation. This indifference cuts two ways, however. At least half of the parents are vocally disposed to accept the Superintendent's and the Board's definitions of what is needed. They are tolerant of authority; they prefer clearly stated, authoritatively designed changes. They *trust* those in control of the public schools, and this trust extends into the area of race relations.

If the Board and the Superintendent announce that specific changes—short of radical revision of the neighborhood concept— are necessary, a majority of the parents would accept this definition of the situation at face value. Moreover, most parents believe that such changes are the province of the Board and the staff—that expert and authoritative leadership is requisite to decisions on problems of school segregation.

There are many ways in which segregation and any attempted resolution of it can touch off older social, economic, and religious tensions latent in the social organization of Little City. Neighborhood residents are aware of minute differences between localities; a sharply stratified class structure exists and will undergo stresses with changing racial balances.

In view of the nature and depth of these attitudes, planning for school integration and implementing even part of the plan must depend upon an exceptional convergence of counterforces. Little City, for instance, began to plan for integration because the State Commissioner of Education pressed for such action, because a secure, long-established local superintendent saw the value of desegregation as one part of a program of educational reconstruction, and because civil rights groups mustered an effective protest. These pressures were checked, however, by the death of the superintendent, by simultaneous changes in the composition of the school board, and through the failure of the civil rights supporters to sustain their protest over a two-year period. In other words, the requisite conditions for surmounting an entrenched partial caste system, even in a single public institution such as education, are so elaborate as to be undone at any turn of events. The attitude structure of the public, Negro as well as white, is an enduring impediment, whether active or passive. In Little City, the views of teachers and other school officers were neither felt nor defined as relevant to the issue.

Fortunately, in the process of persuasion which leads smaller urban communities to decide to integrate public schools, the more salient conditions sometimes compensate for one another. Thus, a highly stratified local population with group interests invested deeply in maintaining school segregation may be moved nonetheless by firm sanctions from a state commissioner or superintendent. In New York State, for example, the present position of the Court of Appeals is that

The Board of Regents, under authority of section 207 of the Education Law, has declared racially imbalanced schools to be educationally inadequate. The commissioner, under sections 301 and 305 of the Education Law, has implemented this policy by directing local boards to take steps to eliminate racial imbalance. These decisions are final, absent a showing of pure arbitrariness. . . . Disagreement with the sociological, psychological and educational assumptions relied on by the commissioner cannot be evaluated by this court. Such arguments can only be heard in the Legislature, which has endowed the commissioner with an all but absolute power, or by the Board of Regents, who are elected by the Legislature and make public policy in the field of education.[9]

Differently weighted influences, then, can combine to induce desegregation of public schools. There is a ceiling on how much any one influence fostering desegregation can compensate for resistances. Even court orders and sanctions from state superintendents are insufficient if no other factors are aligned in support of local change.

Perhaps most important in smaller communities is the fact that technical solutions are available in abundance. Small districts can be merged, zones changed, buses introduced, or schools paired. Old buildings can be revised in use, and new ones can be introduced to provide extra degrees of freedom. Several reasonable courses of action toward school integration are ordinarily apparent.

Moreover, in smaller communities, a board's decision to integrate can be communicated to parents clearly and quickly, in combination with programs of social preparation and civic as well as school staff planning. A touch of ingenuity, or merely the adoption of successful features of neighboring systems, also enables smaller communities to make school desegregation a time for improving educational programs in general—for upgrading the quality of instruction or staff or facilities. This prospect and stories of success in integration are gradually becoming commonplace in the professional journals and newsletters of teachers and schoolmen, so the trend should quicken over the next few years.

The Big Cities

An improved rate of change in school integration in the smaller communities contributes little to the acceleration of desegregation in the great central cities of the North. While the suburb of Englewood, New Jersey, eliminates a single segregated school and, over a period of a decade, evolves better school services as a result, neighboring New York City will continue to be burdened with hundreds of highly segregated public schools.

There are technical solutions to minority school segregation in the great cities, but they are few in number and generally drastic in effect upon both the clientele and the practitioners. Rezoning, district reorganization, pairing, free transfer, and open enrollment are valuable devices, but to have any effect upon the problem as a whole, these schemes must be applied in a system-wide and combined fashion.[10] No one mechanism among these, and no combination of devices applied in some but not all sublocalities, will result in any significant change. Technical solutions attempted in pilot fashion thus far have failed or have proved ungeneralizable, because of population density in the big city ghettos and because of traffic congestion.

Several partially adequate technical solutions have been proposed for each of the larger Northern cities. The simplest of these is rationally planned assignment of pupils. Philip Hauser and others demonstrated in their report on the Chicago public schools that, if pupils were assigned to schools in terms of proximity and with full but not excessive utilization of seating capacities, many all-white public schools which are underutilized in that city would be desegregated, and many mainly Negro schools which are now overcrowded would be integrated and thinned out.[11] Rational use of seating capacity would probably reduce the level of school segregation within any one city by no more than 15 to 20 per cent. But, compared with a condition of no change, that is progress.

A second solution entails revising the building programs of city systems so that the sites of all new and renovated structures are chosen with a view toward integration. This means a moratorium on the construction of schools *inside* burgeoning ghettos. Students would be transported in increasing numbers to schools located outside their neighborhoods. A third solution combines revision of building plans with the reorganization and combination of existing schools through pairing and complexes. In complexes, a series of neighboring schools engages in staff and student interchange.[12]

The two most promising technical solutions are also the most radical. One is the concept of the education park.[13] Here, big city systems would abandon neighborhood schools (or use them for very different purposes, such as community centers) and erect consolidated facilities housing from 5,000 to 20,000 students. Such a campus-style institution would be located to draw its students from a very wide residential base, one broad enough, perhaps, to surmount long-term changes in class and ethnic settlements. A second, related idea is to *merge* mainly white suburban school districts with increasingly Negro inner-city districts. District mergers could be achieved by state authorities and could break through ancient patterns of residential restriction.

These proposals imply enormous transformations in the character of public schools. Under contemporary urban conditions, use tends to follow facility. That is to say, if a new kind of physical plant is erected, whether a park, a parking lot, or a new type of school building, enthusiastic users tend to follow. The programs of instruction within an education park, moreover, based as they would be upon new resources of centralized administration and greater staff specialization and flexibility of deployment, would be a major innovation.

For a time, critics of school segregation in the big cities believed the situation to be fairly hopeless. Imaginable solutions like those mentioned above were viewed as infeasible both politically and fiscally. As discontent with urban public schools deepens, and as federal and state aid prospects grow, radical solutions to segregation which have major implications for quality of instruction begin to intrigue critics, specialists, and policy-makers alike.

Not all modes of desegregation contribute to improvement in the quality of public education, nor are technical solutions, by themselves, sufficient to stimulate either integration or excellence of program. If these qualifications are kept in mind, however, it becomes apparent that durable, system-wide excellence in big city schools cannot be attained without integration, and that integration can serve not only the ideal of justice but also the urgent goal of better public instruction.

Sources of Resistance in Big Cities

Our view is thus that valuable technical solutions have been proposed and that fiscal resources for using them are becoming available. The political dialogue about school segregation rages in the big cities against this background of possibilities. Yet, little or no integration of public schools is taking place. After ten years of talk and five years of visible struggle, only Detroit among the six largest and educationally most segregated central cities of the North has made some progress. New York City, Chicago, and Philadelphia, among other major cities, are more severely segregated today than they were in 1954.

Partly, this is the direct outcome of the continuing northward migration of Negro families and the reciprocal flight of whites to the suburbs. Still, the evidence of virtual inactivity among city school boards (or rather the evidence of *no effort* save experiments with open enrollment, rezoning, and a handful of pairings) calls for more than a demographic interpretation.

We must look to the social and cultural bases of Northern big city life to understand why so little change has occurred. In the case of school segregation, especially, we must take into account the political context and the cultural milieu of urban public education. For example, in the great cities, any force toward desegregation is effectively countered by organized opposition. Big city school superintendents, however, get paid more, have better protective clauses in their contracts, command a greater power base, and receive clearer indications of the educational damages resulting from segregation. If a superintendent of a big city did define school segregation openly as a *major* educational issue, change toward integration would occur. Opposition can be squelched with counter-opposition.

Consider Chicago, where the role of the Superintendent, Benjamin C. Willis, illustrates the big city pattern. Superintendent Willis announced in 1963 that he considered proposals for altering neighborhood school boundaries in order to provide free choice to Negroes, or for transferring white students into mainly Negro schools, to be "ominous."[14] He informed his Board of Education that, in his judgment, the manipulation of attendance and assignment procedures might prove disastrous *educationally*. Radical tensions could increase as a result, he believed, and more white families might move out of the city and into the suburbs.

Plans to desegregate had been accumulating in Chicago since 1960. These were submerged in litigation, direct and occasionally even violent political action, the intervention by invitation and strategic intrusion of social scientists and educational experts from the universities and the nation at large, and upheavals within the Board and the Office of the Superintendent itself.

There emerged from this a characteristic Northern urban pattern. On August 28, 1963, the Chicago Board of Education resolved that some schools in the system were all-Negro in student composition, and that such "separation" might interfere with learning. The Board then appointed a distinguished Advisory Panel, including Philip Hauser, then Chairman of the Department of Sociology at the University of Chicago, and Sterling McMurrin, former United States Commissioner of Education. They directed the Panel to suggest remedies.

The gap between Superintendent Willis and his own Board is suggested by one event at the same August meeting. The Board accepted Superintendent Willis's proposal to allow those pupils in the top 5 per cent of the city's high-school students to transfer to another high school—*if* their present school had no honors program. Even this petty proposal stimulated intense public reaction. After massive white picketing, and after negotiation and review, the parents of several transfer applicants filed suit in the local Superior Court, requesting the judge to issue a writ of mandamus against Superintendent Willis on the ground that he had withheld the certification of transfer. The Appellate Court upheld the order. In reply, Willis resigned in protest over the Court decision in order to show the irreconcilable difference between his Board and himself, for the Board had directed him to transfer the students.

Two days after Superintendent Willis resigned, the Illinois Chairman of the North Central Association of Colleges and Secondary Schools warned the Chicago Board of Education that the city's high schools might lose their accreditation if he ever found that the Board had infringed on the Superintendent's administrative prerogatives. And, two days after this warning arrived, the Board voted to refuse Superintendent Willis's resignation. Later, the Board voted to reconsider its previous order directing Willis to transfer students. Willis then withdrew his resignation.

The Advisory Panel on Integration made its recommendations in the early spring of 1964, after weeks of picketing, boycotting of stores as well as schools, and swirling controversy over this issue. Minor parts of the Panel's proposals were adopted by the Board in the fall, but by 1965 there was no indication that any important reccommendations would be adopted. The report was *not* endorsed by the Superintendent.

A policy stand on school desegregation has not cost a single Northern big city superintendent his job. Superintendent Willis has been attacked politically for four years for his opposition to desegregation, yet these attacks have done little more than tarnish his professional and public image. New York City Superintendent Calvin Gross did *not* lose his job because of his stand on this issue.

More important is the fact that no Northern big city superintendent has committed himself emphatically to the pursuit of school desegregation. The barriers to school desegregation in large Northern cities will remain a subject of moot speculation until at least one such superintendent does take a strong, positive position and allows others to observe the consequences. The policy recommendations of city school superintendents are more than influential. They are profoundly indicative of changes in school practice, even where they are not determinative.

Sufficient Conditions for Inaction

There is probably one condition which is sufficient to maintain inaction on big city school segregation in the North: If preservation of the *status quo* on this question helps to preserve the present distribution of power in the community, the *status quo* will in all probability be maintained, while the dialogue about segregation continues. Public officials, including superintendents, do not take unnecessary risks. They do not press for significant social changes if the effects upon their own access to authority are not predictable and promising.

There may be no change, then, because the ability of the city superintendent and his board to act on any question of general interest in the community is limited by the risks that the central political agency, usually the office of the mayor, is disposed to take. "In order for anything to be done under public auspices, the elaborate decentralization of authority . . . must somehow be overcome or set aside. The widely diffused right to act *must* be replaced by a unified ability to act."[15]

In the case of school segregation, the "unified ability to act" depends upon relations among the superintendent, his board, and the political power structure of the community as a whole. No one of these elements will jeopardize another intentionally, although a mayor or a city council often transfers responsibility for this problem to the board of education in lieu of agreeing to act in unity.

Trivial Institutional Impediments

Teachers and principals play a minor role in the politics of school segregation and desegregation. They are vital to the success of any program of desegregation, for their attitudes and practices either reinforce a positive integrative trend and make an educational opportunity out of it or undermine the worth of any effort.

But their role in the decision process itself is minor. The segregation issue is a general political one, and most school functionaries are disbarred from participation in it except under crisis conditions. Crises include incidents where Negro protest groups have managed to unite with teachers' unions for specific pickets and boycotts; but these are very rare. Moreover, it is seldom obvious in the negotiation of conflicts exactly how the teachers' and principals' own interests are involved. When these are touched upon, substantial mobilization occurs, as with all other urban interest groups.

Junior-high-school principals in New York City, for example, were *not* asked for their opinions about desegregation nor did they place themselves in the dialogue. But when a State Advisory Committee recommended in 1964 that segregated junior high schools should be abolished and the grade structure of all junior highs revised, the stake of the principals was defined. Their current arrangements threatened, these lower-line officers organized and communicated their opposition to change. When the Superintendent made no response, the principals undertook a strong newspaper advertising campaign opposing reorganization.

Headquarters staffs often impede desegregation efforts in less direct ways. The administrative staff officials responsible for planning transportation, pupil assignment, and even renovation and new construction of plants, all make hundreds of technical decisions each year which impede or foster revision of the *status quo.*

Change is costly, not only in money but in demands upon skill. School planners resist alterations in population estimation procedures they have grown accustomed to over the decades "merely" because ethnicity and changes in the distribution of minorities have not customarily been considered in detail. If a program of school desegregation involves administrative decentralization, then accountants, other business officers, and related staff workers must make socially costly adjustments that range from changing daily work procedures to changing one's place of work itself.

No values, and no pressures, dominant in the white majority community reward any readiness to change among staff members. The municipal educational bureaucracy, in short, responds much like any other institutionalized establishment. In the case of staff impediments, however, incomplete information, unimaginative assessments of feasibility, and an inability to innovate discourage desegregation more effectively than does the organized opposition of principals.

These resistances to change are trivial in their over-all contribution to the fate of the segregation question both because lower echelons do not have that much influence in policy decisions and because educators themselves are perplexed by competing messages and by a steady change in the salience of the issue *within* their profession. The National Education Association, the teachers' unions, the United States Office of Education, and some of the teacher-training institutions are now at work, through officers in charge of integration or "equal opportunity," emphasizing the importance of the question and the urgency of resolution. On this issue, these agencies work somewhat like the National Council of Churches in its limited bearing upon local Protestant congregations: There is a low ceiling upon the national association's influence.

Prospects for Northern School Desegregation

My argument has been that Northern school desegregation is not difficult to accomplish in smaller cities and suburbs. Where the school superintendents of such communities have allied themselves with state authority and have responded to the protest from their Negro clientele, desegregation has been proven politically safe as well as technically feasible. Moreover, the educational outcomes of most of the efforts to date have been highly encouraging to professionals. News of the revitalization and improvement of staff morale and daily practices within such changing systems is being exchanged constantly at educational conventions and through the professional media.

The major part of the problem centers in a dozen of the largest central cities. In these, very little movement toward desegregation has occurred. The political risks continue to be too high, and the rewards within the educational establishment have not been worth the effort.

The seasonal campaigns of the civil rights and Negro protest groups have become strategic, though insufficient, as a political force. These campaigns are strategic insofar as they maintain the level of priority on the segregation question and even, on occasion, heighten it. They are insufficient—even with annual improvements such as better publicity, broader constituency, and tighter alignment with other interest groups—because the big cities are too divisive and counter-protest is too readily available.

Moreover, school policy-makers know that very few citizens, Negro or white, are as intensely concerned with the educational question as they are with contending issues of housing, crime, and employment. Finally, there is not apt to be enough unity of leadership among Negro groups and politicians to allow for a much greater focus of effort on the school issue than has been achieved to date.

Nevertheless, some big Northern cities are likely to desegregate their public schools when their fiscal dilemmas intensify. Northern-style school segregation is expensive. In the big cities, school funds have been poured into the erection of expensive new plants to accommodate students in the burgeoning residential ghettos.[16] Funds that would once have been used to improve all-white schools in the developing or most desirable real-estate areas must now be diverted. The new ghetto schools that result, moreover, offer little political reward. They are not appreciated because they reinforce the ghetto and because the immediate electorate is a captive constituency that is apathetic about education. In white suburbs, a Negro ghetto school depresses real-estate values in its neighborhood. It is a standing advertisement *against* the educational magnetism to technical and professional workers seeking an alternative to city school facilities. It is often a sign of decadence and commercial deterioration to most whites.[17]

In the big cities, the issue has unraveled the sleeve of public education as a whole. For state and local policy-makers, and for chief administrators, school desegregation has great potential significance for the merger of school districts, the progressive consolidation of schools, the revision of grade structures, and whole programs of instruction. The issue also stimulates questions about the quality and equal distribution of facilities, the rights of substitute teachers, the assignment of teachers to one school versus another, and the *stability* of a career in neighborhood-school teaching in general. The dialogue in professional circles, particularly in Northern teacher-training institutions and among education reporters, even penetrates to the question of the *viability* of public education as it is now operated. The alternative most often imagined is one in which the public school system of the big city becomes a semicustodial institution serving the clientele of the welfare department, and where the advantaged white majority has elected either the suburbs or the private schools of the city.

The thesis is that, if public education cannot evolve toward its historic goal of *universality*, it cannot be maintained in its present form as a general municipal service. Much more than the question of racial segregation is involved in this conversation, but no other issue exposes the total dilemma so dramatically.

The most likely future response of educators to the problem of Northern school segregation will be to make important changes, but to make them only in the wake of the current period of identification of the problem, exploration of its implications, and political negotiation. The United States Office of Education's survey of the state of equality of opportunity in American schools, to be conducted under a directive in the 1964 Civil Rights Act, should have influence in this regard. The position of ancillary institutions, from the National Education Association to the Parent Teachers Associations, has just begun to become firm, let alone articulate.

When the question is somewhat commonly stated, and when the problem is extensively and authoritatively identified, some change toward desegregation that is more than random, or more substantial than token, will be achieved. In public school circles, this change will be noted first in the increasingly more open espousal of "racial balance" by Northern superintendents. Superintendents in many communities will acknowledge, through their conventions, journals, and professional associations in particular, that a "balanced system" is being defined as an educationally desirable system. "Racial balance" will come to be viewed as "essential" to quality. As the image becomes rewarding, superintendents will pursue it as their own *if* minority pressures are sustained and if majority resistance dwindles even slightly.

The ability to advance desegregation depends mainly on state authority and on board and community politics. No social scientist expects a school superintendent to become a culture hero rather than an administrator of a municipal service. But the option to champion desegregation each year becomes less dangerous for superintendents. We should come to a time soon when only the very largest cities of the North, and only a few unaspiring little communities, will still operate segregated schools. The gatekeeper for the institution will be the superintendent.

REFERENCES

1. *The New York Times,* July 31, 1962, p. 1.

2. Data reported by Herman Long, from survey conducted by the National Association of Intergroup Relations Officials, in *New York State Commissioner's Conference on Race and Education,* State Education Department, Albany, N. Y., 1964.

3. New York State Bar Association, *Racial Balance in the Public Schools: The Current Status of Federal and New York Law* (Albany, N. Y., October 20, 1964), pp. 1-7. For a technical analysis, see Robert A. Dentler, et al., *The Educational Complex Study Project,* Institute of Urban Studies, Teachers College, Columbia University, and New York City Board of Education, 1965 (mimeographed).

4. For a good research summary see the Report of the Advisory Committee on Racial Imbalance and Education, *Because It Is Right—Educationally* (Springfield, Mass., April 1965), pp. 77-86.

5. Robert A. Dentler, Bernard Mackler, and M. Ellen Warshauer (eds.), *Urban Community and Education.* (New York, December 1965).

6. New York State Bar Association, *op. cit.,* pp. 1-7.

7. Adapted from "Chronicle" in *Integrated Education,* Vols. 10, 11, 12 (December 1964-January 1965).

8. The author was State Consultant to White Plains in the planning of school desegregation there.

9. *The New York Law Journal,* July 26, 1965, "Court of Appeals," Matter of *Michael Vetere* v. *James E. Allen.*

10. State Advisory Committee Report (Allen Report), *Desegregating the Schools of New York City* (Albany, N. Y., May 1964).

11. See *Report to the Board of Education City of Chicago by The Advisory Panel on Integration of the Public Schools* (Chicago, March 31, 1964).

12. *The Educational Complex Study Project, op. cit.*

13. Nathan Jacobsen (ed.), *An Exploration of the Education Park Concept,* New York City Board of Education Arden House Conference, 1964.

14. Marcia Lane Vespa, "Chicago Regional School Plans," *Integrated Education,* Vol. 1, No. 5 (October-November 1963), p. 25.

15. Edward Banfield and James Q. Wilson, *City Politics* (Cambridge, Mass., 1963), p. 104.

16. For example, the City Commission on Human Rights found that in New York City 45 per cent of the 1964-65 school budget went toward the planning and construction of minority segregated schools. See City Commission on Human Rights, *Study of the Effect of the 1964-1970 School Building Program on Segregation in New York City's Public Schools* (New York, 1964). Also, the Advisory Panel on Integration of the Public Schools in Chicago found that most of the 243 new schools and additions in Chicago from January 1951 to December 1963 were constructed in Negro areas.

17. This is particularly true where an older but contained little Negro ghetto "suddenly" swells with new arrivals. This was the pattern in Englewood, New Jersey, and New Rochelle, New York.

JOHN H. FISCHER

Race and Reconciliation: The Role of the School

I

WHEN George Counts asked in 1932, "Dare the schools build a new social order?" the response could hardly have been called resounding. A frightened few took the query for a Marxist threat, the Progressive Education Association spent a year reaching a split decision, but the majority even of those who gave it any attention at all dismissed the challenge as educationist hyperbole. Whatever it was the country needed, not many expected to find it in the schools. Two wars, a technological revolution, and a massive social upheaval have put a different face upon the matter. No longer is education the optional affair it was a generation ago. The easy rhetoric about the nation's reliance on its schools has become an uneasy reality.

President Johnson reflected the discovery when he said that "One great truth" he had learned is that "the answer for all of our national problems, the answer for all the problems of the world comes down, when you really analyze it, to one simple word— education."[1] Mr. Johnson is not the first President to speak well of learning. The dependence of democracy on popular education has been a continuing theme in our history. But it was not until the end of World War II that the country began seriously to consider the full implications of that relationship, and later still that it officially acknowledged the corollary proposition that to limit a man's education is to limit his freedom.

The rationale for improving the Negro American's chance to be educated derives from basic principles and well-established practice, but merely to proclaim a new policy of equality is not enough. Steps to equalize the Negro's educational opportunities must be accompanied by prompt and vigorous action to improve his access to those opportunities and to increase the inducement for him to use them. Until, in all three respects, he is brought to full parity with his white neighbor, the Negro citizen will continue to depress the composite level of American society, and the society to diminish his standing as a man.

As the struggle to secure the Negro's proper place in that society gains headway and success, it becomes steadily more clear that the two great educational handicaps he has suffered—segregated schools and inferior instruction—are so closely interrelated that they can be attacked successfully only when they are attacked simultaneously.

This is not to argue that segregation is the sole deficiency Negro children suffer in school or that only Negro pupils receive inferior education. Nor is it true that every Negro child is being poorly taught or that effective learning is possible only in the presence of white children. It is important to set the facts, the probabilities, and the proposals straight. Not every Negro child lives in deprivation: each year more Negro families join the middle class. Nor is every white child raised in a good home. Slums are often ghettos, but the two are not always the same. Poverty of purse and poverty of spirit often go together, but the exceptions are numerous and important. Yet when all the differences have been explained and all the exceptions admitted, the hard facts of racial discrimination remain to be faced.

Until the present generation, almost every action affecting Negroes as a group in this country, whether taken by the government or by private agencies, has been to some degree discriminatory and quite often hypocritical. The Negro's just cause for pride in the fortitude of his ancestors in no way alters the fact that from the moment of his birth he becomes the product and the victim of his people's history. The scars he carries are difficult to hide and slow to heal.

Assuring the Negro his proper place in American society involves more than opening a few doors, giving everybody his choice, and waiting for what is certain to come naturally. Many of the trends that have influenced the Negro individually and collectively have carried him not toward but away from the main currents of American life. The momentum that has been built up suggests a sociological analogue of Newton's first law of motion. Unless the course that the Negro race has followed for three centuries is altered by the application of external energy, its direction cannot be expected to change. The heart of the integration question is to determine what forms of energy are most appropriate and how they may be applied to bring the separate courses together. For some Negroes the process is already under way, but for many more significant change awaits intervention on a scale commensurate with the forces that must be checked and redirected. To serve this purpose no agency offers greater promise than the school.

We can begin on the educational task by considering some facts. One is that a school enrolling largely Negro students is almost universally considered of lower status and less desirable than one attended wholly or mainly by white students. Regardless of the quality of the building, the competence of the staff, or the size of classes, a school composed of three-fourths Negro children and one-fourth white children is viewed by members of both races, virtually without exception, as inferior to one in which the proportions are reversed. Whether all such appraisals are valid remains, at least for the time being, beside the point. So often are "Negro" schools inferior and so long have Negro students been assigned the hand-me-downs that unhappy memories and generalized impressions must be expected to persist despite the occasional presence of really good schools in Negro neighborhoods.

The contention that no school of Negro pupils can under any circumstances be satisfactory unless white students enter it is absurd. The argument insults every Negro child and credits white children with virtues they do not possess. But the effort to establish genuinely first-rate schools in Negro communities has been so long delayed that anyone undertaking to demonstrate that an institution known as a "Negro" school can produce first-rate results must be prepared to accept a substantial burden of proof.

A second impressive fact, closely related to the first, is the unfortunate psychological effect upon a child of membership in a school where every pupil knows that, regardless of his personal attainments, the group with which he is identified is viewed as less able, less successful, and less acceptable than the majority of the community. The impact upon the self-image and motivation of children of this most tragic outcome of segregated education emphasizes the dual need for immediate steps to achieve a more favorable balance of races in the schools and for every possible effort to upgrade to full respectability and status every school in which enrollment cannot soon be balanced.

The destruction of the legal basis of segregation by the *Brown* decision in 1954 marked the climax of an obviously necessary first campaign, but the new problems to which *Brown* gives rise are even more complex than those which preceded it. The task now is not only to end segregation but to correct the effects it has generated. There is little profit in debating whether *de jure* or *de facto* segregation is the greater evil. It was the consequences of the fact of segregation that convinced the Supreme Court that "separate schools are inherently unequal" and led the Court to strike down the laws supporting such schools. Only by a curious twist of logic could it be argued that segregation statutes having been declared unjust, the practice itself may now be condoned.

This is not to deny significant differences between segregation established by law and that resulting from other causes. As the Court itself pointed out, "The impact is greater when it has the sanction of the law." But underlying this greater impact is the Court's finding that "Segregation of white and colored children in public schools has a detrimental effect upon the colored children."

Imperative as the need for prompt desegregation is, it would be irresponsible to attempt to deal with a condition so deeply rooted in practice and custom, and so often due to causes lying beyond the school, without taking account of its complexity. The need for intelligence, imagination, and wisdom in effecting fair and workable reforms can hardly be overstated. Yet, however complicated the situation or the final solutions may be, a firm and forthright confrontation of the problem is essential and is everywhere possible.

Some of the most bitter attacks on school authorities have been occasioned not by their failure to integrate every school, but by their unwillingness even to accept integration as a desirable goal. Among the reasons offered in support of this position, two are especially prominent. One is that the only acceptable basis for school policy is simple and complete nondiscrimination. Unless the school is color-blind, this argument runs, the spirit of the *Brown* decision and the 14th Amendment is violated. What this approach overlooks or attempts to evade is that the consequences of earlier discrimination cannot be corrected merely by ending the practices that produced them, that without corrective action the effects inevitably persist. To teach anyone in a way that influences his further development it is invariably useful and usually necessary to take account of the background he brings to the classroom. So often are the disabilities of Negro students directly traceable to racial factors that a refusal on grounds of equality to recognize such factors in the school is not only unjust; it is also illogical. A physician reasoning in the same way would deliberately disregard his patients' histories in order to assure them all equal treatment.

A second justification commonly offered for not taking positive action to integrate schools is the lack of evidence that better racial balance leads to better learning, and it must be conceded that solid, objective evidence on this question is difficult if not impossible to find. The number of Negro children from deprived circumstances who have attended schools that were both integrated and educationally sound is still so small and the period of integration so brief that neither provides more than a limited basis for study. Because the Negro children with the longest experience in good integrated institutions have more often come from relatively fortunate and upwardly mobile families, their performance, although interesting, is only partly relevant to the task of equalizing opportunities for those who are both segregated and otherwise disadvantaged.

Moreover, even when better statistical data become available, it should not be expected that they will furnish, *per se,* a firm basis for policy. The purpose of school integration is not merely, or even primarily, to raise the quantitative indices of scholastic achievement among Negro children, although such gains are obviously to be valued and sought. The main objective is rather to alter the character and quality of their opportunities, to provide the incentive to succeed, and to foster a sense of intergroup acceptance in ways that are impossible where schools or students are racially, socially, and culturally isolated. The simplest statement of the situation to which school policy must respond is that few if any American Negro children can now grow up under conditions comparable to those of white children and that of all the means of improvement subject to public control the most powerful is the school. The Negro child must have a chance to be educated in a school where it is clear to him and to everybody else that he is not segregated and where his undisputed right to membership is acknowledged, publicly and privately, by his peers and his elders of both races. Although his acceptance and his progress may at first be delayed, not even a decent beginning toward comparable circumstances can be made until an integrated setting is actually established.

Some important gains may come rather quickly in newly integrated schools, but lasting changes in the deep-seated behavior patterns of children and parents of both races cannot realistically be expected to take place overnight. The effects of fourteen generations of discrimination, deprivation, and separation are not likely to disappear quickly. What a school has to boast about at the end of the next grading period is somewhat less crucial than what happens to the quality of living in America during the next generation. School integration will, of course, be more productive when parallel improvements are made in housing, economic opportunities, and the general social condition of Negro Americans; but the absence of adequate effort elsewhere only increases the urgency that prompt and energetic action be taken by the school.

The effort to identify and define *de facto* segregation, particularly where school enrollment is predominantly if not wholly of a single race, has led to the concept of racial "balance." While no single ratio of races can be established as universally "right," there is no doubt that when the number or proportion of Negro children in a school exceeds a certain level the school becomes less acceptable to both white and Negro parents. The point at which that shift begins is not clear, nor are the reasons for the variation adequately understood, but the results that typically follow are all too familiar: an accelerated exodus of white families; an influx of Negroes; increased enrollment, frequently to the point of overcrowding; growing dissatisfaction among teachers and the replacement of veterans by inexperienced or unqualified junior instructors.

Although there are no completely satisfactory measures of segregation or imbalance, several tests are applicable. The simplest is to ask whether a particular school is viewed by the community as a "Negro" school. Whether the school is assumed to "belong" to a Negro neighborhood or merely to be the one that Negroes "just happen" to attend, whether it has been provided expressly *for* a Negro population, or has gradually acquired a student body disproportionately composed of Negroes, the typical consequences of segregation can be predicted.

In gauging the degree of segregation or imbalance, the percentage or number of Negro students in a given building is usually less important than the relation of the school to the entire system of which it is a part. As Robert Carter has so cogently argued, it is the substantial isolation of Negro and white students from each other rather than the numbers involved that produces the implication of differential status and prevents the association that is the indispensable basis for mutual understanding and acceptance.[2]

One set of guidelines for correcting such situations has been proposed by the New York State Education Commissioner's Advisory Committee on Human Relations and Community Tensions:

In establishing school attendance areas one of the objectives should be to create in each school a student body that will represent as nearly as possible the cross section of the population of the entire school district but with due consideration also for other important educational criteria including such practical matters as the distance children must travel from home to school.[3]

Although it would be impossible in a sizable district to create or maintain in every school a student body that reflects precisely the racial composition of the total district, the cross section criterion offers an appropriate yardstick.

Most of the proposals for dealing with the issue attempt to strike workable compromises between desirable ideals and practical possibilities. The same Committee in a 1964 report[4] defined a school in New York City as segregated when any single racial group comprised more than 90 per cent of the enrollment.

A more flexible criterion was used by Robert Dentler in a 1965 study.[5] Using the borough as the reference point, he proposed that a school be considered segregated if the proportion of any racial group in its student body is less than half or more than twice the proportion that group represents in the total population. Thus, in Brooklyn, where Negroes comprise 15 per cent of the population, a school would be classified as "Negro segregated" when Negro enrollment reached 30 per cent. Since Puerto Ricans form about 8 per cent of the borough population, a school would be "Puerto Rican" segregated if it enrolled 16 per cent or more pupils of that background. Conversely, a school enrolling fewer than 6 per cent Negro students or 2 per cent Puerto Rican students would be designated as "white segregated." Dealing with the issue in Chicago, Robert Havighurst[6] defines an integrated school as one enrolling at least 60 per cent white students.

II

The dilemma of definition cannot be entirely avoided, but far more important is the creation and retention of student bodies that will be considered acceptably integrated by the largest possible number of persons in both races. As the New York City report pointed out, an essential test of any plan for desegregation "must be its mutual acceptance by both minority group and whites. It should be obvious, but does not always appear to be, that integration is impossible without white pupils. No plan can be acceptable, therefore, which increases the movement of white pupils out of the public schools. Neither is it acceptable, however, unless it contributes to desegregation."[7]

Of the administrative schemes for bringing children of both races together the most widely used is "open enrollment," under which pupils are allowed to transfer from schools that are segregated or overcrowded to others in the district. The receiving school may be one with a better degree of racial balance, or its enrollment may simply be smaller than its capacity. While open enrollment reduces congestion in the sending schools, allows parents wider choice, and improves integration in the receiving schools, its usefulness, especially for poor children, is sharply reduced unless transportation is furnished at public expense. Freedom of choice is also more effective when it is supplemented by special counseling services and by the careful preparation of pupils, teachers, and parents of the receiving school.

In large cities open-enrollment plans have uniformly been found to affect only a small percentage of Negro students. In Baltimore, where relatively free choice of schools (subject to legal segregation) was standard practice before 1954, open enrollment became the sole basis for desegregation following the *Brown* decision. In the school year 1954-55 only about 3 per cent of the Negro students transferred to formerly white schools.[8] In subsequent years the number of integrated schools and the percentage of pupils enrolled in them steadily rose, but much of the change was due to the continued expansion of the Negro residential areas.

For readily understandable reasons, the free choice policy affects younger and older pupils differently. Most parents, and especially those in restricted circumstances, prefer to send elementary-age children to the nearest school, regardless of its condition. Families in more affluent circumstances are ordinarily willing to accept the added inconvenience and expense of transportation to get their children into better schools, but the regrettable fact is that if opportunity is to be equalized by traveling it is invariably the slum children who must accept the inconvenience of going to where the more fortunate already are.

At the secondary level, distance is less of an obstacle. This is one of the reasons that in New York City in 1963, when 22 per cent of the elementary schools and 19 per cent of the junior high schools were found to be segregated, by the same criteria only one of the eighty-six senior high schools was segregated.[9]

The most tightly structured approach to desegregation, the Princeton Plan, achieves racial balance by pairing adjacent imbalanced schools, the combined attendance areas being treated as a single unit and the pupils being divided between the schools by grade rather than by residence. The advantages are clear: Both schools are integrated, and each is enabled to concentrate upon a narrower span of grades. There are also disadvantages. Travel time is increased for approximately half the children and transportation may be required, each school's established identity and its relations with its neighborhood are altered, and large-scale faculty transfers may be required. In addition, the possibility that white families will choose to leave the community becomes an uncertain hazard in every such situation.

Early and largely impressionistic evaluations of pairing suggest that the device may be more appropriate in smaller communities with only a few elementary schools than in larger places where neighborhood patterns and rates of residential change are more complex. One analysis[10] of the probable result of pairing twenty-one sets of elementary schools in New York City showed that, at most, the proportion of segregated schools would have been reduced from 22 to 21 per cent.

A more comprehensive method of correcting imbalance is the re-zoning of all the attendance areas of a school system in order to obtain simultaneously a viable racial balance and reasonable travel time for all the pupils. Re-zoning and the related practice of revising the "feeder" patterns by which graduates of lower schools move on to junior or senior high schools are usually more practicable in closely populated communities than in less compact suburbs where travel distances are greater.

Among the more recent innovations is the "educational complex" proposed for the New York City schools.[11] The term denotes a group of schools serving differing racial constituencies and consisting typically of one or two junior high schools and their feeding elementary units. The attendance areas of the individual schools are not changed, but within the complex a variety of joint activities may be undertaken to bring the pupils, teachers, and parents into closer association. Programs and services that cannot be offered uniformly in all of the schools may be centered in one or two of the buildings and pupils transported to them as necessary. Faculty specialists may be shared by more than one building and common problems met cooperatively. Parents of two or more of the schools working together may bridge over old neighborhood lines that inhibit communication and joint action. The "complex" offers unusual possibilities for countering the effect of segregated housing. By retaining the advantages of neighborhood schools while introducing the social opportunities of a more diversified community, it offers children and parents a chance to try new experiences without totally abandoning the security of their familiar attachments.

Of all the schemes proposed for desegregating urban schools, the boldest and most imaginative is the educational park.[12] The rationale of the park rests on the hypothesis that the effect on the school of pockets of segregated housing will be offset if an attendance area can be made large enough to include white and Negro populations in balanced proportions. Thus, all the pupils of a greatly enlarged zone, perhaps 10,000 or more (in a medium-sized city, the entire school population), would be accommodated on a single site or park. Within the park, which could range all the way from a 100 acre campus with many separate buildings to a single high-rise structure covering a city block, students would be assigned to relatively small units, each maintained as a separate school in which teachers and pupils would work closely and continuously together. The distribution of students among the smaller units would be made without regard to the location of their homes but with the purpose of making each school as well integrated as possible.

Beyond these general outlines, there is little agreement on what an educational park should be. One view is that the full grade range should be included, from nursery school to community college. Others propose that a park serve one or two levels, perhaps elementary and junior high schools, or a comprehensive secondary program of three, four, or six years. New York City has examined the feasibility of using middle-school parks for grades five to eight, retaining small neighborhood schools for pre-kindergarten, kindergarten, and primary programs.

With such a combination, children and parents would be introduced to the public schools first in their own neighborhoods, where familiar relationships, short distances, and close home-school ties would be at their maximum. In these primary centers each child, depending on his age at entry, would spend four to seven years, and some children a longer period, receiving fundamental preparation that primary education at its best should provide. Remedial services, compensatory curricula, and enriched programs would be available to all who need them. At the fifth grade, each pupil would move on to the middle-school park where for the first time his classmates, now drawn from a much wider area, would reflect the diversity of a truly common school and, hopefully, a genuinely integrated one. All high schools, under this proposal, would operate under a city-wide policy of free choice for all students, subject only to such restrictions as were needed to prevent overcrowding and to respect requirements for admission to specialized programs.

One criticism of the educational park is the excessively high costs that some associate with it. A single site and the construction required to house 10,000 pupils need be no greater, however, than the combined cost of ten sites and buildings for a thousand pupils each. Indeed, a larger site located on relatively open and cheaper land might well be less costly to assemble than comparable acreage in congested sections. The total operating costs for a single, well-managed park should be lower than those for several separate units. In almost every case, however, a large proportion of the pupils would have to be transported and the cost of that service financed as a new expense. As in any other new venture, the increased outlay required must be set against the anticipated return. In a well conceived educational park the better education and the improved social situation that may be expected offer future assets of substantial value.

Beside the possibilities for accomplishing school integration must be set the deterrents that currently retard the process, of which the most visible and powerful is the concept of the neighborhood school. Although the close identification of a school with its immediate community produces results beneficial to both, the battles now being fought in the name of that relationship, and sometimes for virtual possession of particular schools, obscure fundamental principles. The public school is the property not of its neighborhood but of the school district. Since the district itself is created by the state, it is quite reasonable to argue that both title and control rest ultimately with the people of the state as a whole. However commendable the interest of a neighborhood in its school may be, concern is not to be confused with proprietary control. Subject to the state's supervision, the school board alone is legally empowered to determine for any school whose children shall be admitted and whose excluded.

The neighborhood school is essentially an administrative device designed to assure all the children of a district equal educational opportunity and equal access to it. When the device ceases to serve those functions, and especially when its use is so distorted that it frustrates rather than furthers the primary purpose, it is the device rather than the purpose that must give way.

It is a curious coincidence that during the very period that city and suburban neighborhood schools have been gaining an almost sacrosanct status, the rural sections in which such schools were first established have been abandoning them. The neighborhood school in its original and most authentic form, the one-room schoolhouse, has been disappearing from the United States at the rate of 3,000 a year for the last half century. Despite understandable misgivings about school consolidation, rural parents by the millions have exchanged their nearby schools and the intensely local form of control many of them embody for the superior instruction and broader educational experiences more comprehensive institutions offer. They have learned that, despite its relative remoteness from the neighborhood, the consolidated school not only provides a broader curriculum, better books and equipment, and abler teachers, but, by drawing its pupils from a wider and more varied attendance area, also furnishes them an outlook upon the world that is impossible in the more homogeneous society of the local school.

City and suburban schools meanwhile have gone in quite the opposite direction, becoming steadily more segregated not only by race but also by social and economic level. The momentum of this movement creates one of the principal forces opposing integration in schools and communities. Combined with more common forms of racial prejudice, segregated housing, and repressive economic practices, the growing social stratification of the public school carries the most serious implications for the future of American society.

Despite the generous lip service that the common school has traditionally received, it is a clear fact that, in many parts of the country, substantial minorities of American children at both extremes of the social scale have not been educated in schools that could, by any reasonable criteria, be called inclusive. Yet the complementary truth is that the vast majority of our citizens, the white ones, at any rate, have been brought up in schools that "everybody" was expected to attend. Whether the connection between such childhood experiences and the health of a democratic society is still or ever was as close as Horace Mann held it to be, is beyond explicit demonstration. But whether an open society can be maintained and, even more to the present point, whether a hitherto excluded group can be brought into the full enjoyment of citizenship without the instrumentality of the common school, are questions this country cannot much longer evade. On so complex a matter, clear causal relationships are difficult to establish, but the correlation between the rise of the common school and the development of an open society in the United States is, to say the least, impressive. Before we accept by default or support by intent the trend toward stratified public education it would be well at least to project and appraise the probable consequences.

A second force impeding integration, in certain respects the first writ large, is generated by the growth of solidly white suburban communities around the heavily congested urban centers into which the Negro population finds itself channeled and confined. The "white noose" not only prevents the outward dispersion of Negroes but equally, if less directly, discourages white families from remaining in the city. As population density and neighborhood depression worsen, larger numbers of families with the freedom to choose and the power to act abandon both the city and its schools.

The steady increase of urban segregation, the growing ghettos, and the declining attractiveness of the city for all groups produce problems whose magnitude and complexity carry them beyond the control of separate localities. Every day the deteriorating situation emphasizes more strongly the need for a total reappraisal of city-suburban relationships. If the present trend is allowed to continue, the difficulties that now plague the central city can be expected inevitably—and soon—to trouble entire metropolitan areas. The almost total segregation of the incorporated area, the political entity officially called the city, is hardly an acceptable alternative to the systematic desegregation of the total social and economic network that is in fact the city. It becomes constantly more evident that, unless steps are taken to bring about a better dispersion and integration of Negro citizens throughout metropolitan areas, direct action will be required to equalize educational opportunities and the process of school integration between the cities and their surburbs. This responsibility for re-examining urban-suburban racial imbalance and its locus is implied by a sentence in the *Brown* decision: "Such an opportunity [to secure an education] where the state has undertaken to provide it is a right which must be made available to all on equal terms." If the right to equal treatment in the schools, including freedom from racial segregation, overrides, as it does, statutes placing children in particular schools, the question naturally arises whether that right is to be restricted indefinitely by statutes that fix lines between local jurisdictions.

III

Imaginative and forthright action to bring as many children as possible into integrated schools as rapidly as possible is an urgent necessity, but it would be grossly unrealistic to assume that integration can be accomplished everywhere in the foreseeable future. In the borough of Manhattan 78 per cent of the public elementary-school pupils are Negro and Puerto Rican. Immediate and total integration could be accomplished there only by closing most of the schools in Manhattan and distributing their pupils among the remaining boroughs or by setting up a vast "exchange" system to move hundreds of thousands of children daily in both directions between Manhattan and other parts of the city. Quite aside from the sheer administrative and teaching problems such an operation would pose, little imagination is needed to predict the virtually unanimous objection of parents.

Important progress can be made, however, on the periphery of segregated communities, through the procedures described earlier and by energetic efforts to concentrate on the possible instead of deploring the impossible. When all the possibilities are exploited and new ones ingeniously devised, there will still remain many ghetto schools in which integration is simply not feasible. In those places, the only reasonable action is the massive improvement of schools to educate children where they are.

It is unhappily true, as Kenneth Clark points out,[13] that to ask for good schools in the ghetto is to risk the charge that one acquiesces in segregation. Yet, even though supporting better schools in ghettos has become a favorite ploy of the advocates of separate equality, that fact does not justify neglecting ghetto children. Indeed, many of these children are already so badly victimized by deprivation and neglect that, if integration were instantly possible, strong remedial and compensatory programs would still be necessary to give them any reasonable chance to compete or to succeed.

In designing educational strategies to meet the special needs of Negro ghetto children the public schools are undertaking tasks they have never really faced up to before. The curricula of slum schools have almost invariably been no more than adapted versions of those designed for middle-class pupils. Even now, a number of the changes being introduced into slum schools involve little more than efforts to apply to the ghetto, although somewhat more effectively and more intensively, the characteristic practices of middle-class schools: smaller classes to teach traditional subjects; more time for reading, using standard readers; increased guidance service employing the customary techniques.

Such projects to multiply and intensify established procedures are by no means wholly wasteful or necessarily wrong. Kenneth Clark[14] insists with considerable justification that the change most needed in slum schools is an elevation of the teachers' expectations of the children. The main reason, he argues, that Negro students rank low academically is that too many teachers and the "system" as a whole consider them uneducable.

However much ghetto children could gain from proper motivation and a decent respect for their potentiality, strong encouragement and high expectation are not enough. No teacher can hope to teach effectively or fairly unless he differentiates between the child whose environment re-enforces the school's influence and the one whose out-of-school world is rarely even so good as neutral and more often is severely damaging. While much can be said for holding both children to the same level of expectation, it is hardly realistic to assume that both will reach it with equal personal effort and the same assistance from the school. The child suffering unusual deprivation would appear obviously to require—and to deserve—unusual attention. The extent to which the special help should be compensatory, or remedial, or unusually stimulating is, of course, a suitable subject of investigation and debate; but that it must be particularly adapted to the child who is victimized by his environment would seem self-evident.

A growing volume of research not only documents the relationship between a child's cultural environment and his school success but also illuminates with increasing clarity the crucial importance of the early years. Benjamin Bloom[15] has examined many of the pertinent studies in the field and estimates that the difference between a culturally deprived and a culturally abundant environment can affect a child's IQ by an average of twenty points, half of the difference being attributable to the influences of the first four years and as much as six points to the next four. After another comprehensive survey, J. McVicker Hunt[16] concludes that while the notion of cultural deprivation is still gross and undifferentiated, the concept holds much promise. He considers it entirely possible to arrange institutional settings in which culturally handicapped children can encounter experiences that will compensate for what they may have missed. Martin Deutsch,[17] whose work has included extended experimentation with such children, has found that those with some preschool experience attain significantly higher intelligence-test scores at the fifth grade than do children of the same background who did not have the experience.

Opinions differ as to the type of preschool program that offers the most fruitful compensation to slum children. One approach assumes that ordinary home-supplementing nursery schools designed for middle-class children will also help the deprived youngster. A second concentrates on preparing the culturally deprived child for school by teaching him to follow directions and to use such things as toys, pencils, crayons, and books. A third approach begins with the view that the culturally deprived child differs fundamentally from others in self-concept, language values, and perceptual processes and offers specialized programs to compensate for the deleterious effects of his lean environment.

While there are still no systematic comparisons of the relative effectiveness of these different programs, two generalizations can be stated with some assurance. One is that preschool programs do appear to be effective in raising intelligence-test scores, vocabulary level, expressive ability, arithmetic reasoning, and reading readiness.

The second is that the results do not run uniformly in one direction. A study made in the Racine public schools[18] reports that:

Potentially the most useful conclusion which can be drawn . . . is that "one shot" compensatory programs would seem to be a waste of time and money. The fact that differences between groups disappeared and that in several areas the rate of growth of both groups regressed during the traditional first grade years supports this contention.

If these implications are supported by future research, it would seem that curriculum revision over the entire twelve year school curriculum is a necessary part of any lasting solution to the basic problem of urban public school education.

The Racine finding bears out what anyone experienced in slum schools would probably have predicted. Any such teacher knows that the moment the child steps outside, at whatever age, he is caught again in the cultural downdraft of the street and all too often of the home itself. Efforts to compensate within the school must, therefore, begin at the earliest possible age and continue with steady and strong consistency throughout the whole length of the child's school career.

One outstanding example of what may be done in the upper grades was the Demonstration Guidance Project,[19] initiated in 1956 in New York's Junior High School 43 located on the edge of Harlem. The principal aim of the project was to identify and stimulate potentially able pupils and to help them reach levels of performance more nearly consistent with their capacities. The project students, all selected because they were thought to possess latent academic aptitude and most of them from disadvantaged backgrounds, were placed in small classes, given double periods daily in English, and tutored in small groups. Intensive counseling, clinical services, and social work were provided, and regular contact was maintained with the parents. Scholastic achievement was stressed and special efforts made to prepare the students for college or jobs. Visits were conducted to museums, theaters, concerts, the ballet, and places of special interest in New York and elsewhere. The program was continued into the George Washington Senior High School and the last experimental group graduated in 1960. After three and a half years of this special attention, these students, most of whom would ordinarily have been considered poor academic risks, showed substantial gains over their own earlier records, and over the usual performance of students from the same school. Of one hundred five in one group, seventy-eight showed an increase in IQ, sixty-four gaining ten points or more. The median for the entire group rose in the three-year period from 92.9 to 102.2. Against a previous average for their school of 47 per cent, 64 per cent earned high-school diplomas. Three students ranked first, fourth, and sixth in their class; two and one-half times as many as in previous classes went to college, and three and one-half times as many to some form of further education.

On a modified and reduced scale, the Demonstration Guidance Project was subsequently introduced as the Higher Horizons Program to other schools in New York City with results that have been comparably positive if somewhat less spectacular.

IV

Special programs to meet the needs of deprived children have been undertaken in a number of school systems. A project in the Banneker Group of the St. Louis school system has stressed the teaching of reading, English, and arithmetic. Particular attention was directed to the motivation of the pupils, to setting standards of performance. The support of parents was solicited, and their pride in their children's accomplishments was stimulated. By the end of the third year of the project the achievement of Banneker eighth graders equalled or exceeded national norms in reading and language and fell only one month short in arithmetic. In the years immediately preceding, the comparable scores had ranged from one to two years below the national norms. The theme of the Banneker project is expressed by Samuel Sheppard, the administrator who conceived it, in his instructions to teachers: "Quit teaching by I. Q. and the neighborhood where the child lives. Teach the child all you can teach him."[20]

Detroit set up a new effort during the 1960-61 academic year with some 10,000 elementary and secondary pupils, mainly in the Negro residential areas, concentrating not only on the children but also on work with parents and teachers. A principal aim was to modify teachers' perceptions of children with limited backgrounds. The program included curriculum revision, re-organized teaching schedules, tutoring, home visiting, and supplementary activities for pupils during after-schools hours and summer months.

A Pittsburgh project centered in the "Hill" district employed team teaching to improve instruction in reading and the language arts.

Virtually every large school system in the country and many of the smaller ones are now attacking the problem of the culturally deprived child, but the volume of well-intentioned activity still substantially exceeds the amount of imaginative and well-designed research that is being done to analyze and appraise the innovations. Until the quality of experimental design and research matches the quantity of sheer energy being devoted to the task, much of the energy is certain to be wasted and potentially valuable information and insights to be lost.

A field in which further study and fresh thinking are badly needed is vocational education, where the long-standing practice of separating vocational students from those in academic programs has more recently been compounded by the effects of racial imbalance. The result has been to render vocational programs in some schools all but useless. The field has suffered also because many schools have adhered too long and too closely to the concepts of curriculum and organization developed forty years ago. The tragically high rate of unemployment among Negro youth is only one of urgent reasons for the early and thorough reform of this essential part of American education.

In higher education impressive progress in some institutions has diverted attention from the massive obstacles that remain to be overcome. While a detailed discussion of this situation is beyond the scope of this paper it is relevant to emphasize the reciprocal relationship between accomplishments by Negroes in colleges and universities and the improvement of elementary and secondary schools, a prominent element in this relationship being the supply of well-prepared Negro teachers. Hard facts on the relative competence of white graduates and Negro graduates of teacher education programs are not easy to secure, but such evidence as has come to light, most of it subjective, suggests that much remains to be done to equalize the quality of programs and the availability of places in first-rate schools. Despite the fact that thousands of Negro teachers have attained high levels of professional competence and status, many others who hold teaching certificates are unable to obtain employment even in schools that want Negro teachers, because of their inability to compete with other applicants. A largely similar situation prevails in graduate-school admissions.

McGrath's study of Negro colleges[21] provides part of the explanation and suggests directions in which some of the answers must be sought: the prompt and substantial upgrading of faculties, curricula, libraries, laboratories, and physical facilities of the colleges that serve predominantly Negro student bodies and enroll more than half the Negro college students of the country.

Another important part of the solution must be found in programs in high school and between high school and college to furnish the supplemental instruction that many Negro students require in order to qualify for first-rate institutions. The encouraging reports of such programs as those conducted by the National Scholarship Service and Fund for Negro Students,[22] as well as by a number of the institutions themselves, indicate what special effort and thoughtful planning toward that end can accomplish.

"A grand mental and moral experiment," Horace Mann once called free schools,[23] "whose effects could not be developed and made manifest in a single generation."

For the Negro American, the development of those effects has taken a good deal longer—far too much longer—than was required to make them manifest for his white countrymen. The knowledge that the Negro's right to education has been restricted is no new discovery, but what is new is the growing consciousness that what has been withheld from him has impoverished the whole people.

The argument for enlarging the opportunities and enhancing the status of the Negro minority goes far beyond extending a modicum more of charity to the poor. The appeal to equity and to the humane principles that undergird the democratic enterprise is the heart of the matter, to be sure, but the evidence is now irrefutable that until each American has full access to the means to develop his capacities every other American's chances and attainments will continue to be diminished.

That this relationship should become so critically significant in a time characterized by technological progress may seem paradoxical; yet it is that progress and the insatiable demand it generates for intellectual competence that now re-enforces our long-standing moral obligation to re-examine the standards by which we live as a society.

The detailed problems of procedure which flow from this obligation impose a complex array of tasks upon the network of the arts, the sciences, the humanities, and the professional specialities that contribute knowledge and skill to the educational establishment. But here, too—here especially—the prior question and the transcendent issue are moral: What ought we to be doing?

If the educational and political leadership of the country can muster the strength of conscience to face that query forthrightly and honestly, there are abundant grounds for optimism that the subsidiary tasks will become both more clearly visible and more readily feasible.

REFERENCES

1. Lyndon B. Johnson, Address delivered at the 200th Anniversary Convocation, Brown University, September 28, 1964.

2. Robert L. Carter, "De Facto School Segregation: An Examination of the Legal and Constitutional Questions Presented," *Western Reserve Law Review*, Vol. 16 (May 1965), p. 527.

3. New York State Department of Education, "Guiding Principles for Securing Racial Balance in Public Schools," Albany, N. Y., June 17, 1963.

4. New York State Education Commissioner's Advisory Committee on Human Relations and Community Tensions, *Desegregating the Public Schools of New York City* (Albany, N. Y., 1964), p. 2.

5. Robert A. Dentler, *A Basis for Classifying the Ethnic Composition of Schools*, unpublished memorandum, Institute for Urban Studies, Teachers College, Columbia University, December 1964, p. 1.

6. Robert J. Havighurst, *The Public Schools of Chicago* (Chicago, 1964).

7. New York State Education Commissioner's Advisory Committee, *op. cit.*, p. 14.

8. Maryland Commission on Interracial Problems and Relations, *The Report of a Study on Desegregation in the Baltimore City Schools* (Baltimore, Md., 1956), p. 10.

9. New York Education Commissioner's Advisory Committee, *op. cit.*

10. *Ibid.*, p. 40.

11. *Ibid.*, pp. 18-20.

12. Nathan Jacobson (ed.), *An Exploration of the Educational Park Concept* (New York, 1964). The papers included in this report of a conference on the educational park contain the most perceptive appraisals of the concept currently available.

13. Kenneth B. Clark, *Dark Ghetto* (New York, 1965), p. 117.

14. *Ibid.*, pp. 131-133.

15. Benjamin S. Bloom, *Stability and Change in Human Characteristics* (New York, 1964), pp. 68-76.

16. J. McVicker Hunt, "The Psychological Basis for Using Pre-School Enrichment as an Antidote for Cultural Deprivation," *Merrill Palmer Quarterly*, Vol. 10 (July 1964), p. 236.

17. Martin Deutsch, "The Influence of Early Social Environments on School Adaptation," Paper presented at the Symposium on School Dropouts, Washington, D. C., December 1962.

18. R. G. Larson and J. L. Olson, *Final Report: A Pilot Project for Culturally Deprived Kindergarten Children*, Unified School District #1, Racine, Wisconsin (Mimeo, April 1965).

19. Board of Education of City of New York, *The Demonstration Guidance Project, Fourth Annual Report, 1959-60*, pp. 2-15.

20. William K. Wyant, Jr., "Reading: A Way Upward" in *Civil Rights USA, Public Schools, Cities in the North and West* (Washington, D. C., 1962).

21. Earl J. McGrath, *The Predominantly Negro Colleges and Universities in Transition* (New York, 1965), pp. 21 ff.

22. Kenneth B. Clark and Lawrence Plotkin, *The Negro Student at Integrated Colleges* (New York, 1963), pp. 7 ff.

23. Horace Mann, "Intellectual Education as a Means of Removing Poverty and Securing Abundance," Twelfth Annual Report, *Annual Reports of the Board of Education of Massachusetts for the Years 1845-48* (Boston, 1891), p. 246.

CHARLES ABRAMS

The Housing Problem and the Negro

WHEN Hell broke loose in the Watts area of Los Angeles last August taking 36 lives and injuring close to 1,000 people, reporters were astonished and reformers shocked to find that the area which was the scene of the most expensive riot in United States history was hardly a slum in the usual sense. Instead of rat-infested crumbling tenements on littered streets, the section was made up of small homes mostly about twenty-five years old, many of them surrounded by lawns, and only 20 per cent of them actually dilapidated. In the public mind, the Negro housing problem was therefore discounted as one of the causes of the eruption in favor of hoodlumism, anti-white emotionalism, and poverty.

The rioting in Los Angeles highlighted one of the five fictions that surround the Negro housing problem and still condition federal housing policy. One reason these fictions persist is that officials are not eager to probe too thoroughly into the Negro housing issue, while the vocal Negro leadership has relegated the issue to a low priority in the fight for Negro rights. Yet, until these fictions are put to rest, the Negro's housing problem will remain one of the conspicuous failures in the nation's effort to elevate his status in American life.

The fiction which the Watts area exposed is that the primary aspect of the Negro's housing problem is the slum, that is, insanitary or structurally deficient housing. The fact is that many Negroes do live in slums and some do not. The accelerated movement of whites to the suburbs has been providing Negroes with a wider choice among the leavings, while improved income has enabled others to venture into neighborhoods once inhabited by middle-class whites; thus the houses Negroes occupy are no longer all on the other side of the tracks but are now part of a mixed inventory. Despite this, the housing problem persists for most Negro families, and in many places it is becoming worse. About half the nonwhite renters in California, for example, and two-fifths of the nonwhite home owners live in substandard houses in contrast to only one-fifth of white renters and one-tenth of white homeowners. The physical condition of the Negro's homes, however, is only one aspect of the Negro's housing conditions. The neighborhoods are run-down; officialdom is less concerned with their maintenance, and their general atmosphere is demoralizing; the schools are segregated and inferior, and so are the recreational, hospital, and social facilities; there are also fewer new buildings erected in Negro areas, even for those who can afford them. Above all, the Negro is discriminated against in almost every aspect of housing and neighborhood life, and he feels it. Urbanization and suburbanization have recast the American scene and redistributed the population into areas inhabited by a new white "élite" and a black unwanted. If poor housing was not the mainspring that touched off the rioting, it certainly has not been a force for advancing interracial harmony— in California or elsewhere.

The 1961 report on "Housing" by the United States Commission on Civil Rights is punctuated by references to housing discrimination in California. Builders refuse to sell Federal Housing Administration and Veterans Administration homes to Negroes, and lenders are chary of lending them money on mortgages. Negroes have been refused access to houses repossessed by the VA, and the Los Angeles Realty Board has consistently rejected Negro applications for membership. The California Advisory Committee of the U. S. Commission on Civil Rights said it was "almost impossible" for minorities to buy homes in new subdivisions. In Northern California, fewer than 100 nonwhites have been able to buy houses in unsegregated tracts in a period during which 350,000 new homes were built. In a check on 117 advertisements for apartment rentals in Northern California, only two were available to Negroes and both were in Negro areas.

Far more serious, however, are the overcrowding within the buildings the Negro occupies and the high proportion of income he pays for rent. A sixth of Los Angeles Negroes, for example, were crowded into the Watts area in conditions four times as congested as those in the rest of the city. A U.S. census survey in March 1965 in the renewal areas of 132 cities showed 36 per cent of the Negroes paying 35 per cent or more of their incomes for their shelter. Moreover, the isolation of the Negro from the main stream of community life keeps resentment well-kindled and gives Negro mischief-makers little trouble in churning up hate of the white man on the ghetto fringe.

Because official policy still views the slum as a building instead of a condition, a second fiction has worked its way into official housing policy, that the best way to solve the Negro's housing problem is to tear down his slums. Because many of the houses are deteriorated, they have been the primary targets for slum clearance. In the United States, from 60 to 72 per cent of those who have been displaced from their homes by urban renewal projects have been Negroes, while only a tiny fraction of the new houses built on the sites have been open to them. Through May 1962, 5,105 Negro families were evicted by renewal projects in California and 58 per cent of those displaced were nonwhite. In the Western Addition redevelopment area in San Francisco, which had a population of 13,000, about 90 per cent of the children among the evicted families were nonwhite.

The renewal program is not the only or even the main culprit, for code enforcement and displacement for public works have taken an even greater toll of Negro homes. Whatever the motivation, these evictions have been disrupting neighborhood life before it has had a chance to mature. In Stockton, California, a renewal project not only leveled a whole Negro neighborhood but destroyed 32 Negro churches in the process. Negro displacement cannot always be avoided, and renewal of central sections is often necessary to salvage the economies of the beleaguered central cities; but as M. Justin Herman, Executive Director of San Francisco's Redevelopment Agency, told the U. S. Commission on Civil Rights: "Much of the problem is a matter of economics—the inability of families to afford such housing as can be made available in the market today. The biggest problem is the discrimination that exists with respect to non-white persons." Thus, low income, coupled with high housing costs and anti-Negro bias, has been at the root of the Negro's housing problem not only in California but throughout the nation. In 1963, the median Negro income was $3,465, compared with $6,548 for white families, and the Negro unemployment rate was twice as high; as a result, many Negro families have found it difficult to secure decent housing even if builders were ready to offer it to them.

Instead of expanding the number of houses available to the Negro, demolitions have been shrinking the housing supply in sections in which he has established footholds, thereby intensifying his overcrowding. The Negro, crowded into his shelter and paying more than he can afford or facing eviction, continuously eyes the white areas on the borders of his ghetto. This does little to enhance his popularity with his white neighbors—which brings us to a third fiction, that Negroes and whites do not mix and that Negroes will spoil any neighborhood and destroy its social status. This fiction is usually supplemented by claims that, once the Negro establishes a beachhead, more Negroes will follow—which is often the case—causing real estate values to topple—which may or may not be the case.

As long as the Negro had been a small and docile minority in the North, the feeling that Negroes always destroy social status and market values never gained widespread acceptance. "Where the Negro pitches his tent," wrote Jacob Riis in 1902, "he pays more rent than his white neighbor next door and is a better tenant." In Washington, D. C., Baltimore, and Philadelphia, Negroes lived in small clusters near the better white dwellings, and, before 1915, they lived in almost every section in Chicago—a third of the city's Negroes living in areas that were less than 10 per cent Negro-occupied. The Negro's presence in cities rarely caused a white exodus; it would in fact have disturbed the equanimity of the whites in those days if their maids and butlers moved too far from the town houses.

The situation changed in the thirty years following 1910 when 1,750,000 Negroes moved northward. By 1960 the central cities of the twelve largest metropolitan areas accounted for 24 per cent of all United States Negroes. They were then 29 per cent of Detroit's population; 35 per cent of Baltimore's; a quarter of Cleveland's and Philadelphia's; 34 per cent of Newark's; and 55 per cent of Washington, D. C.'s. As the Negroes moved to the cities, they accelerated the white movement to the burgeoning suburbs so that by 1960 less than a third of the urban and suburban whites were living in the central cities. Though they constituted only a ninth of the national population, 78 per cent of all Negroes in the nation's 212 metropolitan areas lived in the central cities compared to only 52 per cent of the whites.

As the Negro's numbers increased and as he moved into the

adjoining sections or made inroads into white sections, the whites moved out in droves. Homes were often offered at bargain prices. Since cause was confused with effect, the Negroes were always blamed for declines in values.[1]

As opposition crystallized, racial zoning became the main device to keep the Negro in his place and, when the courts struck it down as unconstitutional, the restrictive covenant was thereafter written into deeds in the effort to maintain white supremacy in neighborhoods. About 80 per cent of the vacant land in Los Angeles was at one time covered by such covenants. When the courts held racial covenants unenforceable, subtler devices were ushered in, including overrigid zoning ordinances sternly enforced against Negroes but relaxed for whites. Condemnation for incinerator dumps or other public works is another current device, while building inspectors and other petty officials are always on hand to harass the Negro who ventures where he is not wanted. When, for example, a private builder announced he would sell a few of his houses to Negroes in Deerfield, Illinois, his site was promptly condemned for a park. When the Ford Motor Company moved its plant from Richmond, California, to Milpitas, and when the union tried to build houses for its Negro workers, the area was promptly rezoned for industrial use. Thereafter came a sudden strengthening of building regulations, followed by a hike of sewer connection costs to a ransom figure. It is not surprising, therefore, that discrimination in housing also reduces the chances of Negro employment; many suburban firms refuse to hire Negroes either for fear of offending the local community or because they know the Negroes will have trouble finding housing.

The big city has thus been performing its historic role as a refuge for minorities, while the Northern and Western suburbs have become the new Mason-Dixon lines of America; of the total suburban population of metropolitan areas with a population of half a million or more, barely 4 per cent are Negroes and a substantial number of these live either in the South or in little fringe ghettos that have precariously survived suburban engulfment.

A fourth fiction is that the federal government is and always has been the prime protagonist of equal rights in housing. One gathers this impression from hearing so often of the law of 1866 which supposedly guarantees the Negro the right to own and lease real property, or the protections of the 14th Amendment, or the recent liberal rulings of the Supreme Court. But the law of 1866 was soon a dead letter and still is; the 14th Amendment, enacted to protect Negroes, was long used primarily to protect corporations; as for the Supreme Court, up to 1948 it supported the use of the racial restrictive covenant as a private prerogative, and so did the highest courts of twelve states. Although the Supreme Court after 1948 became the spearhead in the drive for expanding the Negro's civil rights, and although general economic improvement has helped raise the Negro's sights, he has made little gain in housing.

One of the reasons is that the federal government, during the New Deal period, not only sanctioned racial discrimination in housing but vigorously exhorted it.[2] From 1935 to 1950, discrimination against Negroes was a condition of federal assistance. More than 11 million homes were built during this period, and this federal policy did more to entrench housing bias in American neighborhoods than any court could undo by a ruling. It established a federally sponsored mores for discrimination in the suburban communities in which 80 per cent of all new housing is being built and fixed the social and racial patterns in thousands of new neighborhoods.

In 1962, two years after he had made the promise to do so, President Kennedy signed an executive order outlawing discrimination in federally aided housing. By that time, seventeen states and fifty-six cities had passed laws or resolutions against housing discrimination. This movement at the state and local levels originated in New York in the 1940's and spread elsewhere partly as a liberal protest against discrimination in publicly assisted undertakings and partly because the minority numbers were beginning to become more politically significant. But the Executive Order was hardly a prophylactic against the virus that now afflicted American neighborhoods. In the first place, it embraced only about 23 per cent of all new housing construction and only 13 per cent of the housing not already covered by state or local action. In the second place, it explicitly excluded the federally regulated and federally assisted savings and loan associations which are the principal mortgage lenders in the nation. It was hardly surprising, therefore, that the order could not crack the vitrified prejudices and fears that had become impacted during the sixteen years of concerted federal anti-Negro policy. Nor has the enforcement of the order done much to secure equal rights to housing in American suburbs. At best, the order manifests a shift from officially sponsored prejudice to an invertebrate morality.

The rising tide of state and local anti-bias laws in housing has insinuated a fifth fiction into the housing issue, that such state and local anti-bias laws provide the means for ending discrimination. These laws have had educational value, have helped create a better moral climate in some areas, have secured housing for a few upper-income Negro families, and have demonstrated that such laws do not adversely affect property values. But they have brought no solution to the Negro's housing troubles. City anti-bias laws cannot affect the suburbs where most of the exclusionary practices exist. As for state-wide laws, it is all but impossible to buck the concerted power of the suburbs to which the political balance has shifted. Proceedings before anti-discrimination commissions are protracted and costly, and, when a Negro complainant wins a favorable ruling, he must be ready after the long delays to brave the pressures of his hostile landlord, neighbors, and local officials. He must be willing to have his child be the lone Negro child in an all-white school. Most important, he must be financially poised to pay the suburban rents or, if he buys a house, to get a mortgage on it—which is still all but impossible.

The slender hope these laws offer the Negro family is again illustrated in the case of California, where there were two state laws, the Hawkins Act which banned discrimination in publicly assisted housing and the Unruh Act which prohibited discrimination in "all business establishments of any kind whatsoever" and therefore applied to discriminatory practices by real-estate brokers. One reason for the existence of these laws is that the state by 1960 had 1.3 million nonwhites and another 1.4 million of the Spanish-speaking minority, composing a formidable force of voters.

The two laws were hardly strictures which a real-estate owner should have viewed with trepidation. But California has had a long history of anti-racial activities dating from the anti-Chinese campaign of the 1870's and the anti-Japanese outbursts in the decade that followed. Moreover, California's real-estate boards, which compose one of the most formidable lobbies in the state, have continuously favored race segregation. When, for example, the Supreme Court ruled against the racial covenant, the Los Angeles Board was the first to broadcast eight ways of evading the decision. It simultaneously sought a state constitutional amendment to validate the covenant but did not succeed.

The situation changed in 1963 when a local ordinance was introduced in the city of Berkeley—a community generally considered liberal—which proposed to ban racial discrimination by property owners. Largely because the bill carried a possible prison penalty, it was defeated. The defeat lent courage to California's real-estate interests and, shortly after the Berkeley fiasco, the California Real Estate Association, representing 173 local boards, announced its plan to initiate a constitutional amendment barring any anti-bias laws in housing. The proposed amendment, cleverly framed, provided that

Neither the State nor any subdivision or agency thereof shall deny, limit or abridge, directly or indirectly, the right of any person, who is willing or desires to sell, lease or rent any part or all of his real property, to decline to sell, lease or rent such property to such person or persons as he, in his absolute discretion, chooses.

The California Real Estate Association was soon backed by the powerful National Association of Real Estate Boards which not only gave its nationwide support to its affiliate but also joined the campaign and helped finance it. An advertising agency was hired to guide the campaign, and a fund reported to run well over one million dollars was raised to assure victory.

California now became the battle ground for a nationwide campaign to end, once and for all, the long struggle for equal access to shelter. Anti-Negro propaganda circulated freely, and fear of Negro invasion of white neighborhoods was whipped up throughout the state. As a prominent industrialist put it: "In the real estate industry there were a number who were motivated by racial bigotry, others by their concern for property values and some who won't buck the stream. But at the bottom of it all is racial bigotry."

Proposition 14 rolled up a surprising 4.5 million votes in its favor to less than 2.4 million against it. The votes for the proposition exceeded those polled by President Johnson by more than 350,000. President Johnson received almost 1.8 million more votes than those cast against the proposition, indicating that many voters saw no conflict in voting against Goldwater while protecting their own neighborhoods against the Negro scourge. "People just voted their prejudice" was Governor Brown's private comment.

Proposition 14 was also a great victory for the National Association of Real Estate Boards. Its official code of "ethics" up to 1950 had barred its member realtors from "introducing into a neighborhood members of any race or nationality, or any individual whose presence will clearly be detrimental to property values in the neighborhood.[3] The association had grudgingly modified its code of ethics in 1950 on the advice of counsel who may have feared that the Board could be charged with conspiring against the Civil Rights Laws. But despite the modification, there was little evidence that the official view had altered, and, nine days after Proposition 14 was approved, the NAREB Annual Convention in Los Angeles openly resolved that "government should not deny, limit or abridge, directly or indirectly, the fundamental right of every person to sell, lease, or rent any part or all of his real property." The Convention called the California victory to the attention of other states "where the freedom of real estate practices may be imperilled."

The battle lines were thus drawn for a nationwide campaign. Detroit and Akron have followed California's example, while in 1965 Ohio, Rhode Island, and Indiana adopted the other course of banning race bias in private home selling and renting, with Maine barring discrimination in apartments only. This mixed record of victories and defeats suggests that, while the average voter will acquiesce when moral leadership is given to an anti-bias law by his legislators or Governor, he will vote his property rights against his moral scruples when put to the test in person. As long as ethical leadership is lacking, the supporters of property rights are in a position to win the tests, particularly if put to the people themselves, as in California.

Access of the Negro to decent housing is becoming the vortex around which his other rights revolve. Without housing in areas of his choice, the right of his child to an unsegregated school is meaningless; his right to a job will be impaired; his right to move and to secure shelter in a decent neighborhood will be an empty shell. The vote on Proposition 14 indicates that racial prejudice is still a potent political commodity in the nation, and it is not at all unlikely that the device may become the legal instrument for pitting the issue of property rights against civil rights in the years to come.

The extent to which the heated contest over Proposition 14 contributed to the anti-white emotions that burst forth into the Watts riot will be hard to assess. But this is certain: housing has and will continue to play a part, if not in Negro outbreaks against the whites, then in white outbreaks against the Negro. American history reveals a long string of such riots, dynamitings, and other forms of violence from the time Negroes began moving North in greater numbers. The toll in deaths and injuries is in the thousands, and property damage is in the hundreds of millions—the Watts riot alone destroyed $50 million in property. So far, violence has been confined mostly to the white sections of cities and to a few communities on the fringe of big cities. But since the urbanization of the Negro will not be complete until he has achieved suburbanization as well, a larger toll of violence can be expected as the Negro improves his income and begins to challenge suburban exclusion.

Although the expansion of the President's Executive Order may bring only a moral victory in the struggle against housing prejudice, moral victories are presently important. As long as the order remains incomplete, there will always be the implication that federal policy is indifferent to housing bias; real-estate groups will continue their efforts to win the right to exclude, school segregation will become the established pattern in the North, and racial frictions will accelerate.

Yet the Negro's housing problem can never be solved by laws and orders alone, for neither laws nor orders can reach the subtler and more effective forms of discrimination. Moreover, since Congress in the Housing Act of 1949 has guaranteed a "decent home and a suitable living environment for every American family" and has become the main force for creating and manipulating environment in the nation, the failure of the federal government to pass laws which relieve the Negro's housing problem is itself a form of discrimination, namely discrimination by omission.

The Negro is only 11.6 per cent of the nation's population, and about half of the American Negroes still live in the South. Although the presence of Negroes appears formidable because of exclusion and their concentration in the major cities, they would hardly be noticed in Northern and Western cities if the suburbs were opened to them, for there simply are not enough Negro families in the country to threaten white areas, even if the Negroes and other low-income families were subsidized to make their move possible.

To deal with the Negro's housing problem—as well as with school segregation—a meaningful housing program is needed for low-income families at costs they can afford. Despite official claims to the contrary, present programs cannot accomplish this. The public housing program hardly scratches the surface, and the local housing authorities that build the projects are generally located in the cities and lack the power to build beyond their legal boundaries. The states which could build without regard to local boundaries will not do so because of suburban opposition. FHA mortgage insurance is designed mostly for builders in suburban areas; besides, the housing it produces is too costly for most Negro families.

The two hundred million dollar authorization in rent supplements made available to families under the 1965 Housing Act represents one of the landmarks in the fight for better housing. Unfortunately, initiation of the housing operations will still depend on the will of private entrepreneurs or nonprofit corporations to venture into suburbia, and it will be a miracle if the program produces more than a token number of suburban dwelling units for Negro families. The best of intentions can always be forestalled by devious zoning ordinances or obstreperous building codes. Much will still depend on how much pressure can be brought to bear on the federal housing agencies so that they will be forced to challenge suburban bias.

The real answer is for the federal government to build directly wherever there is racial exclusion and housing needs for minorities are demonstrated. The federal government should not only insist that equal access to housing be provided in all federally assisted private subdivisions, but it should also combine direct building with rent supplements in order to bring the dwellings in suburbs as well as in cities within the means of lower-income families. Federal home building has a precedent in the housing constructed during World War I by the United States Housing Corporation and in the building of public housing and new towns during the New Deal. After their completion, the houses and new towns were sold as they should be under the formula proposed. Until Congress is ready to move in that direction, Negro slum life and neighborhood and school segregation will persist.

Simultaneously, the federal government must also meet the predicament facing the central cities. The migration into their centers of millions of low-income Negroes, combined with the presence of poor elderly families, is confronting these cities with social and economic problems with which they can no longer cope. Unlike the federal government, these cities cannot go beyond their boundaries in search of new levies to meet their rising costs. Since 1946 their debts per capita have trebled while federal debt per capita has actually gone down. The money which the federal government has given them for public housing and urban renewal is of small help when measured against the new burdens they have had to assume. Nor can they expect much help from the states whose debts have also rocketed and who are similarly limited in their taxing ability.

The much publicized poverty program is less a war on poverty than a series of well-intentioned skirmishes. Unlike the Peace Corps, it is not designed to assist, expand, and improve existing programs, but to innovate demonstration and pilot efforts. What the cities need are federal funds to support and improve their existing school systems as well as more federal help in meeting their housing, policing, relief, and other commitments.

Urbanization has confronted these cities with new tasks that are national in scope and origin. The Negro housing problem is only one of these concerns, and it involves much more than housing. It is also undeniably linked with making neighborhoods livable, safe, and socially solvent; creating schools, playgrounds, and social facilities which are better and more ample; providing homes that are within a reasonable distance of areas of employment and are within the means of low-income families. In short, the poverty of people and the poverty of cities are parts of the same problem. The plight of the city's people can be dealt with only if the cities are enabled to deal with them.

If the Los Angeles rioting reveals the underlying weaknesses of the current federal approach to segregation, poverty, and housing, and if it stimulates some fresh thinking on these problems, it may compensate at least in part for the terrible havoc it wreaked.

REFERENCES

1. There is no single price reaction to minority infiltrations. Prices may remain constant, fall, or rise and depend on a complex of factors, including the social and economic status of a particular minority at a particular time; its numbers in relation to the numbers in the majority group; the latter's social and cultural level; the minority's capacity for social improvement and assimilation; the size of the city and the physical condition of its neighborhoods; the particular pattern of minority distribution; the nature of the then current minority stereotype; the type of social and educational leadership and maturity in the community; and the relationship between the groups in employment. Shortages may intensify competition for dwellings and increase values. Whether values rise or fall may also depend upon the ability of the newcomers to bid up prices. Nor do values automatically collapse because the minority happens to be of a lower economic status. A minority family may be of lower economic but higher social status, and vice versa. See Charles Abrams, *Forbidden Neighbors* (New York, 1955), pp. 285 ff.

2. "If a neighborhood is to retain stability," said the FHA manual, "it is necessary that properties shall be continued to be occupied by the same social and racial classes." (Section 937) Among "adverse influences" was "infiltration of inharmonious racial or nationality groups." Protection against "adverse influences" included "prevention of inharmonious racial groups."

(Section 229) "Presence of incompatible racial elements" (Section 225) and "the social class of the parents of children at the school will in many instances have a vital bearing" on whether the neighborhood is "stable." The neighborhood will be less desirable if there is "a lower level of society or an incompatible racial element . . . in such instance it might well be that for the payment of a fee children of this area could attend another school with pupils of their same social class." (1936 Manual, Section 266; 1938 Manual, Section 951) FHA advocated not only deed restrictions but zoning to bar the wrong kind of people, and it included stables and pig pens in the same categories as sections occupied by· the wrong kind of race. (1936, Section 284 (3f)) It advocated the use of hills, ravines, and high-speed traffic arteries to discourage the wrong kinds of parents and children (1936, Section 229; 1938, Section 935), and even prescribed and urged the use of a racial covenant form in which it left the space blank for the group excluded to be inserted.

3. Violation of the rule exposed a member board to expulsion. Supplementing its official code, the association issued a brochure in 1943 entitled "Fundamentals of Real Estate Practice." This classed the Negro seeking an education with strange company:

"The prospective buyer might be a bootlegger who would cause considerable annoyance to his neighbors, a madame who had a number of Call Girls on her string, a gangster, who wants a screen for his activities by living in a better neighborhood, a colored man of means who was giving his children a college education and thought they were entitled to live among whites. . . . No matter what the motive or character of the would-be purchaser, if the deal would instigate a form of blight, then certainly the well-meaning broker must work against its consummation."

EUNICE AND GEORGE GRIER

Equality and Beyond: Housing Segregation in the Great Society

RIOTS, RACIAL protests, and rising waves of crime and violence in Los Angeles and other cities across the nation have focused attention upon a problem unique to America—and one which, if not dealt with decisively and soon, can wreak wholesale destruction upon the objectives of the "Great Society." The point at issue is the increasing dominance of Negro ghettos, with all their human problems, at the heart of the nation's metropolitan areas. While racial segregation is by no means new to this country, in recent years it has assumed new dimensions. And the long-smoldering difficulties and disillusionments of a suppressed Negro population have simultaneously taken on new and frightening forms of expression.

The newly emergent pattern of segregation is as simple to describe as it is ominous in its implications. Since the end of World War II, Negroes have rapidly been replacing whites as the dominant population of our greatest cities. Meanwhile, the vast new suburbs growing up around these same urban centers—sharing most of the same problems and feeding upon a common economic base, but separated from the cities politically—have become the residence of an almost exclusively white population. Too many of the suburbanites disavow any concern or responsibility for the cities they have left behind.[1]

Yet the ghettos will not be ignored. To the degree that human problems—economic, social, educational, health—are concentrated in the ghetto, they become self-reinforcing. Exploitation flourishes, since "captive" markets can be forced to pay exorbitant prices for inferior merchandise and services, and continuing Negro population growth presses inexorably upon an inadequate and overage supply of housing. Discouragement and bitterness are the natural expressions. As the Negro ghettos have grown in size, these symptoms of the deeper disease have sometimes reached epidemic proportions.

Unless drastic measures are taken, the ghettos and their problems will continue to grow. They contain within themselves the seeds of their own further expansion. The present urban nonwhite concentrations result only in part from the recent migration of Negroes out of Southern rural areas. They are also the product of natural increase (the excess of births over deaths) among populations already in residence. As a result, even if migration were to cease tomorrow, the ghettos would continue to grow. During the next few years, this trend will be rapid as the postwar "baby boom" reaches maturity and has its own offspring. With this expansion are likely to come greater pressures of people upon available space, and probably more damaging racial explosions.

Today there are very few major cities where Negroes do not constitute a significantly greater proportion than the roughly one-tenth they average across the nation as a whole. In virtually every city they are increasing rapidly. During the 1950's alone, Negro populations increased in New York City by 46 per cent; in Philadelphia by 41 per cent; in Washington, D. C., by 47 per cent; in Los Angeles by 96 per cent.[2]

One consequence of this growth pattern is that Washington has become the first important city to have a Negro majority. But it almost certainly is not the last. Baltimore and New Orleans are likely to join Washington by 1970 at the latest; Cleveland, Detroit, Philadelphia, and St. Louis before 1980.

Insight into both the nature and the causes of racial change in America's urban areas can be gained from the example of Washington, D. C. Since 1920, the metropolitan population of Washington (encompassing both the central city and its suburbs in neighboring Maryland and Virginia) has grown more than threefold, from less than 600,000 to over two million. Meanwhile, the proportion of Negroes in that population has remained essentially constant at roughly one-fourth of the total. In other words, Negroes have both migrated to and multiplied within *metropolitan* Washington at roughly the same over-all rate as whites.

Yet within the central city of Washington, D. C. (which now contains only about one-third of the total metropolitan population) Negroes have increased from one-fourth of the total to well over one-half, since virtually all the Negro increase has gone to the city.

At the same time, the proportion of Negroes in the suburbs has declined from 25 to only 6 per cent as an almost exclusively white outflux has overwhelmed long-existing suburban Negro enclaves.[3]

Rapid Negro increases have been almost universal in cities of large and medium population alike. But in proportional terms, the change has often been greater in the middle-sized cities. Syracuse, Rochester, New Haven, San Diego, and Fort Worth all saw their Negro populations approximately double during the 1950's. Thus these cities can no longer look with smug superiority upon a few urban giants marked by the blight and disorder of Negro ghettos. By the same token, Rochester, New York, and Springfield, Massachusetts recently achieved the headlines through racial disturbances.

Not all the predominantly Negro portions of today's cities are decaying, crime-ridden, potentially explosive slums, however. The movement of white families to the suburbs has recently opened up a number of highly desirable living areas for the small minority of Negroes who can afford them. Some of the finest residential sections of cities like Washington and Philadelphia—once predominantly white—now are interracial or heavily Negro. Their physical character and general flavor have changed little. Imposing stone and brick homes still stand on immaculately maintained lawns. Only the color of the occupants is different.

Yet these too are *Negro* neighborhoods, and—like the sprawling all-white subdivisions surrounding the cities or like the less desirable central districts where most Negroes are allowed to live—they betoken the growing segregation which is splitting our metropolitan areas into two huge enclaves, each the territory of a single race. Their continued social and physical stability, furthermore, is threatened by many of the same pressures of population increase and exploitation which beset the Negro slums. Segregation itself may not be new, but never before has it manifested itself on such a giant and destructive scale.

The Growth of Residential Segregation

How did this change occur so swiftly and so massively? Discrimination and prejudice are certainly among the causes, but they are not the only ones. America cannot escape responsibility for the many decades in which the rights of its Negro citizens were denied. Nonetheless, the present situation cannot be fully understood, nor can solutions to its perplexing aspects be found, without recognizing that it was produced and is maintained in significant part by forces that are both broader than and different from racial discrimination.

The background to all that has happened lies in certain facts concerning the rapid urbanization of America's people—facts racially neutral in themselves, but having profound racial effects. As the nation has grown more populous, its inhabitants have located increasingly within metropolitan centers. A century ago Americans numbered 31 million, about one-fifth of whom lived in urban areas. By 1920 the total population had risen to 106 million, and the urban proportion had grown to one-half—a ninefold jump in absolute numbers (from about 6 million to 54 million) in only sixty years.

After World War II, population growth accelerated sharply. The largest ten-year increase in the nation's history took place between 1950 and 1960. During that decade 28 million new citizens were added, a total nearly equal to the entire population of a century ago. About 85 per cent of this increase occurred within 212 metropolitan areas, making about two-thirds of the nation's people urban today.

In addition to increase through births and immigration during these fruitful years, the cities gained also from large-scale population movements from the center of the country toward its boundaries (especially to the seacoasts and Great Lakes region) and from the South to the North. These streams of people, most experts agree, were both "pulled" toward the cities by job opportunities and other urban attractions (especially in the coastal areas) and "pushed" out of the rural areas by shrinking labor needs, especially in the depressed portions of the agricultural South. Negroes and whites shared in the migration—Negroes to a somewhat, but not drastically, greater degree in proportion to their share of the total population.

Migration to the cities helps explain why, after World War II, the nation turned to its suburbs in order to satisfy housing needs which had been accumulating during almost two decades of economic depression and world conflict. The previous growth of the cities had used up most of the land suitable for development within their boundaries. Yet the people had to be housed somewhere, and swiftly. The easiest place, requiring no costly and time-consuming demolition of existing buildings, was the suburbs.

How should the suburbs be developed? In answering this question certain key public policy decisions—involving racial implications which were probably neither foreseen nor intended—joined with private actions to help produce the present situation. Primary among these was the critical decision to allow the private-enterprise system to meet the housing shortage on its own terms. Most of the government mechanisms mobilized to aid in the task, especially the mortgage guarantee provisions of the Federal Housing Administration and the Veterans Administration, served to support and encourage the efforts of private enterprise.[4]

Such a decision was completely in accord with America's social philosophy and economic structure. And, in light of the inherent dynamism of the private-enterprise system, it is not surprising that the home-building industry was able to provide usable physical shelter. Indeed, this success can be counted as one of the major achievements of a nation which has never been satisfied with small accomplishments. Almost every year following World War II more than one million dwelling units were constructed and occupied, a figure which is double the rate at which new families were formed. And, despite rapid population growth during the fifties, the 1960 Census showed that Americans were far better housed than ever before. Overcrowding and "doubling up" (two or more families in one dwelling) had been considerably reduced. So had dilapidated and otherwise substandard housing. To a greater or lesser degree, the entire population benefited from this widespread improvement—even Negroes, though they continued to be less adequately housed than whites.[5]

Nonetheless, the decision to let private enterprise satisfy the housing need carried with it unfortunate consequences for future residential patterns. It meant that the great majority of the new postwar suburban housing was built for those who could afford to pay the full economic price. Thus the basic mechanisms of the private enterprise system, successful as they were in meeting overall housing needs, selectively operated to reinforce existing trends which concentrated low-income families in the cities. At the same time, they encouraged the centrifugal movement of those who were more wealthy to the outskirts of the cities.

Most Negro families were among those with low incomes, the result of generations of discrimination in employment and education. Quite apart from direct racial discrimination, in which the private housing industry also indulged whenever it felt necessary, economics posed a giant barrier to the free dispersal of the growing

Negro populations. The findings of a market analysis conducted by Chester Rapkin and others at the University of Pennsylvania's Institute for Urban Studies at the peak of the postwar housing boom in the mid-1950's were quite typical. At that time, only 0.5 per cent of all dwellings costing $12,000 or more in Philadelphia had been purchased by Negroes—a fact which the authors laid mainly to economic incapacity. This was about the minimum cost of a modest new house in Philadelphia's suburbs.[6]

But this is only part of the story. Federal policies and practices in housing reinforced and increased the separation between the "Negro" cities and the white suburbs. In part, this was intentional. From 1935 to 1950—a period in which about 15 million new dwellings were constructed—the power of the national government was explicitly used to prevent integrated housing. Federal policies were based upon the premise that economic and social stability could best be achieved through keeping neighborhood populations as homogeneous as possible. Thus, the *Underwriting Manual* of the Federal Housing Administration (oldest and largest of the federal housing agencies, established by the Housing Act of 1934) warned that "if a neighborhood is to retain stability, it is necessary that properties shall continue to be occupied by the same social and racial group." It advised appraisers to lower their valuation of properties in mixed neighborhoods, "often to the point of rejection." FHA actually drove out of business some developers who insisted upon open policies.[7]

More recently, a number of studies by competent real-estate economists have thrown serious doubt upon the thesis that Negro entry lowers property values. Laurenti, in his thorough analysis entitled *Property Values and Race,* found that prices *rose* in 44 per cent of those areas which Negroes entered, were unchanged in another 41 per cent, and declined in only 15 per cent. These were long-term trends, and they were measured *relative* to trends in carefully-matched neighborhoods which remained all white—thus obviating any possibly misleading effects of generally rising prices.[8]

Surveying the literature, Laurenti noted similar results from other studies in various cities extending back as far as 1930. But erroneous though the allegation of nonwhite destruction of property values may have been, it nonetheless provided "justification" for widespread discriminatory practices, as well as active encouragement of private discrimination, by agencies of the federal government during a period of critical importance in determining present residential patterns.

However, discrimination *per se* was only a small factor in the impact of federal policies and practices upon racial patterns during this crucial period. Much more important were more basic aspects of the structure and functioning of federal housing programs. Three major programs have dominated the field. The largest and most significant has been the Federal Housing Administration's mortgage insurance program, with its post-World War II counterpart for veterans, the Veterans Administration's loan guarantee program. Both granted their benefits chiefly to the "modal" family recently embarked upon married life, with children already born or on the way, and willing to commit itself to the responsibilities of home ownership with a mortgage. For such families, down-payment requirements were minimal, repayment periods lengthy, and credit restrictions lenient. A certain minimum of present earnings and good prospects for future income were paramount, as well as some evidence of faithful repayment of past obligations. Households which did not fit these criteria—smaller families, older couples, single persons, people with low or precarious earnings, families who sought dwellings for rent rather than for sale, even families dependent upon the wife's employment for an adequate income—all were required to satisfy their needs chiefly through the older housing left vacant by people moving to new homes in the suburbs.

Prominent among those left behind, of course, were Negroes. The federal programs permitted them to "inherit" the cities, along with an assortment of whites who did not meet the conditions for access to the new suburbs: the old, the poor, the physically and mentally handicapped, the single and divorced, together with some persons of wealth and influence who preferred the convenience of living in the central city. The significance of the housing programs for residential patterns, however, lay also in their tendency to pull young and upwardly mobile white families away from the cities and out toward the suburbs.

It may be that a large number of these families, given free choice, would have preferred to remain within the cities, close to work and to older relatives. But the FHA and VA programs generally did not provide nearly so liberal terms on the mortgages of older homes in the cities. Down payments were usually larger; repayment periods shorter; monthly payments higher. For most young families, therefore, the suburbs were the only practical areas in which to solve their housing needs. In this way, the FHA and VA programs, essentially independent of any direct racial bias in their decisions on applications, enhanced the tendency toward white dominance in the suburbs.

The second of the federal government's major housing programs is subsidized low-income public housing, administered by the Public Housing Administration through local housing authorities. Its criteria for admission are based upon *maximum* rather than minimum income levels. Under these conditions relatively small numbers of whites can qualify because their earnings exceed the required standard. In many areas, even where conscious efforts are made to attract an interracial clientele, the great majority of residents are Negro. In further contrast to the FHA and VA programs, most public housing projects have been constructed in the central cities rather than in the suburbs—since one of their objectives is to reduce the incidence of blighted housing.

The differences between the two programs thus reinforce each other in their effects upon patterns of residence. While the FHA and VA have helped promote white dominance in the suburbs, public housing has helped enhance Negro dominance in the cities.

The third of the major federal housing programs is urban renewal. Established by the Housing Act of 1949, its chief goal is to combat physical decay in the central cities. In a sense, urban renewal has worked against FHA and VA programs, since, among other things, it attempts to draw back to the cities the more prosperous of the families who have left it. Until recently, the renewal program has usually cleared off blighted sections and replaced them with housing units priced in the middle- to upper-income brackets. Most often, as might be expected, the occupants of the site before renewal have been low-income members of a racial minority. They have been displaced by housing which, for economic reasons alone, was available mainly to whites and to very few Negroes. Some civil rights groups therefore have dubbed urban renewal "Negro removal."[9]

Renewal agencies are required by law to relocate displaced families into "decent, safe and sanitary" housing. Relocation procedures have recently received a great deal of criticism throughout the nation. Whether or not all of it is valid, it is an undeniable fact that most relocatees move only a short distance from their former homes. One study found, for example, that two-thirds of them relocated within a radius of twelve city blocks. As a result, displaced low-income minorities ring the renewal site.

Sometimes this movement appears to set off a chain reaction. Whites in the neighborhoods to which the displacees move take up residence elsewhere—as do some of the more secure Negroes. The ultimate effect too often is to touch off spreading waves of racial change, which in the end only produce a broader extension of segregated living patterns. Thus, if the FHA, VA, and public housing programs have helped produce metropolitan areas which increasingly resemble black bullseyes with white outer rings, urban renewal has too often created small white or largely white areas in the center of the bullseyes—simultaneously causing the black ghettos to expand outward even further.

Combined with rapid population growth in the metropolitan areas, the interacting effects of federal policies and practices in the postwar era did much to produce the present segregated patterns. But they were not the only factors. Clear discrimination by private individuals and groups—including the mortgage, real-estate, and home-building industries—has also played its part. The activities of the "blockbuster" provide a good focus for examining the way this works.

The *modus operandi* of the blockbuster is to turn over whole blocks of homes from white to Negro occupancy—the quicker the better for his own profits, if not for neighborhood stability. Once one Negro family has entered a block, the speculator preys on the racial fears and prejudices of the whites in order to purchase their homes at prices as low as possible—often considerably below fair market value. He then plays upon the pent-up housing needs of Negroes and resells the same houses at prices often well *above* their value in a free market situation. Often he makes a profit of several thousand dollars within a period of a few days. Studies have indicated that skillful blockbusters frequently double their investments in a brief interval. They can do this only because tight residential restrictions have "dammed up" the Negro need for housing to such a point that its sudden release can change the racial composition of a neighborhood within a matter of weeks or months. Apart from the damage done to both sellers and buyers and to the structure of the neighborhoods themselves, blockbusters have a far wider negative impact. By funneling Negro housing demand into limited sections of the city (usually around the edges of the Negro slums, since these neighborhoods are easier to throw into panic), the blockbusters relieve much of the pressure which might otherwise have encouraged the dispersion of Negroes throughout the metropolitan areas.[10]

Technically speaking, blockbusters represent an unscrupulous minority of the real estate industry—"outlaws" in a moral if not a legal sense. However, their activities would not prove profitable if racial restrictions on place of residence were not accepted and enforced by the large majority of builders, brokers, and lenders, backed by the supporting opinion of large segments of the white public.

By restraining the Negro market and permitting its housing needs to be satisfied only on a waiting-list basis, "reputable" members of the banking and housing industries have helped perpetuate the conditions under which their less-scrupulous colleagues can flourish. For reasons they consider entirely justifiable, they guard assiduously against the entry of Negroes into white areas. In recent testimony before the Commissioners of the District of Columbia, the President of the Mortgage Bankers Association of Metropolitan Washington stated bluntly that "applications from minority groups are not generally considered in areas that are not recognized as being racially mixed." A study by the Chicago Commission on Human Relations found that such a policy was pursued by almost all lending sources in that city. Voluminous evidence from both social research surveys and testimony before legislative and executive bodies indicates that the same is true of most real-estate boards in cities throughout the country.

Supporting this activity is the subjective equivalent of the ostensibly objective economic argument that underlay federal housing policy for years: the belief in neighborhood homogeneity—that is, neighborhood exclusiveness. The general attitude of much of the public (or the most vocal) has been that neighborhoods were better off when the people within them all belonged to the same broad socioeconomic groups and had the same ethnic or racial origins. In practice, of course, this commitment to neighborhood homogeneity has tended to exclude individuals who fell below a certain status level, not those who were above it. The latter, however, usually have "excluded" themselves in neighborhoods restricted to occupants of their own status.

After 1948, when the Supreme Court ruled that racial and religious covenants were unenforceable in the courts, minority groups began to find it somewhat less difficult to obtain access to neighborhoods on the basis of financial status and preference. Still, neighborhood exclusiveness remained a commonly accepted value, widely enforced by the real-estate, home-building, and lending industries. It served as the final factor in the constellation which created the nation's new patterns of residential segregation.

The Shape of the Future

The future shape of metropolitan areas, in racial terms, is outlined clearly in population statistics. The growth of segregated patterns has attained a momentum that now tends to be self-sustaining. Most of the young white families who will provide the future increase in white population have moved outside the city limits. In Washington, D. C., for example, half of the remaining white population (children included) are over the age of forty. Even among the young adults, a disproportionate number are single.[11]

On the other hand, the central cities continue to be the place of residence of Negroes of all ages, including the young couples and teenagers approaching maturity who provide the potential for future population growth. Left to themselves, these population patterns can have no other effect than to swell the ghettos and further exacerbate the color dichotomy between cities and suburbs.

What steps would be necessary to halt or reverse these trends? The magnitude of the effort required is suggested by statistics computed by George Schermer for the Philadelphia metropolitan area. Schermer has estimated that merely to prevent the current areas of Negro concentration from expanding further would require an annual outflux of 6,000 Negro households. To *reverse* the trend and to disperse the Negro population evenly throughout the metropolis by the year 2000 would require the entry of 9,700 Negro households *annually* into currently white districts and the counter-movement of 3,700 white families into areas now Negro. No comparable shift of populations is presently occurring in Philadelphia or in any other metropolis. And, each year that the ghettos continue to expand, these figures grow progressively larger.[12]

The Costs of Segregation

Today's wide-scale patterns of segregation, and the prospect of their further expansion, have several extremely important consequences for the nation as a whole. One of the most dramatic of the current ramifications is the fact that the problems long associated with the Negro ghetto because of generations of discrimination —educational deficiencies, high rates of illness and social disorders, low employment rates, and predominantly low incomes even among those who are employed—all press with increasing force upon the cities as the ghettos continue to grow. At the same time, the financial and leadership resources of the cities have been severely depleted by the middle-class white movement to the suburbs. As a separate political entity, the city has, with growing force, been deprived by the expanding rings of suburbia of the resources it needs to set its house in order.

The newly emergent residential patterns have thus transformed segregation from a parochial concern largely confined to the South (though posing a moral dilemma for the entire nation) into the hardest kind of practical economic problem affecting all the urban centers of America.[13]

But the problem no longer stops at the city line. Today, segregation increasingly threatens the rational planning and development of entire metropolitan areas—a consequence of profound significance in light of continued population growth and the scarcity of urban land, which make it essential that future generations be housed in a less haphazard fashion.

In recent years choice land on the periphery of the larger cities has been devoured at a ferocious rate. In metropolitan Philadelphia, for example, while the population of the "urbanized" or heavily built up area grew by 24 per cent during the 1950's, its geographic spread doubled. This reckless consumption of land cannot continue much longer. Municipalities are already grappling in various ways with the challenge of making more efficient use of the land which is still within feasible commuting distance. The aim of their plans is to keep the metropolitan areas fit places in which to live, with a satisfactory balance of the various elements that together constitute an adequate human environment: homes, commercial and cultural centers, adequate transit facilities, industries, parks, and other necessities and amenities.

In metropolitan Washington, regional planning agencies recently devised a "Plan for the Year 2000." This plan is essentially a general set of principles for meeting the needs of a population that is expected to grow to more than twice its present size before the end of the century. The plan suggests that future growth be channeled along six radial "corridors" extending outward in star fashion from the central city. Highways and transit lines would run alongside the corridors; centers of commerce and various service areas would be located at appropriate intervals. To preserve as much as possible of the green countryside, parks and open recreation areas would be placed between the corridors.

The plan, however, fails to take into account one vital consideration: the effect of race. If the movement of the city's population continues in its present directions, three of the planned corridors will be heavily Negro. They will have their central origins in neighborhoods which currently are Negro and which already are expanding outward in the directions proposed by the plan. The other three corridors will be almost exclusively white, since they originate in the only white residential areas that remain within the city. Thus segregation will be extended for an indefinite period into the new suburbs. If, on the other hand, Negro expansion is cut off along the three corridors which are presently "open," the future population growth will be forced back into the city, thereby intensifying dangerous pressures which already exist.[14]

Still another instance of the way racial segregation thwarts planning can be found in the emerging new towns which, in some parts of the country, at least, may soon begin to offer an alternative to the previous norm of suburban sprawl. These new communities—of which Reston, Virginia, and Columbia, Maryland, both already underway, are two important examples—will be planned and built from the outset as complete urban complexes, with a full panoply of shopping, employment, and recreational facilities. The most comprehensive of the new towns will also contain a wide selection of housing, ranging from bachelor apartments to large single houses, so that the residents will be able to satisfy their changing needs without moving from the community. Over-all population densities in these new communities will be considerably higher than in the dormitory suburbs of the recent past. Yet, through imaginative planning, they can offer their residents an even greater sense of spaciousness and privacy.

Already popular in Europe and Great Britain, the new town concept offers important advantages over the formlessness that characterizes America's postwar suburban development—advantages that accrue not merely to the residents of the towns but to the entire nation. The new towns offer a way of comfortably accommodating population growth while conserving irreplaceable green space. The proliferation of multi-million dollar superhighways can be slowed down. Pollution of the air by exhaust fumes will be reduced. Speedy, economical mass transit systems, now virtually unfeasible in many areas because of the low density and wide geographic spread of suburban growth, will become practical once more. There will even be substantial savings in taxes for municipal services, as well as in utility and commuting costs.

But the new towns, despite the hopeful prospect they represent, also confront the ever-present specter of race. To be successful in realizing their diversified goals, the towns will require a large number of service workers—including manual laborers, domestics, custodians, and sales people, to mention only a few categories. Today, the only significant reservoir of labor available for many of these occupations is the Negro population. Furthermore, civil rights laws now require equal access by all citizens to employment opportunities. Yet, in most instances, the new towns will be located too far from the central cities for easy and economical commuting. Thus, in all likelihood, the workers will have to be housed in the towns themselves.

But on what basis? Will the new towns contain, from the outset, pre-planned ghettos? If not, how is integration to be accomplished, given the differential income levels of the people involved and the many problems connected with providing low-cost housing under private auspices? Even if this last obstacle is overcome—as might be possible if Congress implements new and imaginative forms of governmental aid and subsidy—will white Americans long conditioned with the encouragement of their own government to rigid spatial separation, not only of races but of economic groups, accept any other arrangement?

If, on the other hand, the new towns do not offer accommodations to families of low income, what will happen as they draw away more and more of the cities' remaining affluent residents, while providing no comparable outlet for their growing low-income populations? Will vast new towns then be planned especially for the low income populations, thus extending patterns of racial segregation upon a scale even now unknown? Or will the cities merely be expected to absorb the population increase indefinitely?

Within some cities, the low income housing needs are already reaching crisis proportions. In Washington, D. C., for example, public attention has recently been focused on the problem through widespread civic protests. With virtually no vacant land remaining, and with a population which has grown since 1960 both in total numbers and in the proportion of low-income Negroes, Washington now faces a perplexing dilemma indeed. Virtually every improvement of any magnitude in its physical structure, whether publicly or privately sponsored, further reduces an already inadequate low income housing supply. Development of expressways to relieve traffic congestion has been threatened as a result. Even code enforcement aimed at improving housing conditions is endangered because it often results in evicting poor families with no place else to live. Yet private construction, stimulated by Washington's booming economy and unhampered by considerations that often affect public action, is proceeding apace. Almost all centrally located homes which are privately renewed for occupancy by middle-class families, and many of the sumptuous new apartment houses and office buildings as well, gain their valuable land by removing additional units from the low income housing supply. Some Washington observers are wondering how much longer this process can continue without triggering racial outbreaks similar to those which have already disfigured other major cities.

The complex issues which surround land development, both present and future, constitute only one of the concerns made increasingly problematical by the city-suburban racial split. Paradoxically, it presents obstacles also to current major attempts to aid minority groups in escaping from poverty and deprivation.

A good case in point is the multiple efforts to upgrade Northern public schools in a state of *de facto* segregation. For the most part, these schools are desegregated in principle, but because of surrounding residential patterns have become segregated in practice. A considerable amount of this segregation, it should be realized, occurred during the fifties as a direct result of population shifts. At the time of the Supreme Court decision barring school segregation, Washington, D. C., which is located among the border states, had a completely segregated educational system. Once the decision was announced, the city immediately desegregated. Yet only a decade later, because of intervening population shifts, the school system once again is almost entirely segregated. "Resegregation" is the term some concerned local citizens have coined for this disturbing phenomenon.

De facto segregation tends to create poor, inadequately serviced schools. The concentration of culturally disadvantaged Negro children makes it difficult to provide the intensive programs they need to reach an equal footing with their white contemporaries. In racially mixed schools, their deficiencies are leavened through contact with children more fortunate in background and home environment. One attempted solution has been to bus Negro children to better schools which are underutilized and for the most part are predominantly white. But this approach has met with strenuous resistance from many of the parents (including some Negroes) whose children attend the better schools. Some officials fear that continued busing in the face of such protests would cause even more middle-class whites to leave the cities and thus make the situation even worse in the long run.[15]

The whole problem is exacerbated by the fact that most heavily Negro schools are located in the older and more depressed neighborhoods of the city. Both the schools and their surroundings are often in physical and social decay. Thus, in addition to everything else, it becomes difficult to attract or keep good teachers.

But the nation quite rightly, although belatedly, has committed itself to providing equal educational opportunities for all its citizens. In the face of *de facto* segregation, it is now trying to meet that commitment by a huge complex of experimental programs costing millions of dollars. If the programs are successful, their extension to all those who need them will ultimately mean the spending of many more billions. But aside from the question of money, the nation currently confronts the much more difficult question of whether the programs can in fact work, given the complex of environmental obstacles which exist.

Most of the dilemmas and problems posed by residential segregation in the United States are brought into focus by the current war against poverty. Can poverty among Negroes ever be eliminated while rigid segregation increases within the metropolitan centers? On the other hand, can the metropolitan areas ever be desegregated as long as the majority of Negroes remain poor? As segregation continues to grow and Negroes reach numerical predominance in more and more urban centers, will not the cities which house the majority of the nation's industrial and commercial life find themselves less and less able to cope with their problems, financially and in every other way? What then will be the answer for the metropolitan complexes where two-thirds of America's population currently reside and where as much as 85 per cent of the nation may live by the year 2000?

Aside from these large and basic questions of public policy and social change, residential segregation causes havoc on a more personal and individual level. And the personal damage is not to Negroes alone. Many of the neighborhoods newly entered by Negroes since World War II have been occupied by middle-aged and retired white families who often look upon their current homes as being their last—and whose emotional attachment to both house and neighborhood is based upon ties of familiarity and friendship built up over many years. These occupants feel deeply threatened by the entrance of a Negro family. The result often is mental stress, misery, and loneliness, as well as a sense of overwhelming personal loss at being "forced" to leave a home and neighborhood one had grown to love.[16]

The effects of precipitate change are particularly sad in ethnic neighborhoods where much of the community's life has centered around a house of worship and where neighbors often include kinfolk as well as friends. In such cases, the change is harmful not only to individual families but to institutions and social organizations that can rarely survive transfer to another location. Constant change is normal, of course, and neighborhood institutions should adapt constructively to it and help their members to adjust. Nevertheless, many institutions are unprepared, and the rapidity of racial change often gives them little opportunity to catch up with their responsibilities.

In all these ways, then, residential segregation is or has become central to major domestic problems of the nation. There is no way to determine the ultimate sum of its costs. It ranges into so many areas that it may accurately be designated the key question of our national life in the 1960's.

The Upsurge of Civic Concern

Over the past decade and a half, as the situation has worsened, the significance of residential segregation has steadily been pushing itself into the forefront of the national consciousness. As public comprehension has grown, one response has been a groundswell of concern and action on both public and private levels. This development cannot be overvalued. It is a change of almost revolutionary proportions, a change that has been accomplished not through violence or political disorder but through the constitutional mechanisms of the government and through the exercise of individual freedoms that form the basis of American society. Yet, this counteraction, despite its importance, is in itself presently insufficient for the task at hand. The best way to indicate both the limitations of the current activity and the general direction in which the country must now move is to outline the various ways in which mounting public concern has expressed itself.

Between 1950 and today, the federal government has completely reversed its racial policy, moving from official sanction of segregation to a Presidential order that prohibits discrimination in any housing receiving federal assistance. The first official impetus for this change came in 1948, when the Supreme Court ruled that restrictive racial covenants were legally unenforceable. At first the Federal Housing Administration declared that the decision was inapplicable to its operation. Finally, late in 1949, it removed the model covenant and all references to neighborhood homogeneity from its manual and declared that after February 1950 it no longer would insure mortgages having restrictive covenants. The Veterans Administration and the Urban Renewal Administration both issued similar statements.

Further changes ensued. By 1960, they included the following: both the FHA and VA had ruled that the insured property they acquired (usually under foreclosure proceedings) would be made available to all buyers or renters, regardless of race, creed, or color; the administrative head of the FHA had instructed local offices to take "active steps to encourage the development of demonstrations in open occupancy projects in suitably located key areas"; both the FHA and VA had signed a series of formal agreements of cooperation with state and local agencies responsible for enforcing laws and ordinances against housing discrimination; the government had dropped a system of racial quotas in housing built for persons displaced by urban renewal; and it also had banned discrimination in a special loan program to assist the elderly in their housing needs.

These regulations and directives clearly represent a large stride forward from the directly discriminatory policies pursued before 1950. Yet their practical effect on the rigid patterns of segregation that had developed over the years was very small. In 1962, federal reports revealed that nearly 80 per cent of all public housing projects receiving a federal subsidy were occupied by only one race. Segregated projects were located as far North as Scranton, Pennsylvania, and Plattsburgh, New York—and, as might be expected, in practically every locality in the South. The vast majority of new suburban housing backed by FHA and VA mortgage guarantees was occupied exclusively by white families. A scattering of developments built on urban renewal sites were made available to both Negroes and whites; but they were limited mainly to the largest cities of the North and West and generally priced at or close to luxury levels. Where integration existed, it was largely the result of state and local laws rather than national directives. Only seldom, however, were these laws adequately enforced.[17]

Nonetheless, by 1962, partly because of the ineffectiveness of previous changes, it had become clear that the broad problems of discrimination and segregation were too interwoven to be solved with piecemeal changes in federal policy. The first step toward a more comprehensive approach came on November 20, 1962, when the late President Kennedy issued an Executive Order barring discrimination in all housing receiving federal aid after that date. At the end of April 1964, it was estimated that 932,000 units of housing had come under the directives of the Order. In June 1964, it was estimated that between 12 and 20 per cent of all new residential construction was covered.

But the segregation that had developed in previous years still remained. Charles Abrams summed up both the limitations and the value of the Executive Order shortly after it was issued in the following way:

The Executive Order will . . . touch only a small fraction of the housing market. If any real gains are to be made, its coverage must be widened or more individual state laws laboriously sought. The President's Order is no more than a small first federal step toward breaking the bottleneck in housing discrimination.

Nevertheless, its importance cannot be discounted. First steps in civil rights legislation have often led to second steps when the will to move ahead has been present.[18]

The federal government has also made special, though limited, efforts to mitigate the unintended racial effects of its housing programs. Housing legislation gave the FHA, in cooperation with the Federal National Mortgage Association, the right to issue insured loans from government funds at below-market interest rates for housing to be occupied by families with incomes too low to acquire new homes in the private market. This indirect form of subsidy was intended in part to reach a larger number of Negro families. Urban renewal programs have begun to pay more attention to relocation procedures and to stress rehabilitation of existing dwellings rather than total clearance. In some cities, Community Renewal Programs aided with federal funds are attempting to develop comprehensive plans for housing all groups in the population. In the public housing program, where Negroes predominate, federal action has paradoxically been least decisive. Still, many local authorities have tried to promote racial balance in their projects, and some have been experimenting with various types of nonproject housing scattered throughout the community.

But the fundamental orientations of the federal programs remain today—as do the deeply entrenched consequences of their operation throughout the peak years of the post-World War II housing boom. It will take more than piecemeal efforts to shatter such a solid foundation for the continued growth of segregated living patterns.

While the federal government was moving toward its policy of nondiscrimination in housing, many states and municipalities were moving in the same direction—and, in recent years, at a more rapid pace. Prior to 1954, only a few of the states in the North and Midwest had legislation which barred discrimination in any segment of their housing supply. The laws usually covered only low-rent public housing and, occasionally, units receiving such special forms of assistance as tax exemptions or write-downs on land costs.

As of mid-1965, however, sixteen states and the District of Columbia had barred discrimination in a substantial portion of their private housing supply. At the 1960 census these states together contained about eighty million people, or 44 per cent of the total population. Thus nearly half the citizens of the United States are now living in communities whose public policy is clearly opposed to deliberate segregation on the basis of race—even in housing built under private auspices. President Kennedy's Executive Order of 1962 therefore was basically an extension on the federal level of a principle already gaining widespread acceptance in states and localities across the nation.

However, mere nondiscrimination cannot by itself overcome the problem of segregation. It will take vigorous positive efforts on the part of government and private citizens to halt, let alone reverse, trends now so firmly entrenched.

Contributors to Change

Changes in public policy can usually be attributed to the determined efforts of a small minority of citizens who recognize a need and work tirelessly to bring it to public attention. In no case has this been more true than with residential segregation. Led by the National Committee Against Discrimination in Housing—a small and meagerly financed organization which grew out of the first successful campaigns for housing laws in New York—religious, civic and labor groups in many parts of the country have spearheaded similar campaigns in their own states and cities. The resulting laws have provided a foundation upon which other types of private effort could build.

A second important variety of private effort toward housing desegregation is the intentional development of new housing on an open-occupancy basis. Beginning in 1937 with a small Quaker-sponsored project in southwestern Pennsylvania, the spontaneous development of nondiscriminatory housing by private groups got underway in earnest following World War II. Despite concerted opposition by the federal government, many local governments, and most segments of the real estate industry, a 1956 survey found that some fifty new interracial communities had been produced by private efforts up to that time. Some of them had been inspired by civic and social service organizations to foster racial equality, but a number had been constructed by businessmen for profit. Today, such developments are estimated to number in the high hundreds or even the thousands.[19]

In a third approach, "grass-roots" organizations in many cities across the country have sought to stabilize the occupancy of their own neighborhoods following the entry of Negroes. In numerous instances they have accomplished what many once thought impossible —quelling panic, avoiding possible violence, maintaining sound neighborhood conditions, even bringing new white residents into areas where formerly the prognosis had been for complete transition to all-Negro occupancy.[20]

Finally, in the suburbs of a number of cities, concerned white residents have banded together to help open their own neighborhoods to Negro families able to pay the price. The first of these "fair housing committees," established in Syracuse, New York, in the mid-1950's, was sponsored by the local Quaker Meeting. Religious influence of various denominations remains strong in many of the later organizations, now estimated to number more than one thousand.[21]

These private efforts represent one of the most encouraging examples of the inherent strength of American democracy and its capacity for change. They have helped shatter many racial myths, have opened new housing opportunities for Negroes in areas not previously open to them, and have done much through practical demonstration to alter the attitudes of the white majority toward the prospect of Negro neighbors.

But in the face of population forces, they can have little effect in destroying racial segregation. The point was passed some years ago where either legal bars against discrimination or the best-intentioned of meagerly financed "grass roots" endeavors could accomplish the task. If Americans wish not only to create truly equal opportunity for all, but also to solve the many domestic problems which stem from inequality and the artificial separation of the races, they must now be prepared to move beyond mere nondiscrimination and good will—in a sense, beyond equality—into an area of positive and aggressive efforts to undo the damage already done. It will require a massive national effort, calling upon the full resources of both the public and private sectors.

The Task and the Methods

That the country possesses the fundamental resources it needs to solve the problem is fortunately clear. What is required is less the creation of new mechanisms than the effective harnessing and, where necessary, the reorientation, of those which already exist. Otherwise it will be impossible to meet the goal of rendering segregated housing patterns ineffective as an obstacle to the objectives of the "Great Society."

This aim, it must be stressed, need not be sought through methods which run counter to the basic tenets of American democracy. For example, it need not be attempted through forced redistribution of population. Force is not only intolerable, but unnecessary. The normal mobility of the American people is so great (about half of all households moved during the latter half of the 1950s alone) that redistribution can be achieved through the operation of free choice—if sufficient resources are applied to make socially desirable patterns of residence as attractive to the public as socially undesirable ones have been in the past.

Nor is it necessary to attempt a rigidly planned dispersal of Negro households. The aim, rather, should be to achieve complete freedom of choice in place of residence without respect to racial barriers. Within this framework of unconstrained choice, some substantial concentrations of Negro families would doubtless persist, just as Jews have remained in certain neighborhoods even after obstacles to their residing elsewhere have largely been eliminated. But the present monolithic character of the Negro ghettos, their inexorable growth, and the social evils they encourage would be broken.

The following are some specific measures which would help achieve the goal. The list is not all-inclusive; doubtless many readers will think of others which would be of value:

A central federal agency possessing the competence to plan comprehensively for all phases of urban development and the authority to translate plans into effective action. This agency must have the power to draw together federal operations in such diverse areas as housing, urban renewal, highways, transportation, and community facilities and to guide them toward a set of common objectives. The newly created Department of Housing and Urban Development can be such an instrument—if it can overcome the handicap of its origin in the Housing and Home Finance Agency, a loosely knit combination of essentially independent agencies, and achieve better coordination of individually powerful organizations than has the similarly amalgamated Department of Health, Education and Welfare. This will not be easy.

A total strategy for desegregation. The segregation problem is too complex to be solved without a total approach which recognized all the manifold forces which brought it to its present magnitude and threaten to enlarge it further. This approach must take maximum strategic advantage of all available resources and knowledge. It must be adaptable to varying local conditions and flexible enough to permit changes as "feedback" from early applications dictates. But it must be directed always to a clear and unwavering set of goals.

Broadened federal incentives for effective action by local governments and private entrepreneurs. Incentive programs have proved one of the most acceptable means of applying governmental leverage in a democratic system, for they do not involve compulsion and do not infringe upon freedom of choice. In housing, for example, incentives have promoted urban renewal (through grants to local authorities to clear slum land for redevelopment) and the construction of specific types of housing (through liberal mortgage insurance). Incentives must now be used to encourage comprehensive planning and action toward social goals. For example, suitable incentives can encourage private builders to construct balanced communities serving all population groups, can attract and assist low-income minority families to move to such communities, can stimulate existing neighborhoods to self-renewal and racial stabilization, can encourage local governments to attack segregation in the comprehensive manner it requires by cooperation throughout the metropolitan areas.

Imaginative new forms of subsidy for low-income families. Traditionally, housing subsidies have been available almost exclusively for units built by local nonprofit authorities—chiefly in the form of multi-unit public "projects," which stood apart from their surroundings and amassed the social ills associated with poverty in much the same fashion as did older and less solidly constructed ghettos. More recently, various localities have experimented with methods for widening the range of choice and location in subsidized housing. The Housing Act of 1965 contains provisions which can make subsidies a much more valuable tool in combatting segregation. But their operation toward this end cannot be left to chance; it will require vigorous and imaginative guidance.

Comprehensive measures to increase minority incomes. Any measure which increases the purchasing power of racial minorities will bring a corresponding reduction in the critically important economic barriers to desegregation. Minimum wage floors must be raised; present ones are actually below the level defined by the federal government as "poverty." Federal resources must be directed toward expanding the number of jobs available, particularly for those of limited education. The most important need of the minority poor is for decent jobs at decent pay. Economic measures can and should be tied to housing. For example, low-income minority persons should be trained for the specific kinds of jobs which will be made available in the new, comprehensively planned communities on the outskirts of metropolitan areas. Housing should be planned for them close to these new job opportunities. Similarly, relocation from urban renewal areas should be coupled with a range of services, including training and assistance in finding employment, to help assure that displaced families improve not only their housing conditions but their economic situation as well.

Intensive efforts to improve the attractiveness of central cities. To date, urban renewal, in its efforts to draw middle- and upper-income families back to the urban cores, has focused mainly upon the physical aspects of decay. It is increasingly obvious that social renewal is required also—that many of the economically more capable families, Negro as well as white and especially those with children, will not be persuaded to return to the central areas until they are assured of protection from the social pathology of the ghetto. City schools, for example, must be drastically improved; yet there is growing evidence that this will require not merely replacement of individual buildings and teaching staffs but also comprehensive restructuring of entire school systems. Crime and violence are among the greatest deterrents to affluent families who prefer to live in central areas, and the cities will be at a disadvantage until they prove that they can control both the chronically lawless and those driven to crime by frustration and economic need.

Vigorous enforcement of anti-discrimination laws and affirmative measures to promote equal opportunity. As noted earlier, anti-discrimination laws in themselves are unable to solve a problem which stems from much broader causes. But, if vigorously enforced, they can prove a most important weapon in the arsenal of measures against segregation. Further, as many of the more effective law-enforcement agencies already recognize, it is not sufficient merely to remain passive and wait for a minority conditioned by generations of segregation to recognize and claim its newly guaranteed rights. Affirmative measures are necessary to promote awareness of the law both among those it protects and those who offend against it.

Expanded support for "grass-roots" citizen efforts. While the efforts of spontaneous, citizen-led groups have had impressive success in helping change attitudes, practices, and laws across the nation, these groups have been severely handicapped by their meager resources. A few have been fortunate enough to receive substantial support, usually from local foundations. Where funds have permitted hiring full-time staff, the increase in effectiveness has often been dramatic. Compared to the many millions spent annually by philanthropic organizations on problems of comparable or even lesser importance, the few thousands devoted to housing segregation have been infinitesimal. This is still another way in which available resources must be redirected if the problem is to be solved.

A national educational campaign. For the first time in American history, the majority of the white public appears aware that discrimination and segregation defeat the goals of democracy. But it is a long step forward from this recognition to a vigorous and affirmative effort equal to the need. This will require a type and degree of comprehension and commitment, by majority and minority peoples alike, which are still far from achievement.

National consensus is most readily achieved through full information about the problem and stimulation of public debate on the means of solution. A full-scale campaign to arouse and inform the American people must begin immediately if public understanding and support are to reach the necessary levels before segregation grows so much larger that it appears insoluble to many. The turning point may well come with the 1970 Census. If some tangible progress has not been made—or at least a plan of action proposed—before its statistics appear, discouragement may rule.

The core of organized citizen support necessary to mount such a campaign already exists—in such national organizations as the American Friends Service Committee, the Anti-Defamation League of B'nai B'rith, the NAACP, the Urban League, CORE, and the National Committee Against Discrimination in Housing as well as in the hundreds of citizen fair housing groups across the country. But their efforts must be focused, coordinated, and, above all, adequately financed. And they must be brought into the context of related activities such as urban planning and the war on poverty.

The task of eliminating segregation rests ultimately with the American people as a whole—led, as in every major struggle in their history, by a small group of devoted citizens. If they do not succeed, the result will almost certainly be the continued spread of Negro ghettos; large-scale physical blight generated by population pressures and exploitation; economic loss to many citizens of both races; persistent social disorder; and spreading racial tensions which strike at the very foundations of a free and democratic society. The choice is not merely between segregation and desegregation, but between wholesale destruction of property and human values and the continued growth and security of American society itself.

Contents of this article were basically prepared prior to employment of Mr. George W. Grier by the Government of the District of Columbia and Mrs. Eunice S. Grier by the United States Commission on Civil Rights. The opinions expressed by the authors are, therefore, not necessarily reflective of the views of either the Government of the District of Columbia or the United States Commission on Civil Rights.

REFERENCES

1. There is a vast literature on the implications for local government of the

divergence between population patterns and political boundaries in today's metropolitan areas. For an overview of governmental efforts to cope with the resulting problems, see Roscoe C. Martin, *Metropolis in Transition: Local Government Adaptation to Changing Urban Needs* (Washington, D. C., Housing and Home Finance Agency, September 1963). This study contains an extensive bibliography. An early and prescient discussion of the racial implications of metropolitan population shifts will be found in Morton Grodzins, *The Metropolitan Area as a Racial Problem* (Pittsburgh, Pa., Univ. of Pittsburgh Press, 1958). While Grodzins' prescriptions for solution sometimes seem a bit naive in retrospect, his dramatic presentation of the problem has been amply confirmed by later knowledge. A provocative discussion of the suburbanites' viewpoint toward metropolitan-area-wide cooperation toward solution of urban problems will be found in Charles R. Adrian, "Metropology: Folklore and Field Research," *Public Administration Review*, Vol. XXI, No. 3 (Summer 1961), pp. 148-157.

2. Unless otherwise indicated, these and all other statistics which deal with population and housing characteristics are drawn from the U. S. Censuses of Population and Housing, which can be found in any well-stocked public library. These censuses, taken at the beginning of every decade, are the nation's most valuable storehouse of data on many social and economic problems.

3. For a detailed discussion of recent population shifts and their bearing on racial patterns of residence, see George and Eunice Grier, "Obstacles to Desegregation in America's Urban Areas," *Race*, The Journal of the Institute of Race Relations, London, Vol. VI, No. 1 (July 1964), pp. 3-17.

The topic has received intensive treatment by local scholars in a number of major cities. See, for example: Mildred Zander and Harold Goldblatt, *Trends in the Concentration and Dispersion of White and Non-white Residents of New York City, 1950-1960*, New York City Commission on Human Rights, Research Report No. 14. Also: D. J. Bogue and D. P. Dandekar, *Population Trends and Prospects for the Chicago-Northwestern Indiana Consolidated Metropolitan Area: 1960 to 1990*, Population Research and Training Center, University of Chicago, March 1962.

4. The indirect racial effects of federal housing policies are discussed in Bertram Weissbourd, *Segregation, Subsidies and Megalopolis* (Santa Barbara, Calif., Center for the Study of Democratic Institutions, 1964). Also, in more detail, in an unpublished paper by Eunice and George Grier, "Federal Powers in Housing Affecting Race Relations," prepared for the Potomac Institute and the Washington Center for Metropolitan Studies in September 1962.

5. *Our Non-white Population and its Housing: The Changes Between 1950 and 1960* (Washington, D. C., Housing and Home Finance Agency, July 1963).

6. Chester Rapkin and William G. Grigsby, *The Demand for Housing in Eastwick*, prepared under contract for the Redevelopment Agency of the City of Philadelphia by the Institute for Urban Studies, University of Pennsylvania, Philadelphia, 1960.

7. The federal role in enforcing housing discrimination is documented in Charles Abrams, *Forbidden Neighbors* (New York, 1955). Also in Eunice and George Grier, *Privately Developed Interracial Housing* (Berkeley, Calif., 1960). The latter volume contains, in Chapter VIII, detailed case histories of two post-World War II developments intended for interracial occupancy which were driven to financial ruin by FHA opposition despite powerful private support.

8. Luigi Laurenti, *Property Values and Race* (Berkeley, Calif., 1960).

9. The impact of race upon urban renewal, and vice versa, has been touched upon in many places. Among them: Robert C. Weaver, "Class, Race and Urban Renewal," *Land Economics,* Vol. XXXVI, No. 3 (August 1960). Also L. K. Northwood, "The Threat and Potential of Urban Renewal," *Journal of Intergroup Relations,* Vol. II, No. 2 (Spring 1961), pp. 101-114; and Mel J. Ravitz, "Effects of Urban Renewal on Community Racial Patterns," *Journal of Social Issues,* Vol. XIII, No. 4 (1957), pp. 38-49. For an optimistic view on the consequences of renewal for displaced families, see *The Housing of Relocated Families,* a summary of a Bureau of the Census survey of families recently displaced from urban renewal sites, published by the Housing and Home Finance Agency, Washington, D. C., in March 1965. The "pro-renewal" viewpoint is also presented in *New Patterns in Urban Housing,* Experience Report 104, published by the U. S. Conference of Mayors, Community Relations Service, Washington, D. C., May 15, 1965.

10. Probably the most thorough and telling analysis of the economics involved in racial turnover mediated by real-estate speculators was published by the Chicago Commission on Human Relations, a municipal agency, in 1962. In a single block which had changed from all-white to virtually all-Negro, with heavy involvement by speculators, the differential between the price paid by the speculator and that paid by the Negro buyer upon purchase under an installment contract ranged from 35 to 115 per cent, with an average of 73 per cent. The installment contract itself is a financing device which yields higher-than-average returns to the entrepreneur, so the profiteering only began with the sale. For a graphic description of the activities of these speculators, see Norris Vitchek (as told to Alfred Balk), "Confessions of a Blockbuster," *Saturday Evening Post,* July 14, 1962.

11. Eunice S. Grier, *Understanding Washington's Changing Population* (Washington, D. C., Washington Center for Metropolitan Studies, 1961).

12. George Schermer, "Desegregation: A Community Design," *ADA News,* published by the Philadelphia Chapter of Americans for Democratic Action, July 1960. (Statistics somewhat revised by the author in light of subsequent information.)

13. Municipal governments must now confront the problem of race in many of their decisions. For an overview of local governmental action *vis-à-vis* race as of the early 1960's, accompanied by a good bibliography, see "The City Government and Minority Groups," *Management Information Service,* International City Managers Association, Report No. 229, February 1963.

This report can be obtained from the Potomac Institute of Washington, D. C., which participated in its preparation. See also many of the publications of the U. S. Commission on Civil Rights dealing with local practices in housing, employment, and so forth. But the extent to which racial considerations now affect local decisions in many subject areas is only scantily documented.

14. The relationship of racial factors to the Washington metropolitan plan is discussed in George B. Nesbitt and Marian P. Yankauer, "The Potential for Equal Housing Opportunity in the Nation's Capital," *Journal of Intergroup Relations*, Vol. IV, No. 1 (Winter 1962-1963), pp. 73-97.

15. The problem of *de facto* educational segregation and the civic conflict it often creates has been widely discussed in the public print. The *New York Times Index* is an especially useful source. For more scholarly treatments, see Max Wolff (ed.), "Toward Integration of Northern Schools," special issue of the *Journal of Educational Sociology*, February 1963. Also, "Public School Segregation and Integration in the North," special issue of the *Journal of Intergroup Relations*, November 1963. A provocative view on the feasibility of desegregation will be found in James B. Conant, *Slums and Suburbs* (New York, 1961).

16. The pain caused to long-time residents of ethnic neighborhoods by forced relocation in connection with urban renewal has been documented in Marc Fried, "Grieving for a Lost Home," in Leonard J. Duhl (ed.), *The Urban Condition* (New York, 1963). No doubt much the same kind of agony is caused when long-established white residents feel "forced" to give up their homes in changing neighborhoods.

17. The most complete and reliable source of up-to-date information on the status of housing anti-discrimination laws and ordinances throughout the nation is *Trends in Housing*, published bi-monthly by the National Committee Against Discrimination in Housing, 323 Lexington Avenue, New York, N. Y. 10016. A comprehensive analysis of action at all governmental levels up to the period just before the Federal Executive Order of 1962 will be found in Margaret Fisher and Frances Levenson, *Federal, State and Local Action Affecting Race and Housing*, National Association of Intergroup Relations Officials, September 1962. The texts of state and local laws as of the end of 1961 are summarized in *State Statutes and Local Ordinances Prohibiting Discrimination in Housing and Urban Renewal Operations*, published by the Housing and Home Finance Agency, Washington, D. C., December 1961.

18. Charles Abrams, "The Housing Order and its Limits," *Commentary* (January 1963). For another discussion of some of the limitations of the Order, as well as a legal rationale for its extension, see Martin E. Sloane and Monroe H. Freedman, "The Executive Order on Housing: The Constitutional Basis for What it Fails to Do," 9 *Howard Law Journal* (Winter 1963).

19. A nationwide study which examined the experiences of some fifty private housing developments open from the outset to interracial occupancy is

reported in Eunice and George Grier, *Privately Developed Interracial Housing, op. cit.* A more recent but less comprehensive compilation of experience, which leads nonetheless to many of the same conclusions, is found in *Equal Opportunity in Housing—A Series of Case Studies* (Washington, D. C., Housing and Home Finance Agency, June 1964).

20. The experiences of various neighborhoods with efforts to achieve racial stabilization have been discussed in the public print, oftentimes in local newspapers. Among the more valuable studies on this topic is Eleanor Leacock, Martin Deutsch, and Joshua A. Fishman, *Toward Integration in Suburban Housing: The Bridgeview Study* (New York, Anti-Defamation League of B'nai B'rith, 1964).

21. An excellent presentation of techniques which have been found useful in efforts to promote open housing opportunities in neighborhoods formerly closed to Negroes is contained in Margaret Fisher and Charlotte Meacham, *Fair Housing Handbook,* published jointly by the National Committee Against Discrimination in Housing and the American Friends Service Committee, 1964. See also various issues of *Trends in Housing.*

EUGENE P. FOLEY

The Negro Businessman: In Search of a Tradition

I

FOR YEARS, prominent Negroes have been urging the Negro community to recognize the importance of increasing the number and strength of Negro businessmen. The "Buy Black" movement pointed in this direction and the Black Muslims and various Black African organizations make this a key point in their programs. Yet it is apparent to anyone who has visited a Negro ghetto or is in any way familiar with American business that, irrespective of all the urging and movements, Glazer and Moynihan were all too correct when they pointed out that Negro business has not developed in this country,[1] ". . . despite the fact that business is in America the most effective form of social mobility for those who meet prejudice."[2]

Why is this? If Negroes are simply another immigrant group, why have they not developed a Negro Giannini, or Kennedy, or Rosenwald?

The answer is far more complicated than most Negroes tend to believe. The most common explanations Negroes give for the failures of Negro business development are (1) lack of capital because of prejudice on the part of bankers, and (2) unfair competition from Jewish merchants.

Consider the second argument first. The following statement is much milder than some we have heard: "Another thing I am sick and tired of, I am sick and tired of all these Jew business places in Harlem. Why don't more colored business places open? This is our part of town. They don't live here but they got all the businesses and everything."[3]

In 1947, Fred A. Jones, President of the St. Louis Business League, summed up the situation as follows:

A Negro can hardly rent a store for business in his own neighborhood because the Jew has thought ahead of him. When the Jew sees the drift of the Negro population he steps in and buys up the strategic corners and spots for the Jew. He rents to the wholesalers, to the retail sales outlets. He supplies every Jew store in the Negro belt from his wholesale houses.

There is no doubt that many Jewish merchants are able and effective business competitors and that they abound in the ghettos. Drake and Cayton reported that in 1936 about three-fourths of the merchants in Bronzeville were Jewish.[4] In Harlem, more stores are owned by Jews than by any other ethnic group, and the same is true in Philadelphia's Negro areas. There is a reason for this.

During the middle of the nineteenth century, there was a sizeable immigration of German Jews and the 1880's marked the beginning of the enormous Jewish migration from Eastern Europe. These immigrants settled in the large eastern cities and many established independent businesses, inasmuch as many had been small businessmen in Europe and most other fields were closed to them in the United States.

The Jews moved out of the blue-collared class into the middle class at a surprisingly fast rate. As they did, they abandoned the ghettos they had settled in earlier and moved to more desirable residential areas. However, many retained their businesses in the older sections of the city and continued to cater to its new inhabitants, who in many cases were Negroes. So, a pattern of Jewish-owned businesses in predominantly Negro areas developed. As time went on, other Jewish businessmen established businesses in the Negro area because of their familiarity with the area and the Jewish merchants already located there. But Jewish merchants abound in most sections of any city. As an ethnic group, they are three times as heavily represented in American commerce as any other group[5] and, of course, are located almost entirely in metropolitan areas.

Of all the European immigrant groups, the Jews are the only people with a trading background. The vast majority of immigrants to the United States came from an agrarian society.[6] In 1880, very few immigrants had a commercial background, 3.3 per cent as opposed to 63.0 per cent who were farmers or laborers. In 1900, the commercial category was changed to that of managers, officials, and proprietors. The numbers of immigrants in this category continued to remain low; for the years 1900, 1910, and 1920, the percentages of immigrants in the preceding category were 2.3, 1.9, and 3.7 respectively. During this period, farmers and laborers continued to comprise the majority of immigrants; their percentages for 1900, 1910, and 1920 were 63.7, 65.8, and 42.9.[7]

Compare the following figures for the Jewish immigrants with the general pattern. In 1900, the occupational distribution of Jewish immigrants was:[8]

Manufacturing	59.6
Trade	20.6
Domestic & Personal Service	8.0
Clerical	6.7
Professions	2.6
Other	2.5

In their native countries, most Jews were engaged in trading, manufacturing, or mechanical pursuits. For example, the first Russian census of 1897 showed that one-third of the Russian Jews were tradesmen, another third were engaged in manufacturing and mechanical pursuits, one-fourth were unskilled laborers, and 5 per cent were professionals.[9]

The Jews, therefore, had an advantage over other immigrants in America's business culture. Despite this advantage and the advantage of native whites, there have been many outstanding business successes from each ethnic group, but very few Negroes, and no Negro business successes to match the accomplishments of the other ethnic groups. Furthermore, the strong feelings about the Jews do not explain either the lack of Negro merchants in non-Negro sections of the city or the failure of Negro merchants to exploit their obvious advantage in the Negro ghettos.

The depth of Negro feeling on this subject can be explained by the proximity of Jews to Negroes which causes the latter to manifest their anti-white feeling in the form of anti-Semitism. Drake and Cayton found that in New Orleans, where Italian merchants predominate in Negro areas, "Dagos" are the target of attack.[10]

The other and somewhat more frequent explanation for the lack of significant Negro success in business is the lack of capital available to Negroes because of the prejudice of bankers. The following statement by a fairly successful Philadelphia Negro merchant is quite typical of the Negro businessman's attitude toward banks: "Local bankers have not treated Negro businessmen fairly. Most of the time they are willing to lend money only after you have been able to obtain money from some other source. Most of the time they disregard a good credit experience they have had with you prior to the attempt to obtain a significant loan to promote or improve your business."

But prejudice is not the sole reason for the scarcity of capital available for Negro businesses. Bankers, of course, share in and manifest American racist patterns, but they also make many loans to Negroes. In Philadelphia, one large bank has had a branch in a predominantly Negro area for many years. About 50 per cent of the branch customers are Negroes, as are 50 per cent of the time-payment customers; the branch manager states their records of payments have been good.

In the matter of consumer loans, the bank noticed a trend toward rejections over the past five years. For instance, in January of 1962, seventy-one applications for consumer loans by Negroes were received; forty-two were put on the books and twenty-nine were rejected. These figures have continued downward until now 50 per cent of the applications for consumer loans by Negroes are rejected. The reason for rejection is that, in the bank's view, the Negro applicants have over-extended themselves by buying on credit. The loans they are requesting are too high for their incomes, and some of them have payments outstanding each month amounting to 70 per cent of their income. At times the bank will consolidate their debts, but experience has shown that they often return to the practice of over-extending themselves.

The important point to note, however, is that this bank has been making consumer loans to Negroes for years, and for a long time Negroes have accounted for at least 50 per cent of its consumer lending activity. Contrast this with the fact that this same branch has only two loans to Negro businessmen on its books today. It is obvious that the bank, located in a Negro area and catering heavily to Negro consumer loans, is not discriminating. In fact, all three banks having branches in Negro areas of Philadelphia report they are seldom approached by Negro businessmen for commercial loans.

The financing of home purchases is further evidence that banks and other financial institutions desire to make loans to Negroes. A comprehensive report financed by the Fund for the Republic covering home purchases by Negroes and whites in Philadelphia in 1955 was made by the Institute for Urban Studies, University of Pennsylvania, at the request of the Commission on Race and Housing.[11] Banks financed approximately 10 per cent of the Negro purchases and 18 per cent of the white purchases. (Savings and Loan Associations accounted for the largest share of the financing for each group.) The report reviewed 1,574 home purchases by Negroes and 443 by whites in that year and these 1,574 purchases accounted for 30 per cent of all purchases by Negroes in Philadelphia that year. The report concluded that "Negroes and whites alike were able to obtain very liberal credit terms, particularly considering the age of the properties on which loans were made. Thus, despite the recency of the transition and the racial mixture of the areas, purchasers appear to have had no unusual difficulties in obtaining the necessary financing for the acquisition of their homes." In fact, the records indicate that Negro purchasers obtained mortgage terms which were somewhat more liberal than those advanced to whites. The reason for this is largely explained by the higher proportion of Veterans Administration and Federal Housing Administration loans made to Negroes.[12]

The reason that Negroes can obtain consumer and mortgage, but not commercial, financing lies in the different types of financing involved. A review of the commercial consumer and mortgage lending practices of banks should make this clear. In earlier days banks were generally unregulated, but, when abuses by bankers resulted in losses to depositors, more state and national regulatory commissions came into being to place certain restrictions upon the banking community. Banks are now limited in the amount they can loan to any one borrower at any one time. There are reserve requirements that limit lending power and there are discount rates that restrict loan activity.

The economic trend of a locality or the country as a whole is a factor in determining a bank's loan and investment policy. Because of the dynamic nature of business conditions, changes in particular industries or areas can enhance or jeopardize the liquidity and the soundness of a bank. "A cautious or conservative policy is generally thought the best insurance against possible swings or fluctuations of the economy."[13]

The banking community recognizes that the making and handling of mortgage and consumer loans differ greatly from the making and servicing of the average commercial loans. Regular commercial loan officers are felt not to be suited to installment loan work because of their generally cautious attitude. "Of primary importance in *consumer* lending is the honesty and ability of the borrower; information in regard to the borrower's assets and indebtedness; the source, amount, adequacy and permanency of his income."[14] (Italics added.)

Mortgage loans, of course, are fully secured by real estate. In making commercial loans to very small businesses, the *management ability* of the borrower is of highest concern. The financial factor, while important, is generally the most difficult to analyze properly because of the small firm's chronically inadequate and nonexistent records.

In short, the Negro consumer who has a stable income and is not overextended in his credit can get a consumer loan as easily as any non-Negro with the same characteristics. The same is true of a Negro home owner who can provide a first mortgage on his property, thus fully securing the loan.

But commercial financing, based on the proven management ability of the borrower in a stable industry and a stable locality, is another thing. It is not only Negroes who have difficulty getting such financing. Sixty per cent of *all* businesses in Philadelphia have no borrowing facility from a bank or finance company, *irrespective of race*.[15]

The key then to the lack of financing for Negro businesses thus lies in the characteristics of Negro businesses more than in the fact they are Negro-owned. A study has been made of the characteristics of Negro-owned businesses in Philadelphia by the Drexel Institute.[16] And I have made a study of the history of Negro business in that city in an attempt to discover the sociological and economic forces that have brought about these characteristics in Philadelphia.

II

In 1964, the Drexel Institute of Technology of Philadelphia initiated a massive study of little business and the little businessman in Philadelphia. Among other things, the objectives of the study were to review the economic characteristics and behavior of firms with less than four employees and to explore the special problems of businesses owned and operated by members of minority groups. Most of the material in this section has been based upon Drexel's unpublished studies.

There are thirteen manufacturing concerns, all small, operated by Negroes in Philadelphia. The following breakdown, in alphabetical order, indicates the wide degree of diversification:

> 8 beauty products manufacturing companies
> 1 casket manufacturing company

2 clothing manufacturing companies
1 ironworks manufacturing company
1 meat products manufacturing company

In addition, fourteen wholesale distribution companies were found. They represent five kinds of products.

8 beauty products distribution companies
1 candy, notions, and novelties distribution company
1 casket distribution company
1 clothing distribution company
3 food distribution companies

But, the Drexel study revealed that while there were about ten Negro-owned businesses—insurance, publishing, catering, cosmetic supplies, and contracting—which were quite successful, most of the 4,242 Negro businesses of Philadelphia,[17] comprising 9 per cent of the city's total businesses, were marginal in profit-making, stability, and physical condition.

The type of businesses followed the pattern observable in other American cities. Nearly all were retail and service trades, and most were single proprietorships. Personal services were the more numerous, hairdressing and barbering comprising 24 per cent and 11 per cent, respectively, of the total number of Negroes in business. Luncheonettes and restaurants comprised 11.5 per cent of the total.[18] Many of the businesses would be submarginal if free family labor were not available. For example, median sales for a sample of Negro-owned beauty shops were $2,500, for Negro-owned luncheonettes, $6,800, and for barber shops, $4,400.[19]

Seventy-seven per cent of Negro businesses are concentrated in three of the city's twenty community business areas. (Drexel used the twenty community business areas originally developed by the Philadelphia City Planning Commission.) The largest Negro community business area, Area 13, comprises nine square miles in the north-central part of the city. Approximately 200,000 Negroes live there, representing 69 per cent of Area 13's total population,[20] and about one-third of the city's total Negro population. Approximately 40 per cent (1,615) of all Negro businesses are located here.[21]

Almost all Negro businesses are located in predominantly Negro neighborhoods, but at least half of the businesses in these neighborhoods are white-owned. While the white businessman is free to pass through the walls on either side, the Negro businessman cannot look beyond "his neighborhood."

Community Business Area (CBA) with Significant
Negro Population*[22]

CBA	% Negro Population within CBA	% City Negro-owned Business within CBA
4	7.5	1.1
5	29.7	3.4
8	21.4	3.4
13	69.0	42.4
14	82.9	20.6
15	10.4	2.0
16	27.2	7.7
17	27.5	1.7
18	21.6	2.2
19	25.8	14.5
All others	2.6	1.0
		TOTAL 100.0

* Areas which contained a Negro population of more than 5 per cent were studied by Drexel and described, with the exception of Area 20 which has more than a 5 per cent Negro population but very few businesses because of area redevelopment.

The Drexel survey team took a sample of the various types of businesses in each of the community business areas and rated them by appearance.[23] The meanings of these appearance ratings are as follows:

A. "General appearance of being neat and clean looking; with a large sign and/or window display of some current nature; goods or products properly arranged; appears to have enough stock on hand; not necessarily a new store."
B. "General appearance of being neat, but not eye-appealing to the observer; with a sign and/or window display of relatively small size; appearance implies adequacy."
C. "General appearance of being 'run-down,' untidy and dirty; paint peeling off walls, plaster coming off ceilings, little or no lighting; no displays to speak of; little stock on hand."

A detailed breakdown of the Negro businesses in Area 13 by type of business and appearance of establishment is given in Table 1. Note that, of all the businesses in Area 13, 12.1 per cent fell in Category A (neat and clean), 55.9 per cent in Category B (not eye-appealing), and 32 per cent in Category C (run-down). Of the six largest categories in that area (groceries and delicatessens, luncheonettes and restaurants, candy and variety stores, barber shops, beauty shops, and other personal services), barber shops had by far the cleanest and neatest appearance. Still, only 17.6 per cent of these were in Category A, 60.6 per cent in Category B, and 21.8 per cent in Category C. The fifteen drug stores classified have the neatest and cleanest appearance of all the businesses surveyed: 60 per cent were in Category A, and 40 per cent in Category B. The results in the other two community business areas with a large number of Negro businesses, Areas 14 and 19, were quite similar to the results in Area 13 and are given in Table 2.

The picture, then, of the Negro in business is that of a small businessman—a very small businessman—who is generally not a very good businessman and, frankly, not a very significant factor in the Negro community.

III

Urban life in nineteenth-century Philadelphia to a large extent revolved around the intense competition between Europe's huddled-masses and the fleeing slaves of America, both yearning to breathe free. The simultaneous influx of freedmen, fugitives, and foreigners within a large city resulted in prejudice, lawlessness, crime, poverty, and race riots.

Before this influx of slaves and immigrants, Negroes participated to a surprising extent in business. Many were already keeping small shops in 1789[24] and doing well. A beneficial insurance society was established by Negroes in 1796[25] and a Negro life insurance company in 1810.[26] An exceptional person during this period was James Forten, a Negro sailmaker who employed approximately forty employees, half whites, half Negroes. (Later, his Negro successors were to fail when the growth of steam vessels made the business less profitable).[27] By 1820, the Negro population of Philadelphia was 11,891, and it had about $250,000 worth of free property.[28] An Englishman visiting the city in 1823 reported that a few Negroes in business had amassed fortunes[29] and that they were engaged in almost all the branches of business pursued by whites.[30]

The decade of the 1820's, however, witnessed the first great confrontation of free Negroes and immigrants, a confrontation which continued with rising intensity and without abatement for the next hundred years, until Congress, in the early 1920's, passed the Immigration Exclusion Acts.

A series of riots directed chiefly against Negroes started in 1829, recurred frequently until about 1840, and did not cease until after the Civil War. The sympathy of the general populace was not with the Negro, and legislation was introduced, but failed to pass, to stop further migration of Southern Negroes into Pennsylvania. However, W. E. B. Du Bois stated that Pennsylvanians who were friends of the Negro advised against sending fugitives to the state since the effects would be detrimental to the colored population.[31]

Du Bois spelled the problem out very clearly. Noting the rapid economic changes which accompanied the growing industrialization of the American economy, he said:

The new industries attracted the Irish, Germans, and other immigrants; Americans too, were fleeing to the city and soon to natural race antipathies was added a determined effort to displace Negro Labor—an effort which had the aroused prejudice of many of the better classes, and the poor quality of the new black immigrants to give it aid and comfort. To all this was soon added a problem of crime and poverty. Numerous complaints of petty thefts, housebreaking, and assaults on peaceful citizens were traced to certain classes of Negroes. In vain did the better class, led by men like Forten, protest by public meeting their condemnation of such crimes. The tide had set against the Negro strongly, and the whole period from 1820 to 1840 became a time of retrogression for the mass of the race, and of discountenance and repression from the whites . . . a mass of poverty-stricken, ignorant fugitives and ill trained freedmen had rushed to the city, swarmed in the vile slums which the rapidly growing city furnished, and met in social and economic competition equally ignorant but more vigorous foreigners. These foreigners outbid them at work, beat them on the streets, and were enabled to do this by the prejudice which Negro crime and the anti-slavery sentiment had aroused in the city.[32]

The Negro cause suffered a great legal setback between riots. In 1836, a case came before a state court in Philadephia involving a Negro who had been denied the right to vote. The court decided that free Negroes were not freemen in the language of the State Constitution and, therefore, that Negroes could not vote. The case was appealed without success. Thus, after forty-six years of full American citizenship the Negro in the City of Brotherly Love was denied the right to vote.[33]

The effect on the Negro community was disastrous. The better classes could not escape into the mass of white population and leave the new Negroes to fight their own battles with the immigrants. In terms of the Negro businessman, the impressive developments of the 1790-1820 period fast melted away. In the Register of Trade of Philadelphia in 1838, 344 Negroes—133 women and 211 men—were reported as being in business for themselves.[34] (Most of these operated from stands rather than shops.) A pamphlet issued in 1838 by the Pennsylvania Society for Promoting Abolition of Slavery said, in reference to Negro businessmen, "Here, as in many other particulars, they are met by the prejudice with which they have to contend, which renders it difficult for them to find places for their sons as apprentices, to learn mechanical trades."[35] From what we have been able to determine, there were probably fewer than twenty-five affluent Negro businessmen in Philadelphia in the entire generation preceding the Civil War.

Following the war, the immigrant rate doubled while the Negro population increase was relatively modest. Immigrants vastly outnumbered the Negroes, and each generation renewed the barefisted competition with each generation of Negroes. In the spring elections of 1870, the Irish incited a race riot so fierce that U.S. Marshals were called on to preserve order.[36] By the end of the century immigrants made up over one-fifth of Philadelphia's 1,294,000 population while Negroes accounted for about 5 per cent.[37] In 1896, over one hundred years after Negro enterprise had commenced in that city, there were approximately 300 Negro-owned businesses.[38] The great majority of these were barbershops, caterers, and restaurants—all developments from the Negro domestic servant. Negro business had scarcely changed despite the revolutionary developments taking place in the rest of American commerce and industry. Du Bois, in fact, flatly stated that the Philadelphia Negro in the 1890's "holds no conspicuous place in the business world" and had generally experienced a retrogression as compared to the pre-Civil War period.[39]

Some significant developments took place in the Philadelphia Negro population from 1890-1915. It had grown slowly during the previous part of the nineteenth century. In 1860, there were 22,185 Negroes in Philadelphia; in the next thirty years, they increased at the rate of approximately 6,000 per decade. But the Great Migration, beginning in the 1890's, caused an increase of 23,242 in Philadelphia's Negro population in that decade and another 21,846 in the first ten years of the present century. The important thing about these rapid increases is that the major portion of them took place within very limited geographical areas of the city. There is a direct correlation between this gradual concentraton of the Negro population and the growth of the Negro businesses.

It is more than likely that Negro businessmen, prior to 1890, catered primarily to a Negro trade. However, this is not entirely true, for many served primarily white customers. At least two Negro undertaking establishments lured white patronage away from white competitors, and first-class Negro barbers would not allow Negroes in their shops because of the color prejudice.[40] But, as Du Bois pointed out, "The 40,000 Negroes of Philadelphia need food, clothes, shoes, hats and furniture; these by proper thrift they see ought to be in part supplied by themselves, and *the little business ventures we have noticed are attempts in this direction.*"[41]

The distribution of Negro business establishments in relation to the Negro population seems to confirm this. In 1896, when Du Bois made his study, about 60 per cent of the Negro-owned businesses were located in a small compact area, Wards 4, 5, 7, and 8,[42] which included 35 per cent of the total Negro population of the city.[*] The remaining 40 per cent were scattered throughout the city in small segments somewhat similar to the distribution of the Negro population in the rest of the city. In other words, Negro businesses tended to locate in areas where a fairly sizeable Negro population had concentrated.

By 1913, there were 1,028 Negro businesses in Philadelphia, a remarkable gain of over 700 in just seventeen years. In that year, 67 per cent of all Negro businesses were located in a very concentrated area containing 38.5 per cent of the total Negro population.[43] (Wards 7, 26, 30, and 36; note that, as the Negro migration continued into the twentieth century, the population increases took place slightly south and west of the areas previously mentioned in a section which was fast becoming the growing commercial center of the city.)[44]

With the exception of a second Negro population center (Wards 14, 15, 20 and 47) developing between 1899 and 1913 slightly north of downtown Philadelphia and where 9 per cent of all Negro businesses were found in a concentrated area containing almost 17 per cent of the city's Negro population, Negro businesses in all other wards were few and scattered, coinciding with the scattering of the Negro population.[45]

It was only natural for newly arrived Southern Negroes to move into existing Negro population centers, expanding them rather than starting colonies of their own. The rapid development of these areas between 1896 and 1913 provided new opportunities for Negro businessmen. However, whenever the Southern Negroes moved in, the whites—both native and foreign born—moved out. What was worse,

[*] The percentage of the city's Negro population for 1896 was obtained by taking the mean between the per cent of the total Negro population each ward represented in the 1890 census and that represented in the 1900 census.

as the Negro population soared, not only segregation but bitter racism increased. Vacant houses in "non-Negro" sections were no longer for rent or sale to Negroes. The sudden increase greatly stimulated the movement, which had already started, to segregate Negro children in the schools. Also, such social activities as eating in restaurants or attending white churches and theaters were almost completely withdrawn. While actual conflicts between the two races were not numerous, a race riot did break out in the summer of 1918 in which two men were killed and sixty injured.[46]

The changing patterns of Negro-white relationships, as well as relationships between the native Negro and the migrant, are described for us by a very astute contemporary observer:

The colored people of every class received harsh treatment at the hands of the white public. This was virtually unknown to the Philadelphia Negro, for the city had long possessed a relatively small population of Negroes of culture, education, and some financial means. They had always enjoyed the same social and educational facilities as the whites and courteous treatment from them. But, with the increase in population by a group of generally uneducated and untrained persons, these privileges were withdrawn—the old colored citizens of Philadelphia resented this, placed the blame at the migrant's door and stood aloof from him.[47]

After World War I, segregation patterns grew worse rather than better. Theaters, restaurants, and lunch counters were either completely off-limits for Negroes or were strictly segregated. The YMCA, YWCA, and hotels all refused accommodations to Negroes in the 1920's.[48]

A sharp rise in the number of Negro businesses took place during World War I. Negro business statistics are not available for Philadelphia during this period, but, nationally, the number of Negro merchants grew from 14,181 in 1910 to 23,794 in 1920, a 68 per cent increase, while Negro undertakers at the same time advanced from 953 to 1,558, a 64 per cent growth.[49] A sharp decline occurred after the war. "An investigator discovered that from one-half to two-thirds of the small business establishments of Negroes like butcher shops, groceries, cafes, and tailors, listed in 1910, could not be found in 1927."[50]

The stimulus that the war gave to Negro businesses led to a growth in the size of the largest Negro enterprises. The vast majority of Negro-owned establishments were still very small retail or service stores; but, by the end of World War I, a few Negroes had learned to attract and organize capital.[51] In Philadelphia, the Brown and Stevens Bank, established in 1920, and the Cosmopolitan State Bank, formed in 1923, were both Negro-owned; both fell in 1925.[52] Falling with the Brown and Stevens Bank were the Gipson Stores, a Negro chain with branches throughout Philadelphia, and the Beresford Gale Corporation, a real-estate and investment broker business which had annual gross receipts up to $100,000 before its collapse.[53] The Citizens and Southern Bank, organized in 1920, is still in existence, although several years ago white owners gained a majority control. (Abram Harris, in *The Negro As A Capitalist*, evaluated the Citizens and Southern as the best managed Negro financial enterprise in existence in 1935.)[54]

Nevertheless Negro business was made up almost exclusively of very small operations all through the 1920's and 30's. While precise statistics are hard to come by, it appears there was a gradual increase in the number of Negro businesses during the 1920's, though not proportionate to the population increase. Table 3 makes a partial comparison of Negro-owned businesses in selected categories between 1913 and 1935.

The depression, of course, took its toll. The number of Negro retail stores decreased by 58 between 1929 and 1935. In terms of percentages the number of Negro stores declined 7.6 per cent in this period, compared with 12.8 per cent for white retail businesses, but in volume of sales, the Negro stores fell 48.2 per cent as opposed to 39.4 per cent for white stores.[55]

During this entire period, the Negro wards of the city continued their population expansion. Table 4 shows that by 1920 86.1 per cent (116,199) of Philadelphia's Negroes resided in three of the eight major city sections. For the first time in history, one ward (Ward 30) contained more Negroes than whites (15,480 Negroes; 13,990 whites).

At the same time segregation incidents were occurring monthly. It was not until the Pennsylvania legislature passed the Civil Rights Act of 1935 that there was even a partial diminution in the number of monthly incidents. But the 1935 Act did not end racial conflict. In the early 1940's, white transit workers caused a crippling strike which cost the city $10,000,000 because Negro workers were given the same compensation as whites. In 1950, Negro lawyers still could not obtain first-class office space in downtown Philadelphia and were not accepted into white law firms. There were no housing covenants; but builders and sales agents practiced discrimination.[56]

Executives of white-owned companies still feared employee and customer reaction if they hired Negroes for responsible positions.[57] Since World War I, almost 70 racial incidents, major and minor, have been reported by the Philadelphia *Bulletin*. While the Negro population continued to grow in all wards, the Negro ghetto, as we see it today, did not really take shape until the 1940's. In the 1940 census, only two wards (30 and 47) held more Negroes than whites. Table 5 shows that in 1950, eight wards had this distinction and in 1960, fourteen wards. It was not until 1960 that one of the eight major city sections, the north, held more Negroes than whites.

In other words, the post-World War II development of residential segregation patterns has transformed Philadelphia into almost all-black or almost all-white sections. Concurrent with this has been a decline in the purchasing power of Negroes. In 1946, the incomes of Philadelphia Negro families almost matched the national urban average; by 1959, they were 25 per cent below the median income of Philadelphia whites.[58]

The closing of the ghetto caused a sharp increase in Negro businesses. By 1964, there were 4,242 Negro-owned businesses of all types; 1,759 retail stores compared to 729 in 1935. As shown in Table 6, 86.4 per cent of these businesses were located in the South, West and North, which contained 90.4 per cent of Philadelphia's Negro population. But, the types and character of Negro businesses have not changed greatly since Du Bois wrote *The Philadelphia Negro* in 1899. (See Table 7.)

IV

What is it that has restrained the business development of the Negro? While there are some modest successes among Negro businessmen, almost all of them depend on a predominantly Negro trade, and in neither numbers, stature, nor prestige do they approach the outstanding successes of other ethnic groups. ▬

For one thing, the long competition with the immigrants was a retarding factor, both because the foreigners were "more vigorous," as Du Bois noted, and because natural race antipathies were exacerbated by the social and economic conflicts arising out of the competition between ignorant fugitive slaves and ignorant European immigrants. Thus, after a promising start in enterprise, the Negro as a businessman suffered when "the whole period from 1820 to 1840 became a time of retrogression for the mass of the race, and of discountenance and repression from the whites."[59]

The greater vigor of the immigrants cannot be taken lightly, particularly in view of their propensity for entering business on their own. Immigrant groups characteristically engage in individual enterprise in a higher proportion than natives. Two separate studies confirm this, one, a study of 5,368 heads of small businesses in Poughkeepsie, New York, from 1936 to 1955,[60] and, the other, a study of 110 founders of manufacturing enterprises established in Michigan between 1945 and 1958.[61] In the Poughkeepsie study, it was found that: "The number of foreign born proprietors is out of proportion to the foreign born in the total population. Only 5 percent of the employed native born persons in Poughkeepsie are business proprietors as compared with 15 percent of the employed foreign born."[62]

The same study indicates that the percentage of immigrants entering business declines in the second generation. "The number of foreign born in Poughkeepsie is declining, as it is in the country as a whole. A comparison of the businessmen who started their concerns in different periods shows that the foreign born proprietors have declined from 41 percent of the total of those going into business before 1936 to 28 percent for those starting the decade 1936-1945, and to 20 percent for those starting after 1945."[63]

The percentage distribution of the foreign-born population as of 1940 and the foreign-born proprietors for the 1936-1955 period in Poughkeepsie are given in Table 8. Note that almost 23 per cent of the presidents of manufacturing establishments were foreign-born.

The Michigan study was a survey of 110 manufacturing firms established between 1945 and 1958, almost all of which had twenty or more employees.[64] The report notes: "There was a large percentage of foreign-born. Twenty percent of the entrepreneurs . . . were immigrants to this country. In addition, 35 percent were the sons of immigrants. Thus, 55 percent, or more than half of our sample, were either foreign-born or first generation Americans."[65]

Very likely, immigrant status itself explains the large numbers of Puerto Rican-owned businesses in New York City as compared with Negro businesses.[66] We are not certain whether this strong tendency of the immigrant to become a businessman is an extension of the rebellion begun with the act of immigration, the euphoria of being "free," the resistance to domination by unfamiliar groups, the lack of familiarity with the social roles expected of his income group, or a combination of these with the economic facts of life, or whether it can be better understood through a more elaborate psychological explanation. The facts are clear, however, and they do show a highly disproportionate number of immigrants in business. There are, then, some differences between the immigrant and the Negro that stimulated the former to overcome the lack of a business tradition common to members of both groups.[67] And in that very process, the aggressive efforts of immigrants compounded the many other problems Negroes experienced in developing their own business tradition.

The relatively small number of Negroes compared to immigrants also prevented the former from developing two strong economic and social supports which the latter had organized early and well: namely, ethnic institutions and, through them, political unity and strength. The Negroes, of course, had their churches but they were not then the social and political institutions which they have become. As noted previously, the native Philadelphia Negro possessed a considerably different culture than the Negro newly arrived and resented the latter because his migration in growing numbers caused the native whites to withdraw privileges from the former.[68]

The old colored citizens of Philadelphia resented this, placed the blame at the migrant's door and stood aloof from him. Negro preachers invited the new arrivals into the church, but many of the congregations made him know he was not wanted. In some cases the church split over the matter, the migrants and their sympathizers withdrawing and forming a church for themselves.[69]

Other ethnic groups had similar troubles. German Jews, for instance, resented Eastern European Jews. But in this case, the large numbers of each group and the existence of a strong and ancient culture gave even the divided groups a unity and strength which Negroes could never develop.

The unceasing and unbalanced social and economic competition between each influx of Negroes and each wave of immigrants, together with the relatively insignificant ethnic institutions and political strength of the former compared to the latter, as well as the accompanying "discountenance and repression" from all whites, kept the Negroes from developing a business tradition in the American tradition of business throughout the entire nineteenth century.

The Great Migration of the early twentieth century brought about the paradox of a dramatic rise in the number of Negroes in business coupled with an increased isolation from whites, native and foreign-born. As the ghettos grew, Negro businesses grew, but less and less did they deal with whites. The increase in numbers kindled racial friction which in turn emblazed the racism long smoldering in Philadelphia society. Negroes, still lacking political strength and any significant racial unity, became locked more and more into the modern ghetto and into the emotional moods and habits it breeds—apathy, frustration, fear, hatred, and lack of self-esteem—hardly the climate to foster those traditional free-enterprise qualities of persistence, thrift, initiative, and risk-taking.

In the final analysis, the fundamental reason that Negroes have not advanced in business is the lack of business success symbols available to them. The culture has simultaneously unduly emphasized achievement in business as the primary symbol of success and has blindly developed or imposed an all-pervading racism that denied the Negro the necessary opportunities for achieving this success.

One is reminded of George Bernard Shaw's observation in the introduction to *Man and Superman:* "We laugh at the haughty American nation because it makes the Negro clean its boots and then proves the moral and physical inferiority of the Negro by the fact that he is a shoeblack."[70]

Racism has pervaded the white man's society in the United States ever since the country's founding. The United States Constitution provided that a slave would be counted only as three-fifths of a person in determining the number of representatives which a state would have in Congress.[71] While the free Negro in Philadelphia enjoyed the voting franchise for almost forty years, this was taken from him by court action in 1836 and by the Reform Constitution of 1837. While the main stimuli to the many race riots during the pre-Civil War period were the immigrants, the native white Philadelphians were hardly blameless for, as Du Bois pointed out, the better classes of Negroes "could not escape into the mass of white population and leave the new Negroes to fight out their battles with the foreigners."[72]

Abraham Lincoln himself, at least before he became President, did not believe in the equality of the races. For example, in an 1858 speech, he said:

I will say then that I am not, nor ever have been in favor of bringing about in any way the social and political equality of the white and black races—that I am not nor ever have been in favor of making voters or jurors of Negroes, nor of qualifying them to hold office, nor to intermarry with white people; and I will say in addition to this that there is a physical difference between the white and black races which I believe will forbid the two living together on terms of social and political equality. And inasmuch as they cannot so live, while they do remain together, *there must be the position of superior and inferior and I as much as any other man am in favor of having the superior position assigned to the white race.*[73] (Italics added.)

The 100 years of unremitting competition between the Negroes and immigrants merely served to keep the sore of racism open and festering. "With the abolitionists long since gone, and consciences salved by the Civil War and Emancipation, Northern public opinion took a racist turn: the fact that the mass of poor Negroes had not become cultivated gentlemen in two or three decades since Emancipation seemed to justify all the old notions about inherent Negro inferiority."[74]

The United States Supreme Court gave racism official and legal sanction when it established the "separate but equal" doctrine in the case of *Plessy v. Ferguson.* "If one race be inferior to the other socially," Justice Brown declared, "the Constitution of the United States cannot put them upon the same plane."[75]

There followed the gradual denial of privileges at public and commercial centers in downtown Philadelphia as well as the beginning of the Great Migration, both leading to the birth of the ghetto and the gradual physical separation of the races. We have seen that "the Roaring Twenties" were also "the Warring Twenties" as far as race relations were concerned. And, as the ghetto imprisoned the Negro more and more, frustrations increased. "The Warring Twenties" became the Warring Thirties, Forties, Fifties, and Sixties.

The Negro, therefore, is hardly any further advanced in business today then he was in the 1820's. In the American culture the sovereign specific was the art of making money, and thus the more enterprising immigrants were allowed to break through into the Anglo-Saxon world of commerce.

As Warner and Srole note in the Yankee City Series:

The occupational history of the ethnic groups in Yankee City follows a course which is very similar to their residential history. The workers of the newly arrived groups started at the very bottom of the occupational hierarchy and, through the generations, climbed out of it and moved up to jobs with higher pay and increased prestige. Each new ethnic group tended to repeat the occupational history of the preceding ones. By 1933, most of the ethnic groups had attained positions of the industrial life of the community which approximated that of the original native groups.[76]

But in the American culture the cult of racism was greater than that of money-making since it involved more people and spread to all religious, social, and ethnic groups; and there were no Negro Giannini's, Kennedy's, Rosenwald's, or similar great makers of fortunes from immigrant families. The Negroes, therefore, had no reason to believe or hope that persistence, thrift, or initiative could pay off, nor had they any reason to take unusual risks. Totally limited to a poverty market, the best the Negro could work for was a modest, marginal retail or service operation, hardly an example to cause great dreams or build high hopes, or set fires ablaze in a young Negro's heart.

V

With the passage of the various civil rights acts during the past several years and, even more importantly, with the development of a strong moral climate in the country with respect to equal rights for Negroes, it can be expected that new opportunities will gradually be presented to venturesome Negroes where previously the walls of racism had blocked them off. As in so many other areas of modern life there remains much to be done quickly to enable Negro businessmen to exploit fully the new openings.

Somehow, in the past, enterprising individuals of the various ethnic groups were able to surmount the lack of capital and business experience through unusual determination and superior ability. Because the American culture recognized and encouraged the natural-born money-maker and business-getter, these success stories became well known and encouraged others from their respective ethnic groups. Negroes, as we have seen, could not make such a breakthrough because of an all-pervading racism that permeated white America. Since the progress against racism will probably be gradual, any program of rapid action must confront the traditional capital and management barriers.

In recent years some interesting work has been done in this field. In the fall of 1963 a review was ordered of the loans made to Negroes by the Small Business Administration of the U. S. Government through its Philadelphia office during the ten and one-half years that it had existed. While the Agency does not keep a record of the race of a loan applicant, the number of approved Negro loans had been so small that it was possible to make an accurate account by interviewing the loan processors who had been in the Phila-delphia office during this entire period. The study showed that only seven loans had been made to Negroes during these years, while 425 loans had been made to white businesses.

In an attempt to experiment with a more liberal lending policy for Negro businessmen, SBA launched a "6×6" Pilot Loan and Management Program in Philadelphia on January 28, 1964. With this "6×6" program, a plan involving loans up to $6,000 for six years plus individual management training and counseling, SBA reached and assisted the very small businessman, especially Negro business-men since they own and operate a large segment of the very small business sector. Under the Philadelphia program, SBA in 1964 approved 219 loans totaling $912,547, and, of this number, 98 loans for the amount of $379,657 were made to Negroes. There were 68 loans to established Negro businesses for $272,757, and 30 loans to new Negro businesses for $106,900. Of the 219 approved loans, only 8 were delinquent—6 loans to Negroes and 2 loans to white busi-nesses—and none were liquidated.

SBA overcame traditional bank barriers by considering loan applicants principally on the basis of character, integrity, and ability to repay the loan from earnings, rather than on collateral. Collateral was limited to assets available in the business or acquired from loan proceeds. Prior to SBA's "6×6" Pilot Program, these very small business owners were shut off from the capital needed for improve-ments because commercial institutions generally do not lend to the very small businessman. Furthermore, prospective businessmen could not get capital to begin a new business. This pilot program was a major breakthrough and was subsequently expanded to five other cities. Its success prompted its inclusion as Title IV in the Economic Opportunity Act of 1964 on an expanded basis with loans up to $25,000 for fifteen years.

This liberal financing available from the Small Business Admin-istration under Title IV of the Economic Opportunity Act, together with the management training and individual management counsel-ing, should make it possible for enterprising Negroes to begin in business, modernize, and expand. This has to be done if any start is to be made in creating a respectable Negro business tradition because it can be expected that, as the walls of segregation lower and the incomes of Negroes improve, risk-taking, "profit-smelling" white businessmen will begin to cash in on an untapped market. White businessmen will move in faster than Negro businessmen will be permitted or will feel free to move. In the process, many Negro businesses are bound to fail. In fact, it is estimated that in ten years it is very likely there will be fewer Negro businessmen than there are today. Presumably, those businesses which survive will be stronger, more competitive, and more profitable.

Title IV is a promising beginning; the successes will be more immediate and more visible than those to be achieved under other programs of the anti-poverty campaign. But, it is still not enough. Conditions must be created which will enable the born Negro entrepreneur and risk-taker to feel free to market his services where big money, high stakes, and rich rewards exist. While the ultimate solution is the full and complete implementation of various civil rights acts, it must be taken for granted that this will take some time.

In the interim, a number of actions, in addition to Title IV, could be taken to spur Negro entrepreneurship. Unfortunately, almost all of them are based on the assumption that our cities will continue to have segregated areas. It is hoped that these will soon evolve into the ethnic types of neighborhoods described in *Beyond the Melting Pot*,[77] where some members of the group prefer to live within the confines of the group but are also free to leave and to reside in other sections of the city.

One of the most promising opportunities for Negro businessmen to move outside the ghetto lies in franchising. Under this system the individual businessman gets the benefit not only of management guidance and some financing from the owner of the franchise system, but also the prestige and stature of the franchise trade name. The businessman remains independent and reaps the full reward of his hard work. Howard Johnson restaurants, A & W root beer stands, and Holiday Inn motels are examples of franchising. The federal government through the Commerce Department and the Small Business Administration has already started such a program. The greater the "visibility" attained by Negro businessmen outside the ghetto, the sooner and easier it will be for the real entrepreneur to make his great break-through.

Within the ghetto, a coordinated economic development plan is badly needed, not just to stimulate Negro entrepreneurship (though this will result), but also to create jobs, increase the purchasing power of ghetto residents, and gradually lift the omnipresent cloud of apathy, frustration, and bitter despair that affects not only the Negro's self-esteem, but also his ability and determination to improve his station in life.

A number of new programs suggest that tremendous potential exists for accomplishing this. They all involve construction projects. Apart from the more direct ends being served by each program, such as the need for low-cost housing, equally important and equally direct economic objectives might be obtained if each project were required to utilize qualified Negro contractors, either as prime- or sub-contractors, in a portion of the units being constructed. For instance, a certain percentage of the units could be "set-aside" for Negro contractors living in the affected area in a manner similar to the way federal procurement agencies "set-aside" certain contracts for bidding exclusively by small businesses. In addition, a certain minimum percentage of Negro labor living in the affected area should be employed by all the contractors working on the project. This would involve delicate problems with the labor unions, but it would surely develop that they would be receptive to a portion of new construction jobs for their union membership rather than none at all.

In the 1965 Housing and Urban Development Act, the Small Business Administration is given the authority to guarantee the leases of small businessmen up to ten years. (A small businessman for these purposes is one who grosses less than one million dollars annually.) The great significance in this authority lies in the fact that private mortgage money (insurance companies and pension funds) which heretofore has not been invested in slum areas can be fully protected against any change in the economic or social conditions of these areas or any defaults in rental payments by the small businessman. In other words, modern shopping areas could be built in the Harlems of our nation's cities. Careful planning, of course, is required, but at least the tools now exist.

A valuable program virtually unused in urban areas is the Local Development Company Program of the Small Business Administration. Under this program the SBA lends to a local, non-profit, economic development corporation 80 per cent of the funds needed for land, buildings, and equipment for twenty-five years at 5.5 per cent interest. The maximum allowed is $350,000 per small business aided. If ten small businesses are assisted, the amount can be $3,500,000. Under this program factories, industrial parks, parking garages, nursing homes, and a wide variety of job-creating enterprises have been financed. For instance, last summer a modern twenty-nine unit shopping center was built in South Chicago. This program has great promise if coordinated with an urban renewal program that broadens its interest to include total land use of a slum area and total community needs.

Various construction programs administered by the Department of Housing and Urban Affairs provide similar opportunities for Negro contractors and Negro employees, and for economic development of the ghettos. These include: (1) F.H.A.'s 3 per cent insured loans for the construction or rehabilitation of housing projects designed for low and moderate income families;[78] (2) the new grant program (2/3) for small public facilities, such as community centers and health centers which are related to the community action programs of the Office of Economic Opportunity;[79] and (3) the construction as well as the new leasing program of public housing units.[80]

An important aspect of the ghetto's economic development, as well as the ultimate liberation of the Negro entrepreneur, is the full involvement of normal commercial financial institutions and services in the ghetto. The trade contacts, business opportunities, and local financial assistance they can offer are far greater than anything the federal government can devise. Important among these are the following: (1) Development of high-risk casualty and theft insurance policies by the major insurance companies similar to high-risk automobile collision insurance policies. Most casualty and theft insurance companies do not insure in Negro areas; this applies to white businessmen as well as Negroes. A progressive, risk-taking businessman cannot operate boldly without such insurance; this is true any place, but especially in the ghetto. (2) The banks must be brought into the commercial financing of the very small businesses they historically have not financed. The Small Business Administration has proved that the risk is not so great as feared. And now banks have been offered a further incentive because under Title IV of the Economic Opportunity Act they can obtain 100 per cent guarantees by the Small Business Administration. (3) A retail installment credit institution needs to be created for ghetto businessmen. At the present time both Negro and white stores have difficulty getting credit from banks using a Negro consumer's installment purchase as security. (This is typical bank discount financing.) They are thus forced into the hands of disreputable high-interest installment operators.

Finally, Negro businessmen must organize their own business associations until such time as they are freely admitted into the local chambers of commerce and other trade associations. Such associations will help give the Negro businessman a sense of identity and a channel of communication for success stories. In addition, they provide a vehicle for representing the individual Negro merchant's views and complaints on rent-gouging, licensing, traffic-routing, and zoning, as well as his interests in the anti-poverty program, city hall, and civil rights.

The growing interest in the Negro market should naturally lead to an increased awareness of the Negro as a businessman. A strong Negro business community is one reality which the white power structure will truly respect simply because it will have to.

TABLE 1. Negro Businesses in Area 13 by Type of Business and Appearance of Establishment[81]

Business Type	Total in Business Type	Per Cent of Businesses By Type	A Number of Businesses	A Per Cent of Businesses	B Number of Businesses	B Per Cent of Businesses	C Number of Businesses	C Per Cent of Businesses
Total	1,615	100.0	188*	12.0*	871*	55.9*	500*	32.1*
Retail Trade Establishments								
Groceries, Delicatessens, etc.	211	13.2	20	9.5	132	62.5	59	28.0
Luncheonettes & restaurants	194	12.2	20	10.3	107	55.4	67	34.3
Taverns	18	0.8	not classified					
General merchandise	27	1.7	9	33.3	11	40.7	7	26.0
Apparel stores	52	3.3	9	17.4	18	34.5	25	48.1
Furniture, furnishings, etc.	38	2.4	—	—	5	13.2	33	86.8
Automotive stores	2	0.1	1	50.0	—	—	1	50.0
Gasoline service stations	20	1.3	9	45.0	6	30.0	5	25.0
Lumber, bldg., hardware	3	0.2	—	—	2	66.7	1	33.0
Drug stores	15	0.9	9	60.0	6	40.0	—	—
Candy & variety stores	147	9.2	11	7.5	90	61.2	46	31.3
Other retail stores	17	1.1	6	35.2	4	23.5	7	41.3
Service Establishments								
Hotels & other lodging places	—	—	—		—		—	—
Real estate	12	0.8	not classified					
Funeral directors	26	1.6	not classified					
Barber shops	216	13.5	38	17.6	131	60.6	47	21.8
Beauty shops	271	16.9	28	10.3	181	66.8	62	22.9
Other personal services	240	14.9	18	7.5	126	52.5	96	40.0
Radio & TV repair	33	2.1	5	15.2	17	51.5	11	33.3
Reupholstering & decorating	10	0.6	—	—	6	60.0	4	40.0
Other repair services	9	0.6	1	11.2	4	44.4	4	44.4
Auto repair services garages	39	2.4	3	7.8	16	40.9	20	51.3
Motion pictures & recreation	3	0.2	—	—	2	66.7	1	33.3
Janitorial services & maint.	—	—	—	—	—	—	—	—
Other business services	12	0.8	1	8.3	7	58.4	4	33.3

TABLE 2.   Negro Business in Areas 14 and 19 by Appearance
of Establishments*[82]

	Total in Business Type	Per Cent of Business by Type	A		B		C	
Area			Number of Businesses	Per Cent of Businesses	Number of Businesses	Per Cent of Businesses	Number of Businesses	Per Cent of Businesses
14	784	100.0	118	15.7	390	52.0	241	32.3
19	554	100.0	48	8.9	260	48.5	228	42.6

* The above table is a condensed version of the two original tables of Areas 14 and 19.
The totals exclude businesses unclassified by Drexel.

TABLE 3.   Comparison of Negro-Owned Businesses in
Selected Categories Between 1913 and 1935*[83]

Category	1913	1935
Food stores, including bakeries and caterers.	174	258
Automotive, including accessories, filling stations and garages.	0	36
General merchandise.	3	3
Apparel.	8	15
Furniture-household, including radios.	21	3
Lumber—building, hardware.	0	1
Eating and drinking places.	190	161
Drug stores.	3	27
Other retail stores, including cigar stores and stands, fuel and ice, beer and liquor stores.	102	159
Second-hand stores.	6	66
TOTAL	507	729

* We omitted about one-half of the businesses in 1913 because they did not coincide with the
categories in the 1935 count.

TABLE 4. Distribution of the Population of the North, South, and West Sections of Philadelphia, 1920[84]

Section or Ward	Negro Population	% of Total Negro Population	White Native Population	% of Total White Native Population	White Foreign Population	% of Total White Foreign Population	Total Population
North							
Ward 13	2,095	1.6	9,257	.7	7,607	1.9	18,959
14	4,946	3.7	9,874	.7	3,498	.8	18,318
15	3,766	2.8	31,717	2.4	9,342	2.3	44,825
20	8,269	6.2	25,798	1.9	12,940	3.3	47,007
28	1,813	1.4	41,023	3.1	10,862	2.7	53,698
29	1,716	1.3	23,793	1.8	6,710	1.6	32,219
32	3,926	2.9	34,467	2.7	9,147	2.2	47,540
37	1,126	.8	18,943	1.5	3,167	.7	23,236
38	2,031	1.5	55,268	4.3	15,048	3.8	72,347
47	9,211	6.9	19,625	1.5	4,219	1.1	33,055
Section Total	38,899	29.1	269,765	20.6	82,540	20.4	391,204
South							
Ward 7*	12,241	9.1	10,585	.8	3,471	.8	26,297
1	257	.2	25,847	2.0	19,726	4.9	45,830
2	1,962	1.4	18,120	1.4	15,133	3.8	35,215
3	1,695	1.3	10,863	.8	8,806	2.2	21,364
4	2,619	1.9	7,793	.6	6,419	1.6	16,831
26	5,715	4.2	39,169	3.0	17,577	4.4	62,461
30**	15,481	11.5	10,700	1.3	3,290	.8	29,471
36	13,291	9.9	32,315	2.5	9,619	2.4	55,225
39	799	.6	52,854	4.0	29,056	7.3	82,709
48	23	—	21,747	1.7	4,573	1.1	26,343

TABLE 4. (Continued)

Section or Ward	Negro Population	% of Total Negro Population	White Native Population	% of Total White Native Population	White Foreign Population	% of Total White Foreign Population	Total Population
Section Total	54,083	40.1	229,993	18.1	117,670	29.3	401,746
West Ward 24	8,152	6.1	40,901	3.2	11,355	2.8	60,408
27	2,927	2.2	17,358	1.3	4,005	1.0	24,290
34	3,557	2.6	57,555	4.5	11,214	2.8	72,326
40	3,946	2.7	64,147	4.9	10,807	2.7	78,900
44	3,595	2.7	34,124	2.6	7,748	1.9	45,467
46	1,040	.7	66,354	5.1	10,816	2.7	78,210
51			(This ward was not in existence in 1920.)				
52			"				
60			"				
Section Total	23,217	17.0	280,439	21.6	55,945	13.9	359,601
Grand Total	116,199	86.2	780,197	58.8	256,155	63.6	1,152,551

* For these figures, Ward 7 is being included in the South, although it is shown as part of the Center City section on the map.
** Only ward in 1920 where Negroes outnumber the white population.

TABLE 5.   Wards in 1950 and 1960 in Which the Negro Population
Outnumbered the White Population[85]

| Section or Wards | 1950 | | | |
	Negro Population	White Native Population	White Foreign Population	Total Population
North				
Ward 13	7,859	3,776	1,671	13,306
14	9,604	3,743	828	14,175
20	25,559	13,532	4,753	43,844
32	44,872	12,175	3,813	60,860
47	27,690	8,032	972	36,694
South				
Ward 30	23,789	3,096	323	27,208
West				
Ward 24	36,741	21,908	4,742	63,391
44	23,398	15,569	2,585	41,552
Total	199,512	81,831	19,687	301,030

| Section or Wards | 1960 | | | |
	Negro Population	Native* Population	Foreign* Population	Total Population
North				
Ward 13	5,070	1,631	518	7,219
14	8,560	1,469	314	10,343
20	24,110	6,018	2,257	32,385
28	46,230	3,122	1,264	50,616
29	23,095	4,178	977	28,250
32	52,191	1,567	739	54,497
37	11,284	6,632	822	18,738
47	28,713	2,231	289	31,233
South				
Ward 4	4,055	2,207	709	6,971
30	21,587	1,701	239	23,527
36	23,542	19,477	2,287	45,306
West				
Ward 24	45,666	9,927	2,394	57,987
44	28,598	6,482	1,379	36,459
52	27,975	18,820	5,451	52,246
Total	350,676	101,643	19,639	455,777

* In 1960, the category for natives and for foreign born included all races.

TABLE 6. Distribution of Negro-owned Businesses in Philadelphia by Wards and Sections With Heavy Negro Population, 1964*[86]

Section and Ward	Negro Population, 1960	% of Negro Total Population	# of Negro-owned Businesses, 1964	% of Total Negro-owned Businesses, 1964
South				
Ward 7	6,308	1.2	98	2.3
1	522	.1	5	.1
2	3,006	.6	15	.4
3	3,032	.6	9	.2
4**	4,055	.8	19	.5
26	6,918	1.3	47	1.1
30**	21,587	4.0	248	5.9
36**	23,542	4.4	167	4.0
39	2,917	.6	4	.1
48	1,035	.2	6	.1
Section Total	72,929	13.7	618	14.7
West				
Ward 24**	45,666	8.6	339	8.0
27	4,074	.8	22	.5
34	11,692	2.2	110	2.6
40	4,880	.9	14	.3
44**	28,598	5.4	253	6.0
46	40,171	7.6	293	7.0
51	6,044	1.1	41	1.0
52**	27,975	5.6	255	6.0
60	(Part of Ward 46 in 1960)			
Section Total	169,100	31.9	1327	31.4
North				
Ward 13**	5,070	.9	16	.4
14**	8,560	1.6	50	1.2
15	10,888	2.1	69	1.6
20**	24,110	4.6	106	2.5
28**	46,230	8.7	349	8.3
29**	23,095	4.4	177	4.2
32**	52,191	9.9	337	8.0
37**	11,284	2.1	71	1.7
38	24,505	4.6	160	4.0
47**	28,713	5.4	354	8.4
Section Total	342,857	44.8	1689	40.3
Grand Total	584,886	90.4	3634	86.4

(There were also 2 wards, 22 and 59 in the Northwest, Far North Section, which had, respectively, Negro populations totaling to 19,531 and 8,454 and contained 76 and 60 Negro-owned businesses. The total section had a small Negro population, but Wards 22 and 59 were contiguous to the North.)

* 305 businesses could not be placed in their proper wards because the addresses were not complete. As a result, the distribution and total numbers of the businesses may be slightly conservative.
** Indicates wards where the Negro population outnumbers the white population.

TABLE 7. Numbers of Negro-owned Businesses in Philadelphia in 1964 in Selected Categories*[87]

Category	1964
Food stores...	446
Automotive, including accessories, filling stations and garages..................................	195
General merchandise..	67
Apparel...	122
Furniture...	57
Lumber—building, hardware..................................	10
Eating and drinking places...................................	489
Drug stores...	29
Other retail stores..	344
TOTAL	1,759

* Several categories, in the services especially, were omitted so as to make this count comparable to the 1935 survey taken by the United States Bureau of the Census.
(See Table 3 for comparison with 1913 and 1935.)

TABLE 8. Foreign Born Proprietors and Total Foreign Born Population in Poughkeepsie*[88]

	Percentage Distribution						
	Italy	Germany Austria Hungary	Greece	Other West Euro- pean	Other East Euro- pean	Non Euro- pean	Total
Poughkeepsie Population	3.8	2.4	.4	2.2	2.8	0.6	12.2
All proprietors	8.5	5.4	4.5	1.7	6.5	2.4	29.1
Retail	7.7	5.1	4.1	1.6	8.0	3.3	29.8
Service	12.4	6.5	6.3	1.8	2.4	0.9	30.2
Wholesale	2.1	5.7	2.9	—	9.3	0.7	20.7
Manufacture	3.5	2.1	.7	3.5	9.9	2.9	22.7
Included in retail:							
Grocery	16.2	7.9	1.1	1.9	12.1	5.7	44.9
Clothing	3.4	4.1	—	2.1	17.2	—	26.9
Restaurant	9.2	5.2	20.4	0.7	3.3	4.6	43.5
Service station	—	1.5	—	1.5	0.8	0.8	4.6
Included in service:							
Shoe repair	72.5	—	2.5	—	2.5	—	77.5
Barber	35.9	—	2.9	1.0	1.0	1.0	41.8
Beauty shop	3.8	—	3.8	3.8	—	—	11.3
Garage	3.0	7.5	—	1.5	3.0	—	14.9
Trucking	2.2	—	—	—	—	—	2.2
Number of cases	217	137	115	43	167	62	741

* Poughkeepsie population is as of 1940; proprietors are for 20 years, 1936–1955.

TABLE 9. Comparison of Nativity of Entrepreneurs and Business
Leaders With Nativity of U.S.A. White Population in 1960

Nativity	Percentage of Entrepreneurs	Percentage of Business Leaders*	Percentage of U.S.A. White Population in 1960**
Foreign born	19.8***	5.3	5.9
U. S.-born with foreign-born fathers	35.0****	19.7	15.0
Total	54.8	25.0	20.9

* Business leader data adapted from Table 34 in Warner and Abegglen, *Occupational Mobility in American Business and Industry, op. cit.*, p. 90. Number of business leaders was approximately 7,500.

** Computed from data appearing in U. S. Bureau of the Census, *U. S. Census of Population: 1960.*

*** Number of entrepreneurs reporting nativity, 86.

**** Number of entrepreneurs reporting father's nativity, 40.

(This table refers to the information given in footnote 65.)

REFERENCES

1. Nathan Glazer and Daniel Patrick Moynihan, *Beyond the Melting Pot* (Cambridge, Mass., 1963), p. 36.

2. *Ibid.*

3. Kenneth B. Clark, *Dark Ghetto* (New York, 1965), p. 29.

4. St. Clair Drake and Horace R. Cayton, *Black Metropolis, A Study of Negro Life in a Northern City*, Vol. II (New York, 1945; 2nd ed., 1962), p. 432.

5. Nathan Reich, "The Economic Structure of Modern Jewry," *The Jews: Their History, Culture, and Religion*, Vol. II (New York, 1949), p. 1246.

6. W. Lloyd Warner and Leo Srole, *The Social Systems of American Ethnic Groups*, Yankee City Series, Vol. III (New Haven, Conn., 1945), p. 54.

7. Department of Immigration, *Immigrants by Major Occupation Groups: 1820 to 1957*, Series C, pp. 115-132. The percentages are of totals that exclude the No-occupation category which contained mostly dependents as well as persons who declined to state their occupations.

8. Reich, *op. cit.*, p. 1245.

9. Warner and Srole, *op. cit.*, p. 55.

10. Drake and Cayton, *op. cit.*, p. 432.

11. See Chester R. Rapkin and William Grissby, *The Demand for Housing in Racially Mixed Areas* (Berkeley, Calif., 1960).

12. *Ibid.*, pp. 83-86.

13. American Institute of Banking, *The Fundamentals of Banking* (New York, 1947), pp. 378-399.

14. Carlisle R. Davis, *Credit Administration* (New York, 1949 and 1964), p. 308.

15. Drexel Institute of Technology, *An Analysis of the Little Businessman in Philadelphia*, Vol. I (Philadelphia, 1964), p. 92.

16. Drexel Institute of Technology, *The Census of Negro-owned Businesses* (Philadelphia, 1964), p. ii. This figure was obtained by a team of Drexel Institute researchers who canvassed the entire City and recorded every Negro business no matter how marginal.

    The Bureau of the Census reported in 1960 there were 1,840 (1,370 males, 470 females) self-employed Negroes in Philadelphia. (*United States Census of Population, 1960, Pennsylvania, Detailed Characteristics*, pp. 40-749, male; pp. 40-751, female.) This self-employed figure is only a part of the total number of Negro businessmen, since many appear to have a business, in addition to a full-time job, but reported only the latter. Also, some may not have reported their businesses for tax reasons.

17. Drexel Institute of Technology, *The Census of Negro-owned Businesses, op. cit.*, p. ii.

18. *Ibid.*

19. *Ibid.*, p iii.

20. Philadelphia City Planning Commission, *Population of Philadelphia Sections and Wards: 1860-1960* (Philadelphia, 1963), Table 4, pp. 4-2. Source: individual returns to the United States Bureau of the Census (In all cases, we calculated the native white population by subtracting the Negro and foreign-born from the total population.)

21. Drexel Institute of Technology, *An Analysis of the Little Businessman in Philadelphia, op. cit.*, p. 53.

22. *Ibid.*, p. 83, as taken from The Delaware Valley Market, prepared by *The Philadelphia Inquirer* Research Department, 1963.

23. *Ibid.*, p. 38.

24. Edward Turner, *The Negro in Pennsylvania, Slavery—Servitude—Freedom, 1639-1861* (Washington, D. C., 1911), p. 123, as taken from Brissot de Warville, *Memoire*, pp. 28, 29.

25. W. E. Burghardt Du Bois, *The Philadelphia Negro, A Social Study* (Philadelphia, 1899), p. 23.

26. Turner, *op. cit.*, p. 9.

27. *Ibid.*, pp. 16, 17.

28. Du Bois, *op. cit.*, p. 24.

29. Turner, *op. cit.*, p. 125, in which the quote from the following publication is cited. "In New York and Philadelphia there are many sensible blacks. Some few have amassed fortunes; several conduct their businesses with considerable ability and integrity." I. Holmes, *An Account of the United States of America, Derived from Actual Observation, during a Residence of Four Years, 1823*, p. 334.

30. Pennsylvania Society for Promoting the Abolition of Slavery, *The Present State and Condition of the Free People of Color of Philadelphia and Adjoining Districts* (Philadelphia, 1838), p. 10.

31. Du Bois, *op. cit.*, p. 26.

32. *Ibid.*, pp. 26, 31.

33. *Ibid.*, p. 30.

34. Pennsylvania Society for Promoting the Abolition of Slavery, *Register of Trades of Colored People in the City of Philadelphia and Districts* (Philadelphia, 1838). The information was taken from Census statistics.

    Du Bois, *op cit.*, p. 143. Du Bois notes that during this period, ". . . though the diversity of employment [for Negroes] at this time was considerable, . . . under such heads as 'shopkeepers and traders' street stands more often than stores were meant." (The majority of the women were engaged in dressmaking and/or tailoring.)

35. Pennsylvania Society for Promoting the Abolition of Slavery, *The Present State and Condition of the Free People of Color of the City of Philadelphia and Adjoining Districts* (Philadelphia, 1838), p. 10.

36. Du Bois, *op. cit.*, p. 39.

37. Philadelphia City Planning Commission, *op. cit.*, Table 4, pp. 4-1,-2,-3, Table 5, pp. 5-1,-2,-3.

38. Du Bois, *op. cit.* Du Bois uses two sets of figures. On page 100, he indicated the results of a questionnaire showing 207 Negro men in business in the 7th ward, and on page 103, 63 Negro women in business in that ward. On the other hand, on page 122, he shows the results of an actual nose count of Negro-owned establishments in that ward which comes to 104. The discrepancy can be explained by the fact that, in the latter case, he does not include caterers because, as he says on page 119, "strictly a large part of them are waiters rather than caterers in the Ward who had annual receipts of $3,000-$5,000 and we have included them in the totals." Neither does he include every barber because of their numbers. In addition, Du Bois' footnotes on page 99, referring to the responses to the questionnaires, indicate the probability of bias in some cases. For instance, "a carpenter who gets little work and makes his living largely as a laborer is sometimes returned as a carpenter." On pages 124 and 125, he lists 144 business establishments in other parts of the City. Again, he includes no caterers and only some barbers. He also omits businesses that seem transient. Therefore, we have used the number of Negro-owned establishments rather than the number of Negro businessmen.

39. *Ibid.,* p. 43.

40. *Ibid.,* pp. 118, 116.

41. *Ibid.,* p. 123.

42. *Ibid.,* pp. 115-126.

43. R. R. Wright, Jr., Chairman, John W. Harris, A. C. Taylor, J. H. Williams, and A. C. Nicholson, *The Philadelphia Colored Business Directory, 1913, A Handbook of Information Concerning Professional and Business Activities of the Negroes of Philadelphia* (Philadelphia, 1913), pp. 25-76. (We omitted some business categories which this directory included, the most notable being 72 caterers, in order to make this 1913 count more comparable to the one taken by Du Bois in 1896.); and Philadelphia City Registration Commission, *Board and Division Book of City and County of Philadelphia,* as of July 1964. (For approximately the last hundred years, the Ward boundaries have remained constant.)

44. Philadelphia City Planning Commission, *Population of Philadelphia Sections and Wards: 1860-1960, op. cit.,* Table 4, p. 4-1.

45. *Ibid.,* Table 4, p. 4-2; R, R. Wright, Jr., *op. cit.,* pp. 25-76; and Philadelphia City Registration Commission, *op. cit.*

46. Sadie Tanner Mossell, *The Standard of Living Among One Hundred Negro Migrant Families* (Philadelphia, 1920), p. 9.

47. *Ibid.*

48. Raymond Pace Alexander, "The Struggle Against Racism in Philadelphia from 1923 to 1948," a speech delivered before the Business and Professional Group of the American Jewish Congress (Philadelphia, 1950), pp. 2-3.

49. Carter G. Woodson, J. H. Harmon, Jr., and Arnett G. Lindsay, *The Negro as a Businessman* (Washington, D. C., 1929), p. 26.

50. *Ibid.,* p. 25.

51. Monroe N. Work (ed.), *Negro Year Book, 1921-22* (Tuskegee, Alabama, 1922), p. 14.

52. Abram Lincoln Harris, *The Negro as a Capitalist* (Washington, D. C., 1936), pp. 125-143.

53. *Crisis,* January 1923, p. 124. Information about the Gipson Stores was obtained from William Kelly, President of the National Business League, Philadelphia Chapter.

54. Harris, *loc. cit.*

55. Florence Murray (ed.), *The Negro Handbook* (New York, 1942), p. 24.

56. Alexander, "The Struggle Against Racism in Philadelphia from 1923 to 1948," *loc. cit.,* pp. 15, 17, 18.

57. William A. Reinke, *The Employment of Negro White Collar Workers in the New York-Philadelphia Area* (Philadelphia, 1950), p. 3.

58. In 1946, the income of Philadelphia Negro families as compared to the average for city families in the United States was as follows:

	Philadelphia Negro Families	U. S. Average City Families
$2,000-$3,000	32%	30%
Over $3,000	21%	27%
Under $2,000	47%	43%

Source: Research Company of America and Harry Hayden Company, *The New Philadelphia Story* (Baltimore, 1946) p. 10.

In 1959, the median income for Philadelphia's nonwhite families was $4,794 and for all city families it was $6,433. Source: United States Bureau of the Census, *1960 Pennsylvania General Social and Economic Characteristics*, PC (1) 40 C Pa., Table 78, pp. 40-43; *1960 U. S. Summary, General Social and Economic Characteristics*, PC (1) 1C, Table 148, pp. 1-310. (The figures were taken in 1959.)

59. Du Bois, *op. cit.*, p. 26.

60. Mabel Newcomer, "The Little Businessman: A Study of Business Proprietors in Poughkeepsie, New York," *Business History Review*, Vol. 35 (Winter 1961), pp. 477-531.

61. Orvis L. Collins and David G. Moore, *The Enterprising Man* (East Lansing, Mich., 1964).

62. Newcomer, *op. cit.*, p. 480.

63. *Ibid.*, p. 481.

64. Collins and Moore, *op. cit.*, p. 70.

65. *Ibid.*, pp. 232-233. The comparison of the nativity of the businessmen included in the Michigan sample of Collins and Moore and the business leaders found in W. Lloyd Warner and James C. Abegglen, *Occupational Mobility in American Business and Industry* (Minneapolis, Minn., 1955) is shown in Table 9.

The authors of the Michigan study comment in regard to this Table that: "Only about five percent of the big business leaders were foreign born and an additional twenty percent were U. S. born sons of foreign born fathers. Our figures of twenty and thirty-five percent are disproportionately large. There are almost three times as many foreign born as would be expected from the general population figures and twice as many sons of foreign born." (p. 233)

Gunnar Myrdal, *An American Dilemma, The Negro Problem and Modern Democracy* (New York, 1944, 1962) p. 310. "The foreign-born are 'underrepresented' among industrial entrepreneurs, business-managers, officials, and white collar workers, but they constitute a larger proportion of the retail dealers than corresponds to their proportion in the population. In fact, one out of every three wholesale and retail dealers in the United States in 1930 was a foreign-born person." (Source: U. S. Bureau of the Census, *Negroes in the United States: 1920-1932*, p. 53.)

66. Nathan Glazer and Daniel Patrick Moynihan, *op. cit.*, p. 112.

67. This inclination of the immigrant to engage in individual enterprise may explain the unusually large number of Southern Negro migrants who entered business in Pennsylvania during the 1920's. Between 1924 and 1927, 62 per cent of Negro businessmen in Pennsylvania were born in the South. In 1930, 264,804 (61 per cent) of Pennsylvania's Negro population were Southern born. While the percentage of Southern Negroes in business was approximately even to their ratio within the total Negro population, the fact that there was that high a percentage, in light of the state of Negro business at the time, as well as of Negroes generally, is surprising. Source: U. S. Bureau of the Census; Commonwealth of Pennsylvania, Department of Welfare, *Negro Survey of Pennsylvania,* (Harrisburg, Penn., 1927), p. 28.

68. *Ibid.,* p. 21.

69. Mossell, *op. cit.,* p. 9.

70. George Bernard Shaw, *Man and Superman* (Baltimore, Md., 1952), p. 19.

71. Constitution of the United States, Article I, Section II, paragraph 3.

72. Du Bois, *op. cit.,* pp. 25-26.

73. Charles E. Silberman, *Crisis in Black and White* (New York, 1964), pp. 92-93.

74. *Ibid.,* p. 107.

75. 163 U.S. 537, 552.

76. Warner and Srole, *op. cit.,* p. 63.

77. Glazer and Moynihan, *op. cit.*

78. Public Law 89-117, Title I, section 106.

79. *Ibid.,* Title VII, section 703.

80. *Ibid.,* Title I, section 103.

81. Drexel Institute of Technology, *An Analysis of the Little Businessman in Philadelphia, op. cit.,* p. 53.

82. *Ibid.,* pp. 58, 79.

83. Murray, *op. cit.,* p. 24; Wright, *op. cit.,* pp. 25-76.

84. Philadelphia City Planning Commission, *op. cit.,* Table 3, 3-1,-2, Table 4, 4-1,-2, Table 5, 5-1,-2.

85. *Ibid.*

86. Drexel Institute of Technology, *The Census of Negro-owned Businesses, op. cit.;* Philadelphia City Registration Commission, *op. cit.*

87. Drexel Institute of Technology, *An Analysis of the Little Businessman in Philadelphia, op. cit.,* pp. 41-82.

88. Newcomer, *op. cit.,* p. 515. It should be pointed out that 94 per cent of all business concerns had less than twenty employees and two-thirds had less than four.

VI

TWO SOURCES OF PRESSURE FOR
CHANGE: INTERNAL AND EXTERNAL

KENNETH B. CLARK

The Civil Rights Movement: Momentum and Organization

The History of the Civil Rights Movement

THE AMERICAN civil rights movement in its most important sense is as old as the introduction of human slavery in the New World. From the beginning, the essential conflict of the civil rights movement was inherent in the contradiction between the practical economic and status advantages associated with slavery and racial oppression, and the Judao-Christian ideals of love and brotherhood and their translation into the democratic ideology of equality and justice. The presence of African slaves visibly different in culture and color of skin intensified this conflict which demanded resolution.

One could read the early history of America as an attempt to resolve this conflict by combining both, that is, by continuing slavery while making grudging concessions to religious and democratic ideology. The decision to convert some of the African slaves to Christianity and to teach some to read could be interpreted as the first "victory" of the civil rights movement, but at the same time it paradoxically intensified the conflict. It would have been more consistent logically to leave the African slave heathen and ignorant if he were to be kept in slavery. Yet the economic demands of slavery required that the slaves be skilled, adaptable, and efficient. The fact that such skill could be developed was evidence of the humanity of the African and the beginning of the end of human slavery in a society committed to social and political democracy. The dynamics of the contemporary civil rights movement continues to reflect this same struggle between the desire to deny the Negro full and unqualified status as a human being and the unquestioned evidence that such denial cannot be based upon fact.

Signs of a civil rights renaissance in the North emerged in the

1940's when Negro resentment mounted against segregation in the armed services and discrimination in employment. A new period of overt and sustained protest had begun. In 1941, A. Philip Randolph threatened a march on Washington to force President Roosevelt to issue the first executive order compelling fair employment of Negroes. Testimony to the depth of the ambivalence of the American nation on civil rights was the fact that Roosevelt, himself generally considered one of the most liberal and far-seeing Presidents in American history, only reluctantly issued this order. His noted charm was brought into play in an attempt to persuade Randolph to compromise his demands. He appealed to Randolph's patriotism and his unwillingness to embarrass the nation at a time of dire emergency; only when all of these appeals failed did he accede to Randolph's demand. This conflict between Roosevelt and Randolph marked the beginning of a new militance and assertiveness on the part of the Northern Negro. It has been sustained ever since.

Since World War II, the Negro had succeeded in eliminating segregation in the armed forces, and, unsatisfied with less in peace than he had won in war, he gained a series of victories in the federal courts, culminating in the historic May 17, 1954 *Brown vs. Board of Education* decision of the United States Supreme Court. He developed and refined techniques for nonviolent direct-action boycotts in the South, resulting in the elimination of the more flagrant forms and symbols of racial segregation. The massive legislative commitment to racial reform, codified by the passage of the 1964 and 1965 Civil Rights Acts, had begun. The American press justified and validated the claims of its freedom and responsibility in its generally objective recording of racial injustices, while television brought into American living rooms the stark mob faces of primitive race hatred. The importance of television must eventually be evaluated by historians, but to this observer it appears to have played a most crucial role in intensifying the commitment of both Negroes and whites and increasing the momentum of the civil rights movement.

International politics also played a strong role in the struggle for justice. With the overthrow of colonial domination in the postwar decade, white Europeans and Americans could no longer sustain their political dominance over the nonwhite peoples of Asia and Africa. The increasing dignity associated with the independence of these colored peoples provided a new source of strength for the American Negro. And one should not underestimate the role of the

Communist ideology as an aggressive world adversary of the American and Western concept of democracy. American Communists had never been successful in exploiting the grievances of the American Negro and attracting any significant numbers of Negroes to the Communist cause—probably because their dogmatic inability to understand the subtle but important psychological aspects of the Negro's aspirations and struggles had led them to advocate *segregation* under the guise of self-determination in the Black Belt. Nevertheless, the competitive struggle between world Communism and the American concept of democracy demanded an American response to this embarrassing and easily exploited violation of democratic ideals. America risked standing before the world as a hypocrite or resting its claims for leadership on might alone, subordinating any democratic ideological basis of appeal. The international struggle for the first time clearly placed racists on the defensive, in grave danger of being classed as subversives in their threat to America's ideological power.

One could define the civil rights movement in terms of organized and sustained activity directed toward the attainment of specific racial goals or the alleviation or elimination of certain racial problems. Such a definition, with its emphasis upon organization as the basis for changes in the status of Negroes in America, would suggest that the civil rights movement was synonymous with civil rights organizations. But this definition would obscure the important fact that the civil rights movement had its own historic and impersonal momentum, responsive to deep and powerful economic and international events and political and ideological forces beyond the control of individuals, agencies, or perhaps even individual governments. In fact, the uncontrollable power and momentum of the civil rights movement impelled it to create the necessary machinery, organizations, and leaders.[1]

The History and Character of the Civil Rights Organizations

There is an understandable tendency to think of the civil rights movement, organizations, and leaders as if they were interchangeable or as if they were only parts of the same historic and social phenomenon. But, while there are similarities and overlaps among them, they are not identical, and their important historical and contemporary dynamic differences need clarification if one is to understand the present nature and force of the civil rights movement, or if one is to assess accurately the role and power of the various civil rights organizations and the actual extent of personal decision-making power held by their recognized leaders. Confusion on these questions can lead only to dangerous miscalculations. Specifically, political and governmental leaders may make demands upon civil rights leaders, demands which they genuinely believe can be fulfilled in the normal course of social bargaining and negotiation. The parties to these discussions may enter into such agreements in good faith only to find themselves unable to fulfill them. Those who view the civil rights movement in terms of the model of the American labor movement, with elected labor leaders holding responsibility for negotiating and bargaining for a disciplined rank and file, misjudge the nature of the movement. One obvious difference is that civil rights leaders have not been elected by any substantial number of Negroes. Either they are essentially hired executives, holding their office at the pleasure of a board of directors, or else they emerge as leaders by charismatic power, later creating an organization which, in effect, they control. Whitney Young is an example of the one, Martin Luther King of the other. So far, no machinery exists to enable the masses of Negroes to select a leader, but, if an individual strikes a responsive chord in the masses of Negroes, they will identify with him and "choose" him. So, too, an organizational leader may be accepted as spokesman by default, by the mere fact that he has been able to avoid overt repudiation.

One cannot understand the nature and the problems of contemporary civil rights organizations without understanding some of their individual histories. The *National Association for the Advancement of Colored People* and the *Urban League*, the two oldest, were founded in the first decade of this century in 1909 and 1910 respectively.

The National Association for the Advancement of Colored People

The NAACP emerged from the Niagara Movement of W. E. B. Du Bois and other Negro and white liberals during that period when Negroes were moving North.

A meeting of some of the members of the Niagara Movement was held in 1908, and it was agreed that a call should be issued by whites and Negroes for a conference on the centennial of the birth of Abraham Lincoln to discuss the status of the Negro in the United

States. Oswald Garrison Villard wrote the Call for the Conference which was held in New York City on February 12 and 13, 1909. It read in part:

In many states today Lincoln would find justice enforced, if at all, by judges elected by one element in a community to pass upon the liberties and lives of another. He would see the black men and women, for whose freedom a hundred thousand of soldiers gave their lives, set apart in trains, in which they pay first-class fares for third class service, and segregated in railway stations and in places of entertainment; he would observe that State after State declines to do its elementary duty in preparing the Negro through education for the best exercise of citizenship. . . . Added to this, the spread of lawless attacks upon the Negro, North, South, and West—even in Springfield made famous by Lincoln—often accompanied by revolting brutalities, sparing neither sex nor age nor youth, could but shock the author of the sentiment that "government of the people, by the people, for the people, shall not perish from the earth." . . . Silence under these conditions means tacit approval. The indifference of the North is already responsible for more than one assault upon democracy, and every such attack reacts as unfavorably upon the whites as upon the blacks. Discrimination once permitted cannot be bridled; recent history in the South shows that in forging chains for the Negroes the white voters are forging chains for themselves. "A house divided against itself cannot stand;" this government cannot exist half-slave and half-free any better today than it could in 1861. . . . Hence we call upon all the believers in democracy to join in a national conference for the discussion of present evils, the voicing of protests, and the renewal of the struggle for civil and political liberty.[2]

The Call clearly indicates that, at its founding, the NAACP sensed that the status of the Negro in the North would not be significantly better than his status in the South. The founding of the NAACP anticipated the race riots of 1917, following the clues of the New York City riot of 1900. It was an attempt by the more perceptive and sensitive Negroes and whites to recapture the fervor, the purpose, and the concern of the pre-Civil War abolitionists.

The NAACP, from its beginning, took a more direct and militant stance, in spite of the fact that its founders and its Board of Directors were always interracial. The top staff tended to address itself to legislation and litigation. It pioneered in the use of direct action demonstrations. The more militant approach of the NAACP reflected, among other things, the role of W. E. B. Du Bois, paradoxically both a detached scholar and poet and an intense actionist. The direction and approach of the NAACP, to the extent that they can be attributed to a single person, were determined by his power and personality. In the tradition of a nineteenth-century New England aristocratic poet-actionist-crusader, Du Bois was a dignified intellectual, Harvard-educated, detached, aloof, and cold, but also intensely concerned and committed to the attainment of unqualified justice and equality for Negroes. He may well have been the most important figure in the American civil rights movement in the twentieth century. His importance lies not only in his role in setting the direction and the methods of the NAACP, but in his capacity to understand and predict the larger dimensions of the American racial problem. Like Frederick Douglass, he was a prophet and leader of the movement, but, unlike Douglass, he was a founder and leader of an organization within the movement, capable of articulating the purposes of that organization. Du Bois the scholar gave Du Bois the leader of the NAACP a deeper human understanding, and to the NAACP he gave a significance which a mere organization could not have had without him. Yet his temperament, facing the contradictions and the turmoil necessary to organizational struggle, determined that his role in the organization itself would be limited. One could speculate that the ardor, the intensity, the militance of Du Bois, his inability to tolerate anything other than acceptance of his complete humanity were viewed as a handicap to those willing to make the "necessary" compromises for the survival of the institution. He was a proud and uncompromising man.

The essence of the controversy between Du Bois and Booker T. Washington was that Washington could accommodate and adjust, while Du Bois could not. If the NAACP had been run by Washington, it would have been pragmatic and practical, but not militant or crusading. The clash between Washington and Du Bois was a clash of temperament and principle. Washington was willing to accept qualifications of his humanity; Du Bois was not. Du Bois' dignity and his inability to settle for anything less than total human acceptance set the tone for the approach, methods, and early militant stance of the NAACP.

The Du Bois-Washington controversy could be illustrated by their conflicting views on education for Negroes. Washington's support for a special kind of education "appropriate" to the caste status of the Negro—vocational education, the acceptance of separation (in a sense the acceptance of segregation itself)—was consistent with his pragmatic accommodation. Du Bois' insistence on academic education, his belief that, if the Negro were to progress in America, he would need to assume the same stance as whites, his belief that one could not make judgments about a person's role in terms of his color, his slogan of the "talented tenth," all were consistent with his refusal to allow color to qualify the rights of persons. He took seriously the American ideology. Washington was the realist, the moderate, yet he never founded a civil rights organization, but operated from the institutional base of Tuskegee Institute. He had gained acceptance from the white power controllers without an "organization." It is indeed doubtful that he could have mobilized a civil rights agency. It may be that his power and his usefulness to the equally pragmatic white political and economic structure would have been curtailed by even the semblance of a functioning civil rights organization. That Washington was not a particularly significant influence in the movement during its earliest stages may be due to the fact that his domain by this time was clearly the Southern Negro. The civil rights movement was then becoming Northern-oriented. One could speculate that the doctrine of accommodation preached by Washington and reinforced by white power effectively curtailed the growth of a Negro civil rights movement in the South until the mid-twentieth century.

The National Urban League

The Urban League was founded a year later than the NAACP, in 1910, for the specific purpose of easing the transition of the Southern rural Negro into an urban way of life. It stated clearly that its role was to help these people, who were essentially rural agrarian serf-peasants, adjust to Northern city life. Until the termination of Lester Granger's tenure as director in September 1961, the League announced in its fund-raising appeals and to both business and government that it was essentially a social service agency with a staff of social workers. Its implicit assumption was that the problems of the Negro were primarily those of adjustment and that their need was for training and help. The League summoned whites to demonstrate their good will, relying upon negotiation and persuasion to show white business leaders that it was in their "enlightened self interest," to use Lester Granger's term, to ease the movement of Negroes into middle-class status. The Urban League played down the more primitive and irrational components of racial hostility, depending on the conviction that white leadership, particularly in the North, could be dealt with in terms of rational economic appeals. The League courted the white community through its national and local boards, considering itself an effective bridge between the Negro community and the white decision-makers; to this end, it recruited a staff skilled not only in social work but also in negotiation procedure and style. During the early 1950's, one member of the top national staff of the Urban League described the role of the League as "the State Department of race relations," in contrast to the NAACP, which was characterized as "the War Department." This was more than an analogy; the style of speech and dress and manner of the League tended to be a stereotype of the style of the staff of the American State Department.

NAACP and Urban League: Democratic, Nonpartisan, Conservative

These two civil rights organizations, the NAACP and the Urban League, had in common their Northern base and their interracial character. They also shared a basic assumption that major changes in the status of the Negro could be obtained within the framework of the American democratic system. They sought to manipulate the machinery of government and to influence other institutions. The Urban League's primary emphasis was placed upon the economic, industrial, and social-service clusters of power, while the NAACP's primary interest was in political and legal power, with a major emphasis upon propaganda which sought to reach the conscience of the American people, both white and Negro. The League's appeal was to self-interest—employ Negroes, or you will spawn large numbers of dependent people. The NAACP's appeal was to public and judicial conscience; their argument was that America is intended to be a democratic nation with justice for all.

From the very beginning, both organizations were politically nonpartisan and therefore in some measure effective in flexibility of appeal and action. They could not afford identification with a particular political group, for they faced an always imminent prospect of political changes in government and the possibility of retaliation. Their decision, on its face, seemed quite wise; but it limited the extent to which the civil rights organizations could, in any meaningful sense, be politically or socially revolutionary. They could not or did not identify with labor, and their sense of alienation was stimulated by the political immaturity of the American labor movement itself. The rank-and-file members of organized labor, if not its leaders, were contaminated by racism; thus, the civil rights organizations and American labor could not form a political coalition or develop a significant labor party. It would, however, be inaccurate to say these civil rights groups ever "sought" an alliance with a political labor movement. The mere fact that civil rights organizations were necessary made a civil rights-labor coalition impossible since one of the major sources of racial exclusion has been and remains the organized American labor movement.

The civil rights organizations were never revolutionary. Their assumptions and strategy and tactics were essentially conservative, in that they did not seek to change and certainly made no attempt to overthrow the basic political and economic structure. The social changes they sought were limited to the inclusion of the Negro in the existing society; the Negro wanted his own status raised to that of other American citizens. The NAACP and Urban League staked their strategies on a belief in the resilience, flexibility, and eventual inclusiveness of the American democratic system—in an ultimate sense, perhaps in a pathetic sense, upon acceptance and identification with the articulated American concept of democracy. They took literally the ideology and promises of the system and shared unquestioningly American democratic optimism. They believed in the words of Jefferson, the Declaration of Independence, the Constitution, and the Bill of Rights and asked only that these rights— and nothing less—be extended to Negroes. This was their main source of power. They could be considered revolutionary only if one tortures the meaning of the term to imply a demand to include other human beings in a system which promises fulfillment to others.

To call such modest requests disruptive or radical or extremist is to misunderstand and misjudge the logic of the original American revolution, and reflects the sickness of racism. In effect, a Marxist could justifiably accuse the civil rights movement from its beginning to the present, as well as the American labor movement, of being unrealistic and superficial in its belief that fundamental change for oppressed peoples was possible under a system within which the oppression occurred and was sustained.

The purpose of the civil rights movement has always been to counteract and destroy the lie that the Negro is subhuman, a lie that no one ever really believed, yet one that was reinforced by those with power. The fact that the Negro *is* human made him susceptible to and influenced by the same forces that influence other human beings in his society. Although the Negro's indoctrination in democracy was contaminated by the obvious reality of his rejection and exclusion by that democracy, he did not, astonishingly, respond by rejection of democracy itself. He seemed to show a sophisticated wisdom in understanding that the ideal of democracy itself was not to blame merely because democracy, as practiced, had not, for the Negro, advanced beyond verbal commitments. He sought a continuation of a revolution that had already begun. He desired only to join it and share its benefits.

Probably even more important is the compelling reality that the civil rights organizations could not have afforded to behave in a revolutionary manner. Even if a racial revolution were psychologically possible, it was not statistically possible. Negro slaves in the United States, unlike Negro slaves in the Caribbean or South America, remained a numerical minority. Attempts at rebellion during and after the period of slavery were ruthlessly suppressed and tended to introduce not the alleviation of oppression but a new period of intensified cruelty. The stark fact is that the Negro in the United States was never in a position to entertain seriously any notions of major disruption or changes in the existing economic or political system. If his condition were to improve, it would have to improve within the framework of the existing realities, realities which he could not modify in a fundamental way because he lacked the necessary power.

It may be that the strategies and techniques of the civil rights organizations could have been only more systematic and organizational forms of the very kinds of accommodations that individual Negroes were required to make in the face of the superior power of the white system. As the material economic, political, and military power of the United States increased during the twentieth century, the validity of this strategy of assertive accommodation on the part of the civil rights organizations became even more justifiable, practical, and realistic. It is important, however, to understand that these accommodations were never acquiescence in or acceptance of injustice, but rather tactical maneuvers, strategic retreats, or temporary delays, and the effective timing of demands for specific changes.

NAACP and Urban League: Leadership and Strategy

What were the effects of this strategy? There is no question that the rationale and techniques of the NAACP led to notable successes in the field of legislation and litigation. Civil rights victories in the federal courts, including equalization of salaries for teachers, the Gaines, Sweatt, and McLaurin cases, the restrictive covenant cases, and, finally, the *Brown vs. Board of Education* school-desegregation decision of 1954, are examples of the extent to which the NAACP has removed almost every legal support for racial segregation in all aspects of American life. Probably the only exception to this is the remaining laws dealing with intermarriage, and these laws may soon be declared unconstitutional.

The techniques, methods, and organizational structure of the NAACP in 1965 are essentially the same as they were in the 1920's. If one were to examine the NAACP today and compare it with the NAACP twenty or thirty years ago, the only significant difference one would find is an increase in the number of staff, particularly in the Legal Defense and Education Fund, Inc., staff.

This important legal arm of the NAACP has been officially separated as an independent corporation from the rest of the NAACP since 1939. But by the early 1950's this technical separation had increased in fact. The Legal Defense and Education Fund, Inc., has its own offices, budget, fund-raising program, and Board of Directors and staff. While there has remained a close working relationship with the NAACP itself, this increasing independence of the Legal Defense and Education Fund has made it possible for it to work closely and provide legal services to the newer more activist civil rights organizations such as CORE and SNCC.

The NAACP itself has added some staff for specialized work in such problem areas as labor and housing. The newer and more direct-actionist civil rights groups have forced the NAACP to initiate more concrete measures, but there is reason to believe that this advance was reluctant and that, left to its own devices, the NAACP would have continued to put its major emphasis on its traditional concerns. Ironically, ten, fifteen, or twenty years ago, such concerns seemed to be extreme militance. Today, in the view of the development of more activist civil rights groups, such as the Congress of Racial Equality (CORE), the Southern Christian Leadership Conference (SCLC), and the Student Nonviolent Coordinating Committee (SNCC), the NAACP is seen as a rather moderate, even conservative, organization.

As leaders of the NAACP, Walter White and, later, Roy Wilkins continued the tradition of Du Bois, but they stopped short where he had only begun. There is every reason to believe that Du Bois would have taken the NAACP to the front lines where CORE,

SCLC, and SNCC are now. Walter White developed the method of personal contact and friendship with top public officials, and during his administration an effective NAACP lobby was begun and the legal staff strengthened. Nevertheless this program and his predilection for a "first name" approach to power figures necessarily supplanted direct-action confrontation. It approached the methods of the Urban League and transformed the Du Bois style of militance into one of personal diplomacy. On the death of Walter White in 1955, Roy Wilkins became executive director of the NAACP, after serving as editor of *The Crisis,* the NAACP's official journal. His approach differs little from Walter White's, in spite of the counter pressure of the more militant groups and more activist and impatient forces within the Board and staff of the NAACP. His style, manner, background, and personality are not consistent with a mass appeal. He seems more comfortable in rational discussions with key decision-makers in economic and governmental centers of power than before a mass meeting of his "followers." Wilkins is the personification of responsible, statesmanlike leadership. He jealously guards his belief in the rational and intellectual approach to significant social change and refuses to be pushed even temporarily into the stance of the fiery leader. The value of this approach is clear; its dangers are more obscure but nonetheless real. Its chief danger is that a primary and understandable concern of civil rights leaders for a posture of respectability might make them more vulnerable to the shrewd, psychological exploitation of skillful political leaders. The power of civil rights leaders could probably be more effectively controlled by affability than by racial brutality.

The NAACP either was not able or did not desire to modify its program in response to new demands. It believed it should continue its important work by using those techniques it had already perfected. It may, of course, have been impossible for an old-line organization to alter its course dramatically, and thus it may have been inevitable that new programs would have to stem from the apparently more militant, assertive, and aggressive civil rights organizations.

The Urban League, contrary to popular opinion, has by no means been so visibly successful as the NAACP in attaining its stated goals. Certainly its desire and efforts to aid the smooth adjustment of the Southern Negro who moved to Northern cities, while quite laudable, have not prevented the massive pathology which dominates the expanding ghettos of such cities as New York,

Chicago, Philadelphia, Detroit, and Cleveland. The fascinating paradox is that the very areas in which the Urban League program has been most active—the blight of segregated housing, segregated and inferior education, and persistent and pernicious discrimination in employment—have been those areas in which the virulence of racism has increased in the North. Obviously, one cannot blame the program and activities of the Urban League for this blight. It remains a fact, however, that the approach used by the Urban League has not effectively stemmed the tide nor obscured the symptoms of Northern racism. The goals of the NAACP, resting on the vision and courage of the federal courts, were far more concrete and limited and hence more easily achieved. The ghettos of Northern cities and the forces which perpetuate such ghettos are clearly beyond the scope of an agency such as the Urban League or indeed any private agency. In response to this, there are indications that the League's present leadership is moving closer to direct involvement with governmental power.

It is clear also that the victories of the NAACP in the federal courts, the victories of all the combined forces of the civil rights organizations, leading to the Civil Rights Act of 1964 and the voting rights act of 1965 do not appear to be relevant to the peculiar cancerous growth of racism in American ghettos now spreading from the North back to more "liberal" Southern cities like Atlanta and New Orleans. The difficult truth civil rights agencies must eventually face is that so far no technique has been developed which seems relevant to this problem which now has emerged as the key civil rights issue. Protest demonstrations, litigation, and legislation do not seem to be specific remedies for this pattern of social pathology.

Within recent years, under the guidance of its new executive director, Whitney Young, the Urban League has indicated its awareness of the complexities of the present civil rights problem. The Urban League has joined with more "militant" civil rights groups, associating itself with mass protest movements, acknowledging that a social-service approach is not adequate to deal with the more flagrant predicaments of Negroes in the North and South. It has joined in demands for effective legislation. Whitney Young, probably by force of his personality, his background as an academician and administrative social worker, and his diplomatic skill, has managed to combine the traditional approach with a more dramatic and seemingly more militant stance without major disruption to the Urban League. He has not alienated white supporters; indeed, he has convinced them to increase their contributions. He has demonstrated beyond question that a more assertive insistence upon the inclusion of Negroes in the main stream of American life (his "fair share" hiring plan) and the willingness of the Urban League to identify itself with more "militant" direct-action dramatization of the plight of the Negro have not been at a financial sacrifice. Whitney Young demonstrated in the Urban League a degree of flexibility not yet so clearly apparent in the NAACP.

The Congress of Racial Equality

The Congress of Racial Equality (CORE), like the Urban League and NAACP, began in the North. It was founded in Chicago in 1942 and became a national organization in 1943. From its inception it emphasized direct action and the dramatization of special forms of racial segregation. The founders of CORE were associated in some of their activities with a pacifist-oriented group, the Fellowship of Reconciliation, and the organization was interracial. In the initial stages of CORE, the evolution of a civil rights organization with a larger political commitment seemed possible. The pacifist aura and direct-action orientation of early CORE founders and members suggested a significant divergence from the politically nonpartisan policies and programs of the NAACP and the Urban League. In fact, one of the rationales for the founding of CORE was that it felt that legalism alone could not win the war against segregation.[3]

It is significant that CORE did not become a major civil rights organization until the civil rights movement reached a crescendo after the Brown decision of 1954. Before that, CORE seemed to be a rather constricted, dedicated, almost cult-like group of racial protesters who addressed themselves to fairly specific forms of racial abuse which could be dramatized by their particular method of direct action and personal protest. In 1943, they sat-in at a segregated Chicago restaurant, successfully desegregating it; in 1947 they cosponsored with the Fellowship of Reconciliation a two-week freedom-ride to test discrimination in buses engaged in interstate travel; and through nonviolent stand-ins, they successfully desegregated the Palisades Amusement Park's pool in 1947-48.[4] These techniques could be viewed as the harbingers of the more extensive use of direct action, nonviolent techniques, which, since the Montgomery bus boycott, have become almost the symbol of the civil rights protest movement. Whether or not Martin Luther King, Jr., was aware of his debt to the CORE precedent, CORE set the pattern for Montgomery. The sit-in technique was initially CORE's, and CORE was also the first civil rights organization to rely upon nonviolent political pacifism.

James Farmer, executive director of CORE,* was formerly a Methodist minister. He combines the appearance of personal calm and tolerant objectivity with a surprising forthrightness and fervent commitment. He makes no diplomatic accommodation to power figures, but demands uncompromising equality. In CORE's loose confederation of militant and seemingly undisciplined local chapters under a permissive national board, Farmer is a stabilizing influence, a convergence point; he holds power by virtue of his personal example of commitment. But while he is a symbol of the integrity of CORE and is generally accepted as such by the public and by CORE members, so far he does not seem able to control the activities of some of the more zealous and activistic CORE chapters.

When local CORE groups in Brooklyn threatened to use a dramatic, but seemingly ineffective tactic—the abortive stall-in to keep people from getting to the New York World's Fair in April of 1964 —Farmer was forced to intervene in an unaccustomed show of discipline to save the national organization. He allowed himself to be arrested at the Fair partly to demonstrate his own commitment to the cause but also to divert the spotlight from his unruly locals. Yet, whatever the anarchism of these locals and the inadvisability

---

* Since initial publication of this chapter in *The Negro American—2*, James Farmer has announced his decision to give up his role as executive director of CORE. His public explanation is that he intends to direct a national program to improve the literacy of Negroes and equip them for the struggle against poverty and the pathology of inferior racial status. The question remains, however, whether this decision did not reflect, among other factors, Farmer's awareness of the internal instability of CORE and his own inability as a single individual, even with trusted staff associates, to change this fact significantly. Were these not major considerations in his decision to resign as director of CORE, a national program for improving the literacy and status of Negroes could have been incorporated into the existing CORE program. Certainly the financial supporters of this new venture could have been convinced that it would be more desirable and economical to use an existing agency rather than to set up an entirely new one. The departure of Farmer therefore must be seen as an ominous sign for the future effectiveness if not meaningful existence of CORE.

of demonstrations not directly related to concrete grievances, there is something to be said for the observation that, when multitudes are inconvenienced or threatened with discomfort, the very random quality of the action reflects the desperation of the demonstrators and has some impact, even if only irritation, upon the white majority. To the Negro, white irritation and anger is at least a *response*. And where chaos threatens, more responsible leaders of society intervene. The danger of disruptive demonstration, of course, is that the intervention may be repressive and the repressiveness may seem justifiable in the name of public order. But thus far CORE has not demonstrated that its tactics and methods are relevant to the problems and the pervasive pathology of the Negro in urban ghettos.

The Southern Christian Leadership Conference

The Southern Christian Leadership Conference, which Martin Luther King, Jr., heads, has the distinction of being the first civil rights organization to start in the South. It began in Atlanta in 1957, primarily as an expression of the commitment of nearly one hundred men throughout the South to the idea of a Southern movement to implement through nonviolent means the Supreme Court's decision against bus segregation. This commitment was made concrete by formation of a permanent organization, the SCLC, and Martin Luther King, Jr., was elected its president.

In order to understand SCLC and King, one must understand that this movement would probably not have existed at all were it not for the 1954 Supreme Court school-desegregation decision which provided a tremendous boost to the morale of Negroes by its clear affirmation that color is irrelevant to the rights of American citizens. Until this time, the Southern Negro generally had accommodated himself to the separation of the black from the white society. In spite of the fact that Southern rural Negroes in Clarendon County, South Carolina, were the original plaintiffs in the school-desegregation cases, one could speculate that if the United States Supreme Court had ruled against them, the Southern Negro would probably have retreated into stagnation or inner rebellion or protest by indirection. The leadership of King came immediately, however, as a consequence of a Negro woman's refusal, in 1955, to make the kinds of adjustments to racial humiliation that Negro women had been making in the South throughout the twentieth century. Rosa Parks' defiance was publicized in *The Montgomery Advertiser,* which also revealed the fact that Negroes were organizing. Ironically, the chief boost to the boycott came from the white press. Scores of Negroes, who would not have known about the boycott, learned of it in the Montgomery newspaper and offered help to King and other ministers.

The bus boycott catapulted King first into local leadership as head of the Montgomery Improvement Association, formed for the purpose of coordinating the bus boycott, and then by virtue of the drama and success of that boycott into national leadership. He had responded to forces beyond his control, forces let loose by the early work of the NAACP in clearing away the legal support for segregation, by the urbanization and industrialization of society, and by the pressures of America's role in a predominantly nonwhite world. Here was a man who, by virtue of his personality and his role as minister, did not excite an overt competitive reaction from others. He could and did provide the symbol of unified protest and defiance. As a minister trained not only in theology, but in philosophy and history as well, sensitive and jealous of his understanding of world events and world history, King could develop and articulate a philosophical rationale for the movement, an ideology to support his strategy. Associating his role in Montgomery with the Gandhian philosophy of passive resistance and nonviolence, he emphasized another dimension of the civil rights movement in America, systematically articulating and developing the form of racial protest first used by CORE more than ten years before. The question has been raised whether or not this philosophy and the commitment to love one's oppressor is relevant to the effectiveness of the method itself. What happened in Montgomery was not a consequence of King's philosophy. The Montgomery affair demonstrated rather the ability of King and others to exploit the errors of the whites and to unify the Negroes for an effective boycott. There is no evidence that whites react to philosophy, but they do react to what happens. King's philosophy did not exist before the fact; rather, it was adopted after it was found to be working.

The development of philosophical and religious support for the method did, however, help to gather support for future action by focusing and refining a tactic and by an appeal to the conscience of Negro and white. King effectively turned the main weakness of the Negro, his numerical, economic, and political impotence, into a working strategy. Practically speaking, he could not seek redress by violence, but he did have available resources of nonviolence. Nietzsche said that Christ developed a philosophy of love because the Jews were weak; and that only when Christianity becomes strong can love become powerful. King's philosophy is actually a response to the behavior of others, effective directly in terms of the ferocity of the resistance it meets. It is not only nonviolent; it is also assertive. It depends on the reactions of others for its own strength. King and SCLC sometimes appear, indeed, to be satisfied, as in the case of Birmingham, with negotiations leading to minimal concessions. King does not insist upon total change in the status of Negroes in a community but considers partial change temporarily satisfactory. What he settles for can be questioned in terms of the energy expended and the risks taken.

One cannot understand SCLC solely in terms of its organization, which is amorphous and more symbolic than functional, even though the national headquarters in Atlanta, Georgia, has sixty-five affiliates throughout the South. To understand this organization, one has to understand King, because SCLC *is* Martin Luther King, Jr. King is a national hero, a charismatic leader, portrayed in America and through the world as a man of quiet dignity, a personification of courage in the face of racial danger. He has the ability to articulate a philosophy and ideology of race relations clearly acceptable to the larger society. As far as the general public is concerned, the civil rights movement has converged in his personality. His ability to portray selflessness and to understand other civil rights leaders has made him a suitable person for his role. In the complexities, tensions, and frustrations of the civil rights movement, King fills an important function of simplification through personalization.

The presence of King and SCLC indicates something about the inadequacy or the inappropriateness of the methods and techniques used by the NAACP and the Urban League in the South today. If either the NAACP or the Urban League had been sufficient, King could not have been so successful as he is. King moved into a vacuum that existing civil rights groups did not fill. He mobilized people not in protest against the entire system but against specific injustices. Concrete successes, in turn, raised Negro morale. But SCLC's program, as a means to transform society, is more apparently than actually successful. The dramatization of the direct-action, SCLC-King technique over the mass media leads to the impression that the civil rights movement in the South is in fact a mass movement. In those situations in which white police and political officers do not exacerbate the resentment of Negroes by acts of cruelty and hostility, even King's appeal does not actively involve more than a fraction of the Negro population. It can, of course, be said of any "mass" movement that it rarely involves more than a small minority in direct action, at least in its initial stages.

King himself seems to realize the limitations of his method as shown by his unsuccessful attempt to encourage a less concrete strategy, a general boycott of the state of Alabama. In his plans to extend his program into Northern cities he seems likely to be less successful. In the future phase of the civil rights movement where Negroes confront not direct tyranny but pervasive oppression, King's strategy and charisma may be less effective. Furthermore, it would probably be all too easy to abort and to make impotent the whole King-SCLC approach, if white society could control the flagrant idiocy of some of its own leaders, suppress the more vulgar, atavistic tyrants, like Sheriff Jim Clark, and create instead a quiet, if not genteel, intransigence. Such intransigence presents a quite different problem to the civil rights movement. A philosophy of love or techniques which seem compatible with such a philosophy would seem effective only in a situation of flagrant hate or cruelty. When love meets either indifference or passive refusal to change, it does not seem to have the power to mobilize the reactions of potential allies. Nor does it seem to affect the enemy—it appears irrelevant to fundamental social change.

Gandhi, of course, whose philosophy was one of nonviolent resistance, was the leader of a *majority* in the fight for Indian independence, King of a *minority;* this fact, important in an analysis of power, may be the decisive one in determining whether King can achieve a transformation of American society as deep and real as the Gandhian victory in India. The willingness of an oppressed people to protest and suffer, passively or assertively, without bitterness or with "love for the oppressors" seems to have influence only where the conscience of the majority of the society can be reached. In Hitler's Germany the Jews suffered nonviolently without stirring Nazi repentance; the early Christians who were eaten by lions seem to have stimulated not guilt but greed in the watching multitudes. King's strategy depends therefore for its success not only upon the presence of flagrant cruelty in a society but also upon the inherent good will, the latent conscience of the majority of the

American people, as Gandhi's did upon the British commitment to justice.

In a situation of benign intransigence—like New York City— or a society of gentlemen—North Carolina, for example—a philosophy of love for the oppressor may be less effective than in Alabama. There Negroes do not face overt cruelty but rather the refusal to alter their status. What do you do in a situation in which you have laws on your side, where whites smile and say to you that they are your friends, but where your white "friends" move to the suburbs leaving you confronted with segregation and inferior education in schools, ghetto housing, and a quiet and tacit discrimination in jobs? How can you demonstrate a philosophy of love in response to this? What is the appropriate form of protest? One can "sit-in" in the Board of Education building, and not a single child will come back from the suburbs or from the private and parochial schools. One can link arms with the Mayor of Boston and march on the Commons, but it will not affect the housing conditions of Negroes in Roxbury. One can be hailed justifiably as a Nobel Prize hero by the Mayor of New York City, but this will not in itself change a single aspect of the total pattern of pathology which dominates the lives of the prisoners of the ghettos of New York.

Two recent major developments in regard to SCLC and Martin Luther King, Jr., have contributed to our understanding of their role in the civil rights movement. First, King spoke out against the United States policy in Viet-Nam. His pronouncements on America's role in Viet-Nam precipitated public disagreement from other major civil rights leaders, such as Roy Wilkins, Whitney Young, Jr., and, unexpectedly, even James Farmer. He was the first civil rights leader since Du Bois in World War I to attempt to tie civil rights goals with the broader problems of international affairs. The early Du Bois (in contrast to the later Du Bois who, in disillusionment about the possibility of justice for the Negro in America, turned to communism and eventually migrated to Africa) spoke out in support of America's foreign policy and war effort. King had violated, probably quite deliberately, the tacit agreement among leaders of the civil rights movement that this movement must not only remain politically nonpartisan but also must not confuse its methods, goals, and ideology with other controversial domestic, but particularly foreign policy, issues.

The second recent major development in King's career as a civil rights leader involved his decision to concentrate on Chicago as a base of operation for attacking the basic problems of ghetto living for the Negro in America's urban centers. This decision can be understood only in terms of King's and SCLC's growing recognition of the fact that the civil rights struggle can no longer restrict itself to the techniques of litigation, legislation, and demonstrations and their appropriate goals but must now explore and develop techniques for change in the lives of the masses of Negroes in the slums and ghettos.

The risks inherent in this decision are real. King and his top staff and advisers must have decided to accept the risks of the possibilities of failure and the resulting loss of prestige. The problems of the Negro in urban ghettos are complicated by the role of white and Negro political power and machines and the deep, often obscure, related problems of financial and real estate power, and by the competition among the various ethnic groups for status and political and economic control.

The success of Martin Luther King's new venture will depend upon whether he is able to use his personal charisma as the basis for the creation and development of techniques appropriate to these special problems.

The Student Nonviolent Coordinating Committee

The rise of the Student Nonviolent Coordinating Committee intensified and sharpened the dramatic confrontation begun by CORE in the 1940's and developed by Martin Luther King, Jr., in the late 1950's. The restless young students who originally led the movement used direct assertive defiance and resistance, nonviolent in tactic and yet militant in spirit. They had gone beyond the quiet, stubborn, passive resistance of the bus boycott in Montgomery to a new stage of challenge—no less stubborn but considerably less passive. The first demonstrations in Greensboro, North Carolina, and Nashville, Tennessee, were appropriately in college towns. It was as a result of these that the Student Nonviolent Coordinating Committee was formed.[5] SNCC was organized in April 1960 at a meeting at Shaw University in Raleigh, North Carolina. It took as its original function the coordination of the protest work of the many student groups conducting sit-ins.[6]

This program, representing the impatience of a younger generation, came at a time when more established civil rights groups seemed ready to settle for post-Little Rock tokenism and moderation. During the years since 1954 and up to that time, the letter and spirit of the Brown decision had been effectively eroded. "All deliberate speed" had been translated into "any perceptible movement," or mere verbalization of movement. The presence of a single Negro child in a previously white school was considered a famous victory. But the SNCC "kids" in their worn denims brought new verve, drive, daring, and enthusiasm—as well as the brashness and chaos of youth—to sustain the dynamism of direct-action civil rights tactics. They propelled more orderly and stable groups like the NAACP and Urban League toward increasing acceptance of direct-action methods not only because some of the older leaders found the ardor of youth contagious but also because, after the manner of experienced leaders, they sensed that bolder programs would be necessary if their own role were not to be undermined. The intervention of youth revitalized CORE and sustained the intensity of the direct involvement of King and SCLC. It has helped make possible—indeed it may have played a vital part in—the continuation of King's role as charismatic leader by arousing weary and apathetic Negroes to the imminence of justice, thereby stimulating an atmosphere sympathetic to crusade and sacrifice.

The SNCC uniform of blue denims and the manner of defiance were far removed from the neat white shirt and tie and Ivy League jacket of Urban League workers and the courteous, Biblical eloquence of King. After SNCC's initial stage of urban protest, it decided to move into the deep South and consciously attempted to express through dress, manner, and method a direct identification with working-class Southern Negroes. Nonetheless, many of the SNCC leaders were actually even closer than the SCLC, NAACP, and Urban League leadership to sophisticated Northern campuses where militance previously had been less action-oriented than intellectual.

SNCC seems restless with long-term negotiation and the methods of persuasion of the Urban League, and it assumes that the legislative and litigation approach of the NAACP has practically attained its goals. SNCC has not overtly repudiated King's philosophy of nonviolence, but it does not root its own acceptance of this strategy in love of the enemy. Rather SNCC leaders seem almost nationalistic in spirit, in the sense of pride that they hold, not so much in *being* black (an appreciable number of SNCC workers are white) as in their conviction that justice and the future are on their side. SNCC welcomes dedicated whites and others who presumably share its concern for total justice. The style and manner of the SNCC leaders and workers are not consistent with any overt display of gratitude even to those whites who share their dangers and daily risks. The underlying assumption of the SNCC approach appears to be that the struggle for political and social democracy in the South is the responsibility of all Americans. They approach their programs and tasks with pride, courage, and flexibility and with an absence of sentimentality which those seeking gratitude or deference might view as disdain. They do not seem to be so concerned with the careful political screening of co-workers and exclusion of "radicals" as are the more experienced and "respectable" civil rights organizations. But it would be a mistake to interpret the SNCC style and method of challenge to the racial hypocrisies of the South as evidence of "left-wing" or Communist domination. SNCC is flexible and inclusive—not doctrinaire and dogmatic. Being loosely organized, SNCC has practically no hierarchy or clear lines of authority. The discipline of its workers seems to be determined by each individual's identification with the "cause" and the direct confrontation approach rather than by external controls or organizational structure.

Instead of a single leader, SNCC has many "leaders." Nominally, John Lewis is president of the Board of Directors and James Forman is executive director of SNCC. Actual "policy" and "operational" leadership is not only shared by Lewis and Forman but must be shared with others. Robert Moses, who plays a key role in the SNCC leadership team, directed the activities of the Council of Federated Organizations (COFO) in Mississippi during the summer of 1964. The individuals who coordinate SNCC activities for such Southern states as Georgia, Louisiana, and South Carolina also insist upon being heard in the leadership councils of SNCC. So far no single personality has emerged to speak for SNCC. John Lewis and Bob Moses seem deceptively retiring and soft-spoken in manner, but each is doggedly determined, assertive, and courageous in pursuit of the goals of unqualified equality. James Forman and Donald Harris, formerly SNCC coordinator in Georgia, are more overtly assertive and articulate but are no less likely to assume personal risks. The essence of SNCC leadership appears to be this willingness to assume personal risks, to expose oneself to imprisonment and brutality, and thereby to dramatize the nature of American racism before the nation and the world. Its members play the important role of commando raiders on the more dangerous and exposed fronts of the present racial struggle. This is not to be understood as mere adolescent bravado or defiance. It must be understood as an insistence upon total honesty, unwillingness to settle for anything less than uncompromised equality. It is an impatience with the verbalizations and euphemisms of "the accommodations" of more "realistic" or "strategic" leaders and organizations. This stance could be and has been described as "unrealistic" and "radical."

The fast pace of developments in the civil rights movement is again illustrated by the fact that a major development in the ranks of SNCC has recently highlighted the depth of its "more radical" stance. John Lewis, president of the SNCC Board of Directors, announced publicly that young Negroes and whites involved in the civil rights movement should seek alternatives to the draft and military service in Viet-Nam. This stand was taken with the concurrence of the major SNCC leadership. Julian Bond, director of public relations for SNCC and recently elected to the Georgia State Legislature, stated his general agreement with Lewis' position in a press and television interview. The members of the Georgia State Legislature thereupon voted to deny him his seat. This matter is now before the Federal Courts. Aside from the constitutional issues and the question of justice or injustice of a state legislature's decision to seat or not to seat a duly elected official on the basis of his opinions and public statements, the Julian Bond incident suggests the following important points concerning the nature of SNCC and its role in the civil rights movement:

1. SNCC, like SCLC and Martin Luther King, Jr., has insisted upon broadening the civil rights movement to include the previously taboo area of public statements on international affairs.

2. The fact and the publicity associated with a luncheon held for Bond by some of the African delegates to the United Nations soon after his rejection by the Georgia State Legislature reinforced the reality of the convergence of the American civil rights struggle with America's image in Africa and Asia. Whether or not the direct involvement of African delegates in this emotionally tinged domestic civil rights incident was diplomatically proper remains a question.

3. The Julian Bond incident clearly demonstrates the extent to which SNCC and its leaders have breached the general agreement among civil rights leaders and organizations not to invade directly the arena of partisan politics. The organization of the political machinery among Negroes necessary for the election of members of the legislature is a logical extension of the activities of SNCC in

increasing the number of registered Negro voters in Southern states and in the organization of the Freedom Democratic party in Mississippi. This might be one of the most significant new developments in this most recent stage of the civil rights struggle.

A Variety of Methods, the Same General Goals, and Contemporary Relevance

There are obvious and subtle problems in any social movement when a variety of organizations with different philosophies, strategies, tactics, organizational structure, and leadership all seek the same broad goals. All civil rights organizations are committed to full inclusion of the Negro in the economic and political life of America, without restrictions based on race or color. But each differs from the other in its conception of how this commitment can best be fulfilled.

There is general agreement that the successes of the civil rights movement and organizations have catapulted the civil rights struggle into a new stage with more complex and difficult problems and goals. Martin Luther King, Jr., in an interview with this observer which included other civil rights leaders, sought to verbalize this growing awareness of the fact that the civil rights movement must now address itself to the problem of bringing about observable changes in the actual living conditions of the masses of Negroes. He said:

Well, aren't we saying, gentlemen, that a program has not yet been worked out to grapple with the magnitude of this problem in the United States, both North and South? Isn't there a need now, because of the urgency and the seriousness of the situation, to develop a sort of crash program to lift the standards of the Negro and to get rid of the underlying conditions that produce so many social evils and develop so many social problems?

I think this is what we face at this time, and I know it leads to the whole question of discrimination in reverse, and all of that. But I think we've got to face the fact in this country, that because of the legacy of slavery and segregation, and the seeds of injustice planted in the past, we have this harvest of confusion now, and we're going to continue to have it until we get to the root of the problem.[7]

The disturbing question which must be faced is whether or not the present civil rights organizations are equipped in terms of perspective, staff, and organizational structure to deal effectively with the present level of civil rights problems. And, if not, whether they are flexible enough to make the necessary changes in order to be relevant.

An examination of some of the concrete deficiencies in the organizations themselves shows that the NAACP and Urban League are under the handicap of experience. Committed to a method and a goal, they have not altered either in major ways since their founding. The sweep of the civil rights movement in the past two decades has not significantly affected these two elders of the movement. They still appear to function primarily in terms of personal leadership rather than staff competence. An exception is the expansion of the NAACP's legal and educational fund staff, which still remains largely legal and pays little attention to education. A serious analysis of the way in which the NAACP has attempted to modify its structure to meet the current civil rights struggle would force one to conclude that it has done so to a minimal degree. For example, the staff concerned with the problems of housing is, practically speaking, nonexistent. As of June 1965, and for the previous two years, the position of housing secretary was unfilled. The NAACP staff concerned with labor consists of a director and a secretary. This is true also for education. The staff responsible for public relations, promotion, and propaganda has increased from five to seven persons within the past crucial decade of civil rights activity. These facts suggest that the NAACP has made virtually no organizational response to meet the present increased civil rights demands. The local branches are archaic and generally ineffective, with barely adequate communication and coordination of policy and procedures between the national organization and the local branches. Probably the NAACP's most glaring inadequacy in light of the present and future demands of the civil rights revolution is the lack of a fact-gathering and research staff.

The Urban League seems more modern and efficient in its fund raising, promotion, and public relations and in its relationship with its local groups. It also, however, seems weak in research.

One could speculate that this weakness—which is shared by the newer organizations as well—reflects the difficulty of moving from reliance on personal leadership to the more demanding, less dramatic, less ego-satisfying but imperative staff approach. Now that the maximum gains have been obtained through legislation, litigation, and appeals to conscience, the difficult problem of implementation, of translating these gains into actual changes in the lives of

Negroes, remains. This cannot be achieved by charisma alone. It requires adequate and efficient staffs, working, of course, under inspired and creative leadership.

In spite of these objective limitations, the NAACP and the Urban League are flourishing. In 1962, the NAACP was said to have a membership of 370,000 in 1,200 local branches in forty-four states and the District of Columbia.[8] By the end of 1964, its membership was given as 455,839 in 1,845 branches in forty-eight states and the District of Columbia. An unaudited budget indicates that income for 1964 was $1,116,565.68.

The picture for the Urban League is even more dramatic. Until Whitney Young became executive director of the organization in 1961, the largest fund-raising total in any one year was $325,000. In 1962, contributions were $700,000; in 1963, $1,441,000; and in 1964, $1,650,000. Of particular note is the fact that, prior to 1962, no corporate body had made a contribution of more than $5,000 to the Urban League. In 1964, several donations of $50,000 were received from corporations, and foundations have given as much as $150,000. These impressive accretions are, no doubt, a testament not only to the skill and eloquence of Young but also, as in the case of the NAACP's growth, to the dynamic momentum and strength of the entire civil rights movement. The success of both might be a reflection, at least in part, also of their relative respectability.

CORE's chief deficiencies are its weak organizational structure, the fact that its executive does not have sufficient power, and the problem that it has seemed at various times to be endangered by lack of discipline. However weak in discipline, it is nevertheless strong in enthusiasm and dedication among its members and its locals. It appears to be weak also in its fiscal arrangements, its fund-raising and systematic promotion. CORE is in serious financial difficulties. There is a serious question whether CORE's lack of organizational discipline and structure is an asset or liability in terms of the flexibility necessary for it to be relevant to the present civil rights problems.

Behind SCLC's inspiring reality lie some very real difficulties, many of them quite human. Financially, however, it seems strong; it seems relatively easy for SCLC, through King, to attract a majority of the nonselective contributions to the civil rights movement, despite the minimal organization of SCLC itself. It is reasonable to conclude that if King were not its leader there would be no SCLC. Indeed, it is difficult to understand the role of SCLC's Board of

Directors. It and the organization seem to be dominated by the magnetic appeal of King, by the personal loyalty and reverence of his top aides and of the masses who respond to his leadership. It is reasonable to assume that most of those who respond most enthusiastically to King's and SCLC's leadership are not members of his organization. The burdens of this special type of personal leadership are great if not intolerable. Probably the most desperate need of King and SCLC is for an effective supporting working staff to provide King with the type of background information and program planning which are necessary if this organization is to be relevant and if the type of leadership held by King is to continue to be effective.

SNCC is probably the least organized of all the civil rights organizations, suggesting that the degree of organization is not necessarily related to effectiveness or to the appearance of effectiveness.

As movements become more structured, they fall prey to the problems that plague most organizations, namely, red tape, bureaucracy, hierarchical discipline restricting spontaneous and imaginative experimentation, fear of change and, therefore, of growth. In large industrial, economic, financial, and governmental bureaucracies, and in political parties, major decisions are not personal, in spite of the existence of a charismatic leader. Similarly in the civil rights movement, major decisions must now reflect painstaking, difficult staff work based on fact-finding, intelligence, continuing critical analyses of data and strategies. Institutions tend to repress the rebel and to elevate the businessman-diplomat, yet the civil rights movement is full of rebels and its goal is independence. It is possible that the vitality of all of the civil rights organizations will depend on sustaining certain respectable organizations like the NAACP and the Urban League while stimulating them to pursue new programs and encouraging the fluid realignment of younger, more restless forces from whom the momentum for change must certainly come.

Who Speaks for the Negro?

It would be understandable to succumb to the temptation to rank the civil rights organizations in terms of their degree of militance and effectiveness. And it has been argued persuasively that for maximum effectiveness the civil rights organizations should develop an efficient and disciplined machinery for coordination and genuine cooperation. This tendency and these suggestions, while understandable, would reduce the complexities of the present civil rights movement and the role of the organizations and leaders to a convenient oversimplification. The civil rights problems—the American racial problem—are historically and currently complex and multidimensional. Each approach has some validity and no one now knows which is more valid than others. The ultimate test of a given approach or pattern of approaches will be in the demonstration of observable and sustained changes in the status of Negroes—the evidence that the Negroes are included in all aspects of American life with the equal protection of laws and governmental power. This goal is not likely to be obtained by a single agency, method, or leader. Certain approaches will be more compatible with the temperament of some individuals, Negro and white, than with others.

The civil rights groups vary in organizational efficiency as well as in philosophy, approach, and methods. The rank and file of liberal or religious whites might be more responsive to the seemingly nonthreatening, Christian approach of Martin Luther King, Jr. More tough-minded and pragmatic business and governmental leaders might find a greater point of contact with the appeals and approaches of the NAACP and the Urban League. The more passionate Negroes and whites who seek immediate and concrete forms of justice will probably gravitate toward CORE and SNCC. Obviously one would not offer financial or other support to an organization whose philosophy and methods made one uncomfortable or threatened one's status. Therefore, while the extent of financial support for a given organization may be seen as an index of the degree of the general acceptability of that organization's approach, it is not necessarily an index of the relevance or effectiveness of its program. One is tempted to hypothesize from these data that the financial success of an organization engaged in the civil rights confrontation is directly related to the *perceived* respectability of the organization and its nominal head. Correlative to this would be the hypothesis that the relative financial success of a civil rights group is inversely related to the *perceived* degree of radicalism of the organization and its nominal head.

The question "Who speaks for the Negro?" is real; perhaps no one group can speak for all Negroes just as no one political party can speak for all citizens of a democracy or no one religion can satisfy the needs of all individuals. The variety of organizations and "leaders" among Negroes may be viewed as a sign of democracy, health, and the present strength of the movement rather than as a symptom of weakness. This variety and loose coordination can help revitalize each through dynamic competition. Each organization influences the momentum and pace of the others. The inevitable interaction among them demands from each a level of effectiveness and relevance above the minimum possible for any single organization.

As Roy Wilkins said in response to a question from this observer:

We cannot promise you . . . that there will be a co-ordinated, organized, structural, formalized attack on these matters and that each will be apportioned a part of this task. But we will say this: like Martin (Luther King, Jr.) said, there is more unity than there ever has been before, there's more division of work, and there's more co-ordination and backing up of each other than there has been before. Maybe in 1975, or some other time, there will come an over-all organization, but no other group has managed that, and why should we?[9]

Direct observation and analysis of relevant data and events lead to the conclusion that the stresses and strains within the civil rights movement and within and among the various organizations are real and cannot be denied; and a great deal of energy is expended in preventing these difficulties from becoming overt and thus destroying the public image of unity. But these problems can be seen as symptoms of the irresistible strength of the civil rights movement rather than as signs of inherent flaws or fatal weaknesses of the organizations and their leaders. Furthermore, the power and the momentum of the movement itself seem able to compensate for the present deficiencies in the organizations and leadership. Probably, and paradoxically, the clearest indication of the solidity and rapidity of movement toward the goal of unqualified rights for America's Negro citizens is the fact that civil rights agencies not only have mobilized and organized some of the latent power of committed whites and Negroes necessary for social change, but, in so doing, have now achieved sufficient strength to risk the beginnings of public debate over philosophy, strategy, and tactics. The lie which supports racism is being supplanted by more forthright dialogue and honest confrontation between whites and Negroes, among various classes of Negroes, between Negro "leaders" and their white and Negro co-workers, and within the civil rights movement itself.

REFERENCES

1. For a thoughtful discussion of the Negro revolt, see Lerone Bennett, Jr., *Confrontation: Black and White* (Chicago, 1965).

2. E. Franklin Frazier, *The Negro in the United States* (rev. ed.; New York, 1957), pp. 524-525.

3. Louis Lomax, *The Negro Revolt* (New York, 1963), p. 145.

4. James Peck, *Freedom Ride* (New York, 1962), *passim.*

5. For an excellent study of SNCC, see Howard Zinn, *SNCC, The New Abolitionists* (Boston, 1964).

6. W. Haywood Burns, *The Voices of Negro Protest in America* (London, 1963), p. 44.

7. Kenneth Clark, Roy Wilkins, Whitney Young, Jr., James Farmer, Martin Luther King, Jr., and James Forman, "The Management of the Civil-Rights Struggle," in Alan F. Westin (ed.), *Freedom Now! The Civil Rights Struggle in America* (New York, 1964).

8. W. Haywood Burns, *op. cit.*, p. 19.

9. Kenneth Clark, *et al.*, in Alan F. Westin (ed.), *op. cit.*

RUPERT EMERSON AND MARTIN KILSON

The American Dilemma in a Changing World: The Rise of Africa and the Negro American

FROM GREAT wars come unexpected consequences—certainly consequences unforeseen, and usually undesired, by those responsible for shaping the policies which led to war. Of such consequences none is more striking or more profound in its implications than the change in the relationship between the races that has come in the aftermath of World War II, bearing out the prophetic dictum of W. E. B. Du Bois at the turn of the century that "The problem of the twentieth century is the problem of the color line—the relation of the darker to the lighter races of man in Asia and Africa, in America and the islands of the sea."[1] The peoples of Asia and Africa have risen to demand their own independent and equal position in the world society, and in their revolt against the old order of colonialism they have been joined by the refusal of the Negro American to linger at some halfway point between slavery and freedom. In particular, the relations of Africa and America, of Africans and Americans, always difficult and ambivalent, have taken on new dimensions, some calculable and others lending themselves to no more than an appreciation of general magnitude. The determination of cause and effect and of interconnections on the two sides of the Atlantic, and of the Pacific as well, will occupy the historians far into the future.

The immense impact of the Second World War inevitably had its effect upon the social structure of the United States, and in no sphere more significantly than in Negro-white relations. The ramifications of the attack upon the established patterns of segregation and discrimination are asserting themselves today in a manner that few could have predicted twenty years ago. Perhaps most significant of all, what had been a domestic problem of the United States has become part of a global problem, inextricably entangled with the destiny of other peoples and continents and profoundly affecting America's standing in the world.[2]

The Negro American has played a role in the stimulation and shaping of African nationalism, and the mere existence of the newly sovereign African states, now constituting a quarter of the membership of the United Nations, has changed the nature of the American scene. The restructuring of American race relationships is taking place within a new framework deriving from international situations generated in good part by World War II. The principal elements involved are America's status as a superpower whose interests reach to every corner of a shrinking world and whose actions affect every people, no matter how remote; the coming of the Cold War and the global confrontation with Communism; and the debut of problems of race and color on the international stage consequent upon the rise of postwar Asian and African nationalism.

The high expectations among Negro Americans that the post-World War II era would bring change had their counterpart at the close of World War I, but with the all-important difference that the world was not then watching what was going on in the United States nor were Americans so much concerned with world opinion. American race relations were essentially a matter of parochial concern, interesting relatively few outside this country. Today Negro agitation and the way in which it is handled by the United States, both nationally and locally, is a matter of crucial concern not only to heads of state around the world but also to many millions of people in many countries. What they think of American intentions and of the way in which the civil rights struggle is handled, brought to them in stories on the air and in the press and in appalling pictures, is a matter which Americans can ignore only at their peril. The one world of political unity and peace among men which many hoped would emerge from World War II failed to materialize, but the globe has unquestionably closed in on all its inhabitants. The United States can no longer live unto itself, nor can Asia and Africa be seen, or see themselves, as isolated continents: we have all become integral parts of a single field of interaction embracing all mankind. Certainly no one can contend that the American pattern of racial discrimination was any more morally defensible after the First World War than after the Second, but what the rest of the world was then prepared to tolerate indifferently has now become internationally intolerable. This revolutionary change in the world's climate has imposed upon American political leaders the necessity of taking speedy and radical action in a sphere in which they could formerly delay action from year to year and decade to decade.

With full recognition of this unique difference between the two eras, it is useful to survey what happened in the United States in the aftermath of World War I. The small group of Negro intellectuals and professionals that had emerged before 1914, the new body of skilled Negro laborers produced during the war, and the thousands of Negro servicemen who for the first time saw foreign lands and ways were all hopeful that the war's impact would favorably alter American race relations. Thus in 1918, Du Bois, the ablest spokesman for the Negroes at this period, reflected this hope in the editorial pages of *The Crisis*, the official organ of the NAACP:

This war is an End and, also, a Beginning. Never again will darker people of the world occupy just the place they had before. Out of this war will rise, soon or late, an independent China, a self-governing India, an Egypt with representative institutions, an Africa for the Africans, and not merely for business exploitation. Out of this war will rise, too, an American Negro with the right to vote and the right to work and the right to live without insult.[3]

Du Bois saw rightly what the future was to bring, but it was to come to realization late rather than soon. The Wilsonian call for self-determination and a world safe for democracy was applied neither to the vast colonial sphere nor to the Negro American. The international circumstances which have aided the Negro to breach the ramparts of segregation and discrimination in the last years were virtually non-existent in the interwar decades. The League of Nations was in operation but, save for the Mandates, it paid no attention to the colonial problem, and the later concern for human rights was essentially beyond its purview.

In the United States the expectations of Negroes were shattered by organized white violence, abetted by the inertia or indifference of our national institutions, both governmental and private. In the so-called "red summer" of 1919 ("red" because Negro blood was spilled at the hands of white mobs) such anti-Negro riots as those in Chicago, East St. Louis, Omaha, Washington, D. C., Longview, Texas, and elsewhere were unmistakable signs that whatever the progressive impact of World War I may have been in other parts of the world, its meaning would be denied the Negro American.

This white reaction was a particularly hard blow to the NAACP, whose leaders' faith in American democracy was tried nearly to the breaking point. A great effort was made to obtain federal action to end lynching. In 1922 an NAACP anti-lynching advertisement proclaimed that it was "The shame of America—that the United States is the *Only Land on Earth* where human beings are BURNED AT THE STAKE. In Four years 1918-1921, Twenty-Eight People were Publically BURNED BY AMERICAN MOBS."[4] Basic as the purpose of the NAACP's anti-lynching program was to the fulfillment of American democracy, no such legislation was ever enacted by Congress; nor was the United States internationally pilloried in shame then as it has been more recently.

The even greater Negro expectations for a new deal in the post-World War II period were similarly met at the outset by white violence in innumerable cities and towns. This violence, often directed against Negro ex-servicemen, also sought to cow the Negro, who had been immensely stirred by the war, into passive acceptance of his lot. While the anti-Negro violence that followed World War I largely succeeded in its purpose, the violence at the end of and after World War II was doomed to failure. Why was this so? The reasons are many, and such domestic changes as the increasing concern of our national institutions and the slow but clear assumption by the white upper classes of their proper responsibility in the racial sphere will, in the final reckoning, be given much importance. These changes did not come of themselves.

They became possible in part because the international situation after 1945 provided a new climate of *political necessity*, within which our national institutions, as they relate to the Negro, were given new opportunity (and possibly their last) to fulfill the aims, purposes, and hopes which had inspired the Founding Fathers. Necessity, we suspect, is as much the mother of institutional as it is of technological-scientific innovation. The domination of the world by the Western European white man and his descendants overseas, belatedly joined by the Japanese, was speedily drawing to a close, and the United States was forced to adapt itself to a fundamentally changed international environment. As Harold R. Isaacs has put it,

The downfall of the white-supremacy system in the rest of the world made its survival in the United States suddenly and painfully conspicuous. It became our most exposed feature and in the swift unfolding of the world's affairs, our most vulnerable weakness . . . when hundreds of millions of people all around looked in our direction, it seemed to be all that they could see.[5]

Although the outburst of Asian and African nationalism after World War II was the primary element involved in the great transformation, the racial issue had been simmering internationally for a long time. Japan had already done its utmost to make use of it in the effort to discredit the United States and to subjugate Asia.[6] This undoubtedly predisposed Asians to emphasize the racial element in their postwar response to Western dominance, even though they repudiated Japan's version of Asia for the Asians. Equally influencing this response was the West's own assumption that its hegemony represented, *inter alia,* the natural subordination of "lower" to "higher" races. Shortly after the commencement of the Cold War, Nehru, speaking at a private meeting with Negro and white American civil rights leaders which was organized at his request by Ralph J. Bunche and Walter White, gave the following account of the racial factor in Asian perception of the West:

Whenever I warn against acceptance of Soviet promises of equality because they are so frequently broken, I am answered quite often by questions about America's attitude toward dark-skinned people. The people of Asia don't like colonialism or race prejudices. They resent condescension. When Americans talk to them about equality and freedom, they remember stories about lynchings. They are becoming increasingly aware that colonialism is largely based on color—and, for the first time in the lives of many of them, they realize that they are colored. With what is happening to the dark-skinned native population of South Africa at the hands of Malan and what the French are doing in Indochina our people are developing a sense of sympathy and unity with dark-skinned victims of exploitation all over the world.[7]

African nationalism, of course, was even more engulfed with matters of race in its postwar encounter with the West. Colonial rule in Africa was explicitly associated with ideas regarding the inferiority of black or Negro peoples, which were also an explicit part of American racism, and offered the Communists a magnificent weapon with which to attack the Western, and especially the American, response to African nationalism.

The Communist claim to be free of the racism characteristic of American society has been belied by several incidents of discrimination and even violence against African students in Soviet bloc countries, but the Communists have made good use for their purposes of the sins of the United States and of colonialism, including the crises of white-dominated southern Africa and such Congolese problems as the use of white mercenaries. To lay great stress on the Communist role is, however, to miss the fundamental realities of the situation. There is indeed no reason to think that events or attitudes would have been markedly different if no Communists had existed. Both colonialism and racism spoke for themselves, and no Communists were needed to point out the moral of the widely circulated pictures and stories concerning the shocking inhumanity which has accompanied the desegregation drive in the United States.

The Emergence of Asian and African States

The heart of our theme is not the Cold War nor the success or failure of the Communists in stirring up trouble and capitalizing on the sins and errors of the West. These are matters which are on the fringe of the great postwar development which challenged the white control of the world and brought into being a host of new states almost wholly inhabited by people of color. The membership of the United Nations is only one indicator of the change, but a striking one. At the end of 1945 the U.N. had fifty-one members, of which six were located in the Middle East, four in Africa (including Egypt), and three in Asia. Twenty years later the total had soared to one hundred fifteen, among which the Africans numbered thirty-six, the Asians fifteen, and the Middle East eleven.

A new world of states has come into being, and it will be long before we fully discern its meaning and adapt ourselves to the complexities and new modes of action which are called for, but it is evident that it has already had a great effect on the American domestic scene.

A few basic facts stand in sharp relief. To state the matter in its largest and most neutral terms, the massive emergence of Asia and Africa from colonialism is juxtaposed and coincides in time with the attack upon the segregated and inferior position of the Negro in the United States. The two are separate developments and yet intimately and intricately interrelated. At another level of discourse, the American stance in world affairs has inevitably been affected by the revolutionary changes taking place in Asia and Africa, and these changes have been in varying degree influenced by American attitudes, policies, and activities. The traditional anti-colonial outlook of the United States, however much it may have been muted as an active force in recent years, played its part in creating the contemporary climate of anti-colonialism which facilitated the growth of nationalist movements. American diplomacy both within and without the United Nations has had to take into consideration the multiplicity of new states which open a wide range of new opportunities and of new uncertainties and insecurities. For the 20,000,000 Americans of African or partial African descent a new avenue of experience, perhaps of vital import, emerged when the continent of their origin burst forth in an unprecedented luxuriance of sovereign states, with more still to come.

No more than a most summary review need be attempted here of what the United States has done, and has not done, in relation to Africa. Since the record is an irregular and sometimes internally contradictory one, there is wide disagreement about where the emphasis should be placed. American policy has constantly tended toward a middle course. As a result, the swings to this side and that, could they be charted, might be reduced to a middle line which would have a large measure of consistency; but anyone who so chooses can stress the zigs or the zags and the opposing courses which they represent. Even though the United States may be said to have adhered quite closely to a moderate and responsible position, the partisans of none of the several camps which are involved, including Americans with strong views of any sort, are likely to be much pleased with it. The past and present colonial powers and South Africa tend to see the United States as meddling in their affairs, irresponsibly encouraging the anti-colonialists and nationalists, while the more militant Africans see America at best as a lukewarm supporter of their cause and at worst as an ally and supplier of the colonial powers and South Africa, and as itself a major practioner of neo-colonialism. The widespread African good will on which America could earlier count has receded sharply in recent years. American endorsement of Tshombe's return to the Congo in 1964 and participation with Belgium in the paratroop drop on Stanleyville—which was launched from a British island-base—produced bitter hostility in many African quarters.

For nearly a century starting with the Civil War the American connection with Africa was very limited, the controlling circumstance for most of the period being European colonial domination of the continent. The assumption that Africa was inhabited by primitive peoples who had barely made a start toward civilization rendered all the more tempting the inclination to abstain from concern with the continent. This assumption was primarily responsible also for the widespread tendency of the Negro American to look down on Africa and to be wary of identifying himself with what were reputed to be the black savages across the sea. World War II brought about a new awareness of Africa, politically, economically, and strategically, but it also enhanced the strength of the American bonds to the colonial powers. The onset of the Cold War rendered any change in the status quo suspect of being of possible benefit to the enemy, and the acceptance of anti-Communism as the dominant theme in American foreign policy was, as the Africans and many Americans saw it, an undesirable and irritating substitute for the direct sponsorship of independence and development.

In the 1950's, the decisive decade for Africa, the United States was more a follower than a leader. The independence of Tunisia, Morocco, the Sudan, the Gold Coast, and Guinea between 1956 and 1958, followed by a stream of other countries, forced an almost total recasting of American relations with Africa. The sedate and measured tread which the United States envisioned for an ultimate African advance to the right of self-determination for those mature enough for independence was outpaced not only by the passionate determination of African leaders to be rid of colonialism but also by the actual rush of events accepted, and even abetted, by Britain, France, and Belgium. Washington was confronted by the necessity to make its peace with the African nationalists and with the multitude of new African states.

Without wholly discarding the caution which had characterized American policy, the United States made some drastic changes. The few consulates which had existed in some of the African colonies were now hastily replaced by an embassy in each of the new countries, equipped in the modern style with aid, information, and other services. At home a change of marked significance in the State Department was a gradual curtailing of the control over Africa of the European desks, culminating in 1958 in the appointment of an Assistant Secretary of State for African Affairs heading an autonomous African Bureau. The number of people dealing with Africa at home and abroad had to be increased dramatically, but a distressingly weak point was the failure to multiply adequately the number of Negroes above the menial and minor clerical level in the Department and the several categories of the Foreign Service.[8] With only one Negro in the corps of Foreign Service Officers before 1950, the various urgent calls for the enrollment of Negroes in the Department and abroad, whether in the newly opened African posts or elsewhere, have still not achieved satisfactory results. The first major postwar changes in this sphere came through a few spectacular appointments of Negroes as consultants and alternate delegates to the United States delegation at the United Nations. In the immediate postwar years these included Du Bois, Walter White, and Channing Tobias, all closely associated with the NAACP; and the Eisenhower administration made similar appointments, including two Negro women as alternate delegates.

It remained for the Kennedy administration to initiate a new approach to this problem. In August 1961, at a conference on equality of opportunity in the Department of State, attended by leading Negroes, the Secretary of State, Dean Rusk, explained the context of the administration's thinking as follows:

The biggest single burden that we carry on our backs in our foreign relations in the 1960's is the problem of racial discrimination here at home. There is just no question about it.

We are dealing with forty or fifty new countries that have become independent since 1945, and we are living through a decade of readjustment of the relationships between Western Europe and the rest of the world—a decade when the white race and the nonwhite races have got to re-examine and readjust their traditional relationships.

Our attitude on a question of this sort is of fundamental importance to the success of the foreign policy of the United States.

Although this conference made strong recommendations that the number of Negroes in the upper ranks should be increased through promotion from below and through lateral transfer to the Foreign Service Officer Corps from related services, the results have been disappointing. A major reason for the relative failure of the campaign to draw in more Negroes is undoubtedly the inadequacy of education in Negro colleges and universities, which leads to a low level of success on the Foreign Service examinations; but a more aggressive and inventive attack on the problem should have been able to produce better results. In any case, in 1964, of the 10,987 persons at a professional level in the Department of State and the three categories of the Foreign Service, including the Reserve and the Staff Corps, only 205 were Negroes. Of these 21 were counted among the 3,698 Foreign Service Officers proper, including three with the rank of ambassador. In the two decades since the end of World War II, a round dozen Negroes have been assigned to ambassadorial posts, several in Africa but increasingly in other countries as well, including Norway, Finland, Luxemburg, and Syria, and also as American representative to the U.N. Economic and Social Council. The way in which the process has been speeded up is indicated by the fact that in midsummer 1965 five Negroes were simultaneously serving or had been named as ambassadors, two of them appointed in the present year by President Johnson.

A much debated and still unanswered question, given increased urgency by the emergence of the new Asian and African states, concerns the desirability of sending Negro ambassadors and other high-ranking personnel to posts abroad. It is necessary to consider whether Africans are pleased to see one of their own people, so to speak, coming to represent the United States, or whether they feel that they are securing only second-rate representation, lacking influence in Washington, since Negroes are disfavored at home. The goal here as elsewhere is surely that members of the Foreign Service and others should be appointed to diplomatic posts regardless of color and on the basis of their ability, seniority, and the kind of contribution they can be expected to make. A precondition for the realization of this goal is that the number of qualified Negroes available for such appointments be greatly expanded; otherwise special consideration must inevitably be accorded the few Negroes who can be called upon. The rise of the new countries has called attention to the shortcomings in the racial balance of America's diplomatic personnel, but it is evident that the attainment of an appropriate number of qualified Negroes cannot be expected without a fundamental improvement in the position of the mass of the Negroes in American society. Although the traditional policy of indifference has been discarded, much remains to be done.

The same moral—that no truly satisfactory answer can be found short of a basic change in the status of the Negro in America—attaches to the reverse side of the coin, the appearance in this country of a number of Asian and African diplomats and visitors of many sorts, including a greatly expanded contingent of students. To put the matter in its crudest terms a society in which segregation and discrimination continued to be, in varying degree, a standard feature was suddenly confronted by the need of dealing with a relatively large body of nonwhite emissaries from a variety of countries, who were far from ready to accept being "pushed around" or tolerated as inferiors who should know their place. In point of fact, their inherent demand that they be treated as human beings and as distinguished representatives of their countries was very likely to be coupled with an oversensitivity to anything which was felt to be a slur or insult—a reaction stemming in part from the colonial experience just left behind them. The issue, peculiarly acute in New York and Washington and the much-travelled strip of Maryland lying between the two, was unhappily precisely one of color. *The Washington Post,* editorially chiding Representative Adam Clayton Powell on May 9, 1961, for introducing a bill imposing heavy penalties on any persons who denied business facilities, services, or accommodations to ambassadors, public ministers, and their staffs because of their racial origin, pointed out the sad truth: "The bill seems to assume that foreign envoys travelling in the United States are special objects of discrimination. But the fact is that they suffer discrimination only when they are mistaken for American citizens."

Housing, meals, schools, transportation, recreation—these were all spheres in which rebuffs were likely to be experienced, and apologies after the fact, even when delivered by the President of the United States in person, could not wipe out the incident itself. Nor was it adequate to seek to explain the intricacies of the American federal system and the limited power of the government in Washington to control the attitudes and actions of states, cities, and private persons. Particularly under President Kennedy, in part because of a change in outlook but also because of the extraordinary increase in the number of African states represented in the U.N. and in Washington, very serious efforts were made by the State Department and other agencies and groups to find solutions. No solution was possible, however, unless the American Negro came to be accepted as a person of worth and dignity. The gap between the ideals of which the United States boasted and the social habits which it tolerated was so great as to cast grave doubt on the justification of the American claim to lead the free world; and indignities inflicted upon U.N. delegates and personnel brought demands for a removal of the United Nations from the United States—a United Nations, be it noted, in which the peoples of color played an increasingly decisive role. To maintain its standing in the world the United States had inescapably to deal with the way envoys and others from abroad were treated in American society. In many instances Asians and Africans were not prepared to accept special favors for themselves which were not made equally available to all others: this housing or that social gathering might be opened to Africans of appropriate standing, but were they equally open to colored Americans? Why should the Negro American accept exclusion when the Indian or African was accepted? The ability to escape the consequences of American prejudice by wearing African national dress served only to underline the shoddy nature of the compromise which sustained Jim Crow while evading some of its penalties; and some Africans have refused to avail themselves of the privilege.

Significant headway appears to have been made in dealing with parts of the problems raised by the visitors from the new countries, but no workable or acceptable solution is possible until the racial issue has been settled domestically by ridding American society of segregation and discrimination. What has become inescapably clear is that this is no longer a parochial issue for Americans to settle when they get around to it, but a matter of urgent international importance which gravely affects many aspects of American policy.

Africa and the Negro American

The issues which have just been discussed are, in good part at least, within the realm of the calculable and as such are susceptible of reasonably precise analysis. Another order of discourse is exposed when inquiry turns to the questions of the attitudes of Negro Americans toward Africa and the effect upon them of African independence. Even though exposure to Africa might frequently confirm the conviction of the Negro that he was American rather than African, Africa's liberation has beyond any shadow of doubt helped to liberate the Negro in America as well. Like emancipation from slavery, the breach with colonialism was an indispensable part of the Negro's rise to equality, and its repercussions have been strongly felt on this side of the Atlantic. Two quite different but inter-related propositions are involved. One is that the end of colonialism so changed the balance of forces in the world as to compel the United States to undertake at long last a major attack upon the racial situation at home. Thus James Baldwin, among others, gives primary credit for the civil liberties campaign to the rise of Africa in the context of the Cold War.[9] The other is that the emergence of sovereign states in Africa has changed the Negro American's image of himself and of his place in the world. Israel is not necessarily the homeland of the American Jew nor Africa of the American Negro, but both Jew and Negro have gained in stature from the existence of independent countries created by peoples to whom they have a special relationship. For the Negro in particular it has been a unique and stirring experience to see whole societies and political systems come into existence in which from top to bottom, from president through civil service to office boy, all posts are occupied by black men, not because of the sufferance of white superiors but because it is their sovereign right. In contrast to the Negro's experience of the American society, the control of the new African states and societies is in African hands, and where white expertise is needed it is employed by African governments on African terms.

Africa, in one form or another, has always been a part of the reality of Americans of African descent. The relationship has often been tortuously ambivalent and confused, but given the segregated framework of Negro acculturation to American standards and the influence of white supremacist values, this was not surprising. Nor was it unique to Negro Americans. British and French West Indian Negroes, Brazilian Negroes, and others in the New World had a not dissimilar experience. All have been shaped in their behavior and self-definition by the standards of the politically dominant white populations. Thus the trend among Negro American women at the turn of this century away from forms of African cosmetic standards for treating the hair, which persisted in the American South for centuries, to those of the white women has its counterpart throughout the Caribbean Negro communities, urban Brazil, and, interestingly enough, in urban West Africa.[10] Likewise, the sense of being ashamed of one's black skin, rooted in the Negro American's subordination to white standards and representing the ultimate of self-rejection, has its counterpart in the Caribbean communities and Brazil, and, alas, has not been unknown among acculturated Africans.[11]

The tragedy bequeathed by racist beliefs and practices has in modern times been experienced by no other people, save for the Jews who fell into Hitler's hands, so deeply as by the Negro Americans. Unlike the Portuguese system in Brazil which granted the African slave and his family-unit legal standing, with the result that whole clusters of African culture (language, family organization, religion, and so forth) persist until today, North American slavery, conceiving the slave as chattel—property pure and simple—cut his indigenous organization into shreds. Neither the law, the religion, nor the sense of decency of American slavocracy prevented the separation of husband and wife, mother and child, or tribal kinsmen, as black and white met in the slave-auction market place. Yet not everything African was destroyed among the slaves. An array of persistent Africanisms has been discovered among Negro communities in the rural South,[12] and in the urban South and the urban North, where the Negro's acculturation to American standards was greatest, the Negro subculture maintained a subterranean and private world of rituals, symbols, and motifs, where a bit of Africa persisted through time. In a real sense, however, it was no longer *African*, but *Afro-American*[13]—and more American than African because the ultimate measurement was white America which held the keys to life or death. When this measurement was brought into play, the result was all too often a self-rejection and a rejection of Africa, envisioned as a savage land, but in the Negro's subterranean world sufficent self-value was preserved to make group survival possible.

One aspect of the political significance of these dimensions of the Negro's world is that occasionally the poorer Negro masses and some well-educated Negroes have rallied to the banners of black nationalism.

The greatest movement toward black nationalism has invariably come at moments of high expectations among Negroes that change will occur, on the one hand, and of white America's unwillingness to permit it, on the other. This was precisely the situation after World War I when Marcus Garvey's Universal Negro Improvement Association rallied hundreds of thousands of adherents, and perhaps several million sympathizers, to its black nationalist banner whose aim was to return to Africa. The Garvey Movement never returned any Negroes to Africa, partly because of the inefficiency and corruption of its petty bourgeois, semi-literate leadership, the rock on which most black nationalist political movements in America have foundered and may continue to founder. But it displayed vividly that the Negro's subterranean world possessed enough kinship with Africa to be stirred by a black nationalist defense of her name.[14]

Since the end of the Second World War the black nationalist political response has reappeared, partly as a reflection of the international situations affecting the Negro protest or civil rights movement. The Black Muslims, led by Elijah Muhammad, represent the most articulate of the postwar groups, but a return to Africa is not a part of their program. Unlike the Garvey Movement's hundreds of thousands of adherents and sympathizers, they have little more than 15,000 souls and few keen sympathizers,[15] although they have had a striking influence.

In light of our analysis, this is not surprising. The postwar era has qualitatively altered the response of our national institutions and upper classes to the Negro's quest for equality. Though the intent to move forward is stronger than the actual movement, the Negro has reasonable grounds for expecting bona fide progress. Not only does he expect it, but, unlike any other period since slavery's end, the postwar era has brought all segments of the Negro community, rich and poor, highly educated and semi-literate, into articulate support for equality within the changing American national framework.

Yet the Black Muslims still represent, at the level of the Negro's subterranean world, a force of ultimate significance. This is found in its influence upon the new stage in the Negro's self-definition. This stage, moreover, has been reinforced by the rise of more rational black nationalist conceptions than those represented by the Black Muslims, and all of them have been affected by the debut of African nationalism on the international scene. It exaggerates the facts of the case only slightly to suggest that when Garvey was active the world at large was not listening very intently to him, whereas the murder of even a single dissident Black Muslim leader, Malcolm X, early in 1965 attracted world-wide attention and comment and was seized upon as a vehicle for political propaganda and accusations of various shades and dimensions.

Postwar African nationalism and the establishment of new African states have provided the Negro American his first examples of the black man's full entry into the modern world. Though Liberia, Ethiopia, and Haiti have long been ruled by black or colored men, they were either not effectively in control of blacks or were unhappy examples of modern black rule. No doubt some of the new African states are also not under effective black control, and some will prove sad models of modern government and development. But, unlike the period before the war, the Negro American is himself in movement toward fulfillment within his society. It is, then, this simultaneous movement of all black men (indeed all men of color, including Asians)[16] toward self-realization which renders postwar Africa an unquestioned source of inspiration and pride to the Negro American.

The Black Muslims are only one type of Negro organization that reflects the impact of postwar African developments upon Negro Americans. There are, however, many other groups of this sort, and they are likely to have a more sustained influence upon the Negro's new thrust for self-realization in American society than the Black Muslims. Unlike the Black Muslims these organizations are secular in orientation, intellectually capable of coping with the modern world; and they reject naive political goals like the establishment of a Negro state within the jurisdiction of the United States. The Afro-American Research Institution in San Francisco, which publishes a quarterly journal, *Soulbook*, represents one type of such organizations; it endeavors to apply lessons from African nationalist developments to the Negro movement for equality, emphasizing self-help programs (for example, it runs a technical school for Negro youth) and political action which excludes white participants. Another type of organization is represented by the Freedomways Associates and the Liberation Committee on Africa, both headquartered in New York. Through their journals, *Freedomways* and *Liberator*, they, among other things, orient their readers toward identification with the radical, mainly Marxian-Socialist, tendencies in Africa and in the Third World generally. The Liberation Committee, for instance, supports the Pan-African policy of the Nkrumah regime in Ghana which seeks an immediate union of African states along Marxian-Socialist lines, and has staunchly defended the Castro government in its struggle with the United States—a defense which is greatly influenced by Cuba's governmental policy of upgrading the status of its large Negro population. There is, finally, an array of organizations whose main concern is the redefinition of the Negro's self-image in American society through artistic, literary, and other intellectual activities. The more interesting of these groups include the American Society of African Culture (New York), the Society of Umbra (New York), the Black Dialogue Associates (Los Angeles), the Harlem Writers' Guild, and the Harvard-Radcliffe Association of African and Afro-American Students. The American Society of African Culture, the largest of these organizations, is particularly concerned, in the words of its President, John Aubrey Davis,

to bring to the American Negro . . . an understanding of the continuing value of our gifts and a pride in our origins, so that we may join other Americans who feel secure in the traditions of their past and their contributions to America. Thus, we have sponsored demonstrations of African culture, such as art exhibits; we have encouraged the exchange of views between African and American Negro writers, artists, and musicians both in the United States and Africa; and we have explored the historic relationship . . . between the American Negro and Africa in lectures, panels, symposia, and publications.[17]

Ralph Ellison reports that, significantly, in Harlem the reply to the greeting "How are you?" is very often, "Oh, man, I'm nowhere."

The phrase "I'm nowhere" expresses the feeling borne in upon many Negroes that they have no stable, recognized place in society. One's identity drifts in a capricious reality in which even the most commonly held assumptions are questionable. One "is" literally, but one is nowhere; one wanders dazed in a ghetto maze, a "displaced person" of American democracy.[18]

In the swift cycle of recent events the Negro American's "nowhere" begins to give way to a more concrete and identifiable reality. It is in this context that the Black Muslims and other mainly nonpolitical black nationalist conceptions have their meaning for Negroes. All of these groups assert or seek, in one guise or another, an identification with America, but all of them also have bolstered their formulations through identification with postwar Africa as well, thereby demonstrating Africa's world significance for the Negro American. It is one thing to be the descendant of a slave born in a colonial country of an allegedly barbaric continent, and another to be linked racially to a continent suddenly peopled with independent states making a strident and impressive entry into the world's affairs. The Italian attack on Ethiopia in 1935, it has been said, had the effect of giving large numbers of Negroes a sense of involvement in world events for the first time,[19] even though the Ethiopians were then by no means sure that they wanted to be counted among the black Africans. The tidal wave of independence which swept over Africa from the middle of the 1950's brought to the Negro American a far more vivid and intimate sense of both world and African involvement. Although some Negroes no doubt still repudiate Africa and many know little or nothing about it, something of a new universe has been created for them whether they take any active share in it or not. Let there be no mistake about it: the way both whites and Negroes look at color is inevitably transformed when large numbers of men of color take over positions of great prominence and authority which had formerly been virtually a white monopoly.

Dining with Elijah Muhammad and a contingent of Black Muslims, James Baldwin was struck by Elijah's comment that no people in history had ever been respected who had not owned their own land, to which others at the table responded, "Yes, that's right." Baldwin adds that

I could not deny the truth of this statement. For everyone else has, is, a nation, with a specific location, and a flag—even, these days, the Jew. It is only "the so-called American Negro" who remains trapped, disinherited, and despised, in a nation that has kept him in bondage for nearly four hundred years and is still unable to recognize him as a human being.[20]

For the majority of Negro Americans it is evident that the land and the flag—the nation—which they "own" will not be African, even though increasing numbers find their way to Africa. Short of some unexpected cataclysmic change, no more than a trickle of Negro Americans will decide, or have an opportunity, to cast in their lot with Africa; but for many, and probably for most, a sense of racial community with Africa and of some vicarious sharing in the sovereignty of African States will be a significant part of their social awareness. How significant such a sense will be and what kind of a cultural and political role it will play can now be estimated only on the most meagre evidence. Factors which would have a determining influence are presumably the success of the United States in achieving an open and color-blind society and the success of African peoples in achieving societies which are at once stable and progressive. But it may be that other less calculable elements of attraction or repulsion will bring about results not presently foreseeable, including, perhaps, sharp divisions within the Negro community over such matters as the proper American attitude toward the Congo or South Africa or the extent and conditions of American aid to Africa. Certainly it cannot be assumed that considerations favorable to Africa will necessarily be the dominant ones. It is equally within the realm of experience that Negro American students may resent scholarships and other favored treatment given to African students coming to this country, and that envious eyes may be cast by underprivileged Negroes, whether in Harlem or in the South's Black Belt, on American largesse to Africa. As African states, parties, and ideologies have differed among themselves, so will Negro Americans continue to differ among themselves about attitudes toward Africa and other matters.

The Foreign and the Domestic Scene

The interplay between domestic race relations and American foreign policy in a swiftly changing world was officially perceived immediately after the war, and the awareness of it has constantly grown. Both the Truman and the Eisenhower administrations sought, however fitfully, to give executive leadership to the protection of a wide range of civil rights long guaranteed to the Negro by the Constitution but subverted by the states. No major civil rights legislation was secured from the Congress, but a Civil Rights Commission, now under a Negro chairman, was established which has provided an invaluable body of information by means of investigations and public hearings throughout the country.

Another facet of the impact of the postwar world upon our race relations may be seen in the response of the federal courts to demands to desegregate public education. The judiciary reached its apogee in this sphere with the Supreme Court's decision on desegregation of public schools in May 1954. Long cognizant of the social and political environment within which it functions, the Court's decision in *Brown v. Board of Education* was as much influenced by America's postwar circumstances as the decision supporting segregated schools in *Plessy v. Ferguson* in 1896 was shaped by the post-Reconstruction era. The supporting brief of the Justice Department in submitting the segregation cases to the Supreme Court in December 1952 indicated full awareness of the contemporary international atmosphere and pressures. It declared that

it is in the context of the present world struggle between freedom and tyranny that the problem of racial discrimination must be viewed. . . . Racial discrimination furnishes grist for the Communist propaganda mills, and it raises doubt even among friendly nations as to the intensity of our devotion to the democratic faith.

This observation was further bolstered by a quotation in the brief from the Secretary of State:

The segregation of school children on a racial basis is one of the practices in the United States which has been singled out for hostile foreign comment in the United Nations and elsewhere. Other people cannot understand how such a practice can exist in a country which professes to be a staunch supporter of freedom, justice, and democracy.[21]

A sphere in which desegregation has moved ahead more fully than in the schools is represented by the armed services. In World War I Negro servicemen were organized into four entirely segregated regiments. The 920,000 Negroes who served in World War II had the same experience, although the Army officer-candidate schools were conducted on an integrated basis. But this latter concession to decency in the midst of the worst armed encounter democratic government had ever faced appears small when it is noted that only 2,484 of the 174,000 commissioned officers and 152 of the 6,000 warrant officers were Negro.[22]

At the end of the war the Truman administration moved slowly toward integration of the armed services, issuing an executive order in 1948 declaring equality of treatment and opportunity for all men bearing arms, regardless of race, color, religion, or national origin. The Navy, which did not even deem the Negro fit for recruitment until 1943, moved first toward full integration and was followed by the Air Force. The Army dragged its feet and did not reach a stride comparable to that of the Navy and Air Force until the Korean War, the first major encounter between the United States and the Soviet bloc in the Cold War.[23]

C. Vann Woodward records the Korean War's impact on integration in the Army thus:

With a surplus of Negro troops piling up behind the lines and a critical shortage of white troops, who were bearing the brunt of casualties, one regimental commander in Korea explained that the "force of circumstances" compelled him to integrate surplus Negroes into his decimated white platoons. It worked. Platoon leaders were delighted to have them. Men in the ranks accepted them. The Negroes fought better than they had before. Race relations took a turn for the better instead of for the worse as feared. General Matthew R. Ridgway asked and was granted permission to integrate Negroes throughout his Korean command.[24]

Following these Korean experiences integration was pushed throughout Army units overseas and in training bases at home, with the result that today the armed forces are one of the most effectively integrated of our national institutions. Thus, under the grim necessity of the Korean War, racial democracy did away with the intolerable situation which allowed men to die for their country only on a segregated basis.

It was not until the last year of the Kennedy-Johnson administration that Congress enacted the first major piece of civil rights legislation in this century—the Civil Rights Act of 1964—which was attained under the pressure of the tragic events surrounding the assassination of President Kennedy. The attention and anxiety of the world, and especially of the nonwhite peoples, were centered upon the death of an American President whose administration symbolized as no other in our history the Negro's quest for full status and who had on a number of occasions demonstrated his concern for Africa and the march toward African freedom. Fortunately for the international standing of the United States, Congress did enact the legislation on which the late President had staked a large part of his career.

Equally fortunate for our political system's future esteem in the world's eyes was the result of the 1964 election, which much of the world saw as directly related to the events surrounding President Kennedy's death and the enactment of the Civil Rights Act. In returning Lyndon B. Johnson to the White House the electorate overwhelmingly endorsed a President who stood firmly behind the civil rights program in the face of a political campaign in which a major party, the Republican party, exploited the fears and prejudices of whites regarding the Negro's militant quest for equality.

The international impact of the election was comparable to that of the adoption of the Civil Rights Act. For instance, the normally anti-American press and information media in Ghana took momentary leave of their anti-American line to express gratification at the defeat of Goldwater and the white Southerners whose support he openly sought. Any other decision on either the Civil Rights Act or the Goldwaterites' bid for power would have produced a very different reaction in Ghana and elsewhere in Africa and Asia.

Africa and America

The affairs of Africa and the United States have come in the last decade to be deeply enmeshed with each other, primarily because of the changed role of each in the world but also in part as the culmination of the forced migration of millions of Africans to America in earlier centuries. For good or ill, that relationship is more likely to intensify than to diminish in the years ahead between both governments and peoples. In the latter sphere more and more Negroes, and other Americans as well—more, perhaps, than the Africans will always welcome—will surely concern themselves with Africa and will travel there to see for themselves and, for a few, to settle in with a greater or less degree of permanence. In all probability the reverse flow will also continue to increase as more Africans come to the United States on official business, as students, and as visitors.

Governmental relationships can be expected to be increasingly diverse, complicated, and difficult. At the outset of African independence there were few states to deal with and the rough edges of forthcoming problems were obscured by an aura of optimism. Even though the United States had played no significant role in pressing for self-determination and the end of colonialism in Africa, American good will toward the African states and peoples tended to be taken for granted, and Africans in general welcomed the wider contact with America which independence brought. Aside from the suspicions of a small number of ideologically motivated Africans, the first disillusionment on the African side perhaps derived from the French-inspired delay of the United States in recognizing Guinea's independence when Sékou Touré secured an overwhelming "No" vote in the 1958 referendum on the De Gaulle constitution. Nonetheless, the belief was widespread that the United States would back African freedom and development, just as many Americans generally assumed that the abandonment of colonialism, particularly when it came about through friendly agreement with the colonial powers, would lead to democracy and orderly progress.

The easy assumptions of good will and amicable cooperation are still by no means wholly destroyed, but many events have intervened to challenge their universality and air of innocence. From the American standpoint a significant feature has been the multiplication of African states which has brought a diversity of governmental structures and political styles, including sharp clashes between African states and divergent views on foreign policy. The turn toward one-party systems, usually with one strong man dominating the scene, has undermined the hopes for the emergence of liberal constitutional democracies, and charges of corruption and other abuses are common.

Although the United States has sought to hold itself aloof from intra-African disputes whenever possible, it has on a number of occasions been forced to take sides with one or another state or grouping, as in relation to the Congo and the countries of southern Africa. Since the American position is generally middle-of-the-road, or veering to the right of the middle, difficulties have arisen most frequently with the more militant and left-inclined states, parties, and leaders, who are already the most exposed and most susceptible to Communist denunciation of the United States as the arch-imperialist, the leader of the neo-colonialists. Such attacks are, of course, certain to be amplified by the American left and in particular by the radical nationalist elements in the Negro community. As the world now operates it is virtually impossible for the United States to avoid some measure of embroilment in any major African controversy, and any such controversy is sure to have significant reverberations within this country. Thus the murder of Lumumba and the secession of Katanga became American issues, fought over with bitterness in this country.

The most sustained and vitriolic onslaught upon the United

States was provided by the reactions of the African representatives at the United Nations to the airlift of white hostages from Stanleyville in November 1964, which itself followed the much-criticized American backing of Tshombe when he returned to the Congo earlier in 1964 as Premier. What the United States portrayed as a humanitarian rescue mission was denounced by African spokesmen as premeditated aggression involving the wanton and deliberate massacre of the black inhabitants. The bitter fury of some Africans was reflected in the shrill charge of the *Ghanaian Times* on November 28, 1964, that "after killing thousands to free their few spies, the Americans and Belgians stayed on to aid the already entrenched mercenaries to exterminate Congolese citizens in an effort to reintegrate Stanleyville into the Leopoldville administration."[25] Yet Nigeria and most of the former French African territories either endorsed the airlift or took it calmly. While the militants and "progressives" backed the rebel forces and demanded that the imperialists withdraw their support from Tshombe and his white mercenaries, many members of the Organization of African Unity protested the effort to force them to intervene in Congolese affairs. No matter how the United States played its cards it could not help falling afoul of one camp or the other, even, perhaps, if it had wholly abstained from action in the Congo.

African disenchantment with the United States was at least as multi-faceted as that of the United States with Africa. At the head of the list stood the American handling of the racial problem: stories and pictures of murders, beatings, burning and bombing of churches, attacks by police dogs, and the exclusion of children from schools inflamed African opinion. In good part the African denunciation of the airlift was merely one form of the expression of pent-up African feelings toward the American treatment of black men. Few Africans who have visited or lived in the United States have escaped encounters with racial discrimination, including those escorted around the country by Department of State protocol personnel in hope of special protection. As long as racial discrimination exists in this country we can expect African attacks and, in all probability, proposals to bring the issue to the floor of the U.N.

As many Africans saw it, the American attitude toward southern Africa, including the Portuguese colonies, was quite unacceptable and demonstrated a readiness to accept gross evils thrust upon Africans, while lesser injuries and indignities inflicted by Communist states were subject to stern and immediate censure. The

United States was accused of subordinating the struggle against colonialism to the maintenance of good relations with the NATO allies and to the continuation of its profits from its South African trade and investments. Accusations were made that America was intervening in African affairs and American aid programs were denounced as having strings tied to them and, perhaps contradictorily, as being both subtle instruments of neo-colonialism and too limited in scope.

Image and Identity

In the contemporary idiom, problems of image and identity are crucial in the relations between Africa and America, Africans and Americans; but here it is far easier to ask questions than to answer them. What image does Africa (which, of course, means millions of Africans with divergent opinions, just as America is synonymous with millions of Americans) have of the United States, and what image will it come to have? The United States can be seen as a generous and freedom-loving country, afflicted by a racial conflict which it is desperately seeking to solve in a humane fashion, or as the stronghold of capitalist imperialism, seeking globally to hold down the revolution which threatens its white ruling class and their super-profits. What of the American image of Africa? The rise of the new African states and the unexpected claims to leadership of Ethiopia and Liberia have undoubtedly had a great effect in dispelling the image of Africa as a primitive continent hopelessly behind the rest of mankind. Not only Negro Americans but the majority of white Americans repudiated Senator Ellender when he proclaimed in the course of his 1962 African tour that no Africans were fit to govern themselves and that South Africa was on the right track, and yet he presumably spoke for many of his fellow Southerners and other conservatives. Of one thing we can be sure: he impaired the African image of America. Is it implausible to go one hazardous step further and suggest that the new American image, Negro and other, of Africa still rests on fragile foundations, and that if, say, the Congo were to disintegrate into tribal strife and other countries were to follow suit, the older derogatory image of Africa might seep back in? And, if so, what effect would it have on Negro Americans, on their attitudes, and on their standing in the American society?

The identity of Africans among themselves raises serious and fascinating questions, but they need not concern us here, save perhaps to remark that the concept of pan-Africanism is a product primarily of the Negroes on this side of the Atlantic.

The identity of the Negro American is, however, central to our inquiry. Many people have sought to define it, to distinguish the elements which enter into it, and to determine the many forms and shadings which it can take. Here we can do no more than reiterate that the Negro American's sense of identity has been greatly influenced by the emergence of the new Africa and that it is likely to be more rather than less influenced by Africa as time goes by. Failure to integrate the Negro into the total American society must surely intensify his alienation from that society, and hence make more likely an identification with Africa. It is more dubious that the reverse proposition follows with an equal necessity. For example, imagine the full integration of the American Negro, accompanied by a growing conflict in the Congo and, even more dangerous, open strife and bloodshed, perhaps on an international scale, in South Africa. If the United States should stand aside or, worse, join in the support of white domination—which currently seems an improbable outcome—where would the loyalty of Negro Americans lie, in what fashion would their identity assert itself? Africa is a part of the identity of the Negro American: how large and what kind of a part has varied from man to man and generation to generation. The future destiny of that identity depends on the United States, on Africa, and on the relation between the two.

Conclusion

The twentieth century has not found the answer to the problem of the color line, but it has witnessed a uniquely massive drive in search of an answer. The colonial system has almost been swept away. Aside from stray bits and pieces of empire, what is left is the large and dangerous expanse of southern Africa, white dominated and largely white settled. The resolution of the Negro American's status has been well begun but still has a long distance to travel before it achieves its goals, and, in the present close-knit world, what happens abroad and the way the United States reacts in Africa and elsewhere may have drastic repercussions on the domestic scene. Both at home and abroad major transformations in our policies and in the traditional uses of our national institutions must still be made if we are to meet the present challenge.

The Rise of Africa and the Negro American

The inescapable issue of identity was well posed by Chief S. O. Adebo, Permanent Representative of Nigeria to the U.N., in a speech to the American Negro Leadership Conference on September 29, 1964, in which he pointed out the similarity between the problems of Nigeria and Negro Americans.

A great many of the things that happened to you here, which you thought happened to you because you were a minority people, happened to us in Nigeria. . . . I no longer think simply as a Nigerian; I no longer think simply as an African. I think more as a person of color. And the objective of all of us is to restore to the man of color, wherever he may be, whether in Nigeria, or in the United States, or in Moscow, or in Brazil, the dignity of a human being. That is why we are involved in the same struggle in Africa, here, and elsewhere.[26]

This latter half of the twentieth century has presented us with a different world to live in—a world of color—and the way in which we adapt ourselves to it and make use of our opportunities, or deny them, will in great measure determine our future at home and abroad. The entire context in which we live has changed. Until the day before yesterday some Americans could delude themselves that they lived in a white country which also contained a subordinate minority of Negroes, almost wholly excluded from the serious conduct of affairs. Can we now bring ourselves to see, and to act upon the vision, that America's twenty million Negroes are not to be considered a burden and liability to be shunted off into a segregated corner, but an asset as great as any we possess in our effort to live in the new world which has sprung up about us?[27]

What lies before us is to create, as we have not succeeded in creating in the past, a nation in which all Americans without regard to "race, color, and previous condition of servitude" have equal and unquestioned access to human decency, dignity, and rights. If we can now succeed, spurred on by the rise of Asia and Africa, we will have mastered our greatest problem at home and established our claim to esteem and influence in the multi-colored world which in the last years has swept white domination aside. The challenge to America is immense as the once sharp line between the domestic and the international becomes blurred and fades away.

REFERENCES

1. Harold R. Isaacs, *The New World of Negro Americans* (New York, 1963), p. 211.

2. This turn of events was foreseen by Gunnar Myrdal who was writing his classic study of the American racial problem during the war years. Pointing out that the Negro problem had already become national in scope, after having been mainly a Southern worry, he commented that it had now "acquired tremendous international implications" in the course of a war which could be seen as ending American isolation. "Statesmen will have to take cognizance of the changed geopolitical situation of the nation and carry out important adaptations of the American way of life to new necesssities. A main adaptation is bound to be a redefinition of the Negro's status in American democracy." *An American Dilemma* (9th edn.; New York & London, 1944), pp. 1015-1016.

3. W. E. B. Du Bois, *The Crisis*, 1918.

4. Facsimile of advertisement in James Weldon Johnson, *Along This Way —the Autobiography of James Weldon Johnson* (New York, 1933), pp. 364-365.

5. Isaacs, *op. cit.*, pp. 6-7.

6. Pearl Buck commented in 1942 on Japan's use of race matters in its propaganda as follows: "Japan . . . is declaring in the Philippines, in China, in India, in Malaya, and even in Russia that there is no basis for hope that colored peoples can expect any justice from the people who rule in the United States, the white people. For specific proof the Japanese point to our treatment of our own colored people, citizens of generations in the United States. Every lynching, every race riot, gives joy to Japan. The discriminations of the American army and navy and the air forces against colored soldiers and sailors, the exclusion of colored labor in our defense industries and trade unions, all our social discriminations, are of the greatest aid today to our enemy in Asia, Japan." Pearl S. Buck, *American Unity and Asia* (New York, 1942), p. 29.

7. Quoted in Walter White, *How Far the Promised Land?* (New York, 1953), p. 13.

8. This and the immediately succeeding material is drawn from two unpublished papers, each entitled "The Employment of American Negroes in the Foreign Service of the United States," prepared by John A. Davis for the first and second American Negro Leadership Conferences on Africa, held in 1962 and 1964.

9. "Most of the Negroes I know do not believe that this immense concession would ever have been made if it had not been for the competition of the Cold War, and the fact that Africa was clearly liberating herself and therefore had, for political reasons, to be wooed by the descendants of her former masters. Had it been a matter of love or justice, the 1954 decision [concerning school segregation] would surely have occurred sooner; were it not for the realities of power in this difficult era, it might very well not have occurred yet." *The Fire Next Time* (New York, 1964), pp. 117-118.

10. One of the authors was resident in Ghana in 1964-65 where he heard conversations between urbanized African women about the respective value of "good" hair (meaning straight hair of whites) and "bad" hair (meaning curly or wooly hair of blacks). He found the conversations disturbingly reminiscent of his American childhood when such talk was legion. And there was a certain irony in encountering the urbanized African female adopting the hair-straightening styles of the Negro American female as her model, insofar as the younger generation of college-educated Negro American female, influenced by the postwar militancy of the Negro protest movement, shows a tendency toward discarding these styles.

11. On the interesting features of this problem among Brazilian Negroes who represent nearly 40 per cent of the population, see Donald Pierson, *Negroes in Brazil* (Chicago, 1942). Brazil's most effective exponent of theories of Negro inferiority was himself of mixed blood, and the relationship of most mulatto Brazilian Negroes to the darker Negro is one of rejection. On the Negro American aspect of this phenomenon, see the excellent study by Harold R. Isaacs, *The New World of the Negro American, op. cit.* See also E. Franklin Frazier, *Black Bourgeoisie* (Glencoe, Ill., 1957).

12. Newbell N. Puckett, *Folk Beliefs of Southern Negroes* (Chapel Hill, N. C., 1926). Cf. Melville Herskovits, *The Myth of the Negro Past* (New York, 1941).

13. For a brilliant analysis of this transformation, see LeRoi Jones, *Blues People* (New York, 1963).

14. The best account of the Garvey Movement is E. Cronon, *Black Moses* (Madison, Wis., 1955).

15. See C. Eric Lincoln, *The Black Muslims in America* (Boston, 1961); E. Essien-Udom, *Black Nationalism: The Search for Identity in America* (Chicago, 1962).

16. Asia, incidentally, has figured in a curious way in the ideology of several Negro American black nationalist propositions, and especially that of the Black Muslims. Their Allah, W. D. Fard, the progenitor of the Muslim sect, was supposed to have been born in Asia, not Africa. Asia, or more particularly the Middle East (especially Egypt), is more often referred to as the prime example of the great contribution of black men to world civilization. "Black" in this context is expanded to include all men of color, preposterous as this may seem. Among other things, this use of Asia or the Middle East as the black man's historical reference point reflects more the impact of the American experience upon the Negro than it does of informed history and anthropological knowledge. It is a curious working out of the inferiority complex imposed by white America upon the Negro—a facet of the Negro's ambivalent relationship to Negro Africa's objective position in world history. This position, for the most part, left Negro Africa at the stage of the Neolithic (along with North

American Indians, the aborigines of Australasia, and the peoples of Melanesia and Polynesia). Confronted with white supremacist beliefs and practices, the Negro American and other New World Negro communities quite naturally gave this position a negative valuation. It was not until the post-World War I era that a new evaluation could be hammered out of the existential dialectic of the Negro's subterranean world, which was done in the first instance by the Harlem Renaissance group of Negro intellectuals, and subsequently, in the late 1930's, given explicit conceptual definition by the Negro poet from French Martinique, Aimé Césaire, who invented the term "negritude." This term signifies a meaningful synthesis of the historical experience of peoples of African descent, enabling them to discard the debilitating effects of the inferiority complex. No longer, thus, must one deny history or distort it by claiming for black men what is not theirs, or partake in romantic glorification of a past that, whatever historical research ultimately allocates to it as its true historical position, was no more romantic than any other segment of the human situation. Rather one can now take hold of reality with the aid of that measure of humanity which the Negro can claim, with its own unique twist, along with all other men:

> Hurray for those who have invented nothing!
> Hurray for those who have explored nothing!
> Hurray for those who have conquered nothing!
> But who in awe give themselves up to the essence of things.
> Ignoring surfaces, but possessed by the rhythm of things.
> Heedless of taming, but playing the game of the world.
> Truly the elder sons of the world.
> Flesh of the flesh of the world,
> Throbbing with the very movement of the world.
>
> Aimé Césaire

17. John A. Davis, "An Editorial Statement," *African Forum*, Vol. 1, No. 1 (Summer 1965), p. 3.

18. *Shadow and Act* (New York, 1963), p. 300.

19. Harold R. Isaacs, *op. cit.*, p. 151.

20. *The Fire Next Time*, pp. 100-101.

21. Quoted in C. Vann Woodward, *The Strange Career of Jim Crow* (New York, 1935), pp. 120-121.

22. Florence Murray, *The Negro Handbook, 1949* (New York, 1949), pp. 242 ff.

23. See *ibid.*, pp. 263-265.

24. Woodward, *op. cit.*, pp. 137-138.

25. The virulence of the attack upon the United States appears vividly in *The Spark* (an Accra journal which declares itself to be "A Socialist Weekly of the African Revolution") of February 26, 1965. Here, in an

article headed "Who Killed Malcolm X, a Negro American," W. G. Smith, accuses the "leaders of fascist imperialism who control the invisible government of the United States" of murdering not only Malcolm X, but Lumumba, President Kennedy, three officials of the Congo-Brazzaville, the Prime Minister of Burundi; of bombing Uganda and North Vietnam, of plotting to overthrow the revolution of Tanzania, of toppling the government of the Sudan, and of being linked with the South African Nazi slaughter of the Congolese people. "The death lashes of the imperialist monster, in its long drawn out agony, are sometimes terrible." In an accompanying editorial, *The Spark* accuses the American ruling class of assassinating Malcolm X because nine African states, influenced by him, are to raise the question of American race discrimination in the U. N. "Even a member of their own class, like the millionaire Kennedy is rubbed out because he evinced the slightest desire for changing the tactics of American foreign and military strategy."

26. Photocopy of transcript of speech, pp. 5-6. Chief Adebo also spoke warmly of a speech made earlier at the Conference by Secretary of State Rusk, but objected to the Secretary's assertion that the world's greatest problem is Communism, remarking that "I think we must be pardoned for thinking that the greatest problem of this world is South Africa." pp. 14-15.

27. Seeing international leadership passing to the United States as World War II progressed, Gunnar Myrdal held that all the world would be given faith if America could succeed in integrating the Negro into modern democracy. "In this sense the Negro problem is not only America's greatest failure but also America's incomparably great opportunity for the future. . . . America would have a spiritual power many times stronger than all her financial and military resources—the power of the trust and support of all good people on earth. *America is free to choose whether the Negro shall remain her liability or become her opportunity.*

"The development of the American Negro problem during the years to come is, therefore, fateful not only for America itself but for all mankind." *An American Dilemma,* pp. 1021-1022.

VII

SOME GENERAL PERSPECTIVES AND PROSPECTS

OSCAR HANDLIN

The Goals of Integration

Since 1954, and even more so since 1960, Americans concerned with resolving the dilemma posed by the Negro's plight in a society committed to equal rights have lived in a state of crisis. The destruction of the concept of "separate but equal" in the Brown Case was the culmination of a quarter-century of re-examination of the premise that the colored men of the United States could be held permanently in a position that was actually separate but unequal. The implications of that decision were not immediately clear; nor have they been clarified in the intervening eleven years.[1]

Had the decision been immediately acceded to, it might have been possible to begin at once to explore its consequences. Instead, the necessity for fighting a succession of guerrilla actions behind the lines has delayed any consideration of long-range problems. Attention has been so narrowly focused on tactical issues that there has been no time to consider ultimate goals. The civil rights movement, which is actually a congeries of quite disparate efforts, maintains the pretense of unity only by a resolute determination not to think of long-term objectives.

However, we know all too well, from an earlier conflict a century ago, that battles and even wars can be won and yet the fruits of victory lost through men's haziness about what they are fighting for. In the present situation, the inability to define the ultimate goals of the civil rights struggle is an unacknowledged threat that complicates immediate tactics and that may deprive this momentous upheaval of its meaning.

In the absence of defined goals, it is difficult to estimate the character or pace of change or even to judge its direction. Under these circumstances, organizational controls and leadership weaken. There is confusion about which objectives are salient, and issues tend to crop up of their own accord. Action is sporadic, local, and discontinuous and is not related to any general standard of importance. Explosive activists, always ready to precipitate conflict, find tactical opportunities to determine the questions to be fought over while the established leadership has to tag along to maintain its influence. At the same time, the atmosphere of continuous crisis generates the obligation of solidarity. Those who dissent must be silent or be counted as sympathizers of the antagonists. No one wishes to be known as an Uncle Tom or a white liberal.[2]

Recent demonstrations of solidarity on behalf of civil rights have been impressive. The march on Washington in 1963 and from Selma in 1965 showed the extent to which diverse elements in American society coalesced in support of a common cause. These occasions have ceremonial significance; they manifest the extent to which a variety of people affirm their dislike of brutality and their faith in the orderly methods of democracy. There is no difficulty in eliciting unanimity of support for the slogan of equal rights as man and citizen as long as the terms remain vague and undefined.

But it is erroneous to regard these events or professions of sentiment as expressions of unity with reference to a program of action. The calls for brotherly love sounded on the platforms do not reduce the intensity of the hatreds in Harlem. White resentment at black demands is also stiffening. It is a mistake to judge the extent of backlash by the refusal to commit suicide in 1964; the California vote on Proposition Fourteen that year was more revealing than the national vote against Goldwater. Popular sentiment is still for tolerance and against prejudice; but the time is approaching for a test of the meaning of that preference.[3]

Insofar as the civil rights movement has proceeded beyond the call for brotherly love or for equality, it has ventured upon unsure ground. Civil rights demands in Alabama and Mississippi are comprehensible; the promises of personal security, the ballot, and decent schools are familiar and long overdue. But the issues blur in the newer context of New York or Chicago or Atlanta where these minimal gains are well on the way to attainment. There the failure to define appropriate goals has created future difficulties, the shape of which is already apparent. The new problems are important not only because an increasing percentage of American Negroes live in an urban environment, but also because the range of decisions involved will confront the nation long after the difficulties of the rural South are resolved.

In the earlier stages of the struggle for equality, it was enough to ask that the government be color-blind. The barriers that confined the Negro were the products of law, and it was necessary to demand only the equal treatment that the Constitution guaranteed. Desegregation was the response to segregation; and it was a response that attracted the support not only of other underprivileged minorities but also of many Americans who found it in accord with their own creed of individual dignity and equality of opportunity.

In the past decade, emphasis has gradually and imperceptibly shifted from desegregation to integration, but without adequate awareness of the consequences and often with a profound ambiguity about the nature of the desirable goal.

The term integration sometimes refers to the openness of society, to a condition in which every individual can make the maximum number of voluntary contacts with others without regard to qualifications of ancestry. In that sense, the objective is a leveling of all barriers to association other than those based on ability, taste, and personal preference.

But integration sometimes also refers to a condition in which individuals of each racial or ethnic group are randomly distributed through the society so that every realm of activity contains a representative cross section of the population. In that sense, the object is the attainment, in every occupational, educational, and residential distribution, of a balance among the constituent elements in the society.

In crucial matters of public policy, antithetical consequences follow from the two positions. The one calls for improvements in the Negroes' opportunities for jobs, housing, and schooling even though the group may remain as separate as before; the other puts a primary emphasis upon racial balance.

The civil rights movement has never made a clear choice between these alternatives, nor has any spokesman fully articulated the implications of the two points of view. But increasingly in the past five years, the thrust has been in the latter direction, toward an organization in which every sector of society is racially balanced; and it is in that sense that the term integration will be used in the discussion which follows.

In part the change of recent years was due to the very intensity of the struggle against an intransigent opposition. More important, however, was the perception that the leveling of governmental barriers was in itself inadequate to remove the handicaps under which colored people labored. The vicious cycle of slum housing, poor schools, lack of skills, and low income trapped the urban Negro and widened rather than closed the gap between him and others in the society. Deprivation became a pattern of life that hopelessly handicapped him in the competition for desirable places. The simple neutrality of government would not relieve him of these shackles; positive action to compensate was essential. The state was to intervene to assure the disadvantaged a due proportion of well-paying jobs and to balance the population of neighborhoods and schools in a thoroughly integrated pattern. That assurance was deemed necessary to restore equality to the disadvantaged. Hence the campaigns to destroy *de facto* segregation in the public schools, to secure preferential hiring and job quotas for Negroes in industry, and to manage housing in the interest of mixed residential neighborhoods.

This profound shift in the tactics of the civil rights movement during the past decade has come without any clear estimation of the consequences. To clarify those consequences, it is necessary to resolve the ambiguities in the goals of the civil rights movement. Is the ultimate objective to eliminate the differences that actually divide the population of the United States and thus dissolve its people into a single homogeneous and undifferentiated mass? Or will it be possible to reach toward equality while retaining the social subgroupings produced by a heritage of diversity and by the problems of managing a free population of almost 200 million? The answer, upon which the welfare of all Americans rests, should, to a greater degree than in the past, influence the tactics of the civil rights struggle.

The view of integration as racial balance rests on two fallacious assumptions—that the position of the Negro is absolutely unique in the American experience and that racist prejudice is so thoroughly ingrained in the people of the United States that only positive exertions by the government will assure the colored man his rights. Neither proposition conforms to the evidence.

The Negro is unique, it is argued, because his color sets him off from the majority more decisively than the traits of other ethnic groups did and because slavery crippled him so seriously that he cannot compete on equal terms and needs a crutch to help him along.

Certainly slavery was a more traumatic experience than the centuries of persecution, the hardships of migration, and the generations of depressed proletarian existence from which the Irish peasants suffered. But the argument slights the Negro's powers of recuperation and exaggerates the extent to which the damage caused more than a century ago remains a permanent part of his character. There has been a tendency to underestimate the extent of his achievements even in the fifty years immediately after emancipation, under conditions immensely more difficult than those of the present. When one considers the backwardness of the Southern economy after 1865, the exclusion from political power, the racist prejudices, and the bitterness left by a great war, it was a respectable accomplishment to have formed stable family units, to have developed productive skills, and to have created an array of churches, lodges, and media for cultural expression, with the limited resources the group possessed. Few people released from bondage in any society have performed as creditably.[4]

The disadvantages from which the Negro suffers in 1965 are less the products of the plantation than of the great migration to the city in the past fifty years; and that experience he shares with the other ethnic groups who have participated in American urbanization. Of course the Negroes are different from the Poles or Italians or Jews, just as those peoples differ among, and from, each other. The differences, however, are not of kind but of degree, and they are largely explained by the recency of arrival of the colored men, by their greater numbers, and by their dense concentration in a few cities. The problems of prejudice and acculturation from which the most recent newcomers suffer had their counterparts among the earlier arrivals.[5]

Nor is color the sole and unique sign of ethnic visibility. It is no doubt the most prominent mode of social recognition; but much depends upon the social assessment of this as of other physical traits. The Japanese-Americans are far less visible in 1965 than they were in 1940 although their color has not changed. And the Kennedys are still identified as Irish after five generations in the New World, and despite their wealth, prominence, and whiteness.

The assumption that color has a unique differentiating quality rests upon the argument that American society is inherently racist, its promise of equality reserved only for the white man. It has become fashionable in the past few years to sneer at Myrdal's statement of the American creed of equality and to urge that only forceful measures will restrain the propensity to prejudice.

There was a racist period in American history in the sixty years after the end of the Civil War; but the hatreds of that period were peculiar to the time and place. Much more significant is the deeper tradition of equality before and since that interlude. The agony with which slaveholders like Thomas Jefferson and George Mason considered their own situation, the tortured efforts of early scientists to understand color differences, and the torment the abolitionists caused in the North and the South were the results of the inability to square the existing labor system with the belief in the brotherhood of man and the commitment to equality. And the changes since 1945 have been the result not of fear either of the Negroes or of Africans but of the awareness that equality is a necessary ideal of the Republic.

Furthermore, the Negro, while the most prominent, was not the sole target even in the racist period. Prejudice was not limited by race, creed, national origin, or previous condition of servitude. The majority of the victims of lynchings in those years were Negroes; but there were 1,293 white victims of the rope and faggot as against 3,436 black. Italians in New Orleans, a Jew in Georgia, and Greeks in Omaha also met the fury of mob violence. The Ku Klux Klan of 1924 was more concerned with Catholics and Jews than with colored men.[6]

Above all, the response of Americans to the crisis of the past decade reveals the effectiveness of the appeal to the creed of equality. Even Bogalusa is not South Africa; and the inability of the open advocates of racism to attract support is the best evidence of the extent of commitment to that creed.

In estimating the meanings of integration, therefore, it is entirely appropriate to examine the analogous if not identical experience of other ethnic groups. Their process of acculturation will throw light on the need for defining the goals and the strategy of the civil rights movement.

Barring a major overturn of the American social system, which at the moment appears neither probable nor desirable, change will come within definable limits and will involve choices among alternatives. And decisions on this matter will be more effective if they come within an informed context that makes it possible to envision their results.

The inequities which survive from the past cannot be understood or remedied without a comprehension of the social order that produced them. They are the pathological manifestations of a mechanism of adjustment which permitted that order to function. Their successful removal requires a consideration of the function they serve; otherwise, the alternatives are grim. Either the order will collapse to the injury of everyone, white as well as black, or else uncontrolled alternative modes of adjustment will recreate and perpetuate the diseased condition.

This was the error of most of the abolitionists, who thought they could extirpate slavery without considering the effects upon Southern society. The result by 1900 was the restoration of the Negro's subordination in other forms than slavery.[7]

Hence, the importance, in any effort to foresee future developments, of an understanding of segregation, of its relationship to equality, and of the probable effects of integration.

Popularly speaking, segregation was a response to the dissolution of earlier forms of stratification. In a slave regime, the physical separation of the dominant and subordinate populations was superfluous and inconvenient. In other relatively static societies, where places were rigidly defined and the symbols of status clearly fixed by law or custom, groups could mingle with considerable promiscuity because there were no problems of recognition and no dangers to the established hierarchy of persons and groups.[8]

In the South, segregation was a response to the abolition of slavery and to the threat to white superiority posed by Reconstruction. The pattern that emerged in the last quarter of the nineteenth century used the law to fix the identity of the Negroes and to confine them to inferior social places. To those ends it established a rigid etiquette of behavior and separate institutions that restricted the opportunities of the former slaves for education and employment. Within the limits thus established, residential separateness was unnecessary. The measures that implemented segregation were deliberate on the part of the whites; the purposes were clearly understood at the time. As for the Negroes, their wishes were of no consequence; once they were excluded from political power, violence induced their acquiescence. The result was a kind of order, the price of which was inequality of rights.[9]

In the freer, more fluid, and more mobile sections of the country, segregation was achieved by withdrawal rather than by restraint and was voluntary rather than compulsory. As the Northern cities expanded with the influx of waves of heterogeneous newcomers, the old residents moved away, and the new arrivals sorted themselves out in neighborhoods that reflected their own sense of community. Education, employment, religious affiliation, and associational life fell within lines that were not imposed by law or by violence but were shaped by informal and largely spontaneous connections of kinship or community.

Although the Northern Negro suffered from prejudice as did the Southern, society was not polarized but fragmented; and he found himself but one of many groups comparably situated, some of which suffered from disabilities similar to his own. Negroes did not confront a homogeneous white community with a single chain of command leading up to a unified leadership. They found a place among numerous communities, each with its own power structure and its own leaders.[10]

The function of separateness in this context was not to establish or to perpetuate the inferiority of one group, but rather to accommodate diverse patterns of life that were the products of differences in ethnic and sectional heritage, or in economic and social background. By reducing contacts at the points of potential tension, this adjustment permitted each group to organize its own institutions without the oversight or interference of others, and yet was flexible enough to preserve some degree of order in a highly complex society. Furthermore, the expanding cities possessed enough free space and their organization was so loosely articulated that individuals who preferred not to affiliate could refrain from doing so and could get along in whatever degree of detachment they wished. The ghetto arrangement was therefore totally different in intention as well as in form from the segregation of the South.

Indeed the fact that the pluralistic order took account of actual differences within the population made it possible to preserve the *concept* of equality. Not every man was equally qualified in terms of inherited capital, cultural traits, personality, and intelligence to pursue equally the goals of success in American life. But the pursuit of happiness was not a single, unified scramble in which every individual sought the same prizes and in which only a few could be winners while the rest were doomed to frustration. In the stated beliefs of the society, every boy could grow up to be President—of the United States or at least a railroad. Americans could cling to faith in that useful proposition because they never subjected it to the test of practice. In reality the disparity of aspirations and career lines drew only a few persons into the competition for those lofty places while relatively independent subsystems, with their own values and rewards, provided satisfying alternatives to many more. The children of Irish or Italian parents did not count themselves failures if their lives did not follow a course identical with that of the children of the Yankees. They had their own criteria of achievement and their own sources of gratification.

The result was to take the edge off the harshly competitive psychological and social conditions of an open society. Pluralism permitted the deployment of the population in an intricate network of relationships and associations that facilitated cooperation at some points, but that left large areas free for the withdrawal of individuals and groups and that therefore minimized conflict-provoking contacts. There were manifestations of prejudice, discrimination, and occasional violence among many of the ethnic and occupational groups. Measured against the potential explosiveness of the situation, however, those were relatively minor. Until the migrations of the past half-century, Negro life in Northen cities was not essentially different from that of other ethnic groups. It had some distinctive problems as every other group did; but relatively small numbers and generally favorable conditions permitted an accommodation on essentially the same terms.

Neither in the North nor in the South is integration in the sense of racial balance a meaningful guide to proximate future action. Desegregation is likely soon to eliminate the vestiges of discrimination inherited from the Jim Crow era; and it may open the way to full participation by Negroes in the political and economic life of the nation, but it will do so within the terms of some approximation of the group life already developed. Integration, defined as the elimination of differences, on the other hand, demands of both Negroes and whites an impossible surrender of identity. The deletion of all memory of antecedents, the severance of all ties to the past, and the liquidation of all particularistic associations is not only unfeasible but undesirable. It would curtail the capacity of this society to deal with its problems under the conditions of freedom; and significantly some of its advocates are either altogether nihilistic or else do not flinch from the totalitarian methods and consequences that would be involved in achieving this version of integration.[11]

Only a small minority of Negroes, however, think in these terms. The vast majority understand that they are a group and will remain so; they seek an expansion of their rights and opportunities, but show neither a desire to merge with the whites nor any expectation that that will soon happen. Desegregation is a genuine issue; racial balance is a vague and confusing abstraction that turns their attention away from the genuine political, economic, and social problems they and other Americans confront.

The issue is perhaps clearest in the field of political action. No right is more basic than that to full and equal participation in the governmental process; and Negroes were quick to exercise the privileges of citizenship once they secured access to the ballot either through migration to the North or through the leveling of barriers in the South. Apathy was no more widespread among them than among other voters new to the suffrage. The colored people promptly assimilated the techniques of machine organization, and their power has increased steadily as their numbers have. With the appearance of a second generation, native to the city, they have begun to move into elective office at about the same pace as their predecessors did.

Three related factors continue to limit the effectiveness of their use of political power. The lack of competent leadership has enabled self-serving hacks and demagogues to push to the fore and has wasted on the quest for petty privilege the effort and energy that might have gone into improving the status of the whole group. The modes of collaboration with other blocs of voters have been slow to develop; and since the Negroes remain a minority, the ability to use their strength depends on alliances with others. Finally, Negroes have had difficulty in perceiving where their true interests lay when it came to such complex questions as education, urban renewal, and economic policy. In all three respects, they are repeating the experiences of earlier groups drawn into the processes of American democracy.

Nor is it to be expected that these people will be more enlightened in the use of power than their predecessors. Politics is not the cure-all that some naive observers consider it to be.[12] Post-Civil War Negroes in the South did not use their strength any more effectively than did the Irish of Boston in the first quarter of the twentieth century. The same sentimental temptation to idealize the underdog that once built up exaggerated expectations of the proletariat now sometimes leads to hopes for a panacea in the activities of the Negro citizen. There is no more reason to expect political wisdom from the black than from the white resident of a slum or from either than from the suburban commuter. The vote is not an abstract exercise in either intelligence or benevolence but a means of exercising influence on the processes that shape governmental decisions. For some time yet, Negroes will use it to serve narrowly defined group interests.

The removal of surviving restraints on the right to vote is obviously important; but integration is an irrelevant distraction which disperses energy and inhibits the development of responsible leadership which can take a full and active role in politics at every level. Political effectiveness will grow not through the weakening of the sense of identity but through the development of institutions that can clarify the group's interests, provide organized means of ascent to leadership, and retain the loyalties of the growing middle-class and professional elements in the colored population.

Integration in the sense of the elimination of distinctiveness is no more relevant to the economic plight than to the political plight of the mass of Negroes. The demands for preferential hiring, for assigned quotas of desirable jobs, and for a Black Man's Marshall Plan are sometimes presented as if they were the means of attaining racial balance and therefore of furthering integration. Actually, they are calls for the recognition of the special character of the group; and to the extent that they are heeded, they strengthen identification with it.

Measurement of the rate of Negro progress is difficult because of the recency of this migration to the cities and because gross comparisons of whites and nonwhites distort the actual situation. A large proportion of urban Negroes have been where they are less than twenty years, almost all of them, less than fifty years. The analogous migration from Eastern and Southern Europe began in the 1890's and reached its peak between 1900 and 1910. The mass of Poles, Italians, and Russian Jews even in the prosperous 1920's, much less in the depression 1930's, had not made more rapid progress. Furthermore, the limitations of the census categories which recognize only whites and nonwhites obscure the genuine differences in occupation and income among the former and make comparisons invidious. Unfortunately, more refined data are difficult to come by.

It is undeniable, however, that a large percentage of American Negroes are confined to unskilled and poorly paid occupations at a time when technological changes reduce the demand for their labor. They therefore suffer more than do other sectors of the population from unemployment, low incomes, and the consequent social deprivations. Furthermore, the same economic forces that contract the demand for their services and their position as late arrivals prevent them from developing the protected trades through which other groups maintained quasi-monopolistic control of some employment opportunities.

The difficulty is that no occupation in the United States—hod-carrier, teamster, machinist, shopkeeper, physician, or banker—ever represented a cross-section of the whole population. The social and cultural conditions that influenced recruitment to these callings did not prevail identically in all ethnic and sectional groups. Entirely apart from prejudice or discrimination, therefore, the chances that a given individual would follow one career line rather than another were likely to depend on an environment and on connections shaped by family influences.

Conceivably this pattern of recruitment could change. Since Jefferson's day, various utopians have dreamed of a mandarin system within which all infants start on equal terms and are directed by successive competitive tests of ability to their appropriate niches in life. This is the ultimate model of integration; and it would certainly put Negroes on terms of parity with all others. But, desirable or not, this solution is visionary. It is hardly necessary to attempt to estimate the social and psychological costs of such a system or even to speculate about the difficulty of defining ability (intelligence?) in that context. The dominant tendencies in American life have consistently broken down any effort to create the rigid controls upon which development in that direction depends. The likelihood is slim that those tendencies will change enough in the near future to offer any promise of relief to the Negroes' problems.

A general assault on the problems of poverty may, in time, mitigate the difficulties from which Negroes suffer along with the other unskilled and therefore superfluous elements in American society. But some Negroes at least are not content to wait for that happy outcome and are struggling now for better chances as a group. Pressure on employers to assign a quota of desirable places to colored people may result in a kind of tokenism, advantageous to a few without easing the hardships of the many. But such adjustments do help the few; and both the tactic and its outcome sustain and strengthen the sense of group solidarity. There are already contexts—in some levels of government employment, for instance—

in which there is an advantage to being black, a condition which puts a premium on affiliation with the group.

In the last analysis, the welfare of the Negroes depends upon the health of the whole economy and its capacity to produce and distribute goods according to an acceptable pattern. But the last analysis is remote indeed. In the interim, the Negroes will use what power they can muster as a group for their own advantage. Preferential treatment in some high-prestige forms of employment will be justified not because it will improve the lot of the great mass of the unskilled, but because it is a means of opening some avenues of escape for the most qualified. At relatively little cost in efficiency, this device can create a pool of potential leaders with a stake in social order and at the same time break the identification of the race with poverty.

Hence the importance of education upon which, increasingly, access to the more desirable places depends. The Negroes started with the initial disadvantage of dependence on the weakest schools in the country—those of the South. Migration compounded their difficulties, and the environment of poverty adds to their handicaps. The need for improvement is unarguable.

The methods of effecting that improvement are by no means clear, however. The pressure for integration has called attention to the problem; but it has also confused the solution. For some elements in the civil rights movement, integration in the form of racial balance has become an end in itself more important than the quality of the schools. Martin Luther King's hit-and-run involvement in this issue in Boston, Chicago, and Cleveland shows the danger of the thoughtless transference of the tactics of one kind of struggle to another.

Partly this outcome is the result of the historic development of the school issue in the South, where segregation was a means of perpetuating educational inequality and Negro inferiority. There desegregation was an essential step toward equality. However, the slogans of that effort were uncritically applied to the separateness of the Northern schools which had an altogether different function. The imbalance of the Northern schools was not designed to create or maintain Negro inferiority; and its result was not always to lower the quality of the education available to colored people.[13] Yet there was no forethought about the consequences of the attempt to end what came to be termed *de facto* segregation.

Furthermore, in this matter, there is a striking division of opinion among Negroes, covered up by the appearance of unity on such occasions as the school strikes. The most vocal persons in the civil rights movement are the most mobile, those whose aspirations reach furthest, those most irked by the identification of their color. Integration expresses their not fully understood desire to sever their ties with the past; and racial balance is a means toward that end.

This desire does not reach very far among the mass of Negroes. In such cities as New York and Boston, where open-enrollment plans offered parents an opportunity to send their children outside the districts of their residence, only a very small minority chose to do so. However the lack of response may be explained away, it reveals the limited scope of the appeal of racial balance.

Yet this issue in many places has overshadowed the far more important factors that enter into the Negroes' educational deprivation. And it is likely that time and energy will continue to be dissipated on the question of racial balance that might more usefully be expended on the quality of the schools and on the orientation of the educational process to the needs of the colored students.

The demand for racial balance has sometimes had a blackmail effect; it has forced concessions on municipal authorities willing to spend more heavily on slum schools than they might otherwise have in order to stave off the drive for bussing. But this tactic has also had the adverse effect of exaggerating the deficiencies of schools in Negro neighborhoods and thus of frightening away experienced teachers, of hastening the flight to the suburbs and increasing the rate of withdrawal to private and parochial schools. The insistence upon integration is thus self-frustrating, as the experience of Washington, D. C., shows. Further pressure toward racial balance will certainly weaken the public schools and leave the Negroes the greatest sufferers.

The dilemma is unnecessary. There is no evidence that racial balance itself improves the capacity of the underprivileged to learn; nor that the *enforced* contact of dissimilar children has significant educational advantages. There is abundant evidence that deprived children have distinctive needs that require the special attention of the school. Yet the drive for integration has obscured, and sometimes actually impeded, the task of providing for those needs. Indeed the argument is now often being made that racial balance is desirable to meet the needs of white children.

Here, too, an awareness of the group's identity and a determination to deal with its problems is the most promising path to equality.

The Negro deserves preferential treatment in education because his needs are great. But to receive it calls for the recognition of the special character of his situation, not for costly efforts artificially to commingle his children with others in the interest of the ideal of balance.[14]

Since the desegregated, but unintegrated, school is a neighborhood school, there is a relationship between the range of residential choices and the conditions of education. The Negroes suffer from poverty, from their recency of arrival, and—in housing, more than in any other sphere—from prejudice. It remains unfortunately true that some whites willing to work side by side with the Negro or even to vote for him in an election will boggle at accepting him as a neighbor. That hesitation is connected with the fact that the residential district, especially in the middle-class areas of the city, is also the setting of a distinctive communal life, with group-derived values and activities of its own. The presence of any outsider is a potential threat, exaggerated in the case of the Negro by fears of a mass inundation.

Something has been done—by law and persuasion—to quiet these fears; a good deal more can be done by these methods. But it would help if the fearful were aware that there is no widespread desire among Negroes for residential intermixture as such. Colored people are primarily concerned with the quality of housing; they do not value highly propinquity to whites. Talk about racial balance not only distorts the actuality of Negro intentions, but it heightens the very fears that may limit the freedom of the occasional black family that wishes to move to a mixed neighborhood. A recent study of middle-income Negro families, for instance, expressed surprise at the preference for ghetto residence and suggested that whites be moved in to encourage integration, as if that were a necessary and desirable end in itself. A state legislative committee on low-income housing uncritically adopted the same goal. These proposals repeat the errors of New York City's experiment with benign quotas which deprived Negroes of the quarters they needed in order to save room for whites, all out of the concern with balance.[15]

Integration is a false issue. The problem is housing—how can adequate space up to present-day standards of decency be made available to the poor? How can all other colored families get fair value up to the level of their incomes, without being penalized for their race? For most Negroes these are the primary issues. They are difficult enough without the complications of racial balance. The control of the urban renewal process, the role of government as entrepreneur, and problems of design and form will set the framework within which the character of the Negroes' future housing will be determined. And group cohesiveness will be of great importance in influencing decisions in these matters.

The development and strengthening of Negro communal institutions may also help normalize the situation of the colored family. The disorderly features of that position are well known—the absence of a male head, frequent illegitimacy and dependence—as well as their relationship to juvenile delinquency, crime, and narcotic addiction. But these characteristics have been too readily associated with the effects of the slave heritage. The servitude of the plantation may have left elements of weakness in the families of the freedmen; but the extent to which sound family life developed among the Negroes between 1865 and 1915 is impressive, as is the extent to which it still prevails in the rural South closest to the slave setting.

A more plausible source of disorder is the effect of rural-urban migration with low income and slum housing at its destination. That correlation conforms to what is known about the changes in family life in other societies in which slavery has not been a factor.[16] It conforms also to the experience of earlier groups of migrants to American cities. Less than a half-century ago, the foreign-born residents of Irish, Jewish, or Polish slums faced comparable problems of matriarchal households and delinquency.

It was not alone the tradition of solidarity and discipline that contained the damage among these peoples, but also the fact that their families were encased in social and cultural institutions which imposed restraints upon recalcitrant individuals, established norms of behavior, and disposed of weighty sanctions for conformity. Negroes have been slower to develop similar institutions, partly because this migration came at a moment when government absorbed some of these functions, but also because in their experience separation meant segregation and bore the imputation of inferiority. Yet those men who, in the name of integration, deny that there is a significant role for the Negro press, or for Negro churches, or for Negro associations are also denying the group of its media for understanding, for expression, and for action. They would thereby weaken the capacity of the people who need those media to act on their own behalf.[17]

It is the ultimate illogic of integration to deny the separateness of the Negro and therefore to inhibit him from creating the communal institutions which can help cope with his problems. Delinquency, poverty, slums, and inadequate housing of course concern all Americans; and the attempt to eradicate them calls for common efforts from every part of the nation. But history has given the Negroes a special involvement in these matters; and to deny the actualities of the group's existence is to diminish its ability to deal with them. To confuse segregation, the function of which is to establish Negro inferiority, with the awareness of separate identity, the function of which is to generate the power for voluntary action, hopelessly confuses the struggle for equality.

Clarification of the goals of the civil rights movement has immediate tactical implications. Desegregation is not the same as integration; Selma is not Harlem, Bogalusa, not Chicago.

Where violence, exclusion from the ballot, or state power has deprived the Negro of his equal rights as a man and a citizen, it is his obligation and that of all other Americans to demand an immediate end to the discriminatory measures that aim at his subordination.

Desegregation will not solve any of the other important economic, social, and political problems of American life; it will only offer a starting point from which to confront them. The inadequacies of the political system, unemployment, inferior education, poor housing, and delinquency will still call for attention. In some of these matters the peculiarities of the Negroes' situation call for special treatment. But with reference to none of them is integration a meaningful mode of action; and the call for it which echoes from a different struggle on a different battleground only produces confusion.

Whatever may happen in the more distant future, Negroes will not merge into the rest of the population in the next few decades. Those who desire to eliminate every difference so that all Americans will more nearly resemble each other, those who imagine that there is a main stream into which every element in the society will be swept, are deceived about the character of the country in which they live. As long as common memories, experience, and interests make the Negroes a group, they will find it advantageous to organize and act as such. And the society will better be able to accommodate them as equals on those terms than it could under the pretense that integration could wipe out the past.

REFERENCES

1. I have treated the background of this problem in greater detail in *The American People in the Twentieth Century* (Cambridge, Mass., 1954); *Race and Nationality in American Life* (Boston, 1957); and *Fire-Bell in the Night* (Boston, 1964).

2. The civil rights movement is neither unified nor represented by a single spokesman. The attitudes here discussed reflect a trend expressed in statements of individuals. There are helpful collections of these views in Harold R. Isaacs, *The New World of Negro Americans* (New York, 1963); and Robert Penn Warren, *Who Speaks for the Negro?* (New York, 1965). For the background, see Richard Bardolph, *The Negro Vanguard* (New York, 1959); August Meier, *Negro Thought in America 1880-1915* (Ann Arbor, Mich., 1963). On the extremists, see Irving Howe, "New Styles in 'Leftism,'" *Dissent*, Vol. 12, No. 3 (Summer 1965), pp. 312, 314, 318 ff.

3. See, for example, *New York Times'* survey of whites' attitudes, September 21, 1964; Dean Harper, "Aftermath of a Long, Hot Summer," *Transaction*, Vol. 2, No. 5 (July-August 1965), pp. 9, 10.

4. Reconstruction literature generally focuses on the failures and the missed opportunities rather than on the achievements. See E. Franklin Frazier, *The Negro in the United States* (New York, 1957), pp. 135, 142; W. E. B. Du Bois, *Black Reconstruction in American* (New York, 1935).

5. Oscar Handlin, *The Newcomers. Negroes and Puerto Ricans in a Changing Metropolis* (New York, 1959).

6. Walter White, *Rope & Faggot* (New York, 1929), pp. 20, 227, 230 ff.; James E. Cutler, *Lynch-Law* (New York, 1905), pp. 170 ff.; J. E. Coxe, "New Orleans Mafia Incident," *Louisiana Historical Quarterly*, Vol. 20, No. 4 (October 1937), pp. 1067 ff.; Theodore Saloutos, *Greeks in the United States* (Cambridge, Mass., 1964), pp. 62-69.

7. See Dwight L. Dumond, *Anti-Slavery* (Ann Arbor, Mich., 1961); Martin Duberman, *The Antislavery Vanguard* (Princeton, N. J., 1965), pp. 137 ff.; James M. McPherson, *The Struggle for Equality* (Princeton, N. J., 1964 ; Willie Lee Rose, *Rehearsal for Reconstruction* (Indianapolis, Ind., 1964).

8. See Frank Tannenbaum, *Slave and Citizen* (New York, 1946); Stanley M. Elkins, *Slavery* (Chicago, 1959).

9. C. Vann Woodward, *The Strange Career of Jim Crow* (New York, 1957) describes the process.

10. See T. J. Woofter, *Negro Problem in Cities* (New York, 1928), pp. 177 ff.; Howard Brotz, *The Black Jews of Harlem* (New York, 1964); John Daniels, *In Freedom's Birthplace* (Boston, 1914), pp. 133 ff.; W. E. B. Du Bois, *The Philadelphia Negro* (Philadelphia, 1899), pp. 197 ff., 389 ff.; St. Clair Drake, *Churches and Voluntary Associations in the Chicago*

Negro Community (Chicago, 1940); St. Clair Drake and Horace R. Cayton, *Black Metropolis* (New York, 1962), Vol. I, pp. 174 ff.

11. See, for example, Howard Zinn, *SNCC, The New Abolitionists* (Boston, 1964), pp. 216-241.

12. For example, Charles E. Silberman, *Crisis in Black and White* (New York, 1964).

13. A misleading impression is often the result of gross comparisons of selected Negro schools or school districts with a general white average. It is necessary to take account also of variables other than race that affect performance. An analysis of achievement in Boston district high schools, for instance, shows that schools in certain white neighborhoods are as deficient as those in Negro neighborhoods (reported in *Boston Globe,* December 14, 1964, pp. 1, 13).

14. There is abundant evidence that significant improvement can come in the performance of Negroes in desegregated but racially unbalanced schools. The Banneker experiment in St. Louis, the experience of Washington, D. C., and the results in Louisville, Kentucky, point to the same conclusion. Of course, improvement can also come in balanced schools. However, the essential element is not balance, but the allocation of adequate educational resources to compensate for the disadvantaged situation of the Negro. See also Frank G. Dickey, "A Frontal Attack on Cultural Deprivation," *Phi Delta Kappan,* Vol. 45, No. 8 (May 1964), p. 398; *New York Times,* May 17, 1965. A good deal of the literature is summarized in T. F. Pettigrew, *A Profile of the Negro American* (Princeton, N. J., 1964), although the conclusions drawn are different.

15. Lewis G. Watts, et al., *The Middle-Income Negro Family Faces Urban Renewal* (Boston, 1964); Massachusetts Special Commission on Low-Income Housing, *Summary Report* (Boston, 1965), and *Final Report* (Boston, 1965), House Document 4040, p. 10.

16. See, for example, B. A. Pauw, *The Second Generation: A Study of the Family among the Urbanized Bantu in East London* (Cape Town, Union of South Africa, 1963); Raymond T. Smith, *The Negro Family in British Guiana* (London, 1956).

17. See, for example, Louis E. Lomax, *The Negro Revolt* (New York, 1962), pp. 204, 205.

JOHN B. TURNER AND WHITNEY M. YOUNG, JR.

Who Has the Revolution or Thoughts on the Second Reconstruction

Now THAT injustices to the Negroes have once again eaten deeply into the public conscience of the white citizenry of the United States and the burden of these injustices has become less bearable by the Negro than ever before, and now that the impossibility of continuing the status of Negroes without serious and almost irrevocable damage to the concept of democracy is increasingly apparent—with its unavoidable harm to the political and social future of the United States—many people are beginning to raise the inevitable question: What will the solution to racial injustice be like? How will the future look?

The question of the kind of society we will have when the Negro is truly a full participant is essentially a question of how whites should regard and treat Negroes, of how Negroes should regard and treat whites, of how the Negro should regard and treat himself, and of how the white should regard and treat himself. It is essentially a question of whether people, white and black, can behave in such a way that race and skin color are no longer relevant in human relations.

It must be clear to those with their fingers on the pulse of Negro discontent, those who are not distracted by more visible and purely local discoloration of the civil rights struggles, that anything short of the prescriptions of the Constitution of the United States and of the Bill of Rights will be completely unacceptable to the Negro and that it should be equally unacceptable to white citizens.

The Negro will demand a society that no longer kicks the Negro around, not in a physical sense alone, but in economic, political, social, and psychological senses as well. This society will not be content with the mere cessation of abuse of the Negro. It will seek in fact to allocate its resources so that *all* people now unable to take advantage of an open society because of the evils of the past systems of discrimination and prejudice can develop their talents for becoming contributors to society as well as consumers.

Beyond these architectural benchmarks the elaboration of the ideal into the tangible is much more difficult. A fair amount of disagreement exists among whites concerning how this utopia should look, what it should be like. It exists among Negroes as well. Such disagreement can never be settled by injunction; and if it is lifted to a focal point in discussion, disagreement can greatly slow down efforts to achieve the Negro's full participation in society. It may even immobilize those efforts.

What will society be like when the Negro is a full participant may be a spurious question; and if taken too seriously it could prove to be a millstone around the necks of the very Americans who believe most deeply in our political, economic, and social democracy, those who are concerned to make this democracy work.

At this particular stage of the civil rights struggle, devotees of democracy, Negroes in particular, must focus on the goals, the strategies, and the activities needed to close the gap between the life chances of all minority groups and those of the white majority. It is to this latter problem, the development of an interim strategy, that the major part of this paper is addressed.

I. *The Negro and the Revolutions*

The past twenty years have seen increased activity aimed toward improving the status of the Negro. This activity is characterized by some new inputs that distinguish these twenty years from those preceding World War II. Perhaps the most important new element is the greater predisposition of the Negro to assume risk in pressing for status equal to that of whites. A second has been the positive response of institutions, public and private, which traditionally guard and promote our democratic and moral heritage. Perhaps a third is the still weak but yet impressive show of Negro solidarity and group discipline, which is at best a loose and shaky coalition.

There is a tendency both in literature and in conversation to refer to the current civil rights struggle as a *revolt* or a *revolution*. The label is a comforting one to those who have been concerned with civil rights for a long time, for at the simplest level *revolution* connotes an acceleration of pace. There is nothing automatic or magical, however, about the outcome of a revolution. Revolutions must be planned, must be led to the desired end. To achieve that end, evaluations must constantly be made to determine what is to be done. Therefore, those persons concerned with the management and stewardship of the civil rights struggle should be increasingly accurate in their use of this concept, and must constantly ask how the current civil rights thrust can in fact maintain its revolutionary purpose.

A revolution seeks change through "a sudden and violent break with the past." The temper of a revolution is "not tomorrow but now, not part of the way but all the way." Certainly the civil rights movement has conveyed this notion of urgency through its slogan, "Freedom Now." There is no denying that without the picketing, the sit-ins, the marches the nation would have progressed less rapidly, if at all, to its present position. The protests have provided a visible rallying point for *all* Americans, Negro and white, but especially for the Negro. They have become a source of pride, a builder of morale. Protests satisfy the need to take action to help oneself. When successfully designed, they provide a sense of tangible accomplishment. They have drawn the young and not-so-young intellectuals, Negro and white, who have participated in an effort to rediscover the full meaning of democracy in today's age of scientific discovery. But to what extent do the sit-ins, the lie-ins, the marches, and the other protest and defense activities promise, in the areas where they have occurred, a sustained commitment to increase the pace of action to secure change?

Social revolutions seek change in one or all of the following areas: (1) in the locus of power and control, (2) in the rules of the game or in policy, and (3) in the distribution of rewards within the system for large segments of the population. It must be stated that *if* the civil rights struggle is indeed the current revolution in the United States, it is in many ways unique. At least until now the Negro has not been so much trying to change the American system as attempting to become a part of it. The greatest articulated concern is with just and fair access and with sharing in the rewards of the system. He is not directly seeking to put another class or another political group into power or control. He is concerned with change in those policies which exclude him, legally and extralegally; and he is concerned either with replacing those persons now in power who control such policies or with influencing them to change their exclusion practices and present pattern of reward distribution.

Realistically, though, the possibility of Negroes gaining full inclusion into society cannot be considered apart from other major domestic problems: During this era of unprecedented abundance and affluence, what is to be done with the one-fifth of the nation that is poor, with the second fifth that is economically deprived? Now that almost two-thirds of the nation lives in or near vast metropolitan complexes, what is to be done about the management and control of urban America, its obsolete housing, the increasing need for services, the archaic forms of local government and financing?

It is evident that, without viable solutions to these problems, any attempt to make the Negro part of the system will succeed only partially, thus leaving the Negro outside or forcing him to adopt a strategy to change the system. Viewed in this perspective, the nature and scope of the revolution is less clear, for the problems of automation and cybernation and of urbanization appear inexplicably entwined with that of Negroes being excluded from the main stream of society. If we are to adhere to the political and moral values of this nation, we cannot possibly progress in resolving one problem without making progress in resolving the others. Of course a certain amount of "slack" can be taken up in the system, but deeper and more permanent solutions will not be achieved.

Protest has been the Negroes' major weapon in the past and will continue to be a major part of the arsenal of strategies to win full participation. But the strategy of protest is not equally applicable in all situations.[1] As a means of bringing about a sustained step-up in pace, it has a limited use. For one thing, it is easy to mistake protest for progress, to mistake tokenism—albeit tokenism on a broader basis than ever before—for a sign that reform or revolutionary ends have been achieved. In associating constantly with people who share our convictions, it is, in fact, easy to believe that the walls of exclusion have fallen; having won the opportunity to enter barbershops in one community, it is possible to conclude that barbershops in all communities are open, or, having integrated housing on one street, to think that the street will remain integrated forever. It is easy, having received newspaper, television, and radio coverage, talked with mayors and community leaders, sustained insults and suffered weariness during marches and picketing, to conclude that the revolution is ended. It is precisely this phenomenon that led Hannah Arendt to write in her study *On Revolution:*

> There is perhaps nothing more detrimental to an understanding of revolution than the common assumption that the revolutionary process has come to an end when liberation is achieved and the turmoil and the violence, inherent in all wars of independence, has come to an end. This view is not new.[2]

A revolution is not a special moment in time. There is no such thing as instant revolution. Revolution consists of *before* and *after*. And we have yet to complete the *before*. Wisdom must be developed regarding its scope and the obstacles which it must overcome. Interim strategies and action must be planned to guide it to its intended outcome.

The reasons that, following the Emancipation, the Negro failed to dig in, failed to move more rapidly, are complex, yet as understandable as the slow strides now being made by the newly emerging independent countries of Africa. But to know why an action fails is not to correct it. Our situation today is much different from that of a century ago. In addition to the new inputs already indicated, there are other factors which might suggest a better climate for the efforts of the Negro: (1) Poor as the Negro's education is in comparison with that of whites, it is much better than it was a hundred years ago. (2) As a result of mobility and mass media, the Negro is more aware today of his opportunities, rights, and the discrepancies between his status and that prescribed by the moral and written law of the land. (3) The existence of large numbers of demoralized and alienated people poses a threat to an increasingly urban society. (4) The burden of the unresolved race problem weighs heavily upon the nation's effort to seek and maintain world leadership. All these contribute to the efforts of Negroes and whites to bring about a speedier solution to the race problem.

A hundred years ago the United States stood in the midst of another revolution. Although the Negro American was merely a pawn in that struggle, the expectations were that he would emerge a full participant in society. This he did not do. Most assuredly these expectations were unrealistic, but the warnings and lessons to be gained from the Reconstruction era cannot be ignored today.[3]

Nathaniel Weyl epitomizes the turbulent years of Reconstruction in his view that no leadership worthy of the name emerged among the Negro masses to give them coherence, organization, direction, and goals. The Negro mass itself failed to meet the challenge of the new opportunities. During the hothouse period of Northern military protection the Negro failed to seize his opportunities. Weyl quotes James Ford Rhodes as saying that the fifteen Negroes who served in Congress "left no mark on the legislation of the time." It may well be that Mr. Weyl writes harshly, even unsympathetically, but the accuracy of his conclusions remains largely unchallengeable.

But even though the climate for the Negro's efforts has improved, there is much on the current scene that gives reason for intelligent concern. Within the larger society there is an increasingly visible resistance of the heretofore somewhat latent but hard core of white supremacy. Perhaps the newest acronym in the field of white supremacy is SPONGE, the Society to Prevent Only Negroes from Getting Everything. In a fashion not unlike that of the Reconstruction era the union of white supremacy and political opportunism can pulverize the economically and politically disorganized, the inept, and the naive. Once again, there is evidence of a return to violence to keep the Negro in his place—such violence was a major characteristic of the Reconstruction era.[4] The stiffening of resistance is to be expected. Prediction, however, is not enough; plans must be made to dissolve the resistance.

The larger society is also threatened by the economic and social problems already alluded to—namely, the impact of automation and cybernation upon the economic security of the Negro. Willhelm and Powell aptly phrase the issue in the question "Who Needs the Negro?"[5] Unfortunately, the laws and programs demanding that the employment structure be opened are being enforced at the precise moment when the requirements for entering and remaining in employment are being raised, and at a time when the preferences for manpower are shifting. The undereducated Negro is consequently placed at a disadvantage. Willhelm and Powell suggest that the real revolution is the economic one. They write:

As more of us become unnecessary—as human energy and thought themselves become increasingly unnecessary—the greater will be our social anxiety. Then perhaps we will become aware that racial strife today is not between black and white, but is instead a search for human rights in a world of machines that makes so many humans utterly dispensable.[6]

Within the Negro "group" there are also causes for concern; there is continuing evidence of political naiveté among the leaders and the masses. It is still extremely common to find Negro candidates for political office running in such numbers that they cancel out the chances that any one of them will be elected. Often the Negro electorate fails to support those elected officials who have risked their political lives to help the Negro cause. It is still frequently the case that the Negro electorate uses its vote primarily to veto rather than to seek remedial and corrective action.

At the moment there is danger that the efforts of the Negro to help himself may fall short of their target through over-dependence on protest action. As James Wilson points out in his article "Strategy of Protest," there are conditions which must be reasonably met if protest is to be successful.[7] When inappropriately used, protest fails to achieve the objective; this in turn lowers the readiness of potential supporters to participate. It can also mobilize the opposition prematurely. In a few instances, as one might expect, protest is used to achieve purely individual objectives as opposed to group objectives. Such activity naturally creates doubt and suspicion among those who are called upon to participate; and it also undercuts the legitimacy of the protest in the minds of those against whom it is directed as well as among the general public. Ways must be found to protect legitimate protest from this abuse.

In summary, the current civil rights struggle is indeed revolutionary. First, it is revolutionary because it seeks and must find within the larger framework of social change a solution potentially involving modifications of traditional relations, between man and work and between man and his socio-political environment. Second, the civil rights struggle is revolutionary because, if it is to succeed, it must bring about rapid and radical changes within the Negro "group." These two revolutionary aims are not independent of each other. While it is clear that the major initiative and responsibility for the second belongs to the Negro, he cannot permit himself to become a pawn or onlooker in the broader revolutionary struggle. What strategy and what action is required of the Negro if the revolutions are to be successfully pursued?

II. *The Revolution from Within*

Restating the problem operationally. In describing the racial problem many people confuse their definition of it with its solution. In other words, some people view the problem as the failure of the Negro to achieve integration, while others refer to it as the failure of the Negro to achieve an equal partnership in a pluralistic society. But the issue is incorrectly stated when put into these terms. It is dramatically clear, it is simple to describe, and it can be expressed in terms which do not confuse definition with solution. The Negro's problem arises because his minority status has brought about greatly limited life chances in comparison with those of the white majority. This disparity appears frozen in relation to the majority group. In an address on civil rights to the Congress on February 28, 1963, the late President Kennedy stated this clearly. He said:

> The Negro baby born in America today—regardless of the section or state in which he is born—has about one-half as much chance of completing high school as a white baby born in the same place on the same day, one-third as much chance of completing college, one-third as much chance of becoming a professional man, twice as much chance of becoming unemployed, about one-seventh as much chance of earning $10,000 a year, a life expectancy which is seven years less and the prospects of earning only half as much.

It is not necessary to detail these statistics further, for they are increasingly well known. In any area selected—economic security, citizenship, housing, education, family stability, health, crime—the Negro is subject to grossly unequal life chances. The effect is to reduce his opportunity seriously as compared with that of the white majority. At the same time it adds significantly to his burdens and handicaps as compared with those experienced by whites.

The equalization of life chances for all racial, ethnic, and religious minorities is not only a goal compatible with the values of our democratic system of government and way of life; it must, in fact, be realized if the idea of democracy is to remain viable for Americans. It is necessary if our system of government is to remain a model which Americans aspire to have respected and emulated in the world of nations.

To many people the solution to the problem of equalizing the life chances of the Negro is a simple one. If the Negro really wants to improve himself, it is up to him. If he is down and out, if he has fewer life chances, he has only himself to blame. People who see the cause of the Negro's problem as individual failure say to the Negro, "Learn to speak better, dress well but less conspicuously, become quieter and more moderate in your behavior, work harder, save your money, fix up your property, attend concerts and the symphony and ballet, visit art museums, frequent the theater, meet and know the right people, and your problems will be resolved. It will only be a matter of time. Haven't the Jews, the Irish, the Italians— even the Southern whites—solved their problems this way?" This prescription for solving the Negro racial problem is called acculturation or, more commonly, the "melting pot" approach. People who believe in this approach would seek to help the Negro equalize his life chances by making him a "dark white man."

This acculturation model has not solved the racial problem for two compelling reasons: (1) It is based upon the principle that, if a member of a sub-group can lose those characteristics which set it apart, he will become indistinguishable from the majority group and will thus have the same life chances as members of that majority group. This principle might work were it not for the Negro's skin color, which makes him an accessible target for group subordination and exploitation. (2) The "melting pot" approach is also based upon the principle that, if an individual can succeed in our occupational system, he can rise to the top of our status-hierarchy. But the Negro's efforts to develop economic security have come at a point in history when certain major changes in our economic system all but close the traditional doors to economic security. The day has passed when an enterprising small merchant can expand a push-cart operation into a chain of food, furniture, or department stores. The openness of the employment market is now controlled by a labor movement whose major concern is not the control of working conditions and wages but whether or not there will be enough jobs for its present members.

A strategy for action. If at this time Negroes cannot defend themselves as a group against exploitation by submerging their identity or by becoming indistinguishable from members of the majority group, they must prevent group exploitation by group counter-power. They must be able to deter and to ward off exploitation, to protect their group by creating conflict of interest between exploitative behavior and goals of equal or greater importance to the majority group.

The essential requisites for group-exploitation deterrence-capability are: (1) *power* or *ability* to cause others to act as one desires —even against their wishes if necessary, (2) *the will to use power* for group purposes, and (3) *the capacity to exercise power skillfully.*

The first task in action to equalize the life chances of the Negro as a group must be to mobilize power. There are many sources of power but three are particularly relevant for action—political organization, economic control, and group solidarity.

Operationally, political power constitutes the ability to elect officials, to pass or veto issues voted upon by the electorate, and to procure a reasonable distribution of the rewards of the political system. A prior condition for maximum political power is maximum registration and voter turn-out, disciplined use of the ballot, disciplined use of elected official influence, and the procurement of key jobs in the government.

Economic power means, operationally, the ability to withhold needed purchasing power, to influence vital centers of decision in regard to the allocation of economic resources, to mobilize capital for group interest, to control an equitable share of wealth, to get a fair return on the dollar spent, and to become dispersed throughout the occupational structure, with mobility in each occupational class. Essentially what is required is capacity to exploit economic opportunity and to apply economic sanctions. The Negro must engage in a program of economic development.

Group solidarity is perhaps the most difficult of the sources of power to define operationally. It means, in general, the capacity to mobilize psychological and social resources at the sub-group level. It is rooted in the mutual-help concept characteristic of many families where mother, father, brother, and sister sacrifice to some extent so that one member of the family may go to school, get needed medical care, take a trip abroad, go into business, or seek some other family approved and valued objective. At another level, people from the same neighborhood or city may pool resources to help newer members.

Group solidarity raises the question of group identity, a difficult obstacle for the Negro because it was his identity (color) that created his problem. This is particularly true when acculturation is the preferred method of solving the problem. But in employing exploitation deterrence as an interim strategy, group identification is not only necessary but also more easily rationalized and accepted.

The question whether group identification is an end in itself or a means to an end will also arise. It seems to be clearly the latter, and its mobilization is justified on this ground alone. Whether it should become an end-goal will remain for future generations to determine. What *is* important is that Negroes should have the opportunity at some later date to make this choice.

The mobilization of power is not in itself sufficient for achieving effective action. As we have already seen, there must be the will to use it. The exercise of power is always at a cost, and the Negro group and its leaders must be willing to pay it. The Negro is caught in a vise between the pressure of American culture for individual success and the necessity for individual sacrifice if group success is to be achieved. Until this obstacle is understood and until Negro leaders and the masses place higher value upon group success, Negro group power can never be appropriately utilized for the ends of equalizing life chances. Every Negro institution, beginning with the family, must place high value upon cooperation in attaining group goals, while continuing to promote the idea of individual initiative. This is a complex and difficult assignment. The pattern of cooperation and collaboration must be visible and meaningful throughout the civil rights movement. It cannot be limited to a public facade of "togetherness." Civil rights leaders must be deeply committed to the value of mutual aid as a means of accomplishing the common goal.

Collaborative action will not come automatically; it will be necessary to assign responsibility for its promotion. Nor will collaboration take place in a vacuum. It must take place around tangible, important objectives and, at first, around the more clearly achievable ones; for in learning to value highly cooperative endeavors "nothing succeeds like success."

Finally, power must be intelligently utilized. It cannot be wasted as if it exists in inexhaustible supply. It must be conserved, channeled into priority issues at the precise moment when it can do the most good. There are two major directions for action within which appropriate priorities must be set even though they will require periodic readjustment: efforts to change the rules of the game and efforts to help the Negro play a more skilled game within existing rules.

With respect to changing the rules of the game, the architects of the civil rights struggle must ask what policies, what programs, what practices at the national, state, and local levels are most crucial in equalizing the life chances of the Negro. There should be frequent and regular communication at the national level among the leaders and staffs of the major organizations in the civil rights field to determine the primary areas of policy concern. An elaboration of the prevalence, scope, and etiology of the gap between the life chances of the Negro and the white should specify the most important areas of policy change and policy development. Too often civil rights organizations have been satisfied with playing a monitoring or watchdog role. Such activity is undoubtedly needed, but alone it is an incomplete answer to the task at hand.

To an increasing extent, policy and program issues will not be clearly marked with the label of race. They are likely to deal with long-term plans for the social, economic, and political development of the community. To play a role in shaping such plans so that they do not work to his detriment, the Negro must become at least as knowledgeable about these issues as others are; and obviously it is to his advantage to become even more expert. Also, it will be increasingly important for the architects of the Negro's future to link minority goals to the goals of other interest groups such as labor, business, and religion and also to the goals of the commonwealth.

While community policy is being forged to alter the broad conditions which limit and control the status of the Negro, the individual Negro cannot stand aside and wait. He must make individual decisions within the limits of the present system to determine how best to cope with it. He needs motivation, knowledge, and skill to enable him to cope as effectively as possible with the complex of factors uniquely affecting him. Civil rights organizations must give serious consideration to programs designed to help the Negro deal with life as it is now.

There are two related ideas which should be a major part of such programs. First, the notion of excellence should be seriously reassessed and must become the test of social, economic, and political literacy. It is probably true that, in the past, the Negro has gained little advantage by excelling. Often incompetence became one way of retaliating against the oppressive forces in his life. While these explanations are understandable and were even functional to some degree, in today's society incompetence is highly dysfunctional. The idea of excellence must be disassociated from the idea of occupational status mobility. One need not become a teacher, physician, or judge to achieve excellence. Excellence is more than a demand for mere competence. It is a plea for the highest standards, and it is a plea for creativity.

In his book, *Excellence: Can we be equal and excellent too?* John Gardner points out that "the importance of competence as a condition of freedom has been widely ignored."[8] Opening the doors to opportunity—which is clearly a first condition—will not of itself bring about full participation of the Negro in society. The formula is much more likely to be opportunity plus contribution plus power leads to fuller participation.

It is important that the Negro be identified among those considered to be the most skilled, creative, and qualified, whether he be a garbage collector, housekeeper, engineer, or politician. Some people will ask why the Negro needs to be any more competent than anyone else. The answer is simple: The Negro is not yet able to enjoy the democratic anonymity of being anybody. Excellence will be one component in earning the distinction of being as good or as bad as anybody else. Now the Negro needs to concentrate on being at least as good as and better than most, if he can.

The second idea concerns the assertion or exercise of rights and opportunities. Civil rights programs must help the Negro take advantage of job, business, educational, cultural, social, and political opportunities in tangible ways. Freedom and opportunity must be used, or they wither away. What is needed is a massive on-the-job training program in socialization into society. Such a program should be close enough to the individual Negro that help can be individually tailored to provide a good base for continuing growth. It would demand a new approach to social education outside of the traditional setting, whether in schools or in social agencies.

Of major significance will be efforts to link the Negro middle class with the working class. This is badly needed by both groups. The dynamics of mobility are understandable, but the shaky connection at the present time is dysfunctional. Efforts should be made to strengthen this linkage. Programs designed to bring about social, economic, and political literacy cannot be fragmented efforts but must be built into the Negro organizational structure with the assurance that they can continue for several years.

There are two target groups in the Negro population that require special thought, study, and investment. These are *youth*—the next generation—and *men*. Ways must be found to effect a dramatic increase in our economic, social, cultural, and psychological investment in Negro youth. Likewise, ways must be found to free the Negro male at every social level to assume responsibility up to the limits of his talent. The entire history of the treatment of the Negro is a travesty upon his masculinity. This travesty will not be easy to overcome, but attention to Negro males should rank high on any list of priorities. It should realistically adjust his self-image upward.

There is need for a National Commission on Negro Youth which would pay special attention over the next twenty-five years to the needs of Negro youth. The Commission should be a planning, research, and policy development operation. Its purpose should be to determine the direction and scope of programs designed to assist

Negro youth in becoming full partners in the American system. It should seek to encourage and promote its goals through existing organizations, such as schools, churches, social agencies, certain public media, and to help bring into being new agencies where needed. Such a Commission should seek to sensitize all organizations having Negro youths as members to the need to assist them in overcoming the obstacles to full participation; to include emphases which strengthen the capacity of Negro youths to participate with equality in the larger society; to make use of the existing resources in carrying out these tasks. It is essential that special and combined resources be allocated to instruction, exposure, confidence building, and opportunity linkage.

Efforts must be made to widen public support for improving the quality and quantity of education in every public school district— obviously a first and necessary target. But, in addition, ways must be found to encourage the fullest exploitation of those programs which undergird and extend the work of public schools. Such efforts would not only involve institutionalizing present tutorial efforts for the undereducated, but would also provide a new approach to educative experience for the parents of these children, thus helping to create a more supportive environment in the home for education in general. Remedial and enrichment classes should be undertaken by such organizations as churches, labor unions, and social agencies. Instruction should focus upon full and responsible entry into the economic, political, and cultural activities of our society. These emphases will require that organizations rearrange their present patterns of allocations. Perhaps it will be necessary to offer inducements to organizations to change supplementary funding.

Role identification by contact and exposure remains one of the fundamental ways of motivating to learn. Negro youth are too frequently deprived of effective role models whom they can come to know in other than a superficial and vicarious manner. Youth need to become aware through first-hand experience of the reality of achievement, and to gain true perspective on costs and gains. Negro youth need systematic, repeated exposure—socially, vocationally, and physically—to effective role models as a major means of encouraging the development of their talents. A special fund should be established nationally to make it possible for several of the talented young Negro people in various fields to work and study with outstanding senior people for one or two years. Such a plan might even operate on a local level in some communities.

The theoretical ideas underlying the work of the President's Committee on Juvenile Delinquency and, more recently, the Anti-Poverty Program make clear the importance of actual access to opportunity. Instruction and exposure without opportunity will lead to bitter frustration and conflict. During the next twenty-five years even greater emphasis must be placed upon providing the Negro with truly equal opportunity.

Finally it is important that Negro youth be offered the opportunity to develop a sense of self-respect, worthiness, adequacy, and self-confidence as a human being. To the extent that the preceding conditions are met, self-esteem will grow. But an important additional input is his elders' belief in him, communicated repeatedly during the day-to-day routines of life.

As suggested previously, any serious efforts to help the Negro must take into account the needs of the Negro male, long denied his masculinity in a society which worships it. Reference is made here to two traits, aggressiveness and responsibility. In the past, the Negro male has been punished for being aggressive and prevented from being responsible. This history of castration has played a major role in the structure and dynamics of the Negro family. Certainly there are no panaceas and no substitutes for jobs. But, there must be an effort to rediscover and free the masculinity of the Negro male so that he can take full advantage of equal opportunity. Pilot projects are needed to help determine the most fruitful ways of accomplishing this goal.

In summary, the final section of this paper has suggested that the interim strategy for the civil rights struggle derives from a statement of the problem. The operational definition posed here focuses upon the gap between the life chances of the Negro and the white. It is suggested that where the "melting pot" response is prohibited as a means of defending against group exploitation, the alternative is to develop group-exploitation deterrence-capability. The following elements are fundamental to group-exploitation deterrence: sources of power, will to use power for group ends, and skill, knowledge, and organization designed to change the rules of the system and to teach the Negro to play a more skilled game within the existing rules.

REFERENCES

1. James Q. Wilson, "The Strategy of Protest: Problems of Negro Civic Action,"

The Journal of Conflict Resolution, Vol. 5, No. 3 (September 1961), pp. 291-303.

2. Hannah Arendt, *On Revolution* (New York, 1963), p. 300.

3. Nathaniel Weyl, *The Negro in American Civilization* (Washington, D. C., 1960), pp. 85-118.

4. Maurice R. Davie, *Negroes in American Society* (New York, 1949).

5. Sidney M. Willhelm and Edwin H. Powell, "Who Needs the Negro?" *Transaction,* Vol. 1, No. 6 (September-October 1964), pp. 3-6.

6. *Ibid.,* p. 6.

7. Wilson, *op. cit.*

8. John W. Gardner, *Excellence* (New York, 1961), p. 159.

EVERETT C. HUGHES

Anomalies and Projections

THE PAPERS of this volume present vividly and in detail most of the orders of fact one would want programed into a computer set up to predict the future of American society with respect to race. Some of the interacting variables considered are the development of our population, economy, ecology, and institutions; the distribution of our population among whatever occupations and whatever "non-occupations" there are and will be; the distribution of goods and services among the population; the importance attached to race by various elements of our population as individuals and as incumbents of various roles and offices in our institutional systems; and the part of social doctrines, movements, and law in maintaining or changing the place of Negroes in our American society and economy. Gunnar Myrdal[1] spoke of the place of the Negro in American society as presenting a dilemma. The present volume presents it not as a dilemma, but as a complex of anomalies and paradoxes. My contribution is comment *en marge* on some of those anomalies and paradoxes.

In some respects Negro Americans have got out of the place in which it used to be said they were all right, only to find that, in some respects, the new place is worse or, at least, less comfortable. Their original place was that of cheap illiterate labor on plantations which produced crops for world markets in which they—the laborers—could not buy much. The illiteracy was "functional" for the system as long as it wanted labor more than customers. That "place" is rapidly disappearing by force of economic and technological change. The plantation workers have moved from the cabin and shanty rural slums of the South to the crowded Black Ghettos of converted mansions and luxury apartments in the "central cities of the Standard Metropolitan Areas," which are larger and more nu-

merous in the North. Negroes have become more urban than their
nearest racial and religious kin, the more-or-less Anglo-Saxon white
protestants, who are numerous in Appalachia and other rural slums,
who still own and operate a large proportion of the more prosperous family farms of the country, and many of whom—after success
in urban business and professions—have become the ex-urbanites.
But in course of becoming more urban, the *under*employed, illiterate, ill-fed, underpaid share-cropper or gang-laborer has become
the latterday, unskilled, illiterate, *un*employed of an urban, industrial, and partially post-industrial economy. He has come to the
foot of the ladder only to find the bottom rungs gone.

As the unemployed poor man of the city he is not so ill-fed and
clothed as in his old place; he is enough healthier to produce more
surviving offspring, so that the proportion of Negroes in the population is increasing slightly. He has plenty of leisure, but without
the work that gives it meaning, or the money to make much of it.
The whole country is richer, and so is even the poor Negro, but he
is becoming relatively poorer in comparison to white people. And,
as Esther Peterson of the Department of Labor has so convincingly
shown in a recent report, it costs money to be poor. It also costs
money to be a Negro.

In fact, Philip Hauser shows us that "the cost of being a Negro
increases as his education increases." Education, as everyone knows,
is the American means of climbing out of poverty; it takes more of
it than ever for anyone. It takes still more for the Negro to get the
same benefit in income; the income, in turn, will buy him less housing, services, and goods than it would a white American. Yet a large
number of Negro Americans have risen above their traditional
place by way of education. By tradition and doctrine, every Negro
was supposed to be inferior to the lowest white man in education,
income, and standard of living.[2] There was never a time when all
Negroes were so low as that, but there were and still are—as
Thomas Pettigrew shows—places and situations where any Negro
who wants to live should act as if it were so. The late E. Franklin
Frazier had hair-raising stories to tell of the dangers of talking a
more grammatical English than the Georgia cracker from whom he
had to buy gasoline for his old Buick car. There are more Negroes
of education in this country than in any other. In spite of the strict-
est race line outside South Africa, we have the greatest population
of people classified as Negro who are effectively literate, work in a
modern economy, and want and buy the goods other Western in-

dustrial people produce and buy. Since their wants and ambitions are those of other Americans of similar education and income, it is they who notice that it does indeed cost a great deal—in money and dignity—to be a Negro in the United States. It was the younger among them who first "sat-in" for the right to consume goods and services, including education, as other Americans do. Participation and consumption are much the same thing in our world. Those young middle-class Negroes have since been joined by people of all ages, of other ranks and races, in their "nonviolent" but aggressive battle to destroy their traditional "place." The violent opposition has generally been led by white Americans inferior to "nonviolent" Negroes in education and all status-giving characteristics except race itself.

About one in ten of us United States Americans is known to himself and others, and was probably counted in the census, as a Negro. This fact affects the manner in which that one earns his living and "chooses" his place to live. It will be paramount in determining many of his associations: religious, professional, and social; the more intimate the association, the more paramount is race. But little is said of the nature of the race line itself and of those most intimate and inescapable of all relationships, kinship and marriage. We Americans may have poor relations, if we are rich; rich ones, if we are poor. For people who get ahead in the world do not usually immediately or completely renounce the kin they have left behind; and those who do not get ahead are not inclined to lay embarrassing claims on those who have done so. Compared with the kin systems of most societies, ours is flexible. People are relatively free to set the boundaries of their own complex of kinfolk. If we cannot get rid of relatives in any other way, we can move a thousand miles away from them.

We are also unusually free to choose our spouses. Kinship is reckoned on both sides of the house and kin names are the same on both. As a result our children may have relatives of two or more religions, ethnic groups, and social classes. If the relatives on both sides are very much alike and there are no active feuds, they may comfortably meet on social and festive occasions. The family gettogether, small and large, is a great American institution and at greater distances than ever. But for various reasons the two sides may not be comfortable together, except perhaps at those most universal of festivals, funerals. If a marriage be ethnically, religiously, or otherwise mixed, one side or other—or both—may absent itself from the wedding. A naming (I was about to say christening) calls for a lining up of the forces on the side of the one true faith for the once-and-for-all identification of the child with one side or another. If there be, as often in Quebec, marriage of French with English, the kinship may be bilateral, but not symmetrical. Family gatherings are apt to be lopsided—either heavily French or heavily English. And when the time comes to send children to school, a choice of language must be made.

North American kinship is bilateral and marriage selection is relatively free. People may prefer one set of relatives to another. They may draw the line within which they give mutual aid more or less as they wish. They may and do pick from among their ancestors those who will reinforce the conception of themselves which they wish to hold and have their neighbors accept.

But on one point of difference this grandly flexible system is hard and unyielding. The essence of the race line in North America is that no person identified as Negro will be admitted as effectively social kin of any person classified as white. In those states which have laws against intermarriage of the races, there can be no legitimate offspring of a mixed mating.[4] In all states, the offspring of such a mating are popularly considered Negro whether legitimate or not. What would happen to a white woman who had an illegitimate child of a Negro father today, we can only guess. The treatment might vary according to region, community, class, and family. The result, if not the means, would probably be the same as in the case of the Southern white grandmother of Horace Cayton:[5] complete separation of mother and child. Neither the white mother-to-be of a Negro man's child nor the Negro mother-to-be of a white man's child can invoke the American woman's right to a shot-gun wedding. The Negro mother can at least keep her child. Here is a great American anomaly—a case in which the general rules and duties of kinship are not merely not invoked, but are completely denied. More than denied, they are taboo, even at the graveside. Those who would violate the taboo are cast out from the socially "superior" and more powerful race. They might be killed, in the name of virtue. For with respect to those classified as Negroes, virtue becomes vice and vice, virtue.

This may be illustrated by the phrase, "Would you want your sister to marry a Negro." Its meaning is that if she were to marry a Negro she would no longer be your sister, that her Negro husband would be no kin of yours, and that any children of the marriage, being Negroes, would likewise not be kin of yours. But the shame brought upon you, because of the former kinship, would justify not merely the withholding of the usual aid to kin, but violence, even killing. Thus there is a great moral fault—in the geological sense, and let us not quibble about the other sense—in American society when it comes to obligations to Negroes who would be kin if they were not Negro.

It is a fault that is crucial to any projection of the future of what Talcott Parsons calls "full citizenship" of Negroes or any other Americans of less than full standing. For citizenship as he conceives it, and as Americans generally do, is more than a legal status; a citizen is a member of a moral community. The definition of the white and Negro serves the function of limiting moral obligations of whites to Negroes; it makes the relationship not reciprocal, but one-sided. The function of the American definition of race has been to justify that one-sidedness; and the essence of the justification is exclusion of Negroes from full membership in the "human race." To make sure, all doubtful cases must be cast into the less-than-human group.

The American definition of racial categories—as that of most social categories—seems very odd indeed if considered from any other point of view than that of setting the limits of social obligation. Yet there is a consistency in the definition, a consistency worked out in social history, not in a laboratory or by a scientific taxonomist.

The historical situation in which the categories were worked out has been one in which it was greatly to one's advantage to be classed white, and in which the people already called white had and have power to determine the criteria and to settle disputed cases of identity. If we talk of the future of Negro Americans we of necessity talk of the manner in which Americans are and will be categorized, of the importance which they will attach to the various categories, of the relative power of groups to control the definitions of these classifications and to assign people to them, and of the advantages of belonging to one group rather than another.

If the criteria for classifying us by race remain the same, continue to be applied to all Americans except a few exotics—American Indians and those Asiatics who comprise the majority of the human species but are not at the moment numerous in America—and continue to be important, projection of the relative numbers of Americans of the two major racial categories will be a matter of predicting rates of marriage, including intermarriage, rates of reproduction properly corrected in the many ways required in such a society as ours, and rates and directions of migration. In view of the genocide practiced by the German National-Socialists and occasionally advocated here, one would have to consider the possibility of political and military action—with methods not yet known—of one race against another and would have to predict the winner.

The significance of race in North America and our definition of it have given us sharp and suspicious eyes. Most Americans will immediately place another with but few Negroid characteristics as a Negro. People in other parts of the world may have sharp eyes or ears for people of the categories crucial in their societies, but not necessarily for ours. Once we have placed a person in the Negro category, it takes strong proof to the contrary to alter the assignment. We may even place them without any biological signs. Twice in my career a blond blue-eyed student has drawn my office door shut after her in a way that told me—from experience as a college teacher—that she was about to reveal her troubling secret, and before she could speak I knew—from being an American—what the secret was to be. One, a young woman, had come from the West to Chicago to escape from her Swedish mother and become a Negro —when it suited her. Her father was a Negro jazz musician whom she found fascinating, though he had abandoned his family. The other, a middle-aged woman, had moved North to become white so that her daughter could do likewise. A middle-class woman, she required letters of recommendation; all of hers betrayed that her previous employers had been Negro institutions. I do not go around looking for Negroes behind pale faces and blue eyes, but I carry the experience of America in me. I am quick to classify by race; I do not mean to be, but I am.

Our definition of races is then both complicated and simple. There is no American who could not be a Negro, so far as physique is concerned. In that sense it is complicated. It is simple, however, in that anyone is a Negro if it is obvious that some of his ancestors were Negroid, and in that anyone is considered a Negro if it is known or strongly rumored that one or more of his ancestors were Negroid. The American white race is a residual category whose members have developed an uncanny and suspicious eye for any who do not belong. Such sharpness and suspiciousness of eye can be developed only about something which people regard as of paramount importance. Negroes of course equal, indeed probably

699

excel, whites in their eye for race; they have even greater reason to recognize race. It can mean the difference between friend and enemy, one's own to be trusted or outsider to be feared, between life and death.

The sharpness of eye is developed not merely with respect to physical characteristics. There are findings which show that race is more easily detected, or sought, by the white eye in some circumstances than others. If the Negro does not wear one of the many uniforms of deference or of poverty or play some role in which we expect Negroes to appear, the Negro-ness might not be noticed. On the other hand, there might be situations in which it would be doubly noticed. Imagine a handsomely purple-black Negro woman in a decolleté white gown at the ball celebrating her husband's inauguration as President of the United States. The future of the perception of race is an important part of the future of this country. Television, the founding of new nations, and the United Nations have shown to the world people of every tint and physiognomy in nearly all social roles. This raises again the question of the power of costume, role, and office to determine what we see and accept. The priest, the pope, the king, the supreme court justice—in our image of them does the office outshine race or does race dim the luster of the office? Or might it be that a situation would arise in which race and office would enhance each other? As Negroes appear in a greater variety of prestigeful positions, perhaps whites will allow the Negro-ness to blend into the shadow of the office or role—after, of course, we have given ourselves (the whites) credit for allowing the Negro to occupy the position and after we have given him some condescending credit for his sterling character and hard struggle.

We do not in this country, as in South Africa, have card-carrying Negroes. But the assignment to the Negro race is probably just as fateful, except for the possibility for white Negroes to resign from the race by going where they are not known and denying the bonds of kinship. But we are all card-carriers: social security, insurance, military registration, Blue Cross, Union, credit, driver's license, blood-group, allergies. All of us have our pockets full of them. There are dossiers especially on people of the middle class to which an increasing proportion of us of all races belong. The internal revenue and the FBI know all about us. The Educational Testing Service and the College Entrance Examination Boards have the word on an ever increasing proportion. The colleges of the country and the mail-order houses have the most amazing mailing-lists. By a trick of history racial classification is being left off cards and dossiers just when everyone in the country is getting cards and dossiers. There are few of us who could not be unerringly classified as white or Negro by the IBM machines or computers, because of combinations of characteristics on tapes or cards. The isolated communities where certain groups of peculiar mixtures of ancestry once maintained a special racial status are disappearing. We are all classified. There is no hiding place from our past; the question of the future then is whether those agencies which inquire so relentlessly into our pasts will bother to pay attention to race.

So far as I know there has been no movement in this country for a long time to change the criteria by which persons are assigned to the social category, Negro. There have always been criteria, including color, of distinction within the Negro world. But no one appears to be proposing any elaboration of the racial classification or any new set of devices to determine whether any given individual is indeed Negro or not. As a frontier the racial line is quiet, except for the drive to keep race off documents and even to forbid tell-tale photographs. If the Black Muslims were to gain the day, they would have to set up tribunals to decide who is truly of their morally superior race rather than of the bestial white race. But the general movement is to make race line unimportant, to have Negroness forgotten. Suppose there were no longer any distinct social advantage in not being Negro; suppose, as Edwin C. Berry of the Chicago Urban League puts it, it were really and fully all right to be colored. Suppose the time came when a court would no longer hold it libelous to put it in writing that a white man is a Negro.[6] There might still be a period in which it would be newsworthy to be the first Negro to be named, say, a justice of the Supreme Court or president of the Dupont Company (and the latter might be the more newsworthy!). One's identification as Negro might be used to push a special claim to some position because of previous disadvantage. Those would be passing phases. But would Negroes really want their past as Negroes forgotten in an essentially race-less world? It might be a world in which traditional American claims on social prestige would hold.

For here is a paradox of identity and prestige. Except for being black, American Negroes have most of the symbols necessary for being considered rather more American than average. They were a larger proportion of the population in 1790 than now. Not long ago, the way to find the Negro sections of Northern cities from the census was to look up those tracts with very high proportions of the population native-born of native parents. Negroes are "old Americans," a characteristic that earns one prestige. They are almost WASP's. If only they were not black, some of them would be eligible for the Daughters of the American Revolution; maybe that is why the organization is so adamant on race. Too many of the "wrong" people are eligible. One of my eight great-great grandmothers was held up to a window to see the British soldiers marching in the streets of Philadelphia in the War of 1812. She was the granddaughter of a German bondwoman who had married a veteran of the American Revolution. The bondwoman part can be forgotten or even used as proof of early immigration, but color cannot be forgotten. Yet in this world of prestige by date of immigration of the earliest known American ancestor, the Negroes have one of the valued symbols. Some Negroes have shown themselves all too ready to make the claim, by way of African princes taken into slavery or by emphasizing unacknowledged kinship with white families of renown. It will of course be interesting to see whether Negroes, by the time that there is no advantage in not being one, will want to claim any kinship with the people who so stubbornly denied them the human rights they so loudly preached—for whites only—from pulpit and platform. Perhaps they will ask the Jewish question: If I were not a Jew, what would I want to be? A descendant of the Mayor of Selma, Alabama? Or of any whites, for that matter? One possibility, pleasant to contemplate, is that all of our descendants will have found better canons of social prestige when our eye for race has grown dim. If any emphasis is, in that day, to be put upon descent from those who cleared the land, contributed to America's arts, and struggled up patiently—until they got impatient and got results—from humble origins, the Negroes will have a foremost claim.

Here, earlier, as also in South Africa, some people of Negro descent sought to differentiate themselves from others, thus increasing the number of racial categories and modifying the criteria of racial ascription. That day is past, partly by fiat of the white world supported by bureaucratic identification of everyone, partly by the very definite improvement of the position of Negroes with the promise that integration—tendency toward disappearance of the race line—will continue, perhaps at an accelerated rate. It certainly will not disappear for a long time, but it seems likely that there will be no new movement to multiply the categories or change the criteria. Nor is there any movement to have Negroes rather than whites decide who is a Negro. Perhaps the system has gone on so long, and the web of association and kinship within the American Negro race is so great, that there is essential consensus on who belongs to each race.

If we assume that the races will continue to be defined as they are, what of numbers? That is a problem on which demographers are working. As one extreme model, one might take a situation in which every marriageable Negro would be married to a white and in which those marriages would be as fruitful as marriages between whites. Approximately one white in nine would get a Negro mate and—as now defined—Negro children. In a few generations about half the children born would be Negro by definition, but it would be very hard to tell which were Negro and which not unless a strict record were kept. It would require card-carrying!

Perhaps we should have a geneticist on this problem. If, as some say, the ten per cent of Negroes in our population already carry a gene pool of which approximately one quarter comes from Europe, and if intermarriage were complete, Negroid genes would probably not leave much trace in our population. I set this up as a sort of absurdity. Only a completely totalitarian government could bring about such high intermarriage; genocide has been more to totalitarian liking thus far. The case does indicate, however, how greatly in favor of an essentially white race the proportions in our population work even with our racial definition which eliminates all doubtful cases from the white race.

Suppose even the milder—but equally improbable—case of mathematically random intermarriage between two groups which are in proportions of nine to one. The larger one would exist practically forever as a "pure" group of some size, even if all the mixed specimens were taken from it, while the smaller, even with the addition of all the known mixed cases, would become so diluted that apparently "pure" specimens would become very few and the mixtures who might "pass" would become a great majority of the total population. I apologize for even mentioning this subject. If the demographers and geneticists wish to slay me, let them first set up the various models, probable and improbable, of future breeding and interbreeding of these peculiar categories of people who are, by Americans, classified as of one race or another. The Negroes ought to disappear, but probably will not. Nuclei of people persist even when intermarriage is not strictly forbidden. I am trying only to imagine the genetic situation which would be least favorable to the survival of a large number of Americans discernibly of Negroid descent, perceptibly different, that is, from another large number of Americans.

Suppose we take the much more likely, but still not very likely, case of an America which had become completely indifferent to racial characteristics but which retained its other ways of rating people: education, income, manners, speech, occupation, and family connections. There are societies in South America which are relatively indifferent to racial characteristics, but are exceedingly sensitive to the signs of social class, including "good family" or connection with prestigeful kin-webs. Those societies are economically such that it is much more difficult to get ahead in the world than it is in the United States. A few women, in nearly all societies, have been able by beauty or other talents to rise from the slums to palaces—as in Hollywood. Let us not go into the question of the fascination of the exotic or of the universality of the canons of female beauty. Negro women have not succeeded as young stars in Hollywood; there have been many who would have done so had uncensored male admiration been the only requirement. Perhaps even now a Josephine Baker would not have to emigrate to Paris, but in her earlier years talent cum beauty was not enough. Leaving aside fame by bedazzlement, a very common thing in America, if we became relatively indifferent to race, but kept our other criteria of status and prestige, and rewarded people for about the same activities as now, what would be the future of Negro Americans?

American Negro women have always had more security and less risk of physical and social attack, other than rape, than the men. Already there is a large group of middle-class Negro families in the country. The labor force includes an increasing proportion of people of white-collar occupations and an even larger one of a somewhat lower-middle-class style of life. The Negro family has been stable, but not so Negro marriage. One would expect that with more nearly equal opportunity for jobs at all levels, Negroes might approach white families in their characteristics, become more stable in those matters where they are less stable than white families, and less so where they are more stable than white families of similar class. A real break-through is likely to come only when an interracial marriage could be based on a sound mutual bet that, together, the mates could get on at some appropriate class level in some

American community other than The Village, Chicago's Hyde Park, Cambridge, or their likes and could dare to have children there. A wise and strong Negro woman and a white man who is sensitive and intelligent—and knows some of his own weaknesses—might make a winning combination given half a chance or better. Let us not be over-skeptical of such radical changes. One-fourth of the Jewish men in Germany were marrying Christian women when Hitler came to power; rather, Christian women were winning one-fourth of the marrying Jewish men in a tight market. Those women, given the small proportion of Jews in the population, were—lucky or not—a few.

Even if we were to have a break-through of that magnitude in Negro-white intermarriage, we Americans would still probably consist of a number of endogamous lumps plus certain interstitial, more or less open groups resulting from previous mixtures. My favorite minority people, the French Canadians, have absorbed great numbers of Irish, Scotch, and English, and probably some Negro Americans. Their English-speaking descendants in the United States are probably as numerous as the apparently homogeneous French people of Quebec. Many ethnic and sectarian communities lose large numbers of their children to the "world," yet remain identifiable, endogamous nuclei. Perhaps it will be so with Negroes and whites if, and long after, there is a great deal of intermarriage and interbreeding. As for interbreeding without intermarriage, it will surely dwindle to nothing when the differences between income, power, and social class sharply decline.

The most drastic imaginable change in American race relations would be the full extension of the American bilateral kinship system to include mixed couples and their in-laws on both sides. A mixed marriage—as to race, nation, politics—is often one which ends up not mixed, that is, one in which kin connections are kept on one side only, the other being more or less excluded. Many American marriages are, de facto, like that. The poor, or otherwise embarrassing, relations are suddenly or gradually dropped. The people who make odd marriages of the same kind may in a short time create new homogeneous nuclei of congenial people who hold what are scarcely distinguishable from family reunions. They may hive off and form a new social grouping.

It may well be that, while we will not see new racial categories defined, an increase of intermarriage will be part of that forming of new nuclei of families with common style. Perhaps the common experience of sit-ins, marches, and demonstrations will, as some Southern and other whites predict, create new groups whose common élan and whose common experience of cattle prods and the evil-eye of hatred will lead to continuing associations, including marriages.

Perhaps there will come to be cases where mixed couples and their children will be able to lead normal lives, with real uncles and aunts and cousins on both sides, or at least with those *ersatz* relatives so many Americans have—especially those who have left home and found a breathing place in a moral and intellectual atmosphere other than the one they were brought up in. While we may be a card-carrying people, we appear also to be a people of myriad informal nuclei of common style, fêtes, cuisine, play, and moral causes.

Even if many whites and Negroes were drawn into such common social nuclei, there would remain the problem of the great hang-over from centuries of discrimination. And even if all discriminatory practices based on race alone were to disappear, their accumulated effects would remain. How long would it be before Negroes would have, in the same proportion as other Americans, the characteristics which would allow them to move freely in our society and economy; how long before they would be distributed in the same proportions as others among occupations, and would be like them in income, consumption habits, education, and in all respects but race itself? It would certainly take a long, long time. Many other social events and currents could change the direction and rates of change in the Negroes' condition—and that of others— in the interim.

In the first paragraph of this essay I spoke of the Negroes' place in American society and of the ways in which they have been kept in it. People have searched Scripture and come up with proof that God made the races one day and means them to stay apart—in a peculiar kind of apartness, to be sure, since he equipped them to be strongly tempted and able to get together in the way most fatal to apartness. People have developed elaborate ideologies to justify excluding Negroes from full membership in the human race. Having excluded them from the human race for nobler purposes, we have thought ourselves justified in adapting our legal institutions in whatever ways turn out to be necessary to keep a lower breed in subjection. Thus the sheriff's posse was changed from an occasional device by which citizens might protect themselves from the outlaw into a permanent institution with membership and leadership going from generation to generation—an "almost institution" always ready to mobilize people to keep the Negro in his place and destroy any local whites and to get rid of outside whites who take the Negro's side. A chronically sloppy police in not quite open collaboration with eternally vigilant posses with good horses and guns, back street gangs with old cars and whatever weapons come to hand, and occasional fanatics who are good shots at a distance confront our society with a combination of legitimate and bastard institutions which is very difficult to combat. We have seen some successes of law and vigorous police work against this combination. We must ask whether continued progress against this system of keeping Negroes in their place will result in general improvement of our policing institutions, by which they would approach the quality of policing in England and the countries of western Europe. We must also ask whether increasing application of our constitutional principles to Negroes will be accompanied by a return to the more obvious interpretation of the great documents of the Christian tradition, which are broadly humane. Once there is not even any apparent gain in reading the Gospel backwards will there continue to be great numbers of apparently sincere people who find themselves driven to make that backwards interpretation?

I remember Robert E. Park once saying that even the most benighted Southern Baptist usually gets right on the race question after service as a missionary in Africa. In our own time we have Billy Graham preaching the "Bible" gospel, so cherished as a symbol by many Southern whites, only to integrated congregations. Will increasing integration bring release from those constrictions of mind and sentiment which have certainly had some part in the perversion of doctrines, principles, and institutions themselves? Noble principles have been perverted in defense of vested interests other than those of whites in exploiting the Negro; and noble principles have—with the aid of courageous men—been cleaned, sharpened, and well-used for their true purposes. We have also, in our American institutions, many that have degenerated to very low level without any connection with keeping Negroes in their place. Yet we must ask, at this time of actual and impending great change in the relations of Negro with other Americans, what is likely to be the general effect on our institutions and conduct of this one great change—occuring as I suppose it was bound to do—along with other great changes in our institutions and way of living. Perhaps all that it is wise to say on this subject is that we ought to keep a sharp eye out for the clues to directions of change, take hold of those clues and follow them out quickly and imaginatively, make the most of them in directing social policy and practice, with a sober reminder that we cannot do very well at home unless we do equally well abroad on these matters of humane conduct.

REFERENCES

1. Gunnar Myrdal, *An American dilemma: the Negro problem and modern democracy* (New York, 1944).

2. Robert E. Park, *Race and Culture* (Glencoe, Ill., 1950), p. 242. ". . . the traditional social order . . . assigns every Negro to a position inferior to that of every white man." (First published in *The Annals*, 1928).

3. Horace R. Cayton, *Long Old Road: An Autobiography* (New York, 1965).

4. Charles S. Mangum, Jr., *The Legal Status of the Negro* (Chapel Hill, N. C., 1940), Chap. I, "Who is a Negro," p. 18. "Every court which has considered the question has held that writing that a white man is a Negro is libelous per se. In the case of spoken words, however, the courts have disagreed."

5. Horace R. Cayton, *op. cit.*

6. Charles S. Mangum, Jr., *op. cit.*, Chap. II, "Libel and Slander."

TALCOTT PARSONS

Full Citizenship for the Negro American?
A Sociological Problem

THE DESIGNATION "second-class citizen" has often and with justice been used to describe the status of the Negro in American society. As the British sociologist T. H. Marshall has shown with particular clarity,[1] citizenship is a complicated matter which is by no means exhausted by the more literal meanings of the term "civil rights." I should like to begin this discussion with an analysis of the meaning of the concept of citizenship, leaning heavily on Marshall's work, though attempting to go beyond it in some respects. I shall then attempt to analyze some of the conditions which have been necessary to account for the progress which the Negro American has made so far toward gaining full citizenship—and which, at the same time, the society has made toward including the Negro in that status—and the further conditions which must be fulfilled if the process is to approach completion. In carrying out this analysis I shall pay particular attention to comparing the status of the Negro with that of other groups which have in various analogous ways been discriminated against in American society. I hope that such an analysis will reveal a combination of similarities and differences which illuminates the salient features of the Negro case. Since the other groups have progressed considerably further toward full inclusion than has the Negro so far, their experience may provide certain projective guide lines for considering the Negro case. The relation of the internal change of status of the Negro American to the color problem in world affairs will also be discussed.

The concept of citizenship, as used here, refers to full membership in what I shall call the *societal community*.[2] This term refers to that aspect of the total society as a system, which forms a *Gemeinschaft*, which is the focus of solidarity or mutual loyalty of its members, and which constitutes the consensual base underlying its political integration. This membership is central to what it means to be defined, in the case of our own nation, as "an American"—hence it gives a special justification for the word order in the title of the present issue of *Dædalus,* that it is the Negro American, not vice versa. The Negro slave could have been, and certainly was called, an "American Negro"—he was resident in the United States and owned by American citizens, but was not part of the societal community in the present sense.

Perhaps John Rawls has formulated, in general philosophical terms, more clearly than anyone else the way in which full citizenship implies a fundamental equality of rights—not equality in *all* senses, but in the sense in which we refer to the rights of membership status in the societal community.[3]

From the unit viewpoint, societal community is a category of the commitment of members to the collectivity in which they are associated, and of the members to each other. It is the focus of loyalties which need not be absolute, indeed cannot be, but which require high priority among loyalties of the members.[4] To occupy this position the associational structure must be in accord with the common values of the society: members are committed to it because it both implements their values and organizes their interests in relation to other interests. In the latter context it is the basis for defining rules for the play of interests which make integration possible, preventing the inevitable elements of conflict from leading into vicious circles radically disruptive of the community. It is also the reference base of the standards for allocating available mobile resources in complex communities.

In all "advanced" societies, societal community is linked with political organization, but is also differentiated from it. Although all advanced societies are "politically organized," this aspect of their organization, what we ordinarily refer to, at the societal level, as government, is not identical with community in the present sense. It is precisely when the two are in some kind of conflict that revolutionary situations can arise.

The Nation as Societal Community

In modern Western history, the focus of the differentiation of the societal community lay in the emergence of the nation, hence of "nationalism." Obviously, a similar process is now going on in many parts of the world in the formation of the "new nations." There are three aspects of the emergence of the nation which I should like to note and then briefly spell out for the American case.

The first is the differentiation of criteria for belonging to the nation in contrast to membership in the more "primordial" kinship-ethnic and, often, religious groupings. Here the change is toward the establishment of *associational* criteria. In the case of a total society, as politically organized, it is impossible for membership to be entirely voluntary for all, but it can move very far in this direction, that is, away from a purely ascriptive basis, and has done so. More importantly the status of citizenship comes to be institutionalized in terms independent of the ascriptive criteria just cited, for it concerns above all the "natural rights" so fundamental to American tradition.

Second, the nation is differentiated from its government. This is *not* to say they are dissociated. Rather, this differentiation involves the development of political independence by the societal community so that it is no longer ascribed to any particular governmental leadership, such as hereditary monarchy with full executive authority. The obverse of this development is that government becomes structurally independent in that it is free to mobilize within the society those resources which are relatively fluid, for example, in establishing an appointive civil service free of more particularistic ties and in soliciting support from a range of different groups in the constituency.

Finally, the differentiation of the societal community as nation involves a shift of the integration of the three elements, community, ascriptive bases, and government, in the direction of a synthesis of citizenship and territoriality. This is necessary because the individual is anchored in residential ties, even though there is high residential mobility, because work as well as residence is located physically, and because the availability of resources is territorially anchored.[5]

For the United States, as for many other countries, the consolidation of nationhood was directly connected with a struggle for political independence. It may be said that there was sufficient ethnic and religious uniformity to make solidarity possible, but enough diversity to favor a major shift toward the associational basis of that solidarity, as compared with the European analogues. The core was surely white, Anglo-Saxon, and Protestant (WASP). The Negroes, most of whom were slaves, were not included, and the

Catholic, Dutch, and Jewish minorities were so small as to be structurally almost negligible. However, one of the three components, the religious, had built-in diversity in that there were many Protestant denominations.[6] And, in spite of the prominent involvement of the Anglican church in the colonies, the non-Anglican majority was understandably reluctant to countenance an Anglican Establishment, particularly because of the latter's obvious relation to England.

On the side of values, two particularly important components were the influence of the Enlightenment, with its emphasis on assuring the rights of individuals independently of their ascriptive involvements, and the fact that the most important religious groups involved were in the same broad tradition, which we tend to call "liberal Protestantism" today. The Bill of Rights is the central institutional embodiment of these components.[7]

The new American Union was, however, a *federal* union of a special sort. Though the Constitution prescribed a Republican form of government as well as other universalistic patterns, especially through the Bill of Rights, the states could and did, serve as a strong protector of the particularistic groups and institutions at many levels, from the South's "peculiar institution" before the Emancipation Proclamation and the 13th Amendment to local power interests, police power, and the conservative interpretation of the 14th Amendment.[8] Today we are acutely aware of how hard it has been to overcome the conception that the state was somehow "sovereign" and that we were only a confederation of states, not a federal state. In view of the difficulties of maintaining the Union, not only in the Civil War crisis, but also earlier,[9] it seems probable that this "concession" to state particularism was necessary in order to establish a union at all—*vide* the length of time it took Rhode Island to decide to join.

The essential consequence for our problem is that this version of federalism drastically limited the extent to which universalistic values and normative principles, formulated most conspicuously in the Bill of Rights, could be applied to the regulation of relations internal to a large variety of groups and collectivities. The extension of this jurisdiction has been a long process and is still far from complete. The most visible aspect of the process has been legal, based above all on the post-Civil War Amendments, the 14th and 15th. The legal process has been both cause and effect of a broader process of structural change in the society, several aspects of which will figure in the following discussion. A major force in this process is further societal *differentiation* in many fields, such as property rights and the development of new institutions regulating marriage and education.

Some of the same circumstances established quite firmly the mutual independence of government and the national community. This was a phase which underlay another main source of American strains, namely, the suspicion between the private sector and government. This has had a long-run influence on the Negro problem by minimizing certain kinds of private business support for public action in favor of the Negro. On the whole, the differentiation proceeded faster and further here than in Europe, a fact which has, on balance, contributed positively to the inclusion of the Negro as well as other groups which were originally excluded. The reason for this judgment is that the relatively open and pluralistic situation, although it provided opportunity for much obstruction, has served as a structural base for challenging and overcoming the obstruction. Above all, such structural changes as industrialization and urbanization, which ultimately undermined the obstacles, were favored.

Finally, the new nation began with a unified, territorially based control of resources and of rights, a factor which eventually contributed to the integration of its societal community. The Constitution guaranteed economic unity by prohibiting tariffs between the states and by allowing no limitations on the movement of citizens. Inherent in this guarantee was a general bias against the consolidation of local and regional particularism, even though other powerful forces worked toward it. This was of special importance because it existed in the early phase of a unique opportunity—that of occupying a territorial area of continental scope. The integration of the pattern of citizenship with that of territory in all areas under American control created a relatively uniform standard of citizenship. This meant not the neglect of sectional interests, but the positive establishment of a pattern covering all regions. The special case of the South will, of course, occupy much of our attention.

As Lipset has pointed out,[10] the United States originated as a "new nation" in a way broadly similar to those which have been emerging in our own time. It achieved independence from colonial status. It approached the pattern of association of people who came to implement their own values and goals more closely than could older nations, but it had sufficient initial cultural homogeneity to achieve its initial integration, not without serious internal struggles, but still with a certain effectiveness. This "liberal" tradition, especially as expressed in the Bill of Rights, provided a basis for other groups, culturally and ethnically more distant from those predominant in the founding generations, to be included in the national community.

The consolidation of that community and the advancement of the process of differentiation of the society to the point that a strong national government could take precedence over local, state, and regional particularisms took a long time. Though the most serious crisis was settled by the outcome of the Civil War, as Samuel Beer has made clear, a new phase began in the period of the New Deal.[11] In part, this was a result of our wider sense of national responsibility in world affairs following our involvement in the First World War. As we shall see, it was not unimportant that the process of inclusion of the "new immigration" reached its culmination at the same time that the Democratic party attained its new position of power in the New Deal era. It was not fortuitous that the same transitional period saw the predominant Negro political allegiance shift from the Republicans to the Democrats.

As not only the first, but probably by now the most "mature," of the "new" nations, the United States has, as Lipset emphasizes, a special opportunity to serve as a symbol of the movement of national "liberation" and to assume a role of leadership in this context. This role, in turn, has been intimately connected with the internal structure of the society with respect to liberty and equality. Of these internal standards, those of ethnicity and religion are particularly important. Unfortunately, the American role in international leadership has been severely compromised in the last generation by our competition and conflict with the Communist movement. Our hypersensitivity to the threat of internal subversion places us in danger of being identified internationally with the older European "colonial" powers and their imperialism. The relationship of these issues to race and color is patent. The suggestion will be made in this paper that the movement for inclusion of the Negro into full citizenship in the national community may prove to be a crucial aspect of this complex set of processes, and may present a great opportunity to claim a place of fuller leadership in this setting. This movement, as Rupert Emerson and Martin Kilson show in their paper in this volume, has been stimulated largely by the rise of new nonwhite nations, particularly those of Africa. It is, however, my thesis that its *main* impetus has been internal to the development of American society itself. If the movement, and the forces which favor it in the white community, can succeed substantially, this may prove to have momentous international repercussions. I shall return to this theme at the end of the paper.

I shall conclude this introduction with a brief theoretical discussion. The process by which previously excluded groups attain full citizenship or membership in the societal community will, in this paper, be called *inclusion*. This is, as will be shown presently, a highly complex process. It will be argued that, at least under the conditions which have prevailed in American society, this has been intimately linked with the process of differentiation which has produced an increasingly *pluralistic* social structure. Not only are there many subcollectivities within the societal community, but the typical individual participates through membership in an increasingly wide variety. If interest is centered in *ethnic* groups, membership is necessarily by hereditary ascription.[12] In religious affiliation, a larger voluntary element is common, but most religious affiliations, at least to the larger groups, are *de facto* hereditary and often closely associated with ethnicity.

In a pluralistic social structure, membership in an ethnic or religious group does not determine *all* of the individual's social participations. His occupation, education, employing organization, and political affiliation may in varying degrees be independent of his ethnicity or religion. On the whole, the trend of American development has been toward increasing pluralism in this sense and, hence, increasing looseness in the connections among the components of total social status.

This trend has one particularly important implication for our purposes, namely, that it is essential to make a clear distinction between *inclusion* and *assimilation*. There may be pluralism of religious and ethnic groups among full citizens which cuts across many other involvements of the same people. The prototype was the original religious pluralism within the white Protestant group, which was built into the constitutional structure by the separation of Church and State and by religious toleration and freedom. It has subsequently been extended to include Jews and Catholics through what is usually called an "ecumenical" process.

However, because the United States was originally primarily a white Protestant society, it was often thought that inclusion was synonymous with becoming Protestant or as similar as possible to the Anglo-Saxon tradition. The developments which will be outlined below make it quite clear that this is not the case for the other white groups, and I shall argue that it need not and probably will not be so for the Negro. Full inclusion and multiple role participation are compatible with the maintenance of distinctive ethnic and/or religious identity, though not in the sense which is the obverse of exclusion, namely self-imposed isolation as in the case of extreme Jewish Orthodoxy.

The Components of Citizenship

T. H. Marshall, in his discussion of the development of citizenship in Great Britain noted above, distinguished three components of the status of citizenship, the *civil* (which in an American reference should perhaps be called legal), the *political,* concerned particularly with the democratic franchise, and·the *social,* which refers essentially to the context we defined as "welfare" or, in the terms of our federal organization, health, education, and welfare.

Marshall establishes an important pattern of temporal sequence in the institutionalization of these three components as criteria of membership in the English national community: the civil came first, the political next, and the social last. In England, the establishment of civil rights in this relatively narrow sense was started at the time of Justice Coke in the early seventeenth century, with its consolidation of the independence of the Common Law vis-à-vis government, and extended in various phases through the eighteenth century. The political component began to emerge with the beginning of the development of the parliament's independence from the crown in the seventeenth century, which culminated in 1688. However, for the individual, its institutionalization centered in the franchise extensions of the nineteenth and twentieth centuries— from the Reform Bill of 1832 to the Women's Suffrage Act of 1918. The social component goes back to the factory acts of the nineteenth century, but gathered force in the social legislation of the present century, culminating in the enactment of the Beveridge Plan after World War II. With appropriate adaptations this pattern is applicable both to the American experience as a whole and to that of the Negro.

Before entering into this, further explanation of the meaning of these components is necessary. The civil or legal component concerns the *application* of the value system to the relevant context. This is what is particularly salient in the context of the term, *rights*. Rights indicate that members of the societal community in the normative sense "must" enjoy certain basic freedoms and securities in them. The catalogue is of course familiar. It involves security of each individual and of property, freedom of speech, religion, assembly, and association, and both substantive and procedural equality before the law—components formulated in our Constitutional tradition as "equal protection of the laws" and "due process of law." These rights are to take precedence over any particular political status or interest and over any social component such as wealth or poverty, prominence or obscurity.

It is a very long step from the constitutional and legal enactment of these rights to their effective implementation, and this process is still going on in many sectors of American society, even in some which are largely unrelated to the racial problem. But, the constitutional basis of these rights is firmly established and has served as the most important lever for exerting pressure during the earlier stages of the Negro inclusion movement. The special role of the N.A.A.C.P. has been to exploit this aspect of our citizenship structure in behalf of the Negro.

The political component concerns participation in collective goal-attainment, at the societal level in the processes of government. The differentiation of government from the societal community, as noted above, implies that the average citizen is neither a governmental functionary in any usual sense nor a totally controlled subject of his government. He does, however, have rights of participation in the governmental process. These crystallize at two main points in modern politics. One is the franchise, basically the right of a formal voice in the selection of leadership—leadership being a more generalized and practicable focus than specific policies, even when these are decided by referendum. The other is the right to attempt to influence policy, starting with the rights of free speech and assembly, but extending to the sensitive area of "lobbying." As mediating structures, the party system and the institutionalization of mass media became involved here. The body of citizens needs "spokesmen," the potential influencer needs media for making his wishes and their gratifications known, and leaders need structural outlets for their opinions, appeals, and proposals.

The social component does not concern the opportunity to express and implement the rights derived from the societal values so much as the resources and capacities necessary for this implementation. In this connection the societal community defines and presents standards for the allocation of resources to the community as a whole and to its various sub-sectors. The obverse of this is the definition of the terms on which capacities, as matched with opportunities, can be involved in the process of inclusion. This is a special context of the problem of "qualifying" for inclusion.

There are two categories of resources which must be distinguished for our purposes. In our achievement-oriented society, one can scarcely imagine that justice would prevail if large classes of its members, through no fault of their own, were either denied opportunity for achievement (including the reaping of its rewards) or handicapped severely in gaining access to it. Given the formal status of equality in civil or legal rights and in basic political participation, these rights can be "empty" if opportunity is not equalized.

Of course, discrimination may be abolished or minimized across a whole range of opportunities, particularly in employment. But even absence of discrimination is "empty" if remediable handicaps continue to prevail. These handicaps may be randomly distributed among the categorial grouping with which this discussion is primarily concerned. But if they are linked to the status position of the excluded group, they raise the essential problem of the implementation of the rights of citizenship through the equalization of opportunity and the base from which that opportunity can be exploited.

This is where the distinction between the two categories of resources becomes essential. The first category is mainly financial. For an individual to be able to take advantage of available opportunities he must have not only the capacity but also the financial means to do so. This aspect of the social citizenship complex was paramount in the discussions and measures of public policy during the New Deal era. The second concerns the underlying capacity of the units, especially individuals and their families, to function effectively in the environment in which they are placed. At the level of the individual this concerns above all health and education. There has been so much discussion of all these themes that it is not necessary to spell them out further here. Suffice it to say that, first, increasing attention is being placed on education as the most decisive link between the individual's underlying levels of capacity and his relation to the opportunity structure.[13] Second, the concept of "welfare" is a diffuse one extending from the most elementary financial conditions of subsistence to the problem of the structure of the social environment in which disadvantaged groups are placed. This latter extension reflects the fact, firmly established by social science, that at the bottom of the social scale (as judged by the usual criteria of success, prestige, and so on) there is a vicious circle of cumulative *disadvantage,* which becomes accentuated the more marked the "competitiveness" of the society becomes. This broad tendency is inseparable from the development of individualism, the kinds of citizenship rights we have been talking about, and related matters. It almost goes without saying that the Negro in this country is very deeply caught up in this vicious circle and that Marshall's category of social citizenship is particularly important in the present context.[14]

The three principal components of the citizenship complex seem to constitute not only a rough temporal series, but also a type of hierarchy. With all the differences between British and American societies, they have very similar values. After all, with an important infusion from the French Enlightenment and the Revolutionary tradition, the origin of our own values lies mainly in our British heritage.

We can then say that it is the civil or legal rights which come closest to direct implementation of the values which Myrdal formulated in his famous summary of the *"American Creed."*[15] In understanding what has been going on, it is crucial to remember that the societal commitment to this value pattern has exerted steady pressure toward its implementation in behavior and institutions, though this has often been counteracted in specific ways. These commitments, though they be genuine, cannot by themselves bring about a restructuring of the society. Attempts to implement them will inevitably encounter what Mayhew[16] has called "structural discrimination," which can be overcome only if factors other than the assertion of commitments come into play. Without them, the outcome will be either a stalemate, as it was for so long in the United States, or a traditionalist revolution restoring the ascendancy of the contra-value orientation—a prototype being post-Reconstruction Southern society.

The spread and consolidation of the legal component through judicial process rather than legislation is particularly important in view of the present situation in America. This is a step well beyond a *moral* commitment to the relevant rights, because it places the power of government presumptively behind their implementation. In Little Rock, Governor Faubus was defying not only the "decent opinion of mankind," but also a specific order of a duly constituted federal court. This dramatizes the sense in which the 1954 decision on education was a decisive landmark—yet by itself it produced only a rather paltry "tokenism" in spite of being on the books for a full decade. Clearly something more was required, though this is not to belittle the enormous importance of the legal commitment. This Supreme Court decision was part of a much larger trend in the general development of judicial interpretation of the Constitution, of which more will be said later.

The two other principal factors are, on the one hand, the mobilization of political pressures designed to insure that the excluded group can enjoy both formal rights and actual participation in the political process and, on the other, the mobilization of the governmental apparatus to take the responsibility of implementing these rights. From this point of view, the step from the Supreme Court's espousal of Negro rights to the Civil Rights Acts of 1964 and 1965 was crucial, as has so often been remarked. Both, to be sure, obligate the government. But in the latter case the obligation has been enacted by the elected representatives of the people on the recommendation of a popularly elected President. Hence it can no longer be called the "whim" of nine men who, in the political as distinguished from the legal sense, do not "represent" anyone.[17] Of course there are still many steps which must be taken before effective implementation can be achieved, but the Civil Rights Acts clearly add a major set of social forces to the side of effective implementation.

Even if enforcement were effective, it would still be necessary to bring about the essential set of conditions concerned with qualifications for taking advantage of the opportunities offered. The newly included group must have the capacity to perform its role creditably. The mere statement that justice requires inclusion is not enough because allegations of injustice must involve the capacity factor—namely, that the excluded group could make valuable contributions but is denied the opportunity to do so. Capacity must be asserted on the part of the excluded group, and, insofar as it is not yet present, the larger community must take steps to help develop it.

The hierarchy to which we referred above concerns a relation between necessary and sufficient conditions. With reference to the Negro in the United States, I state broadly that although the institutionalization of both legal rights and political participation constitutes the necessary conditions of much further progress toward full inclusion in the societal community, this is not in itself sufficient. It also requires the implementation of the social component in such a way that the realistic handicaps, so conspicuous in the background, are reduced to the point that, though they cannot be expected to disappear in the short run, they become more or less manageable.

The constitution of a societal community is never static, but is continually changing over time. In my view, the main outline of the American community was established in the broad process of founding the new nation. This basic outline includes the Constitution as well as various aspects of the system as a total social process. At the same time, American society has been subject to major changes. The focus of the present essay is on changes in the composition of its membership through the inclusion of groups previously excluded, more or less unambiguously, from full membership. The Negro, both because of slavery and because of Southern regional isolation, was long kept insulated from the forces favoring inclusion. The groups with which I shall be concerned in the next section, those constituted by the "new immigration" of the turn of the century, were in a different situation.

I shall attempt to analyze the process of inclusion by using a model roughly similar to the "supply and demand" paradigm of economics. There are demands for inclusion—*both* from the excluded group and from certain elements who are already "in"—and there is a supply, which also operates on both sides of the exclusion line. Supply here refers, for the excluded groups, to their qualifications for membership, a matter of their cultural and social structures. Later I shall use the illustration that fully orthodox Judaism, with its rather strong insulation against all but the most instrumental contacts with Gentiles, constituted a formidable barrier to the inclusion of Jews in the American community. The presence of Reform Judaism in the German immigration which preceded that from Eastern Europe provided a focus for the general liberalization of the Jewish community structure. This made it far more amenable to inclusion than the Orthodox structure, as well as far more acceptable to their American hosts. On the side of the receiving community, "supply" consists in structural conditions which create institutionalized "slots" into which the newly received elements can fit, slots structured in accordance with the basic citizenship patterns of the developing community, not opportunities for crude "exploitation" by its members. Supply in this sense refers to a set of structural conditions on both sides of the "equation." This will be analyzed in terms of the factors necessary to extend and consolidate the societal community as such, that is, the commitment to association in a national community, the mobilization of political power and influence, and the establishment of the capacities which have been reviewed in the present section, as well as the underlying value-patterns which are assumed throughout.

The demand aspect concerns the *mobilization* of these factors and their consequences, again on both sides of the inclusion-exclusion boundary. It is a matter first of the existence of attitudes, in both the group "wanting in" and significant sectors of those already in, that the inclusion is normatively desirable and that it *should* be promoted, and then the transformation of these attitudes into various action programs and their implementation. Certainly, much of the actual process often occurs inconspicuously without much of a movement—this, for example, seems to have been the case for much of the inclusion of the new immigration, though by no means all of it. Nevertheless, as expression and implementation of demand in the present sense, the relevant *movements* have a very important place in our analysis.

Such movements tend to gather strength as the strain of conflict between the normative requirements for inclusion and the factual limitations on it are translated into pressures to act. Movements, however, not only express strain in this sense, but "stir things up" further. Thus, their consequences are often relatively unpredictable.[18] One tendency of this type of movement should be noted. The ultimate social grounding of the demand for inclusion lies in commitment to the values which legitimize it. The general reaction to increasing strain is to increase mobilization of such commitments. This in turn is often associated with a demand for direct, immediate, and complete action to implement the values in full. This tendency encounters a problem deriving from the fact that value-commitment, crucial as it is, is only one of the factors necessary for successful inclusion. Strengthening this factor without likewise strengthening the others may lead not to promotion of the "cause," but to a disproportionate activation of the *always-present* factors of resistance, and hence to setbacks. The activists in such movements are above all likely to become impatient with those who would pay attention to the importance of the other factors.[19]

This is the broad paradigm which the reader is requested to keep in mind in reading the sometimes involved discussion which follows.

The American Record on Inclusion Processes

The present crisis over the inclusion of the Negro in the American community has unique features besides its immediacy,[20] but it does not stand alone. A brief review of the larger context of related problems may prove illuminating. Two propositions will introduce the discussion. First as already noted, the core of the American community was basically white, Anglo-Saxon, and Protestant. These three terms, which have become so deeply embedded in the more popular culture, will serve as the axes of our analysis. Second, the United States, in sharp contrast to most of Europe, including our ancestral Britain, has been the proverbial land of open opportunity, welcoming all to join in building a new society in the "New World."

To be sure, this claim was never fully justified. Quite early it was made unmistakably clear that mass Oriental immigration would not be welcomed (note the Chinese exclusion act of 1882). Indeed it may be argued that the Constitutional termination of the Slave Trade was as much an effort to limit the numbers of Negroes in the territorial United States as it was a reflection of hostility to slavery as such. Nevertheless, compared with other societies, especially of that time, the U.S. was notably liberal until the 1924 immigration laws. It placed more emphasis than any other nation of, or before, its time on the view that it was indeed a voluntary association. People were here because either they or their immediate forebears *wanted* to come. And, the proportion of those who came of their own volition was extremely high for quite a long time. The fact that many were escaping from what they felt to be oppressive conditions rather than coming to positive opportunities does not change this pattern. The Negro is the great exception, because his forebears were typically *brought* here as slaves.

Though various early crises of the American nation may be related to this problem, the focus of this discussion will be on the aftermath of the great wave of free immigration of the generation ending with the First World War. This was perhaps, except for the Negro, *the* great test of the norms of freedom for all comers to associate in forming a new kind of nation.[21] Most of the immigrants were a part of the so-called new immigration from Eastern and

Southern Europe, and as such they violated more sharply than previous large immigrations the older WASP formula for the societal community; they were not only non-Anglo-Saxon, but even non-Germanic in ethnic origin, being mostly from the Latin and Slavic countries (especially Italy and Poland). Also they were predominantly Roman Catholic, except for the very large influx of Jews from Eastern Europe. In addition, the Catholics were usually peasants. Earlier, there had been a small element of German Jews, who had become relatively fully included and a larger group of English-speaking Catholics, the Irish, who were marked by a particularly sharp hostility to everything English. These two elements proved in the end to be very important mediators between the older elements and the larger masses of the new.

In this connection the WASP's generally succumbed to the temptation to define their own role on rather aristocratic terms, but on bases so tenuous that they must be considered only a pseudo-aristocracy. This occurred during the period immediately following World War I when economic prosperity was rampant and when "status-seeking" was certainly far more intensive than in the second postwar period. This is the period of the derogatory names like "wops," "polacks," and "kikes," and of the greatest prevalence of "snobbish" anti-Semitism, the deep feeling that having a Jew as a member of your club was totally unacceptable. (It is perhaps significant that such snobbishness was particularly prominent in the younger generation—in fraternities and sororities, and particularly in the Harvard Final Clubs.)

At the risk of typological oversimplification, I should like to deal with the problem of inclusion of the new immigration in terms of two categories, namely, the Jewish and the Catholic groups. It is clear that there is substantial ethnic diversity within both groups. There are not only East European Jews, who are not themselves homogenous, but also the earlier German contingent and small numbers of Spanish-Portuguese origin. The Catholic group is still more diverse. The Irish were the earliest to arrive in large numbers and have been the most influential. They spoke English, a fact which is significant particularly because they discouraged and often as bishops forbade foreign-language parochial schools. Though bringing with them a strong hostility to things English, which was reflected for generations in their tense relations with the WASP's, their long association in Ireland with English Protestantism brought the Irish brand of Catholicism much closer to Protestantism than, for example, was that of most parts of Southern Europe.

Furthermore, an important part of the earlier Catholic immigration was of German origin, which was ethnically closer to the WASP's than most of the new immigration, and therefore was more fully integrated earlier. In some regions of the country, particularly the Middle West, they have played a very important part. The other two largest groups were the Italians and the Poles, which are very different from each other. There were, of course, other Slavic groups, such as the Czechs and Croats, and the two Spanish-speaking groups in the Southwest—those taken over after the Mexican war and migrants from Mexico—and, more recently, the Puerto Ricans, who have begun to diffuse beyond New York City. There are also smaller numbers which are neither Jewish nor Catholic, such as the Greeks, the Armenians, and some other groups who adhere to Orthodox churches. Finally, Protestant immigration has continued, the largest being from the British Isles and still more from English-speaking Canada.

The problem of the absorption of Jews and Catholics resulted in a genuine crisis of the American community; it was probably one of the major foci of social tension and disturbance in this century. The Immigration Act of 1924, with its system of quotas based on the composition of the population by national origin in 1890, was one striking symptom of this strain; it is significant that only now has a serious and widely supported proposal been adapted by Congress to eliminate that egregiously discriminatory policy. The very sagacious French observer of American society at that time, André Siegfried, spoke of the "two nations" and expressed sharp doubt whether they could ever be integrated.[22]

The substantial disturbances and anxieties over the presence of such large "foreign" groups in our midst and their relations to the fears of "un-American" influence and of Communism—from the Palmer Raids and the Sacco-Vanzetti case of the 1920's to the McCarthy episode of the early 1950's—must be understood in this context.[23] Until the crescendo of McCarthyism, the ogre of "Communism" as a danger of *internal* subversion rather than of external threat was increasingly of central concern. Nevertheless it can be claimed that the main crisis over full inclusion of these groups has now passed. I shall argue that the Catholic case was the more serious of the two, and that the election of John F. Kennedy as President, accentuated by the ritual significance of the public reaction to his assassination, put a final symbolic seal on the inclusion of all Roman Catholics, not only the Irish. Perhaps it was also symbolic that the first time Lyndon Johnson left Washington as President was to attend the funeral of a Jew, in a Jewish Temple, namely, that of former Senator Lehman of New York.

Neither civil rights in the legal sense nor political rights was seriously at issue in these inclusion problems. The Jewish ghetto and the status of Catholics in Britain before Catholic emancipation in the 1830's lay far in the background. The problem of acceptance lay more at the social level in the above classification than at either of the others. This we would define as the capacity and opportunity for full participation without informal discrimination, such as ineligibility for certain high political offices or relatively systematic "scapegoating." Nevertheless the problem of discrimination has been serious and, though recently it has changed greatly for the better, pockets of such discrimination remain.

It is necessary to consider briefly a difference in emphasis and, hence, symbolic involvement of these two particularly important white groups, the Jews and the Catholics. Realistically, there has never been much question of Jewish motivation and capacity for achievement in terms of social mobility in America. This applies especially to mobility through educational channels. In any case, the Jewish group, despite having had to contend with serious discrimination, has had an extraordinary success story. From lowly origins in the overwhelming proportion of cases, it has, in general, risen very high in the American social scale in about two-thirds of a century.

The Jewish problem of inclusion has been almost purely one of "acceptance" on both sides. In comparative terms, there has been relatively little serious anti-Semitism, but the Jewish community itself has been concerned about how far "assimilation" should be allowed to progress. The symbolic focus of anti-Semitism has not questioned competence—the Jew has been a *dangerous* competitor. Irrational anxiety has centered about his observance of the rules, which is to say his acceptance of the obligations of solidarity in the national community. To the more discerning, his "unscrupulousness" has not involved a lack of moral discipline, but rather a higher loyalty to an alternative community, the Jewish. In this sense the Jew has often been considered "clannish."

The Jewish community has always been of a special type. It has been a "guest" community within a host society and, therefore, notably apolitical. Its contacts with Gentiles have historically been on the economic level, with strong Jewish emphasis on their own cultural traditions—including, of course, high valuation of learning which could be transferred to the modern professions. Strong solidarity and, in Orthodox Judaism, exclusiveness have been observed in kinship and, indeed, in all relations of intimacy. Jewish communities have been discrete and local, not organized on a national or international basis, and relatively egalitarian in their internal structure.

It seems that the conflict between Jewish and Gentile communities has been most acute where the former represented what could be interpreted as the exploitative aspect of urban society vis-à-vis the rural and parochial, as in the case of Jewish moneylenders or cattle dealers in relation to peasant communities or where, in urban settings, competition at the level of small business was most prominent.

The decline in the proportion of the American population engaged in agriculture and the development of large-scale corporate business have probably contributed to a climate favorable to inclusion. On this level the competition has not been very intense since Jewish business has centered in the small-scale proprietary fields of business—notably the clothing industry—and certain fields of retail trade. It is very likely that the private practice professions, such as medicine and law, have been particularly congenial to the Jews who have sought higher education and that their late entry into the academic profession on a wide scale is not wholly the result of discriminatory exclusion, though that has certainly played a part.

The focus of the "problem" of anti-Semitism has been the conception of the foreignness of the Jews, of their solidarity in a community within the community, from which Gentiles could feel excluded. The pluralization of the general social structure, especially at occupational levels, and the diminishing global exclusiveness of the Jewish communities have set the stage for the progress of inclusion, since many of these groups have maintained their quite distinctive identities and considerable sense of solidarity, both among themselves and with the societies of their countries of origin.

The present essay cannot, however, attempt a generalized analysis of the ethnic and religious composition of American society, but is primarily focused on the problem of the status of the Negro American. It is my contention that, first, the Jewish group has had special significance because of its distinctive historic role and, second, the Catholic groups have been of great importance in spite of the internal ethnic diversity of the Catholic population. It is worth remarking in passing that the largest single "melting pot" in the society has probably operated within the Catholic population through extensive ethnic intermarriage, but much less so across religious lines. Within the Catholic group, the Irish have played a notable role for the reasons mentioned, with the result, among others, that there is a striking Irish predominance in the hierarchy of the American Catholic Church. For the limited purposes of this essay, I shall concentrate on these two considerations which have become the foci of two different problems and symbolic themes which can be contrasted with each other, as well as with the central issue of the Negro case.

The Jew could then be a good citizen, neighbor, business competitor, and occupational associate of the Protestant with neither relinquishing his religious identity. Religious pluralization—long under way in our society—opens the door to a conception of a basis of societal solidarity which makes all these nondiscriminatory relations possible. On the Jewish side, it should again be noted that a relaxation of the predominantly Orthodox separatism of the Jewish subcommunity has been a necessary condition. In America, the Reform movement, which stemmed from the older German-Jewish element, has been particularly important. Primarily by further development in the differentiation of roles, it has become increasingly possible for Jews to participate in more than the economic aspects of the Gentile community without having to relinquish their Jewishness. From a relatively total subsocietal community, the Jewish group has tended to evolve toward becoming a denomination in the American Protestant sense.[24] Socially, American Jews have been included very fully, but have by no means been assimilated to the same extent.[25]

In the symbolism of discrimination, the Jew has tended to serve as the prototype of "foreignness," in the sense that he has been held to be diffusely attached to a community separate from and alien to the American, and therefore presumably untrustworthy in its commitment to the latter. Compared to certain European countries, notably Germany, but also those to the South and East, the United States has had only mild attacks of anti-Semitism. The most serious was in the 1930's (Father Coughlin) and was associated with a general contraction of economic opportunity, a state in which the theme of the dangerous competition of the outsider is more easily made prominent. The more important expression of this complex has perhaps been the diffuse anxiety about foreignness and un-Americanism. The prominence of this theme would seem to fit with an earlier phase of the development of the national community away from a restricted ethnic-religious basis of solidarity—the famous WASP— to a more cosmopolitan one which includes many elements not qualifying on the more traditional grounds.

The next phase of strain in the openness of the American community constituted a further development of the above. If "foreigners" in general—Jews in particular—are to be accepted, should they not conform to certain requirements? In the Jewish-Protestant case there seemed to be a kind of "fair exchange," involving the non-political stance of diffusely organized communal groups on each side. The idea of a Jewish conspiracy was a rather exotic extreme of anti-Semitic phantasy since the Jews were what they were precisely because of their withdrawal from politically significant organization. One might say much the same for the American brand of Protestantism, especially that part which advocated a radical separation of Church and State. On top of this was the pluralism of American political organization, the beginnings of which go back as far as the history of this nation.[26]

It is perhaps not surprising that *any* relatively or apparently monolithic organization should be a focus of anxiety. Compared with American Protestantism, the Catholic Church was relatively monolithic and in part both was and appeared to be so because of defensive attitudes about its minority position in American society. The problem for its members was not only how far they participated in the usual roles in the American community, but also whether, in doing so, they were under the explicit authoritative control of an organization, their church, which was pursuing its own goals and policies independently of, and posssibly in conflict with, the interests of the American community. Put crudely, the Catholic Church could, particularly to non-Catholic Americans, appear to be a kind of state within the state. Sensitivity to this has been heightened by the individualistic cast of American society, with its suspicion of strong central government. Indeed, for special reasons, Catholics, particularly Irish, tended to gain their mobility through governmental channels, starting with the local ones, but extending to the others. Hence they tended to strengthen Protestant suspicion of them. For this reason the symbolic show-down in the election of a Catholic to the Presidency was particularly important.

Two additional facts, besides the nature and position of the Catholic Church, were essential here. First, as will be noted presently, the majority of the Catholic ex-peasants formed the urban lower class. In a sense they played symbolic "proletariat" to the WASP pretensions to privileged social status, a peculiar combination of the European traditions of aristocratic and "bourgeois." Second, the protection of local interests in our constitutional system opened the door, given the democratic franchise (reinforced by corruption), to organizing these new urban masses into the famous —or infamous—political machines of which New York's Tammany Hall was long a prototype. In the decisive period the leadership of these organizations, which tended to wrest immediate local political power away from the WASP element, was predominantly Irish and, of course, Catholic. Hence at a certain level—a highly salient one to the average "old" American—the Catholic Church as a state within a state seemed to have fused with an actual Catholic control of the most important system of local politics of the nation, thus compounding the felony.

The general path of resolution here has been "pluralization" in a political sense. Generally we do not have monolithic or, as Rokkan and Lipset say, "columnar"[27] blocs as major units in our political system. By their continually increasing involvement in American society at all levels, Catholics have come to be widely represented in many different sectors. They are by no means always on the same side in political decision-making. In view of the European experience, it is striking that there has been no strong move to establish a Catholic political party in the United States at either the state or national level. Obversely, the non-Catholic community has been decreasingly apt to relate to Catholics as Catholics rather than on the various other grounds, especially personal competence in specific fields, which come to be so important in the allocation of personnel through the social structure.

Whereas the integration of the Jewish group seems to have been the "simplest," at least symbolically, in that it involved only the "capacity to accept membership," sometimes through renouncing but more importantly through transcending conflicting solidarities,[28] the present case involved a further complication, namely, that the group in question might have a propensity to organize within the community for its own special ends in a way subversive of the community's delicately balanced basis of consensus. This seems clearly to be related to the more general symbol of "Communism" as a source of vague danger. The Communist system is precisely characterized by maximal commitment to effectiveness through collective organization.

What I called the American hypersensitivity to the Communist danger is connected with the problem of inclusion of the Catholic groups. The link between them is highly integrated political organization, internally on a nationwide basis but with an international base centered outside the country. It is particularly significant that the fear in the United States has been primarily of internal subversion. This may have been somewhat plausible in the 1930's, but in the cold war period the strength of the American Communist party had been reduced to practically nothing, even among intellectuals. There is a discrepancy between this internal anxiety—firmly documented in Stouffer's study[29]—and the substantially smaller concern about the really serious conflict with Communist movements in foreign affairs. Communism, however, is a symbol, the latent meanings of which include various forms of collective authority which may be felt to threaten freedom—among which the Catholic Church has figured prominently. Therefore, we can infer that the fear of Communism includes a "displaced affect," the sources of which must be sought elsewhere.

Not only was there the problem of the Catholic Church, but the relevant period, from the New Deal on, was one of rapid increase in the size and functions of the federal government. It is notable that the main internal focus of this increase lay in the strengthening of the social component of citizenship which concerned the status of the largely immigrant urban lower classes. Externally, it derived, above all, from involvement in two world wars and the attendant changes in the level of American responsibility in world affairs.

In these circumstances, anti-Communism could serve as a unifying symbol for two important groups, namely the older "conservative" groups who stood in fear of and opposition to the general trend to "bigness," urbanization, and the like, and the upwardly mobile, largely Catholic, groups. The latter could claim to be more than one hundred per cent American and accuse the "liberal" elements among the WASP's of insufficient loyalty to their own country. The strongly anti-Communist stance of the Vatican before the Papacy of John XXIII presumably also strengthened this attitude.[30]

In spite of the complexities, I think it is justified to establish an equation that connects Communism symbolically with Catholicism, on the one hand, and with big government, on the other, as a focus of the fears and anxieties of a large sector of the American public. It is significant that the relation to Catholicism seems to have eased greatly in the most recent period, especially since the Presidency of Kennedy. This is related to the new definition of the American Right, that is rightward from Goldwater, as quite explicitly connecting the trend to big government and the danger of Communism. The mitigation of the anti-Communist feeling of the Catholic element—in spite of some lingerings in the South—was fundamental in Lyndon Johnson's ability to command a political consensus over such a wide band as he did in the 1964 election. The inclusion of the Catholic component in the anti-Communist syndrome seems to be parallel to the relation of anti-Semitism, again often latently, to the vaguely generalized anxiety about the "foreignness" of the new immigration as a whole, which was so prominent in the 1920's.

There is another aspect of the broadly "Catholic" inclusion problem which constitutes an important bridge to the Negro problem. The elements of the new immigration not only were different in cultural and national origin from most of their predecessors, but also occupied a different position in American society. Virtually all of them became the lower class of the large cities and industrial areas. The Jewish group escaped from this situation very rapidly, while the Catholic groups, most of whom were of peasant origin, did so more slowly. Indeed this circumstance sharply distinguished the United States from the European cases which were the prototypes for classical Marxian theory—there was hardly any indigenous "working class" here and the lower occupational roles were largely performed by immigrants whose eventual group status in the society was still very uncertain. Siegfried put great stress on this fact. With a good many qualifications, it can be said that the urban Negro has inherited this status as the immigrant has moved up. He, too, is by origin predominantly a "peasant," though from the rural South, and has had to undergo many similar processes of adaptation to the urban environment.

In the Jewish case we might speak of the "foreign" community as standing "beside" the main national one. It was difficult to assign it to a hierarchical position, and it was not highly stratified internally. In proportion as the situation just outlined applied to the Catholic group, it tended to bolster the WASP position as an aristocracy in the premodern sense. This tendency was of course most accentuated in the South, particularly vis-à-vis the Negro. But it was hardly unknown in the ·North. Indeed, the kind of anti-Semitism which has been manifested in the exclusion of Jews from select clubs, college fraternities, residential neighborhoods, and resorts is clearly an example of this. Precisely because the Jew has been such a capable achiever by American standards, he has been excluded in order to assert a claim to a status which is not only, or sometimes not at all, linked to achievement.

In the Catholic group, this has been overcome in part by their achieving admission on the most nearly aristocratic terms. The Kennedy story illustrates this dramatically. The elder Kennedy had great wealth which was linked to local political power by his marriage to the daughter of an Irish mayor of Boston. Then not only did his son achieve political success, ultimately the summit of the Presidency, but he partially joined the circle of the WASP aristocracy by attending Harvard College and developing, with his wife, a style of living which was anything but that of peasants.[31] This is an illustration of the process of pluralization. Increasingly the Catholic populations have diffused through the social structure so that there remains little in common among them but their religion and, of course, their Americanism. The great relative growth in the urban population has helped greatly in this by reducing the distinctiveness of a predominantly urban group. The same applies to the Jews.

It was noted above that, partly in reaction to the new immigration, but also to industrialization and urbanization, the tendency toward the turn of the century and well into the present one was for the WASP's to assume something of the position of an aristocracy—a trend related to "snobbish" anti-Semitism. The Jews did a great deal to discourage this through their striking record of upward mobility, especially in educational achievement, the professions, and, latterly, science and the arts. There have, however, been various symptoms of this such as the conspicuous "Anglo-philism" of the upper groups in this period, which has stood in strong contrast to the Anglophobia of earlier phases of our national existence. The England particularly emphasized was that of the "Establishment," the prestige of Oxford education being a prominent symptom. In this situation, it was natural in the North for there to be greater acceptance of the status of the Negro as belonging to a "service" class in a way not too different from the trends of English colonial practice.

The upward mobility of the new immigrant groups and their increasing inclusion in the national community tended to isolate the Negro in this capacity—the virtual disappearance of Irish domestic servants is an index. Such changes as the immense broadening of the pyramid of education—so that virtually the whole age cohort has received some secondary education and a rapidly increasing proportion has been going to college and beyond—have tended to alter this situation. Thus the brief tendency to crystallize a predominantly WASP upper class has increasingly given way to a new egalitarianism—one stressing equality of opportunity, rather than of final status, but definitely covering an ever-widening ethnic-religious range. This trend has made the recent status of the Negro even more anomalous and is part of the setting of the recent phase of the inclusion process.

The Negro Case

If the predominantly Catholic part of the new immigration owed its primary status ascription in American society mainly to its lower-class status, for the Negro this has been almost wholly the case. For our purposes, color will be treated not as a direct component of the social status of the Negro—for in strict theoretical terms it is not that—but as a symbol. On relatively concrete levels, it is correct to say that individual Negroes are discriminated against in various ways solely because of their skin color. This statement is not, however, an explanation of the general phenomenon of color discrimination, as distinguished from individual cases. Unfortunately this vital distinction is often not kept firmly in mind. Our concern is with the general phenomenon.

In this context skin color symbolizes inferiority in the sense that it is purported to justify placing Negroes as a category so radically at the bottom of the scale as to be only equivocally inside the system at all. It will perhaps be illuminating to consider the problem first in connection with the difference between the South and the North.[32]

The Civil War broke out about the time of, and partly as a result of, the process of industrialization and urbanization in the North. This accentuated the difference in social structure of which slavery was a primary feature. The South was largely an agrarian society with a planter gentry at the top practicing an aristocratic style of life, and with the great mass of menial labor being done by

Negro slaves. The principal class whose status was equivocal was the white group which could not pretend to gentry status, but which wanted above all to avoid being classified with the Negroes. It was something like a caste society. Though the slaves were formally emancipated as a result of the South's defeat in the war, the post-Reconstruction reaction confirmed this caste structure with the "Jim Crow" system.

Unlike the Jews and Catholics, the Southern Negro has generally had to start his rise by acquiring the most elementary components of legal and political citizenship. Through court decisions and now increasingly through legislation, this part of the task of inclusion has progressed a long way toward accomplishment. The social component is another matter—inclusion in this area is just beginning to develop, and there is no doubt that it will prove the most difficult of the three processes.

Until the First World War the Negro was scarcely a "problem" in the North, mainly because his numbers were so small. This was changed by the great migrations which began about that time, accelerated by the boll weevil havoc in Southern cotton growing. Of course, this process has now gone so far that less than half the Negro population is resident in the eleven states of the old Confederacy, and the proportion will continue to decline. Moreover, in the South there has been a great deal of migration to the cities, so that the category, Southern rural Negro—once the predominant type— is now a distinct minority.

The upward mobility of the white urban lower groups, the new immigration, has contributed to the fact that, in both North and South, the Negro is predominantly urban and lower class. Today about half of the estimated 20 per cent of Americans who are "the poor" are Negroes.[33] This classifies about 50 per cent of the Negroes as poor, whereas no other group—Irish, Italian, and so forth—has nearly that large a proportion.

In a sense the South has "infected" the North with the virus of the Negro problem, even though its meaning has been deeply changed. It was hardly to have been expected that Southerners would get very much Northern political support for maintaining the Jim Crow system. Even the coalition of Southern Democrats and Northern conservative Republicans has been gradually eroded to the point that, with the mounting pressure and certain general changes, it has almost disappeared. However, the "problem" is now becoming much more uniform throughout the nation—it is becoming an urban class problem.[34]

As noted above, the Jewish inclusion would probably have been much more difficult had it not been for the type of differentiation process in the economy exemplified by the growth of corporate business, and for the great development of higher education, which opened the doors of the professions to considerable numbers of Jews. Similarly, the pluralization of the political system, the breakup of the city machines as the preserves of specific groups, and the decline of the corresponding "better element" sectors of the political structure have greatly facilitated the inclusion of the Catholic groups. I should like to suggest that the "host society" has been undergoing an important process of structural change which is creating essential conditions for the inclusion not only of the Negro, but of the whole lower class in the societal community.

In an important sense, American society has been protected against the urgency of the class problem by the fact that for so long such a large proportion of its lowest socio-economic groups has been of recent immigrant status, especially in the crucially important cities which have increasingly become the structural focus of the newer society. As noted, upward mobility has greatly alleviated the potential class problems, but they are now being brought to an acute and symbolically appropriate focus by the Negro's becoming the prototypical disadvantaged category.

In the broadest terms the incipient inclusion process depends for its success on the much more effective institutionalization of Marshall's social component of citizenship. However, it comprises new movements with respect to all three of the components. It has, for example, been noted that a most important trend in the Supreme Court decisions of recent years is the extension of the Bill of Rights to the level of the states, especially through re-interpretation of the 14th Amendment.[35] Many of these decisions, such as the school desegregation ruling of 1954, have most notably affected discrimination in the South. Others, however, such as the requirement that indigent defendants accused of crime be provided with counsel (the Gideon case), apply more generally. Furthermore, not only legal rights, in the narrower sense, but also political and social rights are affected. Thus the reapportionment cases profoundly affect the franchise and, with it, the distribution of political power; and the school cases impinge on the social component. They seem to imply that government is obligated to provide adequate educational facilities to the whole population—with discrimination by race being only one aspect of the present inadequacy.

Within this framework of legal rights, public policy is attempting to cope with the causes of *de facto* discrimination, not just by color but by any status of inferiority which cannot be fairly attributed to the individual himself. A certain religio-ideological grounding of this first emerged with the prominent Social Gospel movement in American Protestantism in the latter part of the nineteenth century (which, incidentally, had much to do with the establishment of sociology as an academic discipline in this country) and with its role in the development of philanthropy concerned with the disadvantaged classes. The New Deal comprised a second main phase, with the beginning of comprehensive federal social welfare legislation, including the consolidation of the legal status of trade unionism through the Wagner Act and, particularly, unemployment, old age, and other benefits. The opposition of the Supreme Court to such legislation, especially by the states, was also ended in that period. The United States now seems to be well into a third phase. Perhaps its most important feature has been the shift in concern from welfare in the narrower sense to health, education, and the nature of the urban community, focusing most acutely so far upon housing.

By the narrower sense of welfare, I mean that concerned primarily with money income. The older conceptions of lower-class status emphasized lack of financial means as the central feature of being disadvantaged. Hence, stress was put on improvement in financial status. This was reasonable especially when, as in the Great Depression, massive unemployment was the most acute condition needing remedy. However, there has been increasing insight that poverty is a function of other factors such as poor health, both physical and—as has been emphasized more recently—mental, and certain aspects of community structure and the like.

Education has become the most salient link with the occupational system, which is, in turn, the principal basis of financial independence for the individual and his immediate family. There has been a general upgrading of education. On the one hand, this means that larger proportions of the age cohort have been attaining higher levels of education, with the result that the disadvantaged minority, especially the well-known drop-outs, has been separated from the majority with increasing sharpness. On the other hand, educational requirements for good employment have been rising at the same time—most of the present unemployment is found among the poorly-qualified groups, and educational qualifications are becoming of increasing importance in holding jobs. It seems that not only formal opportunity for a relatively good education (that is, at least through high school), but also capacity to take advantage of it, both in individual ability and in motivation, is coming to be as much a requisite of full inclusion as civil and voting rights.

Behind this, as treated in much more detail elsewhere in this issue, is the problem of the social environment of the disadvantaged, the "slum." The central concern is the vicious circle of the factors in *actual* inferior capacity for valued performance, in which poverty, bad health, low educational standards, family disorganization, delinquency, and other anti-social phenomena are mutually reinforcing. This is where the structure of the urban community itself becomes a salient problem focus. The new concern centers on the residential community. In this connection attention has been called to the fact that the Negro is disadvantaged, even beyond other slum dwellers, in many senses besides the color of his skin. First and foremost, he has been peculiarly lacking in relatively strong family organization[36] which could give strong psychological support to the individual, especially as a child. Second, this has been connected in turn with a relative weakness in "community" institutions of mutual support and solidarity, for example, of the sort which have preeminently characterized Jewish groups even before they rose significantly from their initial low status in American society. Even as the victim of the most radical discrimination of any group, the Negro has not only been forced to be subservient, but has also failed to develop, or bring with him from his Southern rural past, sufficient ingredients for socially effective self-help—a question not merely of individual qualities and initiative, but of collective solidarity and mutual support at many levels, particularly the family and the local community. The strongest Negro institutions have centered in the churches, a vital complex which must be preserved carefully against some of the disintegrating tendencies of urban life. The role of the churches in the civil rights movement perhaps symbolizes this best and will be commented upon further below.

Some Highlights of the Inclusion Process

It is reasonable to suggest that, whatever the extent and nature of the responsibility for the many previous failures, the time is ripe for a major advance. The broad tendency of modern society, one in which America has played a rather special role, has been egalitarian in the sense of institutionalizing the basic rights of citizenship in all three categories sketched here.[37] This tendency has become institutionalized over an increasingly broad front, the legal development noted above being prototypal. The basic types of inequality which have continued to be tolerated—in this context rather than that of recognition and reward of achievement—have been justified, when at all, primarily in terms of "paternalistic" immunities of a variety of sectoral types, the status of the child in the family being a kind of model. In case after case, these immunities have been whittled away, so that the universalistic norms of the society have applied more and more widely. This has been true of all the main bases of particularistic solidarity, ethnicity, religion, regionalism, state's rights, and class. The "sovereignty" of the individual American state has perhaps been the most important single bulwark of these particularisms, in the first instance those of WASP's, but potentially of every group. The inclusion of the Jewish and Catholic groups as outlined above fits this paradigm.

Today, more than ever before, we are witnessing an acceleration in the emancipation of individuals of all categories from these diffuse particularistic solidarities. This must be seen as a further *differentiation* of the role-set in which the individual is involved. By being included in larger community structures, the individual need not cease to be a member of the smaller ones, but the latter must relinquish certain of the controls over him which they previously exercised. This reasoning applies to aristocratic groups as much as it does to negatively privileged ones like the Negro. We have been witnessing major steps in the extension and consolidation of the societal community.

Let me emphasize again one particularly important aspect of the present phase, that the more general insistence on the basic equalities of citizenship, which is essential to the inclusion process, cuts across the status of Negro. In its deeper layers, it is a demand not for the inclusion of Negroes as such, but for the elimination of *any* category defined as inferior in itself. For a long time the status of the Negro was a peculiarly Southern problem. Then it became a national problem, but *qua* Negro. Now we are entering the phase in which it is no longer that, but the problem of eliminating status-inferiority as such, regardless of race, creed, or color. The Negro, in becoming only a "special case," even if a very salient one, loses a ground for special consideration which he has enjoyed. At the same time, he has established a position for tapping much wider bases of support than before. He can become the spokesman for the much broader category of the disadvantaged, those excluded on this egregious ground. The Negro movement, then, can become the American style "socialist" movement. This is to say that the basic demand is for full inclusion, not for domination or for equality on a basis of separateness.[38]

At the risk of repetition, I may note that the successful accomplishment of this goal of inclusion depends on a balanced mobilization of four categories of factors. The first is commitment to the values which underlie the assumption that the goal itself is desirable. This has a long history in American society and is clearly of the greatest importance. I have mentioned that it was invoked by Myrdal. Recently we have seen a notable "effervescence" (in Durkheim's sense) with respect to activation of these value-commitments at the requisite levels. Here the Negro movement has played the paramount part, but the activation has extended far beyond the movement itself. Its incidence in religious circles is especially noteworthy, not least in the way it has brought all faiths of the white community, Catholics and Jews as well as Protestants, together behind the Negro cause. The presence of Catholic nuns among the demonstrators in Selma was a new note having a significance scarcely to be overestimated.

Mere affirmation of the values is not enough. If a process of change is to be a new implementation of fundamental values, its basic direction must be articulated. This involves the development of a conception of the societal community in which all elements will be fully included in the sense of this discussion. In our own cultural background, quite different directions have also enjoyed powerful value-sanctions, even if rather insecurely. One example was the conception of the Negro as inherently inferior—indeed, in a certain version of older Calvinism now dominant in South Africa, as rightfully belonging in a subordinated status. It is the basic values, as applied to the developing conception of the American societal community, which together form the normative focus of the power of the movement.

This factor underlies the trend to implement the values by inclusion—the only tolerable solution to the enormous tensions lies in constituting a single societal community with full membership for all. This is a renewal and reinterpretation of the concept of the

Union which was so central for Lincoln. No other solution is tolerable from the American point of view—hence the Black Muslims cannot gain active support in the general community. And despite much ambivalence, it seems certain that the main Negro community is committed to this outlook. The continuing mobilization of these loyalties and commitments on both sides of the racial line seems to be the second crucial factor in the general inclusion process.

It has been very common to postulate and emphasize a primary difference between the "idealists" who hope to achieve integration by asserting the values of, and a willingness for, acceptance, and the "realists" who say that *only* the mobilization of political power and economic interests will help. I should strongly repudiate this framing of alternatives. It is quite correct that the goal cannot be achieved *without* the mobilization of power and economic interests, but it does not follow that these factors are themselves sufficient. It is only a balanced combination of "ideal" and "real" factors which provides the formula for success.

In speaking of political power, I should like to conceive it here more broadly than is usual. Essential as government is, it does not stand alone in implementing major political changes. The political problems of integration involve all fields of organizational decision-making, especially for business firms to accept Negroes in employment, for colleges and universities to admit them for study, for trade unions to avoid discrimination. We have become acutely aware of the limitations of political power. Against a recalcitrant group, attempts to *enforce* compliance are all-too-often ineffective. Nevertheless, at certain crucial points its mobilization is clearly an essential factor, a factor which includes making decisions affecting inclusion processes *binding* as obligations on all members of the requisite collectivity, whether governmental or private. It is particularly important to remember that the use of power has a double effect. First, it mobilizes sanctions against recalcitrants in such ways that they may no longer be able to afford previously feasible resistance. Second, it asserts on behalf of the relevant collectivity that the policy of inclusion must be taken seriously, and hence that noncompliance will not be allowed to proceed with impunity.

Of all the factors favoring integration, economic interests are the most neutral as far as normative obligations are concerned. They involve both the extent to which receiving elements can "afford" the risks involved in taking various steps and the development of realistic capacities to do so—a theme discussed above in connection with the whole complex of inferiority of status. Perhaps most important is that without support from the other three sets of factors, economic interests and capacity to exploit economic opportunities are weak reeds. This has been made vividly clear where state governments in the deep South, backed by what seems to have been a white consensus, have adamantly opposed steps toward integration. In such cases business men simply would not move. But where the balance of the other factors shifts toward integration, economic interests on both sides can provide a powerful reinforcement of the change. It is a question of "getting over the hump."[39]

A Note on Resistance to Inclusion

In American social thinking it is regarded almost as simple common sense to emphasize primarily, when speaking of the resistance to such developments as the Negro movement for inclusion, the material vested interests of the opponents, for example, the fear of loss of real-estate values or the view that "our customers would not like dealing with a Negro receptionist," so we would lose business. Such examples themselves suggest that another set of factors is involved. The structure of vested interests is a function of the structure of values and norms underlying the relevant social interaction. We are in the midst of a process of social change in which these components, and not only the interests, are changing.

Resistance has been strongest in the white South. This is because the structure of Southern society has been more "archaic" than that of the rest of the country. It has, however, been changing very rapidly and has tended more or less to polarize around its more advanced urban, industrial, and partly intellectual sectors, on the one hand, and its more traditional rural and small town sectors, on the other. This very broad polarization is by no means peculiar to the South, but is nationwide. Thus states' rights, the resistance to reapportionment on population bases, and many other issues mark a "conservative" reaction against many of the processes of change in the society at large.

Political developments in recent years bring this situation into sharp relief. The one-party system of the South has been breaking up rapidly, creating an opportunity for the Republican party to gain a major foothold in the South. This in turn relates to the tendency of a major—and the more activist—wing of Northern Republicanism to sympathize with the whole constellation of orientation of which the Southern resistance to desegregation has been a part. Hence that part associated with, or sympathizing with, the more radical Right has been particularly attracted by what has come to be known as the "Southern strategy," which was adopted by Goldwater and his advisers in the 1964 campaign.

Nothing could bring out more sharply the impact of changes in social structure in the last generation or so. The old isolation of South and North has largely broken down. The older Republican party was largely a sectional party, which on the whole opposed the New Deal, especially institutionalization of the social component of citizenship. Now, for the reasons sketched above and others, the Negro has come to the forefront all along the line of the process of social change feared by the "conservative" elements, North and South. Indeed it may be suggested that the affinity between the Goldwaterites and the segregationist Southerners was so strong that they became almost compulsive in their urge to unite. One may suspect that shrewd political calculation played a much smaller part than did this sense of affinity. Yet the outcome of the election makes crystal-clear how impossible it is for a national party which wishes to win nationwide elections to include endorsement of the segregation system in its major policies.

An important underlying aspect of this affinity is the great prominence of Protestant Fundamentalism on both sides of the political alignment. There is strong evidence that such religious orientations are particularly marked among the radical Right, especially in its principal stronghold of the Southwest. Certainly this is true also of the South.

The alignment of the resistance to Negro inclusion, directly or through resistance to various measures essential to its success (such as federal support of education and the war against poverty), with a *generalized* political conservatism is a highly important development. Its obverse is the alignment of the society's more progressive political forces in support of the inclusion process, again both directly and by promoting policies which will provide or strengthen its major factors. Moreover, the more serious of the resistances seem to be located politically rather far on the right, so that it is unlikely that in the near future the opponents of inclusion of the Negro can reach far enough into the political center to mobilize very large political blocks at the national level. Many resistance groups will retain power at the more local levels, but the general trend of weakening parochial particularisms seems to be working in a favorable direction. The strengthening of federal power as such is only one aspect of a much more comprehensive process.

Finally a further word should be said about the symbolization of the resistance to inclusion. I have stressed the theme of inferiority as the most central in defining the symbolic status of the Negro. If this is as important as has often been held, it follows that the main focus of anxiety involving resistance lies in the fear that the quality of the societal community will deteriorate if inferior members are admitted. Here the resemblance to fears of "debasing the currency" through irresponsible monetary management and banking is striking. Sometimes in our economic history such fears have proved justified, but over the long range the extension of credit systems and the like have contributed enormously to the productivity of the economy. The "sound money" people have on the whole fought a rear-guard action against such extensions, one which would have contributed greatly to economic retardation had it prevailed.

The process under discussion here is that of a major extension of full membership in the societal community. If it is done imprudently—as, it might be said, was the completely free immigration before World War I—it may have effects analogous to inflation. But the fears of it are just as irrational as the fears of economic modernization have been, and they can be analyzed in closely parallel terms. The most important single condition of avoiding inflationary "debasement" is the general upgrading not only of the Negro but of all elements in the population falling below the minimum acceptable standards of full citizenship.

The Negro Movement and the Problem of Negro Identity

A particularly conspicuous feature of the recent phase in the changing status of the Negro has been the emergence of a strong movement which has had very extensive and important white support, but which has struck much deeper roots in the Negro community itself than have previous phases. The emergence of the movement is a function of several factors such as the general social changes outlined above, the stimulus of the emergence of African states, the strengthening of the Negro middle classes, with their higher levels of education, and the concentration of Negro masses in the cities, primarily in the North. This essay cannot attempt a more detailed analysis of these developments. I should like rather to state a few of their implications, especially regarding the opportunities they present.

It has been remarked in several papers that the Negro group has generally had less solidarity and weaker organization than the other ethnic groups which have preceded it in gaining inclusion. The growth of the present movement seems to be both a symptom and a cause of a notable strengthening in this solidarity, which is beginning to create a more clearly defined group consciousness and sense of power and opportunity. It presents a new opportunity to shift the definition of Negro status away from its predominantly negative meaning as an oppressed group which is typically excluded and exposed to multifarious disadvantages. The problem is to develop a basis for a more positive conception of group identity in both American and world society. I should like to suggest that there is a most unusual opportunity inherent in the nature of the movement and its situation, the importance of which, however, is not yet widely appreciated.

One major point of reference is that the primary source of Negro grievance, exclusion on the basis of alleged *inherent* inferiority, is the most radical grievance entertained by any major non-WASP group, except possibly the American Indian's grievance of dispossession. It raises a clearer, more drastic *moral* issue than the other cases, one compounded by the status of the Negro's ancestors as slaves in America and by the injustice of using the "trival" symbol of color as a primary basis of exclusion. Given the universalistic and egalitarian elements in our national traditions, both religious and constitutional, it is difficult to find an issue which is morally more straight-forward.

It has been possible to keep the issue relatively insulated for a long time, but recent social changes as well as the movement itself have made this progressively more problematic. Now, in a period of rising economic affluence, and, it may be said, moral ambivalence both about this and about the confusions over the American position in world affairs, the nation has been presented with a notable opportunity to define a clear and *simple* issue of conscience. By and large, the reverberation of the issue in many different groups has been extensive and impressive, in spite of the tenacious resistance just reviewed. Perhaps the issue also becomes more urgent precisely because of the progress made in resolving the other issues of inclusion which we have discussed, since this leaves the Negro even more conspicuously excluded.

It seems particularly significant that white involvement has come so definitely from two sources, the churches, especially the clergy, and the students.[40] Categorizing my examples of non-Negro inclusion problems into Jews and Catholics, rather than the corresponding ethnic categories, was the result of deliberate theoretical choice, not simple convenience. I have long been convinced that the religious background of these problems has been—and remains—fundamental and that both the difficulties of inclusion and the opportunities for its success have been intimately involved with religion. One may say that, for the inclusion of the new immigrants, the problem centered in those elements of the relatively "liberal" Protestant community which were, in one way or another, involved in the tenuous WASP claim to aristocratic status.

I have noted that the processes of social change in the present century have tended increasingly to polarize the society along an axis which includes not only political conservatism in resistance to change but, closely related to this, what we call religious "fundamentalism." In the South the connection between militant segregationism and fundamentalism has been very clear,[41] and I have suggested that a broader connection was certainly evident in the Goldwater campaign.

Generally speaking, there are also important connections between lower-class status in industrial societies, social origins in more "primitive" or "underdeveloped" social settings, particularly of a peasant type, a certain general conservatism (or, as Lipset says, "authoritarianism"), and religious fundamentalism. Indeed, one may say that the predominant kind of Catholicism among the new immigrant urban masses was a form of fundamentalism and that the liberalization of American Catholicism in the last generation is partly a function of the upward mobility and inclusion of these masses. To a degree, the Orthodoxy of so many East European Jewish immigrants was also a form of fundamentalism.

The majority of Negro Americans have been and are, religiously speaking, fundamentalists. But, this fact does not have simple consequences. Undoubtedly, in their segregated and insulated status in the rural South, it helped to motivate acceptance of their lot, as the corresponding features of Catholic and Jewish fundamentalism have done in both the peasant or ghetto circumstances of the "old countries" and in the difficult early stages of involvement in American society as first- and second-generation immigrants.

At the same time, there is the deep-seated Judeo-Christian tradition of religious motivation to preserve integrity, to assert autonomy, and eventually to seek justice through change in the structure of the situation. Here, what I am calling the more fundamentalist orientation has, in the course of history, repeatedly assumed moral leadership, in part facilitated by an unworldly lack of concern for the complexities of process in highly differentiated societies. Fundamentalists in this sense—which includes such "secular religions" as Communism—tend to be direct-actionists, to see issues in *simple* moral terms; and about half the time they have the balance of long-run merit on their side.

However, Negro fundamentalism, like that of the previous immigrant masses, has come to be mobilized on the side of differentiation and inclusion, not of segregation and exclusion. The development of the movement has strongly activated the moral sentiments of the other groups, including very significant groups of non-Protestants. This process has quite directly *split* the fundamentalist element in American religion, with all its important *indirect* relations to politics and other contexts. The *moral* basis of opposition to change in the older and simpler order—so strongly emphasized by our latterday conservatives—is thereby gravely undermined. There has developed, significantly, a strong and sometimes very sharp dialogue on the subject of moral justification between those camps. This brings the process of restructuring the social system to the highest normative level, a level already fully structured specifically in terms of religious and social pluralism. It raises, in a form difficult to evade, the question of the moral basis of the American type of "Free Society."

I should like to emphasize the subtle combination of similarities and differences between the processes of inclusion for the groups of the new immigration and for the Negro. All three have been in certain respects "foreign." They have also come with socio-cultural patterns which have been relatively "backward" by the main standards of the new society—to put it sharply, all except Jews have been "peasants," and they have been small-town bourgeois. All three have had religio-cultural orientations which can be called "fundamentalist." Environmentally, however, all three have been plunged into a converging set of integrating influences, as the most recently arrived lower-class group in the largest urban communities.

In the other context, the three are not only distinct from each other, but constitute a series. The Jews, curiously from some points of view, have proved the easiest to include. This was not the case in

Germany, with its much more hierarchical social structure. But in "individualistic" America, the principal problem was that of defining the legitimacy of, and opportunity for, cultural pluralism without prejudicing the other, more instrumental bases of participation. The Catholics had to overcome high American sensitivity to tightly organized collectivities which might be accused of "conspiracy."

In this succession, the Negro stands at the "end of the line." His is the most serious (hence in some respects, the most plausible) basis of exclusion, namely, his inherent inferiority. The relatively satisfactory—it will not in our time ever be fully so—resolution of the problem of Negro inclusion will certainly be one of the greatest achievements of American society. Moreover, the record of the movement, even up to this point, makes it clear that a very major part of the credit will go to the Negro community itself; it will be *their* achievement, certainly in the sense of direct goal-orientation to a much greater degree than is true of the groups which have already gained inclusion.

This seems to me to constitute a crucially important focus for the future of the collective Negro identity. The Negro community has the opportunity to define itself as the spearhead of one of the most important improvements in the quality of American society in its history—and to do so not only in pursuit of its own obvious self-interest, but in the fulfillment of a *moral* imperative. It is a change in American society which is deeply consonant with our moral traditions, but also one which could not come about without strong, systematically exerted pressures and strong leadership. The resistances are quite sufficient to explain these necessities.

This role of the Negro movement and the community behind it has significance far beyond the internal American scene. The whole world has now become more or less polarized between the developed and the underdeveloped nations. This polarization largely coincides with the freeing of large areas of the world from colonial status, a process which has moved with great rapidity in recent years, and with their emancipation from inferior status in terms of both political dependence and economic and educational development. Not least, this axis also relates very closely to a color line— the Asian and African new nations are largely nonwhite.

It has been stressed above that the American Revolutionary tradition has prepared this country for a position of leadership in the movement toward equality for the new nations of the extra-European world. The internal processes of inclusion of the Jewish and Catholic elements have strengthened the American position in this respect—the vaunted promises of equal treatment have not been wholly worthless. The opportunity, then, is for the Negro to symbolize the completion of this internal process (and to give symbolic promise of the solubility of the world-wide problems) as a massively large colored group which has found its rightful place in American society and has done so very largely by its own efforts.

It has been noted above that, earlier in this century, there was a tendency to define class lines in the United States as more or less equivalent to ethnic lines, with the new immigrants forming the core of the "working class." It is probably true that the heavy influx of immigrants contributed substantially to preventing the crystallization of class divisions in the older community along the European lines stressed by Marxists as typical of "capitalist" societies. In any case, American society has certainly evolved away from, rather than toward, this Marxian model, the inclusion of the earlier immigrant groups constituting a most important aspect of the development. However discriminated against the Negro has been, he has been too small a group to constitute a full "proletariat"—indeed, within the group itself, there has been very strong resistance to this definition of their role, in spite of intensive propaganda from Communist sources.

The whole trend of development in American society constitutes the sharpest challenge to the Communist diagnosis of the modern world, and, increasingly, Western Europe has also moved in many respects in the "American" direction. These trends cannot be explained on Marxist premises. The status of the Negro has been morally the most vulnerable feature of the American society. If, as there seems to be good hope, this can be dealt with effectively, it can have a most extensive effect on the larger world situation.

This is because the Communist trend has been to redefine the crucial "class struggle" as a struggle not between classes within societies, but between exploiting and exploited societies, with the famous theory of "imperialism." Just as successful Negro inclusion will put the seal on the Marxian error in diagnosing American society, so the United States, with strong Negro participation, indeed leadership, has the opportunity to present a true alternative to the Communist pattern on a world-wide basis, one which is not bound to the stereotype of "capitalism." Because of the immensely important role of race and color in the world situation, the strategic position of the Negro American is crucial. This subcommunity of our pluralistic society has the opportunity to be *the* main symbolic spokesman of the possibility of achieving a racially, as well as religiously, nationally, and otherwise, pluralistic world society in which some kind of integration among the racial groups can be developed without a loss of identity and in terms compatible with raising the previously inferior to the status of those fundamentally equal in world citizenship.

Near the beginning of this essay, the distinction between inclusion and assimilation was stressed. The purport of this latest phase of the analysis is to suggest that to identify non-discrimination (that is, inclusion) too strongly with complete "color-blindness" might be to throw away a very precious asset, not only for the Negro, but for American society as a whole. My own view is that the healthiest line of development will be not only the preservation, but the actual building up, of the solidarity of the Negro community and the sense that being a Negro has positive value. In the process there is the danger of cultivating separatism, as most conspicuously exemplified by the Black Muslims. But the pluralistic solution, which has been stressed throughout this discussion, is neither one of separatism—with or without equality—nor of assimilation, but one of full participation combined with the preservation of identity. The American Jewish and Catholic groups have, by and large, been able to achieve this goal.

Quite clearly, the Negro's own associations with fellow Negroes who survive the inclusion process should no longer be compulsory.[42] Each individual Negro should be free to associate with any non-Negro in any legal way he sees fit, and, if he so desires, to give up completely his identity as a Negro in the sense of belonging to a Negro community. But this does not mean that Negro identity should or will disappear. I should envision continuing predominance of marriages of Negroes with each other. I see no reason that some religious denominations should not be identified as "Negro churches," or that, as long as residence there is not compulsory, many neighborhoods should not continue to be mainly Negro, as many today are Jewish.

Once being a Negro loses the stigma of inferiority, I suggest, it is likely that these will cease to be salient issues. After all, color is a *symbol* and, if the context of its historic meanings is sufficiently changed, the prospect is that it will cease to be the basis of a stigma.

Full Citizenship for the Negro American?

The following schematic outline may be helpful to the reader in interpreting the above discussion.

Symbolic Groups in Relation to the Inclusion Problem

Focus of Anxiety	Ambiguously Included	Projected Upon
Commitments outside the community High Achievement capacity plus "clannishness"	The Jews	Undefined Foreignness suspected of "un-Americanism"

Common feature: diffuse foreignness. Dominant circa 1920's, but into 1930's

Commitments to authoritarian, presumptively conspiratorial collectivities	Catholics	Communists

Common feature: organization which might "take over." Dominant a little later, culminating in McCarthy era

Incapacity for full participation	Fundamentalists	Negroes (Color as Symbol)

Common feature: inclusion could debase the quality of citizenship. Dominant since about 1954.

Patterns for Inclusion

Jews—Foreigners: Fully differentiated participation with special reference to the occupational system—differentiating occupational status from ethnic belongingness—acceptance on one side, abandonment of "clannishness" on the other. Organic solidarity.

Catholics—Communists: Pluralization in the analytical-political sense. Movement from *altruisme* to *egoisme* in Durkheim's sense. Acceptance on both sides that citizenship is not ascribed to position in a "columnar" structure a la Rokkan and Lipset. Loyalty problem.

Fundamentalists—Negroes: Upgrading. The development of capacity for full participation after breaking the stigma of inferiority, as sinful reprobates or as biologically inferior. Symbolic animals and children.

REFERENCES

1. T. M. Marshall, *Class, Citizenship, and Social Development* (Garden City, N. Y., 1964), Chap. IV.

2. Cf. Talcott Parsons, *Societies: Comparative and Evolutionary Perspectives* (Englewood, Cliffs, N. J., 1966).

3. John Rawls, "Constitutional Liberty and the Concept of Justice," in C. J. Friedrich (ed.), *Justice (Nomos VI),* (New York, 1963).

4. Edward A. Shils, *The Torment of Secrecy* (Glencoe, Ill., 1956).

5. Talcott Parsons, "The Principal Structures of Community," *Structure and Process in Modern Societies* (Glencoe, Ill., 1960).

6. Richard Niebuhr, *The Social Sources of Denominationalism* (Cleveland, Ohio, 1957).

7. Cf. S. M. Lipset, *The First New Nation* (New York, 1963).

8. Cf. Samuel Beer, "Liberalism and the National Idea," Public Affairs Conference Center, University of Chicago, 1965.

9. Seymour Martin Lipset, *The First New Nation* (New York, 1963).

10. *Ibid.,* Part I.

11. Samuel Beer, *op. cit.*

12. Qualifications must be made, for example, for interethnic marriages where, with or without formal "adoption," the couple functions primarily in one group and, hence, the "inmarrying" spouse may be said to have changed ethnic affiliation, especially if the children identify clearly with the one group.

13. Peter F. Drucker, "Automation is not the Villain," *The New York Times Magazine,* January 10, 1965.

14. Considerable evidence on these points is presented in other papers in this book, notably those by Rashi Fein, Daniel P. Moynihan, and Thomas F. Pettigrew.

15. Gunnar Myrdal, *An American Dilemma* (New York, 1944).

16. Leon Mayhew, "Law and Equal Opportunity: Anti-discrimination Laws in Massachusetts," 1964 Harvard Ph.D. dissertation.

17. Even Arthur Krock, if my memory serves me, was impressed by this point.

18. Neil J. Smelser, *Theory of Collective Behavior* (New York, 1963).

19. An almost classic instance of this is the recent impatience of the ministers, whose commitments to the values of racial equality has been impressively activated, with President Johnson, essentially because he wanted to mobilize strong political support for his more drastic proposals on voting rights before taking his own strong personal stand about the Selma crisis. The proposals were on the whole in favor of immediate and drastic federal compulsion in Alabama, regardless of the possible political costs.

20. Cf. Pettigrew, *A Profile of the Negro American* (Princeton, N. J., 1964).

21. Oscar Handlin, *The Uprooted* (New York, 1951).

22. André Siegfried, *America Comes of Age* (New York, 1927).

23. Talcott Parsons, "Social Strains in America" and "Postscript 1962" in Daniel Bell (ed.), *The Radical Right* (Garden City, N. Y., 1964). Cf. also other essays in this volume.

24. Will Herberg, *Protestant, Catholic, Jew* (Garden City, N. Y., 1960).

25. Thus, the rate of intermarriage with non-Jews is lower than corresponding rates for either Protestants or Catholics.

26. It is notable that by contrast with German Nazism, American anti-Semitism has not strongly stressed the connection of Jewishness with Communism. Similarly, the anti-Communism of this cold war period has dissociated itself from anti-Semitism. Vide the role of Cohn and Schine as lieutenants of McCarthy and the fact that the name Goldwater has not been a political liability in Rightist circles.

27. Stein Rokkan and Seymour Martin Lipset, *Cleavage Structures, Party Systems and Voter Alignments: An Introduction.*

28. On the side of supply for the receiving community, another important consideration for the Jewish case may again be emphasized. This is that the rivalrous incompatibility of the two communities—Jewish and Protestant— seems to be at its height when both sides are constituted mainly of "independent proprietors," farmers, artisans, small businessmen, and private professional practitioners. The danger of acute anti-Semitism in the American system has probably been greatly mitigated by the fact that the central economic organization developed in the direction of a more highly differentiated corporate structure. In this, there is no "individual" proprietor whose interests can seem to be blocked by the competing Jew. Not unconnected with this development is that of a much broadened system of higher education, one that has changed the character of the general American elite, not least that of business men. Jews gradually gained access to this system and performed oustandingly in it, and, moreover, there were various structurally interstitial areas open to them, such as semi-monopolized areas of small business (for example, clothing) and, not least, the professions organized primarily on the basis of private practice.

29. Samuel Stouffer, *Communism, Conformity, and Civil Liberties* (Garden City, N. Y., 1955).

30. Cf. my paper "Social Strains in America," in Daniel Bell (ed.), *The Radical Right* (New York, 1962).

31. Further, the sister of the President's wife married into European aristocracy, taking the title of "Princess," while remaining very close to the whole Kennedy family.

32. Color, in turn, symbolizes *parentage,* since of course the skin color of Negroes varies greatly. The social criterion is that a Negro is anyone one or both of whose parents were socially classified as a Negro.

33. Cf. Pettigrew, *op. cit.*

34. However dramatic, episodes like that in Selma are clearly coming into the category of "mopping-up operations."

35. Erwin N. Griswold, *Law and Lawyers in the United States* (Cambridge, Mass., 1964).

36. Cf. remarks of Clifford Geertz in the 1964 *Dædalus* planning conference.

37. Contrary, of course, to the temporary trend to the establishment of a WASP aristocracy.

38. It could perhaps be said that the claim of Orthodox Judaism for a secure position in the host society is a case of the "separate but equal" principle. Similar things can be said of other ethnic and religious situations, for example the French minority in Canada.

39. It must be understood that the economic factor here includes the whole opportunity-capacity complex, which is especially important for the Negro. For this reason *primary* reliance on economic interests is clearly inadequate.

40. There is no space here to go into the reasons that the mobilization of students in the civil rights movement is so significant. I do not accept Paul Goodman's suggestion that students are the most exploited class in American society, but their position does have some similarities to that of an exploited class. Though their general prospects are good, as individuals they occupy a probationary status, being under rather strong control from their elders and their teachers. They have developed a strong subculture of their own, characterized by a "romantic" simplification of the general word—a part of the "youth culture." When politically activistic, they tend to be "radical," sometimes in a rightist as well as a leftist direction. Especially in "underdeveloped" societies, the violence of student nationalism is well known. This simplification makes them prone to a strongly moralistic stance—perhaps particularly emphasized because of the prevalence of various adult suspicions about their moral integrity. Hence, they tend to be kinds of "fundamentalists" to whom a simple moralistic issue can appeal greatly. But, by the same token, as representing the best of the future of the society, they can play an exceedingly important role in dramatizing really important moral issues. Cf. Eisenstadt, *From Generation to Generation* (Glencoe, Ill., 1956), and my own article, "Youth in the Context of American Society," *Dædalus* (Winter 1961) reprinted in Erik H. Erikson (ed.), *Youth: Change and Challenge* (Garden City, N. Y., 1964).

41. Charles Campbell and Thomas Pettigrew, *Christians in Racial Crisis* (Washington, D. C., 1959).

42. Not only that, but the positive value of a Negro identity in the long run should not be used to justify failing to act to break up *discriminatory* segregation in the more immediate situation.

NOTES ON CONTRIBUTORS

CHARLES ABRAMS, born in 1901 in Vilna, Poland, is Chairman of the Division of Urban Planning of the School of Architecture and Chairman of the Institute of Urban Environment at Columbia University. His principal books include *The Future of Housing* (1946), *Forbidden Neighbors* (1955), *Man's Struggle for Shelter* (1964), and *The City is the Frontier* (1965).

KENNETH BANCROFT CLARK, born in 1914 in the Panama Canal Zone, is Director of the Social Dynamics Research Institute and Professor of Psychology at the City College of the City University of New York. His principal books include *Prejudice and Your Child* (1955) and *Dark Ghetto* (1965). He was the editor of *The Negro Protest* (1964) and co-author, with Lawrence Plotkin, of *The Negro Student at Integrated Colleges* (1963).

ROBERT COLES, born in 1929 in Boston, Massachusetts, is Research Psychiatrist at the Harvard University Health Services, Consultant to the Southern Regional Council, and member of the National Advisory Committee on Farm Labor. He has written numerous articles on the problems of desegregation and on the lives of migrant farm workers and sharecroppers which have appeared in medical, psychiatric, and general publications.

BRUCE DAVIDSON, born in 1934 in Oak Park, Illinois, joined Magnum Photos, Inc. as Associate Photographer in 1958 and was elected to membership in 1959. In 1962 he was awarded a Guggenheim Fellowship to undertake a photographic study of youth in America. He has produced numerous photo-essays, including "The Clown," "Brooklyn Gang," "Fashion," and "England." His photographs have been widely exhibited, and in March 1965 a one-man exhibition of his photographs was held at the Art Institute of Chicago.

ROBERT A. DENTLER, born in 1928 in Chicago, Illinois, is Deputy Director of the Center for Urban Education in New York City and Associate Professor of Sociology and Education at Teachers College, Columbia University. He is the co-author, with P. H. Rossi, of *The Politics of Urban Renewal* (1962); with P. Cutright, of *Hostage America* (1963); with N. W. Polsby and P. Smith, of *Politics and Social Life;* and, with M. E. Warshauer, of *Big City Dropouts and Illiterates* (1965).

ST. CLAIR DRAKE, born in 1911 in Suffolk, Virginia, is Professor of Sociology at Roosevelt University and is presently Visiting Professor of Sociology at Stanford University. He collaborated with Horace Cayton in writing *Black Metropolis* (1945). Among the articles which he has published are "The Colour Problem in Britain," which appeared in the *Sociological Review* of January 1956, and "Hide My Face? An Essay on Pan Africanism and Negritude," in Herbert Hill (ed.), *Soon One Morning* (1963).

G. FRANKLIN EDWARDS, born in 1915 in Charleston, South Carolina, is Professor of Sociology at Howard University. He is the author of *The Negro Professional Class* (1959) and of "Changes in Occupations as They Affect the Negro," in Arnold Rose (ed.), *Assuring Freedom to the Free* (1964). He is a consultant to the United States Office of Education.

RUPERT EMERSON, born in 1899 in Rye, New York, is Professor of Government and Research Associate of the Center for International Affairs at Harvard University. His books include *State and Sovereignty in Modern Germany* (1928), *Malaysia: A Study in Direct and Indirect Rule* (1937), *Representative Government in Southeast Asia* (1955), and *From Empire to Nation* (1960). He was co-editor, with Martin Kilson, of *The Political Awakening of Africa* (1965).

ERIK H. ERIKSON, born in 1902 in Frankfurt-am-Main, of Danish parentage, is Professor of Human Development and Lecturer on Psychiatry at Harvard University. Among his publications are *Observations on the Yurok* (1943), *Childhood and Society* (1950), *Young Man Luther* (1958), *Identity and the Life Cycle* (1959), *Insight and Responsibility* (1964), and, as editor, *Youth: Change and Challenge* (1963).

RASHI FEIN, born in 1926 in New York, is presently on the Senior Staff of the Economic Studies Division of the Brookings Institution. His publications include *Economics of Mental Illness* (1958) and articles in the areas of economics of medicine, migration, and education. His major field of interest is economics of human resource development. He was formerly on the staff of the President's Council of Economic Advisers.

JOSEPH H. FICHTER, born in 1908 in Union City, New Jersey, has been appointed Stillman Chair Professor of Roman Catholic Studies at the Havard Divinity School, 1965–68. His books include *Social Relations in the Urban Parish* (1954), *Religion as an Occupation* (1961), and *Priest and People* (1965). Father Fichter was founder of the Students Inter-Racial Commission, New Orleans, in 1948 and the Catholic Commission on Human Rights, New Orleans, in 1949.

JOHN H. FISCHER, born in 1910 in Baltimore, Maryland, is President of Teachers College, Columbia University. He has written numerous articles which have appeared in educational journals and other periodicals. Mr. Fischer is currently chairman of the Advisory Committee on Human Relations and Community Tensions of the New York State Department of Education.

HAROLD C. FLEMING, born in 1922 in Atlanta, Georgia, is Executive Vice President of the Potomac Institute in Washington, D. C. He is the co-author, with David Loth, of *Integration North and South* (1956) and has written articles for journals, periodicals, and reference books. He is former Executive Director of the Southern Region Council, Atlanta, Georgia, and former Deputy Director of the Federal Community Relations Service.

EUGENE P. FOLEY, born in 1928 in Wabasha, Minnesota, is Assistant Secretary of Commerce and Director of Economic Development. He was formerly Administrator of the Small Business Administration. He began his career in the practice of law in Minnesota.

JOHN HOPE FRANKLIN, born in 1915 in Rentiesville, Oklahoma, is Professor of American History at the University of Chicago. Among the books which he has written are *From Slavery to Freedom: A History of American Negroes* (2nd edn., 1957), *Militant South* (1956), *Reconstruction After the Civil War* (1961), and *The Emancipation Proclamation* (1963). He is the author of numerous articles and is a member of the editorial board of the *Journal of Negro History*.

PAUL A. FREUND, born in 1908 in St. Louis, Missouri, is Carl M. Loeb University Professor at the Law School of Harvard University. His publications include *The Supreme Court of the United States* (1961), *Religion and the Public Schools* (1965), and, as co-editor, *Constitutional Law: Cases and Other Problems* (1961). He is President of the American Academy of Arts and Sciences.

EUNICE S. GRIER, born in 1927 in Stamford, Connecticut, is Acting Director of the Research Division of the United States Commission on Civil Rights.

GEORGE W. GRIER, born in 1927 in Abington, Pennsylvania, is Coordinator of the Anti-Poverty and Social Welfare Programs of the District of Columbia. Mr. and Mrs. Grier have written *Privately Developed Interracial Housing* (1960) as well as numerous monographs and articles for professional publication. They have served widely as consultants to federal, state, and local governments and private agencies on housing, human relations, and urban problems.

OSCAR HANDLIN, born in 1915 in New York City, is Winthrop Professor of History at Harvard University. Among his many publications are *Boston's Immigrants* (1941), *The Uprooted* (1951), *The American People in the Twentieth Century* (1954), and *Fire-Bell in the Night* (1964). He has also written numerous scholarly articles on educational and historical subjects.

PHILIP M. HAUSER, born in 1909 in Chicago, Illinois, is Professor of Sociology and Director of the Population Research and Training Center of the University of Chicago. He is the author of *Population Perspectives* (1961) and edited *Urbanization in Asia and the Far East* (1958), *The Study of Population, An Inventory and Appraisal* (1959), *Urbanization in Latin America* (1961), *Population Dilemma* (1963), and *The Study of Urbanization* (1965). He was formerly United States Representative to the Population Commission of the United Nations.

ADELAIDE CROMWELL HILL, born in 1919 in Washington, D. C., is Assistant Professor of Sociology and Research Associate of the African Studies Center at Boston University. She has been engaged in studies of African women, delinquency among Negro girls, and the Negro upper class in Boston.

EVERETT CHERRINGTON HUGHES, born in 1897 in Beaver, Ohio, is Professor of Sociology at Brandeis University. His books include *French Canada in Transition* (1943, 1961) and *Men and their Work* (1952). He was co-author, with Helen MacGill Hughes, of *Where Peoples Meet* (1952) and, with H. Becker and B. Geer, of *Boys in White: Student Culture in Medical School* (1961). His interest has centered on multi-ethnic societies, and especially on the division of labor in them.

FREDERICK S. JAFFE, born in 1925 in New York City, is Vice President for Program Planning and Development at the Planned Parenthood Federation of America. He is the co-author, with Alan F. Guttmacher and Winfield Best, of *Planning Your Family: The Complete Guide to Contraception and Fertility* (1964), and has written numerous articles on family planning which have appeared in professional journals.

MARTIN KILSON, born in 1931 in East Rutherford, New Jersey, is Lecturer on Government and Research Associate of the Center for International Affairs at Harvard University. He is co-editor, with Rupert Emerson, of *The Political Awakening of Africa* (1965), author of *Political Change in a West African State* (forthcoming), and contributor to James S. Coleman and C. S. Rosberg (eds.), *Political Parties and National Integration in Tropical Africa* (1964).

DANIEL PATRICK MOYNIHAN, born in 1927 in Tulsa, Oklahoma, was most recently Assistant Secretary of Labor. He was co-author, with Nathan Glazer, of *Beyond the Melting Pot* (1963), and has written articles for various journals. Before going to Washington, he was director of the State Government Research Project at the University of Syracuse.

TALCOTT PARSONS, born in 1902 in Colorado Springs, Colorado, is Professor of Sociology at Harvard University. Among his extensive publications are *Structure of Social Action* (1937), *Toward a General Theory of Action* (1951), *Family, Socialization and Interaction Process* (1955), *Structure and Process in Modern Societies* (1959), and *Evolutionary and Comparative Perspectives* (1965).

THOMAS F. PETTIGREW, born in 1931 in Richmond, Virginia, is Associate Professor of Social Psychology at Harvard University. His principal books include *A Profile of the Negro American* (1964) and, with E. Q. Campbell, *Christians in Racial Crisis: A Study of the Little Rock Ministry* (1959). Articles by Mr. Pettigrew have appeared in numerous professional and scholarly journals.

LEE RAINWATER, born in 1928 in Oxford, Mississippi, is Professor of Sociology and Anthropology at Washington University and a research associate in the University's Social Science Institute. He is the author of *And the Poor Get Children* (1960) and *Family Design: Marital Sexuality, Family Size and Contraception;* he is the co-author of *Workingman's Wife: Her Personality, World and Life Styles* (1959) and *The Professional Scientist* (1962).

PAUL B. SHEATSLEY, born in 1916 in New York City, is Director of the Survey Research Service of the National Opinion Research Center at the University of Chicago. He is a contributor to *The Encyclopedia Americana* and *The Americana Annual* and has written articles for such publications as *Scientific American* and *Public Opinion Quarterly*.

JAMES TOBIN, born in 1918 in Champaign, Illinois, is Sterling Professor of Economics at Yale University. He is the co-author, with Seymour E. Harris, Carl Kaysen, and Francis X. Sutton, of *The American Business Creed* (1956) and has written numerous articles for professional and popular journals. He is a former member of the President's Council of Economic Advisers (1961–62).

ARTHUR D. TROTTENBERG, born in 1917 in Rochester, New York, is Assistant Dean of the Faculty of Arts and Sciences at Harvard University. His publications include *A Vision of Paris* (1963) and numerous articles, photographs, and essays on education, arts, and photography, which have appeared in national publications. He is Chairman of the Executive Committee of the Carpenter Center for the Visual Arts at Harvard University.

JOHN B. TURNER, born in 1922 in Ft. Valley, Georgia, is Professor of Social Work at the School of Applied Social Sciences of Western Reserve University and consultant to the National Urban League. Among the articles he has written are "The Volunteer in Intergroup Relations," in Nathan E. Cohen (ed.), *The Citizen Volunteer* (1960), and "Relation of Health and Welfare Planning to Social Change and Social Development," in *Social Work and Social Planning* (1964).

JAMES Q. WILSON, born in 1931 in Denver, Colorado, is Associate Professor of Government of Harvard University and Director of the Joint Center for Urban Studies at MIT and Harvard University. He is the author of *Negro Politics* (1960) and *The Amateur Democrat* (1962) and co-author, with Edward C. Banfield, of *City Politics* (1963). He has also written numerous articles for professional and scholarly journals.

WHITNEY M. YOUNG, JR., born in 1921 in Lincoln Ridge, Kentucky, is Executive Director of the National Urban League, He is the author of *To Be Equal* (1964), and writes a weekly newspaper column under the same title. Mr. Young helped plan the 1963 March on Washington and is a member of the Council for United Civil Rights Leadership, the National Advisory Council of the Office of Economic Opportunity, and the National Commission on Technology, Automation, and Economic Progress.

Fair Employment Practices Commission, 63, 373, 394
Fair Housing Committees, 351, 545
Family: Negro awareness of "normal," 170–171; breakdown of and high fertility, 224
Family, Negro: instability of, 77–79, 90–91, 738; and employment opportunities, 136; crisis in, 147, 157–158; and broken homes, 148, 150–151; autonomy of, 166–167; history of, 167; and relatives in household, 169–170; measures needed to change pattern of, 196–199; size of, 209–210; size preferences of, 213; size of, and discrimination in medical services, 216; per cent with both spouses present, 287; and ghetto life, 287–288; educational level of head of, 288–289; effects of migration on, 291, 674; effect of, on change in U.S., 298; and public assistance, 463; size of and poverty, 467; and development of communal institutions, 674; development of from 1865–1915, 674
Family planning, 291; Negro response to, 214–215; and availability of medical services, 215–217; need to increase services, 218; and better life for Negroes, 219–220
Farmer, James, 609; resignation of, 609; disagreement with King on Vietnam, 614
Farms, Southern: and Negro birth rate, 208–209
Farm Security Administration, 61
Faubus, Orval, 375, 720
Faulkner, William, 265
Fayette County, Tenn.: distribution of surplus food in, 379
Federal aid: and equal treatment, 380
Federal budget: and income allowances, 466
Federal government: and Civil Rights Movement, xiii, xxvii; and civil rights, xx–xxi, xxvi; segregation policies of, 57; and change in race relations, 299; reorganization of its civil rights activities, 1965, 378, 385; and commitment to desegregation, 396; and equal rights in housing, 516–517; and problems of central cities, 522; direct building of housing by, 522; and residential

segregation, 530–533; current housing policies of, 542–544; and incentives to achieve residential integration, 547–548; increase in size of, 731
Federal Housing Administration, 529, 530, 531, 559; and neighborhood stability, 523–524
Federal Old Age Survivors and Disability Insurance, 465
Feild, John, 392
Fein, Rashi, xi, xxii, 456
Fellowship of Reconciliation, 608
Ferguson, Clyde, Jr., 153
Fichter, Joseph H., xxiii
Fiedler, Leslie, 165
Filler, Louis: on racist views of Northerners, 52–53
Fire Next Time, The, 12
Foley, Eugene P., xxii
Ford Motor Company, 516
Forman, James, 617
Forten, James, 563, 564
Franchising: and Negro business, 576
Franklin, John Hope, xi, xii, xxv
Frazier, E. Franklin, 36, 148, 281, 351, 695; on cities and the Negro family, 164; on Negro middle class, 293, 295; on Negro church, 411
Freedom Democratic Party, xvii, 428, 443, 619
"Freedom now," 401, 680
Freedom of the press, 364
Freedom ride, 1961, 386
Freedom rides: clergy participation in, 414
Freedomways, 641
Freedomways Associates, 641
Free Speech Movement, California, 246
French West Indies, 638
Freud, Sigmund, 212, 233, 234, 236; on identity, 230
Freund, Paul A., xxi, xxv, xxvi
"From Protest to Politics: The Future of the Civil Rights Movement," 423
Fundamentalism, religious, 746–747
Fund for Negro Students, 509

Gaines case, 605
Galbraith, J. K., 452
Gallup poll: on integration, 309, 320; on civil rights, 321
Gandhi, Mohandas K., 228, 251, 406;

612; limitations of his method, 613; and U.S. Vietnam policy, 614; his Chicago project, 614–615; on changing living conditions of Negroes, 619; and racial balance in schools, 671

Klansman, The, 56

Korean War: impact of, on integration in the Army, 645

Ku Klux Klan, xvi, 64, 297, 388; in Radical Reconstruction period, 55; revival of during World War I, 60; clergy in, 409; and Catholics and Jews, 664

Labor, mobility of: need to improve, 460

Laborers, Negro, 142–143

Labor force: Negroes in, 80–84

Labor legislation: and New Deal, xx

Labor market, slack: and job qualifications, 456–457; and discrimination, 457

Labor market, tight: importance of to Negroes, 453–457; ways to accomplish, 457–460; and migration from agriculture, 468

Labor movement: compared with Civil Rights Movement, 598

Labor unions: and preferential treatment for Negroes, 292; and equal employment opportunity in federal programs, 383; as political ally of Negroes, 435; and alliances with Negroes, 443

LaFarge, John, 408

Landlord and tenant: legal relationship of, 365

Language institutes: federal financing of in Southern colleges, 379

Laurenti, Luigi, 530

Lawrence, David, 382

Laws: state segregation, 57; and change in human attitudes, 341–342, 369; and civil rights, enforcement of, 386–388, 549

Lawyers' Committee for Civil Rights Under Law, 395

Leadership Conference on Civil Rights, 380, 394

League of Nations, 628

Legal Defense and Education Fund, Inc., 605

Legal representation: and NAACP, 364–365

Lehman, Herbert, 726

Leopard's Spots, The, 56

Lewis, Hylan, 219–220, 290

Lewis, John, 617, 618

Liberals, white: as Negro political ally in North, 437–438

Liberation Committee on Africa, 641

Liberator, 641

Liberty vs. equality: for Negroes, 134; and Negro-white coalitions in South, 431; in North, 438–439

Lieberson, Stanley, 76, 77, 286

Life chances: Weber's concept of, 5; inequality of as Negro's problem, 685; and use of power, 686–688; and group solidarity, 687; and excellence, 689–690; and exercise of rights by Negroes, 690

Life expectancy: Negro-white compared, 20; increase of Negro, 72–73; Negro-white males compared, 106–108, 147

Life Magazine: portrayal of Negroes in, 349

Life styles: Weber's concept of, 5; among 'lower-class Negroes, 194–195

Lincoln, Abraham, 598; urges Congress to colonize Negroes, 51; on equality for Negroes, 53, 54, 572–573

Lincoln University, 331

Lippmann, Walter, 205

Lipset, Seymour Martin, 713, 714, 730

Little Rock, Ark., 375, 720; ministers in, 414

Liuzzo, Viola, 414

Locke, Alain, 61

Logan, Rayford, xii

Los Angeles: Watts riot, 1965, xvi, 36, 322, 512; congestion in Watts area, 513

Lower class: need for housing program for, 521; need for subsidy for housing, 548; and immigrants, 732; and Negro, 735

Lower class, Negro: life style of, 11–12; churches, 12; and employment opportunities, 136; and first marriage, 168; number of children in families, 170; and "normal" family life, 170–171; behavior of adolescents, 171–173; and premarital pregnancy, 173–175; attitude to-